THE OTHER SIDE
OF THE RIVER

Books by Edgar Snow

THE OTHER SIDE OF THE RIVER

Red China Today

EDGAR SNOW

Random House   New York

THIRD PRINTING

© *Copyright, 1961, 1962, by Edgar Snow*

All rights reserved under International and Pan-American Copyright Conventions. Published in New York by Random House, Inc., and simultaneously in Toronto, Canada, by Random House of Canada, Limited.
Library of Congress Catalog Card Number: 61–6243
Manufactured in the United States of America by H. Wolff, New York

DESIGN BY TERE LoPRETE

To Bennett Cerf, Donald Klopfer, Mao Tse-tung, Chou En-lai, Rewi Alley, and Gardner Cowles, who helped make it possible for me to visit China.

And to countless Chinese, Americans and Europeans who contributed in various ways to this report—for which no one is responsible except the facts and myself.

A strange justice that is bounded by a river! Can anything be more ridiculous than that a man should have the right to kill me because he lives on the other side . . .

—BLAISE PASCAL, *Pensées*

Men will not receive the truth from their enemies and it is very seldom offered to them by their friends; on this very account I have frankly uttered it.

Placed between the conflicting opinions that divide my country-men, I have endeavored for the time to stifle in my own bosom the sympathy or the aversion that I felt for either . . .

The subject that I wished to cover by my investigations is immense, for it includes most of the feelings and opinions produced by the new condition of the world's affairs. Such a subject certainly exceeds my strength, and in the treatment of it I have not been able to satisfy myself.

—ALEXIS DE TOCQUEVILLE, Preface to
Democracy in America, VOLUME II

A Note on Chinese Pronunciation

———◆————

It is not necessary to strangle over the pronunciation of Chinese names if one observes a few simple rules in the rather arbitrary but workable "Wade system" of transliteration (romanization) of the language into English. Each Chinese character represents only one sound and homonyms are innumerable. Chinese is monosyllabic, but combinations of characters in the spoken language may form a single idea or equivalent of one foreign word and thus in a sense the spoken language is polysyllabic. Chinese surnames come first, given names (usually two words) follow, as in Teng Hsiao-p'ing. Aspirates are represented in this book by apostrophes; they indicate a soft consonantal sound. Examples:

Chi (as in Chi Chao-t'ing) is pronounced as "Gee," but *Ch'i* (as in Liu Shao-ch'i) sounds like "Chee." *Ch'in* is exactly our "chin."

Chu is roughly like "Jew," as in *Chu Teh* (Jew Duhr), but *Ch'u* equals "Chew."

Tsung is "dzung"; *ts'ung* with the "ts" as in "Pa*ts*y."

Tai is our word sound "die"; *T'ai*—"tie."

Pai is "buy" and *P'ai* is "pie."

Kung is like "Gung" (a Din); *K'ung* with the "k" as in "kind."

J is the equivalent of r but slur it, as *rr*run.

H before an *s*, as in *hsi*, is the equivalent of an aspirate but is often dropped, as in Sian for Hsian.

Single Chinese words are always pronounced as monosyllables. Thus: *Chiang* is not "Chee-yi-ang" but a single sound, "Geeang." *Mao* is not "may-ow" but pronounced like a cat's "miaow" *without* the "i." *Chou En-lai* is "Joe Un-lie" but the last syllable of his wife's given name, *Ying-ch'ao*, sounds like "chow."

Vowels in Chinese are generally short or medium, not long and flat. Thus *Tang* sounds like "dong," never like our "tang." *T'ang* is "tong."

a as in f*a*ther

e—r*u*n

eh—h*e*n

i—s*ee*

ih—h*er*

o—l*oo*k

ou—g*o*

There is also a ü as in German and an ê as in French. I have omitted Wade's umlaut and circumflex markings, which are found in European latinizations of Chinese.

*u—soo*n

These sounds indicate Chinese as spoken in *kuo-yu,* the northern (Peking, mandarin) speech, which is now the national language, taught in all schools. Where journalism has already popularized misspellings or variants in other dialects, such as Chiang Kai-shek for Chiang Chiehshih, etc., I have followed the familiar version.

Chinese words frequently encountered in place names are:

> *sheng*—province; *hsien*—county; *hsiang*—township; *ching* (or *king*)—capital; *ch'eng*—city; *ts'un*—village; *chiang* (kiang)—great river; *ho*—river; *hu*—lake; *k'ou*—mouth; *pei*—north; *nan*—south; *tung*—east; *hsi* (or *si*)—west; *chung*—central; *shan*—mountain.

Such words combine in the following examples:

> *Peking* (properly, *Pei-ching,* pronounced "Bay-ging"), meaning "northern capital." Peking was renamed "Pei-p'ing" (Peiping or, erroneously, Peping), "northern peace" (or tranquillity), by the Kuomintang regime, which made its seat in Nanking (southern capital) but the historic name remained in general use and was formally restored—except at the State Department—in 1949.
>
> *Shantung* means East of the mountains.
>
> *Shansi*—West of the mountains.
>
> *Hankow*—Mouth of the Han (river).
>
> *Sian*—Western Peace (tranquillity).
>
> *Hopei*—North of the (Yellow) river.
>
> *Hunan*—South of the lakes.
>
> *Yunnan*—South of the clouds.
>
> *Kiangsi*—West of the river.

Contents

———◆◆———

Contents

Photographs
  (All photographs not otherwise credited were taken by the author)

THE OTHER SIDE
OF THE RIVER

Introduction

Journey to the Beginning,[1] an autobiographical account of adventures in ignorance (not necessarily all mine), contains enough details of my personal history to satisfy any reasonable reader's curiosity—and considering the subject of this book you have a right to be curious. It tells among other things how I went to China when I was twenty-two and there began my career as a foreign correspondent, with Colonel McCormick's *Chicago Tribune*.

What is relevant here is that I happen to be well known in China because I was the first person to penetrate a civil war blockade and interview and photograph Mao Tse-tung, Chou En-lai and other leaders of the old Chinese Red Army. That was a century ago (1936), a year before the Communists and the Nationalists under Chiang Kai-shek called a truce in their first nine years of mutual extermination, in order to compete in a war of resistance against Japan. I then represented the *London Daily Herald* and the *New York Sun*. My reports on the Chinese Communists also appeared in *Life* and in the *Saturday Evening Post,* for which I later became a world correspondent and then was for many years an associate editor.

Mao Tse-tung told me his own story and the history of the Chinese Communist revolution up to that time, which appeared in my book

Red Star Over China, published in 1937.[2] A Chinese version of that book came out before the English edition and provided countless Chinese with the first authentic information about Chinese Communists. Among those readers were many youths whom I have recently met as second- or third-echelon leaders of Red China today.

This background made it possible for me to be given a welcome, despite official hostility between Peking and Washington, when I returned to China in 1960 for the first time since the end of the Second World War. Relatively few of the small number of Occidentals who have seen Red China ever lived there before the revolution. I believe I was, among resident American correspondents who knew China in prewar days, the first to return.

It might be assumed from the foregoing that it was easy for me to get a Chinese visa, but several years elapsed before my application was granted—only after reaching the highest level of authority. Some of my reports about Stalin's Russia had caused me to be barred from that country and I had expressed views on the origins of the Korean War sharply at variance with the way it looked from Peking. Other comments on Sino-Soviet relations, on Yugoslavia, and on communism in general might have made me *persona non grata* if Peking authorities admitted to China only those who never questioned their official *People's Daily* version of history. As early as 1948 (December 11), I had suggested that Tito's heresy marked the beginning of Communist heterodoxy and foreshadowed today's Sino-Soviet dispute.

"The Belgrade schism," I wrote in the *Saturday Evening Post* at that time, when Stalin expelled Tito and his colleagues from the Cominform,

> provides a mirror which clearly reflects the basic aims and limitations of Russia's policies in Europe [and] likewise gives us a perspective on events now transpiring in China. There is projected, against the screen of the remote future, the real possibility* of war between socialist states even after the "final" extirpation of capitalism. The possibility first impressed me a decade ago in China, where the Communist party was at that time the only one in the world outside Russia which had an army, territory and real administrative responsibilities of its own. Because of that, it seemed likely that the Chinese would become the first foreign Communists openly to place their national interests on a level with those of Russia. But while the Chinese were still deeply involved in a long and complicated civil war on a continental scale, the Yugoslav party relatively quickly won absolute internal victory. It thus achieved all the conditions necessary to enable it seriously to question the paramountcy of Kremlin interests.

* Possibility, not "inevitability." In 1957, Mao Tse-tung himself discerned "contradictions" between socialist national states. See page 387.

As is well known, the Yugoslav Communists were not installed by the Red Army but as a result of a severe internal struggle in which they were armed chiefly by Britain and America. Out of the struggle grew a strong sense of pride and brotherhood bound together in a spirit of self-reliance and self-glorification. Demands imposed in the name of the Kremlin myth [of infallibility] increasingly interfered with the performance of internal tasks which Yugoslav Communists themselves considered necessary to stabilize their power. And it was in bold rejection of the doctrine of Kremlin infallibility that the Yugoslav party reiterated, last July [1948], its conviction that "the national independence of the people of Yugoslavia is the condition for their road to socialism and their progress in general."

As a result there is a head-on collision, not between [Yugoslavian] nationalism on the one hand and [Stalinist] internationalism on the other, but between two sets of nationalisms within the "socialist system of states." And it has come not because of a Yugoslav deviation from the Russian model so much as because of a too exact emulation of it.

Insubordination in Marshal Tito and his party could not long be tolerated without encouraging others to place the national interests of their own countries on a level with those of Russia. For there exists, in every Communist party that possesses even a measure of responsible power, a latent but growing will to free itself of the dogma of unconditional obedience. The heresy of Tito marks the end of an era of communism *as an extension of Russian nationalism.* The Kremlin myth has been defied and the infidel has not fallen dead. Tito is the beginning of a true heterodoxy in the Communist "universal church." The lesson must have penetrated even the thick walls of the Kremlin, to bring about realization that the satellite countries themselves could not be counted as true assets, rather than liabilities, in the event of an early war. In particular, the potential risks of Poland and Hungary—not to mention Soviet Germany—following Belgrade's example must haunt the Russian high command.

How, then, explain provocative Soviet actions at Berlin and elsewhere? Russian tactics can be viewed primarily as heavy-handed efforts to accelerate a basic settlement recognizing international legality of the new status quo. . . . The blockade of Berlin and sabotage of the United Nations' pattern of internationalism [reflect] Russia's growing determination to hold onto and fully consolidate economic and political control over all the territory it now dominates militarily including, above all, Eastern Germany. . . . Russia's second objective is to dis-

engage herself from the war crisis with the United States by
accepting the division of Germany as a legal fact, and the de-
marcation line as basis for a new balance of power system in
Europe. Unless we attempt to drive Russia from Eastern Europe
by force there will be no general war between us in the foreseeable future.

That was published on December 18, 1948. Four months later
(April 9, 1949) I wrote about China in the same precincts:

As a result of the Communists' sovereign victory in China
there now exists in East Asia a new set of circumstances with
significant implications both inside and beyond the Marxist
world. Moscow must deal with a major foreign power run by
Communists possessing all the means of maintaining real equality and independence. This becomes important when it is realized that potential sources of friction between Soviet and Chinese nationalisms already exist in Manchuria, Mongolia and
Chinese Turkestan, where Russian attrition has been going on
for generations. The question is: Will the legacy of past differences, and their influence on the psychology of the two regimes
which now face each other along many thousands of miles of
frontier, be overcome by their adherence to a common ideology? . . .

Far from accepting the role of satellites, either for Manchuria
or for China as a whole, the Chinese Communists look upon
their country as the potential focus of a new federation of East-
tern socialist states, which can exist independently, on a plane
of complete equality with the U.S.S.R. While the Kremlin cannot be much happier over such a prospect than it was about
Tito's Balkan federation scheme, it would be highly illusory to
imagine that the Russians will promptly repeat, in China, the
mistakes which lost them effective control in Yugoslavia. They
will proceed with extreme caution, hopefully waiting for the
Americans to make the blunders on which their own success
could be improvised. . . .

So long as it is true that the United States is the main support of the old regime in China and of any or all anti-Communist parties, groups, politicians or warlords prepared to continue what is now clearly a lost war, Americans will easily hold
their present position as Foreign Enemy No. 1. . . . If the purpose of American policy is to strengthen China's independence
from Russia then it is not likely to be achieved by forcing the
Communists to resign themselves to the terms of Russian alliance in self-defense. . . . In any event, in the long run the
Chinese Communist Party cannot and will not subordinate the

national interests of China to the interests of the Kremlin. *China will become the first Communist-run major power independent of Moscow's dictation. And that in itself would project entirely new perspectives within the socialist camp, as elsewhere . . .* [Italics added.]

Given the opportunity to develop its own resources in arm's length cooperation with other nations such a new Asia might form a bloc of powers important enough to maintain a stable balance between the Russian and American spheres of influence. People accustomed to thinking in terms of ideological absolutes may find it hard to understand how "communism" can be contained by communism or how it could be checked by anything but its exact opposite, which they tend to see as "capitalism." But there are many shades and variations in meaning and growth in words of that type, and there will be more. It is likely that the threat of *Russian* world dictatorship will be checked by rival developments of communist power as well as by social democracy and modified capitalism. History shows us that conquering universal faiths and organizations have been halted before they united the world—or burned it up—by internal rivalries and disintegration more often than by attacks from without.

Following these remarks I was barred from the U.S.S.R. during Stalin's lifetime, and in one Shanghai journal I was called an agent of American imperialism. Washington likewise rejected the views expressed above; United States policy for a decade was based on quite opposite assumptions that the Peking regime was "non-Chinese" and a will-less puppet of Moscow, and that the process of Soviet expansion by such means could continue indefinitely. Twelve years later it had become clear to everyone that disputes and rivalries rooted in conflicts of national interest had arisen between Russia and China, and so respected a diplomatic historian as George Kennan was able to draw the following logical inference without fear of contradiction even by his less discerning colleagues in the State Department:

There is no magic by which great nations are brought to obey for any length of time the will of people very far away who understand their problems poorly and with whom they feel no intimacy . . . or understanding. This has to be done by bayonets or it is not done at all. . . . This is the reason why, despite all that is said about Soviet expansion, the power of the Kremlin extends precisely to those areas which it is able to dominate with its own armed forces without involving impossible lines of communication, and no farther. . . . What I am asserting is that universal world dominion is a technical impossibility and that

the effectiveness of the power radiated from any one national
center decreases in proportion to the distance involved and to
the degree of cultural disparity.[3]

Remembering my "controversial" writings of a decade earlier, the
Yugoslavs and other Eastern European Communists in Peking were
keenly interested in my admission to China in 1960. They attached
significance to it as a straw in the wind of increasingly unfavorable weather in Sino-Soviet relations. In that same year the departure of many thousands of Soviet technical advisers from the People's Republic was to begin to reveal to the outside world the deep
tension and open fissures that had grown between the two giants of
the Communist bloc over just such rivalries as I have mentioned—
disputes formerly held unthinkable by orthodox Marxists, who believed as an article of faith that class solidarity was a stronger cement than the atavisms of tribalism which we call nationalism.

Seemingly unaware of such nuances in the Sino-Soviet alliance, the
State Department had rebuffed numerous overtures from the People's
Republic to reopen communications. My own return provided the most
recent example on record. It was strenuously opposed by the Eisenhower Administration, as had been true of every effort made by Americans on a nonofficial level who understood something of the historical
contradictions, and their portent for the U.S.A., as I have described
them. The State Department actually did everything but compel me to
go to China illegally, if at all.

The road of independent inquiry, seeking some truth beyond the
propaganda, is never an easy one, but I had not expected that my
way back to China would be blocked by our own government.

Certain State Department press releases have given the impression
that the Peking regime alone is responsible for barring Americans
from China. The facts are not that simple. Although today China takes
the position that it is useless to admit correspondents there as long as
the United States is unwilling to discuss ending its armed protectorate
over Taiwan, it must be noted that formerly the Chinese government
did offer visas to many Americans, including correspondents and
writers. It was Secretary of State John Foster Dulles who then forbade
all Americans to visit China. By threatening any violators with loss of
their passports and possible fines or imprisonment—and by instigating direct Presidential appeal to a few important publishers who were
inclined to defy him—the Secretary managed for years to keep
America effectively cut off from any direct news of the great story of
the Chinese revolution.

In 1957, Mr. Dulles finally made up a selected list of "news media"
he considered "qualified" to send representatives to China—if they
could get visas. Peking declined to receive his "accredited" correspondents unless the United States would accept an equal number of Chinese

correspondents. Mr. Dulles flatly rejected that proposal, saying that American immigration laws prohibited the issuance of visas to Communists. The evasion was transparent; exceptions had already been made for Soviet and other Communist correspondents. But there the matter rested until after Mr. Dulles' death.

Meanwhile the Peking government continued to offer visas to Americans who wished to enter China as ordinary travelers, but the State Department would not permit that, either. During the Eisenhower Administration many distinguished Americans, including Eleanor Roosevelt and Averell Harriman,* were offered visas by China but were prevented from accepting them by State Department warnings that to do so would be violating the law. Mr. Dulles' attempt to build a diplomatic Berlin wall around China failed to win support even among the NATO powers, but it effectively prohibited Americans from crossing the border from the free world to study life in the Asian slave world.

As I intend to be candid throughout this book I should here offer a few additional details to explain how I received a Chinese visa. There was no conspiratorial or underhanded arrangement. I had followed events sufficiently to know that in 1958 the Peking government had abandoned what it considered three years of fruitless attempts at conciliation of the United States. Reasons for the change will emerge in these pages. Briefly, as Chou En-lai was later to state to me in most concrete terms in Peking, his government had concluded that it was profitless to discuss concessions to be made by China unless the United States would agree to mutual rejection of the use of force in the settlement of Sino-American disputes *and* simultaneously recognize, *in principle*, the sovereignty of China over the Taiwan territories.

Part of the new "firm" policy meant the refusal to receive "correspondents" of publications and news media "accredited" to China by the State Department. Peking officially had made it clear that China would now seek no exchange of correspondents unless the United States reconsidered its Taiwan policy. Despite past rebuffs, and although it was related to a whole complex of international events discussed herein, the Chinese decision was unwise. (For one thing, it enabled the new Kennedy Administration early in 1961 safely to offer to circumvent immigration laws and to "consider" applications of some Chinese correspondents for visas, with the knowledge that Peking would be obliged to refuse—a response then used to justify continuation of the Dulles China policy.) But my point is that it was already evident, in 1960, that it would be futile for me to apply to enter China as a "correspondent." Instead, I asked for admission as a "writer." I

---

* Mr. Harriman was offered a visitor's visa, but the State Department would not validate his passport. Under pressure he had himself made a State Department-accredited "correspondent." The Chinese then declined his application in accordance with the policy noted above.

was so defined on my passport. At the same time I applied to Secretary of State Herter for permission to travel there in the same category, to gather material for a book. China accepted me, but the State Department promptly rejected my request. My problem then was how to confound beadledom without losing my passport or becoming a diplomatic issue which would cause China automatically to withdraw a visa.

At this point my guerrilla publisher, Bennett Cerf, took charge by selling periodical rights to my potential book to *Look* magazine. *Look* then applied to the State Department to "accredit" me as its "representative."

Look magazine was on the Department's "list," but once *Look* wished to send me to China the publisher was subjected to intense pressure from the Department; certain senators and even the White House were incited to intervene to try to persuade him to withdraw my name. My record was too well known at the State Department for me to be called a Communist. The special reason given for opposing me was that as a correspondent I had known Chinese Communist leaders since my youth, and that I was still acceptable to them; therefore, it was obvious that I could not write a "satisfactory report." Anyone else acceptable to Peking might have met the same opposition in Washington. It seemed that the Administration could "contain" China and its seven hundred millions but dared not risk having even one independent American report printed which *might* contradict Mr. Dulles' conviction that the People's Republic would soon "pass away."

Of course the Department had no diplomatic right to "accredit" or not "accredit" *any* news media or correspondents to a government which it did not recognize, and from whom it could make no demands for the normal courtesies granted American citizens abroad. It is highly doubtful that the Department has any domestic legal right to "accredit" news corporations to operate in China while denying freedom of movement to individual writers. Gardner Cowles, publisher of *Look*, was well aware of these facts. The Department itself in the end tacitly admitted as much in official correspondence with *Look* which conceded that it "had no alternative" but to validate my passport if Mr. Cowles insisted. He did. Very grudgingly permission was finally given for me "legally" to enter China.

After all this difficulty I presented my passport to the Chinese authorities in Europe for a visa. They found that it still included a ban against travel in North Korea and North Vietnam, countries friendly to China, which they regarded as unsatisfactory. Ironically, therefore, they gave me a visa on a separate piece of paper, and thereafter ignored my passport.

Officially, I entered China as a-writer-not-a-correspondent, while in Washington I entered as a-correspondent-not-a-writer.

This book of course concerns a land where a dictatorial government quite frankly decides what is good for people to know and what is not, and where reporters shall go or not go. It is a matter of basic principle with Communists in power that they *must* freely utilize all means of communication in the service of a party which claims identity with the interests of "the whole people" and certainly is identical with the state. Nor is it any news that such control is philosophically justified by a positive faith that communism and public ownership will lead to ultimate human liberation. Just the opposite faith is claimed to be the basis of a democracy, which holds that the truth itself is a greater liberating force than any party and that a free society can exist only if the tools of communication are freely available to all. If by common agreement both the bureaucracy and those individuals who actually own the essential means of communication use them to disseminate only that part of the truth which serves their private interests, however, the cornerstone of what is called "the democratic process" crumbles, and a basic difference in principle between the two systems we are talking about disappears.

In judging China today the American reader can no longer comfortably assume that he lives under a system immune from state intervention between himself and the facts. Still greater conditioning by means of self-censorship is required if the public reflexes are to provide satisfactory responses to stereotyped cold-war idioms increasingly invoked by the state. Following the debacle of the Cuban invasion, which the President was led to support by incompetent advice from his top confidants, the only public rebuke he delivered was aimed at the Fourth Estate. Its error lay in having reported the damaging facts at all.

"While Americans have freedom that few other people ever knew, the clichés that Madison Avenue exploits are distortions . . ." said Mr. Justice William O. Douglas in a recent speech[4] which for obvious reasons went unreported in the newspapers. "We speak of the free press. Yet a man without ten million dollars would have a difficult time to establish a printing plant adequate to compete with our prominent papers. . . .

"We have been so vastly regimented that almost overnight opinion is shaped to fit a synthetic image. Mossadegh—the man who first brought democracy to Persia's villages and who strived to get a constitutional monarchy—became overnight at the hands of our press a clown, a demagogue, a neo-communist. Kassim—an ardent nationalist —was pictured as a tool of communism, when in truth communism suffered in his regime the worst setback it has known. . . .

"Truman and Eisenhower taught us to find security in arms, not in ideas. . . . The man out of step with American free enterprise was a dangerous man. That intolerance of ours was a close competitor to the communist; each demanded its particular type of conformity."

It is true that I might not have been granted a visa by the Chinese

People's Republic but for the accident of the special circumstances I have related. Neither would the information in this report have been made available to a wide American public if the State Department's policy had gone unchallenged at *Look* and at Random House, as it did in recreant quarters elsewhere.

That there existed even one *Look* was enough to prove that state control and self-subjugation of our press were far from complete and far from unified. The area of freedom of inquiry which separates China from the United States is not itself an absolute gulf, however, but a frontier; not something fixed or permanent, not anything ordained by God but a will in men's minds; not a right which may exist forever or has ever existed without constant struggle to maintain it; of wholly negative value if used only to serve narrow interests of private ownership while censoring the general interest of the public enlightenment and welfare; and a freedom which will soon lose all meaning if those who possess it, on the American side of the frontier, do not more energetically use it to reveal the truth about ourselves as well as the black, the white and the gray about people and systems on the other side.

The greater danger which has all along faced America, as Walter Lippmann has eloquently observed, is not communism but whether we can "to ourselves be true," and whether we can "find our strength by developing and applying our principles, not in abandoning them."

Part One

REDISCOVERING CHINA

☆

After I had been in China four months I spent an evening with a Very High Official. He was an old acquaintance and we spoke off the record. He asked what my impressions were and I mentioned several aspects of China's material and cultural progress.

"But that's only a bird's-eye view of the surface of things," I said. "I would have to get a lot closer down to go in deeper than that. What seems obvious is that China is no longer a backward country."

"You are mistaken," he said. "China is still a backward country. It is true that China is in better condition than it was under Chiang Kai-shek, but that is not saying much. The old China could hardly have been worse; some improvement was inevitable. The big change is in the people. I believe they have changed fundamentally for the better. But if we speak of economic progress we can only say that China has laid the foundations for fundamental change. We have enormous difficulties to overcome before we can call ourselves a forward nation."

Yet this "still backward country" will probably explode a China-made atomic device before 1964, and become a full-fledged nuclear power by 1966, according to analyses recently published by able and respected American research scientists and technicians.* Within this major paradox lie hundreds of lesser paradoxes which it is the purpose of this journey to explore.

* See pages 643-644.

I

Arrival in Peking

At 6:30 A.M. on June 28, 1960, I said good-by to Lois and our two children, Sian and Christopher, and left Geneva on a Swiss plane which took me to the sparkling new, all-window Vienna airport, where I changed to an old Czech copy of a Douglas for Moscow. By the following afternoon at about three I had flown halfway around the world and landed at Peking in a Soviet turbojet manned by a Chinese crew.

At the Moscow terminal my luggage was carried in and I had to go through customs and immigration and be weighed out again. As a through passenger I hadn't expected that, and I protested at the weighing process; like all seasoned travelers I was carrying about twenty-five pounds of overweight on my person and thus far had encountered no discourtesies about it. But here a stiff-necked young official made me divest myself of coat, cameras, films and a small box about the size of a baby grand, and even empty my pockets onto the scale. Ignoring my dimly remembered Russian, he made out a receipt for me and kept repeating *"Pláta, pláta, pozhaluista"* (Payment, payment, please). He demanded, at four times the rate charged Communist-bloc citizens, the equivalent of seventy dollars for my excess.

"Be reasonable, comrade," I said. "Every American isn't Rockefeller.

I'm paying fourteen hundred dollars to fly to China and back. Is it fair to charge me seventy extra for a bit of fat to bring me even with your Russian passengers?"

He waved me aside, but I saw a sympathetic look in the eyes of his blond assistant and went on to say that the excess was mostly Swiss toys and chocolate for children of people I knew in Peking (perfectly true), which altogether hadn't cost seventy dollars. "I'd rather leave the gifts here for Russian children," I said, and I began to unpack. A crowd had gathered nearby to hear a Russian woman peasant demand a free taxi ride for herself, a mountain of baggage, and a child, because the airline bus had left without them. Now the audience deserted her to watch me and among them I saw a number of Chinese dressed as students.

The Sympathetic Blonde engaged her superior in animated debate in which two other women clerks joined on my side. The young stiff-neck dismissed them angrily and told me I could do as I pleased about disposing of my excess but if I carried it I'd have to pay. Then he disappeared behind a door marked *Kontora*.

As soon as he had gone the young woman snorted after him, "Huh! The *Chef!*" spoke some fast Russian to the others, and then abruptly turned and packed my things back in the box. "Simply a blockhead!" I heard her mutter. From snatches of conversation I gathered that "the Chief" had arrived just the day before.

Without another word she tore up the receipt he had written out, stamped my luggage and ticket, and passed me through the barrier. Shortly afterward I saw her order a taxi and send the old peasant on her way. Later she came into the café for tea. When I saw her draw out some Russian cigarettes I offered her a package of Camels. She took just one.

"That was a very decent [*prilichni*] thing you did for me," I said, "and very Russian." I asked her if she would permit me to offer her a souvenir from Switzerland and tentatively proffered a box of Tobler's chocolates.

"Thank you, no," she said, exchanging a smile with her colleagues at the counter. "The Chinese need them more than I do. All I want from you is a box of *speechki!*" Evidently Russian matches were as bad as ever.

"*Bon voyage!*" she said as I left, to continue my journey reassured that the sense of humanity is not dead in Russia.

When we took off from Moscow at midnight, one of the Czechs aboard the big Soviet transport spoke to me in broken English. "So, you are an American writer? Going to *China?*" His eyebrows lifted.

As the only "validated" American at large in the People's Republic during the next five months I was to be greeted by many as a subject of mild wonder and speculation. Why was I there? Was I a secret envoy? Did my presence foretell some change in China's policy? Who knew what explanations of a mysterious mission lay hidden in the leather satchel I kept so carefully locked beside me? (Answer: old clippings, a Marxist handbook, Hamilton's *Mythology*, two Chinese dictionaries, a dozen blank notebooks, my toilet articles, a Hermès, and plenty of aspirin.)

I did less to allay the Czechs' curiosity than they did mine. There were six of them, with stout, bourgeois-looking wives (all wearing Bata shoes), on their way to serve two-year contracts as technical advisers in China—replacements, perhaps, for Mr. Khrushchev's Russians who were soon to begin their widely publicized trek homeward. The Czechs settled down to bridge at a few kopeks a point, and for hours I watched the northern lights stretch in a red banner nearly as far as Tomsk. There the true dawn spread over Siberia and its endless dark forests broken by somber black lakes and only occasional signs of human habitation.

We skirted a great new dam and power grid and landed at Irkutsk on a vast field full of the confusion of a half-finished building program. A long wait followed in a barracks-like edifice. Eventually we were fed black bread and a few slices of cold bologna and tea, which reminded me of my wartime days in Russia. Then we slowly passed through customs and immigration. A small host of Chinese youths in dark blue tunics and ballooning trousers joined us and we all entered a Chinese-manned Ilyushin jet, its immaculate interior décor all in familiar Peking style. Chinese stewardesses seated us. They wore dark slacks and high-collared crimson silk Chinese jackets, and their long black braided hair was tied with bright red ribbons. When we were aloft one of them brought me hot coffee and biscuits.

"*Ni hao?*" she said, in the greeting now universal in China. "You are well?"

"*Wo hao, hsieh-hsieh ni.*" My Chinese won a smile. She answered my questions briefly; she was a Peking girl, the daughter of a peasant family, a middle-school graduate, and had been an air hostess for two years. She and her good-looking assistants, who served a savory buffet luncheon, including Chinese wine or beer, made a first impression of courtesy and modern efficiency which I later found to be characteristic of China's main-line air service.

We flew all morning over Siberia and Outer Mongolia but saw only clouds and blue sky until we dropped suddenly over the jade hills of Jehol and crossed the Great Wall. Now the garden-like, well-watered fields of shaded colors and textures and the ancient plaid pattern of rural China unfolded toward the historic capital.

In a few minutes we landed at the new Peking airport, its wide paved runways flanked by a spacious modern terminal building. I knew that no visitor nowadays arrives in China anonymously, and I had supposed that some minor official would meet me. I was touched by an unexpectedly warm reception. Stepping from my plane into the bright dry June day, I saw a small group of people familiar to me from days of auld lang syne. Having been informed of my visit they had troubled to make the long journey out to the airport to welcome me.

I recognized Rewi Alley, a New Zealander who has lived in China for thirty years and has been a Chinese foster father many times over; Dr. Chi Ch'ao-ting, a University of Chicago graduate whom I had last seen in Chungking, where he was adviser to Dr. H. H. Kung and the U. S. Treasury representative; Huang Hua, whom I knew as a student leader when I taught briefly at the American-supported Yenching University; T'ang Ming-chao, whom I hadn't seen since he was editor of the *Daily News* in New York's Chinatown; Israel Epstein, a former United Press correspondent at Chungking and now a Chinese citizen and editor of the Foreign Languages Press in Peking; Y. Y. Hsu, an old colleague from the Chinese Industrial Cooperative days; and Dr. George Hatem, a remarkable American physician whose story I shall be able to tell in these pages for the first time.

We drove back to Peking on a wide macadam parkway, arrow-straight for forty kilometers and bordered by trees and shrubs. Substantial new structures surrounded by thick plantings of willows, acacias, walnut and fruit trees were identified for me: new research institutes, schools, the permanent agricultural exhibition pavilion, new factories, and many community buildings under construction. On the outskirts were long rows of landscaped brick apartments, and soon we passed Wai Chiao Ta Lou, the foreign diplomatic quarter, with its white homes and gardens built in Western style adapted to suit Peking's plans and tastes.

"There are only half a dozen embassies left in the old Legation Quarter," said Rewi Alley. "Eventually they'll all be shoved out here. The Quarter is gradually being rebuilt as the space is needed for more and more government office buildings moving that way." Then he added with a wry smile, "I'm living in Count Ciano's old quarters —the former Italian Embassy—myself. Quite posh. You'll see it."

Rewi and George Hatem were the two I knew best in that group. I had first encountered Rewi Alley in 1929. We became friends, and later worked together to found Chinese Industrial Cooperatives ("Indusco") during the Second World War, when I wrote a great deal about him.[1] Now he is widely known, especially in the British world, for his work in building early cooperative industry in China; for the unique and self-sufficient Sandan community he organized in the Northwest during the war—in some ways a prototype of the commune ideal; for his knowledge of Chinese character and the books he has written about it; and as the man to whom Joseph Needham, Cambridge's noted sinologue, dedicated the latest volume of his monumental work on China. Alley is, incidentally, one of the few British subjects who has turned down a knighthood.

"Fawncy me wearing a garter, now," he said when I asked him

about it. He had not long since returned from his native home in New Zealand, where he was a guest of the Prime Minister.

Alley was now in his early sixties. His blue eyes had lost none of their sharpness, but his red hair was sparse, his rugged frame sagged somewhat under its heavier weight, and his short sturdy legs were no longer the muscular pistons that had driven him across thousands of miles of rural China. Yet just the year before he had made an eight-month trip, he told me, retracing all the footsteps of his youth, to visit every province of the country. I had corresponded with Alley often, and read his books, so that he was no stranger even after twenty years. What had happened to Dr. Hatem since Pearl Harbor was much more obscure to me. I turned to him now:

"What about you, Shag? What have you been doing lately?"

"Married a wonderful girl. Two children, nearly grown by now. Bound up the wounds of the revolution."

"Is that all?"

"I helped wipe out syphilis in China. That's something. You know it's the dream of every doctor to rid a whole country of at least one disease he knows he can beat. We did it! Come over to our institute and I'll show you."

"Institute?"

"*P'i-fu Hsin-ping Nien-Chih-So.* We translate it, Institute of Venereology and Skin Diseases."

We had reached my hotel, the new Hsin Ch'iao (Overseas Guest House), a modern six-story edifice built just inside the Tartar Wall near Hatamen Gate, on what used to be Legation Street. Years ago I would ride down this street on my Japanese bicycle, with my beautiful white Kansu greyhound Gobi pulling me at the end of a leash, on daily rounds to press conferences at the foreign embassies. Now it was all-Chinese, like everything else in China.

"*Hsiu-hsi!*" (Take a rest!) was the welcome advice I was left with at the door. "You'll need plenty of rest to get ready for all that's ahead of you."

For two days I did not make any engagements, while I found my bearings in an old city now thoroughly renewed. Then I had a conference with Huang Hua, Mme Kung P'eng and other officials of the Foreign Office, and we worked out a proposed itinerary for presentation to Premier Chou En-lai. That I had needed "plenty of rest" to prepare for what lay ahead of me was a prophecy abundantly realized.

I cannot complain about lack of opportunity to *see* China. I was to travel, if anything, too extensively in the time I had available. In five months I visited scores of factories, hospitals, schools, urban and rural commune enterprises, projects large and small—dams, reservoirs, bridges and power plants under construction, steel mills, coal mines —from huge machine-building plants to porcelain factories. In many thousands of miles of travel I got close to the Siberian border in Heilungkiang, reached the sea at Dairen, retraced old steps in Inner Mongolia and the Northwest, traversed the Yellow River country and saw Chungking and West China again, spent some weeks in the Yangtze Valley and got as far south as Yunnan, on the borders of Burma and Vietnam. I saw something of nineteen principal cities in fourteen of China's twenty-two provinces before I left. My interviews with China's leaders, from Mao Tse-tung and Chou En-lai to the youngest cadres, numbered more than seventy. And I talked with soldiers, peasants, workers, intellectuals, students, composers, teachers, doctors, lawyers, scientists, journalists, actors, pediatricians, nurses, gardeners, ex-capitalists, lumbermen, nomads, prisoners, priests, ca-dres, ex-landlords, research workers, jailers, ballerinas, union leaders, housewives, movie stars, poets, inventors, acupuncturists, engineers, V.D. specialists, state planners, cancer specialists, former acquaint-ances, harp makers, gentlemen in the park, Mongols, Tibetans, Miaos, Lisus, Mohammedans, assorted foreign diplomats and one ex-emperor.

I talked to many such citizens alone, and often directly in Chinese, but that does not mean that I was given any clairvoyant power to enter into their private thoughts. At formal interviews there was gen-erally an official or an interpreter present, and nobody bares his soul to either one, especially with a foreigner around. Nevertheless, I think I know more about all these people than I could possibly have under-stood had I never returned to China.

2

The Quiet City

At the Hsin Ch'iao a small suite consisting of a sitting room, bedroom and bath cost me 24 yuan ($10)* a day, about as much as a highly skilled Chinese worker can earn in a week. A balcony overlooking the Outer City gave a view of the distant triple-tiered, blue-glazed round roofs of the Temple of Heaven, glistening above the carved marble altars where emperors used to offer annual sacrifices and pray for good harvests. I could see it only when the sun was relatively free of the heavy haze from new smokestacks, however, which was not often. The view was not generally worth the price of the suite, so I shifted to a fifth-floor bedroom and bath which, at about half the price, over-looked Legation Street and gave an opportunity to take note of everybody who entered and left the Hsin Ch'iao.

There are now a dozen substantial modern hotels in Peking, besides numerous inexpensive Chinese-style inns, and many new hotels have been built throughout the provinces. In former days Western-style hotel accommodation was scarce in China beyond the seaboard cities, but now it exists in towns I had never visited or scarcely heard of before. All these hotels are today managed by the China Intourist

---

* The official exchange rate, stable for several years, had been 2.44 yuan to U.S. $1.00. For statistical purposes it was generally figured as 1 yuan = U.S. $0.40.

Bureau, and many were built primarily to house the thousands of
Soviet advisers who once worked for China. Nearly all offered
satisfactory European as well as Chinese cuisine. Food served to foreign hotel residents was not rationed, and I learned that it was often
better and priced much lower in the provinces than at the Hsin
Ch'iao, where my meals averaged three dollars a day.

For the benefit of American tourists planning early trips to Peking,
I may as well add that the Hsin Ch'iao service was fully up to old
standards in politeness if not always in quality. The "foreign-style"
cooks and No. 1 boys for which the city used to be famous have scattered to become *maîtres d'hôtel* in the provinces. They were constantly
training new staffs. In the Hsin Ch'iao, as in other hotels I visited,
kitchens were scrupulously clean and servants were courteous and
conscientious. Quick to respond to appreciation, they politely declined
all tips.

Menials are not called "servants," "waiters" or "porters" (you can't
find a porter at a railway station) but are addressed as *t'ung-chih*,
"comrade," like anyone else.* They are much in earnest. If you want
special attention from a waiter or a room servant it is well to learn his
or her name and use it, and to find out what he is studying. Servants
don't spend their idle time playing mah-jongg now but sit by the bell
boards studying English or Russian, or other textbooks, getting ready
for after-hours classes; or they do *t'ai chi ch'uan* calisthenics. Even
old Fatty Wang, the headwaiter at the Hsin Ch'iao (who used to be
a "boy" at the Peking Hotel), could be seen out on the terrace every
morning at six-thirty going through the balletlike movements of *t'ai
chi ch'uan.*†

"It's good," he told me enigmatically, puffing in at breakfast one
morning, "for personal contradictions."

The hotel staff had its party cells, like all state enterprises. On each
floor there was a committee in charge of a workers' clubroom decorated with the usual posters, photographs, letters of praise (in lieu of
gratuities), wall comments and criticisms, a few pieces of furniture,
books, a radio and a television set which seemed available for general
use when not rented out to some guest. The floor committee held a
meeting once or twice a week and exchanged criticisms and self-
criticisms which I sometimes heard waxing warm when I returned at
a late hour. Warm but not boisterous, I thought to myself, when I

---

* *T'ung chih* is now the common form of address to a stranger. Formerly one could
address anyone in town or country as *Lao Chia*, "Old Family," but this has become
obsolete, just as *lao pai-hsing*, "Old Hundred Names," for "the people," has been
replaced by *jen-ming*, which carries more connotation of "the masses."
† To benefit fully from the seemingly effortless rhythms of *t'ai chi ch'uan* one
must understand something of their underlying philosophical principles, which
are related to Taoist concepts of unity and harmony as products of tension between
opposites. See pages 387-388; see also Sophia Delza's *Body and Mind in Harmony*,
N.Y., 1961.

remembered former Chinese conversations which had often sounded nearest mayhem at their peak of amiability.

Hotel employees also participated in a constant war against flies and mosquitoes, and small boys with butterfly nets competitively chased cicadas in the streets and parks. It was true that these old pests, as well as rats, mice, lice and fleas, were under better control in China than in most countries, and that stray cats and dogs had disappeared. Peking was not only much cleaner, more orderly and more disciplined; it was somehow far quieter. The capital had never rivaled Shanghai or Canton for bedlam, but now that public spitting, yelling, quarreling, gambling, drug dens, brothels, haggling in the market, peddlers' bargaining, and rickshaws had been eliminated, everything was more subdued than I remembered.

After eleven at night theaters closed, the electric buses stopped running, and only an occasional car or bicycle appeared on the brightly lighted broad main streets. Except for a night-long traffic of heavy cargo trucks and endless rubber-tired carts heard on the back roads, it was a silent city until dawn. I missed the old peddlers' chants of daytime, the trained pigeons that used to fly overhead and fill the air with music made by tiny flutes fixed to their tails, and the late-hour noodle vendor with his plangent cry.

Buses were unwontedly chaste and their girl drivers and conductors deferentially polite to the foreigner. Invariably some youth would be stirred to arise and offer me (mistaken for a Russian comrade) a seat which it was not always easy to decline. Buses discreetly sounded horns and pedestrians observed traffic lights and posters instructing them on the right and wrong ways to cross streets. People automatically gave right of way to the two-wheeled miniature buses which carried six or eight kindergarten children tandem behind pedicabs piloted by aging rickshaw men.

Taxis (Soviet, East and West European, and American makes) were available at hotels and the new central railway station. A few two-seater pedicabs also occasionally appeared. Near the Hsin Ch'iao I picked one up, pumped by a neatly dressed gray-haired gentleman who said he had pulled a rickshaw at the old Peking Hotel in the "preliberation" days. I managed a bit of local dialect and he responded cheerfully, to ask me how I liked "new" Peking.

"It's cleaner, more modern, more beautiful," I said. "It also seems very quiet."

"Quiet? Yes, I know what you mean." He laughed over his shoulder. "People are quiet—but the radio isn't quiet!"

I asked him how things were with him and he said *"Ma-ma hu-hu,"* meaning so-so. Then he added, "I couldn't afford a wife in the old days. Now I have a wife who makes a few yuan in the commune [*kung-sheh*] factory. Our daughter works in a nursery [*t'ou ehr-so*]. Who ever heard of a nursery in the old days!"

He went on to say that he hadn't been able to work much lately. He was fifty-eight and he had a back ailment for which he regularly took acupuncture (*hsia chen pien*) treatments free of charge; for he belonged to a union now.

"If only we had more to eat; the imperialists—" he muttered. *"Nin shih na-i-kuo jen?"* (What nationality are you?) he suddenly called back.

"I'm an American," I answered.

He repeated his question and I my answer.

"Shuo li!" (Speak reasonably!) He turned, and seeing that I was serious he then pumped on in silence.

At the end of our trip I paid him the small regulation fare, which he accepted politely. "Truly an American?" I nodded. He smiled, wagged his head and pedaled off.

3

The Big City

After fifteen years of disuse I could still understand simple conversational Chinese but I could not claim fluency. In the written language, all the basic characters which I had once known well enough to translate vernacular literature were now so simplified as to be unrecognizable, and I had no time to learn the new system. Even limited spoken Chinese is useful, however—indispensable as a check on what one is told or not told by interpreters, and to pick up stray bits of conversation here and there.

During my visit no foreigner of any nationality left Peking, or any other city he might be authorized to visit, without a travel permit. Permits were closely restricted in time, space and availability. Every foreigner was regarded as a guest whether he paid his way, as I did, or not. Whether or not travelers spoke any Chinese they were met on arrival anywhere by a Chinese Intourist guide or an official or cadre (state or party functionary) of some kind who escorted them on their scheduled visits. Such attention is not simply surveillance; the average foreign visitor would be completely lost without an interpreter. Where it does amount to interference it is rather pointless; any traveler with good eyesight and some ear for the language learns almost as much that may be unfavorable to the regime as he would learn if he moved everywhere entirely on his own, and sometimes he learns more. One must not forget also that there really are spies in China and elementary precautions are justified. I was spared some of the official overprotection and managed privacy now and then. I also had old friends, Chinese and a few foreign residents, who took time out from busy lives to conduct me on excursions or otherwise serve to alleviate my ignorance. Within municipal limits visitors are generally free to make solo trips, except to a few clearly marked military zones.

The language problem alone is an effective barrier to "individual" research and most strangers perforce keep on well-worn paths. Heart-to-heart political talks with casual strangers are hardly feasible for anyone as conspicuous in China as a Caucasian, a Negro or any non-Mongolian. Much less can any visiting mogul get to the "bottom of things" in five days of banqueting and official interviews. Nor could I in five months.

Invited guests of the state did the routine conducted tours; foreign diplomats often suffered long delays before even seeing the inside of a factory or school. They complained that for them to get to know any Chinese except embassy clerks on terms of some intimacy was very difficult. They rarely got beyond the capital. Clare McDermott, the able Canadian correspondent of Reuters, the only English-language news agency represented in China, had been waiting for weeks, when I arrived, to see his first commune; he was still waiting when I left. The same was true of the Yugoslav correspondents, and the correspondent of Agence France Presse.

To be "confined" to Greater Peking, the political and cultural heart of an ancient civilization, was not exactly punishment, as I kept telling Clare. Now a small state in itself and administered as such, it is five thousand square miles in area, and ranges from the Grand Canal to the Great Wall. As everyone knows, Peking is one of the world's most beautiful capitals, and physical changes wrought by the new regime have not destroyed the inner harmony and integrity of the older city.

The main palace grounds and buildings in the center are intact and well kept. Within them lie the Purple or Forbidden City, and within that the Tartar or Imperial City, which dates back to Kublai Khan's capital, Tatu, and to foundations of more ancient palaces. The central scheme of Peking, a broad south-north road about five miles long, reaches from the Temple of Heaven, through a series of gates in the Outer City, to the entrance of the Imperial City at T'ien An Men (Heavenly Peace Gate), which now faces the world's largest paved public square. Here more than a million people can gather or disperse in less than an hour, between the imposing new Great Hall of the People, where the National Congress sits, the Museum of History, and the Museum of the Revolution. At T'ien An Men's golden-tiled double roofs the central axis pierces vermilion walls and continues through the Forbidden City, flanked by great palace halls, to a series of artificial lakes and wooded hills surmounted by graceful pavilions and temples now used as public parks and playgrounds. Modern traffic circles have been built around the massive gates, but expansion has necessitated eliminating most of the old outer walls, which are being replaced by circuitous new roads. City planning limits building sites and heights and generally seeks to preserve the broad and open beauty of the past.

With a population of about seven million, Greater Peking is three times as large as when I called it home for five years in the thirties. As a "modern" capital it dates largely from the fifteenth century, but it was a political center of North China millennia ago and, if you want to go back to Peking Man, "people" have been multiplying hereabouts for half a billion years. Bits of *Sinanthropus pekinensis* are housed in a special museum, but the skull and the greater part of the once magnificent collection of fossil bones disappeared during the Second World War.

Among the pleasures of living in this old city in my youth I count the highly stimulating friendship of two remarkable men who helped to unearth and identify Peking Man. One was Dr. Amadeus Grabau, who was the real founder of modern Chinese geological study. His "pulsation theory" of the dramatic leaps in geological history—particularly as it applied to the sudden and relatively recent rise of the Himalayas and the Tibetan plateau—also implied a fascinating theory of combined revolutionary and evolutionary mutations of man from the lower primates to the atom-toting personages of today. The other was Pierre Teilhard de Chardin, a lovable French Jesuit who was a brilliant conversationalist. Life for him was a continuous process of reconciling his scientific discoveries and theories (which strongly suggested an arboreal past for early man) with Church doctrinaires firmly determined to permit no monkeys in the family. Both men are honored among Chinese scientists today but (curiously) no attempt has thus far been made to find a place for Dr. Grabau's pulsation theory in the literature of Chinese historical materialism, where it seems to belong.

Peking has its dozen other notable museums, modern and ancient libraries, its score of lake-dotted parks and pavilions, the temple-strewn Western Hills, numerous new and old theaters, cinemas, restaurants and recreational centers. One new stadium seats eighty thousand people and another, built exclusively for table tennis (now second only to basketball as a Chinese national sport), was completed in time to seat fifteen thousand people for the international ping-pong matches of 1961. Wide streets, lengthened vistas, hundreds of new apartment houses and modern government structures—varying from early Stalin-type revolutionary and pretty bad, to later revolutionary (modified Chinese) architecture and increasingly good—extensive networks of extramural roads and highways running in four directions, and scores of new schools and institutes are transforming all but the old inner walled city.

Peking's famous bazaars and shops are no longer a tourists' paradise. I saw fine rugs, ivories, porcelains and embroideries being made here in state and commune factories, but they are mostly for export. The "cosmopolitan charm" visitors loved is gone; this is an all-Chinese city now and the old foreign resident would never feel at home—if he could find it. Much of the attraction of Peking for foreigners lay in the old Peking houses, with their walled courtyards and gardens, many of which have been converted into schools, workshops or multiple dwellings, or demolished to widen streets or erect new edifices that are practical and unaesthetic. Like New York.

Perhaps the greatest physical change is that the Outer City and suburbs have become a major industrial and steel metropolis based on nearby iron, coal and copper deposits. Peking now holds nearly a million factory workers. Housing has more than doubled in area in ten years but the shortage is still acute. Most families live cramped in one or two rooms, although newly constructed flats for state-factory workers are larger and better than anything they have known in the past. Fortunately the spacing and landscaping of "developments" in the suburban city conform to well-balanced zoning plans.

I shall have more to say about Peking, where I could easily have spent all my time without exhausting its interest; fortunately I was not obliged to do that. Travel facilities extended to me were far more generous than those granted even to Soviet Russian correspondents, or so they told me. At the outset I decided to confine my travel requests to the Foreign Office as much as possible to places I had known under Kuomintang rule. As I had roamed widely and to remote corners of China in the past, this would give me plenty of territory in which to judge changes and whether people were faring better or worse. My program seemed reasonable to Premier Chou En-lai. With his help, and with the aid of modern air transport and a much improved railway system, I was able to carry it out.

Before I offer an account of these travels it seems useful to remind ourselves that Red China is no mere compound of Marxist alchemy dating only from 1949. Rather it is the current chapter, and an organic part, of a very ancient and rich history wherein one may find pre-Marxist beginnings even of some institutions built by Chinese Communists of today.

"The entire man is to be seen in the cradle of the child," wrote Alexis de Tocqueville in his classic study of the infant American democracy. "The growth of nations presents something analogous to this; they bear all the marks of their origin." In the exciting and radically new society European immigrants were forming in the New World, which shocked and frightened the crumbling aristocracies of the Old World, De Tocqueville discerned "fundamental causes" in "the obscurity of the past." He observed that not a difference among Americans, "not an opinion, not a custom, not a law, I may even say not an event, is upon record which the origin of that people [in Europe] will not explain."

If that was true of a nation so immature and seemingly free to make its own future as the United States was in 1835, how much more mandatory it is to see China today as a point in time and space reached by a great people who have traversed a long, long road from antiquity.

4

Confucius to Mao

Vast libraries exist to "explain" China, and probably the most enlightening books written to answer the question Why Did China Go Red? are those by the man who led the nation to where it is today, Mao Tse-tung. Few who read these pages, however, will have found time to study even the four volumes of Mao's selected works already translated into English. To attempt to condense China's long history into a brief chapter may be an affront to scholars but excusable as a service to readers unfamiliar with the rudiments of that history. Confucius thought that if he showed a man one corner of a thing he should be able to discover the other corners for himself.

The stage which has witnessed what is to some "the world's oldest continuous civilization" and to others "the world's oldest continuous tragedy" is a multinational country with an area of about 3,705,000 square miles;[1] that is, a country ninety thousand square miles larger than the United States. China reached its present boundaries (including Tibet, Turkestan and Inner Mongolia) many centuries ago; in times past the empire was larger than today. Two-thirds of the People's Republic, however, is mountainous, desert, or land otherwise unfit for cultivation. Slightly less than 12 percent of the total area is now utilιzed as cropland and formidable problems must be overcome before substantially more marginal acreage can be brought under cultivation.* By contrast, 17 percent of the area of the United States is cropland (391,000,000 acres, as of 1959[2]) and a large portion of an additional 22 percent (now in grassland pasture) could readily be cultivated. With close to four times as many people as the United States, the Chinese must feed themselves on 40 percent less cropland. In order to equal American agricultural output, *per person,* China would have to raise her product per acre to almost six times as much—if confined to the present cropland area—as the American output per acre.

If one superimposed a transparent map of China on a map of the United States (see map, page 767), the two countries would correspond fairly closely in latitude and dimensions. Both lie mainly in the temperate zone. In the south, China would extend into northern Mexico and the Caribbean, and in the northeast it would reach far into Canada. China's southernmost point (the island of Hainan) would be at Haiti, and her westernmost area (Sinkiang or Chinese Turkestan) would reach a little beyond San Francisco. Shanghai would lie near Jacksonville, Washington would correspond to Peking, New York to Shenyang in Manchuria, and Los Angeles would be somewhere in western Tibet. The topographies differ greatly. China is landlocked except for her eastern seacoast. The world's highest mountain ranges and plateaus rim her southwest and western borders, and in the north lie the Mongolian desert and a frosty frontier shared with Soviet Siberia.

Until the nineteenth century the Pacific shut China off from, rather than connected it with, the outside world. China looked inward and was a land power, not a great maritime nation. Mountains and desert both sheltered and isolated her from continental neighbors and Europe. Contacts with the West existed but made little impact on the civilization that grew up along the Yellow River—whose origin, on that superimposed map, would be somewhere around Denver, and its exit near Richmond, Virginia. China developed in almost total isolation from the West. The term Chung-kuo, which the Chinese still call their country, means Central Realm. This Ptolemaic conception of the world remains deeply imbedded in Chinese psychology even today.

Legendary Chinese history begins more than five thousand years ago. Dates of the beginning and end of the Shang and Chou dynasties are debatable, but writing on oracle bones and on bamboo offers an increasingly authentic record from the later Shang Dynasty (1523 B.C. onward). The classical period in which the civilization acquired characteristics preserved into our times was the Chou Dynasty (1027-249 B.C.), and K'ung Fu-tze or Confucius (551-479 B.C.) was its

---

* Tibet, Turkestan (Sinkiang) and Inner Mongolia account for a large part of the mountains and desert, of course. Excluding those areas, from 15 to 20 percent of China is under cultivation.

outstanding personality. His teachings gradually became state doctrine, and after the Later Han Dynasty (23-220 A.D.) Confucianism dominated the social and political thinking and the whole form and style of Chinese civilization for twenty centuries.[3]

Lao-tzu (whose name means "Old One"), a whimsical mystic said to have been a contemporary of Confucius, preached a rival philosophy of *Tao*, or "The Way," of harmony with nature, which has little in common with Confucian doctrines. Lao-tzu's teachings embraced a concept of the unity of opposites and dialecticism which had similarities with Platonism and many points in common with Hindu and Buddhistic philosophy. Lao-tzu was not a religious teacher, but his thought was corrupted and combined with traditional geomancy in what became the native religion of China, Taoism. The dialectical nature of the *Tao Teh Ching*, which contains the essence of the "Old One's" philosophy, suggests analogies with the schematic analytical methods of dialectical Marxism. (The authenticity of writings attributed to both Confucius and Lao-tzu is much disputed by scholars. Lao-tzu is far from established as a historical person.)

Confucius was not a religious teacher either. With some reservations it may be said that China was never essentially a religious country so much as a nation ruled by morals, ethics, conventions and philosophy. "Respect the spirits," Confucius is reputed to have said after a dialogue with Lao-tzu, "but keep them at a distance." He was China's first great reformer, a humanistic, practical codifier of the inherited wisdom of the ancients. He sought to "remold" everybody from ruling princes to peasants into "superior men," although he showed less interest in reforming nobles and aristocrats than in "undertaking to make men of humble background into 'gentlemen' able to hold their own in the halls of state with the most polished courtiers," according to one outstanding Confucian scholar and biographer of the sage, Professor Herrlee Glessner Creel.[4] Confucius himself wished "to become a man of perfect virtue and to teach others without weariness."

Confucius lived when the Chou Dynasty was breaking up into the "Warring States," and Chou sovereignty was only nominal over some five thousand petty principalities somewhat comparable to the contemporary city states of Greece. Chinese scholars revere Confucius for having edited the classics and having written the *Spring and Autumn Annals,* a work of literature as influential as the Bible and equally disputed as absolutely reliable history. A generation or more ahead of Periclean Greece, Confucius concerned himself with the same problems of human intercourse. His social and political teachings were moralistic, benevolent, traditional, realistic and authoritarian in contrast with the democratic and republican idealism and lively abstractions of Socrates, Aristotle and Plato. All were equally concerned with the qualities of virtue in rulers and the attainment

of an ideal society, but Confucius found answers very different
from those of the Greeks.

He prescribed a code of behavior between all members of the
family in which women obeyed and deferred to men, younger brothers to elder brothers, sons to fathers, and patriarchs to men of superior rank. All men rendered homage to the emperor, who was regarded as an embodiment of Confucian virtue and innate wisdom and
moral superiority, the Head of the Great Family or Nation. Dynasties
rose and fell but the Confucian pattern was changeless. Administration under the emperor lay in the hands of a small Confucian scholar
class, access to which was in theory democratic. Anyone who could
pass the examinations could qualify, and open opportunity represented the ideal of equality. In practice this meant a monopoly of
power held by a gentry-scholar class over peasant masses organized in
the family system and kept in order by filial piety, ancestor worship
and imperial edicts.

Confucianism provided China with the world's most stable system
of bureaucratic power. It was natural for the Chinese to look upon it
as the only "correct" method of regulation of human relations and to
regard themselves as superior men. China was never challenged by
any advanced civilization until modern times; though sometimes defeated by culturally inferior tribes, she always ended by civilizing
and absorbing them. Chinese civilization made original advances in
the arts, science, industry and agriculture, and Europe borrowed
many of its inventions. Treating their immediate neighbors as vassals,
the Chinese conceived of the rest of the world as barbarians, much as
Rome looked upon the Huns.

Capsulated Chinese history inevitably leaves the impression that
nothing really happened after the Chou and Han dynasties. That would
be as erroneous as to assert that in Europe nothing happened after
Pericles until Copernicus was born. Immensely important changes,
refinements and creative contributions to human culture continued
despite long interregnums of regression under barbarian conquerors.
As instances become relevant, I shall cite a few as we proceed. For the
moment, three examples of Western loss through isolation from the
Middle Kingdom: the Chinese were using elaborate water clocks six
hundred years before one was independently invented in Europe;
water-powered armillaries were turning in China three hundred
years before Copernicus; and the Chinese invented printing roughly
five centuries before Gutenberg produced movable type. China lost
much from isolation also: for instance, Europe invented the mechanical
clock in the fourteenth century, but it did not reach China until the
seventeenth century, and although China invented gunpowder hundreds of years before the West, she failed to develop the uses of her
marvelous firecrackers in time to avoid prolonged humiliation at the
hands of the Christians.

For centuries China had some contacts with the West, but nothing her merchants and travelers reported changed her opinion of Europe's inferiority. Occasional envoys were received as representatives of vassal states and a few early Jesuit missionaries at the Manchu court were tolerated more as curiosities than as cultural equals. China's isolation from the West was finally broken in the nineteenth century, when it was invaded from the sea. From the 1840's onward the British and French wars forced China to permit the importation of opium and other trade with the West. Britain took Hongkong and Kowloon, and extended her control over Burma and Nepal, which had been tributary vassals of Peking. In 1883, France defeated China and ended her suzerainty in Indochina. During the latter half of the century the waning Manchu power was repeatedly humiliated by violence, as China's major ocean and river ports fell under foreign control and she became a semicolony not of one nation but of all the major industrial and naval powers. A series of territorial and political concessions gave the foreigners effective control over China's trade and she seemed destined to be divided among them like India and Southeast Asia.

Objectively, we must not forget the provocations which the Chinese offered to the West. There they sat at home, aggressively refusing to import opium and other useful commodities brought to their doorsteps. What the Chinese tended to consider invasion was fully understood by Western Christians—except for a few sentimentalists like Mark Twain—to be altruistic effort for China's own good and salvation. The mandarins were arrogant, ignorant of modern machines and weapons, and inclined to regard both Western merchants and missionaries as readily expendable whenever they went far beyond the protection of their gunboats. China's laws were severe and punishments were often cruel; no foreigner who had an armed alternative would submit to them. Western historians of the period were therefore quite right when they justified the breakdown of China's seclusion and independence as sanctified by both the Bible and Darwin's laws of progress.

However, the Chinese had to be taught fear and respect before they could realize their own backwardness, before they could recognize the superiorities of Western culture, and before they would concede a few pieces of real estate for the establishment of military bases from which it could be demonstrated that China had a profound need for things which the most-favored nations were determined to sell to her at good profits. Even today she has not fully learned the lesson, as may be seen from continental China's stubborn refusal to recognize that it is the Christian duty of the United States to decide what kind of government should prevail on Chinese territory. Yet there was a time when the Chinese tried very hard to see the Christian point of view.

In the middle of the last century there occurred the T'ai-p'ing ("Heavenly Peace") Rebellion, a titanic effort to overthrow the corrupt

Manchu Dynasty and establish a revolutionary power. The rebellion, which reached the walls of Peking, was led by an able Chinese Christian convert, Hung Hsiu-ch'uan, who proclaimed himself the younger brother of Jesus Christ. Members of the Peace Corps today might tolerate a revelation of this nature by a promising nationalist in the Congo, but it was too much for our rigid nineteenth-century missionaries. They disowned their most promising convert as a sacrilegious impostor. They were even more shocked by some of his Christian reforms. Although there is no evidence that T'ai-p'ing leaders had ever heard of Marx or the *Communist Manifesto*, they had many points of similarity. Reformers in Chinese history from pre-Confucian times had reported (e.g., *Rites of Chou*) early equalitarian societies in which land was held in common and production and distribution were shared by all. T'ai-p'ing leaders made attempts to establish this kind of primitive communism. Land was distributed, with priority given to men between sixteen and fifty. Slavery and the sale of women and children were abolished together with foot-binding, prostitution, arranged marriages and polygamy. The importation of opium was prohibited, and torture and cruel punishments were supposedly forbidden. Armies participated in production and tilled fields in common, much as on a state farm today.

After a decade of civil war said to have cost forty million lives, the rebellion was finally defeated by the Manchus with the help of Western mercenaries, first led by an American adventurer, Frederick Townsend Ward, and later by General Charles Gordon and other regular British army and navy officers, supported by the British government. The victory cost the West its one great opportunity to baptize China in the name of the Christ. It cost the Manchu Dynasty subservience to Western imperialism until it finally collapsed from inner rot, more than from outer assault, in 1912.

Japan had meanwhile joined the imperial overlords; in 1895 she defeated China, seized Taiwan, and ended China's suzerainty in Korea. With financial support from the United States, Japan fought Russia over the Chinese territory of Manchuria and defeated her. As prizes she took over the Russian naval base at Port Arthur, Dairen, and Russian railway rights and concessions in south Manchuria—all of which had also been pried from Peking. Tsarist Russia retained Siberia (annexed the previous century), railway concessions in north Manchuria, and a protectorate over Mongolia—where, however, Peking's sovereignty was still nominally recognized.

All through these years the reformist spirit and patriotism of the T'ai-p'ings continued to seed the underground revolutionary movements, as it later also persisted throughout the Nationalist and the Communist periods. In 1900 the secret societies provided the leadership for the fanatical antiforeign Boxer Rebellion. When the Boxers were crushed by an Allied invasion of Peking, the European powers,

Japan, and the United States together imposed crushing indemnities on the dynasty which robbed it of all remaining prestige. By the time it faded away not only the major powers but small states such as Belgium, Holland and Portugal had become part of the Western dominance which made China a semicolony. The United States took no territorial concessions but fully shared in the whole system of unequal treaties by securing for its nationals all the privileges of the "most favored nation"—a euphemism also reflected in the so-called Open Door policy. Under the unequal treaties foreign nationals had extraterritoriality rights which enabled them to reside and do business in China while remaining accountable only to their own courts.

Following the demise of the Manchu Dynasty, attempts were made to set up a parliamentary republic, for which the nation was wholly unprepared. Western-educated Sun Yat-sen, an exiled hero of the national independence movement, was elected president of the provisional republican government. He lacked armed forces and was obliged to defer to the former chief of the imperial troops, Yuan Shih-k'ai. When Yuan subsequently proclaimed himself emperor he was quickly overthrown by rival militarists. Disunity and chaos reigned as provincial satraps struggled for supremacy and the foreign powers vied with each other to control them. Meanwhile, Sun Yat-sen and the Kuomintang, or Nationalist party, which he had founded, made alliances with various warlords. Repeatedly he failed to establish a stable basis for a successor to the weak, corrupt, semipuppet and largely impotent central government at Peking.

Dr. Sun was spurned by all the foreign powers until after the First World War, in which the Peking government had, as a result of great pressure from the United States in particular, joined the Allies. China had expected that the defeat of Germany would result in the rendition to her of Germany's colonial holdings in Shantung; at Versailles the Allied Powers revealed that they had (except for the United States) signed secret treaties awarding the Shantung concessions to Japan. All Chinese patriots were bitterly disillusioned. These included many youths who had volunteered for service in Europe and had gone there as leaders of China's labor corps. (Chinese were then considered unfit material for soldiers.) Among these were several men prominent in China today—Chou En-lai, for example—who remained in Europe and studied there. Mao Tse-tung also helped recruit such "coolie armies" but at the last moment he chose—a fateful decision—to stay in China.[5]

One of the results of the resentment aroused by the Versailles Treaty was the May Fourth Movement of 1919, led by Chinese students and intellectuals, in which Mao Tse-tung participated. It had important cultural results—a reform in the written language and rejection of many remaining influences of Confucianism—as well as political consequences. In awakening the patriotism of the nation to resist and finally defeat Japan's effort to reduce China to an outright colony (through the 21 Demands) students and intellectuals demonstrated an astonishing moral and political power and foreshadowed an end to warlord rule. By exposing the hypocrisy and cynicism of the Versailles powers, the movement opened all China to the inflow of revolutionary ideas stemming from the anti-imperialist Russian revolution. At this time Sun Yat-sen turned to Lenin for help and there at last he received it.

Soon after seizing power the Bolsheviks had made generous overtures toward China. These included voluntary renunciation of the unequal treaties, the return of territorial concessions, and an offer of joint operation of the Chinese Eastern (Manchurian) Railway. Moscow maintained relations with the foreign-dominated Peking regime, but meanwhile Lenin's correspondence with Sun Yat-sen opened another prospect. It led eventually to the Bolshevik implementation of a new strategy to promote world revolution by supporting colonial nationalist leaders.

It was not until 1920 that the first piece of Marxist literature was translated into Chinese: the *Communist Manifesto*. Out of the intellectual ferment germinated by changes within China and by the October Revolution, the Kungch'antang or Chinese Communist Party arose in 1921. Following the entente between Dr. Sun and the Bolsheviks (represented by Adolf Joffe) in 1923, the Nationalist and Communist parties formed a united front. Its platform was Dr. Sun's *San Min Chu I* or "Three Principles of the People." These principles were known as "nationalism, livelihood and democracy." In brief, somewhat oversimplified terms they meant national liberation and unification; restoration of China's economic independence and the regeneration of rural life; and universal education and enlightenment of the whole nation in preparation for a modern, popular government.

Sun Yat-sen seized a base in Canton and the Russians sent money, arms, military advisers and experts in revolutionary techniques of political organization and propaganda. The Communists were permitted dual membership in their own party and the Kuomintang. In his last days (1925) Dr. Sun said of the principle of livelihood, "It is socialism and it is communism." Chiang Kai-shek, a Japanese-educated officer and one of Sun Yat-sen's young followers, was sent to Moscow and received special training there. Following Sun's death, Chiang Kai-shek was groomed as his successor by the Russian advisers. In 1927 the Nationalist revolution, under the supreme military leadership of Chiang Kai-shek, was victorious over most of China. In the same year Generalissimo Chiang broke with the Communist party and made membership in it a capital offense.

By 1928 four-fifths of the Chinese Communist Party had been exterminated. Forced underground, its urban leaders continued to observe directives from Moscow, while Stalin headed the Comintern, but attempts at proletarian insurrections were disastrous failures. Meanwhile Mao Tse-tung had gone to the deep hinterland, in Hunan, to begin a guerrilla movement with its base in the peasantry. For ten years a civil war as savage as the T'ai-P'ing revolution—and still claiming direct historical descent from it—raged across South China. The basic "three principles" remained the common heritage of both the contending parties. The Communists brought to them a Chinese Marxist interpretation of throughgoing social revolution while Chiang Kai-shek struggled to retain private ownership as the unalterable fundament of all three principles.

Throughout this whole epoch following the demise of the Manchu Dynasty, China's "traditional society" underwent a continuous disintegration. What Chiang attempted was to replace it with a capitalist state in China under a military dictatorship. It is a mistake to assume that his struggle with the Communists was over either the restoration of "traditional society" or its final destruction. "Traditional society" had already been shattered by the impact of foreign industry, science and capitalism. The struggle between the Reds and Chiang Kai-shek was quite simply over whether China's modernization was to be achieved by private enterprise under the dictatorship of a very weak bourgeoisie, or by a proletarian revolution, led by the Communist party, to establish public ownership over the basic means of production and to mobilize "the whole people" and their immense labor power.

Chiang Kai-shek and his bureaucracy were not elected but seized power. Before the Japanese occupation, the Kuomintang (membership about two million in 1938) held the cities against the Communists with armed garrisons, police, and some foreign help. As far as the peasant majority was concerned, "government" simply meant the Kuomintang-appointed county magistrate who ruled as of yore in collusion with the landlord-gentry of the district and their local armed guards—10 to 20 percent of the population.

In the contest between Chiang and Mao, time was decisive. Modern capitalism had begun more than a century late in China. As the nation reluctantly accepted the superiority of science and mechanized industry, intellectuals despaired of ever catching up by emulating the nineteenth-century West and using its agonizingly slow and painful method of "capital accumulation" through the private exploitation of labor and national resources. Even so, Chiang might have won against the Communists had they not received "providential" help from Japanese imperialism.

When Mao said that imperialism had "prepared the material as well as the moral conditions"[6] for Communist victory in China he spoke literal truth. It was not the Communists but Japanese imperialism whose deep penetration and occupation of urban China (1937-1945) crippled the bourgeoisie and destroyed Kuomintang morale. In doing so it opened the countryside to the proselytization and organization of the peasantry by the Communists. Japan's war, originally launched under the slogan "To eradicate communism in East Asia!" had the double effect of destroying Western colonial dominance in China and making it possible for Mao Tse-tung to arm the massive peasant fist of a renewed T'ai-p'ing Rebellion—this time led by Marxists, not Christians.

As early as 1936 Mao Tse-tung had foreseen these consequences as inevitable, and I myself had summarized his convictions in *Red Star Over China:*

> Thus . . . a great [Japanese] imperialist war, which is almost certain to assume the character of a world war, will release the forces that can bring to the Asiatic masses the arms, the training, the political experience, the freedom of organization, and the mortal weakening of the internal police, necessary for a revolutionary ascent to power . . .

In this sense Marx's prophecy that "capitalism digs its own grave" was fulfilled not only in Asia but also in Europe, where two great wars wrecked the old society. As George Kennan recently observed:

> It was not . . . Communist efforts which destroyed the old order in Europe itself in the thirties and forties and eventually delivered the eastern half of the continent into Communist hands; it was Hitler who did this . . . And, similarly, in East Asia, it was not Moscow, and least of all Washington, which really delivered China into the hands of the Communists; it was the Japanese . . .[7]

Mao Tse-tung did not create or command the forces of Japanese imperialism but his understanding of them enabled him to seize leadership and control over the energies of nationalism and patriotic resistance, to win a sovereign victory for social revolution.

5

Paotou Retrospect

In Peking I was invited to a cocktail party to renew acquaintance with some professors, writers, soldiers and other people who remembered me from former days. My host was Liao Ch'eng-chih, with whom I had worked on Mme Sun Yat-sen's China Defense League in days when China and America were allies. Liao is the son of Liao Chung-k'ai, who was Dr. Sun's closest colleague. Today Liao Ch'eng-chih is chairman of the Overseas Chinese Commission, a cabinet-level post, and a director of the China Peace Committee, which might be called the Anti-American-Imperialism Committee.

I found myself talking to a thin, hollow-chested guest who gazed out of lashless eyes behind heavy-rimmed glasses. He had a bad haircut and, in blue cotton work clothes, was the most simply attired person there. If he had not been munching hors d'oeuvres from one hand and holding a glass of wine in the other I would have thought he had wandered in by mistake. Yet he looked vaguely familiar; as I knew most of the guests there I thought I should remember him.

"What kind of work are you doing now?" I probed.

"I am a gardener," he said. "I work in the botanical gardens of the Academia Sinica. I specialize in tropical flowers."

"Oh, you're a horticulturist?"

He spoke some English and must have understood me. He replied, through an interpreter, in self-accusation: "My crime helped to cause the deaths of millions of people. I should have died for it. Instead of that I have been given a chance to repent and to work for socialist construction. I am quite happy at my work, very happy for the first time in my life because for the first time I am doing something useful."

Here was indeed a sinner wearing his remolded thoughts on his sleeve.

"You are," *said the Chinese beside me, having enjoyed my mystification,* "speaking to the former Manchu emperor, Hsuan T'ung." *The boy emperor—P'u Yi. He was now fifty-four. At the age of eight he had been sitting on the Dragon Throne in the Forbidden City when the first revolution forced his abdication. Later he had lived in exile in Tientsin. In 1935 the Japanese spirited him off to set him up as the puppet emperor K'ang Teh of Manchukuo. Captured by the Russians in 1945, he had been returned to China only a few years ago. I had always assumed that P'u Yi had been kidnaped by the Japanese and I asked now if after all he should really feel guilty.*

"Oh, yes," *he told me.* "I worked willingly with them. I felt ashamed to have lost my family's power and I believed the Japanese would help restore it. I cost the lives of millions. Any other country would have killed me. Instead, they have let me work at what was always my hobby —gardening."

He had fared a lot better than the Romanovs, at any rate. Someone later told me that the best of it for P'u Yi was that he had finally been able to divorce two of the three wives to whom others had married him. He was now living the relatively tranquil life of a monogamist.

"And today you support socialism?" *I asked.*

"Yes, certainly!" *he said.* "Socialism is good." *He proposed a toast which was on everybody's lips that day:* "To the friendship of the Chinese and American—people!"

Beginning and end are like a circle, says the Chuang-tzu; *where there is end there is the beginning. P'u Yi had reached the end.*

"Climb in! We're late and trains leave on the dot these days."

Rewi Alley shifted his big frame to make room for me as I got into the taxi, which took us to the new Peking station. Under a wide translucent dome supported by feathery, powerful lattices of steel, stood China's first escalator and other innovations of the large new terminal: public baths, reading rooms, nurseries and laundry facilities for mothers, various shops, a theater, television, and restaurants with Chinese and European cuisines. The food was expensive for most Chinese (three to six yuan a meal), as was true of all off-ration restaurants, but it was still available to those who could pay. A few months later, with the bad news of massive crop failure, most off-ration restaurants were closed down, although meager meals continued to be available in metropolitan railway stations to travelers provided with special ration coupons.*

On the walls of an all-sleeper train of pale green cars, trimmed in yellow, were signs in characters as well as romanized Chinese which casually proclaimed: *Peking-Urumchi Express.* In four days one could now do a twenty-five-hundred-mile overland journey to Chinese Turkestan. When I lived in Peking, Turkestan was accessible only by camel caravan and months of travel across the Gobi.

Alley and I were not going to Turkestan. We were on a four-hundred-fifty-mile trip to Paotou (pronounced Bao Toe), which used to be the frontier end of the line and is now autonomous Inner Mongolia's largest city. I missed by only a year making it the thirtieth anniversary of a summer excursion taken when, still wet behind the ears, I first met Alley during the height of a great famine in the dust bowl of Northwest China, between northern Kansu-Shensi and the Mongolian steppe.

From 1938 to 1941 I had spent much of my time and energy helping Rewi Alley and others promote Chinese Industrial Cooperatives. That had meant raising money abroad to keep Alley in the field as chief technical adviser in the organization of those wartime handicraft production units which later helped to maintain and develop successful guerrilla warfare against Japan. Until recently Alley was director of the Sandan[1] technical training school which he organized in Kansu. It is now headed by one of his adopted children, Alan, a Chinese orphaned by one of the great floods of the thirties. Rewi has many books in print and is constantly writing and translating poetry.

"How do you spend your spare time here?" I asked him.

"Officially I am the New Zealand resident delegate to the International Peace Committee. That makes me chief receptionist to visiting British firemen."

"That's a good idea—peace."

"That's all I've been looking for ever since I got my arse shot up in the First War. But you don't get peace, old boy, without fighting them as wants war."

"Everybody I know agrees on peace—especially on one thing. It's always their neighbors who want war. There's another thing they agree on. Much as they love peace, they love real estate more. I never heard a politician make a speech in praise of peace who didn't end up saying he wouldn't give up an inch of territory for it. Not even one teensy-weensy inch."

---

* Ration tickets were required at this time for grain (raw or cooked), oil or fats, sugar, meat, cloth and a few other items. Rationed items were inexpensive and within the means of all. "Off-ration" restaurants sold food at prices prohibitive for low-income people except as an occasional luxury or treat. Rationing is discussed in Chapters 59, 63, 70, 71. 80 and 81.

"Especially if it's somebody else's real estate. Would you call Taiwan a teensy-weensy inch?"

"Careful, there. That makes you a peacemonger." That's what he was, too. A hard-core peacemonger.

Beyond Peking we passed the growing Shihching Shan (Mountain) iron and steel complex, surrounded by a modern town within sight of the Jade Fountain, the old temples of Patachu, and the imperial hunting parks. All around were green hills now heavily afforested. A new line was being built to encircle and by-pass Peking; this Shihching Shan spur was part of it, an alternate route which now runs to Hualai, on the Inner Mongolia frontier. It was in the process of double-tracking, which involved many new tunnels and bridges to get through the Taiheng Mountains. Hundreds of workers were camped in clusters along the blue-green Yungting River, their red flags flying over white tents or marking the day's advance of battalions on the job. In the early evening their campfires flowered along the river bank and some of the men turned to wave to us.

Rewi told me there were 65 tunnels and 273 bridges between Peking and Changchia Pass (Kalgan), on a hundred miles or so of track. It seemed an understatement. Between blackouts the air was good, cooled by the river and hills freshened by young trees all the way. This country was now well watered by canals and the new Kuant'ing Reservoir, and by the Miyun Dam, beyond Hualai. There, below the Great Wall, we rejoined the main line for Paotou.

Railway mileage in China had about doubled—to 24,000 miles—in ten years and highways had increased by five times—to 270,000 miles—but both were still far behind the need of so large and energetic a country; reservations on express trains usually had to be made far in advance. (In 1959 the United States had 259,000 miles of railroads and 3,510,000 miles of rural and municipal roads.) China's railways are standard gauge and Chinese factories now make all types of rolling stock. The equivalents of first, second and third classes are soft, medium and hard, the last being simply wooden seats, while medium provides narrow berths ranked in tiers of three. "Soft" is a compartment with well-upholstered comfort. Fares are about half those in the United States and service considerably better in both quality and spirit.

We had a compartment finished in blue plush, with a retractable dining table, rose-silk-shaded lamps, and fans. A radio offered Chinese and Western music broadcast on the train, interspersed with pep talks and educational programs; it *could* be disconnected. A hot four-course Chinese dinner (3.50 yuan) was served in the compartment by a waitress, her hair done in pony-tail style, who as usual declined any gratuity. Before you leave one of these de luxe trains the head-waiter brings around his guest book, asks for suggestions and complaints, and beams with satisfaction at a few words of praise.

"It's better than the old gondola I rode in when I first met you up here, remember that?" asked Rewi. "Whatever became of that Kuomintang bantam with you that summer—Napoleon Li, or something like that?"

"Wu—C. T. Washington Wu! Just before the revolution one of his friends told me Washington was a worried man. He had become impotent. Since then I haven't heard of him."

Washington wasn't his real name but it's close enough for a brief recollection, if I may be forgiven for plagiarizing myself by repeating a story partly told elsewhere.[2]

Mr. Wu was a technical expert with the Ministry of Railways. I was working for a paper in Shanghai and doing a series of articles on railways then in use, two years after Chiang Kai-shek had established the Nationalist capital in Nanking. The Ministry had lent me Washington Wu's services but he knew very little about railways. He was a Kuomintang "cadre" of that day, a returned student from America who had been given a sinecure for various family reasons. What Washington lacked in technical proficiency in one profession he more than made up as a connoisseur in another.

At the end of a hard day of sightseeing he would reach his room in a Chinese hotel and shout for the *lao-kuan-ti*, or "old-fix-it." That omnipresent factotum would appear bearing steaming water and hot towels. While Washington was still wiping the dust from his face and hands he would give sharp instructions to the porter, who would *shih-shih* (yes, yes) him and leave. In a few minutes there would be a knock at the door and in would come a young girl or maybe two or three together. Washington would look them over, pinch a behind or two, and make a city man's joke. As a rule he would reject the first offering. "Old-fix-it" would be rebuked for sending in a flower-face (pockmarked girl), and eventually a rosy-cheeked lass would be found acceptable. He would do her the honor and a few minutes later be ready, the technical expert, for an evening banquet.

I smiled in recollection and said to Alley, "Washington told me that the women of Kalgan were supposed to run horizontally—that old smoking-room joke of the West. I can't remember whether he ever found out."

The cities of China used to swarm with prostitutes, and the sale of women was a thriving industry. Girls as well as boys were sold to brokers for indentured labor and pretty girls found ready buyers as concubines, teahouse waitresses, or common street *piao-tzu*. The more talented and stronger became singing girls and sometimes emerged as prosperous house mothers, but the great multitude had a short life as cheap prostitutes and slaves of their owners and procurers.

All over China the poorer peasants were being steadily driven from the land by confiscatory taxes and excessive rents. In the regions of prolonged drought in the Northwest millions were completely destitute and the sale of children was especially widespread. Foreigners in Shanghai would say, "These Chinese are heartless; they think no more of selling a child than a pig." But in an International Settlement where an official burial detail was continuously on duty and used to bury tens of thousands of corpses annually picked up from the streets and canals—they were mostly victims of infanticide—there were worse fates than being sold into service.

Washington had wanted to end our trip at Kalgan but I insisted that we go on to Paotou; I wanted to see the famine country. Not far out of Kalgan we came to a small station on a hot dusty plain and drew up beside a gasping locomotive pulling some freight cars packed with wan, half-naked, hungry children and women. No passenger trains were operating. Our caboose had been attached to a west-bound train made up of a few good wagons and an open gondola or two. Out of a crowd of black-topped Chinese I suddenly saw a carrot-haired foreigner emerge. It was Rewi Alley.

Employed at the time as a factory inspector by the Shanghai International Settlement, he had chosen to spend his annual vacation in the famine region with a handful of foreigners who ran a few soup kitchens and were offering food and shelter to those still capable of working on the Sa Tao Chu irrigation canal near Kueisui. I introduced myself to Alley and after talking to him I asked Washington to let him sleep in one of the unoccupied bunks in our caboose. He refused. He didn't like "imperialists," especially "missionaries," and he had an idea Alley was one of them. They were "always talking about China's backwardness."

We went on to the end of the line at Paotou and to Wu's disgust I spent several days with Alley riding into the ghost towns and the deserts which had once been fertile plains. There for the first time I saw children dying by the thousands, in a famine which eventually took more than five million lives but was scarcely noticed in the West. Seeing it was an awakening point in my life; it remained the most shocking of all my experiences with war, poverty, violence and revolution until, fifteen years later, I saw the furnaces and gas chambers in which the Nazis, too impatient to wait for mere starvation, exterminated six to seven million people.

Except for the International Famine Relief Commission's canal project, run by O. J. Todd, an American engineer, and Dr. Robert Ingram, a medical missionary whose special task was to delouse the labor gangs to keep typhus and plague out of the camps, practically nothing was being done for the hordes of ragged, penniless refugees driven to the dusty mud-walled towns in search of food. Hundreds of last-ditchers sat or lay on the streets or doorsteps dying before my eyes. Relatives were too weak to bury them, but at night they disappeared. Human flesh was openly sold in some villages.

Twenty million people were seriously affected in that winter of

1929-30 and in the equally terrible seasons that followed before the drought ended its three-year scourge. Vast acreage passed into the hands of moneylenders and absentee landlords, from the Great Wall southward to the Wei River Valley. During the next dozen years there would scarcely be a time when famine, flood or war did not strike some large area of China. In every case the same confiscatory economics would be at work, the same exploitation of human tragedy going on unchecked, the same degradation of the farmer, the constant growth of a landless peasantry, and the making of re-cruits for eventual revolution.

That summer Alley adopted his first Chinese orphan, a boy he picked up among the human debris of the famine. He called the child Mike and took him to Shanghai to be educated. I remember him as a little fellow with solemn eyes, then as an honor student at St. John's University, later as a young engineer working with Rewi when he was building industrial cooperatives to help the guerrillas fight Japan. And now I had just seen Mike in Peking, as friendly as ever, tired from overwork, proud of his talented wife and a promising son and charming daughter. He was in charge of an important project in the Academy of Sciences.

Twilight had fallen while Alley and I reminisced. Here and there the fires of coke ovens or small blast furnaces burned through the night. Before them dark figures moved in silhouette, and on the horizon I could see the giant poles of new high-tension power lines with their multiple arms stretched out like the many manifestations of the Buddha, toward the wide steppe beyond.

At ten o'clock the reading lamps on our train were turned off, as is the custom.

"You have a lot more to show for our experience than I have, Rewi," I said. "You made a man out of that famine. A good man and a good family." Alley was already asleep.

6

Steel in Mongolia

Few visitors to this land have been even as far west as Paotou during the past decade. As it has now undergone an astounding transformation, to become China's main heavy-industry base for the development of the Middle Northwest, and is also a principal political base in Mongolia, it is worth some detailed notice here. A few paragraphs of history may help place it in time and space.

Kalgan is the gateway to Paotou and to a million square miles of plateau which form historic Mongolia. Ruled as a single nation under China's suzerainty until late in the Manchu Dynasty (1644-1912), Mongolia was divided when the expanding Tsarist Empire set up a semiprotectorate over the northern or "Outer" half, called Wai Meng Ku. During the revolution the Bolsheviks pursued White Russian leaders into Urga (now Ulan Bator), where they helped create the Mongolian People's Republic after overthrowing the Lama priesthood and the princely descendants of Genghis Khan.

Although the Soviet government continued to recognize China's nominal sovereignty over *all* Mongolia, Moscow made an armed alliance with Outer Mongolia and stationed troops there. Mao Tse-tung said in 1936 that when the Chinese revolution was victorious Outer Mongolia would "automatically become a part" of a socialist federation of China.[1] In 1945, Stalin exacted Chiang Kai-shek's full recognition of Outer Mongolian independence, however, when he signed the Sino-Soviet military alliance against Japan with the Kuomintang government. That alliance died a natural death once Mao Tse-tung achieved victory, but Outer Mongolia retained its independence and is still a military ally of Moscow.

Thirty years ago the Kuomintang government had begun actively absorbing southern or "Inner" Mongolia by incorporating it into Chinese provinces known as Ninghsia, Suiyuan, Jehol and Chahar. The People's Republic formally reversed the Kuomintang's policy of physical obliteration of Mongolia. Under the Communists the frontier provinces mentioned above, together with a large slice of western Manchuria, were "returned" to the Mongols and were combined into today's Inner Mongolian Autonomous Region. In size it is roughly comparable to, and in population (about ten million) nearly ten times larger than, the Mongolian People's Republic.

On a map the Inner Mongolian Autonomous Region may thus impress any Mongols at Urga who might still favor unification with their southern brothers. But the new cities of Inner Mongolia are largely Chinese, so are most of the advanced agricultural lands, and in the whole region Chinese now outnumber Mongols by at least six to one. The great grasslands and plateau are still pastoral domains of the Mongol nomads, and where Mongols predominate they form a majority in locally elected councils. They are all subject to directives from the sovereign Communist Party of China, of course, as is true in all autonomous regions, including Tibet, but each minority nationality has its own party, also. The term autonomous is administrative more than political—they have nothing like independence—but the revolutionary modernization of the Mongols' economy now in process was probably inevitable if they were not to be extinguished as a continuing people.

Possibly more than a third of the population of Inner Mongolia lives in the area served by the Peking-Paotou section of the railway. Beyond Kalgan the two principal cities are Kueisui, officially known as Huhehot and now the capital of Inner Mongolia, and west of it, by about a hundred miles, the sprawling old and new cities of Paotou. Huhehot and Paotou are now joined (via Tsining) by the new railway to Outer Mongolia and Siberia. On our map of China and the United States superimposed (page 767) the location of Paotou would roughly correspond to that of Des Moines, but its climate is similar to that of North Dakota and its place in China's future scheme of economy more like Chicago's or Pittsburgh's.

Passing through this ancient land west of Kalgan I counted fourteen small and medium-sized new iron and steel mills, with power plants and settlements of workers clustered around them. One of these, the Shih Hsuan Hua No. 1 Steel Works, was the focus of an entirely new industrial city built up for about two miles along the railway. Here and there spur lines came in from the north, bringing coal and ore from newly developed mines. Near Huhehot the buildings of a large modern rolling mill, under construction, stretched for nearly half a mile. Around all the metallurgical developments substantial steel and concrete factories and new brick apartments were rising. Little building in the old mud-brick style is done nowadays; brick kilns seem to be everywhere you look.

On this line you are seldom out of sight of a factory smokestack of some kind, and blue-clad men and women working at every conceivable task. It was like the unfolding of one of those old Chinese scrolls which depict the whole life and activity of a community seen in cross-sections. Flags flew before labor battalions digging or building, or moving coal cars up steep trestles to coking ovens; drums throbbed; dust flew. Each of the plants meant swarms of workers drawn to the plateau, housing to be built for them, roads and streets, more transport, and above all, more food demands. We passed many half-finished settlements of red brick planned around town squares with shops, a theater, a school, administrative buildings and public playgrounds.

The old Paotou I remembered was a few thousand tumble-down buildings and a dusty main street. It is now called East Paotou, and the new or main Paotou railway station lies about five miles farther west. The area in between was rapidly filling up with factories, residences and streets connected with the new steel town by a wide macadamized road which would soon be the main thoroughfare of a single city. Scores of tall chimneys on the horizon told the story of the older town changing at a pace to match the new.

In ten years Paotou had grown from a war-torn and famine-ravaged frontier town of 90,000 survivors, to a metropolis of 1,320,000 inhabitants.

We put up at the Kun To Lun, a new hotel which covered a city block. It consisted of one main building of five stories and an annex. Between them lay a spacious garden complete with fountain and plaza. The main building had a hundred large rooms, each with modern bath and each with an all-wave radio set; on mine I heard the Voice of America from Manila and United States Army broadcasts from Tokyo. Among the programs relayed to me here was one which discussed China, the United States and the United Nations. I remember that among the participants was Harriet Mills, who was then teaching Chinese at Columbia University. The daughter of American missionaries in China, Miss Mills had once been imprisoned in Peking, "thought remolded" and released. Despite that experience, her views seemed to me admirably objective and better informed than those of others on the panel.*

* See pages 371-374.

The balcony of my room overlooked, on one side, a range of red-brick apartments; across the road straggled blocks of old adobe huts with clay chimneys, interspersed with patches of sunflowers (grown everywhere on marginal land for their seeds and oil) and green vegetables. Two miles beyond, the new road ended at the huge half-completed Paotou Iron and Steel Works. It was flanked on both sides by more apartments and by public buildings, schools, an opera house, a hospital and modern shops fronted with Mongolia's first plate-glass picture windows. Near a new bridge a stadium had been completed. Masses of tents clung to the outskirts and I learned that more than 100,000 people were living in them. Of these tent-dwellers 17,000 belonged to construction gangs putting up subsidiary buildings for *Paokang*—the steel mill—and more housing for its 66,000 workers.

My informant was Li Chih, the mayor. He had invited us to lunch, together with the deputy manager of Paokang, a Mongol named Wu Lichi Najen, and some other officials. Mayor Li was a wiry Hupeh man of forty-five, with a well-shaped shaved pate burned as brown as his face. He reminded me of Yul Brynner. I knew almost without asking that he was a guerrilla veteran of the old Eighth Route Army, the Paluchun.* There is something different, a quiet self-confidence without arrogance, a genial manner of authority, and usually a sense of humor, which readily distinguishes these older combat Communists from the sedentary party bureaucrats.

"Yes, everybody here was a guerrilla," Li said, his glance sweeping all the Mongols and Chinese at the table. "First we fought the Japanese, then we chased out the Kuomintang. When we had won we laid down our rifles and immediately picked up tools."

Li Chih had been Paotou's mayor since 1951. He said that the Japanese and the Kuomintang had left him with two industries, a power plant of 500-kilowatt capacity and a mill that turned out 200 tons of flour a year. Today there were 273 state and municipal industrial enterprises and more than 1,000 small-scale *kung-shih* production units. Paotou was producing railroad equipment, lathes, heavy machinery, power tools, all kinds of building materials, processed foods (including packed beef and mutton) and textile machinery. Output value in the whole area in 1949 had not exceeded 10,000,000 yuan, according to Mayor Li. The 1960 target was 1,200,000,000 yuan ($500,000,000). "And we'll exceed it," said the same authority.† Quite possibly they did; but the same would not be true in 1961 and 1962, for reasons which develop in further chapters.

---

* After the Nationalist-Communist truce of 1937, the Chinese Red Army was reorganized as the Eighth Route Army. With its base in Yenan, in northern Shensi, it carried on guerrilla warfare behind the Japanese lines deep into northern China.
† The figure would mean a per capita output value of about 1,000 yuan yearly, or, at official exchange rates, something like $416—extraordinarily high for this

Greater Paotou City includes seven *ch'u* (boroughs), and like most
of China's new industrial metropolises it embraces suburban agricultural and natural resources around it. The aim is to achieve integrated urban-rural self-sufficiency. Under Paotou's administration is
the rich new Mongolian iron-mining center of Pai Yun Shan (White
Cloud Mountain), which is directly connected with Paokang by an
electric railway eighty miles long. One whole borough is entirely
agricultural and pastoral. The regional sugar industry, centered on a
large submodern factory far in the suburbs, is also run by the municipality. Mayor Li added that the local beet crop had been largely
ruined by drought and a siege of pests new to the area and immune to insecticides in use there. The mill was closed down.

"No, we can't say we have achieved anything like food self-
sufficiency here yet—though we have a better meat supply than most
areas. Even if we had good weather, farm output wouldn't take
care of the tremendous growth. Farms are short-handed; we're behind on the new Paotou-Yellow River canal, which will double local
production. We haven't had a real rain all summer—and we get only
four months of frost-free weather and one crop a year. It will be a
hard winter for us but nobody will starve. Nothing like you saw here
in 1929. Paotou is no beggar. We're making things farmers need and
we'll trade for food: steel, power equipment, machinery, agricultural
tools. We'll soon be making big locomotives, cranes, trucks, tractors,
too—"

Staples were already closely rationed in Paotou, as elsewhere,
but I saw no beggars, starving people, ragged urchins, or signs of
mass famine. Steel workers, miners and other heavy-industry workers
stand in top priority on rations all over China, of course.

There was also the problem of housing, and in Paotou's long win-
ters shelter was vital.

"Yes, we're behind in housing," Mayor Li went on. "How do you
keep ahead of a city that grows fourteen times its size in one decade?
The Kuomintang left us nine hundred thousand square yards of mud
buildings filled with vermin. Since 1952 we have built five million
square yards of clean brick dwellings with lights and running water.
We have killed the rats, fleas and lice and wiped out epidemics and
venereal disease. But we still have only fifteen square feet of housing
space to a person—and we're expecting four hundred thousand more
immigrants here within two years! Why? To man new factories we are
building, to extend irrigation works, to open up new farms on the
steppe. Your government keeps telling you people that China wants

part of the world, even in an area undergoing rapid industrialization, with emphasis on heavy industry. Here "output value" would be relatively meaningless unless one had an index of commodity prices related to world market values.

war. Oh, I know that, all right, but, Mr. Snow, we simply don't have time to fight any wars—except for living space right here at home. Of course we'll give the imperialists more than they're looking for if *they* start any wars against *us!*"

The personable Mongol manager of Paokang took us to see the mill: five square miles of belching smokestacks, acres of pipes, sidings, cranes, and different kinds of steel processing plants. One of 156 major projects undertaken by China with Soviet aid, and built under the supervision of Russian engineers—all of whom had now left—Paokang had begun producing early in 1960. By now it had a turn-out rate of close to a million tons of steel a year and 700,000 tons of iron. With a target of 1,500,000 tons of iron in 1961 and hopes of 2,500,000 tons of steel in 1962, Paokang would rank as one of China's five major metallurgical centers. The largest, at Anshan, Manchuria, had a 1960 output of about 5,000,000 tons of steel—which Paokang planned to reach by 1965; the other main centers are at Wuhan, on the Yangtze, the cluster of small new mills in Anhui and the large Shanghai mills which in 1960 reportedly produced more than two million tons. Paokang's ambitious targets were destined not to be reached as early as 1962, however.

Slogans on the pipes, walls and buildings exhorted workers to do their utmost, quoting Mao and party texts. Giant white letters on a duct caught Rewi's fancy and he translated them: "Liberated Thinking Liberates Production." As we watched steel poured from a great furnace, drums began to beat and gongs were sounded. A detachment of young women and men in white overalls arrived to present a red banner of achievement to a girl I photographed manipulating a mammoth overhead crane. I was told that she had just completed a thousand "missions" without a mishap.

Somehow none of this meant as much to me as the thousands of shade and fruit trees planted along the highways, around the factories, and running up the low hills. I kept remembering the dying trees, those that were still standing here in 1929, stripped of their leaves and bark for food of sorts, by starving human locusts.

But before I fell asleep that night I thought: It has taken me most of the day to see one steel mill and I know nothing of the communes and the many factories we passed. What one person can learn anywhere in China in one day is sharply limited. I wondered drowsily about how this city of more than a million new inhabitants, dropped suddenly on a relatively backward agricultural base, would be fed. The mayor had said the region could not meet 60 percent of its grain requirements. From how far away would come the needed supply of at least five hundred tons a day? What about other mushrooming cities along this same railway stretching westward to Sinkiang and southward to Lanchow—fifteen to twenty million people probably also tight on food? The new single-track railway was hardly adequate even to carry vital industrial materials and products. Imbalances between the demands of a rapid urbanization and industrialization and the supply and transport capabilities of the grain-rich plains and valleys of central China to meet them were certain to develop, it seemed to me.

7

White Cloud

The mayor assigned Lu Ch'u-tseng to accompany us on a hundred-mile trip into the Mongolian steppe. Lu was a tall, thin Hupeh man who had fought the Japanese around the famous guerrilla base in Wu T'ai Shan, in Shensi, the mountain stronghold of the Eighth Route Army. His dome was shaved smooth as an egg and was shaped like one. He had a friendly grin, large white teeth, and a vast store of energy and local information. Paotou's official chief of protocol, Lu had been chairman of its Support Korea Committee and its Sino-Soviet Friendship Committee. But the Korean War was over and the Soviet advisers had left, and now here he was, a paradox, temporary chairman of the Welcome Old American Friends Committee, membership strictly limited.

We left Paotou in a new green Volga sedan and journeyed northward through dust and construction which reached along twelve miles of paved highway. Then a gravel and dirt road led into a brief stretch of granite hills. A new highway was being built on the flank of a dry river bed, where hundreds of men working on the project were gathering stones by hand. Farther on, turning from an empty country, we came upon a settlement of tents and new brick houses. Everything was covered with red dust, including men and camels hauling loads up a narrow valley stream. On one side engineers were directing work on the scaffolding of a dam and future power plant.

"Iron country," said Rewi, gazing at the broken ferrous earth. "These hills are full of it." Workers stared curiously at our car. Seeing foreign faces grinning back at them, they waved their red arms in greeting. "This is a spot where bandits used to ambush caravans in the past. Safe as main street now." In two days of riding across this country we saw no armed guards. I had no personal bodyguards anywhere on my travels, and saw none.

Abruptly we emerged from rocky hills and arroyos into rolling prairie something like our Dakota country. On these irrigated lands, margins of the true steppe, pastures alternated with fields of buckwheat, oats, barley, sorghum, corn and wheat. The air was fresh and cool. We passed one large state farm where tractors and motor-driven pumps were doing most of the work. Throughout North China generally the old water wheels are rapidly disappearing. Here I remember a photograph I missed: a woman dressed in a gay jacket and red trousers, her pigtails flying and her face flushed as she trotted out of green gardens on a black horse, precariously balancing a huge market basket on one knee and a child on the other. Far on the road we passed a Mongol pony pulling a cart heavily laden with produce on the top of which, unexpectedly, were perched two shining new red bicycles; and I missed that picture too. Christmas for somebody, and nomads on bicycles.

Rounded purple mountains gradually lowered into wide grazing lands, the flat-roofed villages thinned out; for a few miles we saw only grazing cattle, sheep and goats and no houses at all. Then in the middle of a vast plain we saw, several hundred yards beyond the gravel road, a village of new brick dwellings erected in a semicircle around a two-story hall and school building surmounted by a large red star. We stopped and I hauled out my Bolex to take a panorama and a telescopic close-up. From the village a strong young man wearing Mongol boots ambled up the pathway and stood watching me with detached interest. We learned from him that we were at a production brigade headquarters of the Hsing Hsing Hsi Commune made up of Chinese and Mongol farmers and cattlemen. It ran forty miles in one direction and twenty-four in another.

"What do you eat here?" he was asked.

"*Pai mien* [white flour] and greens."

"What's your ration?"

"Not enough."

"What's not enough?"

"Fifty-three catties."

We all smiled and he seemed disconcerted. This was nearly sixty pounds a month, twice the average Peking ration; it seemed nothing to complain about. I did not pursue the matter, but afterward I thought we had not heard his whole story. This was meat-eating country and if he was not getting mutton no amount of flour would substitute.

Mr. Lu had urged us on. We were overdue at White Cloud, the iron mine, still some miles beyond. Late in the afternoon there arose a vision of tall chimneys and moving cranes, automatic shovels and bulldozers creeping over iron hills served by an electric railway. It seemed a mirage on this broad prairie sea, but the mine manager who met us was real enough. Wang Yung-shou looked twenty-five but was also an Eighth Route Army veteran and said he was almost forty. He had never seen a mine until he was sent to Pai Yun three years earlier to build this mechanized little city from scratch.

"There wasn't even a yurt* here when we began," he said.

"How did you learn mine management?"

"Fighting the Japanese—and the Kuomintang." He grinned. "We had some Soviet comrades for technical advisers. I learned from them. They've all gone home now."

A Mongol named Wu Lung was city chairman; he was an ex-guerrilla too, and had been here since the beginning. With pride he took me on a tour. Pai Yun, population twelve thousand, already had a theater, capacity one thousand, a two-story school building and a large workers' club, each building a block long. New dining rooms were displayed; so were the power plant, hospital, new apartment buildings, the small hotel where we spent the night, and the mine itself. Pai Yun's deposits of very rich ore had never been worked before. They were, together with neighboring reserves, said by Director Wang to be adequate to supply Paokang for "many years." Output quota for 1960 was 2,400,000 tons, "which will be overfulfilled." (I can't recall visiting any mine or factory where "underfulfillment" was predicted.)

Pai Yun mine was certainly moving at a good rate. The modern plant seemed adequate to goals set for it, and buildings everywhere were already in full use, although paved streets and sewers were just being laid.

Skilled underground miners in China earn as much as many university professors, who are among the highest paid state employees. Work at Pai Yun was mostly above ground and the workers, in two shifts of eight hours each, received a minimum wage of 36 yuan and a top of 120. Like all state enterprises, Pai Yun offered free medical care and spare-time schooling; unemployment insurance, a pension plan and other welfare benefits were provided by funds to which workers contributed. Rents were minimal and food better than average. Work clothes were furnished gratis. Winter temperatures here reach 40 below Centigrade and fur hats, sheepskin coats, padded suits and heavy boots were also supplied free.

---

* A Mongol tent made of felt and erected over a light wooden lattice, as every crossword puzzler knows.

Rewi hadn't seen Pai Yun before, but he took its sudden appearance from nowhere much more for granted than I did. "You'll get used to this; China has built a hundred and sixty-five new cities since the revolution," he said. "There are also a hundred and forty completely rebuilt cities like Paotou. I spent most of last year looking at them in every province but I still missed quite a few." [1]

I was well satisfied with what I saw of the condition of the Mongols and the respectable role they had in the direction and management of this town and a modern enterprise far beyond their possibilities in the past. At dinner that night I congratulated the young officials, Chinese and Mongol, and Chairman Lu Ch'u-tseng of the Welcome Old American Friends Committee. Warmed by the food and a little wine, my hosts inevitably recited the achievements of socialism, pointed out its obvious peaceful intentions and good will toward the whole world, and then asked me to explain how the American people could tolerate their oppression under an "imperialist government." Out of sympathy with the gross and repeated errors of American policy toward China as I was and had been for years, I nevertheless found these moments awkward. Chinese are no different from other people and most of us find it easier to pronounce judgments than to discuss facts.

An old reporter is always uncomfortable when asked whether his neighbor is still beating his wife. The "American imperialism" question was usually posed in that way. America is a faraway Thingamajig to most Chinese, just as China is to Americans. It is very hard to help anyone understand in a few minutes how a Thingamajig works, if he has never seen one. This is especially true if the person has it firmly fixed in his mind that this particular Thingamajig exists solely for the purpose of launching world wars.

In Pai Yun, I had to solve the problem by bringing up an extraneous matter, the reasons for the problem of overproduction of food in the United States as compared with the current underproduction in China. My hosts were very much interested in what I had to say about the stupidity of the American solution—to subsidize farmers to grow less grain. The reasons why China could not subsidize farmers to grow *more* grain were of course well understood by them—if not yet by me. It was then possible to conclude dinner satisfactorily after I proposed a toast made to me by an old veteran on a collective farm I once visited in Russia.

"To the triumph," he had said, "of all that is good in man!"

"*Kan-pei!*" (Bottoms up!) we all said.

8

Mongol Commune

Up at six, we breakfasted on ham, eggs and a local cheese vaguely like Parmesan. By seven we were on our way to Hsinpailike, or New Wealth Springs, a Mongol commune in the Pailingmiao district of Autonomous Inner Mongolia.

For a few miles beyond White Cloud we saw virgin land being cultivated by Chinese farmers to supply the mining town, still largely dependent on imported grain. More than ten million *mou* (1,660,000 acres) of Inner Mongolia were already planted in wheat, I learned from Lu Ch'u-tseng, and output averaged four-fifths of a ton per peasant cultivator. Most of this lay far to the east of Paotou. The Mongolian economy is being rapidly agrarianized wherever suitable conditions exist; more and more Mongols are becoming settled farmers and animal husbandmen as cattle breeding and a new dairy industry supplant the old nomad economy of camels, horses and sheep. Besides exporting beef and mutton, Mongolia now supplies North China with increasing quantities of milk, butter and other dairy products used largely by nurseries, hospitals, sanatoria and hotels.

By far the greater part of the ancient Mongol domain above Paotou remains wide grassland, however, in which we soon found ourselves.

For an hour we drove across blue prairie and low hills where herds of horses and flocks of sheep grazed. Here and there were clusters of felt yurts, smoke drifting lazily from their campfires. Then far on the horizon a dagoba spire came into view and soon we arrived at a lama temple called Hsila Tulu. We passed four lamas on horseback and drove beyond some cattle barns to draw up before a whitewashed mud wall. Commune headquarters.

Inside the gate we were met by the young chairman, Jenkejin Noru, small, wiry and rugged. He wore a green cotton gown over black boots, and a gray cap with a bellows top and a long bill pulled low upon his smiling eyes. Committeemen around us were clad in short gowns pulled in at the waist by bright sashes, worn over soft trousers tucked into black-leather riding boots. A middle-aged Mongol woman, also in boots, was introduced as a vice-chairman. Her wind-burned face was as dark and seasoned as saddle leather and wreathed by thick hair tightly plaited. On one side of the compound a trio of yurt-shaped whitewashed buildings stood linked together in a row, a doorway opening into the center one. Waiting beside it was a smiling, booted Mongol girl in a long gown of bright green silk, girdled with a sash of pale pink. Her stiff bobbed hair was adorned with another pink ribbon, which matched a silk scarf tied round her buttoned-up collar. She welcomed us at the threshold.

"Our secretary," said Jenkejin Noru.

Inside the yurt we sat on cushions laid on low benches around a hearth in the middle of one chamber. The floor was covered with clean felt and before each of us was a small red-lacquered table piled with Mongol delicacies, "all products of the commune." There were small, rock-like pieces of cheese, fried wheat fritters, brown sugar and a kind of sorghum. All these ingredients, together with some nameless condiments, were mixed in a cup of buttered tea over which the girl secretary, Precious Spring, wielding a giant brass kettle equipped with a foot-long spout, poured a warm, sweet, milky liquid. This was assiduously renewed as fast as any portion of it was consumed. The honorable name for this hors d'oeuvre I cannot now recall, nor do I soon (begging the pardon of my hosts) care to renew an acquaintance. Mongol taste for the ultrasaccharine and for clashing color in costume—like the warmth and earnestness of Mongol hospitality—reminded me of bedouins I had encountered in Arabia.

"I wonder if I could not just have the rest of my share packed for shipment," I said to Alley after a fourth libation from the kettle of Precious Spring, "to Owen Lattimore."

"Lattimore," Rewi responded unsympathetically, "never had it so good on his *Desert Road to Turkestan*."

"I wish he were here to speak to the Mongols for us," I said. It was bad enough trying to learn anything through one translator. Now everything had to be repeated twice. If the commune was having any problems I doubted that Jenkejin would get them past his interpreter to me. (Not that I could have solved them for him!)

Trilingual transmission gradually revealed that New Wealth Springs was a cattle commune regionally administered under the Tao Mao Integrated Banner at Pailingmiao, fifty miles east of us. In 1958 five "advanced cattle cooperatives" here had amalgamated to form the present commune, consisting of four production brigades made up of twelve teams of herdsmen and a few farmers. Population, surprisingly small: 2,200 adults. Animals: 90,000 sheep and goats, 12,000 horses and mules, 7,000 cows, and 2,000 camels. Grazing lands covered roughly 400 square miles and the commune also cultivated 3,200 acres of grain, mostly for consumption by local livestock.

Flocks and herds and yurts here had been restocked and built up with state loans. Ownership of the cattle and livestock was held by the teams but the commune as a whole owned and operated veterinary, artificial insemination and breeding stations, a meteorological post, a hospital and some health stations, one theater, a telephone line, and a small tractor station. A dairy industry produced dried milk and cheese and there was a small garment factory, a brick kiln, a leather tannery and a blacksmith shop.

Here, as elsewhere in Inner Mongolia, it was claimed that about 90 percent of Mongol children under ten years of age were in primary schools. New Wealth had sent 230 graduates to Huhehot and Paotou to learn more about animal husbandry and combustion engines. In the past, literacy among Mongols was confined almost exclusively to the lamas and nobility, less than 10 percent of the population. According to one writer, Inner Mongolia now had 20 "institutions of higher learning"—including medical, veterinary, engineering and normal colleges; of some 10,000 registered students, more than 1,400 were of Mongol or of other nomadic origin.[1] A substantial number of Mongols, both men and women, had already been trained as technicians. I was told at Paokang that more than 1,500 were learning metallurgy there.

"Last year we had 252 live births in our commune," said Jenkejin as he showed me around the village. "In one year before the revolution only one child born in this whole banner lived till the next year. In former times we used to say that we had more women than men, more lamas than children, more old people than young, and always more deaths than births. The animals survived better than people, but anthrax frequently wiped out whole herds. Now things are different. We have modern medicine and hospitalization, our children are healthy, anthrax is under control, plague and syphilis have been wiped out."

Jenkejin was a party member, of course. So was his Chinese deputy chairman, who did most of the interpreting from Mongol, as Jenkejin knew little Chinese. This was his story, as I wrote it down:

"Our banner was led by Prince Chimiteh Jenching Kaoerlo, and my parents were poor nomads under him. Princes were all-powerful then; we were Chimiteh's subjects. He was one of the anti-Japanese princes. When he refused to collaborate the Japanese captured him and carried him off to Pailingmiao. There he was tortured and killed. Chimiteh became a Mongol hero and our people still speak respectfully of him. We have no more nobility now, of course, but Chimiteh's children live here and work like other citizens and are much respected.

"After Prince Chimiteh was killed our people hated the Japanese, and many more of us were robbed, tortured and strangled to death by them. The year before the end of the war, when I was eleven years old, my grandfather was arrested and accused of connections with the Paluchun. He had sheltered a few Red soldiers but that was all. The Japanese tortured him but he could not tell them anything. They let him out, a wreck, and soon afterward he died of heart failure. I was beside him and I wept. The Japanese were slaughtering and eating all our animals and we were starving and had no money. My father died next, then my older brother, then my mother. Finally there was only my sister, my grandmother and myself.

"Then I joined the revolution—that is, the Paluchun. I attached myself to a company of Mongolian Red cavalry led by Paluchun men trained at Yenan. At that time I was so small I could not get on a horse when I was carrying a rifle and comrades had to help me. Soon afterward the Japanese surrendered and Kuomintang troops came to replace them. There was no difference except that the Kuomintang was worse. Anybody who had anything left was called a collaborationist or a Red and was robbed and beaten or killed. We had more than a hundred Kuomintang troops feeding on us here at that time. I went back to guerrilla life with the Paluchun and fought until we finally drove the Kuomintang out of here in 1947."

Back in the commune headquarters we found that a feast had been prepared and set up under the supervision of the versatile secretary, Precious Spring. A baby lamb roasted whole, in Mongol fashion, sat royally mounted on a saddle of white rice. I blanched when I saw it surrounded by more "products of the commune" such as had already somewhat jaundiced my appetite. But this visit provided for my hosts the excuse of a rare feast, I knew, and I dared not slight it; besides, the lamb was irresistible. With it were served bottles of colored liquor which matched Precious Spring's green and pink color scheme. I think it must have been straight vodka dyed and heavily sweetened. Jenkejin tackled it with the audacity of a guerrilla and there was nothing perfunctory about the sincerity of repeated toasts to his guests— including the first American he had ever seen. As Alley would sip nothing but soda water, I had no choice but to respond to Jenkejin's obvious desire to communicate his good will by this most ancient and honorable language of the cup which binds men in true brotherhood.

"To the friendship of the Mongol and American people," said he quite without reservation. "*Kan-pei!*"

"To the Mongol," I returned, "in all of us."

The effects were warm and exhilarating and the aftereffects not as disastrous as I had feared. We were still able to spend the afternoon inspecting some of the nearby herds of young horses and watching exhibitions of riding, led by Jenkejin himself, and demonstrations of the Mongol method of lassoing—by a noose fixed to the end of a long pole.

A man about ten years older than Jenkejin rode up and was introduced as a production brigade leader. He wore a mustache and the general air of bravado about him was enhanced by a fur-trimmed silk hat, topped by a large coral button, which crowned his head at a sporty angle. The button, I was told, was formerly reserved for nobles but now was the mark of brigade leadership.

As we inspected some of the commune buildings I heard reports of rapid growth: cattle and livestock increased five times in ten years, commune income up 45 percent just since 1958, all due to state loans and credits for the purchase of new stock and equipment. "A hospital, schools, a theater, veterinary specialists, telephones!" said the leathery lady vice-chairman. "Whoever heard of that around here in the old days?"

These were new things and good things for Mongolia, there was no doubt. There was also no doubt that the general growth was partly explained by Chinese immigration. The Mongol banner families numbered 1,320 adults, an increase of 130 percent since 1949, but of the total of 2,200 inhabitants 880 were Chinese. They were farmers and construction workers, I was told—all enjoying full residential rights. The construction workers, Jenkejin explained, were temporary; but I had a feeling that more Chinese farmers were on the way.

Late in the afternoon we drove down to visit the lama temple I had asked about. Half a dozen lamas still lived in quarters nearby but the temple was closed. While we waited for a lama I was informed that there were five temples in the commune. When I asked whether any of the small party with me believed in religion or attended services I was answered with smiles and negative headshakes.

"That's for the old people," they said.

"That's for *some* old people," corrected Madame the vice-chairman.

A monk with a heavy fuzz of beard and wearing rumpled yellow robes appeared and opened the temple, smiling obsequiously at us. Everything was intact, including walls filled ceiling-high with dusty sutras, and a roomful of prayer wheels, gongs, gilded gods and candelabra flanked by vases of paper flowers. At my request the monk picked up one of the brass trumpets, carried it out to the terrace with the help of Jenkejin, and blew a deep blast. It caused a horse to shy. The trumpeter was still a young man. I wondered how he could be a lama.

"Why not?" the chairman answered. "He has known nothing else since he was a child."

"But is that still possible today?"

"Certainly not. No children nowadays believe in gods invented by priests. They are taught the truth and know that priests can't help solve man's problems."

"This is a museum, then, not a living church?"

He shrugged his shoulders. "You can see, we don't interfere with anyone who still believes."

As we left they all mounted their ponies and raced beside our car for a few hundred feet, and then suddenly halted, took off their caps, and waved good-by. Behind them the monk quietly closed the doors of the temple.

"Rewi," I said, "do you think they really have as many as 12,000 horses and 90,000 sheep in this commune?"

"More or less."

"But we didn't see that many."

"Do you want to count all the bloody livestock in the commune?"

No. If some refugee in Hongkong wrote a story saying there were no horses or sheep in Mongolia I could tell you that he is mistaken. But suppose he said that there were half as many as last year or that there were a million people in concentration camps here? I could not disprove that. This does not necessarily show that you can learn more in Hongkong than you can in China and Mongolia, but it indicates the limits of education by travel.

Our visit had been so swift I had not really learned anything about how a commune worked or didn't work. I had permitted my attention to be diverted by Mongol gastronomics. I determined to reform.

9

Why China Went Red

"The unfortunate but inescapable fact is that the ominous result of the civil war in China was beyond the control of the government of the United States. Nothing that this country did or could have done within the reasonable limits of its capabilities could have changed that result; nothing that was left undone by this country has contributed to it. It was the product of internal Chinese forces, forces which this country tried to influence but could not."
—Secretary of State Dean Acheson, July 30, 1949

Why Mao himself and other Chinese intellectuals were logically pushed toward Marxism rather than nationalism-capitalism is abundantly clarified in Mao's life story as he related it to me, and in the testimonials of many other Red leaders which I later gathered. A careful study of these documents as early as 1938 could hardly have failed to suggest that the whole national experience of China made a Communist victory inevitable unless the Kuomintang underwent a miraculous transformation. Deep and revolutionary changes were needed, beginning with a redistribution of the land during the patriotic war against Japan.

The plain fact was that in China (as in Vietnam, Korea and other semicolonial and colonial countries) the *Communist Manifesto* had a literal authority which in Europe and America had been lost to Fabian gradualism, evolutionary socialist movements, and Keynesian economic practice. When Marx's stirring call to arms first began to be read by young people in China after the First World War, they did not see in it an analysis of conditions in Europe of February, 1848, but a true description of their own immediate environment.[1]

"The modern laborer, instead of rising with the progress of industry, sinks deeper and deeper below the existence of his own class," said Marx. Even in America, relatively civilized labor legislation is scarcely a generation old. In China, with its child and female slave labor, its twelve- to fourteen-hour day, its starvation wages and the absence of any protection against sickness, injury, unemployment and old age, and no serious possibility of collective bargaining, why should people have questioned Marx's prophecies right down to 1947?

The old security under the clan-family and the guild systems had collapsed and now the have-not was literally worth no more than his price tag in the market, "purely as a means of production." Back of the defenseless position of labor lay of course the breakup of the old agrarian economy under the impact of Western imperialism and the bankruptcy of handicraft production brought on by machine products. Capital levies in the form of ever rising taxes (sometimes collected sixty years in advance) and usurious interest rates, and the consistent plunder of public revenues by thieving bureaucrats and militarists, had by the twenties and thirties reduced the solvent landowning tillers to a minority. Aided by famine and war, this ruined economy threw millions of "surplus" sons and daughters of degraded peasant families onto the swollen labor market of unemployed. This process was prophetically analyzed years ago by R. H. Tawney in his *Land and Labor in China*. The reminder here serves to emphasize that the biography of almost every Red soldier I met revealed him to be a direct product of this mass rural bankruptcy.

To mention but two dramatic examples: Chu Teh, who was the Reds' commander in chief and Mao's military alter ego; and P'eng Teh-huai, Chu's deputy commander in chief. Chu Teh came from a tenant peasant family in which five children were drowned at birth because of poverty. Of the Chu children who survived he was the only one educated; instead of being drowned he was given away to a childless relative who managed to get him into a school for landlords' sons.

P'eng Teh-huai was almost killed for a minor filial offense (he had kicked over his grandmother's opium pot) by a decision of his family counsel, but an uncle's plea saved his life; he was then indentured as a coal miner at the age of nine.

It required no sharp intuition to comprehend why, in a country where child workers of ten or twelve were often locked up at night, to sleep in rags beneath the machines they operated by day, the *Communist Manifesto* was read as gospel. (I saw this even in Chinese-operated shops in foreign-run Shanghai). Nor need one ponder why Chinese who met Western democracy only in its role of foreign policeman, defending "rights and interests" seized by violence in China, could readily accept at full face value Marx's scornful denunciations of its hypocrisy.

China was never a complete colony; rivalries among the European powers and Japan prevented any one power from becoming dominant. But China was treated as the inferior of all and was the responsibility of none. Any foreigner in the "treaty ports"—even a drunken bum—was superior to the most virtuous Chinese; to be treated as inferiors in their own country rankled for many years.

Thus nationalism, the passion to reassert China's ancient role as a great power, initially played a greater part in attracting literate Chinese to Marxism than it did in Russia. In the West the Communist party had no comparable appeal. The Communist subservient to Stalin's infallibility had to learn to despise "national patriotism," substituting for it a religious "belief in a savior abroad." He had to be essentially a mythomaniac—and often remained so even after he became an ex-Communist.

The program which the Chinese Communist Party adopted soon after its founding called for a two-stage revolution, in accordance with Lenin's classical theses for colonial and semicolonial countries. The first stage would complete the "bourgeois-democratic" revolution, with a united front of the progressive bourgeoisie, the working class and the peasantry led by the Communist party. It would end foreign imperialist oppression and win complete independence. In rural China it would abolish rule by the landlord-gentry and equalize land ownership. In urban China it would nationalize the property of native reactionary capitalists held to be collaborators of foreign imperialism. Only when these two aims were accomplished would the revolutionary power move on to lay the foundations for the second stage: building socialism.

Programmatic aims of the "bourgeois-democratic" revolution, as thus defined, made a strong appeal even to Chinese nationalists. Within it, sentiments of patriotism, class war and international communism under Russian leadership were readily reconcilable. It must be remembered that at the outset the party founders' acceptance of Marxism coincided with direct Russian help to Dr. Sun Yat-sen in his struggle against foreign imperialism. The slogans of anticapitalist class war were also rendered more palatable because of antiforeign and nationalist sentiments. The small native bourgeoisie, including the great landlords linked with it, were in truth largely a collaborator class dependent on the imperialist powers, as events were to show. And it was simpler for the Chinese to believe in Moscow, because Russia's foremost antagonists were just those Western colonial powers who were likewise the immediate enemies of independence movements all through Asia and Africa.

China's outstanding Communists were internationalists in ideology but no less national patriots than the Kuomintang "nationalists." They were not proletarians but for the most part came from the less than 5 percent of China's millions who possessed some secondary or higher education. The biographies I collected showed that among the fifty "top" brains of the Communist party and the Red Army only two or three were of true proletarian (as distinct from peasant or intellectual) origin (although by 1945 the proletariat was somewhat better represented). During the united-front period of the Nationalist government at Canton (1924-27) today's Communists were already men of marked ability. If, by some curious digression of history, they had remained in the Kuomintang camp, they might have ultimately provided its top leadership. As early as 1924, Chou En-lai was first political secretary to Chiang Kai-shek when he headed the Whampoa military academy—where Lin Piao (Peking's current minister of defense) was recognized as a brilliant student. Mao Tse-tung was then head of the Agitation-Propaganda Department of the Kuomintang and an alternate member of its Central Committee. (Both Mao and Chou were also members of the Chinese Communist Party Central Bureau.) Chu Teh had already won fame as a Yunnan general. Chiang Kai-shek's own personal aide, named Ch'en Keng, who carried the frustrated general bodily from a field of early defeat, later became a Red field marshal.[2] All these and other able young patriots of that time broke with Chiang Kai-shek, not because they fundamentally differed over national independence aims, but because they became convinced that China could never realize those aims without deep internal revolutionary changes which Chiang Kai-shek and the Kuomintang conservatives were determined to prevent. There was also no essential disagreement between them on the necessity for authoritarian rule, but over how its powers were to be used.

Authoritarianism was, of course, an ancient tradition in Chinese political history. It long predated Confucius, who merely codified the ethics which were subsequently used to rationalize it. Social conduct as the criterion of individual excellence, and the subordination of the individual to the interests of group good and survival, were indeed sanctions of despotism implanted in Russia by (among others) the Tartar khans whose wisdom and political advisers came from China. Although Marx's version of all history as a perpetual class war was an innovation, his dialectical method had deep and ancient roots in Chinese thought, as we have already observed. To Chinese intellectuals Marxist revolutionary dogma as applied to the modern world seemed, like the theory of dialectics itself, more new wine in Chinese bottles.[3]

These men were also in a hurry. Their own experiences, combined with their study of European and American history, made them painfully aware of China's weakness, backwardness and imminent peril of total disintegration. In their search for a means of coping with complex problems of individual and national regeneration, young Chinese men and women of initiative and intelligence gravitated toward an authoritarian *and* revolutionary doctrine because other means had been tried and had failed, because they believed time ruled out gradualism, and because Chinese history had repeatedly sanctioned revolution as a means of salvation.

The usual arguments against Communists as apostles of violence and destroyers of "individual freedom" had small relevance in China's *Realpolitik*. Freedom in the Western sense did not exist and political change was still something attainable only by armed supremacy. Called upon to judge the Kuomintang seizure of power, few Chinese could have distinguished in it any ethical superiority over the attempts of the Communists, who openly sought power in the name of the "have-nots" at the expense of a minority of landlords, militarists, foreign treaty-port bankers and—during the Japanese occupation—outright imperialist conquerors.

Contrary to opinion held in America, the Kuomintang never posed a clear moral alternative to the Communists but competed with them purely on a basis of efficient use of force. For educated youths joining the Communists it was simply a matter of practical judgment whether their method was the only one which would provide a personal solution as well as quickly close the appalling industrial and scientific gaps between China and the advanced nations of the world. Those who became convinced of this in the early days made a discovery which confounded all previous Marxist theory. They discovered that they could bring the "proletarian revolution" to power without urban or proletarian insurrections.

Mao's faith in the peasant as the main engine of social revolution developed from objective experience and was not shared by the Russians. Orthodox Marxists elsewhere also continued to believe that a Communist movement could not succeed without an advanced industrial proletariat as its main force. In the beginning the Chinese agreed. After their initial disasters (1927-30) in urban insurrections, when the party was all but destroyed, they had no choice but to fall back on the rural areas, where Mao Tse-tung and Chu Teh set up its first sanctuaries. Real events thenceforth made the peasants virtually their sole material and mass support. Out of them came the strength which finally carried the Communists to national power, with minimum help from the heavily policed urban working class.

"Whoever wins the peasants will win China," Mao Tse-tung told me in Pao-an. "Whoever solves the land question will win the peasants."

Aristotle's *Politics* says, "Always it is the desire for equality which rises in rebellion." The desire for equality takes many forms, of course. Infinitely complex human needs and aspirations enter into the passions and energies of any revolution. Yet in the East, where starvation was ever present, belly-hunger alone was enough to turn millions of have-nots against have-gots.

The Reds never believed in land redistribution as an end in itself. But they saw that only by preliminary "land reform" could they get the peasants to join in a fighting alliance and later win their support for the main program. Remaining the party of the proletariat in theory and doctrine, the Communist intellectuals became in practice the party of the poorer two-thirds of the peasantry whom the Kuomintang, wedded to its landlord supporters, could not claim to represent.

Parenthetically, I should say that I was one of the few observers in China who as early as 1941 began to warn Americans that "liberals who build up hopes that the Communists of China are 'different' and 'only reformers' and have abandoned revolutionary methods to achieve their program are doomed to ultimate disillusionment." [4] In another book I devoted a chapter to tracing the history of "That 'Agrarian Reformer' Myth," [5] and my own fruitless efforts to reform its perpetrators. Philosophers will understand that this past record will not deter some who may dislike my report from reviving the slander that it was I, on the contrary, who deliberately fostered the myth that Chinese Communists had renounced Marxism to become "only agrarian reformers."

The Communists became in effect a mobile, armed, ubiquitous propaganda crusade spreading their message across hundreds of thousands of square miles of Asia. To millions of peasants they brought the first contacts with the modern world. To youths and women—for the Reds courted them first and last—they opened up unheard-of vistas of new personal freedom and importance. To the poor farmers they promised land and relief from ruinous taxes, usury, starvation, and family disruption. To all they promised equality of opportunity in a new state free of corruption, devoted to the welfare of the common people, and founded on a share-the-wealth and share-the-labor philosophy. *Kung-ch'an-tang* may be translated as "Share-production-party."

The reasons why the fire at first burned slowly in China were the very reasons why it could not be stamped out. Poor communications —lack of roads, railways and bridges—made it possible to create enclaves of armed struggle in the great spaces between the modern industrial centers dominated first by the Western powers, then by the Kuomintang, and lastly by the Japanese. In the hinterland the Reds could offer leadership and objectives to almost universal rural discontent, agitate and awaken new ambitions, and build an army to fight for their goals. When they actually carried out land reforms, eliminated some of the worst inequalities, turned the old gentry-ruled village hierarchy upside down, and took no personal profit for themselves, the have-not two-thirds of the peasants began to accept them and finally merged with them.

"I believe," says the young page in Mark Twain's *Recollections of Joan of Arc*, "that some day it will be found that peasants are people. Yes, beings in a great many respects like ourselves. And I believe that some day they will find this out, too—and then! Well, then I think they will rise up and demand to be regarded as part of the race, and that by that consequence there will be trouble."

What was also novel and appealing to peasants who had never known the meaning of a political party was that they were actually sought as "members." Was it surprising that they began to think of the Communists as "our" party? It did not matter that the new peasant proprietors were later to bear the burdens not only of their liquidation as a class, but of both fighting the revolution and building socialism. What mattered was that it had been found that "peasants are people" and that they were wedded to the party—which replaced the vanished protection of the old clan-family system.

"The people are the water and the ruler is the boat," said the revered philosopher Hsun Tzu twenty-two hundred years ago. "The water can support the boat but it can also sink it."

"We are the fish," said the modern Communist sons of Hsun Tzu, "and the people are the water of life to us. We do not ride over the people but swim with them." And of this they made slogans the peasants understood.

In 1961, Communists of peasant origin still constituted 66 percent of party membership.

10

Aboard the Premier's Special Train

The Chinese seem to like springing an important appointment as a surprise. Late one evening my phone in the Hsin Ch'iao gave a long, urgent ring. I was asked to be ready to leave early the next morning for a day's trip north of the capital.

At the appointed hour I was met on platform No. 1 by Dr. Chi Ch'ao-ting, my old acquaintance of prewar and wartime days. He was now director of foreign trade promotion, but this was no occasion arranged to discuss commerce. He led me into a special train waiting for a very special passenger. Premier Chou En-lai had ordered it for the day. He had invited me to accompany him to the recently completed Miyun Dam, North China's largest reservoir, power-grid and flood-control project, which nestles under the Great Wall near historic Kupei Pass.

An autumn sun flashed on the amber-colored tile cornices of Peking's marble-walled new East Station as the Premier and his wife drove through a side gate directly to the train. Beneath the quais of the new terminal lay the site of my old home on Kuei Chia Ch'ang, beside the Tartar Wall. Originally that house had been the residence of Dr. J. Leighton Stuart, who was America's last ambassador to prerevolutionary China. And to Kuei Chia Ch'ang, when I lived there in July,

1937, had come a brave woman, Teng Ying-ch'ao, seeking help. Now she was my hostess for this day's trip. Her married name is Mme Chou En-lai.

It was a three- or four-car train and Premier Chou and his wife disappeared in one direction while I was shown to an observation car and an air-conditioned stateroom of "my own." It amounted to an exhibit of New China; this was an all-native train. Peking carpeting covered the floor, a large teak desk and easy chair stood under a lace-curtained window, and a full-size bed filled one side of the room.

"A good place to write a book," said one of my hosts, smiling.

Adjoining the stateroom was a bathroom with green tile tub, matching lavatories, and a glass-walled shower.

We went on to the observation section and more heavy carpets, silk curtains, and handsomely paneled walls. There was a buffet and a bar, and the chairs and sofa were luxuriously upholstered.

As the train left noiselessly I searched for the haunted Fox Tower near our old house, but that also had vanished in the maw of progress. I recognized few landmarks in this corner of the old capital so familiar to me for five years; even the moat where farmers used to bring their ducks for a morning swim was gone. I wondered what had happened to Lao Chin, our last cook, and to Lao Han, our dignified Manchu *kuan shih-ti* (major-domo), who had somewhat doubtfully shown into our house, that long-ago July day, a Chinese woman wearing dark glasses and long-bobbed hair.

It was Teng Ying-ch'ao. She had been living secretly in a temple in the Western Hills outside Peking, convalescing from lung trouble acquired during the Long March, of which she was one of a few dozen women survivors. That was the July of the "incident" at Marco Polo Bridge, of which the Japanese made a pretext to attack and occupy Peking, an action which began the seven-year war. Taken by surprise when the Japanese surrounded the Western Hills, Mme Chou had fled, in straw sandals and disguised as a peasant woman, to reach the city just before the gates were closed.

I had met Teng Ying-ch'ao in 1936, during my first trip to the Red districts; in idle hours she had joined poker games with which I had tried to corrupt the revolution. And here she was, a year later, led to my house by Chiang Hsiao-mei, the vivacious little wife of a friend of mine named Hsu Pin, a professor in Peking. It was Hsu who had given me a letter of introduction to Mao Tse-tung which I carried into Red territory. Years ago I described the circumstances of Mme Chou's escape from Peking at a time when hundreds of Reds and alleged Reds were being arrested.[1] She would have been a rich prize. As a foreigner with extraterritoriality privileges I was able to conduct her and Chiang Hsiao-mei, represented as our family amahs, through the Japanese blockade by a "last train" to Tientsin, and thence to safety on a British boat bound for what was then called Free China.

Now, another summer twenty-three years later, we were on a very different train. We went unannounced and no crowds met us anywhere. During the entire excursion, including two hours of boating on the newly created Miyun Lake, I didn't see any armed guards. Once I commented on this to Chou as we climbed a wide flight of stone steps after we had visited Huaijou Dam, en route to Miyun. Our train stood high above us on a trestle spanning a deep ravine; it looked isolated and vulnerable to sabotage.

"All this used to be bandit country when I lived in Peking," I said. "Officials who came here in those days would have been loaded with arms and troops."

"We have plenty of guards, you just don't see them." Chou's left arm took in some masons working on a wall not far off and some peasants cultivating a hillside. "Every able-bodied person in China is a militiaman now. We don't need professional bodyguards." That was but a slight exaggeration.

Our entourage was a modest one. Besides Dr. Chi and his wife there was Yung Lung-kuei, who had been a depot manager of Chinese Industrial Cooperatives[2] and who was now secretary of the State Planning Commission's Research Bureau; Hsu Pin and his wife, Chiang Hsiao-mei, who was now chairman of the Peking Women's Federation; Mme Ch'en Yi, the attractive and well-groomed wife of China's Foreign Minister; Mme Kung P'eng, a student leader at Yenching University when I briefly taught there, later Chou En-lai's "first secretary," and now director of information at the Foreign Office; and a few other old acquaintances of Peking and Yenan days.

Chou En-lai came into the salon car soon after we left Peking. Tanned and healthy-looking, he had only a tinge of gray in his hair and looked ten years younger than his sixty-one. He wore sandals, slacks and a white sports shirt. Remembering our first meeting, I thought how had the mighty fallen since then, and how had the lowly risen.

Chou had been the first important Communist leader I encountered when I crossed the Red lines in 1936. He was in command of an East Front Red Army in a tiny cave village north of Yenan. I had just entered camp when a slender figure in an old cotton uniform came out to greet me, brought his cloth-soled shoes together, and touched his faded red-starred cap in a smart salute. He examined me intently with large dark eyes under heavy brows. His face, covered with a beard of abundant growth for a Chinese, parted in a smile which exposed even white teeth. That was Chou En-lai, the Red bandit for whose head Chiang Kai-shek was then offering eighty thousand dollars.

An odd thing had happened during those first hours I talked to Chou, which I now irrelevantly recalled. Kuomintang propaganda of that day used to issue "eyewitness" accounts of orgies in the Red districts, of naked women dancing, of widespread "rape and free love."

It took only a few days with those impoverished, earnest and dedicated young zealots to prove the irony of such charges. Then, as now,
the Chinese Communists had a puritanical attitude toward sex that
would satisfy Billy Graham, and their army imposed a death sentence
for rape.

But as I sipped "white tea" * in that cave village years ago there
had been a singular interruption. In the late sun a naked, barefoot
young woman strolled into view above a row of caves opposite us. In
Paris you might not give it a second thought, but strip-tease hadn't
reached Shensi, and I never saw anything like it again. I had just arrived and I remembered those propaganda stories. Then I quickly
saw that she wasn't playing friendly. Unbelievingly I watched her
come to the edge of the bluff, where she stood hurling epithets into
the courtyard. Her body looked as strong as an animal's. All the soldiers smiled and waved and then went on about their tasks. She threw
a few stones at the men below and suddenly laughed mockingly and
turned and ran away.

Chou circled his temple with his finger in explanation. "Fa-k'uang,"
he said. "She's crazy." She was very fierce, would let no one near her,
wore no clothes winter or summer, and lived like a wild beast in a
cave in the hills. I learned that years earlier her whole family had been
destroyed in a famine and pestilence which had left her a demented
orphan. Soldiers and villagers used to put out food for her at night
and she would come down, snatch it, and run off to her lair. Apparently no one thought of capturing her or locking her up. Since then
it has always puzzled me whether it is more humane not to interfere
with harmless crazy people, as in this instance, or to pen them up in
agonized restraint, to get them out of our sight and conscience, as
we do in the West . . .

I had spent two days in long interviews with Chou in that outpost
called Pai Chia P'ing, before going a day's journey farther on, to meet
Mao Tse-tung in Pao-an. Chou had told me that the Reds wanted to
end the civil war and unite with the Nationalists to resist Japan. That
would not mean abandoning the revolution, he said, but advancing it.
"The first day of the anti-Japanese war," he prophesied, "will mean
the beginning of the end for Chiang Kai-shek."

A year later, when the civil war ended (temporarily) following the
Sian Incident.† Chou played a key role in negotiations. After he left
the Communist areas to become chief of the Eighth Route Army delegation in Nanking, then Hankow, and finally in Chungking, I saw him
many times. Few Chinese made a more favorable impression on
American officials during the war than Chou En-lai did in Chungking.
The grandson of a distinguished mandarin of the Manchu Dynasty,

* As they euphemistically called hot water, drunk as a beverage; there was no
tea available, of course.
† See page 264.

and a former honors student at Nankai University in Tientsin—where
he met Teng Ying-ch'ao—he had also studied in Europe and knew
some French and English. Chou was thirty-eight when I first met him,
boyish despite the beard, a person of charm and urbanity in control
of a tough, supple and highly disciplined brain.

Now he sat before me, Prime Minister of the world's most popu-
lous nation and widely regarded as one of the ablest politicians alive.
One reason is that he rarely forgets anything or anybody. He saluted
the memory of Agnes Smedley, "a great American," and of Franklin D.
Roosevelt, "another one." He wondered whether if Roosevelt had
been president at the time of the revolution China would have been
better understood. A few days before I saw Chou I had visited Red
China's Arlington, the National Revolutionary Martyrs Memorial Park
outside Peking. Agnes Smedley was one of two foreigners, and the only
non-Communist foreigner, buried there. Above the ashes of this American "daughter of earth" and of poor-white Missouri pioneers (who was
proud to be one-eighth native Redskin) stood a simple marble ceno-
taph inscribed: "Agnes Smedley, revolutionary writer and friend of
the Chinese people."

Chou explained why the admission of American correspondents to
China had now become a question integrally related to negotiations
over the major problem created by an American policy which had established a protectorate over Taiwan, an island which "belongs to
China as clearly as Hawaii belongs to the United States." Until Washington was ready to recognize that fact, Chou declared, American correspondents could not be welcomed by China.

"We don't look upon you as a reporter but a writer," Chou went on,
"that's why we make an exception. We consider you a writer and a
historian, not a correspondent."

"What's the difference? Every good historian has to be a good reporter, whether you begin with Thucydides or Ssu Ma-ch'ien."

"All the same, your visit cannot set any precedent for American correspondents in general. We recognize you as a writer and a historian,
not a correspondent."

Historian, writer, correspondent, who cared? The story was the
thing.

Having satisfied protocol, if that is the word, Chou picked up the
questions I had submitted to him and began our marathon interview.
I soon understood that he had been quite serious about treating me as
a historian. Three hours later we had not got much beyond history
when our talk was interrupted. We had reached Miyun.

"Don't forget your camera," I was told as I left the train. I could
take all the pictures I wanted—but not as a correspondent

II

New Shores on Ancient Mountains

At Miyun's exhibition hall we stood before a large wall map which illuminated Miyun's future as a resort and vineyard country, to add to China's growing wine output. Rest houses and retirement homes dotted the lake; interspersed were beaches and swimming pools, pleasure boats, botanical gardens, parks and camping grounds. It looked much like a week-end scene at the lake of Yi Ho Yuan, Peking's Summer Palace—but Miyun is a hundred times larger. It was all still on paper, except that far up the slopes, above the island-studded inland sea, extensive walnut groves were already planted.

"They tell me I'll live to eat walnuts here in ten years, but I don't think so." Chou shrugged. "It will take thirty years or at least twenty to see all this dream fulfilled. I won't see it, but"—he pointed to comely Mme Ch'en Yi—"she may. Certainly her son will."

Chou remarked that he could be wrong again; they had astonished him with the big dam itself. Originally scheduled for 1965, it had been pushed ahead by five years. Unexpectedly rapid industrial growth in Peking and its tributary farming country had created new demands for both increased water and power. Initiative had also come from nearby communes, which stood most to benefit. Called into emergency council, he said, commune committeemen promised to furnish them enough workers, together with tools, food and wages, to build the entire project. Its importance, he said, had been self-evident to everybody; 200,000 workers had "volunteered" from twenty-one counties in the area—far more than needed.

We drove up to the main dam and a magnificent view of the broad blue lake enclosed by dramatic, sharp-prowed mountains. The reservoir is seventy-two square miles in area. High above it on the west stood the long serpentine of the Great Wall, studded by five watchtowers. Beneath them twenty-two centuries of history had ebbed and flowed since the first emperor of the Ch'in Dynasty, Shih Huang Ti, mobilized China's man power to complete the world's mightiest piece of masonry, more than two thousand miles long. As a defense against the barbarian hordes it was a success, but the Ch'in empire (259-206 B.C.) collapsed soon after the great builder's death.

Today Ch'in Shih Huang Ti is getting better treatment by historians and in literature and drama than in the past. His character is being rehabilitated somewhat like that of Ivan the Terrible in Russia. Chinese scholars depicted Shih Huang Ti as one of the worst tyrants in history; he preserved the Confucian classics in the imperial libraries but he burned them elsewhere and he humbled the Confucian bureaucracy. He was a great despot, and one of the most creative and remarkable rulers of all time. He controlled more territory than Alexander and unified China both geographically and culturally. He abolished ancient feudalism and divided the land; his system of roads, canals and irrigation and his promotion of agriculture, sericulture and architecture rivaled Greco-Roman works of the period. Incidentally, he sent abroad what might be called the first Peace Corps, an expedition of unarmed youths to illiterate, barbarian Japan in search of the elixir of immortality.

"The stones that went into the Great Wall would have made hundreds of Miyun dams," I remarked to an engineer with our party.

"Maybe they will yet," he replied. "Farther west, dozens of smaller dams are being built with those stones where the Wall is disintegrating."

A village near Miyun was named Old Man by the River. The legend is that an old man one morning sent his eldest son across the Pai River on an errand. As the youth started to cross the stream there was a sudden flash flood and he perished. Next day the old man, ignorant of his son's fate, climbed to the top of a hill to watch for him. There he presumably waited till he died. Such was said to be the belief of the 11,000 peasants who dwelt in the villages now permanently covered by the reservoir, for whom homes had to be provided on new land made useful by it.

Droughts, alternating with abrupt torrents which rose in the rainy season, had always been the scourge of Miyun and its vicinity, as in much of northern China. In flood years the Pai and Chao rivers, whose confluence is the site of the Miyun reservoir, used to inundate more than a million acres of farmland. In years of drought the same land was stricken and starvation followed. The eleven new dams of the reservoir now contain 4,100,000,000 cubic meters of water, which provides a regulated supply for that same million acres, much of which has been converted into rice land.

Like many new reservoirs in China, Miyun is also contributing to a new longitudinal canal system which will eventually join Peking, by way of the central provinces, to Canton, thirteen hundred miles farther south. It will parallel the old Grand Canal system which runs through the eastern or seaboard provinces. In 1961 the Miyun-Peking Canal joined the Peking-Tientsin Canal, to provide a waterway deep enough to carry boats of five hundred tons from the Wall to the China Sea.

Primarily a water conservation and irrigation scheme, Miyun also produces 90,000 kilowatts of power to speed up electrification and industrialization. Miyun had already prevented a serious flood, in 1959; in 1960 it minimized regional effects of the severe drought that struck all of northern China.

With its immense basin and eleven dams, the large reservoir was completed in two years, during the first fifteen months of which mainly hand labor was used. Heavy earth-moving machinery arrived in March of 1959, some 8,000 peasants were taught to use it, and a division of troops participated in the final months of work. An example of China's policy of education combined with practical labor, the whole Miyun project, with its miles of walls and spillways, its facilities, locks and canals, was designed by graduate students and professors of the Water Conservation Department of Peking's Tsing Hua University. Student theses provided the thousands of working blueprints actually used in the construction.

Miyun is impressive, but it is a modest project compared to the great dam being erected at San Men Hsia on the Yellow River, which I was to see later, and the projected Yangtze River power complex, said to be the world's largest. The dam Chou had shown me at Huaijou floods 120,000 acres. Chou told me that it was outside the State Plan and that he hadn't known it existed until it was nearly completed—with commune resources alone.

"They sprang it on me as a surprise when I came up here last year."

He turned to speak to the waterworks engineer and then raised his heavy eyebrows.

"I'm out of date again," he said. "The engineer tells me there are four other small reservoirs under construction hereabouts. This county has just sent 12,000 volunteers over to help the next county build its reservoir in exchange for help Huaijou got from them last year."

In random conversation I asked Chou how much land was now

under cultivation in China and he gave me the figure 110,000,000 hectares, about 275,000,000 acres.

"How much has it increased since 1955?"

"Not at all. There was a decrease of about 2,000,000 hectares."

Answering my puzzled look Chou explained:

"The reason is what you've been seeing: new highways, dams, reservoirs, canals; very large urban and rural housing and industrial developments; new streets, schools, hospitals, laboratories; new railways and new double-tracking; large new airports, and so on."

The area of cultivable land in China has been widely disputed by agricultural experts abroad and the question is worth brief comment. Chou's figure would amount to about 12 percent of China's land area, including the mountains and deserts of Tibet, Sinkiang and Mongolia. It seemed fairly probable that the actual cropland in use was even less in 1960; the press several times referred to 107,000,000 hectares (267,000,000 acres) *under cultivation*. Dr. Wu Chen, secretary general of the Ministry of Agriculture, also gave me the figure of 1,600,000,000 *mou*, or about 267,000,000 acres.

The recent decrease by about 5,000,000 acres which Chou mentioned also traced to other factors. In the euphoria of 1958, official policy encouraged communes to seek increased yields by deep plowing, close planting, more irrigation, more fertilizer, etc., and more double cropping on good land, at the neglect of poorer land. While the government's "eight-point charter for agriculture," which included such advice, might be sound enough if applied by experienced farmers, bureaucratic and indiscriminate enforcement was probably costly. Second, some commune administrations in 1958 abruptly curtailed or even ended the cultivation of small plots privately owned by the peasants, and these fell fallow. Third, commune diversions of farm labor to nonagricultural projects often caused neglect of available land. Finally, many communes had simply expropriated good land of prosperous peasants for public works without compensation. With the erasure of the last vestiges of private ownership, inducements were lacking to encourage enterprising peasants to combine to exploit new fields.

Some of these policies were corrected as early as December, 1958, but emphasis on the opening of new land, and provisions for more labor to till it, was not resumed until late in 1960 and early 1961. Chou's comment would indicate that the government had not yet fully digested the lessons of the period in this respect.

Thirty years ago, O. E. Baker put the "ultimate area suitable for cultivation on the basis of climate, land forms, and soils at 700 million acres," but George Babcock Cressey, whose studies were more thorough, concluded that Baker had "greatly exaggerated the agricultural potentialities of China." [1] At that time China was thought to have 207,000,000 acres under cultivation, or about .04 acre per person. Within recent years the cultivated area has been expanded by about 30 percent, but acreage *per person* remains approximately the same. Dr. Wu Chen told me that China can double her croplands within ten to twenty years, and that an additional two hundred million acres of marginal land might be reclaimed with much greater difficulty. Exactly how much new acreage could profitably be opened by *present* available means—before industrialization has reached an advanced stage—is quite another question, however. More than half of the arable land is multiple-cropped, and the *sown* area is more than 500,000,000 acres annually.[2] As long as it requires the labor of twenty to thirty Chinese to produce as much as one American on a modern farm, they may well be more rationally employed on existing croplands rather than on breaking in new low-yield land over really extensive areas.

Nevertheless, very great efforts were renewed in 1961-62 to develop hillside, plateau and desert land now rendered more cultivable by new water conservancy works in the far hinterland, as well as along the southern coast, where rainfall is generally adequate. Swamps were being drained and difficult mountain land terraced in Chekiang, Fukien, and northern Kwantung, where the appearance of regular army labor battalions on a large scale in 1962 aroused fears in Taiwan of an imminent invasion. It takes several years for such land to begin to yield pay-off results, however, and meanwhile the diversion of labor and materials involved often intensifies local food demands.

Chou En-lai continued his remarks to me: "We are not now trying to get a rapid increase in cultivated acreage, although it is going on all the time. You can see"—he pointed to Miyun reservoir—"that we want first to establish effective control over and efficient use of what land is already under the plow—more scientific agriculture in every respect."

That means, first, about twenty times more chemical fertilizer than China produced in 1960—a figure already about fifteen times the 1952 output. It also means about twenty times more mechanization than the present level. Scientific agriculture in every respect means water and soil conservation projects on an immense scale, better seeds, and improved planting and plowing methods. It means general conversion of small-plot farms into large-scale farm-factory enterprises. But of all this, and of communes and their attempts to improvise speedier answers, more later.

Now, in late August, Chou already predicted a tough year ahead. Nearly 40 percent of China's farmland was reported afflicted by prolonged drought, unprecedented floods in the northeast, hailstorms in the south, and other natural calamities. The early crop was far below expectations. In days I could remember this would have meant that famine and death for millions would soon overtake the nation. But

China's food resources and supply system were now well organized, Chou asserted; even if the autumn crop also suffered a heavy shortfall, there would be no famine. Farther on we shall see how the catastrophe, when it came, was met.

Chou had spoken once of the heroic and "progressive" periods of American history—the Revolutionary War, the Civil War, the emancipation of the slaves—which one must understand in order to appreciate the capabilities of the American people.

"For us," he mused as he gazed across the lake, "the darkest time in history was during our Long March, twenty-four years ago—especially when we crossed the great grasslands near Tibet. Our condition was desperate. We not only had nothing to eat, we had nothing to drink. Yet we survived and won victory."

When one thought back to the Long March, things had been getting relatively better for Chou, not worse, it seemed to me. "You must look upon your remaining national problems as by comparison easy to solve," I said.

"Easy! Nothing about them is easy!" Chou responded curtly. "Don't ever quote me as saying anything is easy here. Ten years ago, all China began a second Long March. We have taken the first step, that's all—the first step."

Our barge, pulled along by a motor launch, leisurely crossed the big lake. The steep hills turned deep purple as the sun dropped lower. Presently a squall blew up and a light rain fell. It did not last long.

"These sudden rains are common here," Chou said. "Once I was walking around this lake when I got caught in a storm. I took refuge in a nearby house. The housewife invited me to eat some stewed apricots—very delicious. It was a new house, clean and comfortable, and I learned she belonged to one of the families displaced by the dam. Her family had lived there for generations. She said many of the peasants had opposed being moved at first but now everybody was delighted with the change. No more fear of flood or drought, new and better land, electricity—and lake fish to eat! That was an interesting experience."

That had made him think that the Long Marches, the first one and the one ahead, were worth the struggle, he seemed to say. As he sat relaxed on the deck beside his wife, and a stiff breeze blew from the young walnut groves, I irrelevantly remembered one reason I had thought I might not get a visa to return to China. Several years earlier I had done a profile of Premier Chou and his wife for the *Saturday Evening Post*. I had entitled it "Mandarin in a Red Hat." To my astonishment it came out under the title "China's No. 1 Hatchet Man." Chou had undoubtedly seen the article but he made no reference to it.

Looking at the waves lapping the sides of ancient mountains which had seen many flood waters but had never before had their middle flanks converted into beaches, I said, "What a time to live in! Even a mountain cannot count on dry feet any more." Called upon to write something in the guest book when we touched shore again at a village called Shadow of Nine Pines on a Hill, I could think of nothing better to say than, "Today I saw new shores on ancient mountains."

12

Chou En-lai and America

One might assume that contempt for American imperialism would by now have produced Chinese equivalents of insulting American epithets such as slopeys, slant-eyes and chinks, but such is not the case—not in print, at least. "American imperialism" is translated by paradoxical characters which literally mean, "Beautiful-Country imperialist doctrine"—or sometimes by "Flowery-flag imperialism"—while Britain has its "Brave-Country imperialists," France its "Legal-Country imperialists," Germany its "Virtuous-Country" ditto, etc. This seems oddly consistent with the Communists' oft-asserted principle which distinguishes hatred of a foreign government policy from friendly feelings toward a people and a country.

Similarly, the possibility of educating and redeeming imperialist leaders may be suggested by the Chinese rendering of Eisenhower as "Forest Hero." Somehow the picture of "Forest Hero," chieftain of the "Flowery-flag imperialists," riding a "Beautiful-Country paper tiger," does not quite fit into standard Marxist idiom. Both Mr. Truman and the late John Foster Dulles bore the same surname, Tu, as the illustrious poet, Tu Fu. Truman's given name, Lu-men, means Gate to Lu (Shantung)—Confucius' birthplace and China's "sacred province"—and is highly complimentary.

I had seen Chou En-lai on one occasion before our trip to Miyun and at his request had submitted some questions for an interview. They numbered more than forty. Chou answered most of them while we were on the train and during a later interview I had with him just before I left China. Altogether our conversations covered about twelve hours, not counting "table talk." In our formal interviews interpreters were used, so that only about six hours of straight collo- quy was accomplished, during which I wrote down some eleven thousand words. All Chou's comment was offered *ad lib* except for an occasional reference to notes. I submitted my own version of the interviews and at Chou's request corrected it to conform to the official transcript. The latter followed the language of Chou's inter- preter, Chen Hui, a Swarthmore graduate who nevertheless insisted upon correcting my "Taiwan Strait" to the English usage "Taiwan Straits." The discrepancies between our two texts were otherwise negligible.

Chou gave me the most comprehensive exposition of Sino- American problems and statement of China's policy yet offered in a public interview. It is still basic at this writing and will probably remain so for some time to come. We also discussed Tibet and China's relations with India—difficulties which Chou connects with American influence on New Delhi. Chou gave me the only interview in which any official, Chinese or Russian, has to date publicly dis- cussed the nature of the "Sino-Soviet dispute." I made an undertaking to publish his remarks "in full or not at all," and they appeared, *in toto*, in *Look* magazine, January 31, 1961. At that time *Look* was criticized on the ground that the Chinese press would never publish an interview with a high American official. Peking has since recipro- cated by publication, in the *People's Daily*, of the full text of Presi- dent Kennedy's interview with Premier Khrushchev's son-in-law.

In this context I need not go over all the ground covered by Chou; further reference to it must be made toward the end of this book. Some excerpts are necessary at this point to provide background for an understanding of the deep hostility toward the United States which I must report as affecting virtually all educated Chinese I met. It will be noticed that nearly all Chou's arguments depend on the logic of nationalism, quite apart from communism.

There is no such thing as a "pro-foreign" Chinese, and even if there were, one would still have to expect a continuing ideological antag- onism against the United States among Communists for many years to come. What is probably not comprehensible from abroad is the extent to which even anti-Communist Chinese support Peking on any *nationalistic* issue. The fact that the United States has for a decade followed a policy of armed intervention in China's affairs, that this policy has served to discredit influential Chinese on the mainland once friendly to America and has added great force to Peking's ideological attacks on imperialism—which might otherwise seem as obsolete to Chinese intellectuals as they do to Mr. Nehru—is little understood by those Americans most anxious to bring about the downfall of the Communists.

I shall later have something of my own to say about the contribution which China's policies have made to the embitterment of Sino-American relations. Here I merely act as a reporter, whose job it is accurately to record answers, not to lead a debating team.

Premier Chou considered that my first seven questions were all related and said that he would answer them in a general discussion of the background of Sino-American problems involved, and then in terms of solutions.* The seven questions, in slightly condensed form:

1. Would China take the initiative in summoning a conference to discuss Chou En-lai's proposal for a nonaggression pact to create a nuclear-free zone in the Pacific? (This proposal was first publicized by Nikita Khrushchev in 1958 and in March of that year supported by Chinese Foreign Minister Ch'en Yi.)

2. What could be the main points covered by such a pact?

3. If the President were to invite Chou to the United States to discuss such a pact, would he accept?

4. Would China welcome any envoy the President might designate to visit Peking for the same purpose?

5. Would it be possible for China to sign such a pact as long as the United States pact with the Taiwan regime existed?

6. If China was resolutely opposed to the extension of nuclear arming of the world, why was she striving to make nuclear weapons?

7. It was said that China considered that successful negotiation with the United States would be possible only when China possessed the means of manufacturing nuclear weapons. Please comment.

"The [Pacific Peace Pact] proposal I made at the National Day reception of the Swiss Embassy," † Premier Chou began, "was not a new one. But to mention it again in August had its new significance. Western opinion has been spreading rumors to the effect that China has given up the policy of peaceful coexistence.

"As one who follows political developments in this country, you must have noted that China signed treaties of peace and friendship with three Asian countries this year. A treaty of friendship and mutual nonaggression was concluded with the Union of Burma in January. A treaty of peace and friendship was signed with the Kingdom of

* These interviews took place on August 30, 1960. The italics on page 88 and subsequently are added to express Premier Chou's original emphasis.
† On August 1, 1960.

Nepal during my visit to that country in April. In August, when Vice-Premier and Foreign Minister Ch'en Yi visited Afghanistan, a treaty of friendship and mutual nonaggression was concluded with the Kingdom of Afghanistan. These add up to three already, not to mention the earlier treaty of friendship with the Mutawakelite Kingdom of the Yemen and the joint statements on peaceful coexistence with India, Indonesia, Cambodia and Ceylon.

"The main content of the three treaties this year is based on the Five Principles of peaceful coexistence, which China has all along advocated. You know these principles: (1) Mutual respect for sovereignty and territorial integrity; (2) mutual nonaggression; (3) non-interference in each other's internal affairs; (4) equality and mutual benefit and (5) peaceful coexistence.

"A peace pact of mutual nonaggression among the countries of Asia and those bordering on the Pacific involves the questions of Sino-U.S. relations and of relations between the four countries of China, the U.S.S.R., Japan and the U.S.A.

"*It is inconceivable that a peace pact can be concluded without diplomatic relations between China and the United States.*

"*It is also inconceivable that there can be diplomatic relations between China and the United States without a settlement of the dispute between the two countries in the Taiwan region.*

"These are two important facts. That is why I said that prolonged efforts were necessary to realize this proposal. Since prolonged efforts are required, why have we repeatedly made this proposal? It demonstrates that the Chinese people and the Chinese Government desire to settle disputes between China and the United States through peaceful negotiations, and are opposed to the U.S. policy of aggression against China. But I would like first to cite one proof of this. After the liberation of China the U. S. Government declared that it would not interfere in the internal affairs of China, and that Taiwan was China's internal affair. [Dean] Acheson said so in the White Paper[1] and it was also admitted by Truman later. As a matter of fact, Taiwan was restored to the then government of China in 1945, after the Japanese surrender. It was taken over and administered by the then Governor of Taiwan, General Chen I, who was later killed by Chiang Kai-shek.

"After war broke out in Korea in June, 1950, Truman changed the policy and adopted a policy of aggression toward China. While sending troops to Korea the United States at the same time dispatched the Seventh Fleet to the Taiwan Straits and exercised military control over Taiwan. *Beginning from that time the United States started new aggression against China.* The Chinese Government sternly condemned United States aggression in Taiwan and the Taiwan Straits. Shortly afterwards United States troops in Korea showed the intention of crossing the Thirty-eighth Parallel and pressing on toward the Yalu River [China's frontier], and, because of this, the Chinese Government could not but warn the United States Government that we would not stand idly by if United States troops crossed the Thirty-eighth Parallel and pressed on toward the Yalu River. This warning was conveyed to the United States through the Indian Ambassador. The United States Government disregarded this warning and United States troops did indeed cross the Thirty-eighth Parallel and press on toward the Yalu River.

"The Chinese people could only take the action of volunteering support to Korea in its war of resistance against the United States. But this action *was not taken until four months after the United States stationed its forces in the Taiwan Straits and exercised military control over Taiwan,* and not until United States troops had crossed the Thirty-eighth Parallel and approached the Yalu River.[2] Truman made many statements during these four months to explain this act of aggression against Korea; of course, they were futile. Moreover, he could not justify aggression in Taiwan, nor the stationing of United States forces in the Taiwan Straits. Furthermore, Truman failed to heed China's warning conveyed through the Indian Ambassador.

"After two years of negotiations an armistice was at last reached in Korea. *By 1958 Chinese troops had withdrawn completely from Korea.* But up to now United States troops are still hanging on in South Korea and will not withdraw. Moreover, the United States is still controlling Taiwan with its land, sea and air forces, and the United States navy and air forces are still active in the Taiwan Straits. Isn't this the best proof that the United States Government continues to pursue policies of aggression and war toward China? It is not necessary to cite in addition the numerous military bases maintained by the United States in Asia and the many aggressive military pacts which have China as their main target. *China, on the other hand, has not a single soldier abroad, and the treaties it has concluded with Asian countries are all treaties of peace and friendship.*

"Though the United States committed these acts of aggression against China, *would we use force to settle disputes with the United States? No!* I declared already during the Bandung Conference in 1955 that the Chinese people were friendly to the American *people* and the Chinese Government was willing to sit down and enter into negotiations with the United States Government to discuss existing disputes between the two countries, though the two countries had not recognized each other and had no diplomatic relations. This proposal of ours resulted, through the good offices of Britain, in ambassadorial talks between China and the United States which started August 1, 1955, in Geneva.

"In order to create a favorable atmosphere China released, before the talks began, eleven so-called 'prisoners of war,' following the mediation of Krishna Menon and U.N. Secretary General Dag Hammarskjold's visit to Peking. Why are they referred to as so-called 'prisoners of war'? Because they were not captured on the Korean battlefield. With the exception of a few who chose, of their own will, to stay behind, all prisoners of war captured on the Korean front were repatriated after the armistice. Later, among those who stayed behind, some returned also of their own will. But the eleven so-called 'prisoners of war' were on a United States plane which intruded into China's air space, and were captured after their plane was hit. Both China and the United States had declared that the Korean War was restricted to Korea and did not extend to China. This plane was shot down in China. So China did not recognize them as 'prisoners of war.' Nevertheless, China released them—to create a favorable atmosphere for the ambassadorial talks at Geneva.

"That was the end of the so-called 'prisoners of war' issue.

"Besides the so-called 'prisoners of war,' however, there were two other categories of United States nationals in Chinese prisons. First were United States citizens, guilty of such crimes as sabotage and espionage, or who had in other ways violated the laws of China. Since 1955, we have released twenty-five such United States criminals when their terms were fully served or were granted clemency and released ahead of time for good behavior. One of the twenty-five chose to remain in China after his release. Of this category only three are now still serving sentences in China.

"There are two United States nationals in Chinese prisons of another category—a very special one. They are air-borne secret agents sent by the United States to China, namely, the very famous Downey and Fecteau. Allen Dulles of the United States Central Intelligence Agency could give you all the details, but perhaps he wouldn't want to give the information in such detail as we would. In early 1955, when Hammarskjold came to Peking to discuss the question of the United States nationals in Chinese prisons, even he found it inconvenient to bring up their case for discussion. These two were in no way related to the Korean War, but were on a mission of pure espionage and secret-agent activity. If you are interested, I could show you some portions of the notes of my talks with Hammarskjold for your reference. The notes have never been published.*

"Five years have elapsed since the start of the Chinese–United

---

* The case of John T. Downey of New Britain, Conn., and Richard G. Fecteau of Lynn, Mass., was widely publicized in China during a trial which followed their capture, along with a number of Nationalist Chinese, in an American plane alleged to have been in the act of supplying an espionage and radio communications base, set up earlier by air-dropping Chinese to operate deep within the mountains of Manchuria. On request, Premier Chou furnished the following from notes of his first meeting with Dag Hammarskjold, January 6, 1955: "Hammarskjold said: 'Regarding the other two [Downey and Fecteau], no one had said that they belonged to the United Nations Command; therefore they were not mentioned in the resolution [of the U.N. General Assembly].' " An official State Department letter to me directly contradicts some of Chou's statements on the prisoners issue. See Chapter 15, New China Hands, and, for full text, the Appendix, pages 753-755.

States talks in August, 1955. At the very outset, we proposed that disputes between China and the United States, including the dispute between the two countries in the Taiwan region, should be settled through peaceful negotiations, without resorting to the use or threat of force. The United States blocked all news of this proposal, but China later published it. Why did [John Foster] Dulles reject it? Because Dulles realized that reaching such an agreement implied that the next step would be discussions on how and when United States armed forces were to withdraw from Taiwan and the Taiwan Straits.

"We hold that the dispute between China and the United States in the Taiwan region is an international question; whereas military action between the Central Government of New China and the Chiang Kai-shek clique in Taiwan is an internal question. The United States has maintained that the two questions are inseparable. We hold that they can and must be separated. Since it has been possible for China and the United States to hold ambassadorial talks in Geneva and Warsaw, talks can also be held at the same time between the Central Government of China and the Chiang Kai-shek clique. The former is an international question while the latter is an internal question. Parallel talks can be conducted and solutions reached separately.

"In the talks between China and the United States, agreement on principle must after all be reached first before concrete issues can be settled. The two points of principle on which agreement should be reached are:

"(1) *All disputes between China and the United States, including the dispute between the two countries in the Taiwan region, should be settled through peaceful negotiations, without resorting to the use or threat of force; and*

"(2) *The United States must agree to withdraw its armed forces from Taiwan and the Taiwan Straits. As to the specific steps on when and how to withdraw, they are matters for subsequent discussion. If the United States Government ceases to pursue the policy of aggression against China and of resorting to threats of force, this is the only logical conclusion which can be drawn.*

"This is the crux of the dispute between China and the United States. The activities and direction of United States policy toward China have been aimed at manufacturing 'two Chinas.' In this respect, both the Republican and the Democratic parties aim at the same thing. . . . This scheme would probably be opposed not only by mainland China, but also by the Kuomintang in Taiwan and the Chinese in Taiwan. Therefore such an approach would lead nowhere, but in the solution of Sino-U.S. relations it would tie things up in knots.

"We believe that a solution to Sino-U.S. relations will ultimately be found; it is only a question of time. But there is one point: if the United States does not give up its policy of aggression and the threat of war against China, no solution is possible. We do not believe that the people of the United States will allow their government indefinitely to pursue such a policy. *There is no conflict of basic interest between the peoples of China and the United States, and friendship will eventually prevail.*"

I asked Chou whether the two principles he spoke of had been the topic of discussion for a long time in the Sino-American ambassadorial talks held at Warsaw.

The Premier: "Yes. The first principle was put forward by China at the end of 1955. The second principle was put forward in the autumn of 1958 at Warsaw."

Question: "Does the second principle include as well the question of the time and manner of the withdrawal from Taiwan?"

Answer: "The United States Government must first agree on the principle before concrete matters can be taken up."

Q: "The United States Government has insisted that no agreement is possible without a declaration from the Chinese Government to refrain from the use of force in the Taiwan area, has it not?"

A: "The United States Government has insisted that the United States and Chiang Kai-shek have 'the inherent right of individual and collective self-defense' in the Taiwan region. In other words, it would also legalize United States aggression in Taiwan and the Taiwan Straits, and create the objective reality of 'two Chinas.' This is opposed by the entire Chinese nation. Suppose someone occupied the Hawaiian Islands and dispatched a fleet to the waters between the mainland of the United States and the Hawaiian Islands, or supposing someone occupied Long Island and sent a fleet to the straits north of Long Island, how would the people of the United States feel in such a situation? You can thus imagine how the Chinese feel. Did not the people of the United States rise up against the Japanese after Pearl Harbor was attacked? . . ."

For some minutes a white-jacketed waiter had been hovering discreetly at the door of the salon. When he had finished speaking, Chou looked around and saw him.

"Hungry?" he asked me.

Here was at least one concrete matter we were able to settle at once. I followed him into the dining car, where a table was set for about twenty guests—and one historian.

13

Table Talk

In some respects I learned more while manipulating my chopsticks on that special train than I did while using a pencil.

"What do you mean," I asked the Premier at the table, "when you say you will leave to future negotiations 'the time and manner of U.S. withdrawal from Taiwan,' if the principle is conceded?"

I wondered whether he would informally or formally discuss a solution along these lines: neutralization of Taiwan in so far as military bases were concerned, with a commitment by China not to send arms or armed forces to Taiwan for a stipulated time following a United States withdrawal. During such a period, I elaborated, China, the United States, Japan and the U.S.S.R. would seek to enter into a Pacific nonaggression pact—all this to be premised upon simultaneous arrangements to dissolve military alliances (in effect a disengagement operation) in both parts of Korea and Vietnam, and for China's admission to the U.N. and U.S.-China mutual recognition.

Chou answered that such questions would belong in the realm of diplomacy, once principles were agreed upon.

"You," said he, "are not the United States Secretary of State. I am not China's Foreign Minister."

"That I am not the Secretary of State no one will dispute," I replied. "As for the truth of the second half of your statement I am far from convinced." He laughed.

"Who knows, you may be Secretary of State yet."

"Not," I said, "in my time."

"You are a pessimist."

"No, sir, an optimist."

Our conversation turned to random topics. We spoke about swimming. Chou hadn't been able to catch up with Mao; he had broken his right arm many years ago and it had never been reset properly. We talked of his wife's growing interest in photography, at which she had become quite proficient; she had kept a picture I had taken of them in Hankow in 1938, in "their first home since their marriage." Then Chou told me something about the language reform.

Han-yu p'in-yin—use of the Latin alphabet for phonetic writing of Chinese—was limited to attempts to break mass illiteracy and to help children get a quick start in characters, he explained. Once they knew the characters they dropped the *han-yu p'in-yin*. There was no literature in the new phonetics and there was no demand for one. The Latin alphabet was used, however, in new written languages created for some of China's minority peoples.

Simplification of character writing was quite another thing. People had been writing abbreviated characters for a long time but it had never before been systematized. Now there was a standard set of abbreviations for a thousand basic Chinese characters. Some old scholars had strenuously objected; they thought the art of calligraphy would be ruined by the simplifications. Chou maintained that even the adumbrated hieroglyphics could be written in beauty. I couldn't agree; I was a reactionary.

I spoke appreciatively of China's widespread interest in Western symphonic and operatic music, unknown in the past. Chou demonstrated some intimate knowledge of the careers and idiosyncrasies of John Foster Dulles, of Mr. Nixon, of Mr. Kennedy, and of sundry others, including Chester Bowles, whom he credited with more influence than I did. I expressed doubt that Mr. Bowles's proposal for an independent Taiwan was anything more than a personal view. Chou corrected me by pointing out that Mr. Bowles was chairman of the Democratic party foreign policy committee. That had escaped my notice.

As for Mr. Dulles, he said they had regretted his passing because he had been such a "downright reactionary." He ran so completely true to form that it had never presented any difficulties to anticipate all his "reactions." Nevertheless Mr. Dulles had, Chou admitted, surprised him once. During the Geneva conference in 1954 Chou had entered the lounge of the conference room ahead of time. No one was there except Mr. Dulles, who was "only an observer" at the conference. In a natural gesture under the circumstances Chou extended his hand. Mr. Dulles folded his hands behind his back, shook his head, and left the room. Chou winced as he remembered it. "That was really carrying even reaction to extremes," he said.

The legacy of Dulles' policy, Chou thought, had left the U.S.A. in a precarious position. With more than two hundred bomber bases around the world, "the U.S.A. is now a man balancing an armful of eggs. He can't move or he will lose them *all*." * The United States was overextended and had lost the mobility to achieve effective concentration on attainable goals.

"You can't catch fleas with your fingers," Chou said, using a Chinese epigram. He spread his fingers wide apart on the table. "You can't lift a finger, don't you see, or a flea will get away. Such a man is fundamentally defenseless against all the untrapped fleas, who can choose where and when to mobilize and dine at leisure." Chou clapped his hands together sharply. "That," he said, "is the way to catch fleas."

That was the strategy Mao used with success against Chiang Kai-shek's attempts to catch fleas with his fingers. "Despise the enemy strategically," said Mao, "but pay attention to him tactically." In this connection he had uttered his famous dictum that "all reactionaries are paper tigers." Chiang Kai-shek was his first example. Later he applied it to "American imperialism." This was oversimplified in the West to suggest that Mao was ignorant of the destructive capabilities of hydrogen bombs. He used the expression figuratively in the way Lenin described old-style imperialism as a "colossus with feet of clay."

What Mao actually said was: "Imperialism and all reactionaries, looked at in essence, from a *long-term* point of view, must be seen for what they are—paper tigers. On this we should build our *strategic* thinking. [That is, the ultimate victory of socialism is inevitable.] On the other hand, there are also living tigers, iron tigers, real tigers which can eat people. On this we should build our *tactical* thinking." [1] Old tigers always die, but while they are still alive they are not to be slighted.

The limit to Chou's allegory of the fleas was also plain. In America's case the hands happened to hold down not just fleas but untold megatons of deadly nuclear power. While it is extremely difficult to exterminate a whole species, the lifting of one nuclear finger might release such violence as to destroy not only a flea-harassed U.S.A. but all the precious fleas, both the trapped and the untrapped as well. How far could the man with his fingers down—if his fingers *were* down—be safely provoked?

Was that the essence of the reported disputes between the U.S.S.R.

* The United States has since announced the liquidation of a number of the smaller bases.

and China over theoretical possibilities of coexistence versus the "inevitability of war"? Would Premier Chou frankly discuss a subject then filling the Western press with speculations? I decided to jump across some of my remaining questions when our interview was resumed.

14

Sino-Russian
"Differences"

At meals we had spoken in mixed Chinese and English; Chou's understanding of English is better than his speaking ability. After luncheon Chou, his wife, and everyone else retired for a brief nap, as is now customary in China, not only among officials but among all the people. Then, back in the salon, we returned to formal colloquy through his interpreters, only occasionally interrupting to question the translation of a phrase or two.

The Premier's remarks on Sino-Soviet relations were made well in advance of the stormy conference of eighty-one Communist parties held in Moscow in November, 1960.

I indicated three questions on my list that were related to disputes or disagreements between China and the Soviet Union. These concerned reported differences in the Soviet and Chinese interpretation of the Leninist theory of the inevitability of imperialist war, whether peaceful coexistence between countries of different social systems was the permanent foreign policy of the Communist countries and not merely tactics, and whether peaceful coexistence was unavoidable in a world threatened by nuclear war in which no nation or class could be victorious. And I asked specifically about the "mass exodus" of Soviet advisers from China.

Premier Chou said: "I would like to begin by stating that the Communist Parties and Governments of China and the Soviet Union, as well as those of other socialist countries, all believe in Marxism-Leninism and formulate their policy by integrating the principles of Marxism-Leninism with the specific conditions of their respective countries. Having the same belief and the same system, they share the same overall principles and go along the same general direction.

"But this is not equivalent to saying that the two parties have no differences* in the way they look at certain questions, nor does it mean that there is no difference in emphasis in the policies of the two countries. To have no difference whatsoever is impossible in the realm of thinking. Even in the thinking of a single person, one sometimes looks at a question in one way and at another time in another way. In a specified period of time, it is a natural thing that there are some differences between two parties on theoretical questions and on ways of looking at things. To be exactly identical would indeed be something strange and incomprehensible.

"For example, though there are some differences in the Chinese and Soviet press on how to evaluate the situation with regard to war, opposition to imperialism launching a war is our common point. Take the case of the policies of the two countries. The Soviet Union is in the United Nations while China is not. *Proceeding from this point, the actions of the two governments cannot be the same in many respects.* Both China and the Soviet Union are opposed to 'two Chinas'; both maintain that the Chiang Kai-shek clique does not represent China, and that only New China can represent the 650,000,-000† Chinese people. This stand of the Soviet Union has not yet won majority support although it is backed by all socialist countries and by a number of Asian, African and European countries. So the representatives of the Chiang Kai-shek clique have remained seated in the United Nations. The representatives of the Soviet Union take part in meetings along with them in the General Assembly, the Security Council and subsidiary organs. China, however, in addition to disagreeing that the Chiang Kai-shek clique represents China, will not participate in any meeting or organization in which the Chiang Kai-shek clique is included. If China also took part, it would result in a situation of 'two Chinas,' which we firmly oppose.

---

* In a subsequent discussion of this statement the Premier said that the Chinese word, *ch'a-pieh*, might more correctly be translated "dissimilarities." Here I adhere to the official transcript.

† Official census figures for the year 1957 showed a total of 656,630,000, of whom 340,140,000 were male and 316,490,000 female—not including "Chinese living in Hongkong, Macao and abroad," but including Taiwan (*T.G.Y.*, p. 8). At an increase rate of 2 percent the mainland population alone should have exceeded 700,000,000 by 1963—with another 25,000,000 in Taiwan and overseas. See also Chapter 54, Of Blue Ants and White; and, for a more comprehensive evaluation, Leo A. Orleans, *Professional Manpower and Education in Communist China*, Washington, 1961.

"Here is a case of a difference owing to the different situations of the two countries. . . .[1]

"Many such examples can be cited.

"All the socialist countries, including China and the Soviet Union, practice internationalism, supporting and helping each other and holding unity as their common goal. In view of these principles, should the imperialists try to seek any loopholes for driving a wedge and sowing discord among the socialist countries, they would do so in vain and are doomed to failure. *An imperialist attack against any socialist country would be deemed by China as an attack on China and on the entire socialist camp, and in that event China would never sit idly by.*

"This is the general aspect of the situation. Under this principle, it is permissible to have some differences between the two parties on ways of looking at things and in the emphasis of their policies. There is nothing strange about this. . . .

"The return of some Soviet experts is a natural thing. Having come to China, they are bound to return some day; surely they can't stay here all their lives. They work in China for definite periods of time and have rendered good service. Perhaps it was because many returned this year that it drew the attention of the Western countries. . . ."

Question: "Have you read any of the recent articles which appeared in the Soviet press written by prominent Communists, in which opponents of the Soviet stand on coexistence and against the 'inevitability of war' doctrine were denounced as 'left-wing infantilists,' 'dogmatists,' 'revisionists,' etc.? Though no specific names were mentioned, it was assumed that they must have been directed against some phenomena within the socialist camp, or else they would have been meaningless. Or were they perhaps directed against some strong left-wing forces within the Communist Party of the Soviet Union? How do you explain this rash of articles?"

A: "In the first place, I have not read many such articles. Secondly, China's explanation differs from that given by you just now. We are not left-wing opportunists as interpreted by the Western press. We consider that the Western press has so speculated because they want to lead on to sowing discord between China and the Soviet Union. We are against attempts to sow discord in Sino-Soviet relations. The Chinese Government and the Chinese Communist Party are against the launching of a war by the imperialists and have advocated peaceful coexistence among countries of different social systems. This has been our stand from way back, and this stand has never changed."

Q: "If the comments in the Soviet press are not to be applied to China, what is your interpretation of China's difference in viewpoint from Russia's concerning the Leninist theory of the inevitability of imperialist war?"

A: "On the question of imperialism instigating wars, we hold that the 1957 Moscow Declaration of the fraternal parties of the twelve countries is correct. The Bucharest (1960) communiqué also supports the theses of the Moscow Declaration. We support the Moscow Declaration and stand firmly by it. There should be no differences in standing firmly by the Moscow Declaration. *The Moscow Declaration states that so long as imperialism exists, there will always be soil for aggressive wars.* Imperialism invariably aims at realizing its domination of the world by instigating wars. But the Moscow Declaration also points out that owing to the mighty strength of the socialist camp, owing to the growth of the anti-imperialist and national independence movements of the Asian, African and Latin American peoples, owing to the growth of the people's struggle in the capitalistic countries for democracy and freedom and owing to the development of the movement to defend peace by the peoples throughout the world, *it is now possible to delay and prevent imperialism from launching war. While preventing imperialism from launching war is one possibility, vigilance must be heightened on the other hand to guard against it.*

"Such a thesis is entirely correct. As China sees it, through the people's struggles we strive on the one hand for a lasting world peace, while on the other hand we remain vigilant and on guard against the danger of war. The mightier the forces of the people, the greater the possibility to defend peace, and the greater the strength to avert war. These are the two aspects of the matter. It is also [a matter of] 'walking on two legs.' " *

Our train had been sitting on the platform of the Peking station for an hour and it was now nine at night. The Premier excused himself but left with a promise to complete our interview as soon as he could arrange to see me again.†

Back in the Hsin Ch'iao that night I reviewed my notes and realized that Premier Chou had given me a historic interview. No previous official acknowledgment of any differences or dissimilarities between the two major Communist leaderships had been made by Peking. Chou's statements remain the only ones of their kind on record. They have never been published in either China or Russia.

Since this interview the rift between Peking and Moscow has appreciably widened. Neither side changed its basic position in the Moscow conference; for the Chinese the resolution adopted in December, 1960, merely reiterated the earlier declaration Chou En-lai quoted above. Journalistic oversimplifications to the effect that Khrushchev "wants peace" while Mao "wants inevitable war" are distortions. Neither Khrushchev nor Mao really expects general peace and neither really wants general war. The basic issue between the two goliaths

* See Chapter 28, Two Legs Are Better Than One.
† See Appendix, pages 758-764.

is whether the combined resources of the Communist camp should be used to promote class interests or to serve national interests.

"Walking on two legs"—pursuing formal policies of peace and peaceful coexistence on one leg while the other actively supports "the growth of the anti-imperialist and national independence movements" and "the growth of people's struggle in the capitalistic countries"—continues to be the overall strategy of both Peking and Moscow. Differences between them concern where, when, how and how much to "pay attention to the enemy *tactically*." But tactics and strategy are finally ends and means; changing one in the long run means changing the other, too.

What recent years have revealed is that *nationalism inside the Communist system of states* threatens to be at least as powerful a factor as the bonds of class solidarity which socialist power would theoretically make unbreakable.[2] Premier Chou's statements require further comment—after we have seen more of the conditions inside China which underlie these differences between East and West, both within and beyond the Marxist sphere.*

* See Chapter 83, China and Russia: Point, Counterpoint.

15

New China Hands

I was bound to feel rather conspicuous whenever I was reminded that I was the only "legitimate" American traveler among the seven hundred million Chinese, but there were fifty-eight other American citizens living in China. There were also an undetermined number of persons of Chinese race who may have a valid claim to U.S. citizenship.

Twenty of the fifty-eight Americans were married to Chinese. Premier Chou asserted that all American prisoners from the Korean War had been released. "We have no reliable information to indicate that American servicemen from the Korean conflict are in fact being held prisoner in China," according to a letter to me from the Department of State.* But the Department expressed the belief "that the Chinese Communists must have knowledge of the fate of at least some" of the Americans missing since the Korean War, a number "now reduced to 389."

Twenty-one American prisoners of war refused repatriation at the end of hostilities in Korea, and chose to remain in China. Ten have since returned to the United States, ten are still in China, and one has died. Among the ten apparently "permanent expatriates" four are

* Written by Joseph A. Yager, Director for Chinese Affairs, Department of State, Oct. 6, 1961. For full text see Appendix, pages 753-755.

skilled workers living in North China, one is a chemist, and four are studying in universities. Several have married Chinese.*

Five Americans, tried and convicted of "espionage" and other "crimes against the Republic" were still imprisoned when I was in China. In 1961 one of them, Robert Ezra McCann, was released and has since died from lung cancer. There are two alleged C.I.A. agents who Chou En-lai claimed were shot down and captured together with some Chinese engaged in supplying an espionage base deep in Manchuria. The State Department describes them as "John Thomas Downey, a Department of the Army civilian employee with the Far East Command, who was a passenger aboard an aircraft which disappeared on a regularly scheduled flight from Korea to Japan on November 29, 1952," and "Richard George Fecteau of Lynn, Massachusetts, a Department of the Army civilian employee [who] disappeared together with John Downey." Mr. Downey is serving a life sentence and Mr. Fecteau was given twenty years. An American businessman, Hugh Francis Redmond, Jr., of New York, "was arrested on April 26, 1951, and sentenced on September 12, 1954, to life imprisonment on charges of 'espionage.'"

The only other American now known to be imprisoned in China is a Roman Catholic Bishop, James Edward Walsh, of Cumberland, Maryland, who returned to Shanghai after the war. According to the Chinese he was guilty of heading a Vatican-directed "Catholic Bureau," allegedly an intelligence center "actively engaged in espionage," and a principal instrument in sabotaging organization of the Chinese Catholic Patriotic Church, which severed connections with the Vatican.† The State Department asserts that he "was arrested in October, 1958, and thereafter held incommunicado for seventeen months with no charges having been placed against him. On March 18, 1960, he was sentenced, along with fourteen Chinese Catholic clergymen, after a 'showcase' [widely publicized] trial, to twenty years imprisonment on charges of 'espionage' and 'sabotage,' having been branded a 'veteran United States spy.'"

The State Department does not report whether there are any American missionaries still in China, but there is one former Y.W.C.A. secretary, Talitha Gerlach. An old and trusted friend of Mme Sun Yat-sen, Miss Gerlach returned some years ago to work for Mme Sun's China Welfare Institute, which has done remarkable things in promoting modern techniques of child care and hygiene, set up China's first children's theater, and pioneered other cultural projects. A former Marine captain, Gerald Tannenbaum, has been similarly engaged in assisting Mme Sun ever since the war.

---

* These men have been interviewed by foreign visitors and writers in the past; I also had the opportunity, and it was only because of early preoccupation with other tasks and subsequent lack of time that I did not do so.
† See page 553.

In Peking, two other U. S. Army veterans were working for Chinese organizations. Syd Rittenberg was brought up a strict Methodist by his family near Charleston, South Carolina. During the war the army gave him a quick course in Chinese. In postwar Shanghai he was obliged, in the performance of his duty, he said, to report the involvement of American officers in black-market sales of UNRRA supplies, illegal speculation in gold bars and exchange, and a notorious case of rape. Nothing came of his reports, but for his zeal he received, so he told me, a speedy (honorable) separation from the service and the reward of a farewell tour of North China. It was 1947. In the course of his travels he was much impressed with the probity of Eighth Route Army officers and their administration, in contrast to the Kuomintang. He met General Nieh Jung-chen, who offered him a job as "an engineer of good relations between the Eighth Route Army and the American people," and he accepted. Eventually he married a Chinese student, fathered two children, and took up broadcasting work in Peking. He was, when I saw him, convinced that he was helping to promote "good relations" between the Chinese and the American people—"but not, of course, between China and American imperialism." He had no intention of renouncing his American citizenship.

The other veteran was Sydney Shapiro, a lawyer by profession, also army-trained in Chinese. He now did editing and translating for the Chinese Foreign Languages Press, wrote poetry, did his *t'ai chi ch'uan* exercises like everybody else, and enjoyed family life with his attractive Chinese wife and their children.

Dr. George Hatem, the only American physician who worked with the medical department of the Communist guerrilla armies during the anti-Japanese war, is now an official in the Ministry of Public Health. His story is told in a separate chapter. A few other Americans who worked as technicians of various kinds had entered China without State Department permission but with strong moral convictions of their righteousness.

Perhaps the best known of all American residents of China was Anna Louise Strong, minister's daughter, author and journalist. She once edited the *Moscow News* with Mikhail Borodin, who in 1923-27 was principal Soviet adviser to the Kuomintang. On a revisit to Moscow in 1948, during the last years of Stalin, Miss Strong was suddenly denounced as an "American spy" and expelled from Russia. Soon after Khrushchev's speech which posthumously demolished Stalin, a special Kremlin declaration was issued to withdraw the condemnation of Miss Strong and to "rehabilitate" her. Shortly afterward she left California for Peking and there settled down comfortably, at least until such time as she could return to her native land without losing her passport. At seventy-three, her hair snow white, Miss Strong was no sedentary journalist. She was the only American reporter who had been to Tibet since the 1959 rebellion, and her book[1] on her travels and encounters there is highly informative and certainly unique. Anna Louise Strong was most generous to me with her time while I was in Peking, and I never failed to profit from a conversation with her.

There were advantages to what was called a State Department "validation" of my passport for travel in China, but it left me neither fish nor fowl. I was not one of those Americans involuntarily detained as a "guest of the state," but not one of those traveling "illegally" either. If the State Department looked upon me dubiously because I had been able to secure a Chinese visa, it was only natural that the curiosity of the Chinese, as well as that of foreigners, was equally aroused by my "accreditation" by Washington. The paradox had its uncomfortable as well as its amusing aspects.

Some years earlier the Chinese government had invited me, along with Pearl Buck and some other writers, to visit China as a state guest, an invitation Mr. Dulles obliged me to decline. During the war against Japan I had exerted myself to raise funds and other aid for China and I had many old friends there who were now officials. On my arrival in Peking I was again offered state hospitality, which it was not easy to refuse without offense.

"I'm here as a working writer," I explained to an old friend. "My expenses are being paid by my publishers, who expect me to remain free of all obligations except to report the truth."

"But if Field Marshal Montgomery can be our guest why not you?"

"No one would imagine that Lord Montgomery's views on China could be influenced by your hospitality," I explained, "and he is not a professional journalist. I myself write for a living. Few would be charitable enough to give me that much benefit of the doubt."

I had carried back with me a unique sixteen-millimeter film I made of the old Chinese Red Army in 1936, the first moving pictures ever taken of Mao Tse-tung, Chou En-lai and other leaders. I presented it to the museum in Peking, where it was greatly appreciated; later it was used in television and in a documentary movie. The studios wanted to pay me at the rare-film commercial rate for which I had already sold sections of the film to the British Broadcasting Corporation. On reflection I had to decline any payment. The B.B.C. is also a government enterprise, but if I had sold my rights to my film to the Chinese government I was not sure that I might not be accused of violating the U.S. embargo against "trading with the enemy" and I had no lawyer around to advise me. How the Chinese were supposed to accept a visitor compelled by U.S. legislation to regard them as "enemies" embarrassed them as much as it did me. It was only after I had been in China several months that I finally received a special dispensation from the U. S. Treasury Department which permitted me legally to pay my way there.

It would be naïve to assume that a Chinese from Communist China, traveling in the United States under conditions comparable to my own

in China, would not be the subject of very special interest to agents
who protect Americans from spies and contagious ideologies. Former
President Truman once told me that Democratic boss Tom Pendergast
of Missouri (Truman's original sponsor in politics) was trapped, and
his machine ruined, simply because a smart F.B.I. agent in Washington rummaged through a hotel wastepaper basket one day and found
a crumpled letter which had been written by a Kansas City mother to
her son (a former classmate of mine at the University of Missouri),
who was on a visit to Washington. The lady was married to a Pendergast henchman and her indiscreet letter revealed certain background
facts which eventually sent Pendergast to the penitentiary. As the
F.B.I. would not be less diligent in sweeping the chamber of a
Chinese Communist visitor today, one might reasonably suppose that
I could expect reciprocal attention in China. Having also lived and
worked in Russia for three years, I was not unfamiliar with these facts
of life.

Allen Dulles' C.I.A. was said to have operatives in China and it had
been officially admitted that U-2 planes based in Japan had made
many reconnaissance flights. An extensive American intelligence network functioned in Hongkong and at other points on China's perimeter. At the time of my visit official Chinese protests against flights of
American planes violating China's air space already numbered more
than a hundred. The United States fleet in the Taiwan Strait was
protecting Kuomintang ships at China's offshore islands held by Chiang
Kai-shek's forces. American-backed Nationalist spies and saboteurs
were regularly smuggled into South China. Reports of the capture and
execution of Kuomintang agents periodically appeared in the China
press.

It therefore behooved a traveler in China to observe the maxim
about the better part of valor. Surveillance of foreign residents in the
Hsin Ch'iao was smooth, unobtrusive and probably efficient. No caller
could arrive or depart without being seen, and no one assumed the
existence of any privacy of phone conversation. I was gratuitously
warned by East Europeans that hotel rooms were bugged with micro-
phones and even cameras, and some visitors insisted on having a radio
turned on or tap water running before they would discuss even the
price of rice. As I was engaged in no conspiratorial activity, I felt these
precautions were unnecessarily melodramatic.

It seems only fair to point out certain contrasts. In America I read
the *Peking Review, China Reconstructs* and other periodicals or books
sent from China to the United States. Each time one arrived I was advised by the Postmaster that subversive Communist propaganda had
been addressed to me. In order to have it forwarded I was each time
obliged to write to the Postmaster stating that I would willingly receive Chinese "Communist propaganda." If and when the material
reached me it was months late. While I was in China I ordered copies

of the *New York Times*, the *Herald Tribune*, *Le Monde*, *Time* and other such edifying reading matter sent to me by air mail from Europe. They arrived in a few days and were promptly delivered. I was never required to state that I voluntarily chose to read this "capitalist propaganda." This is not to be construed to mean that the average English-reading Chinese would (even if he could afford it) be able to receive American or European publications—if he wrote to his Postmaster, which he most discreetly would not do! Copies of all important Western publications are available to specialists in various libraries, of course, and complete files of Western news agency reports are distributed daily to select lists of persons "qualified" to read them. For reasons unclear to me I never qualified, and had to depend on the B.B.C.

In America I never got a letter from China that had not been obviously opened and delayed. In China I regularly received letters by air mail from Europe via Moscow in three to five days. Only one letter reached me that had obviously been opened. It was delayed three months and came via Hongkong; within was a printed anti-Communist leaflet presumably inserted by some mail clerk. Telephone service from Peking to Europe was prompt and uncensored. I called my wife in St. Prex, Switzerland, several times and had excellent connections. Rate: 44 yuan (less than $20) for the first three minutes. All-wave radios are sold everywhere in China and most hotel rooms are equipped with them. I heard broadcasts from American stations in Japan and the United States all over the country. To what extent Chinese citizens listen I cannot say, but when my interpreter Yao Wei traveled with me his rooms also had all-wave radio.

Chinese security is built into the society, and not primarily dependent on any clumsy uniformed leather-jackets. There was no need to dog a foreign visitor's footsteps; certainly mine were not dogged. Whenever I had time to roam Peking with a camera I did so, sometimes with a companion, sometimes alone. Small children pestered me to be photographed but adults usually shied away as they always had, except those who used to pose for tourists and demand *chiu-ch'ien* (wine money) for it. Storekeepers objected to inside shots, but one day I stood alone in the market on Ch'ang An Chieh for about an hour taking pictures of shoppers. One couldn't have done that in most Chinese cities without attracting a mob. I photographed the old Y.M.C.A. (closed) on Hatamen Street, the Catholic Cathedral (open) and other churches, and, a nice piece of photographic irony, the new Peking Communist party headquarters, built adjacent to the former Italian Embassy in the Legation Quarter and opposite the Peking Club, the taipans' sanctum sanctorum of yesteryear.

With Felix Greene,[2] a visiting British free-lance writer and photographer who looks like Anthony Eden and is smarter, I spent hours in the streets outside Ch'ien Men and Hatamen (gates) taking movies and candid shots of every aspect of city life, with no difficulty. We had no Chinese with us.

One day I passed a house I recognized and knocked on the door. A woman answered rather timidly, but when I explained that I had once lived there for a year she invited me in and let me look around and take photographs of her and her daughter. Some weeks later I returned with some small gifts. It was a Sunday afternoon, her husband was home, and they offered me a cup of tea. I shall call him Hsu. He was a slight, diffident, polite, middle-aged man who "before liberation" had been a bank teller. They had leased this house two years after I left; he said he remembered having heard of my stay there.

It was a small house with one courtyard and a spirit screen; on three sides stood six rooms, a bath and kitchen, with two small rooms for servants on the fourth side. Mr. Hsu and his family had formerly occupied the whole house and must then have had servants. Now they themselves lived in the servants' quarters and three other families had the good rooms. Hsu had a minor clerical job, of which he said no more; his wife stayed at home with the children; that is, she did not work in a commune factory. She was house gatekeeper. I learned that they had formerly attended Christian services but did not do so now. They "simply had no time for church," he explained in a tone meaning what-would-be-the-point-to-that? I asked whether they didn't feel crowded in such quarters after having had the whole house.

"Our son is grown now, there is plenty of room for the three of us," he responded cheerfully. "We have more space than most families." And that was true. Dr. Chi Ch'ao-ting and his wife lived in quarters only slightly better. Here was a family whose fortunes had obviously declined but who had not dropped as far as the gutters and mud from which millions were rising. But what did I really know of them? Not much. Only that their fate was duplicated in the big cities, especially Shanghai, by many families of China's very small, almost entirely urban, middle class.

Walking alone one day, I stopped to ask an elderly man to let me take his picture. He was in charge of a parking lot for bicycles on a busy thoroughfare. He readily agreed, seeming pleased at hearing a foreigner speak a bit of Chinese. He told me he had once owned a small provision store in a neighborhood I knew well and asked if I remembered it, but I did not.

"Things must have been better for you in those days?" I asked.

"Oho!" He looked down at his shabby clothes. "You'd never have seen me dressed like this, but in good stuff. I was a smart businessman, we used to live really well. Would you believe it?"

"Your shop—taken by the government?"

"No, by the bowlegged ones! The Japanese ruined us, had to close up, paupers . . ." he ended vaguely.

"Did you lose sons?"

"Two—eaten by war."

"Any grandchildren, then?"

"Seven!" He smiled again.

"Yet you're still working, Old Elder Born? How old? Sixty-eight! Don't you get a pension?"

He nodded. "Not enough. I have an old lady, our children can't help much. I get this work to do—it's light work. Not bad at all. We eat—but not enough."

Already a small crowd had gathered, just curious people. The old man blinked at them once or twice, nodded good-by and walked away, making adjustments among his bicycles.

On a hot August day I drove with Clare McDermott and Felix Greene to a large new municipal "bathing park," a triple-pool complex beside a big stadium near the Temple of Heaven. The place was crowded and the water was more of an attraction than even Greene's cumbersome, tripod-mounted Bolex. Few paid him much attention as he went all over the place taking footage to his heart's content. McDermott and I used our Canons taking stills. Some young men in military uniform began to follow us but we carefully avoided photographing them.

"Take my picture, please," a lieutenant said to me.

"You're an army officer? And you want your picture taken by me?"

"Sure, sure, take my picture."

So I obliged. He asked a lot of questions about the camera, insisted on looking through the finder, and then examined Greene's Bolex. Why were we taking pictures of swimmers? For what country? What nationality were Greene and McDermott?

"They're British," I said.

"That's all right. What are you?"

By this time I was thinking of him almost as one of the team. "I'm an American," I responded cheerfully. I can remember a time when Chinese smiled when you said that but made life difficult if you were British.

He came round and stood in front of my camera again, grinning broadly. "*Pu yao tou wo*" (Don't tease), he said. "What nationality?"

"I'm an American, an American writer."

The grin disappeared. Then he asked for my papers. I didn't have a thing with me, and we had no Chinese along to explain.

"Give me my picture," he demanded. I had thirty other exposures on the strip which I didn't want to lose. Felix and Clare grew uneasy. They packed up, ready to leave.

"You asked me to take your picture, remember," I said. "I did not ask you. Give me your name and address and I'll send you a copy of it."

But I had said I was an American and I had no papers. How did he know, he demanded, that I wasn't an American imperialist *t'an-tzu* —a spy?

"We may be in trouble," said one of my companions. "I was told never to photograph a soldier. Perhaps you'd better—"

It occurred to me that the young officer was probably less worried about my being a spy than he was about having himself asked to be photographed—and by an American!

"*T'ung-chih*," I said reasonably, "I know your chief of staff, Lin Piao. I knew him in 1936, before you were born. He knows I am here. Do you want to get in the car with us right now and go down to see Marshal Lin so we can explain everything to him? Or do you want me to destroy that picture?"

He backed away when I urged him to enter the car. "You promise to destroy my picture?"

"Yes!"

He smiled uncomfortably, stepped aside, and we got into the car.

"I wonder," I said bitterly as we left, "whatever happened to British imperialism?"

By the time I left China I had photographed two army camps. That young lieutenant needn't have worried; he came out underexposed, anyway. But he taught me a lesson—as a New China Hand.

Part Two

WHERE THE WAVES BEAT

☆

Mao Tse-tung on Leadership:

Of all things in the world people are the most important. We believe that revolution can change everything and that before long there will arise a new China with a big population and a great wealth of products, where life will be abundant and culture will flourish.

The Secretary of a Party Committee must be good at being a "squad leader." . . .

"Place problems on the table." Nothing is more important than mutual tolerance, understanding, support and friendship between the secretary and the committee members, between the Central Committee and its bureaus, and between the bureaus and the area Party committee.

"Exchange information." This is of great importance in achieving a common language. Some fail to do so and like the people described by Lao-tzu, "do not visit each other all their lives, though the crowing of their cocks and the barking of their dogs are within hearing of each other."

It is necessary to consult the lower levels first. We should "not feel ashamed to ask and learn from people below" [Confucian Analects]. Be a pupil before you become a teacher. Listen also to the mistaken views from below; it is wrong not to listen to them.

Learn to "play the piano." In playing the piano all ten fingers are in motion; it won't do to move some fingers only and no others. But if all ten fingers press down all at once, there is no melody.

"Grasp firmly." One cannot get a grip on something with an open hand. When the hand is clenched as if grasping something but it is not clenched tightly, there is still no grip.

"Have a head for figures." To this day many of our comrades still do not understand that they must attend to the quantitative aspect of

things—*the basic statistics, the main percentages and the* quantitative *limits that determine the* qualities *of things . . . and as a result cannot help making mistakes.*

Don't call a meeting if the preparations are not completed. Be concise and to the point. Meetings also should not go on too long.

Pay attention to uniting and working with comrades who differ with you . . . [including] people outside the Party. There are some among us who have made very serious mistakes; we should not be prejudiced against them but should be ready to work with them.

Guard against arrogance. For anyone in a leading position this is a matter of principle and an important condition for maintaining unity.

Celebration of the birthdays of Party leaders is forbidden. Naming places, streets and enterprises after Party leaders is likewise forbidden.

If [a person's] achievements amount to 70 percent of the whole and his shortcomings to only 30 percent then his work should in the main be approved.

Our slogan is "Officers teach soldiers, soldiers teach officers, and soldiers teach each other."

The ancients said, "The principle of Kings Wen and Wu was to alternate tension with relaxation" [*Confucius,* Book of Rites]. *If a bowstring is too taut it will snap.*

We must firmly uphold the truth and truth requires a clear-cut stand. A blunt knife draws no blood.

Although the Chinese people still face many difficulties and will long suffer hardships from the joint attack of U.S. imperialism and the Chinese reactionaries, the day will come when these reactionaries are defeated and we are victorious. The reason is simply this: the reactionaries represent reaction, we represent progress . . . All reactionaries are paper tigers.

—*Selected Works of Mao Tse-tung,* VOLUME IV

16

The Big Change

Twenty-four years ago I first met Mao Tse-tung in a cave dug into the clay hills of the province of Shensi, within the great bend of the Yellow River, where the long story of the Chinese people began. Mao's headquarters were in a ruined town called Pao-an, not far below the Great Wall. He was then the leader of a band of fewer than forty thousand "remnant Red-bandits" whom Chiang Kai-shek had already chased thousands of miles across China.

When I stood with other guests on the terrace of the T'ien An Men during the celebration which marked the eleventh anniversary of the triumph of revolution I re-encountered Mao for the first time since 1939. We watched half a million people parade past in a pageant of which Chairman Mao was Hero No. 1. All over China there were two days of festivities and thanksgiving.

"I haven't seen you for a long time," said Mao, when he shook hands with me. "How long *has* it been?"

"Twenty-one years," said I, looking around the spacious old palace room and remembering former circumstances. "Your cave has slightly expanded in size since then!"

He smiled. "Things have improved a little." He invited me to come to see him and in subsequent visits we spent about nine hours speaking of things that had happened in intervening years—and a few things that hadn't happened yet.

When I last saw Mao, his country had been described as a "mere geographical expression." Manchuria, economically the most advanced part of China, was a Japanese colony. Below the Great Wall, Japan also held the most important cities and seaboard provinces; the rest of China was weak, disunited and bankrupt. Since then China's Silurian age had ended. "China has stood up," as Mao proclaimed on the birthday of the People's Republic, in 1949. Today Japan has no colonies and, relieved of the costs of a great army and navy, enjoys unprecedented prosperity as a military ally of the United States. Today the People's Republic has eliminated all foreign economic and political control, and is united under a single government for the first time since the collapse of the empire.

Twenty-one years ago the European powers still clung to their colonies in Asia. China was begging the West for arms and money and was getting nothing but sympathy. The United States was selling war materials to Japan but Americans were still personally welcome in China. Today there are no European colonies left on the Asian continent except Portugal's tiny Macao and Britain's Hongkong-Kowloon. America has replaced Britain as China's most hated nation. ("Britain," as Lord Palmerston said, "has no eternal enemies, only eternal interests.") China has close allies in neighboring Vietnam and Korea, is competing with Russia for the leadership of the world Communist movement, and in Albania even has a dependent state in Europe.*

China is now in some vital respects a greater industrial power than Japan and is vastly more important in resources and near potentials. She is East Asia's most formidable military power. In conventional weapons and in men trained to use them China has become one of the three great powers left in the world. With Soviet nuclear support—? Ah, but does she possess that support? That is one of the enigmas contained within two major paradoxes about China which continue to dominate newspaper speculations and puzzle the world.

First paradox: It is known that the Chinese have, in a dozen years, brought their country close to solo point as a major industrial power and a future competitor in the world market. At the same time China is having a painful struggle to feed her population, now believed to be close to seven hundred million. North China's three-year drought finally broke in the spring of 1962, when abundant rains brought a good early crop and filled the reservoirs, giving hope of a fair autumn harvest. From its distance the American press discerned only mass starvation in China, however; some people, believing the food problem unsolvable, renewed predictions of peasant revolt and overthrow of the regime.

* See pages 664-666.

Second paradox: Sino-Russian relations. Mutual dependence of the two powers for broad strategic advantages is enormous and many believe neither power has any real alternative to the present alliance. Until 1960 China's progress relied heavily on technical aid from the Soviet Union and her East European satellites.

In 1960-62 sharp and open cleavages between Moscow and Peking over policy and ideology further raised anti-Communist hopes that the two giant rivals for leadership would yet end their cooperation against American power in Asia and Europe. By mid-1962, Sino-Soviet reconciliation seemed more possible, and replenished Russian credits to China indicated a time for a change. Hard thinkers in the West saw it merely as a change for a time, however, and "heard from far, ancestral voices prophesying war"—this time a *Götterdämmerung* led by "disillusioned" Chinese ready to destroy themselves with the rest of the world.

Gaps in our information on present-day China seem limitless. The true state of China's industrial and agricultural economy, the general standard of living, rural and urban communes and the degree to which they may have added tension to her straining efforts to catch up, developments in science, education and cultural life, how China is governed and security measures used against anti-Communist opposition, the extent of China's military preparedness and self-sufficiency, are all in dispute abroad. They are all matters of which knowledge is essential for any assessment of the two major paradoxes, and for any estimate of the danger China may represent to world peace—or that fear of world war presents to China.

Travel in China provides no magic bag of answers to all those questions. The chief value of an eyewitness report ought to be that it helps to eliminate some elements of fantasy and improbability about ordinary Chinese life and brings its problems onto levels more universally understandable. There is plenty of information available about China in academic publications but the average Occidental sees too little of it to feel really informed. Absence of an informed public opinion in the international area is perilous in a democracy; it is a necessary check on the behavior of policy makers who may otherwise succumb to military and other pressure groups operating at the administrative level. The mere possession of abundant intelligence data by high officials provides no guarantee that their wisdom will always prevail in sound judgments of its meaning. (In March, 1939, John Foster Dulles said, "Only hysteria entertains the idea that Germany, Japan or Italy contemplates war on us.")

The task of any traveler who returns from China with a few useful facts to disseminate is not made easier by the amazing number of things people know about China which just aren't so. I cannot hope to dispel such notions in quarters where they are deeply cherished. The best I can offer, to anybody who refuses to believe that the Chinese have grown horns and cloven feet, and that they live on bark, grass and soya sauce made of human hair (as *Time* magazine reports), is the loan of a reasonably good pair of eyes and ears, trained by years of professional reporting.

To understand where the Chinese have been, what they are doing now, and where they are going, it is necessary to know something about the commanding place Mao Tse-tung holds in their daily lives. He is the central personality in all internal struggles as well as in Red China's disputes with the U.S.S.R. and its attitudes toward the U.S.A. and the West. He is also the least known and least accessible of all world leaders today.

Since the death of Stalin, Peking has recognized no mentor but Mao as a Marxist theoretician and ideologist. Unlike Khrushchev, he has been for twenty-six years the continuous and practically undisputed chieftain of a revolution. Like Tito, he won sovereign victory without Russian armed intervention and like Tito he contrived to retain his independence from Stalin's dictation. Unlike Tito, he was never called a traitor or a revisionist by Stalin—although Mr. Khrushchev has lately begun assailing him (indirectly) as a dogmatist. Under Mao the Chinese party evolved its own interpretations of Marxist theory, its own strategy and tactics, and its own idiom and "line" to fit Chinese conditions. Until recently Mao's voluminous writings were acknowledged even by Nikita Khrushchev to contain "new contributions" to Marxist thought.

The nature of Peking's claims to ideological leadership in recent disputes with Khrushchev over the "correct strategy" on the international front, was explicitly set forth a decade ago by Lu Ting-yi, propaganda chief and Politburo member. He declared:

> Mao Tse-tung's theory of the Chinese revolution is a new development of Marxism-Leninism in the revolutions of the colonial and semi-colonial countries . . . Mao Tse-tung's theory of the Chinese revolution has significance not only for China and Asia—it is of universal significance for the world Communist movement. It is indeed a new contribution to the treasury of Marxism-Leninism . . . *The classic type of revolution in the imperialist countries is the October Revolution [of Russia]. The classic type of revolution in colonial and semi-colonial countries is the Chinese revolution* . . . Study of [Mao's theory] will help . . . achieve the liberation of all mankind.[1] *

Mao holds no official post in the government. He has long made his chairmanship of the Communist Party Central Committee the most important job in China. Until 1959 he was also Chairman of the

* Italics added by the author are indicated in the Notes at the back of this book.

People's Republic; officially, he retired in order to devote more time to "questions of the direction, policy and line of the party and the state." There were, it will be suggested later, other internal reasons.

17

Impersonality
of Power

Few Westerners converse with Mao Tse-tung these days; for him to spare me as much time as he did was very rare. Mao freely answered a wide range of questions but for the most part it was off the record—unfortunately for historians. I remarked that what he said was bound to influence me when I came to write what *I* think *he* thinks, and he conceded that that was probably unavoidable.

Even if I were licensed to record everything I heard from Mao it would not "explain China," however. Mao himself does not believe that he is indispensable. Anyone who has seen a little history made knows how impossible it is for one man to turn the wheel all by himself. Nor does one leader's death basically change all the infinitely complex forces which gave him power. The individual personality adds something to the mixture, but it takes a whole nation to produce a Stalin, a Hitler, a Gandhi, a Kennedy or a Mao Tse-tung. Each man is the logical outcome of a long history which involves the whole world.

Of course the study of an outstanding person can tell us very much about a whole nation if we study the *people* all the way through, and not just seek to deify a saint or burn a devil. The many days and nights I spent years ago questioning the unknown Mao Tse-tung about his youth and the experiences that made him a Communist were far more important than an interview with him today. In Mao's case the early personal history happened to coincide with the feelings of personal frustration, injured national pride and patriotic dedication of a whole generation of revolutionary youths determined to remake China. And if Mao had been killed, as many of his comrades were, someone else would now be Mao, doing and saying many of the same things.

"Do not suppose," I wrote as my first impression of the hunted "Red-bandit" of 1936, "that Mao Tse-tung could ever be the 'savior' of China. There will never be any one 'savior' of China. Yet undeniably you feel a certain force of destiny in him . . . a solid elemental vitality. Whatever there is extraordinary about this man grows out of the uncanny degree to which he synthesizes and expresses the urgent demands of the peasantry . . . who are the vast majority of the Chinese people. If these demands and the movement which is pressing them forward are the dynamics which can regenerate China, then in this deeply historical sense Mao Tse-tung may possibly become a very great man."

There is an impersonality of power which exists side by side with man's need to worship an image of himself perfected. If there were no God, said Voltaire, it would be necessary to invent Him. In politics, when there literally *is* no god it is necessary to invent the Power Personality.

That such a person acts within necessities imposed by a historic impersonality of power and its objectives may easily be illustrated in China by hypothesizing a situation in which Chiang Kai-shek had remained godhead. Chiang was born a decade earlier than Mao; his parents were landlords and Mao's were rich farmers; Mao was a peasant intellectual, Chiang a warlord and neo-Confucianist; and Mao became a Communist Marxist while Chiang was converted to Methodism and capitalism. But there was little fundamental difference between the *national* (as apart from social) aims each man had to pursue, the aims which most vitally affect China's neighbors.

In his book *China's Destiny*, written in 1943, the Generalissimo left no doubt that he not only intended to recover all China's lost territories, including Taiwan, but also to reconquer Tibet. The 1960 China Year Book published in Taipeh showed a border even farther south in India than Peking claims. Chiang also expected to Sinicize Inner Mongolia, to "recover" Outer Mongolia (whose independence he refused to re-recognize in the U.N. in 1961), and to reassert China's ancient close ties with Burma, Vietnam and Korea. If he held power today history would oblige Chiang to support or seek to establish friendly regimes in all those bordering states. He would doubtless be criticized for murdering Communist intellectuals, conscripting labor, and quarreling with India over the Tibetan border states or territories. The impersonality of power would find him demanding unlimited aid from the U.S.A. to feed his anti-Soviet armies and to police starving peasants and Red bandits. And if aid were not sufficiently generous he would probably be blackmailing Washington with threats to join Khrushchev's camp.

The cult built around Mao is also no new phenomenon. Chiang made a fair start toward self-deification; before him there was the Sun Yat-sen cult, and before Sun there were the emperors and emperor worship. Nations which for centuries have been ruled by authoritarianism may cast aside one skin and pick up another but they do not change chromosomes, genes and bodies in a generation or two. Tsar Nicholas II was succeeded by two men as despotic as Ivan the Terrible. The 1960's were ushered in by a gentleman who used his shoe for a gavel. He then exploded a fifty-five-megaton bomb, disinterred Stalin, and made a place for himself beside Lenin.

To call Mao either the saint or the devil of China is relevant only to those who see history as a branch of ponerology. It is more certain that Mao has far greater power to do evil than he has used, however, than it is certain that he has greater power to do good than he has used. Mr. Kennedy seems to have the power to return Taiwan to China; because he does not do so he is evil in the eyes of mainland Chinese. Mao seems to have the power to call off the anti-imperialist campaign; because he does not do so he is considered evil in the West. But neither man really has the power to do either of those things *alone*, any more than he has the power to launch a war *alone*. This may not be accepted by those who seek a single madman or megalomaniac to explain events of which they violently disapprove, but in truth each man behaves within the pattern set for him by history.

Mao Tse-tung remains the giant of his nation and whatever happens to him henceforth, China will never be the same again. But it was not Mao who made China. Marx observed that man makes his own history but he makes it in accordance with conditions of his environment. Before further considering the changes Mao has made in history it is useful to see something more of the impact of past environment on Mao himself.

18

Flashback to Pao-an

In June, 1936, after walking two days across the broken hills of northern Shensi, not far south of the Great Wall, I had entered the straggling village of Pao-an. There a large part of what remained of the Chinese Red Army, as it was then called, had ended a journey across China known as the Long March. The second column of the Red forces was still fighting its way up from the Tibetan grasslands.

At the front, Chou En-lai had supplied me with a small bodyguard. Now as we reached the crest of a knoll overlooking Pao-an ("Defended Peace") a sentry blew a bugle across the valley and below we saw horses and men scurrying up and down the brief main street. Pao-an was the ruin of a once sizable frontier city reduced by years of war and famine. Remains of its ancient fortifications (dating back to Genghis Khan) could be seen far outside the town gates through which we entered.

A curious crowd lined both sides of the street before a few dozen ramshackle huts and shops. Red flags bore the hammer and sickle and the marginal inscription of a recently acquired title: "Chinese People's *Anti-Japanese* Red Army." Banners in English and Chinese were held aloft proclaiming: "Welcome the American journalist to investigate Soviet China!," "Down with Japanese imperialism!" and

"Long live the Chinese Revolution!" At the end of the street waited a group who included most of the Politburo members then in Pao-an. Here also I first met Lin Piao, Lu Ting-yi, Teng Ying-ch'ao (Mme Chou En-lai) and Li Teh, the one foreigner who made the Long March.

Mao did not join us that day until supper. He was then a gaunt, pale figure. Taller than most Chinese, he had large, searching eyes, wide, thick lips, a high-bridged brow and a strong chin with a prominent mole. His black hair was thick and long, on a head for which the Generalissimo was offering 250,000 silver dollars. Mao gave me a firm hand, said a few polite words, and then ambled down the street, stopping now and then to talk with peasants and soldiers out for an evening stroll.

I was quartered in a newly built mud-brick house with a large earthen k'ang but Mao lived in a hillside cave not far down the road. It had a single window and a door that opened on a lane guarded by a lone sentry. There I soon found myself ending every day, or beginning it. Mao invited me down regularly to have hot-pepper bread— or compote made by Mrs. Mao (Ho Tze-nien)* from local sour plums. Afterward we talked for hours, sometimes till nearly dawn.

There was a brief lull in war and politics at that moment and Mao had some leisure. My intense and youthful interest may have won a response in him. I was also a medium through whom he had his first chance, after years of blockade, to speak to the cities of China from which the Reds had long been isolated. He especially wished to proclaim widely the party's new and moderate policy, seeking a restoration of the united front with the Nationalists—a choice which the Japanese invasion itself made unavoidable for Chiang Kai-shek in the following year.

It was only after he had answered scores of questions about many other matters that I finally extracted from him an account of the first forty-three years of his life.

Mao was born in 1893 in the village of Shao Shan, in Hsiang T'an county, Hunan province, south of Hankow on the Yangtze River. His father, Mao Jen-sheng, was an ex-soldier who inherited a small farm but had fallen into debt and lost it. By thrift and hard work he managed to buy back his land and added to it, until he owned 3.7 acres, which gave him the status of a rich peasant. Tiny though his acreage was, labor productivity was so low that he needed a regular hired hand; in busy seasons he took on another. He also used the part-time labor of his wife and three sons, of whom Mao Tse-tung was eldest. The father sold about half his rice for cash and kept his dependents on frugal but adequate rations. Once a month he gave the hired laborers eggs with their rice, "but never meat," said Mao. "To me he gave neither eggs nor meat."

* Divorced in 1937.

The old man regularly beat his children to secure unquestioning compliance. He was himself barely literate enough to keep books. He sent his sons to school, hoping to see them become good businessmen and help him "amass a fortune" by memorizing the *Four Classics* and the Confucian *Analects*. Their teacher belonged to the "stern-treatment school" and beat his students. Mao's first remembered act of rebellion was in protest against such treatment when he was ten years old. He ran away from school but was afraid to return home for fear of another beating. He wandered "in the general direction of the city" until he was found.

"After my return to the family," said Mao, "to my surprise conditions somewhat improved. My father was slightly more considerate and the teacher was more inclined toward moderation."

Mao's mother was wholly illiterate and a devout Buddhist who gave young Mao religious instruction—heavily diluted by his father's skepticism. "She was a kind woman, generous and sympathetic," said Mao. "She pitied the poor and often gave them rice when they came to ask for it during famines. But she could not do so when my father was present. He disapproved of charity. We had many quarrels in my home over this question." Mao and his mother "made many efforts to convert him, without success."

Mao now used political and dialectical terms humorously to depict the "growing struggle" between himself and Paternal Tyranny.

"There were two 'parties' in the family. One was my father, the Ruling Power. The Opposition was made up of myself, my mother, my brother and even the laborer. In the United Front of the Opposition, however, there was a difference of opinion. My mother advocated a policy of indirect attack. She criticized any overt display of emotion and attempts at open rebellion against the Ruling Power. She said it was not the Chinese way.

"When I was thirteen I discovered a powerful argument of my own for debating with my father on his own ground, by quoting the classics. My father's favorite accusations against me were unfilial conduct and laziness. I quoted, in exchange, passages from the classics saying that the elder must be kind and affectionate. Against his charge that I was lazy I used the rebuttal that older people should do more work than younger, that he was over three times as old as myself, and therefore should do more work."

His father devoted more and more time to buying and selling grain and speculating. Eventually he gathered "what was considered a great fortune in that little village." He did not buy more land but he bought many mortgages. His capital grew to two or three thousand dollars.

When Mao was about thirteen his father invited many guests to their home. A dispute arose between them and the old man denounced Mao before everybody, calling him "lazy and useless." Infuriated, Mao cursed him and left the house, threatening to commit suicide.

His mother ran after him and begged Mao to return, but he continued to the edge of a pond and stood ready to jump in.

"My father also pursued me, cursing me at the same time he commanded me to come back. Demands and counterdemands were presented for cessation of the civil war. My father insisted that I *k'ou-t'ou* [knock head to earth] as a sign of submission. I agreed to give a one-knee *k'ou-t'ou* if he would promise not to beat me. Thus the war ended and from it I learned that when I defended my rights [dignity] by open rebellion my father relented but when I remained meek and submissive he only cursed and beat me the more. Reflecting on this, I think that in the end the strictness of my father defeated him. I learned to hate him and we created a real United Front against him." Yet at this distance Mao was able to speak of his father with some objective appreciation. He added that the discipline "probably benefited me. It made me most diligent in my work; it made me keep my books carefully, so that he should have no basis for criticizing me."

The same pattern of father rejection runs through the lives of many revolutionists. Mao simply seemed better able to analyze it, and franker about it, than most Chinese. The dichotomy between his father's harsh conservativism and his mother's kindness and compassion, the sympathy established with hired peasants who supported him against his father, his resentment against male domination of his mother, and her submissiveness to fate, all reflected a generation in rebellion against blind filial piety and Confucian traditions no longer suitable for the nation's needs. An end to the feudal and patriarchal clan-family system, opportunity for the poor peasants, equal rights for women, brotherhood in a new freedom that had to be won by hard struggle for one's rights, by defending the interests of the lowly against the mighty: these were ideas which Mao's early life taught him to share with many awakening youths.

Mao had long since outgrown personal hostility toward his father, whom he now saw as a product of a tough world of cannibalism. It was to the perhaps impossible task of changing that world that he had since dedicated himself. Yet he certainly had not forgotten the Old Man when, ten years before I met him, Mao wrote *An Analysis of Classes in Chinese Society*. In it he defined the poor peasantry as a *semiproletariat* indispensable to the success of the revolution. He sharply distinguished it from prosperous owner-peasants whom he thus characterized:

> People who, by their manual or mental labor, have an annual surplus over and above what they need for their own support . . . are very eager about getting rich and worship Marshal Chao [god of wealth in Chinese folklore] most devotedly . . . At the sight of small capitalists who command people's respect

their mouths water copiously. They are timid, afraid of government officials, and also a bit afraid of the revolution. This group
is a minority among the petty bourgeoisie and constitutes its
right wing.[1]

From such people, who Mao believed had twisted their lives to adapt
themselves to a crumbling society, he had learned that he could
expect no help in building a new one. Poor farmers, oppressed women
like his mother, allies like his younger brothers and fellow students
who thought as they did, "the great majority," as Mao saw it, these
were his friends—and friends of revolution.

An acknowledged beneficiary, in spite of himself, of the petty,
shrewd, Marshal Chao-worshiping peasants whom he despised, Mao
had educational opportunities then shared by very few of his countrymen. Intermittently his father quarreled with him and opposed his
method and subjects of study. Once Mao left farm work and for six
months studied at the home of an unemployed law student. After he
returned "things again improved" for a while, but when he wished to
enter higher primary school in a neighboring town his father made
him put up the money to hire an extra hand on the farm for a whole
year. Mao borrowed the money—twelve dollars—from a cousin. Always among the most impoverished students, he nevertheless managed to scrimp through five years in the Hunan Normal School, from
which he graduated in 1918. In the interim, and while still in primary
and middle schools, he had witnessed famines, revolts, banditry and
executions.

Mao learned to write verse in the classical style but he was bored
by natural sciences and he especially resented a required course in
still-life drawing. "I used to think of the simplest subjects possible
to draw, finish up quickly, and leave the class." Once the "simplest
subject" was a straight line with a semicircle over it. Mao called it
"Half-Sun, Half-Stone," an allusion to a line by Li T'ai-po. During an
examination he drew an oval and entitled it "Egg." Mao's art teacher
failed him. "Fortunately my marks in social sciences were all excellent
and they balanced my poor grades" in art and the physical sciences.

From boyhood on he had memorized episodes from romanticized
accounts of the "Warring States" and other turbulent periods, books
like the *San Kuo* (*Three Kingdoms*) and *Shui Hu Chuan* (*All Men
Are Brothers*). Discussing these legends with old peasants, who also
delighted in them, Mao heard them reminisce about heroes of the
T'ai-p'ing Rebellion, with whom they had sympathized. Like "most
of his schoolmates" Mao could read such forbidden and subversive
works only covertly—hiding them under texts of the classics when
the teacher walked past. It was these epics, rich in details of strategy
and tactics, and the military experience summarized in the works of
Sun Wu Tzu, greatest of the ancient military experts (fifth century

B.C.), which were to provide for Mao, in later life, basic understanding of the arts of defense and offense in the prosecution of revolutionary war.

"I read *Shen Shih Wei-yen* [*Words of Warning*], which I liked very much," said Mao. "The authors, a number of old reformist scholars, thought that the weakness of China lay in her lack of Western appliances—railways, telephones, telegraphs and steamships." His father distrusted such ideas; aside from being downright subversive they were of less practical value than a sound working knowledge of the *Analects*. Mao Tse-tung had to cover up the window of his room late at night when he read *Words of Warning*. He "was much influenced by such books, read at an early age"—and in defiance of filial obedience.

Fired by reading the works of the reformist scholars K'ang Yu-wei and Liang Ch'i-ch'ao, and by Sun Yat-sen's *sub rosa* writings in *The People's Strength*, smuggled into the classrooms, Mao had by 1910 become an antimonarchist in mind and heart. In Changsha he had seen the heads of rebels mounted on poles to strike terror into the people. It was not the first time Mao had witnessed such sanguinary reprisals. As a child he had watched poor peasants, driven by starvation during famine, sack the granaries of the gentry. When leaders of the bandits were captured their heads had also been spiked and displayed as a public warning. By now he fully understood the price of both social and national revolt. But his own principal soon defiantly invited revolutionaries to speak before the students, awaken sorrow and arouse patriotism to "save China from dismemberment." As a gesture of dedication to the cause Mao cut off his own queue and helped sever the pigtails of some students less ardent than himself. In 1911 he enlisted in the republican forces after he had witnessed the seizure of Changsha. Six months later he "resigned"; the emperor had abdicated and a republic was proclaimed. "Thinking the revolution was over," he explained, "I decided to return to my books." After many vacillations Mao determined to become a teacher.

It quickly became apparent that a mere change from dynastic rule to military dictatorship would not end China's decline. Mao began to spend most of his limited cash on newspapers, in order to follow local and national politics. The famous *New Youth* magazine, edited by Ch'en Tu-hsiu, a returned student from France, made a deep impression on Mao and other students of the time. Echoing Ch'en's revolutionary ideas in Hunan, Mao Tse-tung gathered together some friends to form a "discussion group," very serious in intent. In some ways, it was the prototype of the *hsueh hsi,* or study groups, which were to become a standard feature of "thought-remolding" disciplines applied over all China a generation later.

In his college discussion group Mao Tse-tung built up a following among students and asserted his political leadership for the first time.

Everything they did and said "must have a purpose," he told me. They wasted no words on "love or romance and considered the times too critical and the need for knowledge too urgent to discuss women or personal matters. I was not interested in women. My parents had married me when I was fourteen to a girl of twenty but I had never lived with her—and never did. I did not consider her my wife and at this time gave little thought to her.

"Quite aside from discussions of feminine charm, which usually play an important role in the lives of young men of our age, my companions even rejected talk of ordinary matters of daily life. I remember once being in the house of a youth who began to talk to me about buying some meat, and in my presence called in his servant and discussed the matter with him. I was annoyed and did not see this fellow again. My friends and I preferred to talk of large matters —the nature of men, of human society, of China, the world, and the universe!"

More unusual for Chinese students of that time, Mao and his friends became ardent physical culturists. They sought to toughen and steel themselves by taking long excursions, living in the mountains on a minimum of food, sleeping in the open, bathing in cold streams in November, going shirtless and shoeless, "seeing the country," "living as the poor people lived," testing themselves, "body-building." One summer Mao and another student walked across five counties of his native province, "without using a single copper. The peasants fed us and gave us a place to sleep; wherever we went we were kindly treated." It was always the poor peasants, Mao noticed, who were generous in sharing what little they had. Discussing their lives and problems, Mao learned of hardships and injustice beyond anything he had suffered.

In these same counties, and to the homes of many of the same peasants who had sheltered him, Mao would ten years later return to launch the peasant movement which provided the first recruits for the Red Army.

Mao and his group had opened a wide correspondence with students in other towns and cities. This led to the need for "a more closely knit organization." In 1917 Mao helped form the New People's Study Society. Many members later became Communists and "the majority of them were killed in the counterrevolution of 1927." Similar societies were springing up in other parts of China, and sending delegates to Peking. In that capacity Mao Tse-tung made his first trip to the capital, in 1918. That year his mother died and he "more than ever lost interest in returning home."

In Peking Mao tentatively stepped upon the national political stage, at the age of twenty-five. Provincial education in China was sketchy and confused in this time of transition from Confucian teachings to the first gleanings from the Western world, but Mao had already made wide-ranging contacts and done omnivorous reading in the Changsha library. In his self-study he was guided by his favorite professor, Yang Chen-ch'i, British-educated, "an idealist and a man of high moral character." He taught Mao the first (among the few) English words he ever learned. Now Mao found Yang again, as a professor at Peking National University. Through his help the young delegate from the New People's Study Society obtained a job under the university librarian, Li Ta-chao. Here he also fell in love with Yang Chen-ch'i's daughter, K'ai-hui; they were married in 1920.

Both Li Ta-chao and Mao's youthful and beautiful bride were executed a few years later, after membership in the Communist party was made a capital offense.

As an assistant librarian Mao's job was "so low that people avoided him." On his arrival in Peking Mao shared a k'ang with Professor Yang's gateman. Later he lived "in a little room which held seven other people. When we were all packed fast on the k'ang there was scarcely room to breathe. I had to warn people on each side when I wanted to turn over." They could not afford wood for a fire but shared each other's bodily warmth. Among them they had one winter coat, and they wore it in turn when they wished to go out at night.

But "the beauty of the old capital was a vivid and living compensation," Mao remembered. "In the parks and the old palace grounds I saw the early northern spring; I saw the white plum blossoms flower while the ice still held solid over the North Sea. I saw the willows over Pei Hai with the ice crystals hanging from them and remembered the description of the scene by the T'ang poet Chen Chang, who wrote about Pei Hai's winter-jeweled trees looking 'like ten thousand peach trees blossoming.' "

In spite of his poverty and humble occupation Mao managed to meet important leaders of the cultural renaissance, including Hu Shih and Ch'en Tu-hsiu. As an editor and political mentor Ch'en influenced Mao "more than anyone else." Under his spell and that of Li Ta-chao and other senior intellectuals of that time, the impact of the Russian Revolution turned Mao from belief in parliamentarism, bourgeois democracy, gradualism and ethical idealism, toward Marxism and a commitment to socialist revolution. In 1918 he had joined a study group organized by Li Ta-chao and there first read some Marxist classics.

"Three books especially carved my mind," he answered a question for me, "and built up in me a faith in Marxism from which, once I had accepted it as the correct interpretation of history, I did not afterward waver. These were the *Communist Manifesto, Class Struggle*, by Kautsky, and *History of Socialism*, by Kirkup." By the summer of 1920 Mao considered himself a Marxist, and in the following year he joined Li Ta-chao and ten others to found the Chinese Communist Party.

The ensuing years of Mao's life are largely the history of that party. His leadership was not to assume great national significance until after 1926, but in retrospect it is clear that his experience in organizing the peasant unions of his native province came to dominate his own thinking and, ultimately, the course of the revolution.

From its formation throughout the subsequent years of the first United Front with the Kuomintang and down to the break, in 1927, the line and policies of the Chinese party were largely determined by representatives of the Comintern (Communist International), master-minded from Moscow. During the most fateful period of the Na-tionalist Revolution, 1926-27, Josef Stalin (under constant attack from Trotsky) headed the Comintern and its agents in China took directives from him. From afar, Stalin perhaps saw the revolution primarily as a useful weapon with which to strike at Moscow's archenemies, the great capitalist powers, which were considering large-scale armed intervention in China. Until China achieved na-tional unification and independence the revolution should remain under the leadership of Kuomintang progressive Chinese bourgeoisie, Stalin believed. The Chinese proletariat was yet far too weak (fewer than two million industrial workers) to take power alone. In the peasants he had little faith; they were wavering, "petty-bourgeois" in mentality. Subordination of the Communists' ultimate aim to the interests of unity with the bourgeoisie was, thought Stalin, an essen-tial condition of their survival and future success. He somewhat limited, or tried to limit, Communist arming of the workers and peasants and gave major military and financial help directly to Chiang Kai-shek.

Restraints placed upon the Communists were insufficient, however, to lull the fears of the warlord-landlord-banking interests behind Chiang's controlling right wing of the Kuomintang. The Nationalist forces had reached the Yangtze River by 1926. It was not until after Generalissimo Chiang Kai-shek took Nanking that he turned to the destruction of all Communist-influenced troops. Labor-union organ-izers had seized the Chinese city of Shanghai (not the foreign settle-ments) in March, 1927. They were attacked and disarmed in a counter coup led by Shanghai gangsters, supported by the arrival of Chiang's main forces early in April. Thereafter Chiang Kai-shek made war on the labor unions and thoroughly smashed their urban mass organiza-tions. In the countryside, and particularly in the province of Hunan, the extirpation of the peasant associations turned out to be far more difficult than anticipated. Here Mao Tse-tung entered the dispute on high strategy with his first open defiance of a Comintern line which he believed had led the party to disaster.

Of all Mao's writings, probably none is more important for a student of history than his *Report on an Investigation into the Peasant Move-ment in Hunan*,[2] written in February, 1927, and urged upon the Polit-buro, together with proposals to change party policy, in the last days of the United Front. For a few weeks, following Chiang Kai-shek's *coup d'état* at Nanking and Shanghai, a Left Kuomintang regime remained in power upriver at Hankow, where the two-party alliance hung in precarious imbalance. As secretary of the Chinese Communist Party, Ch'en Tu-hsiu was responsible for placating the Hankow militarists. Mao Tse-tung, as head of the Peasant Department of the Politburo, had repeatedly attacked Ch'en Tu-hsiu's vacillating and negative directives concerning the peasant associations, the arming of the peasants, and redistribution of land. Ch'en was not opposed to the arming of the peasants so much as he was concerned with trying to reconcile two contradictory directives from the Comintern, which in essence were: 1) maintain the united front with the Kuomintang by all means; 2) meet the demands of the peasants, especially for land confiscation. The "united front" with the Kuomintang at Hankow rested upon the support of Hunanese militarists who were themselves big landlords. To threaten their land would (and did) end cooperation. In a decisive May meeting Ch'en tabled Mao's report and four months later had him read out of the Politburo. Thus the teacher disowned his disciple; but behind Ch'en loomed Stalin.

Shortly afterward the Hankow regime ordered the Soviet advisers out of the country, severed its alliance with the Communists, and descended upon its mass organizations with a violence particularly savage in Hunan, where numerous peasant leaders and intellectuals were executed. Mao himself escaped, probably only because Ch'en had ordered him not to return to Hunan. Having fulfilled its mission the Left Kuomintang now disintegrated, Chiang Kai-shek emerged supreme, and the Communist party was driven underground.

Mao's 1927 report had been the result of thirty-two days of travel in five counties of Hunan, starting in his native Hsiang-T'an, where he had gathered information to try to convince Ch'en that all the peasants of China were about to "rise like a tornado" of such force that "no power, however great, will be able to suppress it." He announced that the poor peasants of China were "the vanguard of the revolution"—almost a heresy in the eyes of orthodox Marxists; only an industrial proletariat could be the vanguard of a social revolution. Mao reported that "the poor peasants comprise 70 percent of the rural population; the middle peasants, 20 percent; the rich peasants and landlords, 10 percent." What was more: the "enormous mass of the *poor peasants* are the backbone of the peasant associations." Also, "being the most revolutionary, the poor peasants have won the leadership. . . . This leadership of the poor peasants is absolutely necessary, Without the poor peasant there can be no revolution. Their general direction of the revolution has never been wrong."

Mao now and henceforth saw himself as their champion.

Party critics (those who bothered to read him) had called his associations a "movement of the riffraff" and of "lazy good-for-nothings," which unnecessarily frightened the bourgeoisie. But these associations then embraced about half the population of Hunan. Were they all riffraff? Mao listed "Fourteen Great Deeds" they had already accomplished. These items clearly reveal what Mao considered "good" and "bad" for China and the general aims of the agrarian side of the revolution with which he thereafter identified himself. One of the most remarkable things about Mao's report was that it scarcely mentioned Western imperialism, the major preoccupation of Comintern strategy of the time; almost its entire emphasis was on the necessity to over-throw landlord-gentry oppression in order to liberate the peasantry from "feudalism" and inequality.

Greatest of the "deeds" was that the poor peasants had at last actually organized—a miracle in itself—against "the local bullies," the "bad gentry," and "the corrupt officials." Among other good deeds they were smashing the political prestige of the landlords; compelling them to "audit accounts"; forcing them to make contributions to the starving; parading the "most brutal" oppressors through the streets wearing "tall paper hats"; prohibiting usury, grain hoarding, speculation, excessive rents; taking over the offices of police chiefs and electing magistrates; taking command of the landlords' militia and its arms; eliminating banditry (by bringing bandits into the peasant associations!); overthrowing feudal clan tyranny of rich over poor; fining oppressive landlords and helping themselves to their provisions; ridiculing superstitious practices; ending male tyranny over women; spreading knowledge of the "Three Principles"; prohibiting gambling, opium-smoking, sumptuous feasts, expensive weddings and elaborate funerals; sponsoring mass education for illiterates; organizing marketing and credit cooperatives; and building roads and irrigation ditches financed by "contributions" from the landlords.

"No ancestral temple dare any longer, as it used to, inflict cruel and corporal and capital punishments like 'beating,' 'drowning,' and 'burying alive,'" Mao reported. In instances the peasants had found that "the only effective way of suppressing the reactionaries is to execute, in every county, at least some of those whose crimes and wrongdoings are most serious"—of whom Mao mentioned, in his own Hsiang T'an, two men he accused of having "murdered" "more than fifty" poor men "euphemistically described as bandits." [3]

Such was Mao's vision of good and evil in the countryside. Such became the program of history's first Communist-led revolution based on the poor peasantry as its "vanguard."

After the Hankow debacle Moscow blamed the hapless Ch'en Tu-hsiu for misinterpreting Stalin's contradictory directives, but the party line continued to rely on the proletariat and insurrections in the cities. Attempts at armed uprisings in Canton and Nanchang were bloodily suppressed. Moscow-trained Li Li-san regrouped the shattered party underground and, with Chou En-lai at his side, led it in more putsches (aided by the Comintern) which proved disastrous. By 1932 Chiang Kai-shek and the foreign-policed concessions had made the cities untenable for even a skeleton party apparatus. The bulk of the Central Committee then fled to rural sanctuaries meanwhile built up by Mao Tse-tung and others who believed in the "poor peasantry as vanguard."

After the unseating of Ch'en Tu-hsiu, in August, 1927, Mao had returned to Hunan, where, still lacking party approval, he proceeded to follow a policy based on his own neglected report on the peasant movement. Gathering together the pieces of the peasant associations —their local leadership having been decapitated by the Kuomintang— he launched the first armed rural insurrection, called the Autumn Crop Uprising. By September it had developed what was called the First Division of the First Peasants and Workers Army. Besides recruits from the shattered unions Mao brought in some miners from Hanyang unions and some Kuomintang forces which revolted against the Wuhan (Hankow) government.

Inexperienced and poorly armed, the little band was quickly surrounded and forced into disorderly retreat. Mao himself was captured by Kuomintang forces and almost beheaded. While he was being taken to the execution grounds he broke loose and fled into a swamp where he hid himself and eluded pursuers. Fleeing southward at night he emerged, barefoot and with seven dollars in his pocket; by good luck he came upon friendly peasants who helped him reestablish contact with his remnant forces. Rallying about a thousand men, he retreated to a mountain stronghold called Chingkangshan, and there established the first base of the new revolution. In May, 1928, he was finally reinforced by the arrival of troops from Nanchang, where Chu Teh (as Kuomintang police commander) had led the illfated Nanchang Uprising. From this time on Mao had a trained and able military commander beside him, and he and Chu Teh became inseparable. Mao told me:

"Because the program of the Autumn Uprising had not been sanctioned by the Central Committee, because also the First Army had suffered some severe losses, and from the angle of the cities the movement appeared doomed to failure, the Central Committee now definitely repudiated me. [Behind it, still, were the Comintern experts.] I was dismissed from the Politburo and also from the Party Front Committee. The Hunan provincial committee also attacked us, calling us a 'rifle movement.' We nevertheless held our army together at Chingkangshan, feeling certain that we were following the correct line, and subsequent events were to vindicate us fully. New recruits were added and the division filled out again. I became its commander . . . In November, 1927, the first soviet was set up at Tsalin, on the Hunan border."

Another peasant-worker dictatorship was proclaimed as a local soviet on November 18 in an area far removed from Tsalin. This was formed in Hai-lo-feng, on the southern coast, under the leadership of P'eng Pai, one of the members of the party's peasant department who had agreed with the Mao proposals which Ch'en Tu-hsiu had rejected at Hankow. P'eng had actually begun organizing peasants and leading them to confiscate land and take over the countryside as early as 1924. While still in Canton, Mao was impressed by P'eng's successes and hence had followed much the same pattern in Hunan. The Hai-lo-feng soviet was attacked by southern militarists and destroyed before it could spread; and P'eng was captured and executed. The survivors, led by Ho Lung, eventually joined Mao and Chu Teh in Hunan and Kiangsi.

In the winter of 1928-29, Mao's action during and following the Autumn Uprising, and the formation of the Tsalin Soviet and the first Red Army, finally won approval of the Comintern, still bossed by Stalin. It would be wrong to assume, however, that Mao's general line based on the Hunan report was fully accepted. Mao was reinstated in the Central Committee and the Politburo, but his leadership was not to be conceded till 1935. Meanwhile, Mao himself never openly defied Stalin or challenged orthodox Marxist doctrine, which continued to hold that "seizure of power" could be attained by the party only through the urban working class. Mao's problem in semantics was one of loyally upholding Stalin's infallibility, and maintaining an orthodox posture, while the party in practice became almost solely dependent on the peasantry. This he managed to do by means of postulating the existence of a "rural proletariat" and a worker-peasant army under the leadership of the Communist party itself acting as the vanguard of the true (urban) proletariat. That Mao was able to become an innovator, in Stalin's own time, without again being expelled as a heretic, required great skill in dialectical polemics combined with the ancient Chinese art of "appear to move in a straight line while actually taking a curve." Whether Mao made "original contributions to Marxist theory" is consequently now a subject which engages many Western scholars and historians in debates as hotly fought as were past ecclesiastical arguments over the question, "How many angels can dance on the head of a needle?" [4]

19

The Long March

From 1928 onward the peasant war spread rapidly. North of the Yangtze River other guerrilla bases were set up which developed on much the same pattern as those in Kiangsi, and also achieved limited successes. Foremost among the northern partisan leaders was Chang Kuo-t'ao, an old friend of Mao since student days in Peking, and a cofounder with him of the party, at Shanghai.

Mao's own story of the growth of the Red Army, made up entirely of volunteers and based on intensive political indoctrination, with egalitarian brotherhood between officers and men—new ideas in China —has been fully related in *Red Star Over China*. By 1934 six separate soviets, south and north of the river, embraced a population of 9,000,000 people. In the largest area, in Kiangsi, a central government was formed at Juichin. Mao Tse-tung was elected chairman—but he was not then chairman of the party.

The "mass base" of the soviet movement was built upon the organization of workers' and peasants' unions, with the principal role in the hands of the "poor peasantry, the vast majority" led by the Communist party, claiming hegemony over the revolution and its ultimate "proletarian dictatorship." Its radical policy included outright confiscation of landlords' estates and their distribution among have-not peasants, and the establishment of socialist ownership over means of industrial production. "Reforms" included correction of most of the evils of corruption and inequality listed in Mao's earlier report on Hunan. Effective leadership required very strict discipline and moral codes and a readiness to share all the hardships of peasant life.

"Gradually the Red Army's work with the masses improved," Mao recounted, "discipline strengthened, and a new technique of organization developed." As early as the Chingkangshan period the army had "imposed three simple rules: prompt obedience to orders; no confiscations whatever from the poor peasantry; prompt delivery to the government, for disposal, of all goods confiscated from the landlords." Eight other rules were adopted and put to music, to be sung and remembered by all troops:

1. Replace doors when you leave a house. *
2. Return and roll up the straw matting. †
3. Be courteous and polite to the people and help them.
4. Return all borrowed articles.
5. Replace all damaged articles.
6. Be honest in all transactions with the peasants.
7. Pay for all articles purchased.
8. Be sanitary; establish latrines at a safe distance from people's houses.

"Three other duties were taught to the Red Army as its primary purpose: first, to struggle to the death against the enemy; second, to arm the masses; third, to raise money to support the struggle . . . Red tactics, apart from the political basis of the movement, explained much of the successful military development." All the elementary rules of consideration were innovations for Chinese soldiers—traditionally contemptuous of the people and regarded by them as a kind of unavoidable scourge and punishment. (Good iron doesn't become a nail, said an ancient Chinese proverb, nor does a good man become a soldier.)

Four simple tactical slogans were early adopted:

When the enemy advances, we retreat.
When the enemy halts and encamps, we trouble him.
When the enemy seeks to avoid battle, we attack.
When the enemy retreats, we pursue.

Whenever the Red Army departed from them, in general, it did not succeed.

---

* Wooden doors of Chinese peasant houses are hung on pegs and easily detachable; placed on wooden stools they serve as improvised beds.
† Used for sleeping.

"Our forces were small," Mao explained, "exceeded from ten to twenty times by the enemy; our resources and fighting materials were limited, and only by skillfully combining the tactics of maneuvering and guerrilla warfare could we hope to succeed"—in capturing arms and ammunition from the Kuomintang forces, the Reds' "only supply base." "The most important single tactic of the Red Army was its ability to concentrate its main forces in the attack, and swiftly divide and separate them. This implies that positional warfare was to be avoided and every effort made to meet the forces of the enemy while in movement, and destroy them." On the basis of these tactics the Red Army perfected the mobility and power of its "short attack"—rapid engagement utilizing massive superiority in brief decisive battles of limited scope.

Beginning in 1930 Chiang Kai-shek had launched four major "extermination campaigns" against Red strongholds. The net results had been only further arming of his adversaries. Late in 1933 he mobilized 900,000 men and deployed about 300,000 well-armed troops in his most systematic effort to encircle and annihilate the Red forces. This time he was successful—almost. Until the "fifth campaign," which lasted a whole year, the Chu-Mao offensive-defensive had been based on well-developed strategy and tactics of guerrilla-partisan warfare. Now the Generalissimo met them with new methods; he followed the plans of his Prussian advisers, headed by the Nazi general von Seeckt. Instead of rushing into the well-laid traps prepared for him, Chiang slowly built up a series of stone fortresses, extended highways, transported the "infected" population, built more forts, and gradually closed a vise upon his enemies.

To Chiang's new tactics the Reds also responded differently, and also under the advice of a German general, Li Teh, or "Otto," who had been smuggled into Kiangsi by the Comintern. Against the judgment and will of Chu Teh, Mao Tse-tung and most of the experienced native army staff (I was told), Li Teh and the Moscow-oriented Chinese Politburo leaders committed the Red Army (about 180,000 men) to several great battles in positional warfare. They attached excessive importance to holding towns and cities. They "lost the initiative" and were very heavily defeated.

As the steel encirclement narrowed and tightened, and enemy depopulation tactics shrank the "human base" itself, the Red leaders made an agonizing decision. After seven years of fighting they abandoned their hard-won soviet republic. They withdrew their main surviving forces (about 90,000 men), leaving only a few thousand Red "regulars" and partisans to fight rear-guard actions. On October 16, 1934, with what equipment and supplies they could carry on the backs of animals and 5,000 porters, the Red Army began a great strategic retreat by means of which—historic paradox—they eventually "recovered the initiative."

It was only now that Mao Tse-tung at last stood forth as the strongest personality of the party. It is one thing to command men in hope of early victory. It is quite another to lead them into such cheerless prospects as faced the defeated Red Army. Completely cut off from all further contact with Moscow, moving into country where the populace had been indoctrinated to fear and hate them, yet dependent on the people for survival, constantly pursued, obliged to give battle nearly every day, to improvise, to maneuver, to double and redouble their tracks to avoid ensnarement, never sure when they would eat again or where lie down exhausted, these were warriors whose lives hung upon morale alone—and faith in their leadership. Many thousands were to desert or fall by the wayside.

The weakest link in the encirclement lay on the west, where the provincial warlords in Kweichow were unable to prevent a major Red breakthrough.

Moving into that opium-soaked province, the Reds captured the governor's headquarters and seized his residence at Tsun-yi. There a historic enlarged Politburo conference in January, 1935, unequivocally recognized Mao's leadership. As chairman of the Politburo, he assumed supreme responsibility for strategy. Moscow-trained Po Ku (Ch'in Pang-hsien)* and his supporters stepped down and acknowledged their errors. High among them had been turning over strategic military command to Li Teh during the fifth campaign. Now Mao's strategy (in general, one of capturing the countryside to encircle the cities) was held to have been correct. His summary of the lessons of the period, *Strategic Problems in China's Revolutionary War*, was to become a party classic. Together with two other documents,[1] it forms the bulk of Maoist thought and doctrine of "the science of combining political struggle with arming the people in colonial and semi-colonial countries."

Political differences behind them (for the moment), the Reds now advanced upon the great adventure which was to unite them more firmly than any political elite in our times. Ahead lay unknown dangers, exploration, discovery, trials of human courage, ecstasy and agony, triumph and reverses—and through it all an amazing ardor and optimism, as thousands of youths, most of them still in their late teens or early twenties, marched into the western horizon on an odyssey unsurpassed in military annals.

Mao Tse-tung first spoke to me of the ordeal, now behind him, as the *Liang Wan Wu-Ch'ien-Li Ch'ang Ch'eng*—the Long March of 25,000 *li*. With all its twists and turns, advances and retreats, from the farthest starting point in Fukien to rugged eastern Tibet, and then to the end of the road near the Gobi Desert, some men probably did that distance. An accurate stage-by-stage itinerary prepared for me by the First Army Corps showed a main trek of some 6,000 miles—

* Killed in an airplane accident in 1945.

about twice the width of the United States. This journey on foot led across some of the world's most arduous trails, its highest mountains, and its greatest rivers.

The first critical test was the crossing of the upper Yangtze, the "Gold Sand" River. As the Reds pulled out of Kweichow they entered the wild mountainous country of western Yunnan, where the river flows treacherous and swift, through gorges thousands of feet deep. The few bridge crossings had all been occupied by government troops, and all ferryboats had been drawn to the north bank. Chiang Kai-shek was well pleased. Advancing in an enveloping movement, he sought to finish off the Red Army forever in these defiles. Far into Yunnan, the Reds started to build a bamboo bridge. Then a commando force countermarched at night through the mountains, covered eighty-five miles on foot in twenty-four hours, and stealthily seized a small Kuomintang garrison at a ferry crossing. Dressed in captured uniforms, they persuaded troops on the opposite bank to send over ferryboats. Under cover of darkness they then crossed the river, seized the fort, and secured a vital route on which the whole army soon escaped westward.

Another strategic river had to be crossed: the Tatu, in western Szechuan. Here the heroes of the *Three Kingdoms* had met defeat, and here the troops of Prince Shih Ta-k'ai, last of the T'ai-p'ing rebels, had been surrounded and completely destroyed with their leader. Mao and Chu Teh had studied both those campaigns; they knew that the main cause of their heroes' defeat had been costly delay. To beat Chiang Kai-shek to the river, they entered the never conquered and forbidding forest domains of aborigines known as the Lolos. All Lolos traditionally hated Chinese, as their oppressors, but there were White Lolos and Black Lolos. To the Black Lolos the Reds declared that their enemies were the White Chinese; they were Red Chinese and the Lolos' friends, fighting for their freedom. Why not unite against their common enemies, the *White* Chinese? In skillful bargaining led by one commander who knew the native language, the Reds negotiated a treaty and safely passed their whole army through territory the Generalissimo thought impossible for them.

The strategy and tactics by which the dare-to-die band of heroes then seized and captured the last bridge on the Tatu is an exciting chapter in itself. Had they failed, the Red Army would have been forced into high Tibet and there likely have perished in the eternal snows. At the sacrifice of some lives they succeeded. Ahead lay a 16,000-foot pass over the Great Snowy Mountains of western Szechuan, and range after range beyond that. They climbed on. "On Pao-tung Kang peak alone," Mao Tse-tung said, "one army lost two-thirds of its transport animals. Hundreds fell down and never got up again." So did hundreds of the men and women who braved the trek.

In July the survivors finally emerged in the rich Moukung area and debouched into the Sungpan region of eastern Tibet. Here they met the Fourth Front Red Army which Chang Kuo-t'ao had led up from the abandoned Red districts north of the river in the central Yangtze Valley. They had had an easier retreat and had even managed to augment their forces—estimated at 100,000. And now, in Chang Kuo-t'ao, Chairman Mao met the last rival to his leadership.

In armed forces stronger than Mao, and Mao's own peer in the party since the day they both had helped found it, Chang Kuo-t'ao refused to recognize Mao's leadership and abide by other decisions of the Tsun-yi conference, where he had not been represented. A new council was summoned and debate renewed. Chang opposed the advance into the Northwest; he wished to remain in western Szechuan and start a new base there; he fought Mao's leadership on both strategic and personal issues. Finally he bodily seized General Chu Teh and some other high officers and held them hostage while Mao considered his ultimatum. A clash of wills which almost destroyed the party, it was described to me by both Mao Tse-tung and Chou En-lai as the most critical moment in its whole history.

The crisis was broken by two factors. First, the rapid advance of new forces mobilized by Chiang Kai-shek in Szechuan, moving in from north and south, threatened to drive a wedge between the two Red columns. Second, a sudden rise in the headwaters of one of Szechuan's rapid rivers, which then physically divided the two forces, completely cut them off from each other. Chang's forces were left on the southern banks.

Obliged to leave Chu Teh a virtual prisoner of Chang Kuo-t'ao, the main Kiangsi column now continued its northward advance under Mao Tse-tung, accompanied by Chou En-Lai, P'eng Teh-huai and Lin Piao. With them also went Po Ku, Mao's former rival, who, along with most of the Politburo, had refused to support Chang Kuo-t'ao. They resumed their march with only 30,000 men.

Into wild lands inhabited by warring tribesmen who opposed them at every step, in and out of thick, gloomy forests and miasmatic jungles, across more headwater marshlands where comrades sank and disappeared, into deep, narrow passes where hostile natives often ambushed them—uninfluenced by the "Communist policy of equality for national minorities"—they struggled on. For weeks, said Mao, "to get one sheep cost the life of one comrade."

By September they were deep in the Great Grasslands, where they saw no human habitation for ten days. Almost perpetual rain falls over these high swamplands, passable by a maze of narrow footholds known only to native highlanders, whom the Reds had to capture to guide them. More animals were lost, and more men. Many foundered in a weird sea of wet grass and disappeared, beyond reach, into the depth of swamps. There was no dry firewood. There was nothing to eat but wild vegetables and herbs. There were no trees for shelter:

at night they huddled under bushes tied together. Worst of all, they could get no potable water. "On occasions men were reduced to drinking their own urine."

When at last they came down onto the Kansu plain their numbers had been cut to 7,000. Still more critical battles lay ahead before they entered the fertile Yellow River basin. After a brief rest, they broke through weak cordons of Moslem cavalry and replenished themselves. They finally united with local Red forces* in north Shensi, on October 25, 1935, and wearily assessed their achievement.

Out of a total journey of 368 days they had spent 235 in marches by day and eighteen in marches by night. Official army records show that they fought an average of almost a skirmish a day, somewhere along the line, while fifteen days were devoted to major pitched battles. Aside from the long stay in the Sungpan (fifty-six days) they had taken only forty-four days of rest, over a distance of about 6,000 miles—one halt for every 114 miles of marching. The mean daily stage was about 24 miles.

Altogether they crossed eighteen mountain ranges, five of them perennially snow-capped, and they crossed twenty-four rivers. They passed through twelve provinces, each larger than most European countries; they broke through enveloping armies of ten different provincial warlords; they eluded, outmaneuvered or defeated Kuomintang troops numbering more than 300,000. They entered and crossed six different aboriginal districts and penetrated areas through which no Chinese army had gone for many years.

Ch'ang Ch'eng means "Long March" in Chinese; in historical names *ch'ang* evokes a meaning-sense of "immortality." One may reject or despise Communist ideology as a universal religion or political faith, but it is impossible not to recognize the Long March as one of the great triumphs of men against odds and man against nature. In the past three centuries there had been no similar armed migration of a nation in Asia, with the exception of the amazing Flight of the Torgut from the Caucasus to Mongolia. Hannibal's march over the Alps looks like a pleasure excursion beside it. Napoleon's retreat from Moscow ended in the complete destruction of his Grand Army. Xenophon's march of the 10,000 is one of history's few other examples of a commander who withdrew his army from encirclement across a whole hostile territory and brought it to sanctuary with a sense of victory in defeat.

While the Red Army was unquestionably in forced retreat, its toughened veterans reached their planned objective with moral and political will as strong as—probably much stronger than—ever. They declared and believed they were advancing to lead a sacred national salvation war against the invading Japanese—a psychological factor of great importance to the rank and file. The conviction helped turn

* See page 466.

what might have been a demoralized rout into an arrival in triumph. History has subsequently shown that Mao was undoubtedly right in taking the Red forces to the strategic Northwest, a region which he correctly foresaw was to play a determining role in the immediate destinies of China, Japan and Soviet Russia.

In Yenan, while Mao Tse-tung finished his own eyewitness account, the flesh still lean on his bones from the ordeal, far to the west General Chu Teh and Chang Kuo-t'ao (now chastened from the hard winter on the edge of Tibet) were themselves emerging with their own decimated troops from the Great Grasslands and soon to unite once more with the "vanguard of the poor peasantry" who had proved it could be done. Thinking of this happy event, Mao wrote a poem for me which I translated with the help of his English-speaking secretary, Wu Liang-p'ing:

> The Red Army, never fearing the challenging Long March,
> Looked lightly on the many peaks and rivers,
> Wu Meng's range rose, lowered, rippled,
> And green-tiered were the rounded steps of Wu Meng.
> Warm-beating the Gold Sand River's waves against the rocks,
> And cold the iron chain spans of Tatu bridge.
> A thousand joyous *li* of freshening snow on Min Shan,
> And then, the last pass vanquished, the Armies smiled.[2]

In Peking today there is a whole floor in the newly opened Revolutionary Museum devoted to these exploits, now a part of the David and Goliath legend every great epoch creates for itself. Every fifteen minutes, a huge map lights up which traces each stage of the heroic route. A pony-tailed girl guide stands before it and retells the story before yet another audience of youths and wide-eyed tourists.

20

Power Personality

Mao's childhood resentments seem to have been well founded protests against tyranny and ignorance, but we have only his side of the story. On his later years there is much more information. It is difficult to separate Mao's adult behavior or writing from the whole Chinese revolution. Should that be considered one vast delusion of persecution? Is everyone who disdains to compromise with the intolerable a paranoid? That would put Patrick Henry in the vanguard. If, after a nation has been exploited, robbed, opium-soaked, plundered, occupied and partitioned by foreign invaders for a century, the people turns upon its persecutors and drives them from the house, along with the society whose weakness permitted the abuses, is it suffering from paranoia? Or would it be schizoid if it did otherwise? Some grave miscalculations in Mao's later years suggest delusions of grandeur. Could they not readily be matched by blunders of bigoted "normal" statesmen elsewhere which are rationalized as bad judgment? Erik Erikson recently described Martin Luther as a great man whose personality found maximum stability only when he discovered his *adult* "identity" in reasonable heresy; in his rebellion against Rome he found truth in a fully justified, good cause. Thus far, Mao has had little difficulty in uniting his personality as leader of a "just war" of liberation, but it may be a long time before historians or psychoanalysts can agree on final verdicts.

It is not my intention to offer that judgment here, nor to attempt any amateur analysis to resolve the "personal contradictions" of Mao's character. A man who has made a career of nonconformism, he demands from the nation a degree of conformism unsurpassed anywhere. He is as aggressive as any civilized leader alive, and, like the rest of them, not above wanting a bomb of his own. He would never slap his soft-soled shoe on the table to demand attention, but he is not entirely free of the exhibitionism that affects other power personalities. The father of any nation must reflect at least some of the paradoxes of its children as well as those of the outside world.

It was Mao's ability to analyze the experience common to his generation—rather than the uniqueness of his own experience—plus his messianic belief in the correctness of his own generalizations of that experience, which distinguished him from compatriots who became his followers.

There is nothing neutral or passive about Mao, but neither is there any record that he has ever advocated a war of foreign conquest. His concept is that revolutionary war is essentially an offensive-defensive action. When people are held in subjection by armed oppressors they repel them by force. Having "liberated" China by means of "struggle," Mao views the world today as divided between two camps in which justice and right will finally prevail after more struggle. Class war everywhere continues in the capitalist countries; they threaten humanity with imperialist war which can be prevented or defeated only by struggle, as Mao sees it. Because he is the product of a land repeatedly hit by foreign invasion and civil war, and was himself a near-victim of counterrevolutionary violence, life has taught him to rationalize all revolutionary actions as "blows for peace."

"War," he wrote at the time of the Japanese invasion, "this monster of mutual slaughter among mankind, will be finally eliminated through the progress of human society, and in no distant future, too. But there is only one way of eliminating it, namely, to oppose war by means of war, to oppose counter-revolutionary war by means of revolutionary war, and to oppose counter-revolutionary class war by means of revolutionary class war. All counter-revolutionary wars are unjust, all revolutionary wars are just. Our study of the laws of revolutionary war starts from our will to eliminate all wars—this is the dividing line between us Communists and all exploiting classes." [1]

Generations of Western dominance in Asia had brought not peace but a sword, and Mao summarized the lesson for many of his countrymen when he said, "All political power grows out of the barrel of a gun." Not until China had learned to use modern guns effectively did the West begin to respect and fear her. It is therefore not likely, alas, that China will be first to lay down her arms.

To Mao Tse-tung, Western observers who expect China to commit suicide by launching aggressive wars of conquest are hypocrites or fools. "Sooner or later," he said, "these gentlemen will take a look at a map. Then they will notice that it is not China that is occupying Western territory, not China that has ringed Western countries with military bases, but the other way round."

To a man sincerely convinced that revolutions are "blows for peace" —and who has actually seen revolution bring internal peace to China —the question of war and the nature of its causes is bound to look very different from the way it looks to those who believe that counter-revolutions are "blows for peace." Whatever objective results Mao's policies may have in an infinitely complex world, there is in my own mind little doubt that he wishes to avoid war but greatly fears it may not be possible. Still less does he believe that a general holocaust would hasten the construction of socialism—and certainly not in time for him to receive congratulations. Mao is not mad. Anyone who talks to him for a few hours sees in Mao an aging warrior deeply conscious of his mortality and aware that he must soon step aside, leaving behind him the still unfinished edifice of which he has merely laid the foundations. He knows that it will be long in the creation but he does believe that it will create everlastingly. Even without the cataclysm of nuclear war the task will take many years. Fifty? A hundred? What is that, he asks, in the life of nations—and especially in the life of China?

There is evidence that Mao has understood his own country better than any national leader in modern times, but his grasp of the Western world is a schematic one based on methods of Marxist analysis of classes as they exist in backward economies like the one he grew up in. He lacks sufficient understanding of the subtle changes brought about in those classes in advanced "welfare states" by two hundred years of the kind of transformation China is only now entering; just as many well-fed American congressmen consistently fail to understand that starving have-not majorities of poor nations will not wait for two hundred years to see their children fed and educated.

Is Mao a blind and rigid dogmatist? "Dogma is more useless than cow dung," he has said. He stresses the importance of concrete analysis derived from specific and concrete conditions. Does he hold that *only* material conditions determine social behavior and that there is no such force as the spiritual, which preoccupies the idealistic philosophers? No; what Mao said in *On Contradictions* was ". . . while we recognize that in the development of history as a whole it is material things that determine spiritual things, and social existence that determines social consciousness, at the same time we also recognize and must recognize the reaction of spiritual things and social consciousness on social existence, and the reaction of the superstructure on the economic foundation." Between them contradictions are bound to exist.

Chinese Communists appear to us to hold extremely dogmatic positions from which no logic can budge them. That is because, once a party line is formulated, all members parrot it with the same uniformity and seeming lack of individual thought or will. But the line is constantly subjected to re-examination in terms of old and new data. There are repeated examples of changes and reversals of tactical or even strategical approaches to many questions—often accompanied by "rectification" movements and downgrading of "antiparty" elements too slow to move with the times. Chinese Marxists, in kinship with all Marxists, do not disbelieve in change but regard nothing as immune to change. Although they are often slower to modify their analysis to accommodate minor changes than are politicians who lack a basic doctrine—and hence depend more upon improvisation and pragmatism—they can make very sudden and dramatic policy shifts. They may leave an obsolete line hanging on a cliff, to the embarrassment of nonparty sympathizers who supported it for reasons of personal interest or ideals without understanding its transitory character. Acceptance of the new line—which may directly contradict the old—presents no problem to the experienced party member, however, whose disciplined faith enables him to proclaim the reconstructed "only truth" on any question with the same zeal and uniformity as he did the old.

In the past few years Communists have been going through an "agonizing reappraisal" of the "inevitable imperialist war" thesis—one of the very fundamental formulations of Lenin—based on changed world conditions. Mao has been denounced as a backward dogmatist in this dispute. We shall see, farther on, that experiences of China to date give more logical support to his views than many persons living in another milieu can readily comprehend.

Inside China, Mao's record as a prophet is very good but not without blemish. As a recent example of an amazing lapse: his promise made in June, 1958, when he set goals "attainable within one or two years," namely: "that there should be available each year for each person 1,650 pounds of food grains" and "110 pounds of pork." In 1960 he told Marshal Montgomery that such Western standards of diet would not be realized for "fifty years." How to reconcile the two remarks? Mao is a complex man. Neither he nor China yields to any simple analysis, be it by Freud or by Marx.

Serious miscalculations in planning have been attributed to Mao, and he has undoubtedly ignored some good advice. Yet he was not too conceited to adopt the ideas of a trenchant critic* by incorporating them into the national "eight-point charter for agriculture." In their original aims the people's communes were the most radical attempt to uproot man and remake his environment since the Paris Commune. Observers afar tend to blame the entire current food shortage on the communes (which is erroneous) and to hold Mao responsible. The

* Ma Yin-ch'u. See page 415.

communes were not Mao's idea alone, as we shall presently see, yet he cannot avoid responsibility for the costly haste of their beginnings.

Foreign critics accuse Mao of indifference to the possible loss of millions of lives in nuclear war. It is said that Mao regards his own "blue ants" *—a fashionable substitute nowadays for the "yellow peril," which conjures up the same ancient racist fears and hates—as expendable. Yet under Mao's regime very great and systematic efforts have been made to preserve and prolong human life and to educate it for constructive effort.

Mao has been called stubborn, quick-tempered, egotistical and ruthless. Yet some Chinese intellectuals who have used these terms are still walking around free men.† At a moment when Mao stood at the summit of power Liu Shao-ch'i was named his successor and today works as closely with him as formerly. It has been said abroad that Mao's vanity surpasses Stalin's. But in a period when Khrushchev was still dancing jigs to amuse Stalin (according to his own report to his Twentieth Party Congress) and doubtless looking for new rivers to name for the boss, Mao Tse-tung initiated a Central Committee decision to forbid the naming of provinces, cities or towns for himself or other living leaders, and banned birthday celebrations in his honor.[2]

In order to hold power Stalin had to kill or remove nearly all the Old Bolsheviks left behind by Lenin, and now Khrushchev has removed every member of the 1953 Politburo except Anastas Mikoyan. Mao has worked with much the same Central Committee for nearly twenty years. Except for Kao Kang and Jao Shu-shih, who were accused in the mid-fifties of attempting to set up an independent state in Manchuria (possibly backed by Stalin), there has been no split in the top leadership since 1937. The Politburo is composed exclusively of close comrades of a lifetime, but Mao has at times been bitterly opposed and occasionally defeated. He has not shot his opposition. Following his own advice to others, to "use means of persuasion," he has either accepted his defeat or recovered by winning a majority in the Central Committee.

Three men who were Mao's bitterest opponents and rivals for party leadership are all alive. One of them, Li Li-san, fought Mao for years, with Comintern backing. When Mao formed his government he made Li Li-san Minister of Labor. Li is still a member of the Central Com-

---

* The term "blue ants" seems to have been invented by certain French journalists to describe Chinese Communist society. Visiting photographers and writers were reminded of ant colonies when they observed masses of blue-clad Chinese building great public works. Blue is said to have been widely popularized mainly because of the universal availability of a cheap, fast native vegetable dye of that color favored by makers of homespun textiles. It has been in use for centuries. Today Chinese wear garments of many colors and patterns but work clothes are blue— whether worn by peasants, students, intellectuals or officials, male or female. The blue work clothes of French peasants apparently do not make them blue ants.
† See Chapter 53, Counterattack and Paradox.

mittee. Wang Ming, who earlier tried to wrest control from Mao (with Comintern support, also) and is still denounced as "antiparty" in the official records of the period, is today a Central Committee member and Mao still calls him "comrade."

Mao's treatment of Chang Kuo-t'ao offers a dramatic contrast to Stalin's vengeful pursuit of Trotsky. At the time Chang led an armed revolt and schism which almost destroyed the party, during the most critical phase of the Long March, he allegedly executed "hundreds" of Mao's partisans who disagreed with him.* At the end of the Long March he was expelled by the Central Committee in Yenan but retained his post as vice-chairman of the Northwest "border" government. In 1938 Chang crossed the border, unopposed, and joined the Kuomintang. Later he alleged that his bodyguard had been shot to prevent his escape. According to Mao the bodyguard is today an army officer.

After the war Chang became a refugee in Hongkong. When Mao heard that Chang was impoverished and in poor health he sent for Mme Chang Kuo-t'ao, who was still living in China with her children. He told her that a wife's place was beside her husband in adversity and advised her to join Chang in Hongkong. Mme Chang agreed, was provided with funds, and went to Hongkong, taking her children with her. In confirming these facts to me, Mao concluded with a smile, "Yet Mr. Dulles complained that we Communists were separating husbands and wives and breaking up families!"

Although Chang Kuo-t'ao has harshly attacked him, Mao spoke of his former adversary with a seeming absence of rancor. He even appeared concerned for Chang's welfare and not displeased when he learned that Chang was being paid for his memoirs by an American institution. Chang had made his contributions to the revolution in the past, and even his recent writing was "not all bad." Mao's remarks about Chiang Kai-shek revealed no personal bitterness either. Once Chiang had accepted the role of a protectee he was regarded less as a serious contender for mainland leadership than as a latter-day P'u Yi, a victim of fate and a kind of secundine of the revolution. (If Americans find this difficult to understand we might ask ourselves how much chance Jefferson Davis would have had to be elected to the White House if he had established the defeated Confederate government under British protection on Staten Island.) Mao and other Chinese continued to respect Chiang Kai-shek for one thing, however: he had declined to support the "two-Chinas" plan aimed at removing Taiwan from the sovereignty of China. On this point the fallen leader and his successor are united.

"No man can rule guiltlessly," said St. Simon, and least of all can men in a hurry. If the successes of China's revolution may be personi-

---

* So I was told by Dr. Ma Hai-teh, who was with the Red Army in the Northwest at the time. For an account of Dr. Ma see Chapters 35-36.

fied by one man so must its crimes and its failures. Mao has not held power by devouring his closest comrades, as Stalin did, but he is not without blood on his hands. The amount of killing during a revolutionary change of power varies with the intensity of the counterrevolution, and in China that was of long duration. Throughout his twenty-two years of power Chiang Kai-shek was held responsible for the execution of countless rebels and sympathizers, as well as four-fifths of the Communist party membership during his 1927 *coup d'état*. In the same sense Mao is responsible for sanguinary excesses no less severe. During the revolution Mao sanctioned "necessary" executions of "archcriminals." His repeated admonitions against killing without "fair trials" and emphasis on "the less killing the better" are not indicative, however, of a sadist or a man with a personal blood lust.[3]

"Revolution is not the same thing as inviting people to dinner or writing an essay or painting a picture or doing fancy needlework," Mao discovered years ago on his first encounter with rebel peasants in action. "It cannot be anything so refined, so calm and gentle, or so mild, kind, courteous, restrained and magnanimous."[4]

Today's image of Mao among the masses is hardly that of an executioner. What makes him formidable is that he is not just a party boss but by many millions of Chinese is quite genuinely regarded as a teacher, statesman, strategist, philosopher, poet laureate, national hero, head of the family, and greatest liberator in history. He is to them Confucius plus Lao-tzu plus Rousseau plus Marx plus Buddha. The "Hundred Flowers" period revealed that he has enemies as well, yet Mao was the only party boss who ever dared open the press and forum to give voice to that popular resentment.*

Some of the hero worship of Mao may express much the same kind of national self-esteem as British idolatry of Queen Victoria in days when the Empire was shouldering the white man's burden. Victoria did no more to discourage that, it may be recalled, than the press is doing to demolish the Kennedy "image" of today. In so far as the Mao "cult" is reminiscent of the synthetic beatification of Stalin when he was alive, it is to any Westerner nauseating in the same degree. No public building, no commune, no factory or girls' dormitory is complete without its solemn statue or plaster bust of the man with the mole on his chin. They are as much a part of the furniture in any reception room as the inevitable green tablecloth and bowls of boiling tea. In Szechuan I even saw a towering simulated bronze statue of Mao made of lacquer so light that a schoolgirl could easily shift it from pedestal to pedestal as occasion demanded. The extravagance of praise nowadays heard in Moscow for Stalin's successor, however, does not seem to give Mr. K. much advantage in a modesty contest. Consider a sample from the speeches of party delegates to the October, 1961, Congress which hailed the new Oracle:

* See Chapters 50-53.

The planting of corn in 1961, in comparison with 1953, increased almost 7.5 times. We all know that this is the great service of Nikita Sergeyevich Khrushchev. He revealed to the country the valiant strength of corn, made us love it . . . [Deputy Chairman Ignatov, U.S.S.R. Council of Ministers]

The value of a state father image in the "democratic dictatorship" is clearly recognized by the Chinese party. With the break-up of large families as a result of industrialization of both town and country, as well as the replacement of family paternalism by party paternalism, the mantle of national patriarch would inevitably have descended on the shoulders of any leader in a country not far removed from ancestor worship and emperor worship. Mao has now become an Institution of such prestige and authority that no one in the party could raze it without sacrificing a collective vested interest of first importance. Probably no one knows that better than Mao himself.

He has also been his own best propagandist by practicing the rule of "physician, heal thyself." Consider this significant passage:

If you want the masses to understand you and want to become one with them, you must be determined to undergo a long and even painful process of remolding. I began as a student and acquired at school the habits of a student; in the presence of a crowd of students who could neither fetch nor carry for themselves I used to feel it undignified to do any manual labor such as shouldering my own luggage. At that time it seemed to me that the intellectuals were the only clean persons in the world and peasants seemed rather dirty beside them.

Having become a revolutionary I found myself in the same ranks as the workers, peasants and soldiers of the revolutionary army, and gradually I became familiar with them and they with me, too. It was then and only then that a fundamental change occurred in the bourgeois and petty-bourgeois feelings implanted in me by bourgeois schools. I came to feel that it was those unremodelled intellectuals who were unclean while the workers and peasants are after all the cleanest persons even though their hands are soiled and their feet smeared with cow dung. This is what is meant by having one's feelings transformed, changed from those of one class to those of another.[5]

Early in life Mao understood the obvious but neglected facts which brought him to power: 1) that the vast majority of the Chinese people were poor and illiterate; 2) that China's greatest reservoir of creative energy lay in this majority; 3) that the man who succeeded in winning its confidence and effectively organized it could gain political ascendancy; 4) that in this massive labor power lay all the "capital" necessary to industrialize China and make of it a wealthy and mighty nation.

Unlike many Chinese intellectuals who looked upon the huge, illiterate, spawning population as their country's greatest liability, Mao saw their "economically poor" and "culturally blank" condition as China's greatest assets. Because they were so very poor, he said, things could hardly be worse; any party which brought even a modest improvement would win their support and hold their loyalty. Because they were so "culturally blank" they were like a clean new sheet of paper. Whoever made the effort to remold their lives for the better would leave sharp, clean and lasting impressions.

"Ninety percent of the people," Mao often said, "are without culture and education." What distinguished him from all previous Chinese leaders, with the exception of Sun Yat-sen, was that he did not mean merely to utilize the peasants in order to attain power, and then drop them back into the mud. The ex-teacher proposed to end the misery and stupidity of illiterate and invertebrate peasant life itself by lifting the peasants onto high levels of education and access to tools of a new environment.

To convince the peasants that by determined struggle they could own the land they tilled, and then to convert that sense of ownership into energetic participation in the mastery of their fate through the "construction of socialism"—these were the not inconsiderable tasks which Mao and his followers assumed, and the results of which are here being examined.

21

Mao at Home

Every schoolboy in China is familiar with the major events in Mao's own history, yet the average youth of today knows less about his private life either past or present than the older generation did. Mao has never written any autobiography except as he told me his life story, and many details revealed in my own book are no longer available in Chinese.[1] Few of his countrymen know his general whereabouts most of the time. For long periods his activities are not mentioned in the press. They often become a subject of speculation by foreign diplomats, who sometimes start rumors of "serious illness" to smoke him out. A man who walked twenty thousand miles across China, he still likes to keep on the move.

On the day I first visited Mao in the Imperial City I saw only two sentries at the New Gate by which we entered. Just west of it stands the great T'ien An Men, on the wide and busy main thoroughfare called Ch'ang An Chieh (Long Peace Way). Across from it is the marble-columned Great Hall of the People. Mao frequently walks from his home to the Great Hall followed by a few plain-clothes men. Within the compound no guards were visible along a willow-fringed drive that skirted the palace lakes, past beds of gladioli and chrysanthemums, to the graceful old one-story yellow-roofed residence. It is

one of a group of palace buildings formerly occupied by court mandarins and later by Kuomintang officials. Most members of the Politburo are similarly quartered, close to each other. The great chambers
and audience halls of the main palaces are now museums or playgrounds and in one corner of Pei Hai stands a model nursery.

Mao's family consists of his wife, his daughter, and a grown son.
The son is an engineer and now works obscurely in the provinces.
Mao's daughter, by his present wife, is a student at Peking University.
Mme Mao (Lan P'ing), a comely moving-picture actress from Shanghai when she married Mao in 1939 in Yenan, has long been in poor
health and is rarely seen in public. She and the children are seldom
mentioned in the press.

The large, comfortable living room of Mao's home is tastefully furnished in Chinese style; directly adjoining it are a small dining room
and his study and living quarters. The meals he eats and serves his
guests are a few home-style dishes of Hunanese cooking. He drank with
me a bit of *mao-t'ai*, the fiery liquor of Hunan, in raising toasts for
the occasion. He also served the Chinese red table wine which was
for sale (unrationed) in the liquor stores of North China at one yuan
a bottle.

Mao is much heavier than he used to be; he eats moderately and
smokes fewer cigarettes. For a man close to seventy, oftentimes reported dead, he was "holding the status quo," as he put it, and had had
no serious illness for many years. He wore a plain dark gray woolen
jacket buttoned at the neck, with trousers to match; this has been a
kind of official uniform ever since Sun Yat-sen introduced it. Mao had
on brown leather shoes in need of a polish, and cotton socks hung
loosely at his ankles.

I should not say that Mao's home and the homes of other high officials justify the term "lavish" used by Taiwan critics to describe their
way of life. His "comforts" are the rough equivalent of those enjoyed
in a good ranch bungalow by a successful Long Island insurance salesman. Mao has a staff of secretaries but that was true when he lived in
a cave in Yenan. Across the park are imperial Manchu buildings in
which he could outshine the White House, but these are kept for
"people's palaces." Politburo members are not interested in personal
acquisitions. They do have cars and planes at their disposal, and they
can entertain state guests in the Great Hall of the People, which seats
five thousand at dinner, and where honored workers and peasants
are often invited to superlative food.

These Politburo members lived communally and ate in canteens for
twenty years or more; they have done their apprenticeship. But they
still spend a great deal of time together, still work twelve to fifteen
hours a day, and live relatively simply. Their wives dress inexpensively,
and do not own sideline banks and businesses such as engrossed the

former ruling families of China. Their worst enemies do not accuse these men of accepting bribes or having bank accounts abroad. They do not indulge in private exchange speculations with public funds or operate on the black market. If there is any taint of personal scandal in their lives it is kept well hidden. But they all have power, and love it— led by Mao.

Mao can't ride a horse any more or go on long walking expeditions. He exercises by swimming. This may partly explain why Nan Hai and the other imperial lakes are now fed by clean running water and the Summer Palace lake in the Western Hills has become a popular swimming resort. It may also account for a new nation-wide interest in swimming and the many good pools built by cities, schools and communes. In 1957 Mao horrified the Politburo by announcing his intention to swim the Yangtze near Hankow. The State Council even got the Premier to try to dissuade him; there were treacherous undercurrents; it had never been done before.

One of Mao's slogans that dot the landscape is "Dare to think and dare to do." He asked for proof that the Yangtze was impossible to swim. A youthful champion volunteered and succeeded; then a girl did it. Mao followed them and made it easily "by guerrilla means"; he floated with the current, zigzagging over and back again. Pretty soon the river was full of swimmers. So many were observed near Shanghai that a rumor arose from abroad that China was preparing for an invasion of Taiwan. Mao assured one guest that the report was exaggerated; China would not use a swimming force to take Taiwan.

I should guess that one of the great prices Mao has paid for power is lack of personal freedom to see the world. He has often said that he would like to tour America. In Pao-an he told me he wished to see the Grand Canyon and Yellowstone Park; his interest in them may have helped inspire recent developments of great national forests in China. When I saw him this time, he said that he wanted to swim the Mississippi and the Potomac before he was too old. He thought that Washington wouldn't consent to the Potomac idea but probably would be glad to let him swim the Mississippi. "At the mouth," he added, where it is fifty miles wide.

Chiang Kai-shek was always an extremely tense, tight little man. Mao is relaxed, deliberate in his movements, quick to perceive any nuance in a remark, and a man with not exactly a twinkle but a quizzical beam in his eye. He has an infectious laugh and thoroughly enjoys a witty remark. He also has an incandescent temper.

To be a leader dedicated not just to the explanation of history but to the task of changing it—with the lives of a quarter of the human race at stake—is not easy. Jawaharlal Nehru once told me that the only moment he felt "really free" was "on top of a mountain." After

Mao's first swim across the Yangtze, at the age of sixty-four, he wrote
a poem which at a glance might suggest the same escapist longing for
peace:

> I care not that the wind blows and the waves beat;
> It is better than idly strolling in a courtyard;
> Today I am free!
> It was on a river that the Master said:
> "Thus is the whole of nature flowing!" [2]

"The Master" is Confucius, who wrote in the *Analects,* after reflecting
on the bank of a river: "Thus is the whole of Nature flowing *ceaselessly, day and night.*" It becomes evident on closer reading that here,
as in all Mao's poems, there is a political meaning, and that it is far
from idealizing withdrawal. As the wind blows and the waves beat
Mao finds himself in a scene of elemental change; because he is in
the midst of this struggle he feels wholly alive and free.

Mao likes to be his own reporter. He averages only four months a
year in Peking and is free to travel in China if not America. He visits
the big cities regularly and keeps in close touch with provincial party
leaders and also with the lower ranks. He drops in on new projects,
communes, factories, nurseries and kindergartens, and says that he in-
spects reform-through-labor farms. He frequently makes an unscheduled appearance at a local farm or workshop, where he has long talks
with the peasants and tries their food. My talk with him revealed that
he knows close to the calorie what the average child and adult are
eating; in a time of successive natural catastrophes, he knows how far
it is from adequate.

Many of Mao's disappearances from public view are long periods of
solitary study. He may spend as much as a whole week reading, a
habit acquired in his youth. He once left a middle school he was attending because "its regulations were objectionable," and spent the
term "reading every day in the Hunan Provincial Library."

He told me: "I was very conscientious about it, and the half-year I
spent in this way I consider to have been extremely valuable to me. I
went to the library in the morning when it opened. At noon I paused
only long enough to buy and consume two rice cakes, which were my
daily lunch. I stayed in the library every day reading until it closed.

"During this period of self-education I read many books and studied
world geography and world history. There for the first time I saw and
studied with great interest a map of the world. I read Adam Smith's
The Wealth of Nations, and Darwin's *Origin of Species* and a book
on ethics by John Stuart Mill. I read the works of Rousseau, Spencer's
Logic, and a book on law written by Montesquieu. I mixed poetry
and romances and tales of ancient Greece with serious study of history and geography of Russia, America, England, France and other

countries." Much earlier he had been "fascinated by accounts of the rulers of ancient China: Yao, Shun, Ch'in Shih Huang Ti, and Han Wu-ti."

Mao probably has a better knowledge of Western classics, read in translation, than any Western ruler has of Chinese literature. Nor has he confined his reading to political tracts. Recently he surprised a French visitor with an apt allusion to the character of Marguerite Gauthier, La Dame aux Camélias.

Mao was never out of China until he visited Russia and Eastern Europe in late 1949 and early 1950. He has never seen any non-Communist foreign land, not even India or Japan, nor does he speak any foreign language. Up to 1962, only one person in the Politburo, Lo Fu, had ever seen any part of the New World. It is doubtful if anyone on a level lower than the Politburo could make himself heard with theories contradictory to Mao's own concepts of "American imperialism," which are more rigid and oversimplified than on most subjects.

According to Lenin's theses "imperialism" is capitalism in its "highest stage" of development, or "monopoly capitalism," of which the great American banks and corporate empires are held to be classic examples. In this "final" stage capitalism seeks world domination by various means of which the traditional colonial system is but one. "Oppression," "exploitation," "enslavement" and the collection of tribute in the form of super-profits at home and abroad, say Leninists, can be more effectively imposed by the manipulation of money power in private hands which direct the capitalist government, than by direct military or colonial power in the same hands.

Both Mao Tse-tung and Khrushchev regard the United States as the last and dying champion of world capitalism. They differ in their concepts of how the sick man is to be eased out of his misery and who is to administer euthanasia to him to make way for socialist liberation. They believe that American "monopoly capitalists" see, in the break-up of the older colonial empires, great opportunities for the extension of American power—a view still not altogether discounted in Europe.

The American position in Taiwan itself fits definitions of both old-fashioned colonialism and neoimperialist domination.

That may come as a surprise to many readers of these pages, who may also need to be reminded that Mao Tse-tung and other Chinese leaders do know the United States in one direct and negative way, through their experiences with the American army in China during the Second World War. The United States used its influence to prevent Chiang Kai-shek from renewing open civil war while the Japanese occupation forces remained in China, but throughout that period, when the Communists led the fight behind Japanese lines, not a rifle or cartridge or even a bandage of U.S. government aid ever reached their forces; all American equipment was given exclusively to Chiang, who used much of it to blockade and harass the rear bases held by the Communists. (U.S. wartime aid to Stalin, meanwhile, exceeded $9,000,000,000.) America's generous support for Chiang in the civil war, her subsequent alliance with Chiang Kai-shek on Taiwan, the economic embargo which has imposed serious handicaps on China's internal development, American-led exclusion of China from the U.N., and the maintenance of American bases in eastern Asia, have all helped enlist mass patriotic sentiment behind the Communists' ideological distrust and hostility.

The "thought of Mao Tse-tung" as presented to the masses is both complex and simple. It is complex because the politically literate Chinese is supposed to learn to think in "dialectics" in order to follow "the Chairman's" complete meaning. It is simple because Mao's writing makes its points by use of colorful paradox, earthy epigrams and epithets, folklore allusions, imperialist paper tigers, and commonplace examples obvious to all. And all must learn the essence of the teaching. "Not to have a correct political point of view," said Mao, "is like having no soul."

According to Marx, capitalist society is in a continuous state of class war. What the Voice of America calls "the free world against the slave world" is in the idiom of Marxist dialectics an "inevitable" revolution of the working class (led by Communists) against capitalism-imperialism in which any compromise (coexistence) is merely another "stage" of "higher struggle" on the road toward total synthesis—the final victory of socialism. Class struggles are "inevitable," but international war is not inevitable, although the danger of it will exist as long as "imperialism" exists.

Aside from Sino-Soviet polemics over how "imperialism" may be destroyed—or helped to destroy itself—without major war and mutual suicide, for the man in the street in China acceptance of Marxist doctrine means identifying himself with the forces of light and progress led by the party, and living by a high moral code devoted solely to advancing the interests of socialism and the revolutionary classes. Toward the enemy, the forces of darkness, entirely different methods have to be used. As Mao explains it:

> The [Chinese] people's democratic dictatorship uses two methods. In regard to the enemy, it uses the method of dictatorship, that is: it forbids them to take part in political activities for as long a period of time as is necessary; it compels them to obey the laws of the People's Government, compels them to work and to transform themselves into new people through work. In regard to the people, on the contrary, it does not use compulsion, it uses democratic methods, that is: it must allow the people to take part in political activities, and, far from compelling them to do this or that, use the democratic methods

of education and persuasion. This education is self-education among the people, and criticism and self-criticism is the fundamental method of self-education.

That was written in 1952 and quoted by Mao himself in a recent important policy statement.[3] "Democracy" and "self-education among the people" are still going on and so is the "method of dictatorship." This paradox will receive further treatment, as will my impressions of Mao's views of the world outside what is "home" to him.

Part Three

SOCIALIST CONSTRUCTION

☆

. . . In fact, those two revolutions, the agricultural and the indus-trial-scientific, are the only qualitative changes in social living that men have ever known. . . . Industrialisation is the only hope of the poor. I use the word "hope" in a crude and prosaic sense. . . . It is all very well for one, as a personal choice, to reject industrialisation—do a mod-ern Walden, if you like, and if you go without much food, see most of your children die in infancy, despise the comforts of literacy, accept twenty years off your own life, then I respect you for the strength of your aesthetic revulsion. . . . But I don't respect you in the slightest if, even passively, you try to impose the same choice on others who are not free to choose. In fact, we know what their choice would be. For, with singular unanimity, in any country where they have had the chance, the poor have walked off the land into the fac-tories as fast as the factories could take them. . . .

. . . It took the Russians about forty years, starting with something of an industrial base—Tsarist industry wasn't negligible—but inter-rupted by a civil war and then the greatest war of all. The Chinese started with much less of an industrial base, but haven't been inter-rupted, and it looks like taking them not much over half the time.

. . . Much of the suffering was unnecessary: the horror is hard to look at straight, standing in the same decades. Yet they've proved that common men can show astonishing fortitude in chasing jam tomorrow. Jam today, and men aren't at their most exciting; jam tomorrow, and one often sees them at their noblest. . . .

For the task of totally industrialising a major country, as in China today, it only takes will to train enough scientists and engineers and technicians. Will, and quite a small number of years. There is no evi-dence that any country or race is better than any other in scientific teachability: there is a good deal of evidence that all are much alike. . . .

Since the gap between the rich countries and the poor can be re-

moved, it will be. If we are short-sighted, inept, incapable either of good-will or enlightened self-interest, then it may be removed to the accompaniment of war and starvation: but removed it will be. . . ."

—C. P. Snow, *The Two Cultures and the Scientific Revolution*, Cambridge University Press, N.Y., 1959

22

Steel Decade

Collective life in China today is above all change and movement.

Elements carried over from the past are engaged in dynamic combination and recombination with new elements of the time-present which is itself always becoming a future something-else. Last year's slum may next year be a new school or a garden surrounded by the brick flats of an apartment development. Weather hasn't been tamed (as some Chinese boasted in 1958), and flood, drought or storms can in one season turn a prosperous commune into at least a temporary failure. A production brigade that is without modern machines when you first see it may five months later have electric power and tractors. Food, housing, and working conditions vary considerably. "Good" or "bad" generalizations based on several instances in one part of the country may not necessarily apply everywhere.

Speed-up campaigns slow down for "consolidation," then pick up again. Yesterday's mistakes are corrected, to reveal new and unsolved problems of tomorrow. "Rectification," self-criticism, retraining and restudy among party and nonparty cadres are followed by shake-ups which affect millions. Everything is subject to revision except Marxism, the changeless "law of history." But Chinese Marxism, like all dynamic legal doctrine, makes laws to fit its own history.

The place is still China and the civilization is still Chinese, but nothing of the old has been left untouched and nothing of the new is complete. All is transition and transition often seems to be all. The decade of the fifties saw changes more profound than in any epoch of Chinese history since Ch'in Shih Huang Ti completed the Great Wall two centuries before Christ. China was the largest of economically backward countries. Now her leaders are determined to accomplish in one generation what it took advanced Western countries nearly a century to achieve. A hitherto conservative society has been picked up bodily, turned forward, and started upon a double-quick march to commit one man in every four humans alive to a socialist world. It causes an enormous amount of stress and tension, accompanied by massive experiments, massive successes and massive failures. Every major policy enforced in China directly affects more people than the whole population of Western Europe and North America. As in the case of Russia, what happened to China in the 1950's won't be understood in the West until she explodes an H-bomb or sends a man into space. Quite a few years to wait? It may be later than we think.*

China is not simply a different country; its obsessive haste to catch up with history and to become the world's greatest nation (in more than numbers) is positively awesome to those who can remember a passive China in which time meant nothing. The Communists changed China's *ming* or fate when they fought ceaselessly during twenty years of hardship before winning power. For them the condition of combat and struggle became the normal way of life. Because they achieved everything against great odds, it has seemed natural to the Communist veterans that a whole nation should follow in the same paths with discipline and faith matched by high fortitude, and distant glory as the ultimate reward. It has not always seemed so "natural" to the populace. But these are steel decades led by steel men, an era of "continuation of war by other means" against every obstacle standing in the way of building a modern, mighty, socialist state. Because they arose from the peasants, and are convinced that all they do is solely for the benefit of the common people, these leaders may make far tougher demands on their energies than men from the old ruling class.

Probably Russia, Japan and Germany suffered as much damage as China did during the Second World War, but while those countries (much more advanced technologically) were recovering, China went through three years of heavy civil war before rehabilitation could begin in 1949. India's national debt to Britain was actually erased during the Second World War, and the nation sustained no damage. Germany and Japan received billions in postwar subsidies from the United States, and Russia was at least able to collect reparations in Germany, Eastern Europe and Manchuria. The People's Republic had to start off with a bankrupt nation and a currency in total collapse

* See pages 643-644.

following Chiang Kai-shek's flight with China's meager remaining gold reserves.

China had only 12,000 miles of railways and 48,000 miles of usable roads, all in chaotic condition and in need of major reconstruction. Livestock and draft animals had been greatly reduced and canals and irrigation works had broken down. Industrial production had declined by 56 percent and agricultural output by 25 to 30 percent as compared to the hypothetical peak year of 1936.[1] Population had meanwhile increased by tens of millions, to a total of about 550,000,000. Even that "ideal" 1936 peak production would, if it had been available in 1949, and figured in terms of 1949 population, have worked out at an annual output per person of only 3.3 pounds of steel (compared to 1,130 pounds per head in the U.S.A., 111 pounds in Japan and 11 pounds in India), 6.6 pounds of iron, one-tenth of a ton of coal, 10 kilowatt hours of electric power and eight feet of cotton cloth. Output of chemical fertilizer per person would have been at the rate of less than one pound per year, and output of sugar at less than a pound and a half.

The fundamental problem of livelihood in China was (and remains) the imbalance between people and food supply. Despite intensive hand cultivation by intelligent farmers, China formerly never produced better than an average of 3.5 quintals of wheat to an acre, according to a study made by J. Lossing Buck,[2] compared to 8.5 an acre in Britain and 13.2 in Denmark. (Elsewhere, O. E. Baker concluded that China's average acre yields were only 20 percent lower than in the United States.[3]) It cost 34 cents a day to feed a draft animal in China but a man's labor was for hire at 24 cents a day. Until recently human and animal manure were almost the only fertilizer available. If in 1949 China had used chemical fertilizer on the same scale as Japan, she would have required four times the total world output (some 23,000,000 tons in 1947-48). Dr. Buck calculated that it required 26 man-labor days to produce an acre of wheat in China, compared to 1.2 days in the United States; and 23 man-labor days to grow an acre of corn, which needed only 2.5 days in the U.S.A. By 1951, China had only 2,000 tractors, or one to every 120,000 acres under cultivation; the United States had one tractor to 385 acres and even India had one to 20,000 acres. Since the nineteenth century China's harvest had rarely been sufficient to feed her whole population even if output had been equally distributed. For fifty years China had been a net importer of grain, famine had been endemic, and millions had died of malnutrition or starvation.

Before the revolution China had only about 230,000 acres under cultivation; in more densely crowded sections the inhabitants per square mile averaged more than 1,300. Much less than one acre of cultivated land was available for each member of the farm population.[4] In 1955, Mao Tse-tung put the average at 0.5 acre per person.[5] Cropland actually harvested in the United States in 1960 was 311,000,000 acres, or

62 times more per farm cultivator than in China today, when the total is still only about 270,000,000 acres. In the United States 4,600,000 farm families and about 5,000,000 actual farm workers were sufficient, in 1960, to produce abundantly more food than the whole population consumed, while leaving fallow more than as much again farmland as was actually used.[6]

While American politicians continue to pay homage to the mystique of the free farmer as the backbone of rugged individualism, the truth is quite otherwise. For more than a generation the American farmer has been "managed" (and mismanaged) by the state by means of price supports and other controls. With a working force of more than 67,000,-000 today, American farm workers are less than 8 percent of the total, and farm production itself is largely under state and urban-capitalist management and manipulation. In 1962 President Kennedy formally proposed to plan the entire crop production by further reducing acreage. He sought to utilize state subsidy to convert the farm economy into a factory-farm combination basically not very different in content from the Chinese commune goal of integrating industry and agriculture in the countryside.

In 1949, however, the Chinese rural economy was in a primitive, seemingly hopeless stage, with no state management or support whatsoever and with no prospect that parcelized farming could succeed in modernizing the available resources. Redistribution of the land was a means of mobilizing peasant struggle for the revolution; a mere division of that land plainly could do no more than consolidate the political stability necessary to create and utilize altogether new means to solve the food shortage. What was required was combinations of land parcels into large-scale, modern factory-farms, and radically more efficient means and methods of the kind already cited: heavy increases in fertilizer, more widespread irrigation, river control and power facilities, new roads and transport to open up more land and rationalize distribution, better seeds and tools for deep plowing and cultivation, and mechanized equipment. China was very poor; she could not hope to import such means on a vast scale; somehow she had to make them for herself. But irrigation machinery, power plants, railways, bridges, trucks, tractors, combines, chemical fertilizer plants, all spelled machines and machines to make machines. Above all they meant steel and iron. With an output of 158,000 tons of steel in 1949,* China stood at twenty-sixth place in the world.

China *had* to build basic industry, and quickly: steel and iron mills, machinery-making plants, power equipment of all kinds, coal and electric capacities, oil, chemical, communications and transport industries. At the same time the people whose labor was to create these genies had to be fed, clothed, housed, educated, cajoled and convinced that the effort was worthwhile and indeed unavoidable if China and they

* The Japanese-built mill at Anshan, Manchuria, was then out of production.

themselves and their children were to survive, not to mention win the enticing rewards of modern life. This meant that heavy industry had to be coordinated with the development of light industries to provide the means of modernizing agricultural and urban life and to satisfy at least the minimal needs of the people, whose appetites were bound to increase directly in proportion to their own transition from the wooden plow to the atomic era.

China's revolutionary orientation cut her off from American capital and other foreign investment or aid. In 1950 Russia could still offer but modest economic help. What was new about the Communists compared to past leadership was that they saw, in what Western observers believed to be the deepest source of China's poverty—too many mouths to feed—their very greatest source of new wealth: a billion hands to labor. Their task was to put all those hands to work, to turn labor into capital, and to exploit the virtually untouched and as yet hardly explored natural resources of the nation.

That the natural resources required for heavy industrialization existed in China on an adequate scale was for long disputed by foreign economists, particularly Americans. In 1960 the U.S. Geological Survey acknowledged that "extensive prospecting" by "a few well-trained geologists, including some Russians . . . *has shown China to be one of the world's chief reservoirs of raw material,*" with "vast reserves of coal . . . a great reserve of seven billion tons of iron ore in the Shansi area of Central China" and three billion tons of "50 percent iron oxide ore" in Honan. Very rich deposits of molybdenum have been reported, "making China's reserves the largest in the world." [7]

At the start of the Second Five-Year Plan (1957-62) Chinese "verified figures" of "proved reserves" then being "used as a basis for designing capital construction and investment" were given as 8,000,000,-000 tons of iron ore, 80,000,000,000 tons of coal, and 250,000,000 acres of forests.[8] In addition to well-established reserves in Manchuria formerly thought to hold most of China's iron ore, newly discovered deposits have been reported in Inner Mongolia, Anhui, Shansi and Honan. "China has much greater coal resources than any country in Asia . . . probably inferior only to those of the Soviet Union and the United States," according to the studies of Hughes and Luard.[9]

As recently as April, 1960, however, Mr. Chester Bowles, then Under Secretary of State and the Department's Asia expert, expressed the old view of China's natural endowments when he wrote: "The Chinese government today is embarked upon a gigantic effort to industrialize its 650,000,000 people on a resource base which is woefully inadequate." As a result of what Mr. Bowles regarded as an unattainable and foolhardy ambition to industrialize, he foresaw "expansion into Southeast Asia, with its wealth of . . . resources which China badly needs." [10]

Many historic factors would doubtless bring China into irreconcilable conflict with any United States policy aimed at establishing a military hegemony in Southeast Asia, if that is what Mr. Bowles was proposing. But if he had read recent intelligence from the Bureau of Mines of the United States Department of the Interior, the Under Secretary would have learned that his information about China's inadequate resource base was "woefully" out of date. That report, entitled *Rich Mineral Resources Spur Communist China's Bid for Industrial Power,* asserted: "The extent of [China's] resources was largely unknown until extensive geological work, coupled with vast new knowledge gained through active mineral exploitation in recent years, demonstrated that the country has a sufficiently diversified mineral base to become a first rank industrial power." The report continues:

"Communist China appears to be more than self-sufficient in most minerals both for the present and for the future. The coal and iron base is very strong; iron ore has proved to be much more extensive than formerly thought . . . [At present] petroleum is inadequate but extensive exploration in recent years shows that the country will be prominent in this field five to ten years from now." Besides finding China in a "world position of first rank" in coal, coking coal and iron ore, molybdenum, tin, bismuth, mercury, fluorite, graphite, magnesite and minor metals, and possessing "significant" reserves of copper, aluminum, lead, zinc, gold and silver, chemical and fertilizer materials, this Bureau of Mines survey states that China has "the world's largest deposits" of tungsten and antimony.

"Under the Communist regime remarkable industrial progress has been achieved. Within a decade the country has been transformed from an economy primarily agricultural to one bristling with industrial possibilities." This analysis points out significantly that while 80 percent of China's population is concentrated in the eastern third of the country, much of the undeveloped mineral wealth lies in the west. "Inadequate transport facilities are definitely holding back mineral development. [Particularly in petroleum. E.S.] To compensate for this, considerable emphasis has been placed upon building local industries around resources and markets." By 1958, however, "output levels had been brought up so much that even a letdown would still leave fairly high levels of production." [11]

It was not China's "resource base" but her capital base which was "woefully inadequate." In addition to man power plus resources China had one other asset without which the regime would have been enormously handicapped. As an ally of the Soviet Union, China was able to make maximum use of the rich experience of the senior socialist power of the world in the techniques of building a planned industrialization and managing a planned economy. China had to pay in exports of equal value for all the machines and technical help received, but free access to Soviet scientific and industrial knowledge, patents, blueprints and patterns saved her years of trial and error and incalculable amounts of time and money. Farther on I shall have more to say about the meaning to China, in a year of catastrophic food problems and imbalances between industrial demands and agricultural output, of the withdrawal of Soviet technical assistance and the denial of emergency aid, which put to the severest tests the Chinese party's faith in the creative energies of its own "greatest asset."

For of course the true hero of China's first steel decade was the Chinese people. What has been happening in China reminded me, while I was reading James Michener's splendid novel *Hawaii*, of one of his heroines, Nyuk Tsin. An illiterate Hakka slave girl from Canton, Nyuk Tsin began life at the bottom of the ladder in Honolulu. Through prodigious will, energy, intelligence and self-sacrifice, she managed to build a great family out of mud. By means of nothing but her own labor and the labor of her five sons used as capital, by the harshest frugalities and self-denials, by tireless cultivation of her taro and vegetable patches, by single-minded reinvestment of all her earnings and profits, and by systematic investment in good educations for all her children and grandchildren (while she herself went barefoot under her carrying pole), Nyuk Tsin created within her own lifetime a powerful clan of healthy, cultured, rich and able descendants.

What Nyuk Tsin was able to do, just credible in underpopulated nineteenth-century Hawaii, was hardly possible for any single peasant family to achieve in overpopulated China. It is today being attempted for the whole Chinese people. Using labor as common capital, pooling all profits for reinvestment in production and growth, a new national family is trying to emerge from the mud.

There is one obvious vital difference in my analogy. To Nyuk Tsin that modern collective, the nation, meant nothing, the individual family everything. Throughout her life she was motivated by only one idea: the enrichment of herself for the glory of the product of her personal womb. She was Private Enterprise personified and this had been "The Way" of generations before her. What was the nation except that her family prosper? How far can this instinct be sublimated in a new generation of whom it is demanded that it do no less, in the words of Chairman Liu Shao-ch'i, than "reform mankind into the completely unselfish citizenry of a Communist society"—and still inspire men to surpass the energetic individualism of Nyuk Tsin?

23

Reeling, Writhing and Arithmetic

In 1961 there was perhaps no better measure of China's fallen prestige than that this was the year when even the Indian Communist Party "warned" Peking against alleged violations of India's frontier, high in the Himalayas. In three years the government of the People's Republic had lost ground on two vital fronts: internationally, in ideological disputes with its only important ally; and domestically, in its struggles against the calamities of nature and against the nature of its most important internal allies—the peasants.

In 1958 Peking had startled the world with claims of heavenly harvests as a result of the Great Leap Forward and the people's communes. By 1962 the regime's enemies were exulting in the belief that both efforts were grandiose net failures, and that China was caught in a great famine and facing general collapse. If the harvest claims were exaggerated, so were reports of a breakdown in 1961-62. One of the few things I can say with certainty is that mass starvation such as China knew almost annually under former regimes no longer occurs, for reasons fully discussed later.

By 1962 natural catastrophes and disastrous mistakes in take-off phases of the communes had cruelly combined to expose fantastic overclaims for agricultural output in 1958. Repeated poor harvests since then had slowed down the whole rate of economic growth and in certain sectors put it into reverse. Even with favorable weather, several years would now be required to overcome the food shortage. Until then no major new industrial offensives could be expected.

Even before 1958 an extensive literature of controversy existed abroad over the meaning of Chinese statistics. A dusty answer indeed awaits the soul hot for certainty in that world. Keeping up with the controversy today can absorb one's full attention without leading to anything more conclusive than the studies among the lobsters in Lewis Carroll's submarine school of "reeling, writing and arithmetic" —with special attention to attrition, distraction, uglification and derision.

Beneath all the sound and fury there are, however, some solid facts of astounding growth. Summing up the decade as he had reported it, both inside and outside China, one of the most experienced and perhaps the most consistently objective of correspondents, Tillman Durdin of the *New York Times*, wrote late in 1959, a year after the Great Leap Forward:

"By Draconian controls and pressures, the regime has forced, and sometimes inspired, the masses of China into productivity and social change on a scale unsurpassed, in similar circumstances, by any other country . . ." Mr. Durdin pointed out grave weaknesses of the regime, including "unreliable statistics." He concluded: "If unity and the rate of economic expansion continue, this ancient land will rank, within ten to twenty years, with the United States and Russia among the great powers." [1]

Those who have actually traveled in China today are more prepared to accept Chinese statistics for the *main trends* of industrial progress, on the basis of many kinds of evidence, than those who have not had that advantage. I cannot deny being influenced by what I personally saw of new industry, science, housing, water control, agricultural means, and communications; of improvements in the people's health, dress, education, child care; and other evidence on a scale greater than most of my countrymen or even most Overseas Chinese would be prepared to believe without seeing for themselves, and much greater than I had expected to find.

The "mystery" of the gross overestimates of 1958 involved many political as well as psychological, economic and technical factors which will be briefly discussed when we come to the story of the communes. Meanwhile, it should be noted that the highest leaders of the country themselves were apparently deceived.

There was reason for optimism: 1958 was bound to be a bonanza year in industry because many of the 156 major industrial projects built with Soviet material and technical help, particularly in metallurgy, were coming into production for the first time. Years of basic work in subsidiary industries and in irrigation and improved agronomy were ready, in coordination with the "blowing in" of prime heavy industry, for a maximum effort. Above all, for once the weather all over China was nearly perfect. In the same year came the big psychological push of the Great Leap Forward slogans and the launching of rural communes. The whole party apparatus, and much of the population, was brought to a frenzy of mass enthusiasm and belief in the impossible. The party was deceived by its own.

A general state of euphoria affected even visiting scientists as well as top leaders of the government. For example, a sober French agricultural economist who spent weeks in first-hand investigation testified to an increase of no less than "60 to 90 percent" in national food production.[2] One of his colleagues at the Sorbonne, also a respected economist who had visited China, supported him in Le Monde with convincing explanations of how the miracle had been achieved.[3] A year later Premier Chou En-lai had to announce a downward revision of official claims for increases by about 65 percent. Even that was an exaggeration. With the harvest shortfall of 1959 the responsible authorities could no longer ignore the discrepancies, but they were probably still not fully aware of their scope and its significance. A faulty picture was again reflected in overclaims for 1959, although on a much smaller scale, so that only a bonanza crop in 1960 could have adjusted the position. At the time of my arrival in China in June, 1960, a few realists told me quite frankly that food "abundance" was still ten years away.[4] In July, on a visit to the Agricultural Exhibition Building, I was told by the director that, the spring crop having failed, only phenomenally good weather during August could save the autumn harvest, since no rain had fallen over most of the Yellow River plain for more than two hundred days. Yet claims by reputable economists that the weather had been conquered were still appearing in the press at that time.[5]

These aberrations cannot properly be blamed on the Chinese Central Bureau of Statistics, which had steadily improved its reputation for reliability.

Today it is again difficult for many economists abroad to believe even those facts well established before the "leap" years. For this Peking has no one to thank but itself. In 1958 the party made the egregious mistake of placing "politics in command" of rural statistical field workers. Local cadres were directed to follow new methods of ascertaining crop yields by "questionnaires." This change corresponded with unprecedented party pressures for bonanza output; the result was that fact generally lost out wherever it contradicted propaganda or wishful fancy.

For the government the consequences were far worse than mere loss of face. Many communes that had made overclaims of output found themselves obliged to dig deeply into money reserves and grain set aside for consumption in order to meet taxes and fill percentage quotas promised the state by terms of obligatory sales agreements. Later they had to admit their exaggerations and call on the state to return grain in the form of food relief. Accounts became chaotic, the government itself did not know the true situation within a wide margin, and the whole economy was thrown off balance and off schedule.

By late 1960 the planning machinery had to be brought to a virtual halt in order to retabulate and restore a realistic relationship between inadequate agricultural output and heavily increased demands of industry, trade, commerce and human consumption. "Agriculture is the foundation of the economy" became the national slogan as millions of urban workers turned to reinforce rural labor.

It should be said for China's Bureau of Statistics that it is a great improvement over anything known in that country in the past. Kuomintang statistics were about as reliable as distances measured in native *li*. On level ground a *li* is a third of a mile but uphill it could be far less while downhill it might be half a mile or more. Highly logical, but not scientific. "China used to be a journalist's dream and a statisticians' nightmare," wrote Professor John K. Fairbank, "with more human drama and fewer verifiable facts than anywhere in the world." If he had been writing in 1962 he might have omitted the "used to be"; that in 1958 he still employed the past tense indicated the new respect in which the bureau was then held among academic people. Professor W. W. Hollister, of the Massachusetts Institute of Technology, whose recent work on China's gross national product is one of the most succinct and respected analyses of available economic intelligence yet made, expressed the opinion in 1959 that Chinese official reports "give no evidence of deliberate efforts to falsify data," while "the context and the interpretations placed on the statistics are very often distorted." [6] Unfavorable facts are not falsified but usually simply omitted. Allowing for all missing data and distortion, Professor Hollister reported results which he "judged to be reasonably reliable." He was working, however, with pre-1958 data.

For a decade China had been training statistical and accounting personnel with Soviet assistance and a planned economy made some standards of accuracy indispensable. The Central Bureau of Statistics is a large nation-wide organization closely integrated with the State Planning Commission (they share the same offices), and both carry enormous responsibilities for the functioning of a vast, uneven, groping, complicated and "leaping" economy. Staffs of these organizations include some highly trained experts working with very modern tools. Hollerith-type machines made in Czechoslovakia are used, for example, and China herself now makes advanced types of electronic computers. But good machines and knowledge of sound technique at the top could not guarantee the accuracy of data gathered under the political pressures of 1958—as the government itself belatedly realized.

Since 1959 the Statistical Bureau has been liberated from the rural cadres, but it will take years for confidence to be restored in its reports. "Estimates" are no longer published. Late in 1961 I was told by a high Chinese official * that only "harvest weight" figures are now accepted in planning. "Communes which overstate their output by more than 10 percent must suffer by underconsumption." Few figures of any kind have been published since 1960, and responsible officials have shown a healthy respect for understatement. By 1962 it was clear enough that agricultural failures had applied a brake on the entire economy, and that output in industry had also been sharply curtailed and in some items had probably even declined.

The Leap Forward in industry in 1958 and 1959 was nevertheless real enough and would be remarkable even if the advances claimed were only half true. The 1958 agricultural yield was also an abundant one, although much of the harvest was lost, partly because of the confusion created by the hasty imposition of communes—as we shall see. To understand the lopsided nature of China's economic successes and current critical problems, however, it is necessary to glance back over the road she has traveled since 1949.

* In a conversation in Geneva, Switzerland.

24

Of Leaps Forward

With a per person income which in 1949 was probably one-thirtieth that of the United States, China could never hope to modernize by slowly repeating the two centuries of history whereby private ownership in the West accumulated the capital basis of modern civilization. In 1946 the Kuomintang had planned to develop China by state capitalism; the state then owned many public utilities and communications. Nor could gifts of "free aid" from abroad or even outright colonialism ever have sufficed to provide the capital investment required in China, which by 1960 already reached the order of $10,000,000,000 to $14,000,000,000 annually, and was still insufficient to maintain balanced growth.

The Chinese Communist Party had long planned to follow the pattern of socialized industrialization established by the Soviet Union. Its leaders were convinced that in no other way could the rate of production be increased faster than the rate of population growth, to lift the people rapidly from backwardness and poverty to prosperity and economic independence and power. When the party took over in 1949 it immediately sought Soviet advice to help realize such a program.

Party leaders anticipated that it would take about three five-year plans, beginning in 1952, to complete "the marshalling of all efforts and all resources for the development of heavy industry so as to lay down a foundation for an industrialization and a modernized national defence." [1]

By 1967 the country was to be capable of making everything necessary for indefinite future development. Such an objective inevitably meant concentrating on basic means of production, the machines that make all other machines and tools of agriculture, science and modern living. To achieve such a crash program of industrialization the whole nation would have to dedicate itself for nearly *two decades* to an austere existence. It would take about fifteen years—or eighteen years after the revolution—for the people to begin to enjoy the fruits of this titanic effort.

Economic development thus far divides into these periods: 1949-52, "recovery and rehabilitation"; 1952-57, the First Five-Year Plan; and 1957-62, the Second Five-Year Plan, accelerated by the Great Leap Forward, 1958-59. During the first period war damages were repaired, state bankruptcy and inflation were overcome, land reform was completed to create a new popular base in agriculture, former state-owned enterprises were brought into production, and control was established over private banking and business. China also fought the Korean War, a process which hastened nationalization of the economy and brought some special military aid from Russia. Beginning with 1953 the government adopted a fully planned economy. It was still very much played by ear, but by 1957 it was claimed that basic goals had been achieved. Agriculture had been largely collectivized and remaining business and commerce nationalized. In the third phase, or the Second Plan, 1957-62, Great Leap Forward drives quite possibly did achieve the main *industrial* production targets *by 1960*—or two years ahead of time—but results cannot yet be fully assessed.

The ambitious nature of the whole program may be measured by the amount of state investment in capital construction. State investment represents profits or savings—capital accumulated by the management by withholding "surplus labor value" payments, in the form of wages or purchasing power and their equivalent in consumer goods, from farm and industrial workers. Between 1953 and 1957 China invested about $19,000,000,000 in new construction. This amounted to $23 out of every $100 of national income. By 1958 it reached as high as $30 out of every $100. If the U.S.A. invested that percentage of income in new construction it would come to nearly $150,000,-000,000 a year. It was Peking's hope to average an investment of between 20 and 25 percent of ever mounting income annually for ten years.

That was not to be. China's investment dropped precipitately in 1961 owing to farm failures. Before that it had been growing far faster than that of capitalist countries during their early industrialization. Only the Soviet Union, in its Second Five-Year Plan, ever reached as

high a rate of investment. By way of contrast with undeveloped economies, India invested 7 percent of her income during her First Five-
Year Plan, and even with large foreign loans to finance India's present plan, the rate will not reach 10 percent. According to the Ford
Foundation's *Report on India's Food Crisis and Steps to Meet It*, in
1959, India's planning offered little prospect of bringing her food output abreast of the rate of her population increase. Famine instead of
mass malnutrition would be widespread today in India without the
palliative of American wheat gifts and other assistance. By 1960 this
had reached a total value of $1,789,000,000.[2]

The value of China's entire industrial and agricultural output in 1949
was only about $19,000,000,000. Her first five-year *investment* plan just
equaled that amount. Out of the $19,000,000,000 about 56 cents of
every dollar invested went into industry and about 50 cents of every
dollar went into *heavy* industry. Agriculture got only 8.2 percent. As a
result the production of steel and metal-cutting machines mounted
phenomenally, while light industry and agriculture increased just
about enough to keep up with the growth in population.

Professor W. W. Hollister estimated China's domestic investments
in new capital construction at 14.9 percent of her gross national product
in 1952, at 17.6 percent in 1954, and at 20 percent in 1957.[3] On July 20,
1960, I was officially told in Peking by Yung Lung-kuei, secretary of
the Economic Research Department of the State Planning Commission,
that "capital accumulation" in the Chinese economy had "averaged 23
percent during the First Five-Year Plan" and had "appreciably risen
since then." Western economists deplore this as "forced savings" under
tyranny. Yet during their own periods of greatest expansion capitalist
economies grew at rates of investment which entailed comparable sacrifices and withholding of values from the effort of the working population. In their years of peak expansion the owning classes invested
capital at the rate of 17 percent in Britain, 20 percent in Germany, 18
percent in Japan and 15 percent in the United States. At the start of
economic planning in the Soviet Union the rate of investment was
"nearly a quarter of the national income," and it "led beyond 27 percent" just before the Second World War.[4] Until the significance of the
calamitous harvests of 1960 was fully appreciated by Peking's leaders
they were still hoping to equal if not surpass the maximum investment
in the period of the second Soviet Five-Year Plan. As late as October
26, 1960, Yung Lung-kuei (acting as spokesman for the State Planning Commission) asserted to me that China could "indefinitely support a capital construction investment of 20 to 25 percent annually"
and "maintain an annual rate of growth at between 20 and 30 percent."

In 1959 Vice-Premier Li Hsien-nien (concurrently Minister of Finance) announced figures which indicated that state investment in
capital construction had increased by twenty-three times since 1950.[5]
In 1949 state revenues were 6,500,000,000 yuan and in 1959 they rose

to 54,160,000,000 yuan.[6] Li Hsien-nien's use of 1949 as a base year of comparison may be permissible to indicate political success in recovery combined with achievement, but of course it is misleading as a measure of growth under normal conditions. In 1949 production was, as we have already seen, very much below the supposed peak year of 1936. Up to 1958, economists usually reckon in comparisons either with the statistically hypothetical peak harvest year of 1936, or, more realistically, with 1952 or 1953. Output in 1952 in both agriculture and industry was for the first time well above that of 1936, but food output per capita was possibly still behind the peak year.[7]

The difficulty of stating China's gross national product and its rate of increase compared to those of Western economies becomes obvious when one examines the conclusions Professor Hollister recently advanced:

"Valuation [of the gross national product] in dollars overstates China's output relative to that of the United States while the valuation in yuan understates China's relative output, but it is not possible to measure the degree of this theoretical overstatement or understatement." [8]

Mr. Hollister finds that in 1952 China's "consumption expenditures" valued in U.S. prices indicated "an aggregate value of $54 billion and per capita expenditures of $94 (1 yuan equaling $0.37)." [9] On that basis the American per person expenditure was 15 times that of China. But if an American resident in 1952 had paid Chinese prices in China for all goods commonly part of American consumption—such as gasoline, automobiles, freezers and other hard goods—he would have required 4,830 yuan to duplicate average expenditures in the U.S.A.—or 55 times the average Chinese expenditure! Reversing the situation, and putting the Chinese in America (without changing the items or the nature of his consumption account), might require him to spend three to four times as much as at home for the same values. Direct comparison by conversions either in dollars or in yuan inevitably "gives a somewhat distorted impression of the relative productive power of the two countries." [10]

I shall presently cite examples which show that China-produced trucks, tractors and automobiles seem to cost about twice as much as American products. But electric cranes cost less, building and construction of most types costs less, food and housing—far less adequate in China than America—both cost much less, and education and basic defense items cost very much less. How do you compare output values between a China where the average person spends twenty-five cents a day for all his meals, where a college education costs the state less than $100 a year, and where a skilled electrician's labor, product value added, is a dollar a day, and a United States where steak costs a dollar a pound, a college education costs parents $2,000 a year per child, and an electrician gets eight dollars an hour? All these "costs" are themselves relative to many variables. The United States "wastes" infinitely more materials than China but China "saves" by means which often would seem "uneconomical" in America.

Mr. Hollister computes China's gross national product in 1950 at 55,020,000,000 yuan. By 1952 it was 67,860,000,000 yuan, and he places it at 102,420,000,000 yuan for 1957. Using 1950 as a base of 100, he indicates that China's G.N.P. had increased by 86 percent in 1957.[11] China's social accounting supplies no statistics for "gross national product," however, but only for combined output volume and values which omit important items used by Western economists and which might very considerably increase the Chinese total. In Chinese terms 1959 total output value was reported at 241,000,000,000 yuan or about $153 per person in nominal dollar values. We may compare this with American G.N.P., currently approaching $550,000,000,000 or more than $3,000 per head—but that comparison again combines understatement and overstatement.

The truth seems to be that economies changing at different levels and different speeds can be compared only very approximately in terms of gross national product. Economists themselves disagree on interpretations of information about China, and it is "not possible," in this volume, to reconcile the figures I have used from various Western sources, much less to relate them all to Chinese government figures.

For the years 1952-57, China claimed an increase in "combined output" of 76.7 percent,[12] using 1952 as a base. Various Western economists who rather arbitrarily used 1953 as a base cut the rate of increase to between 6 and 10 percent annually. Professor Liu Ta-chung of Cornell reached a rate of 6.8 percent for 1953-57 while Professor Hollister estimated the annual growth rate at 8.6 percent.[13] Let us merely say that 6, 9, 10 and 11 percent are all exceptionally high rates for undeveloped countries. They are nothing to dwell upon, however, compared to China's final claims for 1958 and 1959.

In an official report in April, 1960, the chairman of the State Planning Commission, Li Fu-chun, maintained that China had already fulfilled, in 1958 and 1959, targets set for industry for the whole Second Five-Year Plan, 1957-62. The industrial target for 1962 demanded an increase in output value of industry (at 1952 constant prices) of "about 100 percent," greater than 1957. Li asserted in 1960 that the "gross output value of industry . . . had already risen by 131.5 percent." Meanwhile "national income" was reported as 62.86 percent over the 1957 figure.[14]

The state was then working on revised figures for *agriculture* which were still much inflated. Official claims for *combined* industrial-agricultural growth for the Great Leap are thus highly suspect. Statistics on *industrial* growth are a different matter. Even in 1961, Soviet economists—who had worked closely with Chinese industry—apparently accepted Peking's official output figures released for selected major items.[15] These continued to show exceptional advances.

For a number of reasons it is much easier to verify industrial statistics than those for food output. While Western economists now discount many Chinese values, no serious student questions that amazing industrial progress has been made.

Steel was China's first objective in heavy or capital-goods industry. "China proper," as the provinces south of the Great Wall used to be called, did not smelt enough steel in 1949 to make a skillet per person. Peak production had been 923,000 tons, but more than 800,000 tons of that was made in the Japanese mills at Anshan, Manchuria, which were dismantled by the Russians during their occupation in 1945. In 1949 the all-China output of 158,000 tons was about one-tenth of India's production. By 1951, Anshan had been restored (appropriately with Soviet help) and new mills were under construction elsewhere, but China still made less than a million tons of steel.

From 1951 to 1957 China's production increased by six times, to reach 5,350,000 tons of steel. With Soviet aid, major mills in Anhui and at Shanghai and Wuhan got under way and smaller modern Chinese furnaces blew in the following year. In 1958 steel production reached 11,000,000 tons. In 1959 it rose to 13,350,000 tons.[16] By 1960 China claimed that several large new furnaces—including the modern Paotou plant—together with seventy-three small and medium plants turned out 18,500,000 tons of steel, and the British Iron and Steel Institute conceded her at least 17,000,000 tons.[17] Both figures exclude steel made by "indigenous methods"—that is, back-yard furnaces.

China's achievement in steel takes on more significance when one remembers that Japan's annual steel product at the time of Pearl Harbor was less than 10,000,000 tons. In 1960 China produced about five times more steel than India and edged close to France for sixth place among leading producers of the world. Unlike older industrial countries, China has little scrap iron and much of her steel capacity has been diverted to making pig, or cast iron. In 1960 this reached 28,000,000 tons,[18] an increase of 37 percent over 1959. Although both West Germany and Britain produced more steel than China, her pig iron product was reported at about 80 percent larger than Britain's and 14 percent above Germany's.[19] In that year China exported nearly a million tons of pig iron to Russia.

China had already passed Britain in coal production by 1959. In 1960, with a claimed output of 425,000,000 tons (almost nine times that of India), she ranked close to the U.S.A. and Russia. During the years 1952 to 1960 China's miners appeared to attain levels it took fifty-three years to reach in Britain and twenty-two years to reach in America. About 40 percent of China's coal in 1959[20] still came from small and medium-sized pits, and Western observers have said that much of it was unwashed coal of poor quality. That was true. China is now building complete sets of mechanized mining equipment, however, and I saw large new open and closed mines using it.

What was happening to the steel and coal? By 1958 China was able to make more than 50,000 metal-cutting machine tools. In 1959 she claimed 70,000 machine tools and in 1960 reported an output of 90,000, thus apparently doubling her entire machine-making plant in two years. China was making her own trucks, cars, tractors and jet planes in small numbers, but also substantial quantities of heavy electrical goods and rolling stock—indeed, 80 percent of the equipment needed to manufacture hard and consumer goods of all kinds.

In 1950 China's cement output was 1,410,000 tons. By 1959 she claimed 12,270,000 tons (slightly less than French output), and her target in 1960 was 16,000,000 tons. In 1952 the Japanese locomotive repair works in Dairen had been restored and converted to a producing plant with Soviet aid, and China made her first twenty locomotives. By the time I visited it in 1960, that Dairen plant and others reported a production of 800 locomotives and 32,000 freight cars, an increase of more than 50 percent over 1959.[21] China's textile industry (formerly largely Japanese-owned) increased output from a prerevolutionary peak of 2,790,000,000 meters of cotton cloth to 7,500,000,000 meters in 1959—about three-fourths that of the U.S.A.

China's erstwhile peak of electric power was 5,900,000,000 kilowatt hours. By 1953 its output was 9,200,000,000, and in 1959, 41,500,000,000. In 1960 China produced more than 55,000,000,000 kilowatt hours, or slightly more than three times as much as India, and not very much less than France.

It would certainly be prudent to make large discounts for substandard and defective products in so young a national industry, and for losses due to carelessness or inexperience in handling and maintenance. I myself saw new motors and parts piled up unprotected in the weather and damaged or ruined because of transport tie-ups or lack of storage facilities. Allowing for inefficiencies as well as for probable overclaims, a few Western analysts cut industrial output values by one-fifth to as much as one-third. For various technical reasons it would be impossible to disguise exaggerations of industrial output as high as the "overestimate" of the harvest in 1958. My own belief, on the basis of what I observed, even a year after the "anti-buoyant exaggeration" reforms were imposed on cadres, is that the industrial product for the early "leap" would be more realistically stated at discounts of 20 to 30 percent. If any of these somewhat blind guesses are right, the whittled-down results still remain impressive, even if the pace of growth fell off sharply in 1961 and somewhat retrogressed.

All the items I have mentioned are primary sinews of a modern industrial civilization, the development of which enables a nation to "solo" as a major industrial power. In basic products, except pe-

troleum and locomotives, China in the middle of her *second* five-
year plan period—the twelfth year of her revolution—may have been
ahead of where the Soviet Union was in the middle of her *third* plan,
the twenty-first year of her revolution. Compared to Soviet output
in 1940, China in 1960 made 12 percent fewer locomotives, petroleum output was only 16 percent as much, and that of chemical
fertilizers was about two-thirds as great. But according to Chinese
figures apparently accepted in the U.S.S.R.,[22] China in 1960 was able
to produce more steel, almost twice as much pig iron, nearly three
times as much coal, 10 percent more electric power, a fourth more
machine tools, and 40 percent more cotton cloth, than Soviet output
in 1940.

In all these comparisons one needs to remember that there are more
than three times as many Chinese as there are inhabitants of the
Soviet Union or the United States, fifteen Chinese for every Frenchman, and fourteen for every Englishman. By 1960 China had already
considerably surpassed India in industrial production of nearly everything, but *she still lagged far behind Japan and most European countries on a per capita basis.* Her very low mass standard of living did
not necessarily mean, however, that China could not continue to reproduce her industrial plant at a faster rate than nations with unplanned economies which dispose of large percentages of their steel,
power and machine-making capacity in the production of nonessential,
luxury or waste consumer goods.

Until 1961, the above figures suggested that by 1967 China might
pass Japan and England in steel production and, possibly early in
the next decade, become second only to the United States and Russia
as a great industrial power. However great the present slowdown, it
does not change the fact that—starting at a stage of industrialization far
behind that of Russia—China had by 1960 apparently possessed herself
of more advanced basic industrial means, with exceptions noted, than
those with which the U.S.S.R. met Hitler in 1941—an observation probably not lost on Mr. Khrushchev. But Russia, of course, had done it
alone. China had had a great helping hand in Soviet aid, and Soviet
protection—another observation which Mr. K. doubtless made aloud,
to Mao Tse-tung.

25

And Leaps Backward

"The Chinese people," said Liu Shao-ch'i during the Tenth Anniversary celebrations, "raised the proportion of modern industry from 26.7 percent in 1952 to 40 percent in 1957." By the end of 1959 the proportion was about 67 percent industrial output value to about 33 percent agricultural value.

The state budget provided for an investment in industry seven times greater than that in agriculture, forestry and water conservation. But local investment in the latter areas, made possible by savings imposed on the peasantry, brought the percentage to about one-third the sum spent on industry. One result was that China's irrigated lands more than doubled between 1949 and 1960. They now cover about three-fifths of her total acreage. This of course meant a great increase in *sown* acreage by means of multiple cropping.

Afforestation work is conspicuous to any traveler and amazingly widespread. By 1960 new railways connected all regional capitals except Lhasa and Kunming (of Yunnan), but China's rail transportation system remained far behind her needs. The recent doubling of mileage impresses Westerners less than Overseas Chinese elders who can remember a hinterland accessible only by donkey or boat. China still had less than 25,000 miles of railways, however, and transport remained her greatest weakness. Telephone networks now serve all 24,000 rural communes, navigable inland waterways have been doubled, and public works have seen comparable expansion; but these are amenities long taken for granted in Europe.

None of this could have been achieved on such a rapid scale without Soviet aid, as I have emphasized. Yet the total value of Soviet loans and aid projects in China up to 1958 averaged less than 50 American cents a head annually, compared to the $30 per head which A. Doak Barnett estimated America had invested in nonmilitary aid to Taiwan and its population under Chiang Kai-shek up to 1958.[1] Whatever the exact amount invested in China's modernization thus far, it is certain that nearly all of it has been paid for by the labor of the Chinese people. China received no *free* economic aid from Russia. To date Soviet loans (as apart from trade agreements) have amounted to only $43,000,000 (1,720,000,000 rubles), and all are repayable. United States economic aid to Yugoslavia alone amounts to more than that, and American loans to India have been more than four times as much. Soviet loans and/or "free aid" for military equipment made during and after the Korean War have been variously estimated in the neighborhood of $2,000,000,000. In his book *Communist Economic Strategy* (1959), Barnett suggested that "an overall figure of $2,240,000,000 consisted of military assistance" from the Soviet Union, "and shares in joint companies" liquidated by Stalin when he returned Russia's industrial assets in Manchuria and Sinkiang to China. As Chou En-lai told me that China had received no "free aid" from Russia (apart from blueprints, patents, etc.), it seems evident that Soviet military assistance compensated (at least in part) for China's war effort in Korea.

Net grants and credits (including military) extended to Chiang Kai-shek's government on Taiwan up to 1960 by the United States amounted to $2,937,000,000, or about $293 a head of its ten million population.[2] Adding net grants and credits extended to Japan and South Korea up to 1958 (exclusive of the cost of the Korean War), the total was more than $8,000,000,000. If Chiang Kai-shek had retained control of China and the United States had extended him the same *per capita* aid there as was given to him in Taiwan, the cost of maintaining his democratic dictatorship would by now have amounted to more than $200,000,000,000. (In addition the National Council of Churches was rationing U. S. government food surplus in a "family-feeding program" intended to reach 1,250,000 persons annually, or 12.5 percent of the population. The Council announced withdrawal from the program in May, 1962, because of "black market operations involving the sale of government surplus by the recipients and by some local Protestant and Roman Catholic churches that have been carrying out the distribution." Taiwan officials were reportedly selling or giving the required food coupons to their friends and business partners.[3]) Viewing matters in this perspective, many American taxpayers might conclude that perhaps President Kennedy is quite right in not encouraging Chiang to invade the mainland.

All Soviet loans "were only enough to pay for 31 percent of the necessary equipment and supplies for the original 156 industrial and other projects which the Soviet Union agreed to help China construct," according to one respected economist in America.[4] It was around these 156 very large key industrial plants that China planned her whole development. But Soviet loans covered only "11 percent of China's total imports for the eight years from 1950 to 1957. During the First Five-Year Plan the amount of Soviet *credit* available for new investment (1,570,000,000 yuan) constituted merely three percent of the total state investment (49,300,000,000 yuan). By the end of 1957, all outstanding Soviet credit was exhausted, and since then no new loan has been announced . . . 97 *percent of the investment for basic development came from the Chinese people themselves.*" [5]

The significance of these figures may be fully appreciated when it is emphasized that, reckoning China's whole investment in heavy and light industries (including about 700 major projects), as well as in plant constructed to accommodate it, the Chinese in ten years themselves produced or reproduced the equivalent of Soviet machinery imports at a rate of between twenty and thirty to one.

In cash income the worker's share of the profits in China has remained minimal. Combined output value during the first revolutionary decade increased about four times, while workers' wages rose only about 52 percent up to 1959. It was claimed that farmers' income, counted in grain and cash, increased by a little less. That is probably no harsher a rate of exploitation than in the earlier days of capital accumulation in the Western countries, but in China it is imposed on a far lower standard of living. It is somewhat ameliorated by two factors. Workers and peasants have welfare benefits (education, medical care, old-age assistance and guaranteed employment) which came only much later in countries of private capitalism. Second, the worker and peasant, who understand very well how, and to some extent why, they are being relieved of the profits of their toil, have some satisfaction in knowing that no individual or owning class is getting rich on their efforts and that capital is being collected and invested for the benefit of society as a whole and especially for their children.

China's rate of annual accumulation, or forced savings, grew to such proportions that the 1960 plan called for a state investment in capital construction of 38,500,000,000 yuan—about $15,000,000,000—including 6,000,000,000 allocated to municipalities and rural communes. That sum represented an increase by 21.7 percent over the amount actually invested in 1959. It was eight times as much as China had been able to invest in 1952. More than five times the total of open loans and trade credits made to China by the U.S.S.R. up to 1959, it was also nearly four-fifths as large as the entire state investment program projected over the period 1961-66 of India's Third Five-Year Plan.

China's budgeted investment assumed state revenues which included 65,000,000,000 yuan from state-owned enterprises and 4,000,-000,000 from the rural communes. Indirect capital accumulated from peasant labor was far greater than those figures suggest, however, due to the government's complete control of prices, credit and commerce. The budget was further premised upon growth proportions officially defined as a "continued leap forward" which would "lay the foundations for continued leaps throughout the whole decade of the sixties." [6]

Obviously those expectations were not fulfilled. The year 1960 was not a great leap in the economy as a whole but a mere hop, made largely on one leg, industry, with the lame leg of agriculture dragged behind it.

It is not known to what degree China's agricultural reverses affected industrial plans for 1960-62. It compelled China to expend nearly all her foreign exchange to buy food imports instead of machines. The crisis in agricultural output seriously crippled her export program in textiles and cotton—her most important trade item with Russia—as well as in other processed agricultural goods. China was obliged to default on payments due Russia in 1960 in accordance with Sino-Soviet trade agreements and seek a five-year moratorium on amortizations. Although Moscow granted an extension of time, which the Chinese acknowledged with humble thanks, Mr. Khrushchev confined his contributions to alleviate China's food shortage to a bit of sugar for Mao's tea (500,000 tons), following the ideological conflicts discussed elsewhere.

It became clear that China was now almost entirely on her own.

Scattered figures available for 1960-61 left one even at this writing with no information on actual revenues or on output of such major items as cotton and cotton yarn, tractors and lorries, ships, paper, timber, freight turnover, textiles and light industry as a whole. A Central Committee communiqué issued in January, 1961, claimed that "the gross value of industrial output increased at an average annual rate of more than 40 percent over three years, 1957-60." [7] But increases in 1958 and 1959 were so high that in balance this meant at best an increase in industrial output value in 1960 of only 14 percent —a mere bagatelle by "leap" standards. So great was the decline in agriculture that year that in all probability China's *combined* output value for 1960 was less—and possibly considerably less—than in 1957.*

For China's capital-starved economy that meant an agonizing setback and a minimal investment available for 1961 and 1962. In January, 1961,

* See pages 623-625.

the Central Committee foresaw *"two or three years"* of *"consolidation"* —years of concentration on "strengthening the agricultural front" in a policy of "taking *agriculture as the foundation* of the national economy." [8]

By late 1960 the party had thus clearly reversed itself on the "continuous leap forward" policy in favor of an "undulatory development" of the economy. The new directive meant that until 1963 or 1964 no major new offensives on the industrial front were to be undertaken, and then only if the *agricultural foundations* were secure against future catastrophes. Because of the time lag in communications, however, it was only in 1962 that American cold warriors, taking note of the results of the changed policy while ignoring its sound realism in the reflections of lessons absorbed, renewed their widespread predictions of internal breakdown in China—long after the most critical months had passed.

Farther on we shall see something more of the combined effects of the withdrawal of Soviet aid, of natural calamities, and of human resistance to overregimentation, which thus halted the Chinese Communists in mid-passage to the Utopian Communist goal, "From each according to his ability, to each according to his needs."

26

Yao Wei and Private Enterprise

To accompany me on a three-week trip to Manchuria I was assigned a China Intourist interpreter named Yao Wei, a young Shantung stalwart who had assisted me in several of the interviews I have already recorded. I should have liked to have one of my former translators, *du temps perdu,* but Huang Hua was now an ambassador (to Ghana), Wu Liang-p'ing was a vice-minister of chemical industries, and two others I inquired about had gone with the wind, I know not whither.

Yao Wei was a six-footer who could well have served me as bodyguard, and once or twice I suspected that he considered that a part of his role, too. If his omnipresence sometimes made me feel overprotected and tended to limit my practice of spoken Chinese, I had to concede, after my experience with the young lieutenant who wanted to be photographed—by anyone but an American—that his physique might come in handy in an emergency. (Unfortunately, none arose.) He took care of himself. In his small valise he carried a two-handled steel-spring exercise device with which he flexed his muscles every morning to keep them in condition. He wore his hair Yale crew-cut style and had a Yale man's walk, too, and though he granted that all provinces produced good men he was glad to be from Shantung. Come to think of it, a Shantung man and a Yale man have a lot in common.

It is impossible in China nowadays for a foreigner to hire a secretary or interpreter without getting government approval or, in most cases, going through official channels. This is a handicap compared with the past, when any reporter could choose his own assistants, who were often full of useful information. Even in Russia I once had a secretary recommended to me by the Foreign Office who turned out to be so anti-Soviet she was pro-Hitler. If anything like that happened in China today, one might assume the person to be an *agent provocateur*. I was told of instances in China when foreign visitors actually had Chinese callers who pretended to be very "anti" for the purpose of ascertaining the visitors' real opinions, but none called on me.

If Yao Wei and his friends had any criticisms to make of the regime, I heard nothing about them. He was as reserved on such matters as an advertising account executive for a tobacco company being interviewed on the subject of lung cancer. He was a patient interpreter, very conscientious, a good loser at chess, and helpful to me in many ways beyond the call of duty. He even had a few bad habits, including a nostalgic tolerance for bourgeois Americans, which may have been why he was chosen for me. By the end of my trip we had become good friends, even though I learned little from him by way of inside information. Perhaps he had none. He was not a party man but he aspired to be —despite obstacles.

What I did learn from Yao Wei was something about what had happened to China's "national bourgeoisie." His father, trained as a doctor of traditional Chinese medicine, had a sister who, in the days of the Shantung warlords, had won approval of a rich official named Kao. After she became Kao's No. 2 wife, Kao had made Yao Wei's father chief of the Shanghai bureau of communications under the Kuomintang. Shantung men are enterprising. The doctor quickly amassed a fortune. By 1930, the year Yao Wei was born, his father was able to retire. He had real-estate holdings in Shanghai, Tientsin and Peking, and was the principal stockholder in the Tsingtao Power Company. The family moved to Peking.

Soon after the Japanese seized Peking, in 1937, they began to take control of the schools. To avoid enemy indoctrination Yao Wei's father put him in the American School at Peking, where he learned English at an early age. He made many American friends, including children of embassy officials, but after Pearl Harbor the school was closed. Yao Wei was twelve years old, knew more English than Chinese, and didn't want to go to a "puppet" school. His family sent him to Tientsin to attend the St. Louis Academy operated by the Marist Brothers mission. There he studied Chinese, English and Catholicism until 1947, when civil war reached Tientsin and he went back to Shanghai.

He was seventeen and wanted to do something. A friend whose father was Minister of Finance got him a job as a signal operator at the airport, and subsequently he was shifted to Nanking. During the civil war he found himself in the radio tower giving landing and take-off signals to B-17 and B-24 bombers attacking the Communist armies north of the river, and helping General Claire Chennault's China Air Transport Command ferry men and supplies to Kuomintang troops beleaguered by the advancing armies of Generals Ch'en Yi and Lo P'ing-hui, which encircled and defeated Chiang Kai-shek's forces in the final, decisive battles of the civil war.

Yao Wei hadn't intended to get involved, he said. He was disgusted with the Nationalists and thought of sabotaging some of the bombing missions and joining the Reds, but he didn't know any of them. When Nanking surrendered he faded into the population and eventually made his way back to Peking. There he looked for a job and was assigned to work with a group of normal-school teachers. All of them were required to write a personal history and make a clean breast of things. Yao Wei played it safe by stating that he had been a student at St. John's University in Shanghai during the civil war. Unfortunately some of the group had actually studied there, so his stratagem was quickly exposed.

"What happened?" I asked him.

"Nothing much. I confessed. Some of the others had done the same kind of thing. When I told my whole story everybody just laughed. I had been a child during the war, and it also helped that I had voluntarily returned."

Yao knew nothing about the Communists except what he had learned from an English edition of *Red Star Over China*, which was ancient history by then. After a period of *hsueh-hsi* or "thought remolding" he was assigned to teach English in a middle school. Meanwhile he had married a former schoolmate who was studying to become a Russian interpreter. He showed me their wedding picture, in which he appeared fashionably dressed in a frock coat and wing collar, she in a bridal veil—a pretty girl.

"What about your father, Yao Wei?"

"Oh, he's still a capitalist and doing very well. He's an old man now, retired, lives in one of his houses here in Peking, and has more money than he knows what to do with."

He said his father had been fully resigned to losing everything and becoming a pauper. Instead, he had found himself classified by the Communists as a member of the "national bourgeoisie" and a "progressive capitalist." Throughout the Japanese occupation and during the postwar Kuomintang period he had never drawn a dollar from his big holdings in the Tsingtao Power Company. Soon after the new regime took over the Tsingtao plant he began to receive dividends from his stock (at 8½ percent) for the first time in more than a decade. He also received rents from dwellings he owned in Shanghai and Peking. The sums were substantially more than he could spend, but he could not invest in more property. Judiciously (probably not without sound official advice) he put most of these payments into state bonds or savings banks. He now lived comfortably "on interest"— able to patronize the few expensive restaurants still open, take his friends to the theater, and, according to Yao Wei, to "enjoy life." Yao Wei never introduced me to his father.

Families still receiving rentals or dividends from the state were chiefly confined to a few big cities. Among the *rentiers* was Han Suyin, the talented author of the lyrical romance, *A Many-Splendoured Thing*, and (somewhat more torrid) *The Mountain Is Young*. She brightened life in Peking for me during the few days our paths crossed at the Hsin Ch'iao. Her mother was Dutch and Flemish and her father was Chinese; she was educated in Peking and then went to London University, where she received a medical degree. She married a Kuomintang army colonel named T'ang, who was killed in the civil war. In her book *Destination Chungking*, written during the Sino-Japanese War, she spoke in high admiration of Generalissimo Chiang Kai-shek. Disillusionment in the postwar period left her convinced that "for China, there was no other way than the revolution." After some years she married a British officer named Comber and lived in Malaya, where she has a medical practice. Thus she had a British passport by marriage, but Peking recognized her as Chinese and heir to her late father's property.

Han Suyin moved through her various worlds with the greatest of ease and good humor, adorning and writing brilliantly about each of them, a formidably competent, astute, beautiful and dazzling woman. Had her books been translated into Chinese they would have shocked the Puritan moral sense of the nation. They seemed to be discreetly ignored by Peking, where she annually visited her relatives for two or three months and collected rentals which she did not need or want.

"I've tried to give my houses to the government," she told me, "but they won't have them." One reason for this benevolence may have been that her father was a "labor hero" and was buried in the Revolutionary Martyrs Park. This is one of the many "contradictions in class lines" common in China, which in Han Suyin's case help to make her the most interesting labor hero's daughter around—and the most intelligent interpreter of her homeland at large in the world.

Whether one remained a member of the capitalist class in China did not appear to be exactly a matter of individual choice. Many who waited too long to shed their plutocratic skins had found it difficult or impossible to "become proletarians" after the revolution.

Owing to differences in conditions and to fundamental differences in the history of the Communist rise to power in China, the treatment of capitalists and the managerial class generally did not follow

the pattern of wasteful, wholesale class liquidation of the Soviet Russian revolution. Great and partly successful efforts were made by
Communists to win the support of the "progressive bourgeoisie."
Their policy traced back to the "united front" led by the Communists
against Japan, when Mao Tse-tung promised to protect "honestly acquired private property" and "patriotic" capitalism during a "transitional period." That promise was reaffirmed in the Common Program
adopted to guide construction during the early days of the People's
Republic, which was itself founded by a coalition of the Communists and allied "bourgeois-democratic" parties.

"The aim of the Chinese revolution *at the present stage*," wrote
Mao Tse-tung in 1948,

> is to overthrow the rule of imperialism, feudalism and bureau-
> cratic capitalism and to establish a new democratic republic of
> the broad masses of the people with the working people as the
> main force; its aim is not to abolish capitalism in general . . .[1]
> Circumstances make it necessary and possible for us to win over
> the majority of the national bourgeoisie and isolate the minority.
> To achieve this aim we should be prudent in dealing with the
> economic position of this class and in principle should adopt a
> blanket policy of protection . . . The enlightened [rural] gen-
> try are individual landlords and rich peasants with democratic
> leanings. . . . We unite with them not because they are a polit-
> ical force to be reckoned with nor because they are of any eco-
> nomic importance (their feudal land-holdings should be handed
> over with their consent to the peasants for distribution) but
> because they gave us considerable help politically during the
> War of Resistance and during the struggle against the United
> States and Chiang Kai-shek . . .[2]

Just as the rural population was arbitrarily divided by the party
into great, middle and small landlords, and rich, middle and poor
or landless peasants, so urbanites were classified as "bureaucratic"
and "national" bourgeoisie, petty bourgeoisie, and working class, or
proletariat. In 1949, Mao Tse-tung still held that the national bourgeoisie—"progressive" and "patriotic"—could play a useful role during
a transition from a mixed economy to a socialist economy.

"Bureaucratic" capitalists were another matter. They were mainly
typified by the very rich "big four" Kuomintang families (the Soongs,
Kungs, Chiangs and Chens) and their close associates in banking,
business and politics, who formed an interlocking directorate of
government and business. (There were no government controls to
prevent Kuomintang officials from owning enterprises that did business with the state.) The holdings of such families, together with
those of compradores or agents of major foreign firms, Japanese collab-

orators, usurers, and "counterrevolutionaries" who fled to Taiwan, Hongkong and elsewhere abroad, were expropriated outright and sans compensation.

The remaining Chinese private capitalists and businessmen (numerically the great majority; as many as 26,000 private firms were engaged in "industry" in Shanghai alone, according to one source, while another mentions "165,000 business units," [3]) were encouraged to continue production with state protection. Except for Japanese property, most foreign investment was not seized outright but was retroactively taxed, systematically milched of profits and capital, and denied access to raw materials and markets, by policies which amounted to confiscatory discrimination. The Communists' moral defense of such measures was that "foreign imperialism" had long since recovered its original capital investment many times over by the exploitation of Chinese labor and resources, without paying taxes to China. They thus took over more than a billion dollars' worth of foreign property.

Beginning in 1951 all Chinese private enterprise, employer-employee relations, and distribution of earnings were brought under state control, as those who bothered to read Mao Tse-tung all the way through had foreseen. Late in 1951 the government launched a national campaign (the "Five Anti's"—against bribery, corruption, tax evasion, fraud, and theft of state property and "economic secrets") which indicated that the "transition" was to be much briefer than the more optimistic capitalists had supposed.

There were many prosecutions. Heavy fines were levied. As the campaign coincided with the Korean War, it was helpful in raising needed funds. To pay the fines and back taxes some "guilty" owners of large plants had no alternative but to sell, and the state was the only buyer. Others were obliged to seek state aid and leadership, and as a result of coercion of various kinds, state-private partnerships increased. At this time the Western press reported that suicides among ruined businessmen were common as during the Wall Street crash of 1929.

After some months the campaign subsided. Businessmen's trading and managerial talents were still needed; the government continued to "remold" them ideologically while supplying them with credits, raw materials and markets. In October of 1953, Peking summoned a congress of representatives of industry and commerce and flatly announced their fate: the private sector of the economy was to be completely absorbed, by stages but not without compensation. Their moral and patriotic duty was to cooperate fully with plans for the "reform" (reorganization) of their own plants in order to hasten their assimilation by the state, a process then envisaged as spreading over another fifteen years.

Subsequently the period was shortened by rapid government penetration of private ownership. From 1949 on private owners had been subject to controls exercised by workers' committees organized by the government to "do everything possible to reduce costs, increase output and stimulate sales," while "giving consideration to both public and private interests." [4] From 1954 on "private interests" got short shrift and the party press continuously attacked capitalist incompetence, mismanagement and exploitation.

In 1955, private industrial production was already reduced to 16 percent of the nation's total (down from 39 percent in 1952), and more than 80 percent of this output had become dependent on state markets. At the end of 1955 the process was further accelerated in order to catch up with the socialist transformation of agriculture. A wave of reportedly "voluntary" conversions of remaining private enterprise into joint state-private ownership swept the country. It was reported that in 1955-56 "three million capitalist industrial and commercial enterprises were converted into joint state-private enterprises." [5] By September of 1956 Chou En-lai was able to assert that 99 percent of formerly privately owned enterprise had entered partnerships with the state.

Control of division of profits had already been in force some years when, in June, 1956, the People's Congress approved a policy of payment of "interest" at 5 percent on extant capital assets of private enterprise, without regard to profits or losses. Six months later it was announced that these payments would continue for seven years, or until after 1962, the end of the Second Five-Year Plan. In December another congress of businessmen in metamorphosis gathered in Peking and resolved to speed up their own "self-transformation" and to "devote our technical training and experience to the cause of the socialist construction of our fatherland and be diligently honest, faithful, responsive and enthusiastic in socialist emulation drives" under the leadership of the party and government. [6]

Former owners of stores and plants who continued to function as joint managers or technical directors drew salaries as well as their 5 percent interest. As the state took direct control, however, all real business decisions and generally the active management were assumed by state employees and administrators. In many cases the original enterprise was broken up or completely absorbed into larger state factories or stores. "Capitalist" had by now become a swear word and it was fashionable to be a *kung-jen,* or of worker ancestry. Many ex-owners began to wish to shorten the time period of their own change of identity. It is believable that some may have "voluntarily" requested, as reported by the press, that their remaining interests be transferred to the state without further compensation. In Peking and Tientsin thousands of shops, production units and houses were turned over to the government in less than a week.

By the time of my visit, private ownership of industry and commerce had for all practical purposes entirely ceased to exist. However, Yao

I-lin, now Minister of Commerce, told me in Peking that there were still "about one million people" engaged in petty private enterprise.* They accounted for only a fraction of one percent of output value, were very small "businessmen" indeed, really self-employed persons: carters, carriers, peddlers and a few artisans, in widely scattered areas. Even these were being gradually absorbed by commune factories or the handicraft and merchants' cooperatives organized in 1957, a process partly reversed when the surplus-workers-back-to-farms drive, to alleviate the food shortage, began in 1961.

According to Yao I-lin, "about 300,000" merchants were still collecting their 5 percent interest from trading organizations operated under the Ministry of Commerce. They constituted "about 30 percent" of the overall total of capitalists, including industrialists, who received such payments from joint state-private enterprises.

"Excluding self-employed people, then," I said to Mr. Yao, "China's ex-capitalists number about one million?"

"Not 'ex-capitalists' but real capitalists."

Such they would nominally remain until 1963—providing some sort of economic basis for the formal superstructure of a government which continued to give nominal recognition to eight impotent "bourgeois-democratic" parties in affairs of state.† After 1962 some would continue as salaried government managers and technicians minus the stigma of "capitalist." Meanwhile many joined the working class directly by taking bench jobs (often in shops they formerly owned) and contributing their dividends to the welfare fund. Eventually they might be granted labor union membership and be entitled to unemployment insurance and other welfare benefits such as free medical care and pensions. For those unfit for labor, provision would be made after 1962, according to Yao, either by a further extension of payments or some form of pension. Others might be able to live on interest from government bonds or savings, as in the case of Yao Wei's father.

From a humanitarian standpoint this is a harsh fate for some honest and industrious men who must have felt that their efforts were building up the country, much as Mr. Paul Getty, the Rockefellers, and most large and small capitalists believe. The elimination of capitalists as "an unnecessary exploiting class" was, however, the logical expectation following the victory of a revolution committed to wholly socialist ownership—unless the leadership was to betray the ideology which brought it to power. The gradual liquidation of Chinese capitalism (as distinct from rural landlordism) largely by political pressure rather than violence, left open a way of reconciliation which preserved many skills needed by the country. In some instances it even won genuinely enthusiastic **acceptance** by "reformed" capitalists able to

* Aug. 28, 1960.
† See pages 322, 327.

sublimate personal interests to the Communist conception of the good of the society as a whole.

"Since the state-private joint operation the government has made very good arrangements for the work and livelihood of my family members," wrote Jung Hung-jen, an American-educated scion of one of China's millionaire industrial families in the Shanghai region. "My elder brother Jung I-jen has been appointed deputy mayor of Shanghai and concurrently vice-minister of the textile industry. I myself have been assigned to the post of assistant manager of the Shen-hsin No. 1 Cotton Mill, in charge of management and capital construction. As a member of the Shanghai Municipal Committee of the Chinese People's Consultative Conference I have participated in consultation and discussions on state affairs." [7]

Mr. Jung went on to say that he no longer had to worry about being kidnaped. This had happened to his father, in 1946, when he was forced to pay Ch. $500,000 ransom to kidnapers "in conspiracy with the local garrison commander." It is quite true that kidnapings by Shanghai gangsters were common both before and after the Japanese War and most rich men had a retinue of private bodyguards. In 1960 I was told by the mayor of Shanghai that when the Communists occupied the city they found a roomful of foul-smelling crates in an abandoned godown. The contents proved to be dozens of dismembered corpses, some of which were identified. Investigation disclosed that they were missing victims of kidnapings or assassinations carried out by gangsters who, during the last days of Kuomintang rule in Shanghai, worked with police and army officers to extract as much as possible of the remaining gold and jewels in the city before evacuating.[8]

There are no more kidnapings in China, but it is obvious that Jung Hung-jen and other capitalists enjoy none of the freedom of movement of Texas oil plutocrats. Scores of thousands of respectable businessmen as well as gangsters and racketeers fled from China before the Communists took over, but by far the majority remained. While many thousands of Chinese still come and go, they are a small fraction of the population, as we shall see in a later chapter. Profit-motive man faces a dismal future in China; more thousands of ex-merchants might leave the country if they had capital or if exit permits were more easily obtainable. A few formerly very wealthy capitalists still live in relative luxury and are available to foreign visitors, but I did not take advantage of an opportunity to interview them. In Hongkong, in 1959, I met a former mill manager, Robert Loh, who had recently left Shanghai. Mr. Loh has written in America of his experiences in helping officials to "entertain foreigners on more than fourscore occasions." [9] Following is the substance of what he told me in Hongkong:

"The Jungs and all other rich families may still live in comfort, some of them even in their own homes, but they have no freedom. They cannot join the party but they cannot get away from it. They are always surrounded by party men who tell them whom to see, what to say, and what they can and cannot do. A few may have some real authority in their former businesses but for the most part they are figureheads and display pieces to impress visiting foreigners. Their children may get along if they absolutely renounce their 'bourgeois' pasts, but anybody who does not toe the line will immediately be put through more thought remolding."

Yet numerous "capitalists" still collect "dividends" in China. That at least is more than can be said for the murderous abruptness of the Soviet revolution. Or, for that matter, of the "thought remolding" of the Bourbonites as carried out by the French guillotine.

27

Manchuria:
Industrial Heartland

Yao Wei and I spent twenty-three days in China's three "northeastern provinces," known in the West as Manchuria. Here Japan had set up the puppet empire Manchukuo which dated from her conquest in 1931-32. As a youthful correspondent I covered (and wrote a book about) that madness, to which many people trace the origins of the Second World War. One reason why the psychology of *Tungpei* (Northeastern) people differs somewhat from that of southerners is that they were under Japanese occupation for fourteen years.

Since 1949 part of Heilungkiang province has been amputated and added to Autonomous Inner Mongolia, but Manchuria is still nearly as large as Western Europe without Spain. It was preserved as a homeland for descendants of the nomadic Manchu people who conquered China in 1644 and ruled from Peking until 1912. They severely limited Chinese emigration "north of the Great Wall" almost until the present century. In 1957, census figures for Manchuria were: Heilungkiang (north) 14,860,000; Kirin (central) 12,550,000; Liaoning (southern) 24,090,000. By 1961 Manchuria's population was estimated at 60,000,000, which is relatively sparse for China. Such growth, largely since 1912, gives one an idea of the speed of Chinese settlement of open territory. One is also impressed, however, by the many centuries that elapsed before the Chinese expanded into that neighboring empty, highly promising land—compared, for example, with American settlement west of the Mississippi.

The industrialization of Manchuria was spurred largely by imperial Russian and Japanese railway development when the region was a chessboard of colonial rivalry between them. It has 80,000,000 acres of arable land and abundant iron, coal and other basic resources adequate to support a large-scale regional industrialization. Before the Second World War, Manchuria held nearly half of China's railway mileage and accounted for about a third of her industrial output and exports. It holds one-third of China's forest reserves and still produces a third of all China's coal and one-third of her machine tools. In 1960 Dairen, with 13,800,000 tons of shipping, was behind only Shanghai and Tientsin as a port. The industrial motherland of the nation, these very rich provinces have sent crews of trained technicians and modern equipment to help start key plants in China's four new major heavy industrial complexes, the Northwest, the Far West (Sinkiang), the Central West, and the Southwest.

In 1943 Japanese coal and iron production reached record levels, but at the end of the war the Russians seized most of the rolling stock and modern machinery. Edwin C. Pauley, who headed an American reparations mission to the Far East in 1946, estimated the value of these removals at $858,000,000 and put their replacement cost at $2,000,000,000. It was also reported that the Russians had seized $3,000,000,000 in bullion (a very unlikely figure) and half a billion dollars in Manchurian currency. *Izvestia* ridiculed these contentions and reduced the valuation to $97,000,000 (also unlikely).[1] By 1952 Russia had replaced most of the rolling stock and machinery and today one sees little Japanese equipment in Manchoria. Chinese Communist officials never refer to the original Soviet seizures but only to the "brotherly aid" which came later. If and when Peking presents a bill to Moscow for these past favors one may say the Sino-Soviet dispute has reached a breaking point.

By terms of the Soviet alliance with the People's Republic in 1950, Stalin renounced Russia's historic interests in joint railway and industrial enterprises—which had been recognized by the 1945 Soviet treaty of alliance with Chiang Kai-shek. In exchange Peking reaffirmed the independence of Outer Mongolia, also first recognized by the Generalissimo's regime in 1945. Soviet control over the naval base at Port Arthur and the city of Dairen was likewise to be relinquished, but the Korean War caused postponement. By terms of a new Sino-Soviet treaty in October, 1954, however, Russia surrendered all her positions in Manchuria as well as her shares in Sino-Soviet joint stock companies in Sinkiang (Turkestan).

"The territorial integrity of China is now an ironic phrase," said Dean Rusk in 1951. (He was then Assistant Secretary of State.) He added: "China is losing its great northern areas [Manchuria, Inner Mongolia and Turkestan] to the European empire which has stretched out its greedy hands for them for at least a century." [2] He thought that the Peking regime did not "pass the first test" of a government of China; it was simply "not Chinese." This misconception was shared by the late Secretary Dulles, who continued to base his policy for years on the conviction that the People's Republic was "a passing phase." Yet today, for the first time in a century, China's northern frontier areas have been wholly freed of foreign, including Russian, control. It is almost three hundred years since a strong government has arisen in China capable of turning back the Russian *Drang nach Osten*. A brief look back at that earlier period may help to suggest the relatively unstable and recent arrival of Russian power in the Far East—and one reason for a growing uneasiness in Sino-Sovet relations of today.

In the middle of the seventeenth century the Ming Dynasty broke up from internal decay and corruption and China was conquered by Manchu princes from north of the Great Wall, helped by Ming traitors. They established the Ta Ch'ing (Great Purity) Dynasty. During the interregnum of chaos the Russians had rapidly pushed eastward from Lake Baikal. In 1682, the year Peter the Great was proclaimed emperor, they reached the Amur Valley and built a powerful fort called Albazin in eastern Siberia. In 1683, after the Emperor K'ang Hsi had driven the last Ming general and his Dutch allies from Taiwan, he turned his attention northward to stop the Russians.

Meanwhile, at the Manchu court in Peking, a Belgian Jesuit, Ferdinand Verbiest, had won some tolerance for Catholicism by teaching Chinese scholars Western mathematics and astronomy, but especially advanced European gunnery. By 1685 Father Verbiest had done his work so well that a Chinese-Manchu force of 15,000 men, armed with 150 pieces of field artillery and fifty siege guns made according to the Jesuit's specifications, attacked and destroyed Albazin. The Russians fled west of the Aigun River into the Nerchinsk Mountains. The Tsar subsequently opened negotiations at Nerchinsk, where K'ang Hsi assigned an important role to François Gerbillon, a Jesuit successor to Father Verbiest. By terms of a treaty (written in Chinese, Manchu, Russian and Latin) signed in 1689, the Russian frontier was fixed at Nerchinsk. Manchuria and eastern Siberia remained under the Chinese Empire. [3]

More than a century elapsed before the tsars effectively resumed their march toward the Pacific. It was not until 1858 that the Russians (taking advantage of China's humiliating defeats by armed forces defending the British opium merchants) obliged Peking to cede them vast territory beyond the Aigun and to the left bank of the Amur, down to its mouth. Two years later Peking conceded Russia the Ussuri region, where she boldly christened a new Pacific port "Conquest of the East"—Vladivostok.

I retraced many old paths in Manchuria, from near the Siberian frontier to the sea at Dairen. I saw seven large cities and six urban and rural communes. I put in twelve to fifteen hours a day; I was a slave laborer. My notes on people and places in Manchuria alone would fill a book; no one but a slave reader would read it and I shall never write it. Yet I saw only a small fraction of that vast collection of mechanized aviaries, where human effort never stops. Manchuria has a greater potential than the Ruhr; it is, on a less developed level, China's New York-New Jersey-Pennsylvania-Ohio combined.

The most fun I had was a day of boating on the Sungari River along Harbin's elaborate waterfront park. I also spent a cheering afternoon with the child crews and administrators of the "Peking-Moscow" miniature railway in Harbin. The most depressing sight: half a million refugees marooned by floods in Shenyang and its outskirts. Also: a holiday crowd of workers at a formerly fashionable Dairen beach club. They were all dining on nothing but large *man-t'ou* (steamed rolls) and "white tea." It wouldn't have been poignant if they had not been sitting under gaily colored striped beach umbrellas.

To do any more in Manchuria I should have had to work three shifts a day. I could not see half the things offered in answer to my requests. The following notes describe an incomplete itinerary of my days as a Manchurian investigator:

HARBIN: Population, 1,600,000. Great railway center, northern Manchuria.
1. *Northeastern Agricultural College.* 2,600 students, 5 year course. 2,500 acre mechanized farm; cattle-breeding.
2. *Electrical Machines Mfg. Co.* generators up to 75,000 KW. Soviet project. 9,500 workers, aged 20-30. 3 shifts a day. Average monthly wage Yuan 62. Start at Y. 28.
3. *Ball-Bearing Plant.* Soviet machines. Modern. Huge bearings. Output value, 1960: Yuan 150,000,000. 10,000 workers. Wages same as Electrical Machine Plant.
4. *Electric Meter Factory.* Large, modern, Soviet-built plant. 4,000 workers; 45% women; 40% husband-wife teams. Assembly line working badly. Administrator a party incompetent. Soviet advisers gone.
5. *Hsiang Fang Urban Commune.* Party-organized in 1950. 148 commune-owned factories. Average housewife earns Y. 32. After payments for own food, nursery care, clothes, services, can save 5 to 9 yuan(?). Satellite commune ball-

bearing factory here made 150,000 bearings in 1959, more than China's total production, 1949. [In 1961-62 this factory was placed under municipal ownership.]

TAILING: *Forestry-Timber Station* near Amur River. Magnificent cedar country. 25,000 acres. One of 13 in timber area. Beautifully kept tree nurseries. Friendly enthusiastic people. 30-year tree-renewals; plant for "eternal forests." Tree-felling and planting; 12,000 workers. Railways, power, mechanized. Lumber mills: 4,000 workers and families. Very good Old People's home here. Wage Scale: Y. 20 to Y. 80. Top, Y. 150. A good place to work.

CHANGCHUN: Capital, Kirin province. Vastly expanded industrial, rail, communications center. Population, 1,800,000.

1. *Changchun No. 1. Automobile Plant.* 200 Soviet engineers designed and built it, trained workers, departed; now all-Chinese. Designed to produce 30,000 "Liberation" trucks (comparable Studebaker) yearly. Trucks sturdy and practical: 6 cyl., 90 h.p., 4 tons. Also makes few hundred luxury "Red Banner" limousines, which cost Y. 40,000 each ($16,000!). Trucks cost Y. 20,000 to produce; sell for Y. 24,000. (About $10,000!) Paper transaction with state. Output now up to 100 daily. 23,000 workers; 5,000 women. Management aims to increase output to 150,000 in 1961-62, when cost of production may fall by 20%. Plant in considerable confusion due to expansion and retooling. 1960 output value about U.S. $300,000,000. Average wage here Y. 62.30 (U.S. $24). Top, Y. 105. Engineers, to Y. 230 monthly.

2. *Film Studio.* China's second largest. 1960 output 26 films, 12 documentaries. 160 actors; 1,200 staff. Top pay, Y. 130 monthly. Stars up to Y. 300. Fair equipment, China-made.

3. *Railway Carriage Company.* Newly built, Soviet advisers, now all gone, leaving plant unfinished. Scheduled capacity, 50 cars a day. Current production: five a day. Suspended animation!

SHENYANG (old Mukden): Capital, Liaoning province. Population 2,400,000. With suburbs, 4,000,000. "Pittsburgh of China."

1. *No. 1 Machine Building Plant.* Makes large vertical and rotary drills, lathes and boring machines. Former Japanese plant, rebuilt with Soviet-Czech aid. Three shifts daily: hours 19:00-3:00; 3:00-10:30; 10:30-19. Wages Y. 33 for apprentices; average Y. 70; top 170. 5,000 workers, 16% women. Factory housing; fixed rents at 1% to 1.5% wages.

2. *Electric Cable Factory.* Rebuilt Japanese factory. Six large shops. Cables up to very largest high tension electrical.

Excellent morale. Soviet advisers now left. 3,000 workers. 1960 output value Y. 65,000,000. Apprentices start at Y. 30; average Y. 62; chief engineer Y. 300 monthly.

FUSHUN: "Coal capital of China." Formerly Japanese enterprise. Electric railway to Shenyang and Anshan steel works.

1. *Open-Pit Mines.* 1960 target, 20,000,000 tons; currently well ahead of schedule. 1960 shale-oil output 900,000 tons, 20% of China's total. 100,000 in open-pit mines and serving industries. All-mechanized. (?)

2. *Lu Sang Kuang Underground Mine.* 47 miles of coal galleries; working seams 45 meters thick. "93%" mechanized. Very modern clean mine. Output 1960: 4,300,000 tons. Workers and staff: 14,000. Average wage, monthly Y. 91. Highest: 150. Manager: Y. 250. Three shifts, with team arrivals and departures staggered. Highly mechanized. Budgeted for safety precautions in 1959: average of 43 yuan per worker.

ANSHAN: China's largest fully integrated iron and steel plant. 20 blast furnaces and 25 open-hearth steel furnaces. 1960 output: 4,800,000 tons steel. Current capacity: 6,000,000 tons steel and iron. 70% equipment now China-made. 22,000 workers. Best paid in China. Average Y. 74. Good all around.

DAIREN: Great seaport and Port Arthur (now called Lu Hsun) naval base. City proper: 1,900,000 people. Greater Dairen: 3,600,000, includes five counties. Old Japanese city and industrial base. Fruit country, and famed for maritime products.

1. *Locomotive Works.* Started as Japanese repair shop. Soviets took over and in 1945-46 trained 1,300 C.C.P. cadres here and 3,000 technicians. Main repair base during Korean War. Modernized and fully equipped by 1954 to produce locomotives. First *12-wheeled* locomotive made in 1956. In '59 output was: 300 conventional locomotives plus few dozen diesels and electrics, and several thousand freight cars. 6,000 workers. Wages start at Y. 33, average Y. 64: top is Y. 232 monthly.

2. *Crane Factory.* Founded 1948 under Russians. Now integrated to produce machine tools, metal construction and oxygen equipment. Makes cranes up to 150-ton capacity of all types: magnetic, bridge, steel, cluster, frame, hook, iron and steel, changeable speed. Largest produced yet: 900 meters long. "Crane-breeder" plant. Sent several teams to start new factories in the south. 1959 production value Y. 106,000,000 (1960: 133,000,000) when profit 32,000,000. 88% profit returned to the state; of balance, 40% reinvested in plant, 60% to workers' bonuses, welfare

fund, etc. Average monthly wage Y. 72. 5,300 workers, 30% women. Labor productivity about 24 times wage bill.

FU HSIN CITY: Newest open-pit coal mine, about 250 miles west of Shenyang, on branch line entering Autonomous Mongolia. City predominantly Chinese, surrounding country mostly Mongol. City population: 440,000. Pit is one mile wide by two miles long, very rich reserves said to be more extensive than Fushun. Electrified railways and highly mechanized equipment. A Soviet project but all Russians gone. New oil wells have been opened up west of here and pipes were just being laid in.

I spent many hours in each of these places, questioned management about details of operations, talked to bench workers, visited them in their homes, ate some meals in their dining rooms, saw their children at school and play, and collected many a thumbnail biography. From my notes it is seen that apprentices' wages start at 25-30 yuan per month, and experienced processing workers average 50-70 yuan. Pay scales are based on eight to twelve grades of work; there are several subgrades in each category, depending on the kind of work performed. Medical care for state factory workers is free; it is half rate for their dependents. Welfare benefits for union members include accident insurance and retirement on half pay, at sixty for men, fifty-five for women. Rents and utilities average three to six yuan a room and food costs are a bit less than in the south, or eight to twelve yuan per adult.

All the factories I saw operated nurseries, clinics, hospitals, rest homes and part-time schools; all had clubs, theaters, drama teams and bands. Housing varied from miles of newly built cheap brick apartments with modern plumbing (some with shower baths and private toilets) to ramshackle tenement structures. "Clubs" and theaters might be in buildings specially constructed for the purpose or in old converted houses or shops. Where the service was not covered by the welfare fund (as in state factories) the cost of nursery care (including noon meal) varied from six to ten yuan a month. Nurseries and kindergartens were sometimes well housed in former homes of the rich; others were in mud-brick huts.

In large factories I saw what might be called "milking stations," to which working mothers came at regular intervals to breast-feed their babies—whom they carried home at the end of the day. A nurse or two or baby-sitters cared for the infants while the mothers, nearby, operated machines. Mothers receive fifty-six days of maternity leave and get extra food allowances; those I saw looked healthy. Some factories have their own dairies and supply milk rations; most of them operate vegetable farms and piggeries and poultry pens.

The workers were paid a "norm-wage" in accordance with their "grade" and also received variable bonuses for over-norm piecework production. There was an eight-hour day and a six-day week in most state factories I saw. Plants worked two or three shifts. Housewives working in municipally owned shops as a rule spent only four to six hours on bench work and two to three hours in spare-time schools learning characters and Marxism.

All state and municipal plants have branch party committees whose cadres are responsible for overall management. Administrators are graduates of courses in factory management. Sometimes a plant technical director may be an important party leader but more often he will be nonparty or of a rank subordinate to a party veteran in charge. Most large plants I saw were jointly run by engineers and party administrators; technical operations were controlled by the former and management-personnel problems were in party hands. More often than not the party man does all the talking in an interview. Where the relationship between political leadership and technical management is a close one the engineer may speak quite freely, and it is usually these plants that are running well.

"Union committees" of workers exist, and plant managers and party leaders are required to consult them in periodic meetings. Production quotas, accounting and all major executive decisions are finally decided by the party committees, however. Both technicians and administrators are required to do shop work one or two months a year, depending on circumstances; in practice that means four or five days out of a month. In large plants "administrators" are merely chairmen of administrative committees; deputies take over during their back-to-the-bench days.

Manchuria still holds only about one in ten of China's population but its importance in industrialization has been about as one is to three. Before the end of the century this region may contain as many people as Western Europe does today. Its ultimate imprint on the formation of modern Chinese character conceivably may be no less important than the influence of the western frontier on American history, as depicted by Frederick Jackson Turner and his eloquent present-day disciple, Walter Prescott Webb. Yet I devote less space to this region than such a role might seem to justify.

In my view the industrialization of Manchuria is, despite its youth as a frontier of mass Chinese immigration, the continuation of a known story. The transformation of some older regions south of the Great Wall to which I direct more attention is much newer and more significant.

One must emphasize that in one of history's ironies Manchuria owes much to legacies of tsarist and Japanese imperialism. When as a youth I first saw cities like Dairen, Shenyang, Changchun and Harbin, as far back as 1929, they were already far more advanced than most places of comparable size south of the Wall. They trained many Chinese technicians. Today everything in the Northeast is on a much grander scale but it is still more of the same, to have been expected whatever regime had recovered the territory for China. Nearly twenty years ago Japan's mill at Anshan already produced close to a million tons of steel a year. It is not so dramatic to find Anshan now turning out five or six times as much steel as it is to see Chinese peasant girls assembling tractors in a backwater town like Loyang. The Russian-built Changchun automobile plant is new to Manchuria but I was more impressed by jeeps and buses and generators I saw made in Chinese-built plants in Kunming, where no motor of any kind was produced before the war. Electric lights in the caves of Yenan, and a print of Botticelli's "Birth of Venus" in a worker's room in Chungking, meant more to me than a 150-ton multipurpose crane I saw made in Dairen.

Chinese have taken many foreign visitors to see Manchuria. Some of them, not realizing its industrial history, have attributed all its wonders to the revolution. Those wonders have been too well publicized, in any case, to require the detailed treatment I have reserved here for such advances as a steel plant and an electrified railway far on the Mongolian steppe, which no other American has seen. Similarly, the forest belts I saw in northern Shensi, and the spectacular water conservation works in the Yellow River Valley, represent wholly new victories won in China's three hundred centuries of struggle against nature.

28

Two Legs Are
Better Than One

Making use of the armed forces in construction is one means of exploiting China's rich resources of man power and native ingenuity. "Walking on two legs" covers another big chapter in China's transition.

That may sound naïve in Madison Avenue English, but China still has partly bound feet. The bound feet must help the free feet move faster. During guerrilla days the Communists learned to use both feet. I remember when women in Shensi were classified as "free feet" and "bound feet," with appropriate work assigned to each. "Bound feet" spent most of their time sewing or in the fields collecting fertilizer.

"Walking on two legs" in 1958 meant starting tens of thousands of small brick blast furnaces or "back-yard" hearths. Millions learned the importance of smelting ore. The Western press made sport of the effort, which produced low-grade and often useless pig iron. It caused serious dislocations in the normal routine and interfered with agriculture. Most of the furnaces were abandoned the next season but quite a few, with improved methods, continue to produce iron for locally forged agricultural tools. A more practical result was that many workers trained at these primitive furnaces combined forces and started small modern mills on a wide scale. These are now making fair quantities of pig iron.

Another interesting consequence was the growth of a school of metallurgists who are fostering a whole network of new small and medium-sized blast or electric furnaces. They use advanced methods and processes now carefully guarded as state secrets. China's few modern steel complexes took years to build at great expense. But Yap Chu-phay, an American-trained engineer well known to many wartime residents of Chungking and long a prophet of the small steel furnace for China, is getting his way in plans for future expansion. In 1960 China had 73 small modern plants using converters with capacities as low as one ton and with annual outputs ranging from 25,000 to 200,000 tons.

On the outskirts of Chengchow I visited a plant built to produce 100,000 tons of iron and steel annually. The manager took me to watch from a distance as iron was poured from one of three open-hearth furnaces which together had a daily capacity of 120 tons. He would not explain the process to me—"a technical secret." This was Chengchow's first iron-and-steel works. In 1958 the plant site was a vegetable field. Peasants in the commune villages built 223 native furnaces during the big leap, and in the process hundreds learned something about the technique. Their cooperatives chose 500 people to send to study steel-making in Anhui. One graduate of the Peking Iron and Steel Institute was then assigned by the state to help construct a township plant.

After scrapping most of the native hearths, the commune and township used the materials and combined to finance and construct the new plant. Land was furnished by a nearby village which shared in ownership, I was told. The site covered 1,667 square meters of land where new brick buildings now housed 4,343 workers. A coke-making plant, repair shops, and a small cement works were also operating. In three years "No. 1" had trained more than a thousand "relatively skilled" workers. Both ore and coal were in adequate supply locally and a small railway ran from the mines direct to the plant. Wages were lower than in state steel plants, the average being only 45 yuan monthly.

This small-plant trend may be significant for capital-poor underdeveloped countries with limited transport facilities bent on speedy acquisition of a heavy industry. Small plants can be built in a quarter of the time required for a big one and bring immediate return. The giant furnace requires a big capital outlay, although its advantage, of course, is much greater ultimate output as well as economy of production. Small furnaces and native hearths produce from 30 percent to 40 percent of China's steel and pig iron. Chinese engineers and metallurgists say that output is of high quality and costs only slightly more than the product of Anshan.

The new technique seems smart for any country with so backward a hinterland as China's. It makes possible a geographically balanced development of heavy and light industry even before adequate transportation develops. Today every province and autonomous region of China already has its own sources of steel. Military advantages of this decentralization are obvious.

"Walking on two legs" campaigns recruited many peasant prospectors who were able to furnish useful leads to resources long known to them but hidden out of superstition or fear of losing their land. Geological surveys had scarcely touched China's surface. By 1960 China's "geological prospecting personnel" numbered 420,000, compared to about 8,000 in Kuomintang times. During the past decade China has spent more than 2,000,000,000 yuan on surveys, prospecting, pit testing and drilling. A by-product of "walking on two legs" is the output of cultural treasures. Earth removals for construction of 180,000 miles of new roads, 12,000 miles of new railways, foundations for countless new buildings, reservoirs and thousands of local dams, canals and irrigation works, have done incidental spade work for archeologists, anthropologists, and general sinologists which would have required vast outlays and might not have been undertaken for years. In 1959 the published figures for earthwork and masonry completed on water conservation projects since 1952 were equivalent to the building of 960 Suez canals, or 400 Panama canals. Allowing for some exaggeration, that would still amount to digging more than 1,000 elevator shafts from Shanghai through the center of the earth to New York.

Everywhere I saw modern industry working across the street from makeshifts of all kinds. Large modern plants in Changchun and Peking were making trucks and cars on an assembly-line basis; in the machine shop operated by Tsing Hua University, midget cars were being made by the students, and I saw others made in Kunming and Shanghai. In 1960 China produced her own jet planes; she also turned out 10,000,000 rubber-tired handcarts. China had two legs, with one foot still bound, the other wearing winged sandals.

In Manchuria and elsewhere I saw in production generators up to 75,000 kilowatts in capacity; high-precision meters and fine X-ray machines; ball bearings from microscopic to giant sizes; 2,500-ton hydraulic forging presses and television sets; 150-ton cranes; all-automatic cotton-spinning machines; vertical lathes you could drive a fire engine through; complete sets of mechanized coal-mining equipment; and 8,000- to 10,000-ton motor ships built in Dairen.

Yet 94 percent of China's land is cultivated without mechanized equipment, and man power still does most of the hauling. The story is told in those 10,000,000 carts mentioned above. Note that they are rubber tired. China has become a quieter country—after street radio exhortations are turned off at night. Rubber tires also make an easier life for the cartman, who today may be anyone from a former rickshaw coolie to a professor or a commune chairman doing his stint of manual labor.

Workers and peasants have contributed many practical ideas to an economy halfway between manual labor and mechanization. Of numerous rice-planting machines invented by peasants the most popular is operated by two people and is said to transplant more rice seedlings per hour than ten men working by hand methods alone. (China has presented all rights to manufacture this machine to Cambodia, Burma and other countries in Southeast Asia.) Greater availability of power and motors encourages practical innovations. Primitive time-saving conveyor systems are used in many kinds of earth-moving work.

In a crowded rope-making shop run by a neighborhood factory in Loyang I saw motor-driven machines made entirely of wooden parts. Here unskilled women workers learned the rudiments of automation. An ingenious amateur had rigged up an assembly line operated from a central switchboard, where he controlled half a dozen machines up to the final operation of swinging the balls of rope out a window of the shop, across a drainage ditch, and into a mat shed where women packed them for shipment. This shop had earned enough in two years to invest in a new brick building with modern machinery. Elsewhere I saw insecticide sprayers, threshing machines, seed drills and fertilizer-spreading machines made entirely of wood. Peasants had rigged up small diesel engines on flat cars to pull miniature trains along wooden rails. Near Yenan I saw one that had already shifted to hard rails and durable rolling stock which brought commune produce into the town.

In a Shenyang cable factory I saw a woman operating an old power drill she had converted into an automatic nail driver. It neatly fastened up cable bobbins she had been putting together by hand.

On a large poultry farm a worker invented a stuffing machine which lines up ducks on a treadmill, thrusts a wad of food down their gullets, and rolls them on, dazed but happy, in a process repeated until they are fat enough to be consumed in the dish that made Peking famous. A cook in Shanghai became a national labor hero by inventing a noodle-making machine, and a woman bank clerk drew a large bonus and the same honor by her invention of a bill-counting machine.

In Harbin I saw an ultramodern railway-carriage factory where beautifully finished fittings were being delivered at one end of a working assembly line—by donkeys.

Labor productivity in many of these small industries was very low. In a competitive economy many could not survive. The Chinese didn't seem concerned with rationalizations of this kind. China had no capital to spare for imports that could be made at home by idle labor using scrap materials. However high the costs of production. they were less than costs of human maintenance without any production. As capital accumulated, better machines would be purchased and labor productivity would improve. It was low-level growth but better than stagnation and immobility.

But there are practical limits to the application of the best of ideas. When cadres carried the urban commune workshops to extremes—as happens with most directives—too many skilled handicraft workers were drawn into them from rural areas. Thousands had to be resi-phoned into the agricultural economy again in 1961 and 1962.*

* See Chapter 76, Szechuan, "The Heavenly Land."

29

High Society

Back in Peking, when it became known that I had spent a few hours with Mao Tse-tung and Chou En-lai, the diplomatic circle, which carries on an old tradition of hospitality under austere circumstances, became mildly interested in me. The diplomatic circle was a square. In one corner were the few representatives of NATO powers; in another were the neutrals, East and West; the third corner was held down by the Russians and the European satellite powers; and in the fourth corner was a door, often closed, to China.

In the last days of the Victorian hangover of prewar foreign society in old Peking, the foreign dowagers—wives of diplomats or ex-diplomats or wealthy (relatively) heads or former heads of foreign business firms—used to consider that a great honor was bestowed when they invited carefully selected Chinese ladies and gentlemen to their parties, and likewise if they themselves accepted a Chinese invitation. Now that has all changed. Western diplomats are never invited to Chinese homes, while their own invitations even to third- or fourth-ranking officials are usually declined and often unanswered.

It is true that Western diplomats are invited, with bland irony, to attend banquets in the Great Hall of the People held to acclaim visiting anti-imperialists such as Sekou Touré of Guinea and Ferhat

Abbas of Algeria. About the only other social life they have with Chinese of ministerial rank, or any rank at all, is on the occasion of an embassy's party or reception to celebrate its own national holiday. Whether the Premier or some other member of the Politburo attends in person or sends a minor deputy seems regarded as a barometer of Peking's degree of satisfaction with a particular ambassador and his mission.

Representing "the West" there were the British, the Swedes, the Finns, the Dutch, the Swiss and the Danes. Australia, New Zealand and Canada did not recognize the People's Republic but their nationals visited China as tourists and businessmen; members of the Commonwealth, they shared (as did Malaya) in the benefits of British recognition. In 1961-62 China became the greatest market for Canadian and Australian grain exports. Trade union groups and intellectuals from all Commonwealth countries visited China. Trade with Western Europe had gradually increased, West Germany vying with Great Britain as a leading trade partner. All the nations of eastern Asia except Japan, the Philippines, Thailand, and the southern portions of Vietnam and Korea, now had diplomatic representatives in Peking. So did the countries of the Middle East, except Jordan, Saudi Arabia and Lebanon—which had trade agreements with China—and Iran, which had no contacts at all.

Peking was first to recognize the provisional government of Algeria, and also exchanged diplomats with Morocco, Guinea, Tunisia, the Sudan and Somaliland. Plans for recognition of the Congo were interrupted by the assassination of Lumumba. After China established close relations with Cuba, Peking's activity throughout South America intensified and Latin-American visitors and residents in Peking increased.

By 1957 Britain had already renounced any serious attempt to enforce the U.S.-backed trade embargo against China, and most countries followed suit. (A British merchant I met in Peking told me that he had counted eighty-four items on the United States embargo list of "strategic machines or materials" that were being manufactured in China and exported. China can and does buy American products from branches or representatives of U.S. firms incorporated abroad.) By 1959 China had signed trade agreements with ninety-four countries, the majority of them bilateral trade pacts renewable annually.[1] Nationals from all those countries come to China to "talk trade or culture." The People's Republic has never banned visitors from any nation; State Department regulations prohibited Americans from traveling in China, not Chinese law.

Foreign newspapermen have a semidiplomatic status in China, as in Russia. Apart from those of Communist countries, representatives of the Western Communist press appear from time to time; the Canadian *Daily Worker* (Toronto) has a resident correspondent. The resident Western non-Communist press consists only of Reuters and Agence

France Presse correspondents, but the Yugoslav Tanjug correspondent is usually classed with the imperialists. A *Times* special correspondent left China shortly before I arrived and Lord Montgomery had just been in the country writing for the *Sunday Times*. Two other British writers and photographers, Felix Greene and Stuart Gelder, traveled in China while I was there, and at least one Frenchman arrived. Raoul Levy, the French producer who discovered Brigitte Bardot, tried to persuade the Peking authorities to let him bring B.B. over to play in *Marco Polo*, in the role of the Mongol princess whom Kublai Khan entrusted to Marco Polo to ferry back to the Shah of Persia. (The Foreign Office turned down the offer, which shows how little coexistentialism there is in Peking.) Soon after I left, the general manager of Reuters made a trip through China, followed by Marshal Montgomery on a return visit. Two French Swiss writers, Fernand Gigon and Gilbert Etienne, visited China not long after I was there. The Fourth Estate is relatively poorly represented in China, but it has never been as completely closed off to the West as many Americans suppose.

Although the British had the largest Western diplomatic establishment in Peking they were still, after a decade, without an ambassador there. The Chinese had declined to exchange representatives on an ambassadorial level. This was particularly distressing to Hongkong officials, who tended to interpret it to mean that their colony and its status were not fully recognized by the Peking regime—which indeed they were not. During my stay, the British mission was headed by a chargé d'affaires, the able and somewhat frustrated Michael Stewart. He was assisted by a dozen or more Chinese-language specialists who pored over such local papers, magazines and books as they could buy, which they translated and analyzed. From this staff the British had probably the best intelligence on China possessed by any Western nation.

All Western observers were regarded as legal spies by the Chinese (perhaps not without reason) and they had few China contacts beyond the printed word. From the Chinese, Western diplomats heard nothing at all about any problems of coexistence with the Russians. But they observed; they exchanged gossip with non-Chinese Communist diplomats; they composed their dispatches; they talked of almost nothing else. Much outside speculation about the Sino-Soviet "cold war" can be traced to Peking's diplomatic circle, where contributions are made by both East and West. Some Eastern Europeans seem even more alert to adverse reports than Westerners. One night I was introduced to a senior Polish attaché who at once excitedly demanded of me: "What do you think of Chou En-lai now? Not the man you used to know, eh? And China? Did you ever think it would come to *this?*"

I said that Chou was twenty years older, that physiologists tell us everyone changes organically every seven years. Otherwise the country was following pretty much the same pattern I had seen in prototype years ago in the Northwest. The Pole probably took me for Dostoyevsky's Idiot. He gave me a disgusted look, shook his head and turned away abruptly; I saw him several times after that, but he never spoke to me again.

One evening at a cocktail party the atom bomb entered the conversation. I repeated a chilling comment made to me by a Chinese "high official" after I had mentioned a responsible Western physicist's estimate that the world then possessed a nuclear weapons stockpile roughly the equivalent of forty tons of TNT for each person alive. Wasn't that enough? I had asked. How much longer could nations behave as if anyone could be a victor in atomic war? "No," I quoted my "high official" as having answered, "I'm afraid it is not enough. It may go on another ten years—until there are four hundred tons of TNT per head."

The diplomat to whom I was talking at once left me to confer with one of his staff; then they drew in diplomats of two other countries. A few nights later at another reception the bomb came up again and I asked an Asian diplomat his guess as to when China would make it.

"They're very near it," he answered. "A high Chinese official just told a friend of mine that China won't join any nuclear weapons ban for ten years. She wants to wait until she has four hundred tons of nuclear TNT for every living person before she even talks about a ban. That means China believes war is inevitable."

On one occasion, at an embassy dinner, I sat next to a certain Western diplomat and a Russian ditto whose conversation, conducted in the best of good humor, went as follows:

Western diplomat: I believe you once had twenty-two thousand advisers in China, but this year they all seem to have finished their tasks at once. How do you explain that?

Russian diplomat: No, not *all*. We still have about twelve hundred experts here. The Chinese are almost self-sufficient in technique, you know.

W.D. I know they are becoming very Red and very expert, but does that apply to physicists, too? Physicists, perhaps, capable of making atomic bombs?

R.D. I must remind you, sir, that my interests here are purely cultural.

W.D. But, sir, education is culture, and physics is an educational subject. Surely you know whether they are culturally capable of making an atomic bomb?

R.D. I don't doubt that the Chinese have very competent physicists. We work with many of them.

W.D. Capable of making the bomb—or perhaps culturally guided rocket missiles? By the way, did you happen to hear anything recently that sounded like a dud missile explosion in this neighborhood? (The Chinese were rumored to have had several rocket-launching failures.)

R.D.   I am a sound sleeper.

W.D.   But your alliance with China is very close, is it not? And you wish to help her in every way possible?

R.D.   Oh, yes.

W.D.   And you support the People's Government position that Taiwan belongs to China and the U.S. must get out?

R.D.   Definitely. The Chinese won't compromise on this question, and they are absolutely right.

W.D.   Then why don't you tell them how to make atomic bombs and strengthen their argument against the United States?

R.D.   I am interested only in cultural questions, but I can tell you that our policy is for the elimination of nuclear weapons, not spreading them; for disarmament, not more armament; for peaceful co-existence, not war.

The "twenty-two thousand advisers" figure mentioned by the Western diplomat in this authentically reported conversation was not disputed by the Soviet diplomat, but the usual estimate was ten to twelve thousand for the period of maximum help. In 1959 Chou En-lai gave an official figure of 10,800 Soviet experts and 1,500 from Eastern Europe sent to China during the decade.[2] How many remained after the major exodus of August, 1960? Guesses by East European diplomats and by the Finns were between five hundred and fifteen hundred. They also said that Soviet technicians assigned to China to supervise installation of the seventy-eight new plants or complete sets of machinery being imported under the terms of the 1959 Sino-Soviet agreement would remain until the machines were in working order. By 1962 very few, if any, senior Soviet technical experts remained in China. Some had been replaced by Czechs and other East Europeans.

It was the underdeveloped, anti-imperialist Africans, Asians, and Latin Americans, not the overdeveloped imperialist Western diplomats, who got time and attention from the Chinese, including mass audiences with the highest chieftains. At the Hsin Ch'iao hotel there was a continuous pageant of short-time visitors representing labor, writers, peace committees, lawyers, scientists, teachers, students, merchants, and rebel leaders from Iraq, Jordan, Afghanistan, India, Mali, Libya, Kenya, Egypt, Uganda, Tanganyika, the Congo, Bechuanaland, Nyasaland, Nigeria, Niger, Guinea, the Gold Coast, Algeria, Morocco, Japan, Burma, Indonesia, Cuba, Argentina, Mexico, Brazil, and Africa and Latin America generally. European clothes were often conspicuous exceptions in dining rooms gay with every color and costume and coiffure, and skins from jet black to gold to vanilla. There were parties of tourists from Russia, Mongolia and the Eastern European countries, and robust teams of ping-pong, basketball, and track athletes—Slavs, Germans, Poles, Koreans. Sekou Touré got the biggest hand of anyone that year, with a million flag-waving people lined up from the airport to the T'ien An Men. Premier U Nu and his party of bewitching Burmese dancing girls came next. Among Latin Americans the Cubans were foremost; there were Mexicans, led by a general; there were Canadians; and there were also a few Britons, Frenchmen, Italians and Swedes. There was a little of practically everything from everywhere—except from the United States, the Philippines and Puerto Rico.

Not many of these visitors stayed more than a week or two. One of the few long-term residents of the Hsin Ch'iao was Professor Leiv Kreyberg, the world-renowned Norwegian cancer specialist, who delivered some lectures at Peking Medical College. I dined with him a few times. He was making a comparative study of the incidence of cancer in all countries. For him China had been one of the blank spots. He was gratified now to be getting full cooperation from the Chinese Medical Association. After visiting a number of hospitals around the country he told me that from what he had seen of the skill and equipment available in China for cancer diagnosis, treatment and research, both were about on a par with Europe's.*

"Incidence of cancer per capita in China," said Dr. Kreyberg, "is about the same as in the West; there are differences in types prevalent. Cancer of the breast and the uterine cancers are about the same. Lung cancer is much less common in China and this is not surprising. There is no longer any doubt that smoking is one of the main causes of lung cancer; the percentage of heavy smokers in China is much lower than in the West. Cancer of the brain may be a little more frequent in China. For some reason cancer of the penis is common here—a type very rare in the West."

"If one stops smoking in order to avoid cancer of the lung, Dr. Kreyberg, what would you recommend for cancer of the penis?"

"You'd better start with cigarettes."

So I gave up smoking; it was easy, as Mark Twain said; he had done it so many times.

A visitor of more dubious background was a Dr. H., of Cuban-Jamaican parentage, who was studying acupuncture in Peking. He was in his thirties, tall and ruggedly built, very dark, and he liked Chinese brandy. In the Hsin Ch'iao bar he explained that he had a practice in Mayfair, London, where he was a kind of chiropractor. He specialized in "back treatments." When he became interested in

---

* He referred to the skill and equipment of top-level scientists, of course. Mass medicine in China is still dependent on primitive means.

China he wrote to the Chinese health ministry to offer to teach his technique free, if they would let him. Months passed and one day he received an invitation to visit Peking to study acupuncture for four months as a state guest.

"I was curious about acupuncture, too," he said, "and I supposed that when I got here I would lecture on my own specialty. Not at all. Every time I mention it they say, 'Later.' I haven't been asked a word about it—after three months."

"You've been attending classes all this time?"

"Oh, yes, every day. Myself, some Russians and an Indian doctor."

Dr. H. never graduated. On his way to school he used to take a certain bus, and on this bus there was a pretty girl conductor. She knew no English, but his Indian colleague knew a few words of Chinese and helped establish some rudimentary understanding between them. After a preliminary meeting shared with the Indian and some others, Dr. H. wanted her to dine at the hotel and go to the theater with him. One day she agreed but said she would first have to inform the work team of which she was a member. The next morning when he eagerly climbed into the bus, a new and very businesslike conductor met him. His girl had been shifted to another line and he never saw her again.

Shortly afterward Dr. H. was told at the school that he had finished his course. He packed up and left. He never did get an opportunity to explain his technique for sore-back treatment to anybody in Peking.

East Europeans also complained that they found it difficult to meet and know any Chinese; few of them spoke the language, and there were no more pillow dictionaries in China. At the universities, marriages between foreign Communist students and Chinese were rare, although one did occur while I was there. And will this change? Yes, it will change—but not very soon.

Among the Hsin Ch'iao's guests I also learned something from a Swedish engineer and from a Swiss watch salesman. The young Swede had supervised the erection of a large modern fiberboard plant at Ichun, in northern Manchuria. It made a special type of hard board which had required imported Swedish machinery at a cost of eight million dollars.

"My company has already set up twenty-two such plants in Russia since the war," he said. "So you might say Soviet production of this item is at least twenty-two times greater than China's. On the other hand, from what I've seen of industry in Manchuria, I'd say China is now able to copy, from our installations, practically all the plywood-making machines Soviet industry is producing. China won't have to import such machines from Russia."

The Swiss watch salesman reported that he was doing a brisk business with regional purchasing agencies, but confined mainly to one item: cheap and serviceable but expensive-looking watches. He could no longer sell any good clocks, nor could he sell the cheapest watches; the Chinese were making these for themselves, and were beginning to export them.

"How long will you have any market left here at all?"

"Five years—but it's good while it lasts. After that they'll probably compete with us in every line. And why not?"

30

Science and Education

China's advances in the education of specialists in applied technology have been extraordinary. Between 1949 and 1960 she graduated 230,000 engineers. Progress in advanced science is far less
spectacular. Before 1950 fewer than 3,000 Chinese had doctoral
degrees in any branch of science and no more than half of them were
in China. Only 862 were listed on the roster as natural scientists
when the new government was established.

In 1955 the Peking government first seriously confronted the problem of rapidly training advanced research scientists when it drew up
a Twelve-Year Science Plan with the help of a large panel of Soviet
experts. This calls for 10,500 graduate (doctoral level) students in the
sciences and two million graduate engineers by the end of 1967. Up
to May, 1957, Red China had 7,705 students doing graduate study in
fourteen countries; the great majority were in the U.S.S.R. The goal of
the Twelve-Year Plan is to catch up with the world "in those branches
of science and technology which are essential to our national economy." Research in scientific theory or "pure science" is of low priority.
The allocation of some 500 top scientists and 800 engineers estimated
to be required for China's priority atomic energy projects[1] makes it

likely that she will lag behind in new theoretical contributions for some years.

China has the latest research equipment, imported from Russia, and is now able to make delicate and complex instruments, including those needed in nuclear research. Adequate scientific libraries have been acquired from abroad. The major emphasis continues to be on research institutes connected with industry and communications. In 1958 these were reported as 415 in number, with 14,700 research and technical personnel. In 1959 the Chinese Academy of Sciences (see page 748) had 105 research institutes to Russia's 87, but only 7,000 members on its research staff, compared to Russia's 14,000.[2]

China's severe shortage of senior scientists may persist for a long time, particularly in view of atomic energy construction requirements. The government has been heavily dependent on Soviet aid in the field of science. If existing Sino-Soviet cooperative projects were scrapped China would be gravely handicapped; she has had no important working contacts with non-bloc countries. Even today 150 of her 180 top scientist academicians who sit on high departmental committees are men educated abroad, among whom 80 studied in the United States. (After the 1961-62 Sino-Soviet controversy, Khrushchev was rumored to have asked for the withdrawal of Chinese atomic physicists in Russia, but renewal of trade and cultural agreements in 1962 apparently provided for continued if limited scientific cooperation.*)*

Popular or "mass line" science is represented by the China Federation of Scientific Societies, which includes 40 groups ranging from senior scientists to an Agricultural Machinery Society that recently admitted 36 "peasant inventors." On a still broader scope, the China Association for the Dissemination of Scientific and Technical Knowledge has a membership of 300,000 professors, engineers, researchers and technicians. It publishes several mass-circulation popular science magazines. An example of its work: 160 lectures on space satellites were presented by its members to the public in one year in Shanghai alone.[3]

Before the revolution no systematic census was ever taken in China and no exact data on illiteracy was available. Official estimates varied from 85 to 95 percent, but probably well over 90 percent of the rural population was illiterate, while in a few cities it was possibly as low as 70 percent. Kuomintang statistics offered shortly before the Japanese invasion showed 13,000,000 students in primary schools, or 13 to 15 percent of children of school age.[4] Even this low level dropped precipitately during the war. In 1949 it seemed probable that not one in ten adults could read and write.

The growth of educational institutions and literacy in China is

* See Chapter 83, China and Russia: Point, Counterpoint.

bound to impress any visitor. My conclusion after visiting many higher, middle and primary schools is that China has made greater progress in liberating masses of people from illiteracy and bringing millions some knowledge of scientific and industrial technique than any nation has ever done in so short a time. The emphasis has been quantitative rather than qualitative, but standards comparable to those in Russia and the West are now imposed in all fields of advanced study.

One of my most profitable days in Peking was spent interviewing Tsui Chung-yuan, Vice-Minister of Education.[5] Mr. Tsui, a graduate of Peking Normal College, was in his early fifties, spoke a bit of English, and suffered from eyestrain. He told me he had been working twelve to fourteen hours a day. At the time I first went to the Northwest he had been a young teacher in Sian. After the Sian Incident he joined the guerrilla forces and for many years thereafter did educational work among the peasants.

As in the U.S.S.R., the State Budget of China lumps expenditures on "social services, culture, education and science" as one item, and in 1960 that amounted to 8,620,000,000 yuan, or 12 percent of all expenditures. In 1953 the state budget for education and science amounted to 1,864,000,000 yuan. By 1960, according to Mr. Tsui, 6,400,000,000 yuan (about $2,600,000,000) was devoted to education and science, or 50 percent more than the direct budgetary military expenditure. Factories, communes and other enterprises spend about an equal percentage of their local budgets on education (assertedly), so that the total invested might well amount to 15 to 20 percent of the national income.

In 1960 United States expenditure on education at all levels was less than 4 percent of the national income, or slightly less than the $18,000,-000,000 Americans spent for alcoholic beverages and tobacco. The significance of this comparison is somewhat modified by the fact that in China the state budget lumps together both the cost of educational operations and investment in capital construction for educational institutions. Thus in 1960 there was a 47.1 percent increase in expenditures for "social services, culture, education and science" as compared to 1959; "of this sum the investment in capital construction increased by 65.7 percent," according to the report of the finance minister, Li Hsien-nien. It is likewise important to remember, as pointed out in an excellent study by Leo A. Orleans, of the Library of Congress, that while "the Communist Chinese have in fact made great progress in expanding the educational system of the country," in their concept education "is not distinguishable from "indoctrination, propaganda and agitation." In the words of *Shih-chieh Chih-shih* (*World Knowledge*), quoted by Mr. Orleans: "Everything that produces an impact on the minds of men and brings about changes in behavior and thought must be considered a phase of education." [6]

In a general survey Minister Tsui divided educational developments during the past decade into three periods:

First Stage, 1949-52: "It took us three years to rebuild the economic basis of education. Everything from transport to schools was broken down. The nation was bankrupt. Money was useless; we were reduced to a barter system. All schools were closed. Our task was to put teachers back to work, in both public and private—mostly missionary—schools. We did this by appeals to patriotism and promising regular pay—mostly in rice—and full cooperation, without much change in the system."

Second Stage, 1952-57: "This period coincided with the First Five-Year Plan. We now began to unify and systematize in preparation for socialist construction. There were twenty-one missionary colleges and higher institutions, more than five hundred private middle schools, and twelve hundred primary schools. Many were using French, English and Japanese texts with little relevance to China. It was necessary to nationalize them and bring them into the broad curricular needs of the nation's public schools.

"In this period we set up a number of specialized schools of higher learning, giving first priority to science and engineering. Our old colleges taught a smattering of everything but prepared very few specialists. We began to emphasize intensified study for practical work. For instance, our old colleges offered only one general course in metallurgy; today we offer eleven courses.

"Our second aim was to decentralize and universalize our higher-education system. Formerly about 70 percent of our college students were concentrated along the coastal regions of East China. Now we have institutes and colleges everywhere; in 1957 some 45 percent of our students were already studying in the interior.

"The third thing we accomplished in this period was to train both teachers and students in socialist philosophy and morality. This was a big task in itself—not yet completed, but well along."

Third Stage, 1957 to date: "At the beginning of the Second Five-Year Plan, the year of the Great Leap Forward, we adopted the motto: 'Educate students for overall development—with equal emphasis on mental, moral and physical training.' We sought to make every student a worker, and to make students from workers. We stressed theory combined with practice.

"In the past only 18 percent of our students studied technology and engineering as against 36 percent studying art, law, history and social sciences. That was wrong. Today more than a third of our students specialize in the physical sciences and engineering. Together with normal-school students they make up 60 percent of the student body. We have introduced many new branches of engineering—fifteen altogether. There are eight branches of geology and survey, instead of one. We have students in schools and institutes specializing in four- or five-year courses never offered before: in mining dynamics, metallurgy, tool building, electronics, power apparatus, heavy engineering, light industry and synthetic fabrics, geodetics, transportation, communications, aircraft, atomics, computer techniques and advanced mathematical engineering. No one can be good in all these. This is an age when we must specialize."

My questions elicited from Mr. Tsui the following miscellaneous statistics, as of 1960:

There was a total of 814,000 college students, of whom 660,000 were full-term (four- or five-year) students and 154,000 were short-term (two- or three-year) students enrolled in the equivalent of junior colleges or polytechnical schools. Full-term college enrollment had increased by more than 400 percent over the Kuomintang peak year.

Among full-term university-level students 283,000 were engineers, of whom 17 percent were women; 119,000 were normal students, of whom 24 percent were women; 77,000 were medical students of whom 40.2 percent were women. The total of women among full-term college students in all categories had risen to 23 percent in 1958. Among agronomists, incidentally, 28 percent were women.*

In twenty years of Kuomintang rule China graduated a total of 185,000 college students, as compared to 431,000 graduated during the first ten years after "liberation." Mr. Tsui estimated that 69,000 full-term college students would graduate in 1961. By the time this sees print China should have well over 700,000 college graduates, including more than 200,000 engineers and 50,000 scientists educated since 1949. Again one should emphasize that, while the best of these graduates would compare favorably with Western counterparts, the need has been for quantity and the average technical level is still low.

In the organization of her new graduate educational system China made use of 694 Soviet Russian lecturers and specialists, 17 Germans, 10 Czechs, and 5 Indians. In 1960 there were fewer than 100 foreign teachers—mostly in engineering and higher physics courses—left in all China. Foreign language study is compulsory from senior middle school onward but it is rudimentary until college. In the higher institutes Russian and English predominate and in English literature nineteenth-century classics are used as texts alongside translations of Mao and other masters of Marxism. Science students study technical texts in foreign languages, of course, and specialists attend institutes of foreign languages.

Schools of higher education in 1961 included the following: 61 general universities; 271 engineering; 142 medical; 174 normal; 99 agricultural; 14 forestry and mining; 5 foreign language; 5 finance

---

* In an interview with the vice-minister of agriculture, Mr. Chen, I was told that China had trained more than 200,000 agronomists by 1959.

and economics; 33 art, drama, and music; and 29 institutes offering courses of specialization in law, politics—or physical culture. Their combined teaching staff "exceeds 100,000."

Full-term middle school students in 1960 numbered 12,900,000. This figure included 7,743,000 students in junior middle schools, a category equivalent to higher elementary school in many countries, for youths aged thirteen to sixteen. (Part-time and work-study middle schools are discussed in the next chapter.) The middle school system employed 350,000 teachers.

China's primary school students in 1959 formed a vast children's army of "nearly 91,000,000" enrolled in 737,000 schools, with 2,500,000 "teachers and staff." * Mr. Tsui said that primary education was now compulsory in all except the more remote and backward regions, notably certain minority nationality areas. In 1953 China's census showed a total of 89,500,000 children up to four years of age. Anticipated 1960-61 *new* enrollment in primary schools was 21,000,000. Eighty to 90 percent of China's primary school-age population appeared to be getting at least some elementary education. This is well above average among Asian countries except Japan. Fewer than one in four of India's school-age population were in school, for example, and fewer than one in five in Pakistan.[7]

In 1957 Premier Chou En-lai estimated illiteracy over the whole country at 70 percent. Mr. Tsui said that by 1960 the percentage had been reduced, through all efforts (including adult education courses), to about 66 percent for the rural areas and 24 percent in the cities. Few industrial workers are illiterate or remain so very long. In advanced cities the literacy rate is high. Mr. Tsui estimated illiteracy in Peking as "less than 20 percent" among persons of school age or under forty. If as much as 34 percent of the entire population was literate there were about 235,000,000 literates in 1961. That indicated a high percentage of literacy in the age group under seventeen—which accounted for 41 percent of the population in the 1953 census. Some 70,000,000 adults were exposed to spare-time mass education between 1949 and 1959 but by no means all of them possessed the ability to retain the characters (the test for literacy is the ability to recognize 1,500 characters). In addition, some 47,000,000 persons graduated from spare-time elementary schools. If the current rate of advance in mass education is maintained, illiteracy will be rare among persons under the age of forty by 1967.

As a group, university professors are among the most highly paid employees. In 1960 they were divided into twelve grades, with salaries ranging from a top of 345 yuan down to 62 for student instructors. A teacher's grade is determined by technical ability, years in service, and general standing, including political factors. Some professors are able to keep private cars at their own expense and many augment

* Figures for primary schools may include some adult students.

their incomes by writing articles and lecturing for good fees, and with royalties earned from books. Middle school and primary teachers are divided into ten grades, with a salary range of 26.50 yuan, for beginning kindergarten assistants, to 149 yuan for senior teachers.

Retirement age for women professors is fifty to fifty-five, for men sixty to sixty-five. "Many choose to continue teaching after retirement age," said Mr. Tsui. "They may do so, if their health permits. Pensions are 45 percent of the wage income after ten years, up to 80 percent of income on retirement after twenty years."

There is considerable confusion abroad about the work-and-study system in China. Mr. Tsui explained: "There are three different schedules in use, depending on the type of study. Obviously a student agronomist will spend more time working on a farm than a physics or chemistry research student. The first schedule calls for a one-month holiday, four months of field work, seven months of classroom study. The second schedule provides for a one-month holiday, three months of field work and eight months of classroom work. The third calls for a two-month holiday, one month of field work and nine months of classroom study work. We call the first schedule '1-4-7,' the second '1-3-8' and the third '2-1-9.'

"Field labor actually means field practice. Engineering students work in the construction of dams, bridges, power plants; geology students do prospecting or field analytical work; pre-med students work in clinics and hospitals; chemistry students may help build a chemical factory; and so on. Some colleges operate their own farms, vineyards and dairies. Some have steel plants.

"In middle schools, students do eight to ten hours of labor weekly, wherever they are needed. We start early. Primary school students get in four to six hours a week at school shops or chores assigned by their teachers."

"Political study goes on all the time, I suppose—field or classroom?"

"More or less. In classrooms about one hour in ten is devoted to socialist education, both in basic Marxist texts and in lectures." *

"In general, what percentage of a student's university time is devoted to classroom study, apart from labor and politics?"

"About 60 percent to 70 percent—not less than 60 percent." 8

Tuition is free in all schools, including higher schools, and there is no room rent. The majority of university students draw a state stipend which pays for their food and gives them a small pocket allowance.

Very few students from peasant or working-class families ever reached college in former times; as late as 1960 only 20 percent of party members had been to high school or college. The situation had been drastically altered: in 1959 "slightly more than 50 percent" of

---

* This is probably an understatement. It has certainly been much higher in the past.

all college students came from families of peasant and working-class origin—as distinct from "brain workers" and bourgeoisie. If true, this is a revolutionary change the consequences of which may not be fully understood in the West for another ten years. Adult peasants are encouraged to aspire to high school education through state aid. If they reach college level all expenses are borne by the state, which in addition grants a stipend of 40 yuan a month, enough to provide for family care during their period of study.

"What causes your worst headaches, Mr. Tsui—aside from eye-strain? I mean, what are the ministry's hardest problems of the moment?"

"We have plenty of them, mainly deriving from a tremendous four- to fivefold expansion of the educational system in ten years. By 1959 we had constructed more than 44,000,000 square meters of floor space in new school buildings—one-third of it for institutes of higher learning. That's forty-four times more than we built in 1951, but it is still behind the need. Our primary schools are crowded and must soon be replaced or extended.

"The second problem is teachers. Classes are much too large. Our best professors are overworked. Quality of teachers, like school buildings, varies from very poor to very good. We are training and retraining as fast as we can.

"Probably the biggest problem of all is synchronizing educational output with the needs of science, industry and agriculture. We can't keep up with the changes in demand. A few years ago we faced a trying shortage of engineers. That's why we needed so many foreign advisers. We're beginning to catch up with those needs but we're far behind in pedagogues and specialists in natural sciences.

"What will our needs be in 1965 and 1966 for the students we enroll in college next year? We get close guidance from the State Planning Commission at all times, but no plan is good nowadays for more than a year. All kinds of unexpected shortages develop. The year 1958 changed the balance of educational needs in many unexpected ways. We have to be able to shift students from one line to another in a year or two to fill new gaps that may appear quite suddenly. To do that without upsetting and confusing the whole curricular system is a delicate task."

"College applicants don't get to make their own choice of a career or specialization, then?"

"Not always. Category quotas are set in high school, of course, and students begin fairly early to aim at one thing or another. They all get to express preferences, but the decision is made by the authorities, on the basis of the national need. If the quota for one particular field is filled, then the student gets his second or third choice—or may be sent into some entirely different line. It depends first of all on the national need, and then on the student's general rating."

"He also goes where he is sent?"

"He can express a preference but the authorities decide. Generally speaking, a student with highest scholastic standing will get the best chance of priority rating. Students are taught to take an unselfish attitude and accept the decision in good spirit."

In ten years the primary school annual enrollment increased by almost four times, the number in middle schools by ten times, and the number in higher institutions by about seven times. A primary school student now has one chance in seven of entering high school and a high school student has about one chance in sixteen of reaching college. This is truly a great improvement in opportunity. But the literate base of the education pyramid has so vastly expanded that competition for available places in secondary and higher schools is extremely severe. Scholastic qualification alone is not enough to guarantee success. Between two students of equal scholastic competence, it is obvious from the following official criteria, the preference goes to the one most "politically advanced":

> In order to guarantee quality of new students, authorities and institutions of higher education in various localities should, in accordance with the unified regulations, strictly examine the political background, academic standing, and state of health of new students, and give priority to their admission on this basis. After new students have been admitted the institutes of higher learning should also conduct a re-check of their *political and health standards*. If they prove unable to meet requirements in these *two respects* they shall be disqualified from continuing study.[9]

It should be noted, however, that at no time has Red China barred children of "class enemies" from access to higher education, as was true in Russia until just before the Second World War. There is also no restriction excluding non-Chinese nationals from universities; a number of foreign students have been admitted, including several ex-G.I.'s who changed hats in Korea.

China has a National Enrollment Committee which each year confers with the National Planning Commission to decide how many students are to be admitted to various higher educational institutions, and for what branches of study. The N.E.C. issues annual enrollment regulations which inform candidates of the subjects on which they will be examined, the time and place, how to secure travel allowances, room reservations, and so on. The time is usually July 15-August 1, and in 1957 there were about ninety-one examination centers.[10] Since 1958 the selection system has been somewhat decentralized. Provincial and institutional authorities now have a much larger voice in enrollment planning and distribution of students.

In 1958-59 more than 35 percent of all university students were in teacher training courses. Engineering came next, with 31 percent; agriculture and forestry were third, with 6.9 percent; and medicine and other branches of science came fourth. (By 1961 medical students were more than 10 percent.) Fine arts was last, with less than half of 1 percent of all students. Total new enrollment of students in higher educational institutions rose from 65,900 in 1952 to 280,000 in 1960.[11]

Candidates for college entrance need a diploma and written permission from their middle school authorities to continue their studies. Examination subjects are: Chinese language, politics, mathematics, physics, chemistry, biology, history, geography and two foreign languages—as a rule, Russian and English. Foreign languages and geography are not required for entrance into engineering, and certain science subjects may be omitted for students of literature and the arts. Although students are required to enter the schools designated for them, they may, as Mr. Tsui stated, express preferences—three in fields of study, and five in institutions—which are taken into consideration.

Outside the examination system a small percentage of older students have been admitted since 1958 from among military and civilian party cadres and outstanding workers and peasants, on recommendation by their organizations. They are required to take tutorship to make up their deficiencies and may study longer than the prescribed number of years to complete their courses.

"What would you consider the greatest mistake made in this decade of new education?" I asked Minister Tsui.

"We made one big mistake and are correcting it. We tried to build up a huge mass educational system without sufficiently integrating it into the needs of production. Today we have 91,000,000 children in primary school, next year it will be more. Logically, we should expect that within ten years 50,000,000 or more will be in high schools. But obviously our economy could not tolerate the withdrawal of so many people from the labor force.

"From now on secondary and higher education has to be combined with rational solutions of man-power-distribution problems in our basic socialist construction. In the future there will be more labor-and-study combinations, not less. Experience has taught us that is the only way. It is the fundamental concept of our educational system today."

Fifty million high school students! United States enrollment in high schools in 1960 about equaled that in secondary schools in China. If China's rate of increase in the fifties continues, however, she will by 1970 have five or six times as many high school students *and* college students as the United States. Who would feed them? It was now fully realized that the rate of growth of the economy cannot support any such massive sacrifice of labor power to a wholly food-dependent educational system.

The enforcement of universal compulsory primary education within only ten years brought about serious contradictions between the demand for higher education and the state's continuing need for farm labor and increased need for skilled industrial labor. In old China even primary education was so rare that any graduate was considered an "intellectual." Now many new graduates are discovering that they must go back to the farms and shops.

"Several years ago," wrote the editors of *China Youth* in an attempt to explain the change to the Class of '61, "almost all senior middle school graduates were admitted into universities and most of the junior middle school graduates were enrolled in senior middle schools. This was because at that time general education had not caught up with higher education. Today the . . . special situation has gradually disappeared. In 1959 . . . there were altogether 90,000,000 primary school students of whom some 10,000,000 graduated. If all of the graduates were admitted to enter middle schools . . . there would have to be built at least 10,000 new schools! Correspondingly, several hundred thousand new teachers would have been required." The article listed still more impossible demands for colleges, the cost of their support, and the effects on capital accumulation and retarded construction, which in turn must slow down further growth of better social and educational facilities, etc. "*In the final analysis education must be made to serve production.*"

Newspapers have had to exhort high school graduates not to "look down on" farm and factory labor, to remember their own origins, to realize that everyone cannot become a cadre or a bureaucrat, to understand that all *kanpu* hereafter must do physical labor also, to forget their "pride as scholars" and begin to learn life from experienced old farmers and shop workers. Parent-teacher meetings are called to enlist parental support in achieving "readjustment" of their children graduates to labor tasks. The old peasant attitude that no "scholar" should soil his hands but only become an official and glorify the family is still strong.

Probably nothing has been more misunderstood or distorted abroad than the attempt in China to combine practical work with education and to fit education to the realistic needs of a country engaged in a transition from semifeudal society. Blunders and stupidities occur in implementing the slogan, "Intellectuals become manual workers; manual workers become intellectuals." It may be doubted, for instance, that any good was accomplished by sending a microbiologist I know to dig latrines in the countryside. But the law of gravity itself would prove an erroneous directive in the hands of some Chinese bureaucrats I have seen. The principle of respect for toil and of combining book knowledge with related practical work is sound and necessary in China. If it does nothing but prevent the return of a small elite literati with notions that manual labor is beneath it, the effort will be worthwhile. This disdain for labor and the peasantry was the curse of the rulers of Kuomintang China almost as much as among the Confucian mandarinate (and the Brahmans of India), and it explains much about the near-downfall of the nation.

The aim is not to reduce intellectuals to the level of laborers, but to teach them the meaning of labor. The "workers become intellectuals" slogan means to lift the working class to a level where comprehension of the work of intellectuals and its practical applications is possible for all. For this purpose there exists in China a parallel system of schools—highly improvisatory as yet—called Spare-Time Education, of which little is known abroad.

31

"Ministry" of Spare-Time Education

"Trade union bosses in America would tell you that our unions are run by Communists, that they are tools of the Communist party. Is that true? Yes, it is absolutely correct. We are tools of the Communist party. In America I doubt if any union leader would say that about his union?"

Vice-Chairman Li Chi-po, of the All-China Trade Union Federation, grinned at his little joke. It was eight o'clock in the evening in the big trade union headquarters building on Peking's Fifth Avenue, Long Peace Street. Li was in his late forties, a ruggedly built man in a dark woolen tunic, matching trousers and black leather shoes. A young woman sat taking notes and doing side errands until we finished talking at midnight. He had already had supper in his plainly furnished office. He noticed me looking at a cot in an adjoining room.

"I'm going to sleep there tonight," he said, motioning toward it. "I often work sixteen hours a day—my regular office duties, and then all the meetings. I have been talking all afternoon to some provincial union leaders and we finally agreed at supper and now they've gone home." I learned that Li was a veteran of Yenan Academy who had specialized in labor affairs for twenty years as a protégé of Liu Shao-ch'i.

He went on: "The reason our unions are under Communist party leadership is that it is the workers' party. If union leaders in America told the truth they would say that they are under capitalist leadership; they are tools of capitalism. Under capitalism, even honest craft unions can do no more than carry on struggles for small temporary gains which cost the capitalists nothing; they merely pass on increased wages by raising prices at the expense of society as a whole. Under socialism, manager, workers and government all belong to the working class; they cooperate for the benefit of society as a whole."

"I understand the theory," I said, "but what happens if, say, a union of shoemakers wants to strike for higher wages to make shoes for the army?"

"You understand the theory but you don't understand that under socialism the unions' main task is educational. Let me explain it. We operate almost as many schools as the Ministry of Education. In fact, you might call the Trade Union Federation a ministry of part-time education. Our schools have two main purposes. The first is to provide political education, which means education in socialist history and principles, in Marxism-Leninism, in the theory and practice of Mao Tse-tung, and in state policies and contemporary affairs. The second purpose is to provide technical and cultural education. The end objective is to prepare men and women who are politically, technically and culturally fitted to manage the national economy.

"We have two auxiliary tasks: to organize the workers in support of production movements in every way, to maintain morale and enthusiasm. Our four guiding principles in this work are: compare yourself with others; study constantly, never stand still; emulate those who are more advanced than you are; help those who lag behind you. This is the philosophy of our educational effort and what we seek in daily life."

Good Boy Scout principles, too, I thought. Incongruous as it may strike many, a lot of China is like that.

"Our other task is to raise the living conditions of the working class both materially and culturally. We propose wage adjustments and work out wage systems with the government. Because of our work wages have doubled in ten years."

Li asserted that campaigns in the federation's *Workers Daily* had exposed some sweatshop working conditions in both state and private industries which had led to important reforms, including the eight-hour day. (With periodic overtime labor and spare-time study many workers are still committed, however, for ten to fourteen hours a day.) In 1955, for example, the *Workers Daily* revealed that alleged gains made in "speed-up" drives by shocking overuse of labor were more than offset by heavily increased losses in man-power output due to sickness, accidents and absenteeism. An excerpt from that period:

There has been no limit to the prolongation of working hours; individual workers have worked continuously for 72 hours through additional shifts and working hours. As a result of exhaustion, sickness and casualties have been serious. There are quite a few cases in which, owing to exhaustion, workers have fainted, vomited, or even died.[1]

The outside observer may reasonably doubt whether such reports actually provoked subsequent reforms or were merely pseudo-events created to support practical decisions reached earlier inside the party labor bureau. Li also credited the federation with improvements in workers' housing and in safety measures. Undoubtedly the labor press is a main source of information to Chinese as well as outside observers concerning malpractices past and present, and innumerable criticisms do appear in it. A safety drive was demanded in 1955 by Lai Jo-yu, chairman of the A.C.T.U.F., who asserted that too many accidents due to bad management were blamed on "carelessness of the workers."[2] The *Workers Daily* accused "some units" where cadres had penalized workers "already injured" and cited an instance of a worker who had lost both fingers being "fined one month's wages and made to criticize himself in public."[3] Others had been sent to jail for allegedly causing "serious losses" in production while "nothing is done to management." Press criticism also preceded a general wage increase when it was reported that "labor productivity in the whole country was raised by 15 percent in 1954 but the average wages increased by only 2.3 percent. In 1955 labor productivity was raised by 10 percent but average wages increased by only 0.6 percent."[4]

"Are managers actually members of trade unions?" I asked Li.

"It depends on the trade. In some cases everybody in the government ministry is a member: for example, the Minister of Railways and all his staff are union members."

We did not get back to the shoemakers' strike for a couple of hours, until after Vice-Chairman Li—obviously an executive of great energy and detailed grasp of his work—had further explained his main preoccupation with *yueh-yi,* or "spare-time study."

Prewar unions were nearly all under Kuomintang control, as they are now under Communist control. Their 1947 membership was about 5,000,000. Today there are "about 40,000,000 members" of trade unions. That included 4,000,000 urban handicraft workers and 17,000,000 members in heavy or state industry—as apart from office workers and employees in "local" enterprises. About 25,000,000, or 60 percent, were receiving education of some kind in trade union schools which reduced illiteracy among organized urban workers from 85 percent in 1949 to 15 percent by 1961, according to this Walter Reuther of China.

At the lowest level are literacy classes in which workers learn the

1,500 basic characters required to read a newspaper. Not all workers can pass the course, said Li. Many have to repeat and people above fifty often find it impossible. Those who succeed go on to:

1) Elementary primary schools where 13,000,000 literates were taking streamlined courses in literature, mathematics, natural science, geography, history and politics (Marxism). "No time for singing, dancing, music or sports," said Li gravely. Fast learners finish in two years, some take four. State regulations require that workers and peasants in such schools be guaranteed at least 240 hours a year for study.

2) Elementary middle schools and technical middle schools. Four million workers were being taught essential mathematics, science and shop engineering combined with politics. The courses last eighteen to twenty-four months and graduates continue to

3) High schools, for another eighteen to twenty-four months. Courses offered: math, science, engineering, accounting, shop management, plus lectures in history and Marxism. Here 1,500,000 workers were enrolled in preparation for

4) Spare-time colleges, with a current attendance of 400,000 and five to six years of advanced study for those capable of covering full college-level curricula. From these would come technicians, engineers, scientists, factory managers, mathematicians, planning experts and full-fledged Communists.

In spare-time higher education an academic year runs from thirty-eight to forty weeks of study, for an average of nine hours per week. Classroom attendance is required three days a week; three hours of homework are prescribed six days a week. Graduates should have an education, it is claimed, comparable to that of the fourth year in standard institutions.

The spare-time educational program began as early as 1951, but the present system, which covers peasants as well as workers, traces to 1955. A joint conference called in that year by the Ministry of Higher Education, the Ministry of Education, and the Trade Union Federation adopted plans aimed at eradicating illiteracy in a decade. In January, 1960, the State Council set up a spare-time education committee (representing the Ministries of Education, Culture, Science, Economics, Defense; trade unions; and party and other organizations) to unify all such activities throughout the nation. Six months before I interviewed Mr. Li it was reported that 130,000,000 peasants were enrolled in literacy and primary spare-time schools, made possible largely by newly opened commune mass-education facilities.[5]

Radio and television are being increasingly used for supplementary instruction in correspondence courses offered by some universities and colleges. In Peking in 1960 China's first Television College was opened. It offered courses at primary and middle school levels to workers, soldiers, miners and government employees who were prepared to devote eight hours a week to study. The teaching staff was provided by Peking University, the Teachers University, and the Peking Teachers Training College faculties.

"Do you think you can turn out really competent scientists and engineers from a spare-time education system of this kind?" I asked Li.

"We have made studies of the class backgrounds of fifty great scientists and inventors," he replied. "Forty of them—including your Edison and Ford—came from the working class and were largely self-taught or spare-time students."

In fifteen years, he went on, they believed they could "elevate the working class to a general level of middle-school education. Within ten to fifteen years we hope to graduate about five to seven million students from our spare-time college courses or approximately the same figure the regular university system will then be producing. In this way we hope to hasten the elimination of differences between manual workers and mental workers. We aim to combine the maturity and experience of working-class leaders with a high level of technical and cultural education."

Extension study is nothing new in the modern world, of course, but there may not be anything elsewhere quite as intensive as this on a mass scale. Students spend two to four hours a day in classroom work and study. Added to the shop day that means ten to twelve hours of work six days a week—which burns up a lot of calories. Teachers also put in at least that many hours and possibly more. The whole program has a full-time faculty of only 30,000. All China is teacher-short and the union schools borrow, from the Ministry of Education, 70,000 professionals for part-time work (at extra pay). Li said that there were now "*yueh-yi* normal schools" in every province. Nonprofessional specialists in various techniques were being groomed to do their bit to help "elevate the working class" in the shortest time possible. A few schools had different shifts to accommodate both day and night workers. I saw many spare-time schools. As a rule they use clubs or factory dining or recreation rooms, but often the workshops themselves become classrooms. I saw workers holding meetings in corners of machine shops, apprentices being lectured by veterans around the lathes they are learning to operate, groups of workers conferring over blueprints on the grassy lawns of new factories, and party leaders delivering Marxist courses under the scaffoldings of new bridges and dams. Every worker carries a notebook and pencil and often you see a textbook protruding from his back pocket.

For those who do not qualify for higher education, there is a gap between the elementary graduation age of thirteen, and the lower middle school graduation age of sixteen, and the legal minimum full-time working age of eighteen. Half-time work-and-study schools continue the education of adolescents, who spend half-days in shop or farm work. These students may also alternate work and study for full days, or spend three days at the bench or plow and three days in school.

Two other types of experimental schools were run under federation auspices, both for sixteen- to eighteen-year-olds: "school-factories," of four hours shop work and six hours study, and "factory-schools," which combined six hours of shop work with four hours of study. In the factories with a six-hour work day, there was no lunch period and workers got a full day's pay. "Production," said Li, "is not less than in eight-hour factories, efficiency is at a higher level, and enthusiasm is maximum. So far the experiment has involved only 100,000 workers in industries of a high technical level."

Included among the federation's activities is the operation of 32,000 workers' "palaces" or clubs. Some of them are no more than barns but all new satellite towns have clubs of a sort. In Port Arthur I visited a maritime workers' social center with a 2,000-seat theater, a large library, a cafeteria and a big hall for weekly dances. On the Sungari River at Harbin I saw a tile-roofed structure really elaborate enough to be called a palace; it combined boating, swimming, ping-pong, dancing and other recreational facilities with various "cultural" attractions. Unions have organized 39,000 amateur drama and opera groups; the accent is quantitative, to involve as many people as possible. There are 200,000 athletic associations with 3,000,000 participants and about 30,000 union libraries with 84,000,000 books. Unions also operate 210 rest homes and sanatoria. I saw a rest home for miners on the Dairen waterfront comfortably installed in a former brothel for Japanese officers. Another home had once been a club for tired Japanese businessmen.

Important benefits of union membership are free medical care, spare-time education, accident insurance and old-age and sickness insurance. Unions in China are financed by a small percentage of profits remitted to enterprises by the state at the rate of .015 to .03 of the total wage bill. Members pay a registration fee of 25 fen* to one yuan, depending on their wages. Dues are one percent of a member's wages. Unions operate canteens at a small profit and derive some income from sports meets and theatrical performances. They also profit from the *Workers Daily, China Labor Monthly,* and other periodicals owned by the federation as well as from publishing firms which bring out millions of volumes of technical and labor books annually. Quarters and materials are furnished by the state.

All union activities are closely coordinated with the Communist party and Young Communist propaganda campaigns to arouse and maintain enthusiasm for the fulfillment of production quotas and organizational directives. Every union and branch union has its committees to prepare banners, placards, wall newspapers, drawings and cartoons which echo the party line on everything from "factory front

* One yuan equals 100 fen.

support agricultural front" to the current phase of the struggle against imperialist aggression and the battered American paper tiger in Taiwan. They form teams to strike gongs and drums to applaud and congratulate labor heroes during shop hours. They keep account of each person's rate of progress right down to the latest item of piece-work and post notices and awards of honors won by fast quota-makers. They fill the factory with music and slogans and they are tireless organizers and joiners.

Unions are formed in accordance with the Trade Union Law of the People's Republic. Elections follow the same pattern as the state elections. Any place with ten or more workers or employees may set up a union and elect a chairman and subcommittees. Union sub-branches elect delegates to local labor federations or congresses who in turn elect regional and municipal congresses, and so on to the top. The National Labor Congress elects an executive committee which runs the All-China Federation and has broad supervisory powers to dissolve or reorganize any union. At every step workers are led by cadres and altogether they form an administration which corresponds to labor bureaucracies in other countries. In China, however, all union accounts are audited by the government and union chiefs are in every way responsible to supervisors in the party labor department. Federation leaders and the Ministry of Labor are also practically indivisible.

What about that shoemakers' strike? The answers I got may be condensed as follows:

The right to strike is guaranteed by law and there have been occasional strikes on a local scale. Labor disputes in China are "contradictions among the people," however, not class struggles. When an unsettled grievance leads to a strike or slowdown it is due to faulty leadership on the basic level and differences are settled at the next level. A national strike is inconceivable. "Strikes for higher wages cannot occur if workers have been properly educated to understand that wages are based on fair standards of values of production set by the state, which makes no profit for itself but merely acts for 'the whole people' to reinvest national savings for the future enrichment of all." But if shoemakers still want higher wages? Their views will be considered when general wage adjustments are made. Meanwhile, the shoemakers may need more political education. They can also work harder for bonuses or attend spare-time schools and learn higher techniques and perhaps qualify for better-paying jobs.

"Labor unions cannot fight for the narrow interests of any particular craft union at the expense of the whole people." The unions are tools of the Communist party, as Mr. Li said, and the party represents "the whole people." That's the theory, anyway, and I gathered that if I didn't understand it I might need more education.

But education of the workers is not a one-way street, as Mao Tse-tung

No. 1 Electrical Machines Manufacturing Plant in Harbin, Manchuria—one of 156 major projects installed by Soviet engineers (1957).

Cave kindergarten-nursery in the Yenan hills. Children's melon output is on the ledge.

Street scene, Chungking suburbs: schoolchildren in November.

Chow time in a Loyang kindergarten.

Hatamen Ta Chieh, Peking. Shorts are new; sans shorts (infant), old style.
(*Felix Greene*)

Hsia fang! City women, Hankow, en route to spend a few weeks "down on the farm."

Chengchow: Suburban housing, and a park turned into vegetable gardens.

Cotton mill in Sian: all made-in-China machines. See page 460.

Pumpkin Lane, Shanghai, a former slum and still a slum—but paved, tree-planted, and somewhat scrubbed. (*Felix Greene*)

Primary school shop worker assembling radio.

Why it's hard to find an idle pedicab.

Great Hall of the People, Peking. October Anniversary Day. The hall was built in seven months by the collective labor of Peking citizens.

Two Dragon Lane urban commune dining room, Peking. July, 1960.

New canal in an Anhui rural commune. (*New China Photos*)

Dining room—theater, Horse Bridge Commune, Kiangsu.

Formerly privately owned restaurant, now production brigade dining room,
Jungkuei commune, Shunteh county, Kwangtung. (*N.C.P.*)

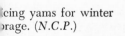

icing yams for winter
orage. (*N.C.P.*)

Hill terracing for water storage and prevention of soil erosion in the Yellow River Valley. (*N.C.P.*)

Kunming girl and popsicle, outside an industrial fair.

has often stressed; the educators themselves must be educated by the workers:

> In 1956, small numbers of workers and students in certain places went on strike. The immediate cause of these disturbances was the failure to satisfy certain of their demands for material benefits, of which some should and could be met . . . But a more important cause was bureaucracy on the part of those in positions of leadership. In some cases, responsibility for such bureaucratic mistakes should be placed *on the higher authorities,* and those at the lower levels should not be made to bear all the blame . . . In the same year, members of a small number of agricultural cooperatives also created disturbances, and the main causes were also bureaucracy on the part of the leadership and lack of educational work among the masses . . .
>
> The guiding spirits in disturbances [including strikes] should not be removed from their jobs or expelled without good reason, except for those who have committed criminal offenses or active counter-revolutionaries who should be dealt with according to law. In a big country like ours it is nothing to get alarmed about if small numbers of people should create disturbances; rather, we should turn such things to advantage to help us get rid of bureaucracy.[6]

32

Who's Hu?

The evening before I visited the Iron and Steel Institute I saw in a Peking theater a contemporary drama about two girls, two boys and a commune against a swamp. The swamp lost; one of the boys was a party veteran and naturally he won the confidence of the peasants and with their faith and his courage they drained the swamp just before the winter frost set in. Humor was provided by the Intellectual, a malingerer afraid to soil his hands by labor; nobody was surprised when it turned out that his father had been an oppressive landlord. A Student Agronomist who knew her books but not life was now learning the hard way, from the Wise Old Peasant. The W.O.P.'s daughter was ambitious; she wanted to drive a truck, a tractor, or anything at all as long as it gave her equal status with a man.

All these were stock caricatures, but the next day I met a girl at the Iron and Steel Institute who was exactly like the peasant's daughter. Her name was Chiang Chu-hsing and I nicknamed her Hsiao-shan or Small Lightning. Her story literally corresponded to that of the character in the play, but in this case life was larger than "art" and more interesting.

I spent the morning talking to the director, Hu Ying, and inspecting the institute. It was one of twenty wholly new universities and colleges, built north and west of Peking, with a combined enrollment which exceeded the total number of students on that level in all prerevolutionary China.

Every province has its own higher educational system, but Peking is still regarded as the Athens of China and attracts more than 100,000 college students, or about 15 percent of the current national enrollment. They still tend to think of themselves as China's intellectual *crème de la crème*. Old Peking had eleven colleges and about 10,000 students, and foremost of the colleges was the Pei-ta, Peking National University, which produced the foremost founders of the Communist party. Pei-ta is still the goal of ambitious arts and sciences students and graduate research workers. Enrollment was now about 11,000. Outside the city, near the Summer Palace, was the "rich man's university" of Yenching, founded by missionaries; nearby was Tsing Hua, which also had a foreign background. Yenching had now been absorbed by Tsing Hua, a greatly enlarged university with an enrollment exceeding 7,000. I revisited both of them, and went on to the new institutes north of the city walls.

The focus of this recently developed university city is the Chinese Academy of Sciences, which embraces institutes of meteorology, economics, geophysics and physics, linguistics, philology and others. Around it are the spacious new campuses of universities, institutes and colleges which specialize in medicine, normal training, petroleum technology, aeronautics, agriculture, mining and metallurgy, music and art. As an illustration of their impact, the new geological institute now had more students than the total number of graduate geologists produced in all the years before 1949.

At the Iron and Steel Institute, Hu Ying was both chief administrator and party leader, a combination I had learned to welcome. One could accomplish one's business much more smoothly and rapidly wherever a party man was in titular as well as factual control rather than operating under some euphemism such as secretary. The party man may or may not answer all one's questions, but he is in a better position to make the decisions. Hu Ying proved so cooperative that I returned to the school a second time to get a picture story of student daily life.

Director Hu was a Manchurian, born in Fushun, the coal town, and educated at Shenyang Normal College. As a young teacher during the war he had joined the anti-Japanese underground, at first simply as a national patriot, so he said. Later he escaped to the hills and the partisans and there became a Communist and fought with the guerrillas until victory. Assigned to help establish the Iron and Steel Institute in 1953, he had been there ever since. The chancellor and vice-chancellors were professional engineers, but Hu Ying was boss. Wearing blue slacks and a blue cotton shirt, Hu received me in a spacious reception room furnished with semimodern Chinese furniture, the walls decorated with Sung and Ming paintings, the windows draped in silk with golden bees embroidered on it. He offered me innumerable cups of scalding tea served by a student assistant.

The institute's well-landscaped campus covered thirty acres and its plant included forty-one completed buildings, with eleven more under construction. It had 6,000 students, of whom 916 were women. The largest institute of its kind in the country, it had a staff of 700 professors, assistants and instructors. It operated fifty-seven laboratories, more than ten experimental factories, and a small modern steel plant with an electric blast furnace where men and women students were trained. The plant had a 1962 target of 100,000 tons. In the middle of the campus were adequate athletic fields and a large swimming pool built by spare-time student labor—as was common now at many universities.

"Our curriculum includes twenty-three subjects," said Hu, "and all varieties of steel processing. We train research specialists and teachers. The full course is five years and we offer one and two years of postgraduate work. There are more than thirty different student activity organizations such as photography, radio, dancing, opera, dramatics, orchestra, chorus, Chinese and Western music appreciation—"

"How about cooking—or is it going to become a lost art in an age of communal eating?"

"There is a cooking club; also a sewing club."

Hu went on to say that tuition and rent were paid by the state, and that 80 percent of the students drew a stipend which covered the cost of food—twelve and a half yuan a month—and provided pocket money of three yuan for undergraduates and five yuan for graduate students. The other 20 percent of the students, who came from families with an income of more than sixty yuan per month (that excludes most peasants), were obliged to pay for their food in whole or in part, "depending on circumstances." Institute students included forty-three Mongols and "about fifty" assorted Moslems, Uighurs from Turkestan, Chuangs from Kwangsi, and Thais from Yunnan.

"There must be stiff competition to get into a school like this. How are students selected?"

"That's right. The demand is greater than the supply. High schools annually yield from two to three hundred thousand graduates who are qualified to apply, but our own institute can't admit more than about fifteen hundred a year. Applicants are judged by scholarship, character and health status."

"Children from ex-landlord families, too?"

"Yes, we have some. But most of our students come from peasant and working-class families. We also admit a limited number of students who are substandard in scholarship—most of the minority nationalities students, for example. They get special tutoring or spend an extra year or two with us. An especially promising peasant from a revolutionary family, or the son of a veteran, naturally has a good chance to be recommended."

"By the party?"

"By the party—and the school authorities, too."

"Your teachers must average out pretty young?"

"Most of them are under forty. Quite a few were educated in Russia. We have about sixty 'old boys'—over forty—trained before the war."

"Would you say your teaching methods follow Soviet lines or develop independently?"

"In some basic respects they are the same; we use a lot of translated Russian texts. But the teaching revolution going on here now is our own development. We call it a three-in-one technique. It combines, in all grades, teaching, practical research work, and actual production. All students spend some time in our factories where we make some of the materials used in the buildings you see being constructed here. We designed and helped build our steel plant. You'll see it, if you wish. We are working on more than a hundred research projects—real, exciting, practical problems passed on to us by various industries. We also send students to outside factories to study and work."

"How many months a year?"

"It depends on the kind of work—whether it's a special project, a whole class under the guidance of a professor, or a student's combined research-and-work project—what his year in school is—and so on. Some students spend most of their four weeks' vacation time working. In 1958 practically all of them did."

"Why 1958?"

"We sent two thousand students to build small blast furnaces during the first Great Leap Forward drive."

"Do you count that a waste of time, materials and money? Critics said the people fell behind in their regular work, the back-yard furnace product was useless, the whole thing had to be abandoned. What about that?"

"You have to remember two things. First, our steel output in 1957 was less than a fourth of this year's target. The movement was launched in a countryside where the level of understanding of industry was very low. Many peasants looked upon steel-making as a mystery; they were afraid of it. When the campaign ended, millions of people had learned the principles. Do you know how to smelt iron or steel, Mr. Snow?"

"Never touch the stuff."

"Well, lots of our peasants are ahead of you. You may not need to know, that's true, but in a socialist country just beginning to industrialize, it's important for the people to know what's going on, and what they're working for."

"But your government admitted that 3,000,000 tons of the pig iron smelted was unfit for industrial purposes."

"Yes, there was waste, but not all waste. Don't forget, China can always use scrap iron. We have a big shortage. The educational result of the campaign was not the only thing. Our two thousand students helped build 25,000 furnaces—"

"Out of 600,000 all told, as I remember the claim?"

"Most of those were tiny brick hearths intended only for demonstration purposes. With the furnaces our students built we trained 67,000 skilled workers. The best furnaces were then combined and modernized. Last year China's small blast furnaces made 5,000,000 tons of usable iron and steel. That's more than our whole national production a few years ago.

"Another permanent result of the Great Leap Forward was that we discovered new sources of ore. A few of our students went as far west as Sikang and Chinghai and came back with rich ore from deposits we didn't know existed. Thousands of peasants helped us."

Hu took me through some classrooms and labs. They were less impressive within than outside; interiors were cheaply finished and furnished and classroom equipment seemed mediocre, if adequate. The labs had good instruments; China now makes most of her scientific equipment, including microscopes and some fine lenses. The library held 300,000 books, with journals in foreign languages.

Men's dormitories were two-story brick buildings where students lived in cramped quarters: four to six in a room, with double tiers of bunks, and not much working space. (Not much more, in fact, than I later saw in the Peking jail.) The showers and washrooms, dining rooms and kitchens were clean, Spartan and as dreary as army barracks.

This was the school routine:

5:30 A.M.	Ablutions, dress.
6:00— 7:00	Physical exercise, en masse.
7:30— 8:00	Breakfast.
8:00—11:30	Classrooms, lab, or workshops.
11:30—13:30	Lunch, rest and study hours.
13:30—16:30	Classroom study or workshop.
16:30—17:30	Play or study.
17:30—18:00	Supper.
18:30—22:30	Study, club meetings, political lectures.
22:30	Curfew.

Saturdays and Sundays are free days used for study, club activities, sports, theater or special group projects. There was a college dance every Saturday.

"Would you like to see the girls' dormitories?" asked Mr. Hu as I was about to leave.

I hadn't talked to a girl engineer since I left Russia. I had never talked to a Chinese girl engineer. I said, "Of course." That's how I happened to meet Small Lightning and her roommates.

33

Steel, Sex and Politics

Hu Ying led me down a willow-lined path to a girls' dormitory, a long brick building with a simulated tile roof and numerous casement windows. Two girls in maroon slacks and white cotton pullovers, their hair braided, were hanging laundered underwear on the unpainted wooden stairway banisters. They looked up and laughed confusedly. The student house chairman appeared and led us to the second floor, where some girls skipped past, their long hair damp from a shower.

"Is it all right to just walk in like this—?"

"They're expecting us," said Mr. Hu. The house chairman cried out our arrival and mobilized girls in half a dozen rooms that were in order; she invited me to inspect any of them. I looked into two or three, and their occupants bowed invitingly. Then a girl with an engaging smile above two pigtails called out, *"Wo-men ch'ing nin tao li-pien lai,"* welcoming me to visit them, and three roommates behind her nodded affirmation.

Inside were two sets of doubled-tiered bunks in a room ten feet by twelve. Under the French windows and between the bunks was a work table covered with a white cloth and on it stood a small lamp and the usual teapot and statuette of Mao Tse-tung. Under the bunks was just enough space to store the regulation small canvas or wooden traveling boxes which contained the girls' personal belongings. There were two cheap chairs and another small table. From the white walls in rough plaster hung a few dresses, slacks and coats. Overhead there was one unshaded light bulb.

The girl who had beckoned to me was slightly pockmarked and not very pretty, but she radiated personality. She had bright, merry, bold eyes—not so much bold as direct. Women of her province, Honan, are not shy or cringing but are noted for their independence. Most Honanese women are also large and deliberate in their movements, but this girl was diminutive and quick; she was Chiang Chu-hsing.

I asked the same questions of six girls who crowded into the room and here quote their answers, from my notes.

First (Chiang): Born near Chengchow (northern Honan, central China). Age twenty-two. Daughter of poor tenant peasants. Neither could read or write; mother now just able to read Small Lightning's letters. Two brothers, one sister. During childhood Chiang Chu-hsing worked as a scullery maid in local landlord's house. One year's schooling before "liberation" (1949), when she was eleven. "Liberation" obviously had literal meaning for her. She had worn only rags till then. She remembered a famine year of a diet of tree bark. Never owned a dress. (Now owns three.) Her parents got some land and security; she was sent to school; life completely changed, "like crossing a bridge to heaven." Worked hard, with party support. Now a sophomore, three years older than average in her class. Will graduate at twenty-six. She belongs to the Communist Youth League.

Second (Ho): Born Hopei province (where Peking is situated). Age nineteen. Parents small landlords; left home and went to Tangshan, mining town on the Hopei coast, during war. Land confiscated; they stayed in Tangshan. Now both parents work in factory there. "They like it."

Third (Lin): Born Hunan (South China). Age nineteen. Pretty girl. Daughter of small landlords. Land redistributed—taken by village cooperative. Parents went through six months of "re-education" and then rejoined community. No discrimination against her? (She would have been a small child at the time.) Not at all, she says. Went through regular schools, won place at institute on high scholarship after close examination. Now in her third year.

Fourth (Sung): Born Kiangsu (where Shanghai is located). Age twenty. Father an "intellectual." Meaning, middle school teacher. Nonparty but helped revolution. He now teaches in Yangchow. Three younger brothers. She is sophomore—and a Young Communist.

Fifth (Wang): Born Shantung (east coast). Age twenty. Third year. Father a railway worker. Two brothers, also railway workers, both party men.

Sixth (Hsu): Hopei girl, age eighteen. Father was scavenger—peddler of coal balls (made of coal scrap) in Tientsin. After liberation he became skilled worker. Mother and father both work in factories, have good three-room apartment, new building, living "better than ever dreamed."

"Why did you choose to become engineers?" Some answers:

"We want to build socialism." "Heavy industry is the foundation of socialism." "We want to build China into a strong, modern nation and help the world get rid of imperialist oppression." "Engineers are the spine of a modern nation."

"Those answers are out of a book," I said. "Before you ever heard of heavy industry, socialism or imperialism, you must have formed an ambition. I met a nurse at a hospital recently who told me she had begun to long to be a nurse from the moment when, as a small child, she first saw a woman wearing a cool, crisp, clean white uniform, 'looking like one of the immortals.' Don't any of you remember wanting to be an engineer before you knew the country needed them?"

Small Lightning spoke up, the most articulate of the group.

"When I was a very small girl I saw a truck for the first time in my life. I said, 'I'd like to drive that truck.' My older brother laughed at me. For a long time I was determined to be a truck driver. After liberation, going to and from school, I saw many trucks, tractors and bulldozers working on a dam but I saw that it was the engineers who told them what to do, and where to put their loads. I knew that I couldn't compete with those strong men driving bulldozers, but by using my brains I could become an engineer."

Freudians may recognize some familiar patterns in that frank statement.

"Many men would say that women shouldn't be engineers," I said provocatively, "especially iron and steel specialists. The work is too tough. Research, draftsmanship, building design, maybe, but can women really do the heavy jobs?"

They all heatedly asserted that they did everything men students did. There was a tendency to give them light work but they all did their time at the furnaces, the same carrying work, the same risks; they wanted complete equality in work assignments. Did I know who was the first volunteer to carry a cable across the Yellow River rapids at San Men Hsia at the start of the big dam there? A woman engineer!

They were beginning to boil when I apologized by saying that I had already heard from factory chiefs and engineers that women make better operators of heavy-duty cranes than men and are more reliable at tasks where a precise sense of timing may mean the difference between life and death. I quickly put myself on record as being in favor of women engineers.

"I hope you will admit," I said, shifting to safer ground, "that two sexes are better than one. Better a two-sex institute than a one-sex institute, for example? There must be advantages in being a girl student in an institute with nine males for every female?"

Nobody denied that coeducation was a good thing. "Much better than an all-girls' school." "Very nice!" "Sex doesn't come into our work here. We are all engineers!" "There is no sex discrimination here."

"Do many girls get married while they are students?"

"Very few. Usually we get married right after graduation." The others laughed at the pretty Hunanese girl, Miss Lin, who said that. "You mean *you're* going to get married," they said. Student marriages were distinctly discouraged now. Although the legal age for marriage is twenty for men and eighteen for women, these young ladies considered the "correct" age to be at least twenty-two or twenty-three for a man and twenty or twenty-one for a woman.

They said they usually dated for Saturday night dances, for Sunday walks, for games or sports like swimming. They often paired up on "teams" for field-work assignments. "We have most of our fun in collective living rather than dating."

Mr. Hu had gone off somewhere, so I asked my interpreter's advice about whether anyone would be offended if I asked their views on birth control. He thought I might try.

"Do any of you object to family planning?"

"Certainly not," said Miss Chiang. The rest looked blank.

"Let me put it this way. How many children do you intend to have when you get married?"

"That won't be my decision alone but my husband's—and the needs of socialism," said the Shantung girl. "Personally, I think two are enough."

"Two!" "Three!" "Two!" The small family was definitely preferred.

"What if you have two or three and they're all daughters? Won't you need at least one boy?"

"That's feudal thinking! We don't make such distinctions any more," said the little Honanese spokesman. They all joined in pouncing on the old attitude that males have superior value.

A few more questions elicited the information that birth control techniques were understood by all, from group discussions on social hygiene. It was also pointed out that the "facts of life" were discussed on daily radio programs which explained contraceptive methods, for listeners of any age, in most precise detail. I was tempted to solicit their views on premarital relations, but this was not a clinic. I had already learned that such questions were often regarded as too prying and rather shocking even to some fully matured adults. I deferred them for another occasion.

"This is too one-sided," I said. "You're doing all the answering. Would you like to ask me any questions for a change?"

They shouted in a chorus and held up their hands.

"You said you lived in Peking before, and taught at Yenching University. How do things in New China impress you?"

"Infinitely more opportunity for the poor, that's obvious. Certainly a poor peasant woman in college was almost unheard of. College was mainly for the upper class."

"How is it in America? Can women study engineering in your schools?"

"They can, and do, but I'd say the cards are stacked—I mean there's a lot of prejudice against that. On my plane to Moscow last June I met an American woman engineer from San Francisco—a Mrs. Henry Taylor, whose husband was a doctor. She was the only American woman engineer I ever heard of. They exist, but they're as scarce as hens' teeth." *

They all smiled. It was what they had expected to hear.

I asked, "Do you think you are happier than American students?"

Howls of derision greeted this, laughter and exclamations of surprise. "What an odd question!" "How could American students possibly be happy—slaves of American capitalism!" "We feel sorry for them; they have yet to win their freedom." "How different it is with us, who are free and have a glorious and victorious future ahead of us!"

"I must tell you that most American women students would say they feel sorry for you. Some might also tell you that the proportion of women to men college graduates in America is still higher than it is in China. There it is about one to two while here it is still one to four, is it not?"

"But here we are changing that very rapidly," said Small Lightning. "We will soon make it fifty-fifty. Besides, in your country only daughters of the rich get to college. Would any peasant have a chance?"

This was going to be a hard one. How explain that the average American farmer never thought of himself as a peasant? That it takes only about 5,000,000 farmers to produce more than enough to feed America? That on the same percentage basis only 20,000,000 farm workers should be needed to feed China instead of the 200,000,000 to 250,000,000 now required? Well . . .

"Yes, farmers go to college—yes, they do. Probably in a higher proportion than urban people. I'm not sure."

This was news a little beyond their information and was received skeptically.

"*Poor* peasants can go to college?"

"Not so many poor peasants—I mean poor *farmers*. Of course it takes money to go to college—"

"That's the difference. Here education is free, it's for the working class. In America colleges are run for the rich—and to make money."

"No, it's more accurate to say they are run to teach *students*

---

* Not quite: in 1958-59 6,755 master's degrees in engineering were granted, 24 to women; 121 women and 38,013 men received bachelor's degrees as engineering majors. One woman and 713 men received doctor's degrees in engineering. (U.S. Office of Education, World Almanac, 1961.)

how to make money. But let's not forget that America had a free educational system long before any other country. We have free primary and high school education—compulsory, in most places. Even in higher education there are some tuition-free local colleges. But good colleges and universities charge heavy tuition—too heavy for most families to bear. Students have to pay for their room, board, everything. That's where discrimination in favor of the rich comes in."

"Naturally," said Small Lightning. "Marx said that bourgeois education means bourgeois class domination. Bourgeois education seeks to perpetuate the enslavement of the working class. That's the kind of system we used to have in China."

"A high percentage of Americans from working-class families get through college with the help of scholarships and part-time jobs. It's quite possible. You believe in struggle, don't you?"

"Struggle is important but it has meaning only if it's conscious class struggle. Individualistic struggle in bourgeois society only means that the one who succeeds joins the exploiters."

"Not always. Sometimes it produces a Lenin or a Mao Tse-tung, does it not? The real weakness of education run by private enterprise, like the real weakness of an unplanned economy, is the amount of sheer waste involved. Someone here in China quoted to me a statement he had read, by an American admiral, Rickover, complaining about the fact that half of the top-ranking students in American high schools never get to college or are forced to drop out. It was an anomaly that America, the richest country in the world, able to spend billions on bombs and nuclear weapons that could be used only in mutual suicide, could yet not afford to provide a proper education for its best brains."

"The people can afford it but monopoly capitalism does not want to educate the poor. That is inevitable under an imperialist system," Small Lightning recited.

Curiously, and to my relief, they had spared me questions about segregation in the South. My last remark had put them back on terra cognita and it would have been an appropriate moment to leave. The normal suppertime had come and gone and I had been pressed to eat with them. Each time I was invited I had declined, because I had a late dinner engagement, but whenever I rose to leave they insisted that I stay. They were genuinely curious, perhaps even more curious about me than I was about them; three of them had never seen an American. I could not leave without finding out a little more about how well they had learned their Mao Tse-tung.

"It may surprise you," I said, "to hear that few American youths believe they live under a system of imperialism. The average American believes imperialism means owning colonies, and Americans think they own no colonies. Students of history might ask you why, if America is an aggressive imperialist country, it supported Russia during the war against Hitler. After victory America had half the wealth of the world, fresh armies of fifteen million men, the best navy, the strongest air force, and men in occupation of a dozen countries and colonies. Why didn't America hold them and build a colonial empire?"

"The imperialists were afraid of Russia."

"Russia was bleeding then, and truly very weak. And she had no defense against the atom bomb."

Hu Ying had returned, but he was taking no part in the students' responses. I got the impression that such a question had never been raised for them in just that way.

They were silent for a moment. Then one of the younger girls, who had said little, remarked thoughtfully, "The American people would not have supported such a thing." To me that was a heartening statement.

Small Lightning would not leave it at that. "Of course imperialism is not just owning colonies in the old way," she said. "It means monopoly capital ownership of the means of production in countries economically colonial to it. It means keeping economic control and enslavement of peoples in order to make great profits. The people's revolutions were becoming powerful in some countries and American imperialism's role was to prevent revolution and to support counter-revolution, in that way maintaining its control.

"America did not really leave any of those countries. She tried to defeat revolution in China and she failed—except in Taiwan, for the moment. She tried to defeat it in Korea and failed. She is trying the same kind of aggression in Vietnam and Laos and she will fail there, too. There are American advisers and bosses in Pakistan and others in India, giving Nehru money to fight socialism. America has two hundred military bases, all the way from Germany to Japan, combining its forces with the native reactionaries to protect U.S. investments and profits and to hold down the people. What we don't understand is why American students tolerate all that—and the great risk of war that goes with it."

"Why? Some of them would agree with some of what you say, but most would say that these bases are necessary defenses against the danger of Communist aggression—"

"Communist aggression! Is China's fleet occupying Hawaii, or is China flying planes over America? Are Chinese troops in Canada or Mexico? No! We haven't a soldier on foreign territory. Are Americans in Taiwan, Japan, Laos, Vietnam? Yes!"

What about Korea? Yes, what about it? That could have meant another six hours and it was really late. I had heard enough to know that these young people, the generation being prepared for leadership, were well indoctrinated in the politics of the land. They had answers to all the questions—or thought they had.

I promised to continue the discussion when I returned on Saturday, but that day was full of activity. Small Lightning was the star in a picture story I did of a day in the life of a student. She was a good actress: getting up, eating breakfast, working in the lab, walking in the park with a boy friend. She wore a light summer frock and black pumps and had her hair put up. In the afternoon we went to the steel mill, where she donned white overalls, helmet and glasses and pulled out half a dozen testings of flaming metal before it was poured. I went with her to the swimming pool, which was crowded with students. Finally she took me for some shots of her, with another partner—she was not sticking to one—dancing decorous fox trots and waltzes.

All this, I had persuaded her and the college authorities, would greatly interest youth in America, and help to correct some distorted impressions there about the slave lives of Chinese students. The pictures were not bad, but American magazine editors did not consider them worth using. Like the Chinese students, they already had the right answers—though not the same ones.

34

Swan Lake in Peking

Performing artists in China today enjoy high social prestige. Many younger artists have reason to be grateful to the new state, which has welcomed talent and opened wide opportunities for it to develop. More than 80,000 professional artists and musicians are guaranteed full-time employment, above-average wages,* special privileges and continuous higher studies. Mei Lan-fang, the world-renowned female impersonator, was allowed to keep his own sumptuous residence, drew a handsome income and—though a party member in his late years—was said to be the only rich man left in China. He died in 1961.

In China, of course, all forms of artistic expression have an ancient history, to which the Communists have been adding new content and reviving some old. Foreign visitors may disagree about other things there today but few would dispute that theater, dancing and music are reaching the masses of the people as never before. Certainly the party recognizes entertainment as a prime means of propaganda.

---

* A graduate of the Peking School of Dance, for example, or of the Conservatory of Music, starts off at a monthly salary of 80 yuan, which is equivalent to the salary of a young doctor or an army captain and four times the wage of an average factory apprentice.

But classical as well as contemporary themes are innumerable and much theater is offered in its "pure" form.

Every state factory of any size has an amateur dramatic club and so have colleges and middle schools. There is an average of seven amateur performing groups in each of the 24,000 communes. Hundreds of new theaters have been built in China. In Manhattan we have a struggle to keep the Metropolitan Opera open; Peking has half a dozen opera houses and many first-class companies perform there and on the road. Nearly every province maintains at least one company to carry on its own opera in the several regional styles, dialects and traditions; these also tour as far as Yunnan and Manchuria. Best seats in Peking may cost as much as a dollar (2.50 yuan) but fair seats there and in the provinces sell for thirty or forty cents and movies cost as little as ten fen. Clubs get reduced rates for bloc seats and free tickets are awarded to outstanding workers.

The spoken drama flourishes; considering its infancy in China, technique and acting ability are promising. Propaganda is much more overt and blatant in drama than in the older opera, with which the audience is too familiar to tolerate much tampering or extraneous moralizing. A Western visitor cannot quickly judge the extent to which the heroic themes of "socialist romantic realism" meet or do not meet the "demands of the masses." The spoken play has the appeal of novelty and of raw materials close to everyday experience in contrast to the historical subtleties of the opera. While contemporary themes are usually handled in crude distortions of black and white (with little of the gray nuances of traditional Chinese painting) they are at least filled with vigor, youth and affirmative hope for man (Socialist man).

But I began this chapter to say something about Chinese ballet.

I apologized to Miss Chen Chiang-ching, vice-director of the Peking School of Dance. "I appreciate your letting me come here on such short notice."

"It's true that ordinarily you might have had a long wait," she replied, not smiling. "We have had so many visitors we must ration ourselves to only a few now."

"I read your book, *Travels in the West*," [1] she said unexpectedly. "In a way you might say that is one of the reasons I am here." Her eyes smiled very faintly but her face did not open.

"That is gratifying news—especially if I could think it had any remote connection with the *Swan Lake* I saw done by your students last night."

"Perhaps, a vague connection. In 1938 when I read your book I was a normal-school student in Shanghai. Soon afterward I went to Yenan. I worked there all through the war. Chairman Mao took a keen interest in promoting dancing but in those times we were limited chiefly to folk dances of the Northwest."

She was of medium height, about forty, slender, bobbed haired, rather severe in manner, olive skin drawn tightly over high cheekbones. Probably once pretty, now Authority. She had been a specialist in folk dancing but here she was the responsible party administrator.

"Until now, you never had any ballet in China, did you?"

"No Western ballet. Of course every province has its dance groups but ours is the first school to specialize in ballet. We teach other kinds of dancing, too. Dancing is an art; art is to serve the people. We train teachers as well as artists to meet the demands of the masses."

"Does that include ballroom dancing?"

"Yes, our people like mixed dancing. There are other instructors to teach that."

I remembered then that in the Hsin Ch'iao hotel as well as in hotels in the provinces I had several times watched dances in ballrooms reserved for the evening by clubs of office and factory workers. Taxi dancers and night clubs had disappeared, but social dancing was more widespread. China now makes all Western band instruments, and each of these parties had its own offerings of Chinese versions of swing, fox trot and even calypso. Square as could be, that's true. No twists and no cheek-to-cheek business, but some attractive young people in their party best. In Changchun I had tried to crash such a dance but was politely told it was a private affair, Sino-American peoples' friendship notwithstanding.

Miss Chen had been with the Peking School of Dance since its inception in 1950; straight from Yenan, she had helped recruit teachers from all over the country. They had begun ballet in 1954. The ballet master was a Moscow student and some other teachers also studied there. A few Russian instructors who came to Peking had since left. Now the school had 340 students. For the 1959-60 term, about 90 new students were accepted, 60 of them to specialize in ballet, 40 in folk and social dancing. The school admits children of the primary school ages, eleven to thirteen. They spend six to eight years as boarding students, in arts and sciences courses and dancing and theater techniques. A tough regimen keeps them busy ten to twelve hours daily.

The "plant" consists of a four-story building around which are grouped brick dormitories and recreation grounds. The discipline is strict and violators are quickly eliminated. Students learn stage technique in the school theater, which occasionally gives public performances. The Peking ballet company made its debut in 1957 and later won acclaim on a tour to Moscow and Warsaw.

Something about that performance of *Swan Lake* had puzzled me. It was in one of the new Peking theaters—seats hard, furnishings simple but adequate, orchestra fair, lighting and staging excellent, costumes brilliant. The dancing was technically perfect, the leaps and pirouettes as lively as any I had seen. Yet compared to a Bolshoi or a City Center performance it was strangely lacking in force, oddly innocent and unevocative. Probably virgin is the word for it. I now learned that all the dancers were still at school and their average age was seventeen. The oldest, Miss Pai Ssu-hsiang (now the celebrated prima ballerina of China), was twenty. I met some of them during their workouts. Miss Pai was there—lovely in face and form and a beautiful dancer but still not quite a woman. She did a *pas de deux* for me with her athletic young partner from *Swan Lake*.

Miss Chen permitted herself a brief smile at my comment. "They aren't fully mature, of course. Our dancers have been doing ballet six years—the Bolshoi a hundred. When ours are better we may do a world tour. By then we hope to have perfected some all-Chinese ballets we're now rehearsing. Some things closer to our own people and the revolution."

As happens everywhere else, hundreds aspire to the stage in China for one who qualifies for a scholarship. Here, too, fond mothers press the case for their offspring, of real or imagined talent. Many runaways turn up at Miss Chen's school, begging admission.

"Usually we send them back after a scolding but there are exceptions." Good! I thought. "The teacher you saw leading the second dancing class is one. She ran away from her home in Szechuan when she was fifteen, to come here. She was good and we couldn't refuse her."

In general, students are recruited through recommendations made by athletic directors, in all parts of the country, who look out for comely children with long straight legs, supple waists and good shoulders.

"Does your experience at all bear out the traditional belief that China's most beautiful women come from Soochow?"

"In a sense it does. We find more girl students in that region than anywhere else. Why? I don't know. They have beautiful legs and flexible bodies; for some reason they seem to have a wider leg stretch than most girls. But look at Miss Pai. She meets your approval? She came to us from Manchuria—transferred from a children's school of music and dancing in Shenyang. We find them everywhere. The physique of our young people is getting better every year."

Indeed, the increased stature of Chinese youths is striking to returning visitors who expect to see runts produced by years of starvation diet. Several times I found myself traveling on trains with girl basketball teams beside whom I felt a dwarf; they averaged around six feet. In Peking, lonely foreigners find it refreshing to wander outside Hatamen or in the parks to watch tall young women athletes pacing each other in sweat shirts and very short shorts displaying magnificent long legs. Ballerinas tend to be on the petite side compared to Russians, and China may never produce a figure like Lepeshinskaya's in her prime. But China intends to have, and indubitably soon will have, not one but several ballet companies with their own Oriental style and grace. I predict they will captivate balletomanes all over the world.

Miss Chen wanted one thing understood. The aim is not simply the attainment of perfection by a few professional performers. It is to train great numbers of instructors who can bring to the multitudes of China's youth—from childhood up—the bodily graces and disciplines that come from actual participation in some form of dancing.

"What is good dancing," asked the mistress, "except skill and discipline contributing to a collective artistic achievement? Dancing is good socialist training."

Schools for artists and teachers of opera, drama and music in Peking and in some provincial cities, echo the same philosophy. "Art is to serve the people." And socialism.

35

Doctor Horse

I spent several days with Ma Hai-teh, a quiet, gentle American physician with whom I had shared a great adventure.

Dr. Ma—who was born George Hatem, in Buffalo, New York, in 1910—knows more about Red China and its leaders than any foreigner alive.

Ma means "horse" and is a family name especially common among Chinese Moslems, but Ma Hai-teh is an American of Syrian descent. *Hai* means "sea" and *teh* means "virtue." The term could mean "great virtue" but in this case the combination was probably intended to imply "virtue from overseas." These two words are also a phonetic rendering of the surname Hatem. Why Dr. Hatem was y-clept Horse in Shanghai I do not know, but his nickname was Shag, and something about his thick black hair, a beard which the closest shave could not altogether efface, and his large, dark, warm eyes, did remind one of a Mongol pony.

In the hot June of 1936, when I met George Hatem in Sian, the capital of Shensi province, he began a journey which entirely altered his life. Had he not undertaken it he would never have met Chou Ssu-fei, one of the most beautiful and charming women in China, nor would they today have a daughter called Liang-p'i, or "Second Horse," and a son, Yu-ma, which means "Little Pony."

Elsewhere I have told how I made contact with the Red underground in Peking in that same year,[1] and was given a letter to Mao Tse-tung, written in invisible ink. Armed with that, I went to Sian and put up at the Guest House, where I was told to expect a call from a certain "Pastor Wang." He would arrange to have me smuggled through the Nationalist lines into the Red districts, a hundred miles to the north. Soon after my arrival George Hatem introduced himself and told me that he was aware of my mission; he was also waiting for a call from "Pastor Wang."

Shag had been in Shanghai a couple of years but had seen nothing else of China before this trip. I liked him. He hoped that we were "going in" together and so did I, but we didn't know. For two impatient weeks we spent most of our time playing rummy and talking. Few foreigners except missionaries then visited Sian, and to satisfy the hotel manager's curiosity we told him we were going on a scientific expedition into Chinghai as soon as the rest of our party arrived. I was after a story. Dr. Hatem was a missionary in search of a mission.

A healthy, uncomplicated bachelor of twenty-six, Shag possessed a shrewd intelligence that had already penetrated the glossy surfaces of society to its ugliest sores. Beneath a superficial cynicism he was serious about one thing. He wanted to find some purpose to his work as a doctor. Hitler had also sent him up to Sian—as, in a way, he had sent me. The world was no longer a pretty place for young people who understood where Hitlerism was leading it, and in the East the Japanese, going in the same direction, threatened to take Chiang Kai-shek (who at that time had German and Italian fascist advisers) with them. At that time communism seemed about the only force interested in fighting fascism. Since Hitler and Japan hated communism so much, Shag thought there must be some good in it. He had also developed a strong distaste for existing society in Shanghai.

"My father didn't starve himself to educate me for what I've been doing," he told me.

"Meaning?"

"Fighting V.D. with a pea shooter. Now, venereal disease is one thing that can easily be prevented and can be cured. Shanghai exists to breed and spread it. It's a big business there run by organized gangs with the full protection of the police in both the foreign settlement and the Kuomintang-run Chinese city. There's a lot of money in the doctor's end of that business, too. I could make a fortune there treating nothing but chancres and blueballs for the rest of my life. In fact I've been doing very well. But I didn't spend my old man's money learning to become a V.D. quack for a gangster society. Maybe these people up north are interested in putting an end to the whole business. I want to see what they're like."

It was not Marx but life experience that had made an emotional radical out of Dr. Hatem before he reached China.

At the turn of the century a labor contractor paid a small sum of
money to an impoverished illiterate family in Lebanon. In exchange,
George Hatem's father, then a boy of fourteen, also illiterate, was
shipped to Massachusetts to work in a textile mill in Lawrence.
After paying off his parents' debt Hatem became a wage-earn-
ing apprentice and then a skilled worker. In a few years he saved
enough to return to Beirut to find a bride. He took her back to settle in
Buffalo, went to work in another mill, and started an American family.

"Life was a succession of good times when we had enough to eat,
and bad times when there were layoffs. My sister became a permanent invalid because of lack of nourishment and medical attention
we couldn't afford. Probably that's why the old man wanted me to
become a doctor. My sister and I were very close. In a period of prosperity in the early twenties my father saved enough to start me in
medical school. I finished my pre-med work in three years and won a
scholarship to the American University in Beirut, where I studied until
I won another scholarship to the University of Geneva. I didn't have
money for railway fare but I had a bicycle and I rode it all the way to
Switzerland."

Besides learning medicine—in Latin, Greek, French and German—
Shag managed to have a lot of fun. During summer vacations he
waited on tables in tourist hotels and then cycled through Europe with
schoolmates. In 1933 he and two other young American doctors in
Geneva decided to set up practice in China. Why China? From
Oriental students at the University of Geneva, Shag had heard a lot
about China, which had come to fascinate him. He wanted to get to
some place where basic medicine was needed. One of his classmates
had wealthy parents. He put up the money to finance the trip to
Shanghai, and to open a joint office.

"We discovered that V.D. specialization was the quickest way for
young doctors to get started in Shanghai. Our practice flourished,
but first one of my partners went home because of family troubles
and then the other followed, to marry a rich girl and become a society
doctor. I stayed on, and took a job as staff doctor for the Shanghai
International Settlement police force. Examining girls from the brothels and cleaning them up till the next dose. A lot of the cops were in the
same clinic. They wanted *their* whores clean."

Shag helped write a pamphlet on health conditions in Shanghai and
through that he met Agnes Smedley, then correspondent for the
Frankfurter Zeitung. Miss Smedley had gradually established contacts with the Chinese Red underground, through whom she got more
information about the civil war than anyone else. One day she introduced Shag to a young Red engineer named Liu Ting, who "awak-

ened" him with accounts of egalitarian life in the forbidden Communist areas. Doctors, he learned, were desperately needed in there. He was about to go home, but after long discussion and thought he determined to go to the Northwest to see whether people there really were trying to do something as worthwhile as the engineer had made it sound.

As we waited, a strange city smoldered around us. Sian was then headquarters of the "bandit extermination" (anti-Red) forces of the Northwest, under "Young Marshal" Chang Hsueh-liang, who was the Kuomintang's deputy commander in chief for all China. His 150,000 troops were exiles from Manchuria, whence the Japanese had driven them in 1931. They weren't really interested in fighting other Chinese, even Reds; Japan was their enemy. The local warlord governor, Yang Hu-ch'eng, was also more interested in keeping the Generalissimo's troops out of Shensi than continuing the civil war—especially after the Reds offered to join in a "united front" against Japan.

"Pastor Wang" finally appeared and took charge of us. Shag and I soon learned that highly important Reds were secretly living in Sian under the personal protection of Chang Hsueh-liang and Yang Hu-ch'eng. General Yang's chief Communist liaison was the son of a sworn blood brother. His name was Wang Ping-nan, and he had been a student in Germany. (In recent years he has been Peking's ambassador to Poland.) Living in Marshal Chang's own house was a person of no less consequence than Teng Fa, chief of the Chinese Red Army's internal security forces, on whose head Chiang Kai-shek had set a price of fifty thousand silver dollars.

By the time we left Sian for the North, the budding conspiracy was obvious to us. Within six months it was to erupt in the "Sian Incident," when Marshal Chang and General Yang led a mutiny, seized the Generalissimo and his staff during an inspection tour, and held them captive for two weeks.* They changed the face of China. As a consequence of the "Incident," Chiang Kai-shek had to postpone his "final extermination campaign" against the Reds and in another year Japan launched her major invasion. The Nationalists perforce once more became temporary allies of the Reds.

Shag and I carried these secrets, unknown to the outside world, with us when we entered Red China. I also agreed to keep Shag's own whereabouts completely confidential, even from his family. Nor could I, for a long time, reveal the manner in which we were smuggled northward in a Nationalist army truck and dumped at the edge of no man's land, which we crossed on foot.

I was "going in" as a correspondent observer. George Hatem was

---

* Marshal Chang personally flew the Generalissimo back to freedom in Nanking; he was arrested and remained Chiang's personal prisoner until 1961. General Yang was later assassinated in Chungking. A contemporary account of the Sian Incident appears in *Red Star Over China.*

taking much greater risks. America was not fighting Communists just then, and in a few years would become an ally of Russian Communists and send them a great deal of aid. Nobody could foresee that, however, and Dr. Hatem was acting on his own conscience alone. He was not a Communist; he spoke no Chinese; he really knew nothing of what faced him; and for a young doctor just beginning life he seemed to be burning a lot of bridges behind him. Naïve? Foolhardy?

"I don't give a damn for a doctor who lives high by pampering the neurotic rich," he said in a serious moment. "The medical profession is a failure if we can't give all children of even the humblest parentage an equal start in life—the same food and proper care that only the wealthy can afford now. If that's what these people up there are aiming at, I'm with them. Anyway, I want to see for myself."

George, as I said, was a missionary: the only American missionary who volunteered for service "on the other side of the river" in China.

36

Sino-American Romance

In the small living room of an old Peking house of two courtyards standing on Hou Lake, north of the Winter Palace, I sat sipping Chinese brandy with Dr. Horse one afternoon in what he liked to call his stable. We spent hours talking about our experiences together and bringing his story up to date since that high summer when I had left him, a mere quarter of a century ago. Mrs. Ma sat beside him.

"I don't think I ever shook inside more than I did in that first Chinese village when we crossed to the Red side," he said. "No one knew who we were or what we were doing there. Huddled up on that k'ang in a cave, surrounded by a bunch of strange peasants. They kept looking at your cameras and our watches. I told you they looked like bandits to me."

"They were bandits," I said.

"That's right, Red bandits. Red Spears, they called themselves. But there were White bandits around too. That was why we had missed the escort Chou En-lai sent out to meet us," he explained to Ssu-fei. "They ran into some White bandits on the way and had to chase them. We heard that later."

"What bothered me was that these peasants kept saying '*Hai-p'a*,' and *hai-p'a* to me meant 'I'm afraid.' It upset me like hell. Why should *they* be afraid?"

"You told me that, all right," Shag said. "Then we went on with one muleteer who left us in a temple in the woods and disappeared for the night. At dawn he came to wake us up and tell us we'd better get a move on. I was really low then. I realized for the first time we'd put our lives in the hands of people we knew nothing about. Maybe we would end up in a couple of cannibal pies. A few hours later we met our first Red soldier on the road and from then on everything was okay."

"I finally learned that *hai-p'a* in north Shensi dialect means 'don't understand.'"

Ssu-fei laughed. She said she had been fooled the same way when she first arrived in Yenan.

"I still meet people in the villages," said Shag, "who take one look at me, assume I don't speak Chinese, and from then on don't hear a word I say. Sometimes I have to repeat, 'I'm talking *Han-hua! Chung-kuo hua!*' several times before they begin to listen."

Shag and I had traveled together for two months and he had sat in on many of my interviews. We were each given a horse, an automatic, and a cotton uniform.

"You were the only person around who managed to put a hat on Mao Tse-tung," Shag remembered. "His hair was very long then and he wouldn't wear a hat."

"I forgot about that."

"Yes, you were taking photographs and insisted that he put on a hat. He didn't have one and you put yours on him because it was the only one that looked at all like an army hat. That was the best picture ever taken of Mao. It's been in books and papers for years, and now it's in the Revolutionary Museum."

We had ridden over northern Shensi, Kansu and Ninghsia together, with P'eng Teh-huai's army. Then Shag went on farther west to meet the Fourth Front Army, breaking through from Szechuan at the end of the Long March, and I went back to Pao-an. On the road Shag taught me how to use a hypodermic needle. I practiced by jabbing him with plague and typhoid germs we had brought along as vaccines.

"I still feel that first needle you gave me. Wham! You left a bump the size of a duck egg," he said now.

Visitors were expected to sing a song or two at army pep meetings then, and Shag and I had alternated with "Yankee Doodle" and "The Daring Young Man on the Flying Trapeze." Luckily, we were never asked for encores. At the start Shag couldn't ask for a bowl of water without my help, but in an amazingly short time he began speaking some Chinese. He had a gift for languages, a good ear for them. Almost at once he felt completely at home. He became popular with the "little Red devils" of that youthful army—the orderlies and mess boys, who used to hang around us and listen and laugh and try to pick up a few words of our ridiculous language.

"I wonder what happened to Shang Chi-pang, that little Beau Brummel orderly of Li K'o-nung's. Remember him?"

"Sure! They used to kid him by pronouncing his name in the wrong tone, so it meant 'penis.' "

"He asked me to be sure to spell his name correctly when I wrote about him—just as if he were a general."

"No idea where he is, but I can tell you where Tai Ch'un-ch'i is. Remember him? A bright kid, medical orderly in P'eng Teh-huai's camp in Ninghsia? He looked like a baby but he must have been fourteen or fifteen by then. You took some pictures of him."

I did vaguely recall Tai. "What about him?"

"He's a doctor now, working right here in the Skin Diseases Hospital with me. Deputy director, no less, and a crackerjack skin-cancer specialist. You'll meet him."

Before I left Shag that summer he had made up his mind that that was the life he wanted. His arrival doubled the Western-trained medical force. The only qualified doctor in the whole army then was Fu Jen-chang, a product of a Methodist missionary hospital in Kiangsi. Medical teams were made up of male and female nurses with rudimentary knowledge of modern practice, assisted by even more sketchily trained orderlies. Shag was a much overworked man until the outbreak of the Japanese war, when the Yenan Hospital was set up with the help of funds raised abroad by Mme Sun Yat-sen. Some Western-trained Chinese and a few foreign doctors went in to augment the force.

A remarkably ingenious Canadian heart specialist, Dr. Norman Bethune,[1] organized front-line guerrilla medical services for the Eighth Route Army. He did the work of twenty men until he died of septicemia for lack of penicillin. Renowned as a surgeon with the anti-Franco forces, Bethune had offered his services to China after Spain was submerged by Hitler and Mussolini. His name is now a legend revered and memorialized throughout the country.

There were years when amputations and other operations on wounded men were performed without anesthesia, as in American Civil War days. After 1940, Chiang Kai-shek's forces had restored a blockade around the guerrilla base in Shensi, and their denial of simple medicines cost the Eighth Route Army thousands of unnecessary deaths, like that of Bethune. The Paluchun had to depend on supplies captured from the Japanese, or smuggled in, or on native remedies. Many a battle, Shag told me, was fought to capture Japanese penicillin and other medicines.

Shag also did his muleback medical assignments at the front, but his main work was in the organization of the army's base hospital and medical training system. It was in Yenan that he met his wife, when she came up as a volunteer. In prewar Shanghai she had been a movie star.

He said, "The minute I saw Ssu-fei I dropped whatever I was doing, yelled 'There goes my wife,' and got on my horse to follow her. She was training theatrical troupes and hardly noticed me. I kept after her for weeks and made no headway. Every bachelor in Yenan had the same idea and I was an ugly American. I was getting desperate, when her best friend went to the hospital to have a baby. It was a difficult birth and I was called in. Ssu-fei watched me deliver the baby and it made a big change in her. She must have decided I was useful for something."

"I didn't think any foreigner could be that gentle," said Ssu-fei, laughing and blushing.

"It was the most rewarding delivery I ever made. Ssu-fei couldn't understand half my Chinese then, but we were married a few days later. She's been teaching me ever since—says my tones are still lousy."

"What do you call him?" I asked her. "Hai-teh?"

"No, just Ma."

"Just—Ma?"

"No," she corrected me, pronouncing it in the third tone, "*Ma!*"

After Japan's surrender there was a period of nearly two years when Communists and Nationalists coexisted and attempts were made to form a coalition government. The United States put military teams around to observe and help enforce a cease-fire between the two Chinese armies. UNRRA brought in relief supplies and medicines which were supposed to be divided impartially, but they were distributed by the Kuomintang-controlled CNRRA. Dr. Ma became Dr. Hatem again briefly when he represented Paluchun's relief organization for the guerrilla districts—which were called "Liberated Areas," then meaning areas recovered from the Japanese.

"We had no luck with UNRRA," Shag went on. "Some of the Americans wanted to help us but the Kuomintang controlled everything and either kept it or sold it on the black market. After a year in Peking all I got was four hundred tons of supplies which turned out to be two-thirds toilet paper. Toilet paper! We still had people dying for lack of penicillin. Six hundred UNRRA workers protested against the scandalous corruption and sale of their supplies on the black market. It all came out in Mayor La Guardia's report when he resigned as head of UNRRA—and it had no effect in China. After the truce broke down I went back to Yenan. Civil war began again.

"That was in 1947. By March, Yenan was surrounded and we had to evacuate and start donkey-back medicine again. Mao Tse-tung gave us a picture of Chiang Kai-shek's strategy, and his own. We had already lost Kalgan and were evacuating most of the cities and railways we held. The Nationalists were bombing hell out of us in their American planes. Naturally I was worried about Ssu-fei and the children. After Mao finished listing all the places we were giving up, things looked pretty grim to me.

" 'We're winning!' Mao said. 'If Chiang goes on making mistakes like this he will be finished in three to five years.' Just before Yenan was evacuated a meeting of delegates from all the liberated areas agreed on a draft constitution for the People's Republic.

"By the winter of 1948 our forces were back in Yenan and I was sitting in the Summer Palace, outside Peking, waiting for Fu Tso-yi to surrender peacefully. We occupied the capital without a battle. So—here we are."

"And it's time for dinner!" said Mrs. Ma.

We sat down to a simple family meal prepared by Mrs. Ma and her wisp of a mother, nearing seventy, who lived with them. "Little Pony" joined us, a dark boy of seventeen with Shag's eyes and his mother's looks and already half a foot taller than his father. He was in high school and going to be he didn't know just what—maybe even a doctor. His sister was nineteen and boarding at college, where she was studying to be a horticulturist. Mrs. Ma was now directing her second moving picture following a big success with her first.

After dinner we walked through the courtyard bordered by giant sunflowers. Three families shared the house. Each had a wing of several rooms but they used a common kitchen. The charm of the old Peking house appealed to all of them and they had no desire to move to a modern building even for more space. We went on to the lakeside and Shag showed me where they went swimming—"after dark, or early in the morning. You're not supposed to swim here but nobody objects."

Shag had never been back to America and he was full of questions. He had some recent books but nothing that explained it all to him. How could people still tolerate racism? What about McCarthyism? Neglecting schools and public health while the state paid billions to farmers not to grow food? What was wrong with youth? Juvenile delinquency? Beatniks? No motivation for life? How could labor tolerate American policy toward China?

I noticed a copy of C. Wright Mills's *The Power Elite* in his small library and I asked Shag if he had read it. He said he had.

"That answers your questions better than I can."

"Yes, another philosopher who explains the world. What are Americans doing to change it?"

"Who said Americans want to change? Who really wants to change when he's convinced he's holding the better end of the stick? Haven't we got the highest standard of living in the world? To accept the Chinese revolution requires too big an act of imagination from a country that has not suffered, itself, for nearly a hundred years. We've been lucky—but luck has a way of changing. Anyway, you've been detached from the American scene for a long time, Shag. Your interest must be mainly academic by now. I suppose you're a Chinese citizen, aren't you?"

"Certainly not." He went to his desk and came back with a fresh green American passport. "I got it just before I left Peking for Yenan, in 1947," he said. "At General Marshall's headquarters. Fellow named Walter Robertson* gave it to me."

I looked inside the cover and saw that it was *not* stamped *verboten* for travel in China, since it had been issued before Mr. Dulles' ukase on the subject. I smiled. "Nobody can say you are not a legal resident here."

"I'm here legally and still an American—unless it's treason to wipe out syphilis."

Dr. Hatem had even more than that to answer for.

---

* Walter S. Robertson later became Assistant Secretary of State under John Foster Dulles. Presumably Mr. Robertson procured Dr. Hatem's passport for him from the U.S. Consulate General in Peking.

37

Small-Devil Doctor

The next day I went over to visit Shag at the Institute of Venereology and Skin Diseases. Laboratories and hospital employed a personnel of about six hundred and Dr. Hatem had been the institute's chief of staff during a successful national war against syphilis and gonorrhea. He was now a deputy director and engaged in campaigns against skin diseases and malaria.

At the door I was introduced to a tall, thick-haired, good-looking Chinese wearing a white uniform. He stared at me intently and shook his head.

"No, I wouldn't have recognized you," he said. "You had a beard when I met you in Ninghsia with Dr. Ma."

"I have no advantage over you, Dr. Tai. You came only to my shoulder then. Your uniform was two sizes too large and you wore a cap that hung down over your ears."

Dr. Tai Ch'un-ch'i, now also a deputy director of the institute, was the grown-up "little devil" whom Shag had mentioned to me. After Director Fu Ching-kuei and other members of the staff had taken me through the institute I heard some of Dr. Tai's story.

He was a native of Fukien, on the South China coast, one of four children born in a family of poor tenant peasants. The Tais were ragged and hungry when Red partisans briefly occupied their village in 1933. The landlords fled and the Reds gave land and food to the peasants. Everything "turned upside down" and life suddenly became "lively and hopeful." When the Reds were driven out again, Tai and some other children ran off with them.

"In a better time my parents had managed to send me to school for two years, so I knew characters. That's why I was put in the Juichin base medical school and given a few months of training as an orderly. I was thirteen then. After a year of changing bandages and giving injections I returned to Juichin and spent six months studying elementary anatomy, biology and pathology. Then we were surrounded and began the Long March. At the end of it, when I met you, I was fifteen. I was a full medical assistant under Dr. Fu Jen-chang. You remember him, the ex-Methodist? He's Vice-Minister of Public Health now."

Tai went on to say that from 1936 until 1949 he had had no more classroom training. He read a few books but otherwise learned everything in the field, where he had to treat all kinds of cases and do minor surgery, as well as fight. He acquired the title "acting doctor" and went all through the anti-Japanese and revolutionary wars without a scratch. "I was lucky. Most of the orderlies you met in the Northwest are dead." In 1949 he was finally sent to a medical school in Shenyang, Manchuria, where a few other surviving "little devils" got their first real medical education.

"Of course I had a big handicap, studying with young people who had had full premedical educations. For two years I don't think I slept more than three hours a night. I had so much to learn: biology, medicine, math and physics. But I did have two assets." He smiled. "I didn't have to spend much time in political training classes. And after the first two years, when we got into clinical practice, I was far ahead of the others. Even the teachers often had to ask me for practical advice."

While he was at medical school Tai found a wife. "Ten years behind Dr. Ma," he said. "But on children I'm already one ahead of him." Dr. Ma and Dr. Tai had been with the institute since its inception in 1953, and from then on their story was a joint one. Several years earlier, however, Shag had helped to begin the war against V.D.

"Our first goal was to eliminate the chief carriers, the prostitutes," said Shag. "We started off in the Peking-Tientsin area, with a team of about a hundred doctors and assistants. Women party workers first went into the brothels and explained the program. It wasn't hard to win support; most of the girls were slaves who had been sold into the houses. In some instances women party cadres went in and lived with them to gain their confidence. The seriously ill were sent to hospitals immediately but the rest were allowed to receive guests for a while, until the younger women were organized and ready to burn their contracts. They told their stories and what they would like to do. No guilt was attached to anyone and no punishment involved.

"When everything was prepared we closed down every brothel in Peking in one night. The women were taken to hostels specially set up for them, where they were thoroughly examined and treated. Most of the brothel owners and pimps had fled; a lot of them went on to Shanghai and later to Hongkong. Those who remained were rounded up and treated. About 80 percent of the 70,000 whores in the Peking-Tientsin area were infected with V.D. My own team treated and cured as many as 1,200 cases every two weeks. That's about all it takes with penicillin: ten to fifteen million units does the job. The follow-up work took a lot longer, of course, but that wasn't our responsibility."

"What did happen to all these Suzie Wongs?"

"Some went back to their villages, some to work in factories, quite a few were young enough to be sent to primary school. We made medical helpers out of the more intelligent. We produced several very able laboratory and research workers from among them. Nobody refers to their past and there's no stigma attached. Many of them have married."

The campaign was soon duplicated in Shanghai, Hankow, Canton and two dozen other cities. In the process medical assistants were trained in the techniques of diagnosing and treating syphilis and gonorrhea, and the anti-V.D. forces quickly expanded. Within two years most of urban China was cleansed of the chief carriers. Work was extended to the rural towns and then to the whole country.

"I read a story about a reformed sing-song girl," I said, "who has just been made a hero of labor in Shanghai. She's in charge of a sanitation squad. Sounds kind of dull after the bright lights."

"That's naïve, my friend. I'll bet that girl had V.D.—that's why she's in a clean-up squad. Most of them were really slaves, owned body and soul by the brothel keeper. A few high-class singing girls, a few women kept by rich merchants, that was different. Those went off to Hongkong with the brothel keepers and opened business there."

"Where do the unmarried men go now for what Dr. Kinsey called 'outlets'? Unmarried women are certainly not getting any more promiscuous and permissive!"

"Promiscuity? Very rare. So is premarital intercourse. Social discipline is all against it. What's different now is that everybody gets married—so-called coolies, too. You know coolies and poor peasants couldn't afford a wife in the past. They used to save coppers for weeks to get ten minutes with a two-bit lay. Now you will find very few men or women still unmarried at twenty-five. Before that, they do without—they're kept busy, no time to fool around, minds and bodies occupied."

I learned later, in the Peking prison, that the horizontal type of livelihood had not absolutely disappeared, but it must take an extremely clever woman to succeed at it in present conditions.

"While we were getting rid of V.D.," Shag went on, "the Ministry of Health organized mass campaigns for personal hygiene, and against pests and epidemics. With the backing of the whole government we have now got control over flies, mosquitoes, bedbugs, rats, mice and lice. Mass vaccination was carried out against smallpox, plague, cholera and typhus. We haven't had a case of cholera or plague for years—1951 was the last I remember*—and smallpox and typhus are extremely rare. Malaria is greatly reduced.

"Parasitic and skin diseases are still a major problem and that's where the institute comes in. After we were set up we divided into teams to do combined research and pilot projects in field mass medicine. We began this as continuation of the anti-V.D. campaign into the villages. Our first big experimental center was set up in the county of Ningtu, in Kiangsi."

"Wasn't Ningtu one of the model counties in the old soviet districts before Chiang Kai-shek drove the Reds out of South China?" I broke in.

"Right. That's why we chose it. People there were proud of their tradition, well organized and politically conscious. High literacy rate —about 50 percent. Ningtu has a population of about two million people and it's a typical South China agricultural area. We thought it would take our small team of ten people two years to make Ningtu the first completely V.D.-free county in China. We accomplished it in forty days. What we learned there made it possible to chase V.D. out of the whole country in two years. Want to hear how it was done?"

* A cholera epidemic was reported in Canton in 1961 but was quickly brought under control.

38

Subversive Medicine

We examined the institute's large basic medical library, which included many Western scientific journals, and then we made an aromatic visit to the department of research in Chinese medicine. Thousands of catalogued boxed specimens stood row upon row: countless varieties of tree ears, fungi, wild spices and herbs, dehydrated seeds and leaves—and doubtless bats' ears, wasps' stings, linnet hearts, tiger bones, dragon dung and other choice items (by hearsay) in the Chinese pharmacopoeia. Among them Western doctors had discovered the rare chaulmoogra nut, the oil from which supplies what was for long the only known cure for leprosy (a specialty of the house, in this case), and ephedrine, a plant extract.

When we sat down again Shag went on with the story.

"In 1949," he said, "China had fewer than 40,000 trained doctors. That included army doctors such as Dr. Tai and wartime trainees who had had only three or four years in medical schools. If we confine it to doctors who'd had six years or more in college, we started with fewer than 10,000. Four years later we still had only about 50,000 doctors but we had 70,000 'middle-doctors' or assistants with two or three years of training each, and about 60,000 nurses. In that year all the villages of Ningtu were organized as advanced agricultural cooperatives, and each of them had some kind of medical team—say, one or two doctors, or just doctors' assistants, for every 5,000 people.

"Our institute team of specialists set up a mobile demonstration center where we gathered the Ningtu local medical teams to instruct them. We used lectures, slides and moving pictures to show symptoms of the disease and how it develops, and then demonstrated treatments. We combined training and retraining courses with practice. We got each village medical team to bring in a dozen to fifteen men and women—both medical and nonmedical personnel—and ran over the routine with them.

"We got the technique down to where we could teach the average fifteen-hundred-character person the whole thing in three days. That included learning how to take blood tests and urine tests, and how to diagnose V.D. We had the full cooperation of local peasant leaders, leaders of the women's organizations, and branch party secretaries, of course. Women and men were divided into separate groups; women wouldn't discuss symptoms before men, naturally. Resistance to examination was overcome until no one felt any disgrace involved. Well, as I said, we covered the whole two million population that way in forty days."

"I think you'll find a lot of skepticism in the West about such claims, Shag. Even with a disease as relatively easy to diagnose as V.D., the margin of error among amateurs must be pretty high."

"We thought so too. So we spent another forty days spot-checking all over the county. We tested the 'trainees' and then the results. We did find that our method wasn't perfect. The percentage of misses was about 15 in 100. But nearly 80 percent of the cases overlooked were latent. That average would not be high anywhere—except for venereology specialists. On the basis of our findings we ran the whole process once more. After that, I'd say Ningtu was about Ivory-Soap pure. There were probably only a few very latent cases left."

The institute team quickly repeated the experiment in widely scattered areas, while other medical groups sent observers with them. Branches of the institute were established in every province, under the provincial health ministries. These branches now trained medical cadres to teach more village health teams, until the practice became universal. They made full use of about 300,000 Chinese-style doctors.

"Gradually we sent teams to the remotest parts. My own team traveled into Mongolia, Kansu, Chinghai, Kwangsi, Yunnan—many tribal areas where we had only native doctors and midwives to work with and had to spend two or three months training young personnel in hygiene and elementary matters.

"By 1957 our national and provincial teams had covered the whole country except for Tibet. The Dalai Lama opposed examination and treatment there on religious grounds; he claimed there wasn't any

V.D. in Tibet. Last year for the first time our people started working there. They've found syphilis widespread."

Director Fu Ching-kuei had come in on his American colleague's story. "Yes, there is practically no venereal problem left," he said. "Dr. Ma has done such a good job, professors in medical schools are mad at us. They say that since 1957 they can't find any more active venereal cases even for classroom observation work. We've had to import some from Tibet!" He added soberly, "We've got plenty of diseases to conquer yet. Some of them are going to take many years. Get Ma *Tai-fu* to tell you . . ." His voice trailed off as he left us.

My friend from Buffalo continued: "In 1957 we took a large institute team back to Ningtu county, to try to develop a method of mass treatment of the six common skin diseases. These are kala azar, schistosomiasis, filariasis, hookworm, ringworm and leprosy. Using the technique we had developed for venereal disease we worked out basic means for easy identification of these parasitic diseases. We used the stages of approach as before. This time people were organized into small teams of a dozen families, each under a discussion leader, to carry out the diagnoses. In this way a competitive spirit was aroused between the small teams to see which would be the first to be declared cured and completely healthy. They made a game out of it.

"I don't know whether it would work anywhere else, but it worked here. In one month we were able to diagnose and begin treatment of 300,000 cases."

"Does that mean that 15 percent of Ningtu's population was infected by one of the six parasitic diseases or malaria?"

"That's right."

"How many could you cure?"

"We cleared up nearly everything but schistosomiasis and leprosy. The number of lepers was very small. Our surveys show leprosy is less prevalent than was thought in the past. There are probably not more than 350,000 cases in all China and they're practically all known now and already under treatment. We have stopped the spread of the disease. The same goes for schistosomiasis—and kala azar. But to stamp them out altogether—as we did V.D.—will take more time."

"Are you talking now about just one county, or Ningtu, or all China?"

"The whole country is now following Ningtu's example—but much streamlined. We had spent several months working to diagnose Ningtu this second visit. We thought it would take twenty years to carry out such a program over the whole country. China couldn't wait that long!

"Our problem was how to cut down on time of diagnosis, how to run more and faster tests, and how to get these diseases under control more effectively and more quickly. That's when we developed what the ministry calls the 'mass line in medicine.' We worked out a very much simplified system of elementary diagnosis for parasitic diseases. We boiled it down to a set of only *one dozen questions.* With this questionnaire as the basis, our institute became the training and the testing center for a great new experiment.

"We brought in all medical and paramedical personnel from the communes throughout Hopei province. We staged them through quick courses of training and retraining in the Ningtu technique. The ministry supplied all the educational materials needed, gave them full support, and sent them back to conduct mass training and enlist the whole people in what amounts to mutual disgnosis. Absolutely unorthodox! All positive cases were reported to medical teams. Qualified doctors then of course made final blood, urine and other tests and checks on diagnoses.

"After a few months we went into the field and spot-checked results, as we had done in Ningtu before. Again we found that the margin of error by omission was only about 15 percent. When the Ministry of Health was satisfied that our questionnaire system was effective it was adopted over the whole country.

"What the mass line in medicine means is that millions of people are getting an elementary understanding of what public health work is all about and the important part every one of them plays in it. With full understanding of the peasants we get cooperation never possible in the past. The villages are now able to make serious attacks on the breeding grounds of snails and sandflies, worms and malarial mosquitoes. Snail-infected canals and ponds and swamps are being drained and filled in and latrines properly sanitized. New cases are diagnosed quickly and isolation and quarantine are enforced because everybody is taking part.

"This is even true of lepers, who used to hide and were shielded by others. Now they know they are not going to be punished or made into pariahs. Our system of handling lepers is to keep them integrated in useful social life. We help them build clean new villages right in the midst of production brigades. They run their own communities and take part in farming and other work while they are being treated."

That about completes the subversive-medicine story of Shag Hatem from Buffalo. At a minimum, the counts of indictment against him would have to include participation in the service of China against the following foreign powers: syphilis, gonorrhea, malaria, kala azar, ringworm, hookworm, schistosomiasis, filaria and leprosy. Not to mention his voluntary contribution of two sturdy young *ma* to the Chinese cavalry.

As I write this I realize I forgot to ask him how much money he made. He did mention that as a foreigner he got a special meat ration. He was fifty years old and he looked in very good health. He asked me to tell his family in America, if I saw them, that he was "a very lucky and happy man."

I had many meals with Shag at his home and in the hotel. Mao Tse-tung invited him to dinner with me; so did Chou En-lai. He was quite at home with them in his now colloquial Chinese. Mao had not seen him for several years and he inquired about his work and listened with attention. (He asked Shag whether it wasn't time for him to visit America. Shag thought it better to wait until he could be sure he could make a round trip.) I spoke to this old friend of my youth for many hours, alone, in his home, in the park, beside the lake waters behind his house, with his family on excursions to the Western Hills, and I had no doubt that he was a happy man. He had difficulty, however, in believing that I could achieve that condition living in a still unredeemed society. Repeatedly he expressed the warmest and sincerest kind of concern for his fellow countrymen in America, who had yet to begin the ascent toward an enlightened civilization and objectives such as he obviously fully approved of, in China.

Talking to George Hatem was more illuminating than I am able to convey here; he helped me understand the logic of some things that had puzzled me in China. He knew the faults and failures of the regime but he also knew the misery of Old China and the enormity of the problems it presented. Because he is the one American who has for twenty-five years intimately shared the ordeals of the men and women who fought for the responsibility to bring China to her feet, his continuing faith in what they are doing merits attention.

"China simply could never have stood up in any other way," he said. "Nearly everything done has been necessary and nearly everything necessary has been done. And all in all it's a success."

Full stop and question mark. From afar, China's failure seemed more evident than its success. It was seen abroad as a land of starvation, overwork, commune blunders, cultism, belief in "inevitable war," shrill propaganda reflecting the fears and tensions of a harassed leadership, forced labor, brain washing and persecution of individualism. American cold-war propaganda overstates these charges but perhaps no more than Communist propaganda distorts its picture of the American scene by overemphasis of news on crime, racketeering, government corruption, racial oppression, narcotics addiction, juvenile delinquency and commercialized pornography.

But in the quiet of Dr. Hatem's tiny garden beside the still lake I was reminded of something overlooked by those who mistake China's current food crisis as the sum total of the revolution. That is the simple fact that behind all the propaganda stand millions of unknown and unsung men and women who have successfully and devotedly carried out the real work of releasing half a billion people from a heritage of dense ignorance and superstition, widespread disease, illiteracy and universal poverty. The task is far from accomplished, but the *foundations* of a modern civilization have been laid, with little outside help, and against handicaps to which Americans have made heavy contributions. These foundations will last regardless of what government rules in the future—unless, of course, it is destroyed by war and all people perish with it. China is bigger than any government. Because this government has been doing things for China it has been able to command support even from many who are opposed to communism.

39

I See the Army

Outside Chungking I visited the Szechuan Art Institute, where large white letters on a huge red pylon proclaimed: "Art to serve the masses, art to serve socialism!" That eliminated quite a few questions about art to serve art.

The school was divided into two departments, "creative" and "applied" art. On a large campus thickly planted in vegetables, eight main buildings housed four hundred high school art students and two hundred advanced students enrolled for four-year terms. Graduates become teachers (starting at 50-60 yuan) in schools or state institutions, including factories, where workers attend spare-time art courses. Peking has always had good art schools but today every province has one or more and the Chungking institute ranks high among them.

Courses in traditional art include Chinese painting; oil painting; carving in wood, stone, linoleum and metal; and sculpture. Applied arts are: design in all materials; lacquer work; porcelain and pottery; decorative and folk art; and furniture-making. China now bakes porcelain as fine as any in her history. Old masters of color and composition are honored and have spread their knowledge widely. I saw superb porcelain exhibited in Peking, Shanghai and Hankow. Most of it is exported or goes into state buildings. High

*quality is also being attained in lacquer, ivory and other applied arts
—as demonstrated in the magnificent interior decoration of Peking's
Great Hall of the People.*

*"Paint" is a different story. No masterpieces have yet appeared
among works of "new ideological content." No one can surpass Chinese
painters in technique, however; tractors and power plants may be
dull subjects but the execution of them is often very good. Stylistic
imitators of Ch'i Pai-shih's enchanting flower and insect paintings
are legion, as are those of Hsu Pei-hung's thrilling horses. Both Ch'i
and Hsu are best-sellers in China as well as abroad. At one lithograph
shop I visited in Liu Li Ch'ang,* Peking's street of art, I learned that
Hsu's most famous horse has been master-blocked there for print
reproductions no less than eight hundred times in ten years.*

*In that large plant half the effort was devoted to reproduction of
the work of living and dead painters in the traditional styles. I saw
three artists doing a copy of a T'ang classical roll scroll by Ku Kung-
chun (910-980) which had occupied them for more than two years. It
measured thirty feet long by a yard wide and one print from it would
sell for eight hundred dollars. I also saw scores of cheap full-size reproductions of Ch'i Pai-shih and Hsu Pei-hung, as well as of classical
paintings, on sale for as little as five cents each in bookstores and art
shops. Many peasants now have lithographic copies of good Chinese
paintings in their huts. Ten-cent prints are also sold of Italian Renaissance painters and a few French impressionists.*

*"Art to serve the masses" inevitably becomes highly pictorial, and
poster art in China today shows greater vigor, imagination and talent
than more ambitious efforts. Traditional Chinese symbolism and impressionism require a high degree of intellectual participation for full
enjoyment. Here is a nation not yet literate, but now becoming literate in Marxist language which has little to do with the mysticism
and philosophical concepts underlying much of China's classical art.
Is it surprising that literal coinages, à la Norman Rockwell, really do
serve mass taste better than abstract concepts?*

*While the Marxist vision of the perfect society is probably the
ultimate abstraction, few men engaged in building the stairway to
it appreciate abstract art. Stair building is an intensely concrete task.
"What does it mean?" Chou En-lai asked me about abstract art. "If
it has no meaning, what value has it for the people?"*

Is it really sinful that the Chinese at the moment have little place

* Outside Ch'ien Men, the great "front gate" which leads to the Forbidden City,
Liu Li Ch'ang was famous for its shops where merchants displayed the finest
works of Chinese arts and applied arts: painting, sculpture, porcelain, jade, ivory,
cloisonné, lacquer ware, silks and satins and embroidery of designs and stitches for
which Old Peking was noted. In the thirties one could still find, in the bazaars
of Liu Li Ch'ang, ancient bronzes, early glazed porcelain, and pottery dating back
to the Chou Dynasty. The state now buys up nearly everything of artistic or
historic value, but all the traditional handicraft arts are being revived; their output
goes principally to the export market.

for nonfunctional art or even for the impressionism which their Taoist mystique first introduced to the world? Abstract and nonobjective art began years ago in the older industrialized societies as a rebellion against realities of a kind not necessarily duplicated in the Chinese society emerging today, which is preoccupied with matter and machinery seen as means of mass *liberation. Conceivably, individual Chinese artists may later skip over the current phase of Western art and develop original works of protest out of paradoxes not yet discernible by us or by them.*

"What contemporary European painters do you study?" I asked an instructor in oil whose students were painting an old peasant model.

"Very few," he said. "We have a long history of art experience and we are trying to develop our own schools and techniques in oil, too. But we do admire Picasso."

"In what period?"

"We like his Peace Dove," he said.

My request to interview and photograph the army was ignored in Peking until one evening I met a high official and said: "I spent four months with the old Red Army in days when you had only one rifle for two or three men and were all in straw sandals. I don't think it did you any harm. How is it that you won't let me see your army now when you've got much more to show?"

He thought it over and smiled and said: "Yes, you are right. Why not? Ordinarily we don't permit foreigners on army reservations for reasons of security, but there are exceptions." I was then told to get ready to spend two days with the army. I expressed interest in seeing a mechanized force and/or an ordinary infantry training school. One late October morning at seven the Hsin Ch'iao room boys were greatly impressed when four officers called for me, led by Colonel Li Hsin-kung, army liaison officer of the Foreign Ministry, and Captain Kuo Kung, an English-speaking graduate of the Foreign Languages College.

Once the decision was made, the army received me courteously and even warmly. I was the first Westerner permitted to take still and moving pictures inside Chinese military establishments in many a year. Except for those who were Korean veterans most of the officers had never seen an American, and for the veterans I was the first specimen of Americana they had encountered outside a hostile field.

On every occasion when I could talk long enough to get past formalities I found much greater curiosity in them, from generals down, about how America really "worked" than I usually encountered among civilians. Coupled with this was an eager determination to have it understood that the army was *not* anti-*American* and did *not* seek a war with the United States. Naturally, that in no way affected their solid support of China's stand against "American aggression." They (as distinct from the government) seemed convinced that if the American people could just be made to understand the necessity for the United States to pull its armed forces out of Taiwan, Japan, Korea and South Asia generally, world peace could be assured. Of the absolute reasonableness of these demands they had, of course, no doubts.

It was a modern army I saw and—if we omit nuclear weapons for the moment—representative of probably the third greatest military land power in the world.

This remarkable transformation had happened even within my own memories of China. In the thirties Evans Carlson and Joseph Stilwell were the only U. S. Army observers who took China's military potential seriously. Both believed that the Chinese fighting man "could become the equal of any in the world," and both said so for the record. Chiang Kai-shek had made the first attempt to prove this, with Soviet Russian aid (1924-27) before he broke his alliance with the Communists. From then on he still tried to unify China largely by military means. Throughout his struggles with provincial warlordism, "communist-bandits," and finally with the Japanese, Chiang remained essentially an old-fashioned militarist. He was never able to subordinate the Bonaparte in himself either to the political discipline of a Napoleon or to the needs of mass support. With all the money and arms given to him by Americans he failed to reconcile the existence of a personal army with the requirements of a modern revolutionary state.

This was always Chiang's chief handicap in coping with the old Red Army and later with the People's Liberation Army. From the guerrilla beginning of the Communist forces on Chingkangshan in 1927 the military head was subordinated to the political brain. The relationship was very close between Chu Teh, the army commander, and Mao Tse-tung, the party leader. They jointly signed all orders and for years the press referred to "Chu Mao" as the "commander leader" of the still little known "communist-bandits"; many people believed they were one. Throughout Communist history a party political commander has stood beside every operational commander, and the "Chu-Mao" twinship symbolized the ideal.

Now, in this pattern the military arm is regarded as only one of several means; it can be effective only when coordinated with economic, political and social factors synthesized by broad strategic planning under party leadership. All military operational concepts and principles and general battle orders derive their authority from the party leader—although they are actually the product of joint thinking of army and political specialists. Of further significance: Mao Tse-tung, as de facto commander in chief, has never taken a military title.

In this fundamental relationship the People's Liberation Army of today is not different from the Red Army of the thirties; it is still the right arm of the party brain. That coordination is by no means perfect or without its own inner "contradictions," however.

My first day with the People's Liberation Army was spent at a tank school near the Marco Polo Bridge, where the Sino-Japanese War began. Part of the barracks here traced to Japanese days. The establishment had been greatly enlarged to include tank practice and gunnery fields and a farm which supplies part of the school's food. A military expert would have learned much more; I myself could bring only a correspondent's amateur view with a general sense of military efficiency picked up from observation of many armies in many countries.

I was probably not shown latest weapons. Those I did see were Chinese variants of standard training equipment in use by Soviet or American forces up to the missile age. Tanks, now made in China, were copies of the Soviet T-34, with long low bodies, wide double-mesh tracks, and a 45-degree climb capability. I was told a later model (T-54?) was in production. Tanks in maneuvers looked effective. Well armored, with a speed up to 50 kilometers an hour, and carrying 85-millimeter cannon, those I saw were manned by expert crews. It was claimed that armor, engines, guns, sighting and firing mechanisms, ammunition, were all made in China.

Before the Korean War, China had no tank command school. The Marco Polo school was founded under Russian advisers in 1950. China's modern tank artillery and jet aircraft industries were begun in 1954 with equipment and advisers also furnished by the Russians. At both the tank school and an infantry regiment I later visited I was told there were no more Soviet advisers.

The 1,200 students here were junior officers of platoon and company grade and three cadet groups in the training department. Two other departments were command and political; they offered twelve courses including tactics, gunnery, signal, mechanical, and ordnance. There were also "cultural" courses. All students had had battle experience but their "knowledge of mechanization and their cultural level" was low, I was told. Classrooms I saw in cheap brick buildings were spick-and-span, battlefield models for tactical study were well mounted and electrically animated, and weapons and ammunition models in cross-section detail were also well arranged for dismounting and assembly practice.

The commandant here was Chao Chi, from the old Fourth Front Red Army; his vice-commandant was Ho Feng, also a Long March veteran. Both had had special training under the Russians. As in other army camps, students spent two to three months of the year on "socialist construction" jobs and working on the school farm. Officers were supposed to participate in rank and file projects of this kind but I have no way of knowing how much was token work and how much realistic practice.

My stay at the tank school was cut short by a phone message which called me back to Peking for another interview with Chou En-lai.* The day after the interview I went with Colonel Li Hsin-kung and Captain Kuo Kung to visit an infantry regiment stationed about ninety miles east of Peking. We drove on a narrow macadam road that skirted the Peking-Gulf canal and in about three hours reached the suburbs of Tientsin. En route, I briefed myself with information available on the People's Liberation Army.

Until 1950 the P.L.A. remained essentially an army of irregulars, chiefly dependent on captured American and Japanese equipment. In its ranks were many ex-Nationalist troops, still poorly indoctrinated and assimilated. The Korean War was a baptismal encounter with a first-class Western army equipped with the latest weapons, which taught China many lessons. Obsolete equipment and ex-Nationalist troops were expended. Material losses were made up by Russia while the P.L.A.'s most reliable cadres were trained in modern technique and re-equipped with up-to-date weapons. Manchurian war industry and transport were also restored by Russian wartime aid, the exact amount of which remains unknown. East European estimates given to me placed it as high as two billion dollars.

Today the army has been streamlined, considerably mechanized and motorized, and equipped with standardized weapons. It is supported by high-priority military industries which maintain the supply and modernization of basic weapons of conventional warfare. The pre-Korean army depended largely on volunteers. Conscription began during the crisis and was regularized in 1954. Officially, today's regular army totals about 2,500,000; foreign military observers believe it does not much exceed that. The air force is estimated at a quarter of a million and naval personnel at about the same. *All* citizens between eighteen and forty are now subject to conscription, and in addition a reserve of many millions of "citizen militiamen" is being built up. Army service is for three years, air force four years, and navy five.

Conscripts for the regular armed forces do not, I was told by Chinese officers at Fangshun, exceed one in twelve of the eighteen to twenty-five group. Between five and six million young men reach eighteen each year; the army chooses its conscripts from the pick of the physically fit, literate, and otherwise mentally qualified. There are many advantages of military service in China for both the soldier and his family. The "selected" are genuinely envied and congratulated by their native villages and service is regarded as an honor, not a sacrifice. The army is popular and officers are held in a kind of awe which in the U.S.A. is reserved only for headwaiters, church trustees, Elizabeth Taylor and the *Wall Street Journal.*

Just outside the headquarters of the 196th Division at Fangshun we passed a long caravan of rubber-tired, wheat-laden army wagons

* See Appendix, pages 758-764.

pulled by horses boosted by many windmills—the only time I saw use of the old land sails in China; evidently motorization of supply is still far from complete. Then we were surrounded by broad fields ribbed by settlements of the new motel-like barracks, and cottages where officers lived with their families. In a moment we entered the outer gates of the reservation and were met by the division commandant, and by Colonel Li Yung-kuei, commander of the 587th Infantry Regiment. Colonel Li took over my tour and acted as host.

The 196th Division consisted of "not over 12,000 men" organized as follows:

> Regiments: 3 infantry, 1 artillery, 1 tank.
> Battalions: 1 anti-tank, 1 medical, 1 engineers, 1 signal.
> Special companies: 1 reconnaissance, 1 anti-gas, 1 chemical
> warfare, 1 vehicle training, 1 artillery command.
> 1 training group.

This is a regular division. China experimented with separate tank and artillery commands but has returned to divisional integration. The navy and air force are also under unified top army command, which is directly responsible for weapons concentration on the corps level.

Obviously I could see only a small part of these components in the ten hours I spent with the officers and men at Fangshun. I watched a machine-gun company maneuver in a sudden snowstorm, saw some engineers throw up a bridge, took some movies of a headquarters battalion "march past" and some more footage of artillery drill; inspected barracks, classrooms, a theater, mess rooms and a museum of divisional battle history. (The division was organized in 1945 and had fought thirty-two engagements.) I saw part of an artillery park and a small-arms and automatic-weapons depot. A wide variety of weapons that I saw—ranging to 105-millimeter cannon—were all China-made and seemed precisely tooled, true and clean. Weapons were well kept and buildings neat. Training routine (reveille, five-thirty, taps, nine-thirty) and the general appearance of the layout reminded me of my last visit to Fort Bragg, but minus most of the gingerbread: quarters for both men and officers were austerely furnished buildings of plain construction. Another notable difference was that I don't recall anybody harvesting carrots at Fort Bragg, and I photographed a battalion doing so on an army farm at Fangshun, with officers' wives and children assisting.

I learned no military secrets here but I had a good look at a lot of fighting men. I picked up some miscellaneous information which might interest humanists and sociologists.

Item 1. By a rotational system the division was cultivating about 1,700 acres of land and had built a reservoir stocked with ten million fish. Everybody in the division was "normally" required to work one month a year in the fields, and one month in army shops or on state construction projects. All the vegetables and meat and "part of the grain" consumed by the division was produced by its own labor, with the help of a few thousand full-time resident peasant families.

Item 2. The guaranteed daily food allowance was 3,200 to 3,400 calories per man, or about one-third more than the basic food ration over the country as a whole. This included 1.6 pounds of grain products and 1.6 pounds of vegetables per day but only half a pound of meat and six grams of oil per month. The average recruit weighed 120 pounds on admission and had gained 10 to 20 pounds on his separation. Soldiers averaged 5′ 7″ in height (well above the Chinese mean), six-footers were common, and general physical condition seemed equal to Western standards. If their food consumption is typical, my calculation shows that between four and five hundred thousand acres are required to produce food adequate to supply the armed forces.

Item 3. Marshals and generals are the highest paid of government employees. The monthly pay scale given to me may be converted into U.S. dollars as follows: privates start at $2.50; corporals get $4; platoon leaders, $5; second lieutenants, $20; first lieutenants, $24; captains, $29-$33; majors, $39-$44; lieutenant colonels, $51-$60; colonels, $62-$64; senior colonels, $62-$84; lieutenant generals, $144-$160; full generals, $192-$236; marshals of the army, $360-$400. (There are at this writing eight active marshals, seven of whom are members of the Politburo.) All food, uniforms, quarters and transportation expenses are, of course, provided gratis, and general officers have the use of a car. This was no longer the egalitarian army of guerrilla days, and yet the tradition was kept alive when officers did their annual month in the rank and file.

Item 4. There wasn't a fall-out shelter in all of Fangshun—nor in all China as far as I could learn. The People's Republic was as backward as Europe in this respect.

For two hours I questioned four husky soldiers (eighteen to twenty), and a sergeant of twenty-five. I asked each about his background and education and then collectively about army training and their ambitions. They were all from poor peasant families, parents illiterate; they themselves had all been to primary schools. They were "happy" to be chosen for the army; "satisfied" that their families were being well cared for in the communes; "grateful" to be getting "better" education (political, technical and cultural) than they would have got at home; and enjoyed sports and were certain that "socialism is good." All had memories of hunger and poverty in their childhood. I asked one how he explained his fine white teeth if he had been undernourished. (They all had good teeth.) What had he eaten as a child? "Kaoliang"; that was all he remembered. Sons of ex-landlords are not accepted by the army, I learned, but there is no bar against sons of ex-capitalists. Women are not recruited for combat training except as parachutists (why, I don't know) but a few are used in auxiliary tasks, like WACs.

"Do any of you gamble?"

They did not understand the term. The interpreter gave an elaborate explanation. Yes, they played cards, but they had never heard of playing for money.

"I know you may not believe that," said Colonel Li Hsin-kung, the Foreign Office liaison, who was more sophisticated than anyone there. He smiled. "I saw American soldiers gambling when I was at the Panmunjon truce talks. Your officers' drivers spent their waiting time throwing dice and gambling for money. When one of them lost he would swear and get angry and red in the face. Our drivers watched them and couldn't understand but thought it very funny. I explained that it was different in the American army from our army. The American soldier is worried about his future security so he tries to get together a lot of money, hoping to buy a small business when he gets home. In our army every man is guaranteed good employment when he leaves."

I could not help laughing at the picture he drew but I said that American soldiers I knew would probably say they'd prefer to take their chances with the dice. "Isn't a little sideline gambling to be expected inside the bigger gamble of the combat zone itself?" I ventured. A good commander never gambles with the lives of his men, I was reminded in fine copy-book phraseology; Communist leaders are not gamblers or adventurers, like monopoly capitalists.

"What about the woman problem?" I asked. It existed in all armies I had seen, including the Russian. Here also the soldiers mingled with the people—in the fields and at entertainments. (Chinese don't use the old word *ping*, or "soldier," any more; the P.L.A. has only *chan-shih*, or "fighters.") What happened if a soldier got a local girl "in trouble"?

My question elicited stunned silence. The green youths looked genuinely puzzled. The officers exchanged glances as if something indecent had happened.

It was Colonel Li, smiling but serious, who again had the answer:

"You may find this hard to believe, too, but that is no problem with us. A man is free to marry at twenty.* Before that he is kept too busy to think about it. General opinion is very strongly against anyone playing with women. In our army men are taught a stern moral code; we still follow the 'Eight Rules of Good Behavior Among the People' which you knew in the old Red Army.† A man wants to marry a pure woman, he doesn't want to have someone else spoil his wife. An army

---

* In practice this usually means what the Chinese consider twenty-one, since Chinese traditionally count a child one year old at birth, reckoning age from the time of conception.

† The Eight Rules (revised since Kiangsi days) are now: speak politely; pay fairly for what you buy; return everything you borrow; pay for anything you damage; don't strike or swear at people; don't damage crops; don't take liberties with women; don't ill-treat captives. They are still a popular army song.

with socialist ideals won't dirty its own nest. Men in our army are intelligent. Our people don't want to ruin themselves by misconduct which would shame them before everyone. I won't say it never has happened but it really is very rare." He turned to the regimental commander, who added stiffly: "We have simply never had a case of the kind in the five years I've been here."

A situation which I am more convinced the young soldiers had never heard of was "conscientious objection." An officer took a long time to explain "C.O." to them. I heard him saying that this was something that used to happen in the old Kuomintang armies as well as in the United States. The men exchanged glances, in some awe, as if to ask each other whether the American army could really be as bad as that.

I asked whether they had ever heard the expression, "My country, may it always be right, but right or wrong—my country." This took plenty of explanation, too. Then I said: "Could you imagine your country being wrong? Would you still fight for it?"

Here was something that obviously had never arisen in political discussions or "self-criticism" meetings between men and officers. They were all struck absolutely dumb. How could Mao Tse-tung, the party and the army leadership ever be wrong in any war? China would never start a war but China would always destroy any invader. To try to explain that a C.O. would not fight for his country even if he believed it to be "right"—? It was inconceivable. I wonder what they would say today if someone told them that an American general named Walker was led by his patriotism to teach his troops to despise his own government's leaders. They wouldn't believe it. After all, how many "contradictions" can the mind of a simple soldier (or a simple general) be expected to absorb?

40

The Family: Fact and Fancy

On the long midnight drive back to Peking I rode in a new Simca sedan with Colonel Li Hsin-kung. We had dined well and had drunk a number of cups of *mao-t'ai* in apolitical toasts to peace, to the brotherhood of man, to the friendship of the Chinese and American peoples, and to the "restoration of normal relations between countries." *Mao-t'ai* is a rice brandy with a strong sting, and the best quality comes from Kweichow; sealed in attractive earthen jugs, it is in growing demand abroad. Mellowed as we were by the wine or by the bright moonlit autumn night, our conversation took a personal turn.

"How many children do you have?"

"Five—four girls and a son."

"The son was No. 5, I suppose?"

Li nodded and grinned with some embarrassment at this revelation of ancestral atavisms. "How many children have you?"

"A boy and a girl."

"That's just ideal!" he exclaimed, holding up his right thumb. "You're very lucky. I'd have stopped right there if the boy had come earlier."

"Are you having any more?"

"No more! We have adopted absolutely foolproof precautions," he said. "Double insurance."

Not unimpressive in his well-tailored uniform, with braided epaulets, Li looked his role of diplomatic military attaché. He was proud of his guerrilla past. Born into a rich peasant family of Shansi, he had enlisted in the Eighth Route Army in 1937, when he was seventeen. From 1938 to 1940 he studied at the "Anti-Japanese College" in Yenan; afterward he joined the staff of General Nieh Jung-chen.

"My family married me when I was sixteen, to a woman fourteen years older than I. It was a kind of swindle. The woman was my cousin by marriage and her mother, my aunt, had land and money. This aunt wanted her daughter married off to someone she could control; she was afraid of fortune hunters. She thought her daughter would be safe with me and my mother thought it would be a good thing for our family, financially. I refused to live with this wife. The marriage was one of the reasons I left school and joined the guerrillas. After the war I married a woman of my own choice, a teacher at Tsing Hua University. It has been very successful."

"Suppose it were not a success, would you get a divorce?"

"How could it fail? We knew each other, we chose each other of our free will, we were not oppressed. Of course it had to be a success." It is difficult to get a well-trained Chinese Communist to answer a question which hypothesizes a situation he knows to be the incorrect outcome of reform.

"Arranged marriages existed in the past because of social and economic oppression," he explained. "Parents betrothed daughters at the earliest opportunity rather than risk seeing them end up as spinsters. Now girls legally marry only at eighteen and do not rush into marriage until they know their own minds. Poor peasants formerly sold their daughters to pay off debts to landlords or to raise cash. It happened many times in my own town. If parents waited too long to betroth their daughters then the landlords sometimes claimed first rights. After that, who would marry them? Yet to sell them as concubines might be better than having them go into prostitution. Marriages to strike a good bargain, to acquire land, to pay off debts, to gain family position, to buy sons out of the army, without consulting the feelings of the betrothed, with great differences in ages and temperaments—this is what caused misery in the family. Now we don't have any of that."

"Yet a man might still fall in love with another woman. Could he divorce his wife?"

Li was silent for a moment before he answered quite seriously: "Legally it is possible to dissolve any marriage by mutual request. If there are children and there is no mutual consent it is another matter. The kind of divorce you mention would be capricious and not liked. I know it sometimes happens but it is very rare. It is like adultery and premarital sex. You asked about that earlier. These things do happen but I have not experienced a case among comrades personally known to me."

"I remember hearing Westerners in China in the past say that early betrothals and early marriages prevented homosexual and other sex deviations and were intended to do so. What about that?"

"There are fewer unmarried men and women now than before. Since women are not treated as property or commodities, since everyone can afford a wife, everyone can get married. For a man not to be married is looked upon as abnormal. People feel sorry for him and try to help him find a wife. This is a new society with a new moral code. We are all influenced by socialist ideals. We are against bourgeois decadence of all kinds."

One of the fables of Leonardo da Vinci tells us of a discourse between an old elm and a fig tree. The fig tree shook its young figs vainly and belittled the barren elm, saying that it did nothing but cast shade which cut off needed sunshine. "Soon you will be surrounded by many new fig trees." The elm remained silent. Just before the young figs fell to the earth some soldiers swept that way and left the proud fig tree stripped and dying. "How much better it is," said the elm tree, "not to have offspring at all than to see them bring one such suffering and sorrow." In the past, few Chinese would have agreed with the moral.

"To have no posterity was the greatest of all filial sins, according to Mencius," I reminded Li. "Everyone used to approve if a man with a barren wife took a concubine or a second wife, and often his first wife would be the one to suggest it. Is that a justification for divorce?"

Li squirmed uneasily. "We Communists look upon children from a Marxist point of view—not as a man's personal property but as wards of society as a whole. To love children one need not bear them; we love others' children as we love our own. Discarding a wife because she does not bear offspring is not a good reason for divorce." I knew childless party people whose marriages had lasted for years—among them, Chou En-lai and Teng Ying-ch'ao. Yet Li was aware of the contradictions in his own practice; had not that personal son been a matter of necessity for him? The instinct to maintain the patrilineal descent was still strong among both party and nonparty people.

Since the introduction of the reformed marriage law in 1952 much has been said abroad about the Chinese Communists "breaking up families" and "destroying the fine old family system." In a very real sense the whole Chinese revolution, beginning in the nineteenth century, has been a revolt of sons against fathers—against various evils traced to patriarchal tyranny and attributed to "Confucian ancestral worship." (There is little evidence that Confucius himself was interested in the so-called joint family.) Chinese Communists, like Marxists everywhere, accept Engels' classical analysis of the origins of the family, seen as a basic production unit, with both matriarchal and patriarchal power historically founded on ownership and control of the means of production. To say that the Communist aim is to destroy the stem family or the conjugal family or to "separate husbands and wives" is, however, akin to folklore about "common wives" in Russia. Communists do teach that the individual owes his first loyalty to society as a whole (to the state and the party), as Colonel Li said. They are by no means the first to reject ancient codes of filial rites and a joint family system which disintegrated long before 1949.

No perfect or ideal family system ever existed in China outside the pages of Western fiction, such as Nora Waln's *House of Exile*—one of the most charming compilations of anachronisms and sociological misinformation ever produced. Dr. Hu Shih, long respected among Chinese historians, and an embittered anti-Communist until his death in 1962, tried to demolish this "ideal family system" myth for many years, with indifferent success. More than a generation ago he wrote: "The Chinese family of old times rarely, if ever, possessed the virtues which have sometimes been attributed to it or read into it." Life in the joint family was marked by "frictions, suspicions, intrigues, oppression and even suicides." The much idealized virtue of the sacrifice of the individual to filial piety never went much beyond mere ritual and "in those rare cases where it was consciously cultivated the price paid for it was nothing short of intensive suppression resulting in mental and physical agony." [1]

In *My Country and My People,* Dr. Lin Yutang criticized family cultists for the absence of Chinese civic pride, indifference to the sufferings of others, bribery and nepotism. "Seen in modern eyes," he wrote, "Confucianism omitted from the social relationships man's social obligations toward the stranger, and great and catastrophic was the omission. . . . In the end, as it worked out, the family became a walled castle outside of which everything was legitimate loot." The American-educated sociologist H. D. Fong concluded that the "walled castle" was "one of the most serious obstacles to industrialization." [2]

Anyone who wishes to understand the "fine old family system" as it actually appeared to Chinese even half a century ago should read Pa Chin's shattering descriptions of its tyrannies and stupidities in his novel, *The Family.*[3] Even the medieval classical family novel, *Dream of the Red Chamber,* depicts heroines who so abhorred the conventional marriage relationship that they preferred to be nuns, while in the nineteenth century a "girls' revolt" against family-arranged matches became so widespread that the government was obliged to set up separate homes for virgins who refused such contracts.[4]

Historically, China had three basic types of families: the conjugal or nuclear family of husband, wife and children, if any; the stem family, which consisted of parents, their own unmarried children, and no more than one married son and his wife and children; and the joint family, of parents, their unmarried children, several married sons and their wives and children. In a few enlarged joint families a fourth or even a fifth generation, and sometimes one other fraternal stem family's descendants, might live under a single patriarchal rule or that of an eldest surviving son.

The enlarged joint family practically disappeared in China two thousand years ago, at the time generally reckoned as the end of the true feudal period, when the Ch'in state abolished the nobility, broke up the great estates, and divided the land among the tillers. Thereafter, although wealthy landed families arose again and tended to be larger than poor ones, "the family for the overwhelming majority was relatively small," usually five or six persons and seldom more than eight living in a household corresponding to the conjugal or stem family.[5]

The conjugal family is today the commonest form in China, as in most countries; there are also very many stem families. Close extra-familial ties exist between kinfolk in villages, of course. Formerly a loose clan organization was maintained by the gentry, who exploited their control of ancestral temples (now disappearing) as a means of autocratic authority. Even now, in thousands of Chinese villages named after a distant common progenitor (among the some 470 "old families"), a majority of the citizens may have the same surname although they have long since lost track of their direct blood ties. No doubt these ancestral clan traditions were often effective in preserving cultural cohesion and continuity in times of catastrophe and foreign conquest, but their parochial virtues weakened and dissolved under the impact of capitalism and machine invasion and had to be superseded by broader concepts of solidarity.

The entire revolutionary process since 1911 has vastly raised the horizon of political consciousness for the half-billion people now dwelling in the rural areas. Japan's invasion drove millions into the hinterland and the process has been greatly accelerated since 1949. Tens of millions of young people have migrated or been sent from the seaboard into western China, to open up new resources and build wholly new cities in the spread of industry, education and science across the broad land. Turned upside down, greatly diluted by new arrivals and by dispersals of their descendants, the old rural clans nevertheless remain basically the *lao pai hsing*, or "old hundred names." A feeling of historic kinship in most areas makes cooperative economic and social life a more natural evolution than in the West, and particularly in a new nation like the United States, where families have no antiquity and multilateral relationships are very limited. The Chinese commune, therefore, may actually come nearer to achieving the ancient ideal of family "mutual help and mutual benefit" than ever really happened when it was a matter of what Chinese call *yu-ming wu-shih* or "the name of a thing without the reality."

Remembering the reforms of the T'ai-p'ing Rebellion we know that efforts to end parental despotism, to liberate women, and to replace Confucian concepts with higher-than-family loyalties had been embattled slogans a century before the Communists appeared on the scene. The first modern civil code to embody such aims was promulgated by the Kuomintang regime, in 1931, when the whole legal structure of the family was nominally altered. Ancestral worship was abolished, along with male authority and male worship; equality in property rights, inheritance and divorce were promised to women. As with many Kuomintang decrees, however, "The new legislation . . . had little actual effect on the traditional family system because the laws remained largely on paper," according to reflections which appear in *China*, a symposium by Chinese and American scholars.[6]

The basic family law (called the marriage law) of the People's Republic went much further and it has been energetically, if not completely, enforced. It does not at all abolish the family but rather explicitly defines its basis in a marriage contract freely made between individuals whose equality of rights as citizens is guaranteed. The law bans arranged marriages and matchmakers, concubinage, bigamy, child betrothal, and sale of daughters and wives. Spouses share ownership and management of family property, and responsibility for the care and support of their children as well as aging parents. Today's law thus sanctions both the conjugal and stem family household.

The right to divorce is guaranteed both parties; vigorous campaigns to encourage its use by discontented women resulted in a total of 409,000 divorces in 1951—a rate almost one-third as high as that in the United States. Violent reactions among some rejected spouses were strongly suggested in a government report, in 1952, that between seventy and eighty thousand people were killed or committed suicide in a single year in China over marriage difficulties, according to Hu Chang-tu.[7] The party propaganda campaign to encourage divorce abruptly ended. In recent years the rate has greatly declined and—as Li's comments indicated—divorce is now distinctly unfashionable among the party elite.

More important than any mere law in changing the marriage relationship was the distribution of land equally among men and women. Following that, collectivization deprived the male of opportunities to use ownership as a means of oppression or exploitation. Women's equality in the right to education and equal pay for equal work further established their "independence." Among young people the evidence of a new mutual respect is everywhere apparent.

A new usage which indicates change in status and feeling between men and women is the word *ai-jen*. It has replaced the exalted *fu-jen*, *t'ai-t'ai*, etc., formerly correct when a member of the gentry referred to another person's wife, as well as such terms as *lao-p'o*, meaning "old stick," when a person hypocritically disclaimed any distinction in his own wife. *Ai-jen* means "beloved." It is now nearly universal among young people when either spouse speaks of the other. Old Communists introduced it, as it was long common usage among the leaders. "Where is your beloved, Comrade Mao?" is perfectly acceptable—though a bit shocking to the "old sticks."

Few who have seen China today doubt that the regime's success in deeply involving women in all the nation's work and social life has enormously enriched it culturally as well as economically. All these factors, combined with the general economic and social integration of rural and urban life after industrialization by socialist means, have virtually ended any surviving idealization of "the family system." In politics the evils attributed to that system—nepotism, bribery and embezzlement— have not entirely disappeared, as constant rectifications have shown. But today's vigilance is unprecedented and deviations among senior officials are virtually unheard of, whereas they formerly provided the worst examples. Chicanery is practically impossible in a state where money cannot buy lawyers or judges, and so is the sale of office. It seems a real handicap rather than an advantage to be a sibling to a high official, and none achieve prominence because of family connections. Even Chou En-lai refused to interfere to save his obscure older brother's father-in-law from village prosecution and punishment as an alleged oppressive landlord.

Winding up our conversation, on the way back to Peking, the young army officer remarked: "For China, government by the family system ended with Chiang Kai-shek. Chiang and all his in-laws and sworn blood brothers—the Kungs, the Soongs, the Chens—ruled by the feudal codes of family first. They became millionaires by robbing poor families also named Kung, Soong and Chen. China is through with family-system government."

Impressive corroborative data to the same effect is now available in the 1,953 pages of official State Department reports[8] which cover the history of American attempts to save the last family dynasts of China. Nor does anything in those volumes give much cause for optimism about the ultimate results of the current United States repeat experiment with the family system under the Ngo dictatorship in Vietnam.

Back in the Hsin Ch'ao hotel I met some Canadian visitors, among whom was the distinguished child psychiatrist, Dr. Denis Lazure, of the University of Montreal. During his numerous visits to Chinese schools, nurseries, crèches, hospitals, public parks, private homes and communes, Dr. Lazure was making a special study of changes in child attitudes toward the family and state as a result of twelve years of revolutionary orientation. He was able to conduct thematic apperception tests (T.A.T.) on a number of children aged ten to sixteen. He questioned them individually about their values, actions, dreams, memories, choices, anxieties, passions, sentiments and wishes. I need not here intrude a layman's interpretation of his arresting discoveries, which are now medical literature.[9] A mere sampling of his observations may at least help fill in the pattern of youthful thinking in China which has replaced overdependence on the family.

On the basis of "most frequent answers" to his questions, Dr. Lazure found that "adolescents seem to place particular value on patriotism, diligence in their studies and in their work in general, altruism, and accepting constructive criticism." Among "best acts" they could perform, typical were to "help an old person carry his packages," "to return a lost article to police" and "to contribute to the success of the agricultural plan by growing a garden." As for sins, "It is impossible for a Pioneer or a good student to commit a bad act," the psychiatrist was repeatedly told, until he conceded a widespread "unconscious denial of all unacceptable behavior" which "astonishes most Western visitors to China."

Among fifteen subjects he questioned individually only two admitted having any "feelings of sadness." One, a girl, said, "I feel sad when one of the leaders of our country or another socialist country dies." A boy of sixteen reported a dream in which he was playing "but the next morning I was too tired and got up too late for school. I was very sad." Worries? "All subjects replied that they had none." Typical was the answer of a girl of thirteen, who said: "I have no fear or worry. I know that Chairman Mao and the Party are concerned with my welfare and can protect me against any danger." Hostility normally directed against parents or the environment seemed to Dr. Lazure to have been successfully transferred and projected against capitalism and American imperialism, as "symbols of aggression and cruelty." There also "seems to be a remarkable capacity in these subjects to sublimate their aggressive impulses in hard work and for personal improvement and for advancement of the country."

Parental figures "are constantly perceived as affectionate and supportive, in marked contrast to the T.A.T.'s of North American adolescents." There were some indications of "excessive tension and anxiety" (facial tics and nail-biting), but neurotic dreams and certain other symptoms "very frequent among North American children such as enuresis, nightmares, stuttering and juvenile delinquency, seemed very rare." Dr. Lazure told me that he was quite astonished at a rate of mentally disturbed children in China apparently far below that in the West. As the practicing director of the child psychiatric department of the Ste. Justine Hospital of Montreal, he found it difficult to believe all the Chinese psychiatrists, psychologists and educators whom he interviewed when they unanimously "maintained that there were practically no mental defectives" and "denied having ever seen a case of infantile psychosis in China."

What Dr. Lazure described as his "most significant conclusion" about Chinese youth was that "their leaders have very effectively accomplished the revolution of transferring the emotional investment formerly reserved for the family to society as a whole and to the role which the individual will play in building his society . . . The family as an institution has certainly lost importance in all socialist countries based on the Russian model but this is even more true in China . . ." On the other hand Dr. Lazure dismissed the belief that "the mass exodus of women to the factories and fields" is a "principal factor in weakening family ties." He observed that the mother is now "able to devote her time entirely to her children when she arrives home from work. I was particularly impressed to see, for example, that even very young children accompany their parents in the evening on trips to the local park or a movie theatre . . ."

"The child and the teenager appear to be more concerned with socio-political themes than with conflicts which would exist in their relationship with their parents." There seemed "little variation in the theme frequency of psychotic conditions" as compared to the West, but there was, paradoxically, "probably a marked decrease in psycho-neuroses, character disorders, and anti-social behavior."

Dr. Lazure found a "fairly remarkable civic pride but at the same time a stereotyped attitude in thought and behavior. The State does not place itself between the child and his parents but rather above the latter. Understandably such a society has assigned to each individual a definite role: and this structure, at least in this phase, appears to be a favorable factor in the mental health of the Chinese."

A note of warning. No one should take adolescents' claims that they have "no problems and no worries" at face value nor imagine that China "has achieved a utopia" for them. "It is more realistic," Dr. Lazure emphasized, "to presume that the State has been highly successful in creating an image of happy youth and that the young people, in their desire to conform, have accepted that illusion." Their goals and ambitions showed a "remarkable diversity of choices" of future careers but it should not be supposed that they are any less outer-directed than the status-seeking sons of Madison Avenue. Dr. Lazure observed that it is precisely "in these countries, China and the United States, that the adolescent of today experiences the strongest pressures toward conformity. For the American teenager the norms of the peer-groups are all-compelling, while the young Chinese wants at any price to be identified with the norms of the Five Year Plan and the Party slogans."

41

Medical History, Personal and Otherwise

I had four occasions to make some use of Chinese medical facilities. On my arrival at the Peking airport I discovered that my immunization card was missing; apparently it had not been returned with my passport in Moscow. I signed an affidavit declaring that I had received all necessary innoculations; they were repeated at the airport by a Chinese doctor, and in twenty minutes I had a new certificate. Charge, one yuan, or forty cents.

In Changchun, Manchuria, I consulted a hotel physician about an eye infection which looked like possible trachoma. He diagnosed it as conjunctivitis but as he was only a "middle doctor" he called in a neighborhood specialist. She quickly and efficiently confirmed his diagnosis, dressed the eye, provided me with a bathing solution, and left within ten minutes. Charge, twenty cents. She had no time to stay for a cup of tea because she was due at a clinic where "fifty people" awaited her. My eye was well in two days.

In Peking I had a recurrence of a latent infection, the history of which traced to that same city far back in 1936. I had had a small kidney stone removed cystoscopically at the Peking Union Medical College. The operation was a success but postoperative treatment was inadequate and it took months to cure an infection. Ever since then there had been recurrences under conditions of extreme fatigue. On my return from Manchuria the bug made a particularly painful reappearance. I went back to the old PUMC, now part of the Peking Medical Institute. When I entered the office of the chief urologist he had before him a file of my complete medical history to 1937, the year I had left Peking. He reminded me of a lot of complaints that I had forgotten and of some false alarms, including suspected TB on my first consultation there, in 1929! He then gave me a thorough examination, complete x-rays on the latest Chinese machines, found nothing serious, prescribed some antibiotics, and I was well again in a few days. Fees, $2.00, standard rates for the noninsured.

While visiting Peking's Chest Surgery Hospital, a new and ultramodern institution, which trains two hundred internes a year and has American-educated surgeons among its directors, I discovered a small dental clinic in one of its ten wards. The equipment was up to date ("jet-powered" drills), all made in China. I sat down in a chair and asked a doctor to take a location-shot picture of me. A young dentist not only posed with me but took advantage of the time to look over my mouth; to his satisfaction he found trouble between two back teeth. He x-rayed me and made an appointment. I returned and he did a difficult excavation of a tiny needle-like cavity that ran to the very edge of the root canal. When I had to ask for novocaine he was astonished. I heard him say to the nurse: "These foreigners can't stand the slightest pain. No Chinese would feel that!" He completed the work expertly and I have had no trouble since. Charge, $1.00, at standard rates.

The reader now has my medical history up to my departure from China and, I am happy to add, up to this writing. As a nonpatient I visited a dozen other large modern hospitals in or near Changchun, Shanghai, Paotou, Wuhan, Kunming and Chungking, as well as rural health stations and clinics beyond recall. I had an unusual experience at the new and large (900 beds; 3,800 students) T'ung Chi Medical College and Hospital in Hankow. There I watched, through glass theater ceilings, five operations going on simultaneously, three of them for cancer of the esophagus. One was conducted by a woman surgeon with four women assistants.

The rate of death in childbirth has been reduced to about 32 per thousand in urban China, according to the head of the pediatrics department at T'ung Chi, where the rate is "under 20." (It is much higher over the nation as a whole.) Obstetrics facilities and maternity care there appeared to be almost as good as at Doctors Hospital in New York, where my own children were born. Control of preventable and communicable diseases combined with state protection and care of mothers has sharply reduced the adult death rate while increasing live births. Critics who yesterday condemned backward China as shamefully indifferent to excessive mortality now express concern that too many Chinese go on living.

As a layman with no medical knowledge I realize that my own observations are of limited technical value, but many foreign doctors have now been to Communist China. Apart from Soviet accounts of the work being done, there are numerous eyewitness reports on health and medicine written by non-Communist Asians and Europeans. Many have criticized China's emphasis on quantity production rather than quality and questioned the continued emphasis on traditional Chinese medicine in education and practice. None has failed to note immense advances in almost every direction.

Nine British doctors who toured China in 1957 largely confirmed basic Chinese claims in public health. Among the lengthiest and most enthusiastic of their reports was that of Dr. T. T. Fox, distinguished editor of *Lancet*. He considered the Chinese even then ahead of British public health work in certain aspects of "mass line" effort. In one area, for example, infant mortality had been reduced to 22 per thousand births, as contrasted with about 25 in London.[1]

Detailed evidence was also reported by American doctors at an American Association for the Advancement of Science symposium. Using both his personal knowledge of China and an examination of data from foreign doctors recently there, as well as research in specialized medical journals of China (twenty-five of "major importance"), a senior surgeon of the U. S. Public Health Service, Dr. William Y. Chen, summarized for the symposium the staggering dimensions of the historical problems faced by the Communists as well as some results of their efforts.

"Before the Communist regime took control . . . in 1949," writes this authority, "medical and public health organizations were still in their infancy and far below modern standards. Poverty and disease were the rule." [2] Four million people a year died from "infectious and parasitic diseases" and sixty million people required "facilities for daily treatment." The scope of the problem is indicated by Dr. Chen's estimate of China's needs at what he considers "a minimum standard" of one doctor for 1,500 people and five hospital beds for 1,000 persons. *That would mean 466,000 doctors and 3,500,000 beds for China's population.*

"The total number of scientifically trained doctors [in 1949] was estimated to be only 12,000; for about 500 hospitals, the country was only capable of producing 500 medical graduates per year . . ." and it had a total of 71,000 hospital beds.

"Because 84 percent of the total population in the rural areas was incapable of paying for private medical care, the only early solution of such a tragedy was believed to be a system of state (or socialized) medicine." That opinion was held by leading Chinese doctors as early as 1937,[3] and "the idea of the county health centre system was planned, shaped and conducted mostly by American-trained doctors; many of them are now still living in China and, in fact, form the backbone of China's medical and health structure."

Dr. Chen does not understate the case when he says that "the Communists were desperately in need of medical man power." He goes on to report their use of the "370,000" (today 500,000) traditional (herbalist) Chinese doctors, as Dr. Hatem has already explained. At the same time they emphasized "quantity rather than quality" in the medical colleges. Dr. Chen reports 43,000 graduates from higher medical colleges in the first ten years and 153,000 "graduates from secondary medical schools and secondary public health schools, which provided only two to three years of medical training." (Ministry of Health records for 1959 showed 48,474 medical college graduates and 263,000 "middle doctors" with "four years" of medical training. By 1960 there were 1,200 hospitals with 467,000 beds, as distinct from about 200,000 clinics and health stations in the rural communes.[4]) Dr. Chen described in detail rural health facilities which now fulfill the county health center system about as originally planned by the American-trained doctors.*

Hospital beds and doctors qualified in Western terms thus increased four to five times in ten years. This is far below Dr. Chen's "minimum standard," but he reports "greater strides in the improvement of sanitation, health education, and prevention [work] . . . Typhus, relapsing fever and other 'notifiable' or 'reportable' infectious diseases have been brought under control. Great improvements have been made also in the control of major parasitic diseases . . . Millions of malaria patients have been treated and its incidence rate has apparently dropped to less than a 3 per cent level."

Dr. Chen reports 36,000,000 patients cured of hookworm.

The mortality rate of tuberculosis has also dropped rapidly. For example, TB declined from 230 per 100,000 in 1949 to 46 per 100,000 in 1958 in Peking. Syphilis and gonorrhea are no longer menaces to health due to the proper practice of personal hygiene and effective treatment . . . Extensive medical and industrial health work has been done to check the widely prevalent silicosis, and much progress in its diagnosis and treatment has been related. . . .

Having been successful in combating infectious and parasitic diseases the Communists have also realized the importance of preventing and controlling chronic diseases. Recently they launched a vigorous anti-cancer campaign. Although their achievements in cancer research have not been of great significance, yet the scope of this problem in a country with such a vast population warrants our attention. Mass detection of cancer, especially of the uterus and cervix, oesophagus and naso-

* Much pioneer work in this field was done with the help of funds and technical assistance from the Rockefeller Foundation under the direction of Dr. John B. Grant.

pharangeal cavity, was started in 1958 . . . The Communists have also paid great attention to the problem of liver cancer. Thirty-eight medical colleges have conducted intensive investigations of this problem.

British medical reports are informative on results of "the successful control of flies, the litterless streets and fanatical household cleanliness." Professor Brian Maegraith, dean of the Liverpool School of Tropical Medicine, found that they were "having a profound effect on the spread of gastro-intestinal infections." He described the mass work of village health committees and street sanitation and hygiene enforcement much along lines already mentioned by Dr. Hatem. A single paragraph may be particularly arresting to anyone who knew the squalor of rural China of the past. Dr. Maegraith says:

One further method of control [of schistosome snails] which goes on all the time, illustrates the degree of general cooperation obtained [from the people]. Until artifical fertilizers can be developed on a big enough scale, human excreta remains the cheapest and most valuable manure. Fortunately the dangerous schistosome eggs do not live long if left in faeces without contact with water. Storage thus renders the material non-infective. Thanks to skillful propaganda, this essential conservation of night soil is becoming an economic and social fact. Each family now has its own privy, a portable gaily-colored pot. Every morning the contents are poured into large communal earthenware containers, which are sealed when full and left for the appropriate time necessary for the ammonia generated to kill the eggs, after which the faeces are safe for use in the fields. The collection of family night soil is assured by paying the family for it pro-rata, so many cents a day per person, according to age. This scheme is also being used for the control of water pollution by fishermen, for each boat now has its own collecting pot, which is regarded as a source of income.[5]

42

From John D. to Acupuncture

A generation ago the Rockefeller Foundation established the Peking Union Medical College and brought over a small staff of American doctors and teachers to work in its new Chinese-roofed buildings off Morrison Street. John D. Rockefeller had various reasons for setting up his foundation, but he might have said the heck with it and just let the Treasury Department collect inheritance taxes on his estate if he had known that Chinese Communists, acupuncture and moxibustion were to end up as his beneficiaries. Traditional Chinese medicine was looked upon by the founders of the PUMC in much the same way missionaries regarded Confucian rites as paganism.

I learned something about the renaissance in the Chinese empirical sciences when I returned to the PUMC for a long inspection tour and discussion with its vice-director, Dr. Hsu Hung-t'u, and his staff. Dr. Hsu was a small, dynamic, cheerful man, who continually rubbed his head and grinned, exposing some missing teeth, whenever he was perplexed. He had graduated from the old Medical College of Peking National University and was now in his fifties; his professional qualifications were probably inferior to those of many of the younger doctors on his staff. He indicated quite frankly that his duties as staff administrator were more political than professional.

The PUMC is still an important hospital. It is now one branch of the large China Medical College, which is one of ten divisions of the Academy of Medical Sciences. These divisions scattered around the nation include colleges, hospitals and institutes with the following specialties: biological research, in Yunnan; parasitic diseases, Shanghai; blood diseases research, Tientsin; and labor hygiene, pharmaceutical research, antibiotics, skin diseases and venereology, clinical medicine research, pathological and physiological basic medicine, all in Peking. Three departments formerly in the PUMC were removed to provide the core staffs of new hospitals for tumor and cancer, plastic surgery, and chest diseases. All the institutes have provincial branches. Like the other hospitals and medical colleges in China, they are under the general administration of the Academy of Medical Sciences, which is itself part of the national Academy of Sciences or Academia Sinica (see the chart on page 748.)

Since 1958 most medical colleges have offered six- and eight-year courses, but the majority of students are still graduated as "secondary doctors" after four years. This will continue as long as the emergency demand exists in public health and hygiene work. Secondary doctors take spare-time courses and may later return for advanced academic work. The China Medical College (about 3,600 students) and some provincial affiliates now offer eight-year courses only: three years in basic sciences; two years in basic medicine; two years in clinical medicine, including Chinese medicine; and one year in field work. Russian and English are required subjects for all medical students. As in other professions, medical and pre-medical students must do their "down on the farm" period. Each year they spend two months in the villages assisting rural medical workers; they eat and live as peasants do.

The former PUMC, now Peking Hospital, is not a college any more but a large polyclinic combined with an institute of gynecology and pediatrics. New buildings have doubled the number of beds (560) but there is little more room for expansion. Newer hospitals and institutes are centered in the suburbs and around the headquarters of the Academy of Sciences. About one-third of the doctors of Peking Hospital were educated under the American PUMC administration. For the interest of "old Peking hands," the latter include section chiefs Lin Shao-chih (gynecology), Cheng Ch'ao-chien (medicine), Tseng Hsien-chou (surgery), Chang Tsing-tsun (E.E.N.T.) and Tou Tsung-shen (ophthalmology). The whole staff consists of about 250 doctors, nearly half of whom are women.

At its peak the PUMC used to handle 100,000 patients a year, according to Dr. Hsu. It was then the only first-class hospital in all North China. Now this hospital was "processing" 500,000 people annually. That was nearly one in fourteen of the Peking population, I pointed out. Dr. Hsu explained that it was 100 percent of Tung Hua, the only district for which the hospital was now responsible. Doctors here work in close collaboration with neighborhood street committee health and sanitation teams, and "processing" does not necessarily mean treatment.

Each block of residents elects persons to organize and carry out the daily removal of garbage and refuse, to keep sidewalks and pavements swept, and to supervise sanitation and hygiene routine in dining rooms, nurseries, schools, and so on. Under the supervision of the municipal health authorities these teams also cooperate in immunization work of all kinds, and periodic pest-clearance drives. Each family is required to report all illnesses to these street teams, which diagnose where possible, and arrange for clinical examination or hospitalization. Public health is supervised in this way by hospitals in different districts of the city. The same system has been built up around county hospitals and beneath them are the rural district health centers, and commune, production-brigade and village health teams.

"How much has this cut down on hospital efficiency?"

"If we look at it only from a technological standpoint," answered Dr. Hsu, "the level is lower. That is, the few specialists might be better equipped than our present average. If we consider the total number of patients handled and the average level of community health or the recovery rate, it is much better. In the past the recovery rate of hospitalized patients was less than 30 percent. Now it is above 82 percent. Of course we are taking in many more patients than formerly and many patients who would never have been admitted."

Hospitalization and medical care are free for those with full union sickness insurance. Emergency patients are admitted at once. Other cases are registered through street committees or the patient's employing organizations. For private patients ward beds cost a yuan a day— and wards I saw were extremely crowded. Dr. Hsu said, for example, that an appendicitis operation and hospitalization averaged 20 to 30 yuan. A childbirth averaged 5 yuan; if difficult enough to require a week's hospitalization it would be 15 yuan. These fees are higher than prevailing rural rates. Medicines here as everywhere are sold at cost or below cost: penicillin and antibiotic preparations, for instance, at 10 to 20 cents a prescription. But doctors' salaries are also low. The assistant chief of surgery, Fei Li-min, an American-trained PUMC doctor, got 150 yuan a month; his wife, also a doctor, got the same.

The hospital thus offered one doctor for every 2,000 persons in the Tung Hua district, and fewer than two hospital beds per thousand. The rate was higher for Peking as a whole because of numerous smaller clinics and specialized hospitals in addition to general hospitals. Of the latter the best is probably the large (600-bed) Friendship Hospital built and staffed by the Russians for their advisory community; it has been turned over to all-Chinese personnel.

"Another reason we are able to take care of more patients," went on Dr. Hsu, "is because we combine traditional Chinese medicine with Western practice, and because our doctors are trained in dialectical materialism."

"How's that again?"

"Chinese medicine and a knowledge of dialectical materialism help a great deal in diagnosis and therapy."

I learned that since 1958 all Western-trained doctors have been required to devote at least six months to the study of Chinese medicine. During my visit two department heads at the Peking Hospital had been detached from duty to attend courses in the Traditional Chinese Medical Institute.

For three hours I questioned Dr. Hsu on theories of Chinese herbal medicine, acupuncture and moxibustion.* During my former residence in China I had never made a serious attempt to understand any of this; I considered it quackery, as did most foreigners. Dr. Hsu reminded me that it has a written history of 2,200 years and includes thousands of volumes of medical writings, prescriptions and empirical treatments. (The most famous written compilation of the period, the *Nei Ching*, or *Canon of Internal Medicine*, was a textbook on physiology and the treatment of disease.) All science is basically empirical, he pointed out; what is accepted as scientific at any time is only that which has proved effective by trial and error. Anything which had kept up a vigorous growth for 2,200 years must have something of value, the Chinese concluded.

I think I can handle the general theory and how it fits into dialectical materialism, but for scientific comment on Chinese medicine it is best that I refer to the U. S. Public Health authority whom I have already quoted, Dr. Chen. His report states:

> Traditional Chinese medicine is an empirical healing art based on 4,000 years of practical experience. Its simple concept of health and disease is the functional bodily harmony or disharmony between two forces, Yin (the negative) and Yang (the positive). Anatomically and physiologically traditional Chinese medicine has practically nothing to offer; yet the vast volumes of herbs and drugs and medical treatises recording observations of diseases are precious. The results of the use of these drugs and healing art of acupuncture, moxibustion, massage and breathing therapy certainly have their empirical value. . . .
>
> Acupuncture . . . which is quite a controversial subject . . . is a healing art peculiar to China. It was practiced as early as 200 B.C. It consists of the introduction of hot and cold needles

---

* "Moxibustion" is derived from a corruption of the Cantonese word *mongsa*, for Chinese wormwood (*Artemesia moxa*). The leaves of moxa are prepared in a soft woolly mass and used as a cautery for burning on the skin, as part of an ancient empirical science similar to the cauterization healing said to be still practiced in parts of Europe.

into the body at specific points. The needles may be either fine or
coarse, short or long (from 3 cm. to 24 cm.). The application is
based upon the old Chinese medical theory that internal organs
and different body parts are intimately related and work in harmony for the maintenance of health. These organs and body parts
are hypothetically connected by twelve channels (*Ching*). When
the needles puncture and stimulate different tissues or organs at
various depths, they cause physiological reactions and thus produce healing results.[1]

Acupuncturists are now required to learn aseptic techniques and
basic anatomy and science in courses comparable to those given
"secondary doctors." They practice only in hospitals, nearly all of
which now have acupuncture specialists. Many of them use low-
voltage electrically charged needles. Treatment is sometimes combined with radiotherapy. Dr. Chen goes on:

> Acupuncture was carried from China to Japan at an early
> period but was not introduced to Europe until later. Remusat
> published a long analysis for and against this practice at the
> beginning of the last century. Later . . . Sir James Cantlie tried
> it successfully in several cases of rheumatism and sprains . . .
> In 1956 the Russians sent a group of doctors to Peking to study
> the art of acupuncture. At present intensive studies on the un-
> known mechanism of acupuncture are being conducted in Mos-
> cow by Soviet and Chinese doctors.
>
> *The hypothesis is that stimulation from punctures is con-
> ducted from the peripheral nerves to the brain cortex and
> suppresses pathological irritation in the brain. Such an explana-
> tion seems to be in harmony with the Pavlovian theory of con-
> ditioned reflex.*
>
> Acupuncture has been widely used in practically all kinds of
> diseases ranging from surgical conditions such as appendicitis
> to chronic conditions such as diabetes. It is believed that it pro-
> duces best results in illness of the nervous system or those of
> neurological origin. Good results have been reported in the
> treatment of facial paralysis, arthritis and eczema. One Russian
> physician reported that his long history of miserable arthritis
> was much improved by acupuncture. A doctor from India who
> went to China and studied acupuncture in 1958 entertained
> certain doubts as to its value at first. However, he believed
> afterwards that the integration of traditional medicine and
> western medicine had already accomplished remarkable success.
> He was also treated successfully by acupuncture for his acute
> sinusitis.
>
> Dr. Wu Lien-teh [an American-trained doctor, at one time

Minister of Health], the great plague fighter, during the severe Manchurian plague epidemic half a century ago, said in the preface of his book *History of Chinese Medicine* that "Chinese medicine, to be understood and its significance appreciated, must be studied as one whole. In no other field of endeavor in this country has the experimental method realized such concrete and far-reaching results as in the domain of medicine." [2]

Chinese medicine obviously has its limitations but there are many borderline cases, and here the patient's choice apparently is decisive. Dr. Chen, in the same report I have quoted, mentions the use of empirical methods "with good results" also in the treatment of liver cirrhosis, bronchitis, pulmonary tuberculosis and hypertension heart disease. I myself met patients in hospitals in Peking, Hankow and Dairen being treated by traditional means for appendicitis, eczema, rheumatism, sinusitis, tuberculosis, migraine headaches, bronchitis and various kinds of neurasthenia. All expressed preference for the Chinese-style treatment and several were in satisfied convalescent stages. In Hankow I met a patient who had arrived at the hospital unconscious with what Western-trained surgeons had diagnosed as acute appendicitis. Treated by empirical medicine and acupuncture, he was being dismissed as cured.

Coexistence of the supposedly black art and scientific medicine side by side in modern hospitals strikes the foreigner as bizarre. At the Chest Surgery Hospital I saw a patient receiving acupuncture treatments for bronchitis. In the same hospital two heart surgeons showed me a convalescent child who had had an unusual and successful heart operation to relieve a "tetralogy of Fallot," or blue-baby condition, involving a "right ventricular hypertrophy, pulmonary stenosis, interventricular septal defect and overriding aorta." The operation had required prolonged use of both an artificial heart and lung. The child told me, incidentally, that his father was a maritime worker in Dairen and that he had been sent all the way from their home at union expense. The operation mortality rate at this new hospital was given as 4.1 percent for 1959.

Chinese herbal medicine and acupuncture work together and herbalists are often needle men as well. Semantics renders it impossible quickly to explain Chinese medical theory, but the *yin-yang* concept of "contradictions" is basic. The body is an organic unity; illness is caused by imbalances between different organs or their extensions, and cure consists in restoring balance and harmony. This is done by relaxing "antagonisms" among eight principal lines of tension which are: *yin-yang* (negative-positive), *piao-li* (outer-inner), *leng-je* (hot-cold) and *hsu-shih* (empty-solid).

Without getting in any deeper it may be said that the body is charted in terms of those principles and of "life forces" of balance between them. Normally "contradictions" of a nonantagonistic nature exist in an equilibrium. When "disunity" (disease) occurs, one organ or set of functions has been overworked, overstimulated, injured or otherwise disturbed. The doctor's task is to restore the balance by removing the cause of the antagonism or congestion.

"Diseases have inner and outer causes," said Dr. Hsu Hung-t'u, who had got himself into a great sweat to explain this much to me. "The higher nervous system of the brain affects the general physiology, of course. What we call *ni-ch'u chung-kuan* [anger-in-a-state-of-fury-burns]* may cause organic pains and injuries elsewhere. A patient may arrive complaining of pains which a Western diagnosis may show to be heart hypertension but a Chinese doctor may treat by a combination of medicine and acupuncture.

"A Western-style doctor often only asks the medical symptoms and medical history. A Chinese doctor looks upon the person as a unity subject to both outside and inside tensions. He wants to know about the person's family, his relations with his parents, whether he likes his wife, how his work goes, what his personal resentments are, where disharmony exists in his life, whether he is a native of the city or is a southerner or a northerner. All these go into diagnosis."

"South or north? That makes a difference?"

"Yes, certain medicines 'hot' for a northerner give the southerner a 'cold' reaction."

"Such an inquiry would also have to touch upon the patient's political thought, I presume?"

"Of course—conflicts of all kinds are discussed."

From this and subsequent conversations it became clear to me that the Chinese pathologist is something of an analyst and psychiatrist as well and that acupuncture is often used as shock therapy. Whether illnesses caused by unresolved stress or anxiety are greater in China than in the frenetically competitive system of America I do not know. Dr. Chen reports that the incidence of heart hypertension—for whatever this proves—is about the same in both countries.[3] I have no statistics on neurasthenic diseases in China but the number of cases I encountered in hospitals and sanatoria seemed very high. The inner tensions caused by social pressures of the kind of system Communists are trying to create are obviously severe, outlets are few, and it is not surprising that the demand for consultations with Chinese therapists is great.

Communists reject Freud, and many Freudian postulations may be rendered obsolete *if* communism succeeds. Meanwhile, something like a substitute for the couch exists in the kind of diagnostic approach described by Dr. Hsu. Obviously the "contradictions" theory of Chinese therapeutics is especially attractive to native Marxists. It also suggests another reason why dialectical materialism found pre-

* The general idea, not an exact translation!

conditioned soil in Chinese historical thinking. Doubtless because this indigenous medical theory tends to support dialectics, as well as because traditional Chinese doctors are needed to meet present emergency requirements, they are not only being utilized but increased in numbers.

"Whether the Communists will succeed in their ambitious endeavor to produce a new Chinese medical science by incorporating traditional medicine with modern scientific medicine only time can tell," concluded Dr. Chen. "Whatever the outcome, its development is worthy of our constant attention."

Aldous Huxley recently reported that "International Congresses of Acupuncture are now convened (the last was at the University of Clermont-Ferrand)," and that several hundred European doctors are trying to "combine the science and art of Western medicine with the ancient science and art of Chinese acupuncture." He continues:

> That a needle stuck into the outside surface of the leg a little below the knee [elsewhere, needles may penetrate much deeper; expertly handled, they draw no blood] should affect the functioning of the liver is obviously incredible. . . . In the normally healthy organism [the Chinese maintain] there is a continuous circulation of energy. Illness is at once a cause and a result of a derangement of this circulation . . . Acupuncture re-directs and normalises the flow of energy.
>
> This is possible because, as a matter of empirical fact, the limbs, trunk and head are lined with invisible "meridians" related in some way to the various organs of the body. On these meridians are located specially sensitive points. A needle inserted at one of these points will affect the functioning of the organ related to the meridian on which the point lies. By pricking at a number of judiciously selected points the skilled acupuncturist re-establishes the normal circulation of energy and brings the patient back to health.
>
> Once again we are tempted to shrug our shoulders and say that it makes no sense. But then, reading the proceedings of the most recent Congress of Acupuncture, we learn that experimenters have been able, by means of delicate electrical measuring instruments, to trace the course of the Chinese meridians, and that when a strategic point is pricked with a needle relatively large changes of electrical state can be recorded.[4]

Huxley relates that among the pathological symptoms "on which the old Chinese methods work very well" are "various kinds of undesirable mental states—certain kinds of depression and anxiety, for example—which, being presumably related to organic derangements, disappear as soon as the normal circulation of energy is restored. Results which several years on the analyst's couch have failed to produce may be obtained, in some cases, by two or three pricks with a silver needle." [5]

I had no ailments susceptible to acupuncture treatment, but a woman doctor at the Peking Hospital gave me a demonstration. Taking a sterilized needle the thickness of a hairpin she deftly punctured me and guided it halfway through my wrist. I sensed little pain but in about a minute there was an active "gathering" feeling. She withdrew the needle bloodlessly. Patients I saw being treated all told me they felt no pain from the needle but only relief.

My experiences with Chinese herbal medicines were also limited. Everywhere salad and raw vegetables were available I had enjoyed them without any mishap until, on my way back from Chengchow, I experienced the usual agonizing symptoms of indiscretion in the East —what the G.I.'s called Delhi-belly. Rewi Alley was with me on the train. He brought out some Chinese pills of a bilious hue and I trustfully consumed them. After three doses I returned to normal. On a trip to Szechuan I woke up with all the symptoms of a severe cold— fatigue, headache, drip. A Chinese doctor gave me a herbal preventive which has the opposite effect from antihistamines. My nose opened up and I sneezed for hours but otherwise felt physically well. In two days the dripping ceased and I was all right. I supplied myself with a quantity of this preventive and have since used it with repeated success. A friend of mine is now having the pills chemically analyzed, and we expect soon to make a fortune by launching them on the market as anti-antihistamines.

I don't want to leave anyone with the impression that I have switched to Chinese pharmacology and acupuncture, or that all Chinese Western-trained doctors have been converted. Enthusiasm for the therapeutic benefits of both acupuncture and herbalism may be kept within bounds when it is remembered that Chinese medical literature offered scarcely any knowledge at all of such basic sciences as bacteriology, microbiology, parasitology, epidemiology, endocrinology, venereology, etc., and only primitive conceptions of asepsis. Chinese medical doctrine was virtually useless in the prevention of smallpox, typhus, tuberculosis, plague, dysentery, cholera, tetanus, kala azar, malaria, filariasis, syphilis and other deadly diseases. It is too early to say whether those in China who oppose the policy of integration of native and Western therapies may not be proved justified in their prejudices. It seemed to me that some I encountered in hospitals were embarrassed by the prestige being given to traditional methods. All must resent the *compulsion* to study them. (Something like requiring all American doctors to learn osteopathy?)

Dr. Fei Li-min, the assistant chief of surgery at Peking Hospital, obviously was no enthusiastic supporter of the policy. (Admittedly, surgeons are least likely to sympathize with any un-anatomists.) He was a Shanghai man—gaunt, solemn, in his thirties, and to me he looked very tired. There were thirty surgeons and they needed sixty, he said, and twice as many beds. He had graduated from the PUMC when it was located in Chungking during the war, and later had come to Peking when the hospital was used as truce-team headquarters by Generals Marshall and Wedemeyer in 1946-47. He had also briefly studied Chinese medicine. How had he found the time?

"Do you function more efficiently than you did before?" I asked him. He understood English but he answered—or evaded—my question through an interpreter.

"Our technical equipment and operations are all about the same as before," he said. "What has changed is our relationship with the patient. Formerly the doctor decided what to do and that was that. Now if a patient doesn't like it he tells us so and we try to find some other way. Take colostomy. People don't like it. In the past if they wouldn't accept it we would send them home. Now we have to explain, persuade—or find other means.

"Like acupuncture?"

"Yes, sometimes."

"Do you ever recommend it?"

"They use it for appendicitis and hemorrhoids. It's good for relief of pains in the gastrointestinal tract. It helps overcome postoperative spastic condition in the ureter." (That I was told everywhere.)

"But do you personally function more efficiently than before?"

There was a long pause. I repeated the question and the interpreter repeated the question.

Finally Dr. Fei said, "The relationship has changed between the doctor and the patient. If the patient cooperates we can do a good job. If he wants to argue there is much wasted time."

Dr. Hsu was still smiling but his face was flushed.

"Would you say it is less efficient?" Translation again. Pause. Repeat the question.

"In past years the head surgeon had time to talk to his staff," said Dr. Fei. "Now everyone in the hospital has a voice in meetings, even the lowest member of the staff. We accomplish less." He obviously preferred staff meetings of the former type, confined to discussions by technically qualified personnel—and no doubt less concerned with thought reform.

Speaking of mortality rates in operations Dr. Fei said they were 5 to 7 percent in the past and about the same now. "We can't compare it with the past. We used to limit admissions to those with a chance to recover. Now we admit people in the last stages of lung cancer."

"But the rate of recovery in cirrhosis of the liver is much higher than before!" Dr. Hsu broke in, still smiling but still red. "Even with cases we wouldn't have admitted before."

Cirrhosis of the liver can be treated by acupuncture. Obviously some patients would express a preference for it, even if Dr. Fei were of another opinion. Who would decide the issue? I had penetrated, if only slightly, into unresolved contradictions between partisans of *Han-yao* and *yang-yao*, Chinese and foreign medicine.

My question had beaten a sparrow out of a tree but decent consideration of my hosts required that I let it go. I changed the subject, to the evident relief of both doctors.

Part Four

THE
DEMOCRATIC
DICTATORSHIP

☆

"The Kuomintang was the precursor of the Chinese Communist Party in seeking to train a new type of scholar-bureaucrat in a new ideology, so as to revive the functions once performed by the Confucian literati and the classics. . . . Mao in his turn unified the country as a hero risen from the people, like the founders of the Han and Ming [dynasties]. . . . His ideology claimed the Mandate of History if not of Heaven.

"The reader can continue for himself to recognize echoes of the past in China today. C. P. Fitzgerald, for example, has summarized the traditional social concepts as embracing 1) a single authority conterminous with civilization, 2) a balanced economy basically managed by the state, 3) an orthodox doctrine which harmonizes and guides all forms of human activity, including the selection of intellectuals for state service . . . As of 1952, he suggests that these concepts, destroyed during modern times in their traditional form of expression, have found expression again under Communism.

"Since the patterns of the past cannot be entirely expunged, they remain curiously intertwined with new motifs. Peking today has a Marxist-Leninist-Maoist ideological orthodoxy as Confucianism used to be; but it believes in progress toward a future millennium, not cyclical repetition descending from a golden age. Dynastic absolutism has been replaced by party dictatorship, the imperial family-clan council by the central executive committee, the scholar-elite by a party elite, tax-gatherers by cadres in the countryside, Confucian classics by Communist classics, written examination by group discussion, scholarly self-cultivation by guilt-ridden self-criticism. . . .

"[But it would be] simple-minded to conclude that it is merely another in a long succession of dynasties . . . Ancient evils of bureaucratism lie in wait for Peking's mammoth administration at any time its morale declines . . . Secondly, Communist China's methods for ensuring universal conformity . . . are far more intensive than anything old China ever devised . . . [but] a third and conclusive con-

sideration, which seems to lock the Chinese people irrevocably into their struggle to increase production through their conformity and at the expense of personal freedom, is the rate of population increase. Every year, famine waits around the corner . . . Like it or not, there is no alternative [to some kind of centralized and dictatorial planning and controls] by which to feed them, employ the youth, and satisfy the national pride."

—JOHN K. FAIRBANK, *The United States and China,* Harvard University Press, Cambridge, 1948, 1958

43

State and Superstructure

Some differences in the theory and structure of the People's Republic of China and the U.S.S.R. trace in part to the prolonged "united front" policy pursued by the Chinese Communist Party during the war against Japan (1937-45). In modified form the policy was continued during the subsequent struggle for power against Chiang Kai-shek.

"The New Democracy," [1] which Mao Tse-tung wrote in 1940, sought to win the support of all "progressive elements" in a Communist-led war, first to defeat the foreign aggressor and then to eliminate "feudal forces" inside China. In 1945, Mao's "On Coalition Government" [2] foresaw a long period during which the Communist party and the "bourgeois-democratic" parties would work together in a reformed presocialist society. After the revolution both theory and practical experience taught the necessity for a policy of limited class collaboration until the peasantry could be won over to collectivization and a new generation of workers indoctrinated to build toward communism.

In 1949 the Communists summoned a meeting in Peking of the Chinese People's Political Consultative Conference—which had first been organized under Kuomintang auspices. Attended by 662 delegates nominally representing all the anti-Chiang Kai-shek forces, classes, professions and nationality groups in China, and excluding only landlords and "bureaucratic capitalists," that conference adopted an Organic Law for its own existence, a preliminary Organic Law of the People's Republic, and a "Common Program." These three documents were the fruit of many earlier discussions between the Communists and their non-Communist supporters. They embodied Mao's concepts of a future constitution to provide for the state superstructure of a "democratic dictatorship." The term "The People's Republic of China" had been used in Mao's address to the preparatory committee of the "New People's Political Consultative Conference" in June, 1949.

Thus the new Peking government was provisionally set up on the basis of organic laws adopted by the P.P.C.C. During the next four years the government tried out and gradually stabilized an administrative apparatus adequate to carry out the tasks of the "Common Program." Meanwhile the people were organized at the village level to elect congresses which could choose delegates to district, regional and provincial congresses and, finally, delegates to a national assembly. In his last hours in China, Chiang Kai-shek had attempted to hold a national election but virtually no preparation was made for it at a mass level. The Communists were the first to create an electoral machinery as an organic part of the state. The party was at all times in control of that machinery, but it worked with considerable success to enlist nonparty people to help operate it.

By 1953 the government was ready to draw up a formal charter of state. Under the existing organic laws it formed a constitutional drafting committee with Mao Tse-tung as chairman. The committee had thirty-two members, of whom nineteen were leading Communists and thirteen were non-Communists chosen mostly from members of the P.P.C.C. and of eight "bourgeois-democratic" parties. In the spring of 1954 the committee adopted a constitution and announced that elections would be held in September, to choose a National People's Congress. Registered voters numbered 323,000,000 and it was claimed that 85 percent cast ballots. (Nearly 10,000,000 ballots were invalidated on the basis of an electoral law[3] which disqualified landlords and other "class enemies" not formally rehabilitated. Many—perhaps the majority—of those disqualified in 1954 have since received full citizenship rights, but their behavior remains under close scrutiny.) On September 20, 1954, the First National People's Congress adopted the present constitution of the People's Republic of China.

Of the 1,220 deputies elected to the first congress, 680 represented villages and rural towns as against 300 delegates from urban areas and 150 from the minority nationalities; armed forces were represented by 60 and Overseas Chinese by 30.

The Chinese constitution is closely patterned after but not identical to the constitution of the U.S.S.R. A preamble defines the Chinese People's Republic as "a people's democratic dictatorship." In the text of the constitution it is "a people's democracy . . . based on the alliance of workers and peasants." The U.S.S.R. is a "socialist state of the workers and peasants" founded on "the conquest of dictatorship of the proletariat," but the Chinese constitution eschews that phrase and states simply that "all power belongs to the people." The bicameral Supreme Soviet provides for a separate house to represent the constituent republics and nationalities in a "unified multinational state."

Here it is worth noting that use of the word "unified" in the foregoing phrase carries with it a distinction of high significance to Chinese Communists. They maintain that China has not been an "imperialist state" since it was unified by the Han Dynasty more than two thousand years ago. Until the revolution all China was a semicolonial, oppressed nation. Today all its minorities are of dual nationality; they have a local or subnationality, but they are *Chinese* nationals. Chinese Communists assert that Russia is an example of proletarian revolution in a modern "imperialist nation" which oppressed colonial peoples, and that China is an example of revolution in a semicolonial country oppressed *by* imperialism. Relations between the Russians and ex-colonial peoples are thus different from those between the Han majority and the China minorities. Hence there are no national autonomous *republics* in China; there is only one "unified" republic in which all are equal.* This distinction also explains why the Chinese officially use the term *"national* minorities" instead of "minority nationalities." As far as is known, this theory is unique to China among world Marxists.

From the National People's Congress all authority—legislative, judicial and executive—is constitutionally derived. Also, the Chinese constitution recognizes three kinds of ownership: state (ownership by the whole people); cooperative or collective (ownership by "the working masses" at basic levels of production); and capitalist (private ownership by individuals). Nevertheless, this constitution clearly provides for a managed transformation "by law" of the entire economy, "gradually replacing capitalist ownership with ownership by the whole people." Constitutional amendments to conform to growing realities of almost complete state ownership may soon bring changes in some of the foregoing wording, to correspond somewhat more closely to Soviet idiom. It seems less likely, however, that any major alterations will occur in the state administrative structure in China for a long time to come.

The People's Republic is now organized politically and administratively at four basic levels: 1) villages, under district or commune (township) governments; 2) counties, municipalities, provinces and

* Interpretation based on an interview with Prof. Lin Yao-hua, director of the History Department of the Institute of National Minorities, July 9, 1960. See Chapter 78, National Minorities.

autonomous regions; and 3) large municipalities and autonomous areas directly under the 4) central authority. There is direct election of government at the lowest level, where congresses (commune councils) are chosen every two years.* Every four years these congresses elect delegates to a new county congress; county congresses elect provincial congresses; and so on. Representation is thus escalated right up to the National Congress. Official administrative bodies are formed when congresses at different levels elect executive councils. These councils in turn choose chairmen from village heads to mayors and governors. This system is hierarchical or "democratic centralism." The central government has broad supervisory and veto powers at all levels, and each executive council has similar power over councils on the next level below it. (If you want to find any final authority in China look for the "central" in "democratic centralism.")

The National People's Congress elects its own chairman, who becomes head of an elected Standing Committee which serves as a supreme executive council. In practice the Standing Committee has little real power, although it acts for the Congress as a whole when it is recessed—which it generally is except for a week or two once a year. Both the National Congress and its Standing Committee are dominated by a Communist majority which serves as a transmission belt for directives handed down from the party. The nominal authority of the National Congress and its Standing Committee is transformed into realities of power only in the person of the Chairman of the Republic.

Russia has no exact equivalent of the Chairman of the Chinese People's Republic. He is elected once every four years by the National Congress. Once elected, he alone can form a government. Neither the Congress nor its Standing Committee has any power to nominate a premier. It can only approve (theoretically it can also disapprove) a premier nominated by the Chairman of the Republic. The Premier— now Chou En-lai—then nominates his ministers to form the State Council, and the Congress or Standing Committee approves them.

The State Council, which is the cabinet, includes a minister of defense. But Liu Shao-ch'i, as Chairman of the Republic, is the commander in chief of the armed forces and head of the powerful National Defense Council. Only he can summon a Supreme State Conference, enlarging the Congress membership at his discretion. He can remove the Premier. He can also remove the Defense Minister or any minister. He has broad "democratic centralist" powers of supervision over the entire government.

On paper the Chairman of the Republic looks like the final boss. But in practice nearly all important legislative, budgetary and planning decisions, as well as judicial appointments, originate in the Polit-

---

* The special municipalities and areas directly under the central government also hold elections biennially.

buro. Mao Tse-tung was the first man to serve (1954-59) as Chairman of the Republic under the constitution. The office seemed designed for him especially—to combine first responsibility for the state super-structure with top leadership of the ruling party. When he declined to serve a second term but retained his chairmanship of the party, however, it became obvious to anyone who doubted it that party leadership remained paramount over any administrative office.

The outsider may say that all the constitutional electoral procedure is therefore an irrelevant swindle because in practice the chairmen of both the National Congress and the Republic, as well as the Premier, are first of all chosen in secret by the Communist party Politburo, of which Mao is chairman. (The Politburo is in effect the executive council of the Central Committee and is thus the highest organ of party power.) Every official of ministerial rank is also carefully se-lected by the Politburo. The same principle of party paramountcy ap-plies at every level of government and corresponding level of party organization, and even in state factories and other government enter-prises.

Yet neither the Chinese nor the Soviet constitution gives any specific authority to the Communist party. The Communist party holds its authority by claiming for itself, in theory and practice, the sole right to represent the "workers and peasants"—the immense majority. By a combination of persuasion and coercion it monopolizes political lead-ership—but not necessarily political or managerial office—at every point.

Marxists refer to the government administrative apparatus as a "superstructure." Mao Tse-tung defined it as including "our state in-stitutions of people's democratic dictatorship under the guidance of people's democratic dictatorship and its laws and socialist ideology under the guidance of Marxist-Leninism." Its sole purpose is to play a "positive role in facilitating the victory of socialist transformation and establishment of a socialist organization of labor . . . suited to the socialist economic base." [4] There is no room at all here for parlia-mentary opposition nor is such intended. In the Marxist-Leninist theory of the state no government can "stand above classes" but is bound to be an instrument of class rule—either the dictatorship (hidden or masked) of the bourgeoisie, under capitalism, or that of the prole-tariat, in preparation for universal socialist democracy. Only when classes are "abolished" by communism can the superstructure be elimi-nated—a millennium described as "the withering away of the State."

China is in theory still a "unified front" government, but in practice the state apparatus and the party administrative apparatus are, as in Russia, practically identical. There still are, however, a number of nonparty persons in high office, and persons who are party members but of low rank. When a responsible official is not also an important party person he follows directives issued by a party deputy at his side, his alter ego. In practice the party is the real superstructure, the government its instrument, and the substructure is the production system or basic society itself.

The extent to which the party permeates and directly controls offices of the highest rank is indicated by the official positions occupied by the nineteen members and six alternate members of the Politburo. Mao Tse-tung himself is the only one who does not hold either a ministerial or cabinet post or the rank of marshal of the army. (Seven Politburo members are marshals.) China has *sixteen* vice-premiers, almost one to every province or nearly one to every two ministries. Of these, eight are Politburo members while the other eight are, with one exception, party veterans directly in line to fill Politburo vacancies when they occur. Of the thirty-four ministries and four commissions of cabinet level, fewer than ten are ever run by non-Communists or Communists below Central Committee rank.

To repeat an earlier question, then: are not all the popular elections simply irrelevant façade? The answer must be that they are not. The picture I have shown much resembles, it is true, the superstructure of Chiang Kai-shek's government as set up by his own Kuomintang party political committee; Chiang also borrowed techniques from the Russians. But the significant difference lies in the manner in which vast numbers of nonparty people at the mass level are brought to participate in and to become psychologically committed to the Communist administration. Behind this difference, of course, lies the truth that the Kuomintang military dictatorship was always controlled by a small have-got minority seeking to protect private ownership privileges against equalization with the have-nots—whereas the Communist dictatorship has organized its bases among the have-not peasants and working people and deeply *involved* them in the revolutionary economic, social, political and administrative tasks of building a socialist society.

Whether one happens to regard socialist aims as a good thing or a bad thing, this mass involvement remains an objective fact and something new in China. The peasant may have nothing to say about the choice of the Chairman of the Republic, but he participates in the choice of local administrations; by that action he commits himself to the whole process of power delegated by proxies to the higher administration.

Mao Tse-tung's theory and deep conviction—tracing back to the united-front days when even landlords' views were heard in "the new democracy"—is that his government does not merely represent the majority; it "unifies the whole people." And membership in "the whole people" is denied only to open enemies of socialism—the "counter-revolutionaries," the truly irreconcilable "antagonists."

The Chinese constitution is designed to involve not only all the have-nots; it also seeks to reconcile and positively involve the "re-

formed elements" of the former owning classes—capitalists, intellectuals and other middle-class people "tainted" by bourgeois mentality.

The eight small "bourgeois-democratic" parties which still exist in
China supposedly speak for such minorities—but they do so under the
guidance of the united-front department of the Communist party! In
civil war days these parties sided with Mao Tse-tung against Chiang
Kai-shek and later helped form the first "coalition" government. Today
the party could easily snuff them out but sees a real necessity for
their preservation as long as "remnants" of bourgeois thinking survive.
The most important of them are the Revolutionary Kuomintang Committee, which includes many former Nationalist generals and officials,
and the Democratic League. Some of their leaders hold cabinet posts.
With representatives of the six other splinter parties they are allowed
several hundred seats in the overwhelmingly Communist-dominated
National People's Congress. Many more sit separately in a People's
Political Consultative Conference, which has no power but holds sessions when summoned by the united-front department of the Communist party.

The role of Mme Sun Yat-sen (Soong Ching-ling) as second vice-
chairman of the government (Chu Teh is first vice-chairman) is of
moral and symbolic importance. Mme Sun was long a person of rank
in the Kuomintang and retained her seat in its Central Committee
throughout Chiang Kai-shek's era. As the widow of Sun Yat-sen her
presence in the People's Government places upon it, and upon Communist claims to represent a union with the *revolutionary* Kuomintang,
a certain stamp of validity, of descent from the First Republic led by
Dr. Sun. He is still honored in today's China as a national hero. To
understand Mme Sun's significance one only has to imagine the effect
on the prestige of Peking if she had gone over to Taiwan with her sister,
Mme Chiang Kai-shek, and the moral strength which her adherence
might have given to Chiang's own claims to be the true political heir
of Dr. Sun. Her lifelong championship of women's rights to equality
makes her a world figure as well as an Asian heroine.[5] For this reason
John Foster Dulles' refusal to permit Mrs. Eleanor Roosevelt to accept
Mme Sun's invitation to visit China as a guest of the women's organizations was an affront even to many anti-Communist Overseas Chinese.

The continued existence of the Kuomintang Revolutionary Committee and participation by its leaders in the National Congress and the
government provides a device that will be useful if there should ever
be a pro-Peking *coup d'état* on Taiwan. The Generalissimo himself has
been offered a post as a vice-chairman of the Peking government or
a governorship, I was told by General Ts'ai T'ing-k'ai, vice-chairman
of the Kuomintang Revolutionary Committee. A generation ago General Ts'ai was a true national hero when he and his Nineteenth Route
Army defended Shanghai against the first Japanese attack. He still enjoys high prestige among Overseas Chinese. Ts'ai said he had "never

been so happy" as since his return to Peking in 1949. "There is only one way for the Generalissimo to wipe out his national disgrace and rehabilitate himself," according to Ts'ai, "and that is to restore Taiwan to China peacefully and join the People's Government." Incidentally, General Ts'ai was the only Chinese military man I heard maintain that because of her numbers China need not fear atomic bombs. I also remember hearing him give "numbers" as a reason, during the Shanghai war thirty years ago, why Japan could never conquer China. He is over seventy now and still going strong, but Japan has left; perhaps he was right.

(General Ts'ai maintained indirect contacts with Kuomintang officials and generals on Taiwan, through the Communist leadership itself. The possibility of an agreement between Peking and the Generalissimo for peaceful unification could never be ruled out. It is hardly conceivable that such a concord would not have to precede or occur simultaneously with any restoration of United States relations with the mainland. Following the Sino-Soviet-American covenant concerning Laos, in 1961, this possibility became rather more of a probability, as it was apparent that neither Chiang nor Mao would agree to any "two-Chinas" solution or a permanent separation of Taiwan from the motherland. A discussion of this subject appears in the Appendix, pages 765-766.)

Nominally, the splinter parties also represent the non-Communists among the intellectuals carried over from the previous regime. "Intellectual" is loosely used in China to describe practically anyone who earns a living by brain work rather than manual labor. Mao Tse-tung in 1957 stated that "several million intellectuals who worked for the old society" had come over to socialism. Actually the highly qualified older intellectuals and scientists who studied abroad or in state or missionary-sponsored Chinese colleges number scarcely 100,000. Most of them have been exposed to anti-Marxist thought and most have close enough ties with the ex-owning classes to make difficult their entrance into the Communist party. Out of disgust with the Kuomintang, or sympathy with the Communists, or for patriotic or other reasons, about 90 percent[6] of China's intellectuals stayed on after the revolution.

While building up a new generation of university-trained cadres the Chinese Communists wooed these precious brain workers and made heavy use of their scientific or administrative skills and talents. Today some of the ablest are nearing retirement age. By 1958 some 431,000 Communist-indoctrinated college students had been graduated from institutes of higher learning, and the figure is nearing 700,000 now. But the older intellectuals are still needed for their experience, especially in scientific research and teaching.

No one knew how far the thinking of any of the "bourgeois-tainted elements" had been changed by years of ideological remolding efforts. Party control of communications provided little if any possibility for voices of dissent to be heard openly. Two years after the adoption of the constitution, its guarantees of work, sex equality, educational and welfare benefits and electoral machinery had been at least partly fulfilled, but a certain Article 87 bore no semblance of life whatsoever. Article 87 unequivocally guaranteed all "citizens" rights of "freedom of speech, press, assembly, association, procession and demonstration." Any Western-educated person had to regard this article as at worst a cynical fraud or at best a mere expression of distant aspiration.

Then, early in 1956, Communist leaders suddenly began to urge intellectuals and prominent nonparty Chinese to exercise these freedoms. Mao Tse-tung himself appeared before a Supreme State Conference of party and nonparty leaders and invited critics openly to express themselves in a campaign designed to rectify party mistakes. It was a bold experiment, without precedent in the history of any Communist country, and one that revealed, among other things, the extraordinary degree to which traditional and national concepts of correct relations between the rulers and the people have survived the invasion of Marxist thought and given to Chinese Communist ideology certain national characteristics found in no other Communist party.

44

The 800

What lies beneath the surface of the political soil in which dissenters were urged to cultivate the gardens of their private thoughts?

Mao and other top leaders often say that "nine-tenths of the people are with us, only 10 percent are opposed to us." During the brief open season for critics far less than 10 percent raised their voices in public protest. It was a minority more significant than its numbers but it did not necessarily prove or disprove whether the rest were for or against. What the experiment undoubtedly did prove was that no dictatorship, however "democratic" (or republican, for that matter), can safely permit even a minority to carry on prolonged debate about the basic contradiction of its physiology: the necessity to monopolize power and the demand for free and spontaneous unity.

If no more than 10 percent of the population of China were opposed to the "democratic dictatorship" that would be astonishing. By the Communists own reckoning 20 to 30 percent belonged to the "exploiting classes" and suffered material losses (or worse) in the upheaval. Ten percent or even 30 percent is a negligible opposition in most nations, but 10 percent of China exceeds the populations of Great Britain and Canada combined. Ten percent of China's *adult* population (eighteen and over) is a formidable figure—say 40,000,000.

How large a percentage of the people is actually made up of the ruling leadership and its dedicated followers? The size of the organized base of the pyramid would surprise people who suppose that the truth is just the opposite of Mao's statement and that in reality only 10 percent of the people support the regime. It is far more than that. But how much more?

A man very high in the party remarked to me in a moment of reminiscence: "There were 50,000 of us at the start of Chiang Kai-shek's counterrevolution in 1927. After the killings there were only 10,000 left. Today there are about 800 of us—survivors of all the years between. By and large the country is being run and for some years will be run by those 800."

That is as candid a definition as one could get of the meaning of "democratic centralism" and of the enormously important role played by the top hierarchy of the party in relation to its rank and file and the country at large. Decisions that matter are finally made by "those 800": near the summit, 180 members of the Central Committee (or about 500 in "enlarged session"); directly beneath them, the reserves of veterans ready to succeed them in the years ahead. At the very peak stands the chief Democratic Centralizer; forming the summit around him are the eighteen other members and six alternate members of the Politburo.

The Standing Committee of the Politburo consists of Mao Tse-tung, Liu Shao-ch'i, Chou En-lai, Chu Teh, Ch'en Yun and Marshal Lin Piao. Teng Hsiao-p'ing is also a member as Secretary-General of the Politburo. This Standing Committee controls the fate of more millions than any similar governing body in the world. With Chairman Liu Shao-ch'i clearly designated as Mao's "logical successor," Chou En-lai is obviously No. 3, although in public he defers to Marshal Chu Teh. The usual seating arrangement and order of photographs puts Marshal Lin Piao in fifth place but sometimes it is Ch'en Yun or Teng Hsiao-p'ing. They are all of about equal rank below the top level—except that Lin Piao is not there because of his political fluency or following but as the top leadership's current choice as the army's spokesman.

Liu Shao-ch'i took Teng Hsiao-p'ing with him as first deputy to the important Moscow conference in November, 1960, and some people drew conclusions from that. Eastern European gossip in Peking was that Chou En-lai did not go to the conference because he was even more hostile to Khrushchev's international line than Liu Shao-ch'i and Teng Hsiao-p'ing. Yet it was Chou who attended the October, 1961, congress of the Soviet party—where he walked out in protest against Khrushchev's surprise expulsion of the Albanian party from the comity of Communists—the Albanians being the only European group that had supported Peking's line of opposition to Khrushchev's alleged "soft" policy toward imperialism.*

* See pages 664-666.

Certainly both Liu Shao-ch'i and Chou En-lai are several steps above any conceivable rivals. Marshal Chu Teh is still a patriarchal figure of importance but is even older than Mao and for other reasons not a "logical successor." Lin Piao is in poor health and, as remarked, primarily a military man. (The party will never run the risk of being dominated by the army.*) Teng Hsiao-p'ing is badly crippled and both he and Chen Yun are much junior to the others. Younger men such as P'eng Chen and Ch'en Yi, just below the top seven, are of growing importance.

"Consult others first," "don't gossip behind comrades' backs," "exchange information," and "don't call a meeting until preparations are completed," are among Mao's precepts of leadership. Years ago I was practically Mao's next-door neighbor for some weeks in Pao-an. Preceding any important Politburo meeting I used to see members visit Mao's cave, one by one at first, then two or three together, for discussions which lasted several hours. When Mao called a meeting he knew how to present a synthesis to include different points of view. The full meeting usually took less time than meetings between individuals.

Yet the Politburo has frequently been bitterly divided over domestic and foreign policy matters; deadlocks have been carried to the Central Committee to bridge differences. This is not a faceless rubber-stamp committee packed with yes-men, but is made up of strong personalities many of whom have commanded troops in battle and have at times held discretionary power over forces that could have destroyed or overthrown Mao. It is clear from party records that Mao has sometimes been defeated and has had to accept compromises. By keeping opposition inside the highest party organs rather than forcing it outside or underground Mao has been able to bridge most differences and maintain an outer front of unity.

At its highest level of leadership the party thus has an impressive record of unity. There has been no open split for twenty-five years, although there was a severe splintering. No member of the Politburo has a party history of less than thirty years, and this would apply to most members of the Central Committee as well. The spectrum covered by their common experience is narrow. Nearly all the higher echelon are men educated empirically by revolution and a closed system of thinking. Yet in a postrevolutionary crash construction period, united and positive action in support of a clear-cut program has a better chance of success, even if some of its assumptions are wrong or oversimplified, than the vacillation, delay and disunity which failed in China again and again.

Disagreements on tactics and personality rivalries obviously exist. The "severe splintering" in 1954 involved a dozen men in very high positions. Kao Kang, a Politburo member and former chief of the

* See pages 636-638.

regional government of Manchuria, was chairman of the State Planning Commission. His vice-chairman, Jao Shu-shih, former head of the East China regional government, was also head of the powerful party Organization Bureau. These two were the only members of the Central Committee expelled (Kao Kang committed suicide), but five governors and several former regional chiefs were also dropped from the party.

It is a curious and as yet unexplained fact that Mao Tse-tung took no public part in the entire attack on the "Kao-Jao clique." Except as he was a member of the Central Committee which expelled them in March, 1955, there is no record that Mao personally pushed the campaign. Even in his important speech on cooperatives four months later, when Mao referred at length to an antiparty situation in Manchuria, for which Kao supposedly was to blame, he did not mention Kao's name. Liu Shao-ch'i initiated the whole attack, led the purge, and himself took over the supervisory committee which replaced Jao's Organization Bureau.

Kao was formally charged with warlord ambitions in Manchuria and foreign reports suggested that he had Stalin's backing in an attempt to displace Mao. No doubt Soviet relations were involved but the intraparty struggle went much deeper than that. It seems unlikely that either Kao or Jao—whose following among lower cadres extended all over North China—had any ambitions to overthrow Mao. Competition with Liu Shao-ch'i for control of the younger party cadres could well have existed without implying disloyalty to Mao, and a certain balance of power among the three men might not have been entirely undesirable for him. In any case it was Liu who benefited. He clearly emerged as No. 2 in the Politburo and in effective supervisory control of party organization.

Does Mao initiate all major policy decisions and domestic programs and decide the manner in which they are carried out by the cadres? These are questions not so easily answered. Although the "Mao cult" has grown enormously since 1949 there are indications that he has not held, and may not even have wanted, the role of absolute power often attributed to him.

During the war Mao was supreme commander in chief and sometimes made critical decisions alone. In September, 1948 (eight years before Mr. K.'s "collective leadership" speech), when it became apparent that national power was within grasp, the Central Committee passed a resolution, *under Mao's chairmanship,* which declared:

The Party-committee system is an important Party institution for ensuring *collective leadership and preventing exclusive control by any individual.* It has recently been found that the practice of exclusive control . . . by individuals prevails in some leading bodies . . . This state of affairs must be changed. Hereafter . . . all important matters must be submitted to the committee and fully discussed by the members present.[1]

Six months later another Central Committee meeting, "at the suggestion of Comrade Mao Tse-tung," made the decision prohibiting birthday celebrations for party leaders and the use of party leaders' names to designate places, streets and enterprises. Speaking in 1956, Teng Hsiao-p'ing recalled that this decision had "a wholesome effect in checking the glorification and exaltation of individuals."

It had "become a long-established tradition in our Party to make decisions on important questions by a collective body of the Party and not by any individual." Violations had been "frequent" but "when discovered" had been "criticized and rectified." History is "made by the people," not by individuals, but Teng went on to say, in the only official explanation ever offered for the glorification of Mao:

> Marxism never denies the role that individuals play in history; Marxism only points out that the individual role is, in the final analysis, dependent on given social conditions . . . Undoubtedly their authority, their influence and their experience are *valuable assets to the Party,* the class and the people . . . Such leaders emerge naturally . . . and cannot be self-appointed . . . Precisely because of this they must set an example in maintaining close contact with the masses, in obeying Party organizations and observing Party discipline. Love for the leader is essentially an expression of love *for the interests of the Party,* the class, and the people, and not the deification of an individual . . . Of course the cult of the individual is a social phenomenon with a long history, and it cannot but find certain reflections in our Party and public life. It is our task to continue to observe faithfully the Central Committee's principle of opposition to the elevation and glorification of the individual . . .[2]

If the contradictions in that speech clearly showed that the tendency of one-man rule was ever present and had more than once been curbed by Mao's colleagues, it also revealed not only that Mao himself recognized the danger and had concurred in its "rectification" but that the party had a vested interest in Mao as an Institution. Promotion of the cult of leadership is by inference acknowledged to be inherent in the system of "democratic centralism" itself. Since then the cult has grown rather than diminished. Today, during the current double crisis of China's relations with Russia and internal economic problems, Mao's infallibility has been invoked by the party as never before.

I can affirm that Mao Tse-tung was recently asked, in a direct question, what lessons he personally drew from Khrushchev's speech denouncing the cult of Stalinism. Mao's reply was that two articles in the *People's Daily* exactly expressed his impressions. The articles were entitled "The Historical Experience of the Proletariat," "based on" discussions at enlarged meetings of the Politburo held in April and December, 1956.[3] Since Mao often writes for the official party paper, it may reasonably be surmised that the following excerpts reflect his own thoughts on the problem of the cult of personality:

> Marxist-Leninists hold that leaders play a big role in history . . . But when any leader of the Party or the state places himself over and above the Party and the masses instead of in their midst . . . he ceases to have an all-round, penetrating insight into the affairs of the state. . . . Leaders of Communist Parties and socialist states are duty-bound . . . to be most prudent and modest, to keep close to the masses, consult them on all matters . . . and constantly engage in criticism and self-criticism. . . . It was precisely because of his failure to do this that Stalin made certain serious mistakes . . . became conceited and imprudent . . . made erroneous decisions on certain important questions . . . exaggerated his own role and counterposed his individual authority to the collective leadership . . . accepted and fostered the cult of the individual and indulged in arbitrary actions . . . took more and more pleasure in this cult of the individual, and violated the Party's system of democratic centralism . . . failed to pay proper attention to the further development of agriculture and the material welfare of the peasantry . . . made a wrong decision on the question of Yugoslavia . . . showed a tendency toward "great nation chauvinism" . . . even intervened mistakenly, with many grave consequences, in the internal affairs of certain brother countries and parties. . . .

In all this criticism there was implicit and explicit recognition of the same dangers arising in China. "The cult of personality is a foul carry-over from the long history of mankind [and] . . . even after a socialist society has been founded, certain rotten, poisonous ideological survivals may still remain in people's minds for a very long time. . . . We must therefore give unremitting attention to opposing elevation of oneself, individual heroism, and the cult of the individual." How was this to be done? By firmly adhering to the "mass line" on the question of leadership, as defined in a Central Committee resolution recalled from 1943:

> . . . Correct leadership can only be developed on the principle, "from the masses to the masses." This means summing up (coordinating and systematizing after careful study), then taking the

resulting ideas back to the masses, explaining and popularizing
them until the masses embrace them as their own, stand up for
them and translate them into action by way of testing their correctness. Then it is necessary once more to sum up the views
of the masses . . . and so on over and over again.

Despite these grave criticisms the articles assessed Stalin's career as
"nevertheless the life of a great Marxist-Leninist revolutionary." If a
person's "achievements amount to 70 percent of the whole," according
to Mao, "and his shortcomings to only 30 percent, then his work
should be in the main approved." Is that the margin by which Mao
wishes to be judged? Probably. "There has never been a man in the
world completely free from mistakes." Stalin's crimes were not viewed
as inherent in any contradictions of "democratic centralism" itself, but
as the failure of the party properly to apply the "mass line."

What I have already noted as an irreconcilability between the
necessity to monopolize state power and the search for spontaneous
unity or mass approval is of course not a phenomenon confined to
Communist countries but applies everywhere in varying degrees. In
America it is resolved by the use of law and the force behind it in
instances of "clear and present danger" to the existing state superstructure—for example, by the effective denial of freedom of speech
and organization to the Communist party—whereas in Spain it involves the physical suppression of all discontent, in France it is overcome by mass approval for the emasculation of the legislative assembly in favor of rule by one-man administrative decree, etc. The
problem was already old when the most democratic republic of
antiquity consisted of 20,000 free men of Athens who ruled over some
330,000 slaves. How Mao Tse-tung and the Chinese Politburo seek to
resolve it by means of the "mass line" will shortly be examined in
detail.

Meanwhile, despite all the self-criticism implied in the foregoing
reflections, it should be emphasized that no intelligent person in China
imagines that Mao Tse-tung has not used the cult of his own personality to impose his will inside the party. That would require a
non-ego or a Taoist recluse seeking oblivion; even Mahatma Gandhi
repeatedly used his own mass cult to overrule his colleagues. That
there is a governor at work inside Mao, however, which has thus far
saved him from megalomania and enabled him to maintain an equilibrium between personal dictatorship and group leadership is also evident. He may not be swayed as often by colleagues as Mr. Kennedy,
but he obviously spends much more time listening to them than General de Gaulle wastes on the French assembly. The clearest expression
of Mao's awareness of his own vulnerability and replaceability was the
party's choice of a successor during Mao's lifetime.

Until Liu Shao-ch'i was nominated Chairman of the Republic in

Combination afforestation and erosion-prevention work in the Northwest.
(*N.C.P.*)

Many parks now converted into vegetable gardens still keep a corner for children's jungle gyms.

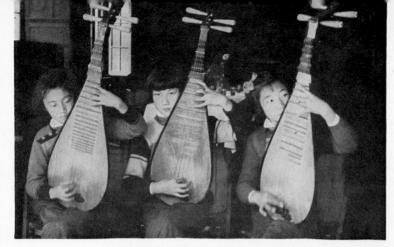

P'i-p'a players, Shanghai Conservatory.

Peking rugs are now mass produced, chiefly for export. Finishing room.

Magazine and book store, Kunming.

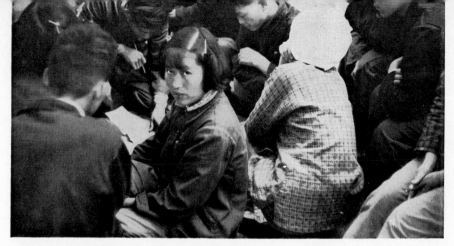

Common scene: Workers and student workers confer on factory schedule and production plan. Chengchow textile machinery plant.

Housewife inventor in a cable factory in Shenyang, Manchuria, operating drill she converted into bobbin riveter.

Part of the Loyang Tractor Plant.

At the tank school, Hopei province; with Yao Wei.

Here the Yellow River has turned blue.

Section of the San Men Hsia Dam, now completed.

Spittoon-cleaning time. Street sanitation worker in Shanghai.

Dr. Ma Hai-teh (George Hatem), center; "Little Pony," left; Chou Ssu-fei (Mrs. Ma), right.

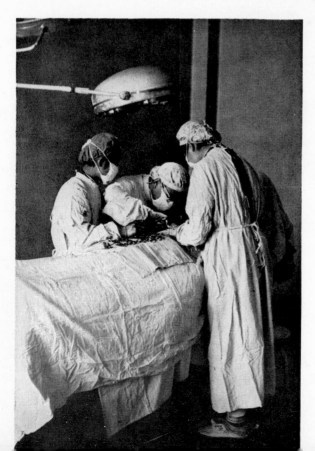

Women surgeons operating on a cancer of the esophagus, T'ung Chi Hospital, Hankow.

Liu Shao-ch'i, Chairman of the People's Government of the Chinese People's Republic (left); Mao Tse-tung, Chairman of the C.C.P.; historian. October, 1960. At this time Mao was reported abroad to be dying. (*N.C.P.*)

Silhouette at Miyun Dam: Premier Chou En-lai and Madame Chou (Teng Ying-ch'ao), chairman of the Women's Democratic League.

Mao Tse-tung at the end of the Long March, Pao-an, 1936. At this time Mao was reported abroad to be dying.

Youthful tourists at Pa Ta Chu, where the Sleeping Buddha lies. Western Hills, Peking.

Pedibus, for kindergarten and first-graders, takes priority over all traffic.

Part of the medical staff at the large new T'ung Chi Hospital, Hankow.

Chiang Chu-hsing, "Small Lightning" (left), with one of her five roommates at the Iron and Steel Institute, Peking.

Close-up of an Engineer.

A Saturday dance.

Small Lightning showers before an afternoon plunge into the college pool, which she helped to build.

The institute's own steel plant: our heroine doing the testing.

1959 many foreign observers believed Chou En-lai was the heir apparent. That Mao also permitted it to be made known that Liu was his successor to lead the *party* was even more significant. No man suffering from Stalin's paranoia could have made such a gesture of confidence in his closest colleagues. One reason for it obviously is that he has not established a habit of having them executed or stuck in the head with ice picks. All members of the Standing Committee have worked intimately with Mao for most of their adult lives. Yet Chou En-lai was once his senior in the Politburo and in opposition to him. Liu Shao-ch'i also worked briefly with Li Li-san, when Li had Mao expelled from the Politburo. Since such events of three decades ago all these men have endured great tests together and have a common memory of hazards shared during the Long March which is a bond as close as ideological ties.

Liu Shao-ch'i is the only leader besides Mao who has in effect already managed a Politburo—actually, a "branch Politburo." In the last war with Chiang Kai-shek, Liu was chairman of a group of Politburo members, including Chu Teh, who were sent from Yenan to take charge of party affairs in the Central Plains and Manchuria. Earlier, Liu had been party chief over most of the guerrilla areas during the anti-Japanese war. He built up the machine in a vast territory stretching from the Yangtze Valley to Manchuria and from the China Sea to the Yellow River while party membership increased from 40,000 in 1937, to 5,800,000 by 1950. The great majority of these "new" members—today already veterans—were trained and won promotion under Liu Shao-ch'i's chieftainship of the northern and central China bureaus. During the same period Chou En-lai headed the West and South China bureaus. Underground recruitment inside Kuomintang territories was much more difficult than behind the Japanese lines where Liu operated; consequently Chou's following among new recruits was much smaller than Liu's.

In former years I wrote biographical accounts of Chou En-lai, Lin Piao, Chu Teh, P'eng Teh-huai and other members of the Politburo based on interviews with them, and this data was later expanded, largely by Nym Wales and Agnes Smedley.[4] I need not here repeat or paraphrase these stories (a task to which others have helped themselves) but something may be added concerning Chairman Liu Shaoch'i, who is less well known abroad. I did not meet Liu until 1960, having missed him during my first visit to the Northwest; he did not rendezvous with other veterans of the Long March there until late in 1936. Yet it was (I only recently learned) Liu Shao-ch'i who authorized the "invisible ink letter" of introduction which I carried to Pao-an, although it reached me by the hand of Hsu Pin, then a professor at Northeastern University, in Peking. At that time Liu was head of the party's North China bureau and was living deep in the political underground.

Liu Shao-ch'i was born only a short distance from Mao's home, in 1898, in Ninghsiang county, Hunan. His father was a primary school teacher. Liu attended Hunan Normal School (where he enrolled after Mao had left) and joined the Young People's Study Society. He and Mao did not meet, however, until shortly after the party was formed, in Shanghai, in 1921. Five years younger than Mao and a year older than Chou En-lai, he is thin, wiry, gray-haired, with a rather sharp face, and is slightly shorter than Mao. Like Mao, Liu was a rebel against parental control; he was first married by a family arrangement which he refused to recognize. His second marriage was dissolved in divorce. He is now married to an attractive Peking college graduate.

Like Mao again, Liu came from a rich peasant family. Too young to participate in the 1911 revolution, he was by 1914 a radical student; in 1920 he joined the Socialist Youth League, a precursor of the Communist party. After entering the party the next year he was assigned to the secretariat of the China Labor Federation and began his career as a labor specialist.[5] In 1922 Comintern representatives in Shanghai sent Liu to Moscow, where he studied for more than two years. Back in Shanghai, he worked closely with Chou En-lai during the organization of the revolutionary trade unions, until their suppression in 1927. There was a brief return to Moscow; then, back in China, Liu led the underground labor movement while the party was headed by Comintern-trained Li Li-san. Following Stalin's directives, Li attempted urban insurrections, which were disastrous, and Liu is said to have opposed Li's line. Since he is a fellow Hunanese with much the same background as Mao, it seems likely that he may have sympathized with Mao in favor of rural soviets based on peasant support —as the party states today. (Some of the Hunanese miners Liu helped organize were recruits to Mao's first peasants and workers army.) But Liu did not openly join Mao until 1932. In that year he entered Kiangsi Soviet with Chou En-lai, Po Ku, Lo Fu, and other members of the Politburo, to which Liu Shao-ch'i was elected for the first time. In Kiangsi he became head of the trade union federation (consisting mostly of rural workers, the "semiproletariat") and was closely associated with Mao Tse-tung. Thereafter he remained steadfast in his support of Mao and backed his rise to supreme leadership at the Tsun-yi conference in 1935.

Liu began the Long March but en route was sent to contact the guerrilla forces north of the Yangtze River and to head the party underground in North China. He was partly responsible for preparing the way for Mao's arrival in Shensi. In 1935 he ousted the anti-Mao factions in northern China and from then on headed the party's underground in Peking and Tientsin. He again joined Mao, in Yenan, and sided with him in the expulsion of Chang Kuo-t'ao from the Politburo in 1937. From this time on Liu's position as urban spokesman and chief of the North China organization in the "white" areas steadily improved. After the Japanese invasion he took charge of party affairs in enemy-occupied areas. In 1943 he was elevated to the seven-man secretariat, or inner Politburo, where he replaced Wang Ming. Throughout the war with Japan and the subsequent civil war, he was the Politburo chief (or first commissar) among all the Communist forces in eastern and northeastern China.

Relatively little known to the Chinese public until he was chosen vice-chairman of the provisional government in 1949, Liu became a figure of international importance in communism when he was elected chairman of the Reds' world trade union federation. Since then he has been quietly revealed in humanizing stories, anecdotes, and reminiscences by comrades, all well placed in the press. Primary school textbooks now contain many heroic tales about Liu; to some extent the same is true of Chou En-lai, Chu Teh, Lin Piao and lesser figures around Mao. Since 1958 a planned effort has been apparent to prepare people for eventual acceptance of Liu as a party chieftain. Even now such a transition might not greatly affect the administrative apparatus, since many governors, important mayors, ministers, and probably a majority of the Central Committee could be termed "Liu's men"—although their primary loyalty remains of course to Mao Tse-tung.

Liu has the reputation of being a severe disciplinarian and taskmaster but is said to give generous support to his subordinates. Although scorning the term "idealist," he would yet "reform mankind into the completely selfless citizenry of a Communist society." Belief in hard work as the proper therapy for everything from juvenile delinquency to "contradictions among the people" is no less firmly held by Liu than by Mao Tse-tung.

The Western press has depicted Liu as a fanatic. As distinguished from whom? In one period Liu's subordinates were criticized for "ultra-leftism" [6] but his writings show no significant deviations from Maoism. He seems to have called the pace before anyone else for the demoniacal speed-up of the Great Leap Forward. He is on the record far more explicitly than Mao in support of the communes *as a short-cut to communism* as well as in defense of the precipitate haste of their launching. In both instances he may have been fronting for Mao—although there are reasons to doubt that.* Liu is the only man besides Mao whose doctrinal works, such as *On Inner Party Struggle* and *How to Be a Good Communist*,[7] are now basic catechismic texts.

Less frequently quoted is Liu's *Internationalism and Nationalism*,[8] written in 1948, which is a straight orthodox Marxist statement of the distinction between bourgeois nationalism and international proletarianism. Bourgeois nationalists "do not hesitate to pursue a policy

* See Chapter 56, At Whose Demand?

of aggression against other nations," which leads to imperialist war. "The proletarian international concept is diametrically opposite . . . fights not only against the oppression of its own nation by any other nation but also against its own nation oppressing any other. . . . No nation which oppresses others can be free." Liu's work then defined Titoists as "bourgeois nationalists"; they "rely on imperialist aid," they "adopt a policy of national seclusion and chauvinism," they "harbor distrust and unfriendliness toward the Soviet Union"; they thereby "betray the basic principles of proletarian internationalism."

By 1962 Poland was also accepting "imperialist aid" and Khrushchev was sending complimentary tanks to Belgrade, while China was accused by some comrades of "seclusion," and of "distrust" of Moscow. Liu would not use quite the same words today, but others, in a speech he made a year later, are still highly pertinent. They contain much of the living essence of Sino-Russian ideological disputes in a nuclear-oppressed world trembling under a precarious balance of terror. Speaking before a conference of Australasian trade unions called in Peking, in 1949, Liu Shao-ch'i had provided a kind of "export formula" that embodied what the Chinese see as the lessons of their own revolution most applicable to colonial and ex-colonial countries. Its four points can be summarized as follows:

1. The working class must join all other classes in a nation-wide "united front against imperialism and its lackeys."
2. The united front must be organized by the working class under its own party, the Communist party, and not by wavering nationalistic elements in the bourgeoisie.
3. Long struggles are necessary to build up and educate a Communist party capable of correct leadership for such a revolution. For this purpose
4. It is necessary to set up a Communist-led army. Mass struggles may be conducted by other means but "armed struggle is the main form of struggle for national liberation in many colonies and semi-colonies . . . This is the basic way of Mao Tse-tung which may also be the basic way . . . where similar conditions prevail." [9]

That remains a key to Liu's thinking to this day but it is also a key to the rest of Politburo thought. All Chinese foreign policy, however it veers or tacks, has been aimed at facilitating use of this strategy in the underdeveloped countries, which Mao Tse-tung has long seen as decisive in changing the world balance of power. It was one nexus of Mao's quarrel with Khrushchev that in these areas Mr. K. followed policies which *divided* the united front against imperialism.

If Mao won his position largely as a peasant leader, Liu Shao-ch'i's support derives more particularly from his knowledge and control of workers' organizations and urban China. If China is moving rapidly from a predominantly peasant economy to an industrial economy it may be logical that Liu should be Mao's successor, rather than Chou. Aside from Liu's strong personal following in the party Chou has a great handicap in being a gentleman born, the grandson of a mandarin—having what he himself sometimes self-consciously refers to as a "feudal background"—and having been a prewar bourgeois college student. It would of course be foolish to assume that because of any of this or Chou's natural urbanity he would be any more accommodating in dealing with "imperialism" than Liu or Mao. More likely he would tend to compensate for his bourgeois heritage with even greater severity.

Foreign diplomats who have spoken with Liu Shao-ch'i consider him a first-rate politician—shrewd, practical, clear-thinking, unemotional and exceptionally able in the quick analysis of complicated problems in simple language clear to all. For example, the Indian Ambassador, Shri G. Parthasarathy, told me: "Liu Shao-ch'i at first gives a superficial impression of mediocrity. Five minutes of conversation reveals a man with an extremely logical mind capable of quickly penetrating to the heart of a question and organizing his answers simply yet with great force and thoroughness."

China's leaders are accused of ignorance of the outside world, but eleven Politburo members traveled or studied abroad before the revolution. Although none of the "top seven" has ever seen America except in movies, Premier Chou En-lai knows English and Foreign Minister Ch'en Yi studied in France. (Has the United States ever appointed a Chinese-speaking Secretary of State?)

"The 800" leading old Bolsheviks are men (and a few women) now in their late fifties or past sixty. Second and third waves of party leadership consist of the younger survivors of the Long March (not over 10,000) and veterans of both the war against Japan and the "liberation war"—about one million. It is these men, now in their forties, who hold jobs of top responsibility everywhere in the state and production. They rely for immediate assistance on the youngest generation of "combat Communists"—veterans only of the last civil war and the Korean War, mostly now in their late twenties or early thirties—who number four to five millions.

Anyone who has outgrown childhood myths knows that in final analysis nearly every land is ruled by a very few. During the Roosevelt era a popular book called *America's Sixty Families*, by Ferdinand Lundberg, purported to show that the decisive policy-making, legislative and police power in the United States was controlled by fewer than a thousand men who held the reins over more than 90 percent of the nation's productive assets. That may be an exaggeration. More recently a deeper analysis of the techniques of control in a plutocracy was contributed by C. Wright Mills in his *The Power Elite*. In China "the 800" have greater power over management and profits than the combined interlocking directorates of all American corporations. Yet there also stability ultimately rests on organized mass support. Of what does it consist?

45

The Party and the People

"Our party," said Chairman Liu Shao-ch'i on June 30, 1961, "now has more than 17,000,000 members. Eighty percent of them have joined the Party since the founding of the People's Republic of China and 70 percent have joined since 1953. They are the Party's newest blood but lack experience and many of them have not yet had a systematic Marxist-Leninist education." [1] This high percentage of youthful members also underlines the necessity for "democratic centralism" in maintaining senior leadership.

If Chairman Liu's figure did not include party "alternates" the total party members and candidates might exceed 20,000,000. But in October, 1960, Premier Chou En-lai furnished me some data on current membership which included a figure markedly below 17,000,000.* An extremely intensive membership drive must have been

---

* These data were supplied to me at the Premier's request by Mme Kung P'eng, chief of the government information department, who put the October, 1960, party membership at "not over 13,000,000." Her figure would indicate a drop of one million since 1959, when party membership was reported at 13,960,000 (*People's Daily*, Sept. 28, 1959). Asked for an explanation when she was attending the conference on Laos in Geneva, one year later, Mme Kung P'eng replied that the figure given to me in Peking was up to date but had not included "candidate" or "alternate" members, "many of whom were admitted to full party membership during the past year." Possibly the 1959 figure had included both members and alternates.

quietly going on during subsequent months. I was at that time also informed that there were "more than 25,000,000 Young Communists" (aged fourteen to twenty-five) and "more than 50,000,000 Red Pioneers" (nine to fourteen). According to the same source, Communists of "intellectual" background (defined as "teachers, students, engineers, technicians and professional people") had increased from about 5 percent since 1956 to about 15 percent in 1960. Working-class membership was also 15 percent and "minority nationalities" accounted for 4 percent. Peasant membership still heavily predominated but had dropped from nearly 70 percent to 66 percent. All peasant members were listed as "educated" but "very few in a formal way." In all, less than 20 percent of party members had attended high school or college. With an inrush of younger members that percentage has doubtless risen. Changes in this respect seem to be following the same trend noticeable in Russia, where before the war party members with high school or college education were in the minority but today are a majority.

Party membership is not forced on anybody in China but is a highly selective process. A reading of Liu Shao-ch'i's *How to Be a Good Communist* shows that it demands discipline and ardor akin to that of a religious order. Nevertheless, recent pressure on intellectuals, particularly among students in state institutions of higher learning, probably accounts for the sharp rise (to an indicated 2,550,000) in their membership. The increase is also notable in view of the party's continuing campaign against "rightism"; among intellectuals, nonmembers are obviously being increasingly isolated. If it is also true (as I was told on what ought to be good authority) that as many as a million party members were dropped or put on probation during the 1957-58 rectification campaign, subsequent increased membership combined with a higher educational level may be reflected in a gradual growth of maturity and sophistication in the party personality as a whole.

If the "Establishment's" support were limited to party members these figures would not be numerically impressive, but the extent of its organic control goes much beyond that. No one knows the exact size of population today; expert foreign demographers who spend most of their time analyzing available data are as far apart as 50,-000,000.[2] For reasons stated earlier, 700,000,000 is as good as any until there is another national census. Allowing a plus or minus margin of 10 percent, it may be crudely estimated that about 4 in 100 Chinese adults over the age of eighteen are now party members. But about 7 in 100 between eighteen and forty are party mem-

If Liu Shao-ch'i's "17,000,000" included only full party members then it might be surmised that an additional three to four million "alternates" had since been recruited. It is just as possible that Liu's figure included both alternates and full members.

bers, and about 14 in 100 in the fourteen-to-forty age group are either party members or Young Communists. If combined Communist, Young Communist and Red Pioneer membership now amounts to 90,000,000 to 100,000,000, that is probably more than 20 in 100 of the ten-to-forty age group.*

Any estimate of basic Communist strength would also have to consider 21,000,000 members of the industrial trade unions,† 3,000,000 to 4,000,000 in the armed forces and public security units, and in excess of 25,000,000 in the armed militia and reserves. Allowing as much as 20 percent for overlapping party membership, those organizations might augment the ranks of the "dependables" by about 40,000,-000. One must also include another 19,000,000 persons in the nonindustrial trade unions and remember the support of activists among the scores of millions of members of the All-China Federation of Democratic Women, and of secondary party aspirants, or dependents of party members. Those under direct *organic* response to the Communist hierarchy in all ways would amount to more than half the "effective" population of the country. Beyond that it would be sheer guesswork to estimate how many people who have no particular emotional commitment to "build socialism," and may strongly resent hardships imposed on them, would still prefer the Communists to the old regime. One thing that may be stated without fear of contradiction by anyone who has been in China recently is that not one adult in ten would cast a vote in an absolutely free election for the return of the United States congressional candidate for Chairman, Chiang Kai-shek.

China used to be a country ruled by venerable gentry; now it is a land where youths in their twenties have greater authority and responsibility than anywhere in the world. Many Chinese youths of twenty are now better trained than their fathers and can produce and earn more. The condition of "youth in command" is as universal as "politics in command." Average life expectancy in China is believed to be still under forty,‡ and population distribution is heavily weighted on the side of youth; 41 percent of all Chinese are under the age of seventeen. *In this group, memory of a pre-Communist period is already dim or nonexistent.*

Men who at forty-five are still outside the party and have no technical qualifications obviously do not have much influence. No longer a landowner and nowadays often having little more earning power than his wife, the older male has a much narrowed economic base for his

---

* These very rough estimates of my own are based on China's 1956 census data. There is a great deal of overlapping membership between the party and the two Communist youth organizations, with perhaps 10 percent of Red Pioneers concurrently in the Young Communists, and 10 percent of the latter in the party.
† According to figures given to me by the vice-chairman of the All-China Trade Union Federation, in an interview on October 26, 1960.
‡ But the last census showed 1,850,000 persons more than eighty years old, and 3,384 over a hundred. One was registered as born in 1798!

senior authority. In spite of the great efforts being made to reduce the intellectual gap between educated youths and older workers by the vast expansion in part-time educational facilities, this general perspective suggests that discontent among people over forty or forty-five is much higher than among younger people. Ex-landlords and former "rich" or "middle" peasants, men and women who ever knew any prosperity but now find themselves looking on the downgrade of life —with another decade or so of hard work ahead—have lost the patriarchal satisfactions of ancestor worship, without being able to look forward to living to see the fruitions of socialism. This would apply less to the many millions of formerly completely impoverished peasants. Retirement pensions or lighter work for the aged, medical care, recreation and entertainment facilities, rest homes and the "iron rice bowl"—filled at least to subsistence level—have done much to make growing old less frightening for the poor.

"Youth in command" in industry and science is probably inevitable in a country which had to start almost from scratch, but in agriculture there is often no substitute for experience. Learning Mao Tse-tung by rote cannot provide talent where it is lacking, or the imagination to "fit directives to local conditions" and "combine flexibility with firmness," as is constantly demanded of cadres. One of the party's problems in personnel management is the millions of primary and middle school graduates who don't qualify for higher education and must be reintegrated with the working class and the peasantry at the "basic level of production"—that is, hard labor. Even though entering the party does not relieve them of work at the bench or in the field, many of them seek to become cadres for prestige and an ultimate future as an office bureaucrat—a tendency which Teng Hsiao-p'ing deplored several years ago.[3]

Liu Shao-ch'i was not exaggerating his problem. Of the many contradictions among members these may be listed: between the growing number of scientists and engineers now in the party and the absence of adequate representation in its top echelons; between veterans and combat Communists and Johnny-come-latelies; between genuinely dedicated socialist patriots and opportunists seeking prestige and promotions; between men of natural managerial ability and born bureaucratic blockheads; between the party's demand for "initiative" and "flexibility" and the party's demand for strict obedience to "democratic centralism."

If 20 percent of the members attended high school that is well above the national average, but it means that 80 percent have gone no further than primary school, although younger members would average higher, and nearly all party members are required to "raise their cultural level" by attending spare-time "Red and Expert" schools. General directives issued in Peking are broken down into simpler lan-

guage for peasant cadres. Yet consider what a party secretary of provincial level had to bear in mind and *reconcile* in practice in 1960.

In 1960 we should further affirm agriculture as the foundation
and industry as the leading force in the national economy,
combine the *priority* development of heavy industry with the
rapid development of agriculture and correctly handle the relations between agriculture, light industry and heavy industry;
we should mobilize *without exception* the forces of the industrial, communications, commercial, cultural and educational
departments, to give vigorous support to *agricultural* production; we should go all out for mechanization and semi-mecha-
nization and automation of all trades and strive for higher
labor productivity; we should carry through policies of *simultaneous* employment of modern and indigenous methods and
simultaneous development of big, medium-sized and small enterprises; we should further consolidate and develop the rural
people's communes, take active steps to set up people's communes in the cities, organize in a comprehensive way the production and people's livelihood in both urban and rural commune areas and consolidate and develop community dining-
rooms; we should make vigorous efforts to *increase production*
and *practice economy,* mobilize the broad masses against *corruption, waste,* and *bureaucracy,* conscientiously *rectify the
style of work of the cadres* and raise the level of their political
understanding and the ideological consciousness of the masses.
In this way it will be possible for us to catch up with and out-
strip Britain in the output of major industrial productions in
less than ten years and to fulfill ahead of schedule the tasks set
in the National Program for Agricultural Development [1956-
1967].[4]

One should think so! At the same time, however, "all our economic
work is subordinate to politics" reads another directive. One must
"dare to think and dare to act." "With regard to the system of distributing goods for individual consumption, the Party and the Government carry out the principle 'to each according to his work' while at
the same time teaching the masses of the people to struggle for great
future objectives *without being particular about personal remunera-
tion."*

Criticism and self-criticism through large-scale airing of views
and opinions, big debates and putting up *dazibao* [posters in
large characters] are carried out in government and people's
organizations, in schools, enterprises and undertakings, as well

as in the people's communes for the self-education of the masses. This guarantees that every man can constantly keep up plenty of enthusiasm and drive, stoutly surmounting all difficulties and be boldly creative.[5]

It takes either a highly talented magician or a doggedly devoted and sincere cadre to combine those two sets of directives into the kind of local leadership to inspire "boldly creative" enthusiasm for the masses. In his dreary nineteenth-century novel *What Is to Be Done?*, Chernyshevsky drew a contrast between what he saw as the faceless Chinese and the Europeans who appeared to the Chinese all alike, hairy foreign devils, but who were in reality infinitely varied and sentient personalities. Today it is still true that European nationalities seem alike to the Chinese, while to most Europeans, Chinese are so many blue ants. The truth is, of course, that beneath the superficial sameness great differences of appearance and personality exist in China: the hot-tempered and the cool, the warm-hearted and the cold-hearted, the passive and the passionate, the taller, slower, more Mongoloid northerner and the smaller, enterprising, aboriginal-mixed southerner, the opportunist and the devoted, the weak and the strong, the mediocre and the gifted. All are represented in a party in which struggles of personality continue, as mutual criticism meetings constantly testify. While the party demands a "completely selfless" generation of youths willing to carry out the work of bureaucrats in a nonbureaucratic way, there are as many failures as among youths struggling in the bourgeois competitive world of business.

The leadership is constantly in danger of falling victim to cadres' misleading reports of success. Ninety-five percent of the party cadres work at the county level * or below, and at every stage there have been peasant cadres holding back or sabotaging on the right, as well as "overfulfilling" enthusiasts bearing too hard on the left. After land distribution many cadres were found to have become rich peasants, exploited hired labor "under the pretext of mutual aid," refused to join mutual aid or cooperative groups themselves, worked solely for personal gain, used their position to seize control of cooperatives and make money, and even engaged in usury. On the left, *kanpu* have ignored the principle of voluntary participation and mutual consent, forced peasants into cooperatives instead of "educating and persuading," and collectivized by "commandism" far beyond the party's intention.[6] Such problems are not confined to the lower level; the same tendencies have appeared among senior cadres. Rectifications ("You're fired," or "Improve, or you're fired") are therefore inevitable and frequent.

The ability to steer a middle course, to hold the sympathy of one's

* The "living allowance" (wage) of a party secretary at this level is 140 yuan monthly, or the equivalent of a doctor's wage.

fellow workers yet meet party quotas and demands, to balance persuasion with coercion and retain majority support, to be a good politician without ever being corrupt, to be thoughtful without ever being in opposition to the leadership or finding its directives unworkable—all this is not the kind of ability found every day or universally, especially among twelve million peasant-born cadres!

The party control committee spends much of its time in rectification work: evaluating and criticizing the performance of members, retraining some, and weeding out others. Yet there are always more waiting in line to join.

46

Security

The 24,000 communes, although now largely relieved of many of their former controls over production, are still the basic administrative units (townships) of rural China. Scarcely a person is not answerable to or dependent upon some subcommune authority in the countryside or its equivalent in the urban areas. China is now a living colossus none of whose organs, including the whole vast external surface or skin, can be touched without sending a message through the nervous system of the giant.

Under the Ministry of Public Security* there are police offices at every administrative level down to the village, but security does not depend solely or even primarily on professionals. Parallel to the police there are "people's security committees" led by cadres in every factory, production brigade, commune and government office. In the cities their function is performed by street committees and subcommittees. They maintain order, mediate disputes, and may even undertake local thought remolding of individuals. They help gather the census and keep a record of each family. Their offices are not secret but elective. They do humble chores such as checking on sanita-

---

* Its total force is 1,700,000, according to the Minister of Public Security. It also has available the citizens' militia force.

tion and street cleaning, family health, school attendance and equable rationing; they help straighten out domestic quarrels and distribute special rations or fuel to needy people. Like the police, they provide social services combined with social supervision.

"Basic level" public security personnel are required periodically to call mass meetings in order to hear complaints as to whether they are violating any of the "eight rules and ten points" of good police behavior. In February, 1961, during the traditional Spring Festival, public security departments and committees launched a "love the people month" to express their friendly sentiments and invite criticism. For example, in Shenyang, Manchuria, the center of 1960's disastrous floods, "more than 70,000 good deeds for the masses" were reportedly performed. Services over the country included distributing extra grain and vegetable rations, cleaning up rubbish and delivering vast quantities of manure to calamity-zone communes. Thus security personnel doubtless manage to combine good intelligence activity with good works. Like much Chinese Communist idiom that causes merriment abroad, "love the people month" illustrates both the intimacy of security links with the household and the party's basic assumptions as father and protector.

China has known close security systems in the past. During his visit to Cathay in the thirteenth century Marco Polo noted that every household had to display on its portals the tablets of identification of everyone resting there for the night. Chiang Kai-shek also revived the ancient *pao-chia* system whereby every 100 households were organized under a street chief held answerable for the political loyalty of each member. But probably no security organization in China's history has equaled the present one in efficiency.

It is extremely difficult for anyone to get lost in this country. Everybody and everything are accounted for. Why steal a car? It is impossible to drive it without papers and gas coupons. A stolen fur coat or a bicycle would at once be noted. How did the owner get it? A hoard of food, a sudden splurge of spending, or an unexplained absence from work or home, are soon known "on the street." People can travel freely from city to city but they can't stay long anywhere without a valid reason. The inn or hotel wants papers and explanations. A private guest is soon known to neighbors. A person looking for work must register with the labor pool. Where would a murderer hide? What would a bandit do with his loot? How would an embezzler invest or waste his money? How could an illicit affair long transpire in a communal flat without being observed? The party, its satellites, and the security committees, permeate all society.

Thieves and pickpockets were formerly as common in Chinese cities as in America today. Now, when I left money and valuable articles in various rooms I occupied, I never locked a door. My luggage may have been searched but I never missed anything. I discarded a fountain pen in a hotel room in Shanghai; it was handed to me a few days later in Hankow. Two or three times I forgot or misplaced pieces of equipment; invariably they were found and returned. Others I questioned had similar experiences. Back in rich and brain-free New York, I thought of this when I entered the third-floor loft of Douglas Gorsline, friend and artist; he had this notice tacked on the studio door:

> The hi-fi set and typewriter have already been stolen and only a worthless AM set remains. Please save yourselves time and save me the cost of another lock.

It had taken several men and much labor to break the stout lock and remove the heavy hi-fi console, which was carried off in broad daylight. My report will surprise no New Yorker, but many will find it less believable (yet it is a fact) that if such an incident occurred in China it would shock a whole street into immediate action.

Several years ago a clever and desperate man in Peking forged Premier Chou En-lai's name to a check on a state bank for a large sum of money, cashed it, and escaped. Full details were broadcast, including a careful description of the miscreant; the case was unique and attracted wide attention. Within forty-eight hours the unhappy man was turned in by his street committee, the money intact. Yet crimes still occur and only a minority of them, it is claimed, are of a political nature.

Nowhere today are people more regimented, more disciplined, and more quickly brought to order by other citizens in instances of public misbehavior. There is very little overt sign of armed force. I never saw armed truckloads of gendarmes or riot squads rushing through the streets. One does see small squads of citizen militia drilling but not making armed demonstrations of terror. Security troops are strategically garrisoned of course, but seldom in evidence. During parades crowds are held back by civilian monitors or Red Pioneers. Most of the uniformed police are traffic cops and the majority seem to be young girls in long braids. This is a well-patrolled society—from within. No policeman ever interfered with my taking pictures but twice I was firmly ordered to desist by housewives acting as voluntary street officers. This happened to me in Dairen, where I was told by the mayor that the regular police force numbered "no more than 600." (The population of the greater municipality was given as 3,600,-000.) He quickly added: "It is the duty of every Communist, Young Communist and Red Pioneer—indeed, of every good citizen—to maintain order and respect for the law."

The People's Republic publishes no comprehensive crime statistics. I asked Judge Wu Teh-fang, chairman of the association of politics and law, why it wasn't done. His reply was, "The figures are so low that they would not be believed abroad." There was Chou En-lai's statement several years ago that 830,000 "enemies of the people" had been "destroyed" during the war over land confiscation, mass trials of landlords, and the subsequent roundup of counterrevolutionaries which ended, as a "campaign," in 1954. (Incidentally, the term *hsiao-mieh*, usually translated as "destroyed," literally means "reduced," "dispersed" or "obliterated," but not necessarily physically liquidated.) This figure, according to the Chinese, was merely used as a basis for "fantastic distortions and exaggeration by our enemies."

No nation ever resorts to violent revolution unless the old order has exhausted all its means of orderly solutions. Class war is the most tragic of all wars. It can be justified only if, as with all emunctory processes, nature itself finds no alternative for survival. There was a bloody civil war and class war combined in China which took millions of lives on both sides* and the wounds are far from healed. Hundreds of thousands of ex-Kuomintang soldiers who allegedly turned bandit after the war were reported as "destroyed"; yet many of them were later sent to Korea. Since the early and party-led mass trials and executions of landlords, scores of thousands have been punished in varying degrees by "people's courts" during half a dozen campaigns against "counterrevolutionaries," "rightists" and private businessmen.

Eight hundred thirty thousand is far from a bagatelle in human life, but the figure, *if true,* is not large in proportion to the population— about 14 per million†—compared to the costs of other catastrophes, such as the American Civil War, the French Revolution, and the Russian Revolution, not to mention Hitler's Germany. Counterrevolutionaries are still being arrested. I was told by Judge Wu that they are executed only if their action has caused the death of a citizen. Notices of executions appear in the provincial newspapers—apparently *pour encourager les autres*—and Western correspondents keep a tally on them. In 1960 these executions varied from eight to twelve a month, mostly cases of allegedly well-paid assassins and saboteurs caught in Fukien or Kwangtung, across the strait from Taiwan.

There are two other types of capital crimes: 1) murder or assault with intent to kill motivated by class hatred, or violence of an especially cruel nature; and 2) rape, of a victim under the age of fourteen. In such cases the death penalty is now said to be suspended for

* In reply to an inquiry I made concerning the total casualties on *both* sides during the two civil wars in China, Rewi Alley, who was in China throughout the whole conflict, wrote to me from Peking on May 19, 1956: "I have myself estimated that the deaths through political executions, Kuomintang 'cleaning up' in Kiangsi, Fukien, etc. [1930-34, during five anti-Communist expeditions], in man-made famines [blockades] in Hunan, Honan, etc., in 'incidents' [armed clashes or 'border warfare' before the outbreak of renewed major civil war in 1948] and following the KMT-CP breaking of armistice negotiations, then in the general [civil war] struggle subsequently, all add up to something like fifty million from the break [counterrevolution] in 1927 up until 1949."
† On a population base of 600,000,000,

two years, during which the prisoner may repent and reform. At the end of that period his case is reviewed and he may receive a reduced sentence.

Certainly no one outside the Ministry of Public Security could effectively confirm or dispute whatever crime statistics the government might choose to release. Neither could I do so with the assertion made by Judge Wu that the total prison population of China is "well below a million." Without attempting to assess his figure I should say from what I was able to see or learn in conversation with other foreigners that statements made abroad of "twenty-five million" or "fifteen million" executed in China can only be guesswork of the highest subjectivity. When *Time* magazine used such figures a few years ago my own pursuit of documentation from the editors revealed that their cover story on the subject was based on a few speculative remarks by Henry Cabot Lodge, which he in turn traced to a personal estimate offered by an aging Kuomintang diplomat, Wellington Koo, who had not been in China for many years.[1]

Despite all I have said of the tightness of organized security, despite Wu Teh-fang's claims of a greatly reduced crime rate, and despite every appearance of a matchless tranquillity of public behavior which very few visitors ever see disturbed, it is obvious that repressive measures are still carried out on a national scale. The law provides for "reform through labor" institutions and they exist in every province and near every large city. These are both urban and rural and industrial and agricultural prisons. All inmates, both ordinary and political, are required by law to work. To say that it all adds up to "one vast slave labor camp" is another matter. There are many contradictory aspects of the term "forced labor" in China, as I shall suggest in the next chapter.

Wu Teh-fang was a delegate to the National Congress but also to the People's Political Consultative Conference, so I assume that he was a nonparty man. He had been mayor of Hankow until 1954 and was now on the Wuhan University faculty. He told me that there are three thousand Chinese lawyers, all of whom have teaching jobs and spend only a few days a year in court.

Three thousand lawyers for 700,000,000 people? Some explanation lies in the Chinese court system. At its apex stands the Supreme Court, made up of a president and associate justices all elected by the National Congress and its Standing Committee. Under it are local, special, appeals and provincial courts, with their presidents and associate judges elected by local congresses and councils. Any literate citizen may be elected. On the same levels there are the Supreme People's Procurator and local and regional procurators and their associates, chosen by similar means. The chief procurator is roughly the equivalent of an attorney general and local procurators act as district attorneys.

Chinese law follows the French code in that once a person is arrested he is presumed guilty until proved innocent. If the police find a case against a citizen, the procurator draws an indictment and holds an examination. The great majority of minor cases are decided at this level. If the crime is serious or the prisoner maintains innocence there is a court trial. The accused may select his own lawyer or ask the court to appoint one or call upon the services of a friend to defend him and summon witnesses. He pays his lawyer five yuan to draw up his brief and five yuan a day expenses. If the defendant cannot pay, the court bears the costs.

There is the right of one appeal—to the court of the next highest level. According to Mr. Wu, only about 5 percent of the verdicts are appealed and "not over 20 percent" are reversed. That is, once on trial the defendant's chance of acquittal is one in a hundred. Whenever a case is ready for trial it is heard at once and few trials last longer than a day or two. There is no backlog of cases and courts are recessed for days at a time because of no business. I was told this in every city I visited; Shanghai was the first place I managed to find a court in session and was able to hear a trial.

Three kinds of detention are provided for: imprisonment in a municipal jail; work on a state reform farm; and restricted freedom or work under surveillance. Prisoners up for less than three years or more than ten are put in standard jails; those serving between three and ten years are assigned to state reform farms or mobile labor teams based on them; those sentenced for less than a year usually get "work under surveillance." This third category is for first offenders and minor crimes. The transgressor returns to his usual abode and work, but he is accountable for his daily behavior and movements to his street security committee or a group of ten fellow workers.

Well over 90 percent of all Western courts spend their time hearing litigation over property ownership and types of cases which no longer appear in Chinese courts. Chinese individuals cannot sue the government against any kind of socialization of ownership authorized by law. Property disputes now usually involve petty theft. Theft of state property is more serious than theft of private property, and theft for resale is a graver offense than theft for personal use. Many crimes have ceased, according to Mr. Wu, simply because of the elimination of private estate ownership. I thought of this while I was marooned by floods in a small Manchurian town where I found in a hotel library two volumes of Sherlock Holmes stories. After reading them all I went back over the plots and confirmed an impression: without exception, every murder or *crime passionnel* solved by the master mind of Baker Street was directly or indirectly motivated by greed or covetousness.

Whether a society can long exist without the motivation of material aggrandizement (under control) remains an unknown of the Communist future, and I don't wish to draw any scientific conclusions from Conan Doyle. But the effective denial to the would-be criminal of any market for his plunder (or at least any market commensurate with the risks involved) is one reason why gangsters and racketeers have virtually disappeared in China. Even more important as a deterrent is the knowledge that no amount of wealth or expensive legal talent can influence the courts. There is also very little crime reporting; this has its bad features (publicity, of course, is one way to awaken citizens to the need for vigilance in enforcement of the law and justice) but it eliminates the commercialization of crime publicity and its appeal to notoriety seekers and potential criminals.

Yet it is obvious that the judiciary in China is subject to the same "democratic centralist" principle of party magistry as the legislative and executive authorities. Mme Shih Liang, the Minister of Justice, has said that "as the People's Tribunals are one of the weapons of the democratic dictatorship of the people, we could not take up and use, unaltered, the reactionary institutions of the old-time courts, but were obliged to destroy them completely." Party members are no exception to the law, however; if arrested they are suspended and if convicted they are expelled. For all criminals incarceration is the beginning of a long period of "education or re-education in the morals and purposes of socialist society." It is not enough that the sentence be served. The prisoner's jailer-teachers have failed unless he emerges a completely reformed man able "to distinguish between right and wrong" and ready to restart life with "the desire for unity." Is not this doctrine right out of old Calvinism—the supralapsarian conviction that Destiny (History) ordained the fall of man in order to create the opportunity for his redemption?

But the concept of law as an instrument of reform, education and ethical indoctrination is not wholly alien to traditional patterns of Chinese thought. Confucians generally believed that those who understood the difference between good and evil had the duty to teach others by positive example, as well as the duty to manage society, especially during periods of crisis. Mao's sense of ethical values churns the content of old teachings, but he also holds that man can be perfected by education. In this he is closer to Mencius, who believed that most men are inherently good, than he is to Han Fei-tzu, who believed that nine out of ten are bad, but even Han Fei-tzu agreed that man can be taught to be good—which is the underlying principle of thought reform.

In a casual conversation during my recent visit, Mao remarked (but without any reference to Confucian concepts), "Most men are good; only the minority is bad. Even bad men are not bad all the time and can be made better, just as good men can be made bad by negative example. The difficult thing is to discover what is good and how to teach it to others."

It is of course impossible for revolution to break all connections with the past. The Chinese Communist attitude toward the processes of justice as sanctions against enemies of socialism may also readily be compared with supralegal or extralegal sanctions imposed in Confucianist society. In old China there was no tradition of civil liberties, trial by jury, or of certain tenets of Western law descended from Roman times. Litigants carried their disputes before formal courts of the official magistrates only as a last resort. Mediation, arbitration and penalties in the great majority of cases were handled unofficially by the gentry (scholars, landlords and merchants) in the interests of hierarchical and class stability. Except for a brief period when "Legalist" philosophers dominated, centuries ago, justice was theoretically based on the Confucian classics and commentaries which expounded *li, yi, lien* and *ch'ih*—the four principles of right relationships between men, and between man and the sovereign power. Decisions of the local gentry were socially binding on the majority of poor illiterates, who could not quote the Books; usually, only the rich and powerful dared to use the more formal courts.

On paper, the Kuomintang promulgated a Western-style legal code, but most litigants still followed the old practice, especially in rural China. There is thus a distinct connection between the traditional system of discipline imposed extralegally by the gentry, and the discipline now imposed by the group under party leadership. Marxist-Maoist doctrines of "right relationships" and the party have replaced Confucian doctrine and the gentry. Both reflect the past—but as two planets reflect the sun.

47

"Slave Labor"

I saw thousands of men and women engaged in major construction jobs on roads, railways, dams and other projects. If they were prisoners there were no armed guards around them. Who could speak to them all personally? Twice during about 11,000 miles of travel inside China I saw groups of a dozen or so men being marched along guarded by a soldier or two. I was told that they were regular prisoners from state reform farms assigned to field work. I did not see anything that looked like the barbed-wire-enclosed concentration camps I frequently saw in Stalin's Russia, guarded by high towers with machine guns. They might easily exist behind those occasional signs marked "military-restricted: no admission without a pass." In two such areas where I was admitted, however, I found only Chinese military personnel.

The round number of "twenty-five million" slave-laborers in China was offered as a Kuomintang guesstimate submitted by the Taiwan government to a world study of that subject made by the International Labor Organization and published by the United Nations in 1957. The I.L.O. report itself assumed no responsibility for the Taiwan document, and noted that no nonpartisan source and no government having diplomatic relations with the People's Republic transmitted corroborating information. The figure "twenty-five million" was nevertheless widely quoted in the press as supposedly authenticated by the U.N. On the basis of information other than the Taiwan document, however, the I.L.O. did conclude that the People's Republic had "set up a highly organized system of forced labor in prisons and labor camps, for the purpose of political coercion and education," and was using the system "on a vast scale for carrying out State programs of economic development." [1]

How "vast"? Also, just what is "forced labor"? Does it include everybody obliged to do work he does not wish to do, or only those formally sentenced to "corrective camps" without pay? Even the Kuomintang's own "twenty-five million" guess included three million homeless refugees from flood areas and eight million "civilians used as corvée labor." Why stop there, suggested a Chinese writer in a scholarly symposium[2] issued under American academic auspices. He argued that corvée labor (defined as forced labor) ought to include millions rallied to water control projects, highways, railways, "heavy work in collectives," manure collecting (seventy million), afforestation work (two hundred forty-six million) and other construction projects. His figures aggregate more than the adult population of China. And what of the labor of the entire population when mobilized to kill rats, flies, mosquitoes, lice and fleas—with the result that many preventable and epidemic diseases have virtually disappeared?

Nearly everybody in China *is* obliged to do some kind of manual labor, from the professor to the coolie. Whether it is voluntary or involuntary depends somewhat on the person's state of mind. But this part-time communal labor is obviously not the Western conception of slave labor. On the other hand there is an unknown number of "irregular" persons, who, although they may never have been convicted of a political offense or a criminal felony, are doing full-time compulsory "education through labor." This is acknowledged by a State Council decision enacted as law by the National Congress of 1957.[3]

According to this law, "to transform idlers into new men" and "to promote order and favor socialist construction" persons may be "taken in hand and subjected to education through labor" without incurring criminal liability if they are found to engage in

> vagrancy . . . violate the rules of public order and do not mend their ways despite repeated efforts to educate them; b) having been expelled from [their] organization, group, enterprise, school or other body to which they are responsible, have no means of existence; c) refuse over a long period to work although they are fit to do so, or who violate discipline and, having been expelled, have no means of existence; d) do not conform to the provisions concerning work and assignment to other work, or who refuse to be directed in production work, who in-

terfere with public tasks . . . and who do not mend their ways
despite repeated efforts to educate them. . . .

Education through labor is a way of achieving compulsory educational reform; it is also a way that makes it possible to
provide offenders with an occupation.

Such persons "receive a salary in accordance with their work." They
must provide for their families or save in order "to found a family."
They are educated in "socialism," in "patriotism, and glory of work,"
to become skilled in "techniques of production . . . and self-supporting."

This may explain what has happened to some professional beggars,
malingerers, truants, recalcitrant landlords, "troublemakers," and those
who formerly "lived by their wits." It is clearly also a powerful deterrent against people who won't work where and when they are told to
work and against habitual nonconformist "noncooperators" or "violators
of discipline" in general. Not only the Ministry of Public Security, but
any head of family, street committee, organization, school, or group
to which the offending person belongs, can place him in this category
of reform-through-labor service, subject only to the approval of local
governing bodies and without going to court.

Such persons may either be assigned under surveillance to special
work in organizations from which they have been expelled or they
may be used in labor construction teams. According to Judge Wu the
maximum period of labor surveillance is one year. If the person deserts his tasks he is tried by the courts and sentenced to a regular
prison term.

It is hardly necessary to point out that the law to "transform idlers"
may also be applied to expelled party members. It is equally obvious
that it is wholly irreconcilable with the existence of civil liberties or
guarantees against search or seizure without a warrant—despite the
constitution.

According to the "State Regulations on Reform Through Labor" [4]
adopted in 1954, prisoners can be used in any kind of work for "nine
to ten hours a day." By a supplementary law [5] such prisoners "may be
kept on by the Labor Reform Group and re-employed" even after they
are released and their rights restored. This may be at the prisoner's
request or if "the prisoner's sentence has expired in a vast, sparsely
inhabited region, where settlers are needed to work and found families." Since a party member must go anywhere he is sent, says the
party, why not an ex-prisoner—or anyone else? Reform through labor
is justified as more humane than enforced idleness. In a report which
accompanied the Regulations the Minister of Public Security, Lo Jui-
ch'ing, declared:

There have also been established a good number of labor corps which undertake hydraulic works, build railways, fell trees and build houses for the nation. All the production work is not only directly profitable to the development of the various construction undertakings of the nation but also saves the nation great expense and is a real source of wealth.

The use of prisoners for labor of all kinds is thus beyond dispute; the only questions are how many and under what conditions. From an ethical standpoint such information may seem no more relevant than in many other countries where the same practice is followed but in China it is politically significant.

As I have said, no outsider can *know* the answers to those questions. Since Khrushchev has confirmed the worst reports about Stalinist concentration camps in Russia (and from what is known of camps in South Vietnam under Ngo Dinh Diem) and Eastern Europe no one is entitled to assume that "reform through labor" in China is administered by humanitarians. A self-constituted "International Commission" in Europe published a *White Book*[6] about persons who had been released by or escaped from Chinese mainland prisons up to 1953. Of the "hundreds" of alleged former prisoners whom investigators claimed to have interviewed, they apparently found only eighteen "case histories" suitable for presentation in the *White Book*. Among these, the majority were former officials or soldiers or affiliates of the Kuomintang. Half a dozen witnesses whose testimony seemed less self-serving than that of the others included a Belgian Jesuit priest. A most sincere and dedicated anti-Communist, he revealed that he was incarcerated as a spy, along with another Jesuit arrested earlier. The latter had "confessed" not only that he himself was a spy but that all Jesuits were spies; his rationale was that things went hard with those who denied the charges and that salvation lay in prompt confession. The Jesuit who testified said that he had nevertheless persisted in his denials of espionage. He was never physically abused but had to undergo prolonged thought-remolding courses. Throughout them he maintained both his innocence and his religious and philosophical opposition to Marxism. He himself was allowed to volunteer for factory work and was eventually released, unharmed. His unfortunate fellow Jesuit had to remain behind to supply details missing from his false confession, which the jailers found unconvincing and evasive.

Obsolete and inconclusive for a nation of 700,000,000, this *White Book* is nevertheless valuable for its compilation of legal and historical documents and official statements. These leave no doubt about the thorough integration of the prison system with both production needs and the ceaseless campaign to bend men's minds and wills to serve the ends of the regime.

Yet a visitor to China finds paradoxes even in the jails. The *White Book* compilation includes a map which lists 292 "concentration camps" alleged to have existed in China. Locations of most of them suggest that they may have been temporary construction camps; others are in the neighborhood of state farms. One is shown at Sanmoshu, a suburb of Harbin. It so happened that I visited a large state experimental farm near there. It was a hurried trip and I had seen so many farms and farmers that I neglected looking into the workers' living quarters but spent my time inspecting the poultry breeding and automatic pig-feeding "innovations." As I left I noticed two armed sentries at the lower gate. It occurred to me only later that mixed prison and free labor may have been employed there. The law quoted above gives reason to suppose that mixed labor is at least sometimes used on state farms—a fact which was officially confirmed for me.

How then does one fit the following phenomena into the conventional idea of a "concentration camp"? 1) I was told that prisoners, paroled prisoners and free peasants all work together on the so-called factory farm at Ch'ing Ho, run by the Peking security bureau. 2) In a conversation I had with Mayor K'eh of Shanghai he said that ex-prisoners settle down in new villages on the reform farm in Supei, which is run by that city.* No Soviet official in Stalin's day would ever admit the existence of even one detention camp. Yet products of the Ch'ing Ho reform farm are even advertised in the Peking newspapers. There seems to be no secret about it.

Curiously, the *White Book* itself contains a description of a reform farm which closely corresponds to that given to me by Mayor K'eh and by prison officials. In some notes written for that compilation a former inmate of the Peking municipal prison, when interviewed abroad, spoke of reading a newspaper called *The Garden of Transformation*, which was composed and printed at the Ch'ing Ho farm. The farm was where the "normal future" of well-behaved prisoners lay.

"An agricultural colony of at least 50,000 acres near the sea, and formerly uncultivated and saturated with salt," much of it had now been drained, irrigated and put under cultivation. "Rice is the principal crop," according to this ex-prisoner. The income from rice alone "represented four or five times the value of the food consumed by the prisoners."

He continues: "Various workshops are attached to the camp," both inside the colony and "near the town." Many workers were employed on "construction work in the town, for example, the new municipal theater of the Bridge of the Sky . . . Members left their lodging every day at about 7:00 A.M. and returned at about 6:00 P.M. or a little earlier. They also often worked on Sunday." There was daily (one to two hours) study of Marxism and, at intervals, criticism and self-

* See page 547.

criticism meetings. Food reportedly was "somewhat better" than in municipal jails, with "meat once or twice a week, and also rice and wheat bread more often." The whole system is designed to "raise production" and inducements are cash prizes and remission of sentences. "When their terms have expired, prisoners are permitted and encouraged to remain in the camp as salaried 'free workers.' Later their families may come and settle there with them." [7]

One thing may be reported with reasonable certainty: there are no more child slaves in China. Before the war legions of children were sold to owners of mines or shops or into household drudgery or prostitution. This practice was also general in French Indochina, and still continues in South Vietnam. *All* the miners in Yunnan's tin mines were formerly boy slaves.[8] In her absorbing prewar Mather Foundation (Yale University) study, *Chinese Family and Society*, Olga Lang reported that: ". . . child labor represented 7 percent of the total employed in Shanghai textile factories but many small workshops . . . employ children almost exclusively. 'Many of those local industries were confining adult labor to the management and clerical staff,' says the Report of the Industrial Section of the Shanghai Municipal Council." Children of farm laborers and poor peasants began farm labor "at the age of 7, sometimes even earlier," while others were sold to labor merchants on "contracts concluded with their parents [which] make them virtual slaves for at least three years. . . . Many receive no pay at all—only food and lodging and a few cents on New Year's Day. Only a few of the Peking apprentices receive as much as 50 cents or a dollar [yuan] a month. . . . Beriberi, scurvy, and other diseases caused by malnutrition are common," and little workers "sleep on wooden planks . . . or under the tables which other shifts continue to use for their work; others sleep on the streets." In the mines near Peking, Miss Lang saw (as I had) children who "emerged from the dark shafts almost completely naked, their thin bodies showing through their skin . . . carrying on an average 35-pound loads. The boys looked not older than 9 or 10 although there were some 14- and 15-year-olds among them. Their usual pay was 10-20 cents a day." [9] Such was life in the thirties, when Miss Lang also reported widespread sale of widows and poor men's wives as well as girl children to become household slaves, prostitutes and concubines.

Alas, these well-documented conditions did not then arouse any more excitement in the free world than did the existence of slavery in Tibet, where half the population were serfs. Nor is there any record of Western protests against widespread mass conscription of labor under the Kuomintang. Millions of peasants were forced into labor service; in the countryside I often saw (as did many other foreigners) men yoked together like cattle, with ropes tied around their necks, being dragged along by military police. No foreigner I met in present-day China had seen anything like that. We also forget that the Kuomintang introduced "thought correction" camps as early as the mass depopulation of Kiangsi Soviet and Hupeh, in the thirties. Official correspondence released by Washington in 1962 revealed that in 1943 the State Department was aware that "'thought correction' camps exist in at least nine provinces in Kuomintang China." They were not used for labor reform but solely for detention; "torture is practiced" and it was reported that those fortunate enough to be released were "usually broken in mind and body." [10]

48

Hsueh-Hsi and Reform-Through-Labor

I was told, and resident foreign diplomats believed, that the entire Peking area has only one prison. There is also a mobile labor brigade of "a few hundred" and there is the state reform farm; both are also under the Peking security bureau. Wu Teh-fang told me the farm had about 2,000 prisoners. That was the same estimate made for me by a resident diplomat. A number of foreigners have seen it; apparently it is not very different from any other state farm. It was only the day before I left Peking that I learned that I could visit the Ch'ing Ho farm—a description of which I have just quoted. I had to omit this opportunity, but I was told I would be able to see a similar institution near Shanghai.

Besides the main prison there was also a "detention house" in the Peking inner city, near the National Library, in Ts'ao Lan Tze Hu-t'ung, the Lane of the Grass Green Mist. Here some two to four hundred political prisoners were held for interrogation and thought reform prior to a formal trial and verdict. During this period the prisoner was given an opportunity, by study and self-examination, to arrive at feelings of repentance and develop a political awareness. Prisoners often went through *hsueh-hsi* in this manner for as long as several years. The results could materially reduce sentences or even bring a dismissal,

while failure to make any progress due to recalcitrance might increase
the severity of the sentence. The trial itself was usually a formality in
which the prisoner might either be given a term in another institution
or released and returned to society.

Harriet Mills, whom I quote farther on, Father Harold Rigney and
Allyn and Adele Rickett, all Americans, were imprisoned at 13 Lane
of the Grass Green Mist for four years, during and after the Korean
War. Here also the two American flyers, John T. Downey and Richard
Fecteau, were kept (and at this writing still are), together with Chinese captured with them. Downey and Fecteau were tried in court-
martial two years after their arrest.*

Only relatives or close friends of inmates are permitted to visit this
prison. While I was in Peking, John Downey's mother arrived for her
second visit (by special permission of the State Department), of two
weeks. She saw her son almost daily. (His brother also visited him
twice.) From her I learned that he was not permitted to do shop or
other work—regarded as an earned privilege—but he exercised regularly and she found him in good health and good spirits. He was able
to receive books and parcels of food through the Chinese Red Cross and
kept up a correspondence with friends at home.

I could have found the Peking jail without a guide if anyone had
told me that it was the old "model prison" I had last visited in 1935,
when some students I knew were incarcerated there. It was built
sixty years ago, a great improvement over the filthy windowless dun-
geons then in general use; that particular prison reform did not spread
very far. The prison stands beyond the eastern suburbs and from a
distance seemed unchanged: the same gray brick walls. But the outer
gate was now open and I saw no sentries until we reached the inner
wall, where one soldier stood in a pillbox. An unarmed guard opened
the iron gate and Yao Wei and I passed through a flower garden into
a reception room which fronted on part of the inner prison walls.
The deputy warden, Mr. Wang, was a serious-minded party man in
his mid-thirties who had had "special training" for his job. He offered
me the usual tea and preliminary briefing.

There were "about 1,800 prisoners" of whom about 40 percent were
"counterrevolutionaries" (aged mostly between thirty-five and forty-
five); more than a hundred prisoners were women. Sixty of the
inmates were under suspended sentences of death. The prison population had been as much as 3,000; in 1960, "more than a hundred" prisoners were released as contrasted to "seventy to eighty" new arrivals.

The prison operated three factories: a hosiery mill, a mill for
plastics articles, and a machine and electrical shop. I was told that the
prison routine was eight hours of shop work, two to three hours of
study and lectures, eight hours of sleep, four or five hours for din-

* See Appendix, pages 753-757.

ing, physical exercise, reading, recreation and "discussion" (thought remolding). Prisoners got one holiday every two weeks, when they could receive visitors or do as they wished. They had their own band, an opera troupe, an outdoor theater, and movies once a week. Men and women ate in the same dining rooms and could attend plays and sports contests held inside the prison compound.

With that said we toured the prison cells and then the shops. The buildings were one-storied and made of brick, with two rows of cells on either side of a central aisle. I noticed that all bars had been removed from the windows and that every cell door was open. The rooms, with two to four long k'angs in each, were white and clean, and all had neat piles of bedding. One man, off on a free day, was lying in bed reading; his door was also open. He was in for two years for embezzlement of state funds.

The shops were all mechanized. Machinery was antique but better than in most urban commune shops I had seen. Women handled the knitting machines and a few worked in the plastics rooms with the men. They wore blue or black cotton clothes issued by the prison, with no special markings to differentiate them from other working people. They paid strict attention to their machines and did not look at us except when I paused here and there to ask a question; then they replied politely and not sullenly. I saw no marks of physical violence and people seemed in average good health. Some of the young women were rather pretty. I asked one of them why she was there. "Fraud," was the answer I got. I was puzzled, but the deputy warden later enlightened me.

What was different here was the "open door" policy, the absence of an armed-camp atmosphere. Shops were run by prisoner foremen supervised by prison staff members; I saw no armed guards among them. Prisoners also managed their own barber shop, mess rooms, a canteen, shower baths and a library. In various courtyards and grounds I saw half a dozen soldiers, but none was posted in guard towers or on the walls which enclosed gardens where prisoners cultivated vegetables. Perhaps the other guards were removed for my benefit? Perhaps. But Sing Sing would consider that rather risky as a public relations stunt.

"It looks easy enough to get out of here," I said to Wang. "Do many try it?"

"We've had several runaways in the past year. Usually they are brought back by their families."

Beside a round-roofed pergola in one corner of a compound near the clinic, half a dozen women were eating rice with their chopsticks, laughing and chattering. They didn't seem to belong.

"They are ex-prisoners," Wang explained. "Two of them work in the clinic, another is in charge of the laundry, one works in the office."

I stopped to take some pictures, to which they made no objection; one or two gave embarrassed smiles. They confirmed that they had stayed on voluntarily after their sentences expired and were working for wages. They felt "at home" here. One was a married woman who lived nearby; her husband worked in a neighborhood factory. I had no time to pursue what might have been a fascinating study of the psychology behind their choice of a place to work—if it was their choice. (Miss Mills later told me that she was prepared to believe it *was* voluntary.)

Around the basketball court and a stage which prisoners had built were bulletin boards posted with *ta tzu-pao* such as you see before any Chinese factory: essays, rhymes, praise and mutual criticism, lists of model workers and their awards. Prisoners got no wages but received an allowance of three yuan a month pocket money, which they could double by outstanding work. The money bought a few cigarettes or other items in the canteen. The kitchen was preparing a noon meal of soup, spinach and steamed bread which looked like a Salvation Army handout.

Back in the reception room to ask more questions, I learned that the political prisoners were generally serving long sentences up to "suspended death"—alleged Kuomintang agents, spies, saboteurs or "despotic landlords" sentenced by "people's courts" in their villages. Many had been here since the revolution, while others had "awakened," completed reduced sentences, and been released. I had been told by Wu Teh-fang that to be arrested as a counterrevolutionary in China one must take some overt action against the state, not merely express a reactionary opinion. Membership in a subversive society or an illegal group would be considered overt action if the clear intent was sabotage. There were some prisoners here in that category. But suppose, I asked, that someone merely expressed verbal support of Mme Chiang Kai-shek's statement broadcast on the American radio in which she advocated dropping nuclear bombs on China. Would that be subversive? According to Mr. Wang such a person would not be sent to jail but to a mental hospital.

Among civil felonies the commonest was theft of state property for resale or personal use; next came embezzlement, chicanery, forgery and the usual crimes of violence: assault, rape and robbery. There were "very few" new cases of murder. More than half the women prisoners were in for *p'ien-lai lao-ti*, which means to "obtain something by fraud." What was it they had obtained? I asked Mr. Wang. Money, clothing, provisions, gifts of all kinds. And by what means?

"An adventurous woman pretends to be in love," he said, "with several different men at the same time. She does it solely to get money. She goes from one man to another, deceiving him, but she won't marry any of them."

"That sounds like a very ancient profession. Isn't prostitution the word?"

"No, no, it isn't prostitution," he insisted stiffly. "It is just fraud. There is not necessarily any sex involved. There are many different kinds. These women are very clever at it. They are put in prison only after repeated offenses."

I should have liked to pursue the matter in a personal interview with one of the defrauders. Mr. Wang said that the women would be embarrassed and besides it was their noon rest period (quite true), so I can offer no further particulars, except that they get light sentences, one to three years. When asked whether I would like to question any other prisoner I chose a political offender under suspended death sentence.

He was a Shantung man, rugged in build, heavy-featured, middle-aged and solemn. I asked him what he had done. He answered that as a Kuomintang policeman in Tsinan he had led an anti-Red squad and arrested many suspects. Urged by Wang to elaborate, he added, face downcast, that he had personally killed four revolutionaries, one of whom was a pregnant woman. His crime was graver because he had not come forward after the revolution when everyone was given an opportunity to confess, repent, and ask for punishment. Instead, he had gone north, taken a job in a Peking textile mill and pretended to be an ordinary worker. One day in 1958 he was recognized by another Shantung man who denounced him and had him arrested. Did he feel he had been fairly treated?

"I ought to be dead," he said. "I deserved death but instead I have been given back life. I am being educated and I can now handle machines and do useful work. I am doing my best to remold myself to show my gratitude." He seemed thoroughly humbled and remorseful, and deep tension was written on his face. One needed little imagination to share some of the awareness that must have filled his days that one bad mistake might be his last. To know with reasonable certainty that salvation depended entirely on his own repentance and reform must in some ways have placed far heavier burdens on him than would be on a condemned man in an American prison. Realizing that nothing he can do by way of inner awakening can alter matters, the latter need not undergo the agony of attempted self-reform but can hold society or his lawyers at least partly responsible for his fate.

When the prisoner and his unarmed escort left, Wang said that he was a good worker. He had been in jail for two years; his sentence would probably be altered to life imprisonment.

The theory holds, and the law supports it, that the starting point for all prisoners is sincere repentance, recognition of the crime, and welcome of the sentence as "good." Until this happened they were kept under stricter confinement. The next step was the "genuine desire" to reform. Many prisoners were "really ignorant and understood nothing about the revolution or what the government was trying to do for the people." Tours were organized to take them to visit communes, factories and schools, to show them the good things being done and to awaken "a sense of shame." Illiterates were taught to read and write and all attended political lectures. Much of the education and indoctrination was done by "advanced" prisoners put into cells with new arrivals and backward ones. Truly "reformed" prisoners received special privileges; the more successful their political work the better their chances of release. By means of cadres organized within the prison blocks, order and disciplined study were maintained. Political prisoners did the same shop work as others but were subjected to much more intensified thought remolding in cells led by reformed "politicos."

Mr. Wang said that in the great majority of cases prisoners who made political progress were also the best shop workers. Their chances of getting good jobs on release were improved by both their technical education and their ideological remolding. Stubborn cases might take as long as a year or two before beginning to see the light. In only a few instances did prisoners refuse to "recognize the roots of their errors"; if these silent resisters worked well and were not political prisoners they would also be released when their sentences expired, although there was no chance for a shortened term. Punishment consisted of overtime work or loss of holidays, but Wang maintained that violence was never used and that solitary confinement "in no case exceeded a week."

Obviously his statement is no proof that Chinese jailers are any exception to the general rule in prisons everywhere: "no force, absolutely, when anyone is looking." I have been through many jails and reform schools and have yet to find a "good" one. The Peking prison looked like a tolerable fate but who can know from the outside looking in? I am much aware of the testimony of Chinese who have been through the wringer of thought remolding, and I have talked to several Americans who were also subjected to it.

The threefold nature of Reform Through Labor and Education is specifically prescribed in the Regulations already mentioned. Article IV declared:

> Organizations responsible for Reform Through Labor shall, as regards counter-revolutionary and other criminals, carry out fully the following directives: co-ordination of punishment and supervision with reform of thought; co-ordination of productive work with political education.

In a recent book an American psychiatrist, R. J. Lifton, has made a study of brain washing which attempts a Western scientific explanation of its pathological and psychological effectiveness.[1] It is worth noting in passing that in the twenty-five cases Dr.

Lifton examined he found that curiously even among those who remained most hostile to the Communists nearly all said that they had
in some ways personally benefited from the experience. Dr. Lifton
was unable to trace any pattern of influence by Freud, Adler or
Pavlov in Chinese thought-remolding techniques, which seem to depend primarily on guilt associations with traditional ethical concepts
and fears rooted in Chinese psychology.

Probably no American is better qualified to testify concerning
thought remolding than Harriet Mills, who went through four years
of the process. I first met her in New York soon after her release from
jail in Peking in October, 1955. She was born in China, in a family of
Presbyterian missionaries, and spent twenty-five years of her life there.
A graduate of Wellesley College, she was back in China as a Fulbright
scholar when arrested and charged with espionage, in 1951. Today she
teaches Chinese at Cornell University.

In "Red China," a special issue of the *Atlantic,* ably edited by another China-born American, Peggy Durdin, who has made important contributions to the cultural community of her two worlds, Miss
Mills described the remolding process with great authority. She wrote:
"The Communists know that only if people are truly persuaded of the
justice of [their] position will they release their spontaneous and creative energy and cooperate not from necessity but from conviction." [2]
Physical violence cannot achieve genuine moral reform and sincere
changes in *thinking,* which are basic objectives. "In serious cases where
criminality is involved thought-reform and punishment are combined
but the essential aim remains *redemption through criticism* . . . [Orig-
inal emphasis.]

"They are determined to negate a fundamental tenet of Chinese
thinking formulated by Confucius 2,500 years ago: 'Who works with
his mind rules; who works with his hands is ruled.' Reform by labor
goes hand in hand with reform through study in rehabilitation of prisoners [and] the right to labor comes only after a certain level of reform
through study has been achieved."

In her article Miss Mills traced "two main lines of experience" in
the techniques of group study. The first derived from the Communists'
twenty years as guerrilla fighters when recruits had to be taught to
"use weapons, obey commands, live together, and protect the country
people," making sure that "each man understood not only how but
why." Small groups (of six to ten) went over all questions until everyone understood. By similar means the program of land and social reform and future benefits was patiently explained to the peasants.
"Thus, they persuaded the peasants to cooperate in resisting Japan
or the Kuomintang," and the result was "high morale."

The second method, the organization of party cells for group study
of Marxist ideology, is standard among Communists everywhere. From
"the fusion of these two traditions—Chinese persuasion and Commu-

nist dogma"—evolved the "ubiquitous working mechanism of thought reform in China."

All study groups report to the party and *no* citizen is exempt from participation. There is no freedom of silence. Parroting answers is not enough; one must apply the new theory and self-knowledge as a continuous life process. Criticism is the main weapon. Those who resist or lack sincerity may face *tou-cheng* (struggle) with the rest of the group—"a humiliating combination of loud criticism, interlarded with sarcasm, epithet and—very rarely—with minor violence." Ostracism from the group is the worst punishment.

Self-criticism is even more important than criticism of others. And self-criticism in public, a form of confessions of all one's doubts, waverings, weaknesses, bad habits and antisocial tendencies, is the most effective form of self-criticism.

"Group study can even be exhilarating . . . a sort of catharsis." The most difficult to redeem have been the higher intellectuals. Communist policy toward this strategic group "has consistently aimed at securing effective utilization of their knowledge. Zigzagging steadily toward this goal, the Communists have now attacked, now united, now criticized"—while training their own "new group both Red and expert."

"Tense and painful as it often is," Miss Mills found group study "effective" for four reasons.

> First, there is the essential need to belong, to achieve and maintain emotional balance. To be unprogressive in China is not simply a political verdict; it is social suicide as well. Second, the constant repetition of correct ideas and particularly the application of them to the public analysis of one's own and others' problems mean that one is forced to give them detailed scrutiny. The Communists are conscious of the value of this. "From habit or pretense," they say, "it may become real." Third—and this is all too often neglected by outside observers—it is the crusading idealism, the strong moral note, that runs through all discussion of political, social, and economic steps. Since it is obviously right that China should be made new and strong to assume its long overdue place as a major power, it is right to collectivize so as to mechanize and increase agricultural production. It is right to be Spartan and not demand higher wages so more effort can go into new plants, right to report opposition to the Party that is bringing medicine, schooling, and security to half a billion peasants, right to resist the "aggressive designs" of the United States in Korea, right that women should be emancipated. Fourth, there is the universal knowledge, as the highest spokesmen of the Party have frankly admitted, that in the long run no course but the correct one is open. Attempts to avoid

the tensions of group study by tacit compact to go through the routine or to stick to pleasantries are blocked not only by the fact of the leader's relations with the authorities but by the ever-present possibility that some member, whether motivated by genuine change of heart or by a selfish attempt at winning official favor, might report the group. Thus, there is tremendous pressure both to fall in line and to want to fall in line.

Finally, and "most important of all," is the appeal to

a sense of nationalism, a patriotic pride in China's new posture of confidence and achievement. That China, which in 1948 was economically prostrate under runaway inflation, maladministered by a weak and corrupt government totally dependent on American aid, incapable of producing motorcycles, much less automobiles, can . . . fight the United Nations to a draw in Korea, maintain the world's fourth largest air force, produce trucks, jet planes, even establish a nuclear reactor, is an intoxicating spectacle to the Chinese. This pride, in turn, has generated a remarkably effective and spontaneous code of public honesty, courtesy, and civic sense unknown in old China.

To be asked whether an incorrect idea is really worthy of the new China can make one feel guilty. Thousands have asked themselves, "What right have I to disagree with those who can achieve so much?" As a professor of English, remembering China's internal disintegration and international humiliation, explained to me in the spring of 1951, "Now we can again be proud to be Chinese!"

This condensation of Miss Mills's article unavoidably omits much of the nuance and paradox of the original. She wrote primarily of *hsueh-hsi,* or the technique of thought reform—not of reform under coercion. *Hsueh-hsi* in principle is the same wherever practiced, but in prison there is the omnipresent *threat* of force and humiliation, combined with the demand for self-regeneration. In conversation with me, Miss Mills has further emphasized the distinction between prison reform and the ideological remolding undertaken by social organizations in a kind of group therapy.

As Mao said, "Revolution is not the same thing as . . . painting a picture or doing fancy needlework . . . mild, courteous, restrained and magnanimous." Nor is "corrective imprisonment" any exercise in non-violence. Armed guards, handcuffs, "solitary," and standing motionless for long periods may all be used "on occasion," but the assault on the human sense of social guilt is the basic means. According to Miss Mills, food is never withheld or used as a weapon and physical punishment is not practiced as an end in itself. But the knowledge of it held in reserve certainly sharpens the prisoner's response to accusations of his selfish behavior, and the combination leaves him aware that his only hope of redemption lies in a genuine soul-searching and exposure of past errors. Most people have some sense of guilt if they really face the truth about themselves. The paradox Miss Mills discovered was that "even strong-willed persons who might never bend before force, alone, did undergo slow, stage by stage, and finally dramatic and wholly convincing transformations."

Mr. and Mrs. Rickett are also now college teachers in America. Mr. Rickett, an ex-marine trained as an intelligence officer, was still in the reserve at the time of his arrest but was not engaged in espionage as he understood it. A book written by the Ricketts is a fascinatingly honest document of self-examination which leaves no doubt that *hsueh-hsi* transformed much of their thinking.[3] Miss Mills and the Ricketts spoke Chinese, admired Chinese culture, and had wide contacts among the people. Father Rigney did not know the language and his views were rigidly pro-Western. His services to China were related to the activities of the Legion of Mary, an anti-Communist youth organization which he would consider it absurd to link with sabotage or espionage. He "benefited" not at all from thought reform and his report corresponds closely to the conventional Western impression that the process is unadulterated hell—without any choice of the salvation offered by the Inquisition.[4]

Incarcerated in the same prison cells with the Americans were a number of Chinese who had engaged in espionage, sabotage and intelligence work for foreign powers and the Nationalist government. Their own stories of the techniques they used to gather and transmit information, and of trips to and from offices in Hongkong, were related in convincing detail. One of the most colorful cases involved Tuan Yuen-p'eng, famous as the "flying" or wall-scaling thief turned agent and saboteur. The Ts'ao Lan Tze prison held many merchants, housewives, innkeepers, former prostitutes, fellow thieves and others who had assisted him in his various terrorist attempts.

That men and women interned under such grave conditions might yet manage literally to "rethink their way out" and eventually be assigned to reform through labor was gradually seen by most of them to be a "marvelous thing." They then tended to become strongly competitive in their desire to be recognized by the interrogator-confessor as "more progressive" than their cellmates. They became genuinely proud of their own "creative efforts" in the process of re-examining their past to qualify themselves for a return to society. Finally to be given the right to work, unguarded, on a dam or a bridge or something else "useful to the people" whom they had "wronged," could (in the objective opinion of Miss Mills) then indeed mean a kind of "freedom" in which they might rejoice as a reward, not a punishment.

"A paradox which comforts while it mocks"? So it would seem to free men. On the other hand, could it possibly be a stage in advance of chain-gangs in our southern states, for instance, where prisoners are regularly returned to a society they still despise, having meanwhile merely become better mentally conditioned to criminality than they were when their legs were first locked together? Or is neither method any more civilized than the other? Dr. Lifton offered no clinical answer to this question, and it ill behooves a layman to venture where psychiatrists fear to tread.

49

Pre-Teen Delinquents

I spent an afternoon in the "Children's Study-Work School" where 185 children between ten and fifteen were being reformed by gentler methods of thought remolding. Peking had one other reform school, with about 100 juvenile delinquents aged fifteen to eighteen, which I did not see. The Children's Study-Work School had some notable features worth reporting. Its roomy compound was in a good residential neighborhood not far from the Winter Palace. There were no guards except one elderly gateman and no special precautions to prevent escapes. "Usually they come back voluntarily," I was told by Mme Wang Ssu-yen, the principal. She was a diminutive woman dressed in a white blouse and dark skirt, her black hair bobbed and caught in curls behind her ears. Her energy and enthusiasm for her job, in contrast with her stature, reminded me of my own spirited grade school principal.

"The methods we follow here," said Mme Wang, "are in accordance with the principles laid down by Mao Tse-tung for all primary school teachers. We must love our students like parents, combine affection with strict justice, respect them as much as adults, understand each one as a distinct individual, and inculcate in them socialist ideals of service and unselfishness. The cause of delinquency in children nearly always lies with their parents. All our teachers here realize that the most important thing is to set an example. We participate down to sharing the dirtiest chores such as cleaning floors and toilets. All the work in the school is done by the children and teachers."

Mme Wang considered that her charges were all reflections of the failure of the "old society" and "hangovers of capitalism," but "class background" figures she gave me did not seem conclusive evidence. According to her, 40 percent of the little delinquents came from working-class families; 20 percent were orphans or from broken homes or had lived with old people too disabled to work or look after them; 25 percent were the children of *kanpu;* and 15 percent were from homes of "former capitalists or policemen." I expressed interest in the quarter from families of cadres. Forty-six in a city of more than seven million was not many, but the relative percentage was high. Weren't cadres themselves supposed to be models of deportment?

"They may work for socialism but still be bad parents," she said. "Remember that they also come from the old society and may backslide in their domestic life. When parents are too busy to look after their children, when they neglect to give them love, the result is always the same; the children become willful, spoiled, aggressive, and do things to win attention. They begin to lie and steal and get into trouble."

The delinquents here had been habitual thieves or had committed acts of vandalism, cheated or caused disturbances in schools, refused to study or work, or had violently quarreled with their grandparents, who, in some cases, had asked that they be put into the school. (Mao Tse-tung was a rebellious child. What would have happened if he had been sent to such a school? The party's answer would be that Mao lived in a feudal society against which it was morally correct to rebel.)

"The majority of our children are unusually bright, not stupid." Mme Wang spoke of their "unusual pride" and "vanity" and how readily they responded when given recognition and responsibility. One "bad" boy had refused to study or work for two months. "I can stand sitting through just one class," he said. "Then I have to hit someone." One day he contrived to tie his teacher's feet to his desk so that when he tried to stand up he was thrown to the floor. The boy expected to be beaten but the teacher dismissed class to talk to him. The teacher thought that he was a clever boy to be able to do that trick without being detected. He thought he had ability and would like to help him. The boy had been abused by his father and hated him, but gradually the teacher won his confidence. A year later the same boy found a gold watch on the street (children are allowed to return, unescorted, to "home" or the equivalent for two days once a month). He was much tempted to sell it or to take it apart. He was a very curious boy. Instead, he brought the watch to his teacher. When the owner recovered the watch he came to congratulate the youth and they became good friends. By the time he graduated after three years he was chairman of his class.

Mme Wang told several more stories of this kind to support her account of their successes, which seemed to owe much to two basic control devices. There was a pupils' association with many management tasks. Among these was responsibility for helping the "new ones" learn correct behavior. The "new ones" were put on two months' probation by the "old ones." If they were then voted into the organization they received emblems of membership. If their performance was unsatisfactory they were put on probation for another two months. To be accepted as a "full pupil" was a "glorious moment," said Mme Wang. The elite of the students belonged to the Young Pioneers—32 out of a total of 150 boys and 35 girls. Membership was extended to students who received "Five S's" or superior marks in study, athletics, workshop, recreation and hygiene-sanitation, and socialist study and consciousness. These Young Pioneers seemed to play a role similar to that of cadres in adult life.

Shop work was required for two hours in the afternoon: carpentry for boys, sewing and embroidery for girls. The rest of the day was devoted to the usual primary school subjects: classroom from 7:30 to 12:00 in the morning, athletics and recreation for two hours in the afternoon. I visited the shop, where boxes of various sizes were being made to fill commercial orders; the boys worked under the supervision of a male teacher. Half the money earned for their products was kept in a welfare and recreation fund, the other half distributed as wages and bonuses. From the welfare fund they had bought instruments for the school band, which did a march and savaged some military airs for me.

Here, also, tours to factories, farms and museums were arranged and movies and speakers were brought in. The children preferred to listen to military heroes, said Mme Wang. They were very patriotic and most of the boys were especially interested in aviation. They get more than an ordinary dosage of political indoctrination in the spirit of socialism, of course. Gangsterism? Yes, there was always that tendency among new arrivals. The staff depended upon the monthly meetings of the pupils' association and on Young Pioneer leadership to break it up. Once troublemakers were criticized and called upon by the group to explain themselves they began to see the advantages of "membership" and compliance with the rules. Much depended on the way teachers helped to support adolescent leadership at such meetings; it was important for the pupils themselves to be in charge.

After graduation from higher primary grades here, students were eligible either for middle school or for half-work, half-study jobs in factories. Would they be admitted to regular schools without discrimination? Mme Wang smiled confidently. "Our students are especially welcomed—those who have the necessary qualifications.

Among Peking schools with Five-S students ours ranks among the top ten. It is well known that during the steel-making campaign in 1958 we built four furnaces in three days and two nights and smelted 2,962 catties [one and a half tons]—the record amount produced by any primary school." Drawing herself up to her full five feet, she glowed with pride as she concluded: "On top of that, the Children's Study-Work School is famous for having won, two years in a row, the West Peking Red Banner for primary schools in sanitation work!"

It was not easy for a stranger to question these children about their past errors—for which they were far from fully responsible—without embarrassing them, and I soon desisted. They seemed to work well together and were cheerful and looked healthy. "Disturbed children" and "incorrigibles"? No, said Mme Wang, they had no special methods for handling them, except plenty of *ai-hsin* (love) and "to follow a cool line" with them. They responded to the reward system as the others did. Teachers (three male and four female) were all qualified normal school graduates who had been given special training in a party school before coming here, but they were not using any foreign or Russian system of child psychology. The worst form of disapproval was the threat of expulsion from the pupils' association—loss of "membership," ostracism and disgrace. Mme Wang said that in three years she had never had to expel a child from the school itself. That was fortunate, she added; she would have to turn him back to the courts and she was not clear herself about what would then happen.

On further reflection the principal said that yes, there was one particularly difficult case of a "disturbed" girl. She was seventeen now and the oldest child there; she had failed in her studies and had had to repeat. She was not really stupid but incredibly shy and reticent; her real reason for failing seemed to be fear of returning to "the outside." She had had a completely loveless childhood, full of beatings and abuse, had been raped when a small girl, had never known a home before she came here, and now dared not face the world. She was pointed out to me at one of the sewing tables. She held her head down and I watched her embroider for a moment; her work was exquisite, far more skillful than the others'.

"What will you do with her?" I asked when we moved on.

"I don't know yet. We are trying to decide." Mme Wang obviously took a more than casual interest in this young woman. I wondered what kind of childhood she herself had had but I never found out. "If Lin-ling were a little brighter," she went on, "we might find some kind of assistant's job for her here, but maybe that would be begging the question. However, we'll find a solution."

Thought remolding has its limitations no less than "the couch."

50

Prelude to the
Hundred Flowers

A small mountain of foreign commentary has grown from the unique "Hundred Flowers" period in China when the Communist party urged "the people" to express themselves freely and made available "the necessary facilities." Because the hiatus occurred there is less mystery in China today than in most Communist countries about what both people and "unpeople" find unbearable. One cannot count the opposition but there is plenty of evidence of its character.

Some Western scholars believe simply that Mao Tse-tung committed a "colossal mistake" based on illusions that his regime enjoyed overwhelming popularity; that this method of rectifying party errors will never be repeated; and that "the Mao of today lives to reproach the Mao of yesterday." [1] Whether these estimates are correct may continue to be debated. It remains mandatory for anyone who wishes to understand something about the why and the how of Red China and the theory, technique, psychology and philosophy of its leadership to know at least the main facts, motivations and objectives behind this daring departure from the norm.

How daring was it? True, nothing like it has been seen before or since under any dictatorship; but it would also be highly unusual in any land where the "necessary facilities" for the expression of public opinion are owned not by the state but by private capitalists. Something like the equivalent of China's 1957 "rectification" method would occur if the millionaire owners of America's largest, nation-wide means of communication turned them over entirely to the views and demands of nonowners: working men, peacemongers, socialists, students, scholars, intellectuals, professional people, farm laborers, Negroes and other minorities—advice and dissent from "the whole people" including John Birchites and "comsimps," but drawing the line at outright Communists.

Wholesale withdrawal of advertising subsidy and financial ruin would doubtless follow and the political repercussions would be very interesting. We are not likely to see a "Hundred Flowers" of this kind in the West, but the rough analogy makes the risks courted by Mao Tse-tung seem all the more remarkable.

The Chinese Communist press is never completely devoid of self-criticism. Policy mistakes, blunders, incompetence, dishonesty and cases of bullying of the people by cadres are frequently exposed, and the open publication of such material forms the basis of many of the foreign attacks on the regime. Party "rectification" campaigns, launched periodically ever since 1942, have often revealed much inner strain and dissension. At such times there seems no attempt to conceal the worst facts against some party members, and they are often more damaging than any isolated refugee tales. During the 1953 rectification campaign, for example, cases of village cadres who had beaten up and robbed peasants, raped their daughters, and driven others to suicide, were widely publicized in the open government press. But never had the leadership invited such wholesale public denunciation as it did in 1957. Why?

One must briefly recall the circumstances. For Communists the world over, 1956 and 1957 were years of confusion and intense crisis. Khrushchev made his Twentieth Congress speech denouncing Stalin as a murderer and overthrew "the cult of leadership" with devastating effects on the monolithic structure of Stalinist communism. While Khrushchev consolidated his own power in Moscow the controls loosened over satellite Eastern Europe, where Stalinist bosses fell before the assaults of "revisionist" opponents seeking "different roads to socialism."

Stalinist icons had already become fewer in China when Khrushchev made his speech before the Twentieth Congress in February, 1956. Since the Soviet party itself was wholly unprepared for it, obviously Peking was still less so. The complete text was never published in China (nor was it ever openly published in Russia). The first news reached the Chinese public when *Pravda's* famous article denouncing "the cult of personality" was reprinted in the official press in March. By then the Politburo had adjusted itself. Subsequent articles "reaffirmed" the collective leadership principle in the Chinese party. That in no way negated Mao Tse-tung's "great role," however—as the leader of the collective.

In 1956 the Chinese party had anticipated Khrushchev by absorbing some lessons of the post-Stalinist period. Witnessing Mr. K.'s murderous fight within the Soviet Politburo following the despot's death, Mao had begun to think of avoiding a repetition of it by dividing his own power and naming a successor in his lifetime—as he did two years later. Observing also the demoralizing consequences of too rigid suppression of opposition opinion, Mao had already (January, 1956) declared it his party's intention to invite criticism and debate in an attempt to resolve "contradictions among the people"—a promise made at a Supreme State Conference of 1,800 members of the National Congress and party and nonparty representatives. After congratulating the nation on its unity and rapid advance toward socialism, he enigmatically discussed a policy of "letting a hundred flowers bloom and a hundred schools of thought contend." This was a month before Khrushchev's denunciation of Stalin.

A year earlier (1955), when the party was exhorting the nation to "combat the bourgeois idealism of Hu Feng"—a prominent writer who had called Mao Tse-tung an "imbecile" and a "rotten beast" and was subsequently denounced as a rightist—the official daily had declared:

> There are about five million people who can rank either as intellectuals or as cadres of a certain level of culture, both within the Party itself, and in the various political and cultural organizations. Most of them, let us say three millions, are capable of acquiring a fundamental knowledge of Marxism-Leninism, of understanding the difference between materialism and idealism, of grasping the essentials of dialectical materialism, and *of educating the broad masses of the population which are still on a rather low cultural level.* All the Party committees, at all levels, must take up this matter seriously.[2]

Nowhere had the leadership more frankly acknowledged its dependence on the intellectuals' support nor more clearly indicated its hope to create from them "a new type of scholar-bureaucrat" to serve the functions once performed by the respected Confucian literati and the classics.

Now, in 1956, Chou En-lai surprised the nation's top scientists and scholars at the Supreme State Conference when he even more warmly appealed for support. He said:

> The very large majority of intellectuals have become State officials; they are serving the cause of Socialism and already form a part of the working class . . . Among the front-rank intellectuals [about 100,000] 45% are progressive elements actively

supporting the Communist Party, the People's Government and socialism, wholeheartedly serving the people . . . Among the others, 40% have travelled only halfway . . . 10% are . . . either politically unconscious or definitely opposed . . . A very small number can be classed as counter-revolutionary.[3]

Mao's speech of January, 1956, was not published but Lu Ting-yi, the party propaganda chief, assumed the task of explaining. He declared that Mao had meant: "To artists and writers we say, 'Let a hundred flowers bloom.' To scientists we say, 'Let a hundred schools of thought contend.' " [4] He defined this as "freedom among the people," and predicted that "as the people's political power becomes progressively consolidated such freedom should be given even fuller scope." Science and medicine were declared "to have no class character." But art and literature must avoid "art for art's sake" and be certain to serve socialism and the masses. Remember that this was *before* Mr. K.'s anti-Stalinist speech. Mutual criticism conferences between party and nonparty people were called. The press published mild attacks on the *kanpu* for holding too many meetings, pushing the formation of cooperatives on unwilling peasants, etc.

A drive against excessive bureaucracy had also begun. It branched out slightly to include criticisms of modern China's excessive conformism. An article in the *Ta Kung Pao*, a nonofficial paper, carried the embittered comment that "Chinese intellectuals who have recognized their own future will no longer think of the question of freedom, a term in vogue before liberation." [5] Satire was again raising its head. Official reporters ventured to quote a comment made at a meeting of the Chinese Writers Union. "The themes of literary works should be unlimited," said the speaker. *"One may either praise the new society or criticize the old."* [6] In these words all China recognized a parody of Lu Hsun* in his best "wild grass" period of anti-Kuomintang irony. In an official paper, also, a writer complained that "if everybody is made to conform to the same pattern it will not only violate the laws of objective beings but also be detrimental to the cause of communism." [7] He denounced party bigots who looked upon bookworms as "bourgeois individualists."

Still, Lu Ting-yi's "interpretation of Mao" was not taken seriously. He had both raised and dashed hopes of a "new freedom." His speech was too ambiguous to smoke out twice-bitten intellectuals harboring grievances. Whether the "Hundred Flowers" would have gone beyond party self-criticism had it not been for the Hungarian uprising is debatable.

Peking had welcomed Khrushchev's early attempts at reform. At the same time the party pressed for greater recognition of its own posi-

* Lu Hsun, often called "China's Gorky," was the most influential literary figure of the revolution until his death in 1937. He remains a national hero.

tion as a political co-equal and sought to fill the vacuum of theoretical leadership left by the collapse of Stalinist absolutism. Khrushchev had yet to make a significant statement as a Marxist theoretician. It was not until the Hungarian events that China's importance to Khrushchev's fight for supremacy became apparent.

Peking's reaction to the first phase of Hungary, in October, 1956, was one of sympathy for those who overthrew the Stalinist leadership there. That the East European parties were satellites in a colonial relationship toward Russia was of course well known in Peking, but Chinese theorists could not reconcile it with Marxist theory. Khrushchev's decision to pull out Soviet troops resolved the contradiction for them. In welcoming the restoration of sovereignty in Hungary, Mao's press went so far as to describe the former Soviet position as one of "great power chauvinism" that was fairly close to imperialism itself. China for once echoed criticisms from Belgrade.

But Mao Tse-tung and his Politburo could not really be expected to understand a Hungarian party which had had no experience at all in leadership but only in obedience. They could not foresee that when Khrushchev momentarily left the helm the junior party would be lost. Having won power by their own independent struggle the Chinese found it difficult to follow the dilemmas of Hungarians obliged to administer a revolution without the prestige of having won a revolution. Once the Budapest Communists lost control and were forced to form a coalition which transferred elements of real power to petty bourgeois, anti-Communist and pro-Western groups, Peking abruptly changed tune. The Hungarian nationalist revolution threatened the dissolution of the whole Communist world bloc. Continued unity and the economic support of the bloc seemed indispensable for the stability of China's own leadership.

Chou En-lai was called back from a trip to Indonesia and India to rush to Budapest. Chou then also threw his weight against anti-Soviet party forces in Warsaw. The Premier's arrival on the Danube marked the first intervention of an East Asian power in Europe itself since the days of Genghis Khan.

51

Unity-Criticism-Unity

The downfall of Stalinism, Khrushchev's on-again, off-again flirtation with heretic Tito, the uprising and spreading disaffection in wavering Poland, with echoes in East Germany, and the naked exposure of the Hungarian regime's dependence on Soviet arms alone: all these occurrences could in no realistic sense be reconciled with orthodox Communist dogmas of the past. Circumstances had compelled Khrushchev to relax tensions within the satellite empire; yet as soon as he had done so events had proved how much mightier were the forces for national freedom within the captive states than any proletarian loyalty to the Soviet ideological pattern. Fighting for his life in the Kremlin, Mr. K. was unable to offer any adequate theoretical formulation of his difficulties.

Now an answer was advanced in China when, on December 29, 1956, the second and much longer part of the official treatise, *The Historical Experience of the Dictatorship of the Proletariat*, appeared in the *People's Daily*. By this means Mao presented an international doctrine essentially evolved from his 1937 lecture *On Contradiction*, which he had delivered at Yenan, to analyze the class forces then at war with each other in China. "Contradictions," said the 1956 thesis, exist not only inside bourgeois society and between socialist forces and

capitalist forces, but contradictions also exist between government bureaucracies and the people inside socialist societies, and exist even between fraternal parties and socialist states at different levels in their
growth toward communism. When such contradictions are allowed
to reach the point of "antagonism" or violence even a socialist state
could be overthrown by its own people—misled and confused by foreign imperialists, of course.

Following Khrushchev's revelations of the Soviet party's isolation
from the people under Stalin, Mao Tse-tung had ordered a widespread check on his own cadres and their "style of work" with the
masses. Under circumstances similar to those in Budapest could counterrevolution possibly occur in China, too? How dependable were
the people, the intellectuals, the students—some of the responsible
leaders themselves? How incompetent were the cadres? Conflicts
were reported in many areas where collectivization was being pushed
too rapidly. How many people had been alienated by Khrushchev's
abrupt demolition of Stalin, by Hungary, or by the Chinese party's
own mistakes? How much could the leadership depend upon reports
it got on all such matters from its own cadres? How could anyone
know unless dissenters were induced to speak truthfully under guaranteed immunity?

Tensions of this nature under Stalinism had always been resolved
by secret arrests, mass purges, deportations and executions. Mao Tse-
tung took a new and subtler approach when he elaborated, at the
Eleventh Supreme State Conference of party and nonparty representatives on February 27, 1957, on his speech of a year before. As later
published (June, 1957) it bore the title *On the Correct Handling of
Contradictions Among the People,* and it is a document of first importance in the literature of contemporary Marxism.

Two points might be stressed before considering Mao's speech.
First, it was the opening shot of an official *cheng-tun tso-feng* movement (usually shortened to read *cheng-feng*). The exact meaning is
"evaluate-rectify work-style." The word evaluate is often overlooked
but the purposes of these movements have been threefold: to assess
results, to recognize merit, and to expose and correct mistakes. They
aimed primarily at *party* purification.

On at least one occasion, Mao Tse-tung himself emphasized that
cheng-feng has been misinterpreted abroad because foreign students
fail to comprehend its positive and continuing aims. Many see in it
nothing more than a periodic purgative process. The rectification campaign conducted in 1942 (which became a model for cyclical repeti-
tions) is described by a party historian as follows:

> Under the Leadership of the Central Committee all Party mem-
> bers, by practising criticism and self-criticism, made a thorough
> analysis of their own thinking and work, and examined the Party

leadership, special emphasis being laid on opposing tendencies to subjectivism, sectarianism, and [meaningless] Party jargon. Mao Tse-tung's lectures entitled *Reform Our Study, Rectify the Party's Style in Work, Oppose the Party 'Eight-Legged Essay'* and *Talks at the Yenan Forum on Art and Literature,* and Liu Shao-chi's speeches, *How to Be a Good Communist* and *On Inner Party Struggle*—all played an important role in guiding the campaign.[1]

The second point is that Mao made the first (and thus far the only) attempt by any major Communist leader to draw a lesson from and provide a theoretical explanation for the Hungarian events. In doing so he evolved a kind of coping mechanism to enable his party to maintain national unity while avoiding the gross errors which he believed had led to the Hungarian uprising or, as Communists see it, "counter-revolution."

Mao reasserted that "contradictions" or conflicts of interest exist not only between the socialist state and its class enemies at home and abroad, but also "among the people." They exist between peasants and workers and between the working class and intelligentsia. By extension, they may also exist between socialist-communist governments. In Mao's own words:

> Contradictions do exist between the government and the masses. These include contradictions between the interests of the state, collective interests and individual interests; between democracy and centralism; between those in positions of leadership and the led, and contradictions arising from the bureaucratic practice of certain state functionaries in their relations with the masses.[2]

These truths were later rejected by Khrushchev, who in effect held them to be local problems of the Chinese Communists only, not applicable to Russia and its subordinate states.

If such terms are not to remain mere mumbo-jumbo to the non-believer it may be useful to recall again, briefly, how Marxist dialectics find tangents in traditional Chinese thought. Greek dialectical method, which Marx borrowed via German Hegelianism, had its counterpart in Chinese philosophy before and during the time of the ancient "Warring States." Thoughts attributed to Heraclitus of Ephesus (examples: "Everything is on the move"; "God is day-night, winter-summer, war-peace, satiety-famine"; "Tension or strife of Opposites . . . out of this, harmony is created"; and "Beginning and end are general in a circle") are remarkably comparable to those of the Chinese Taoist sages.[3] The phrase "Let a hundred flowers bloom, let a hundred schools of thought contend" is a quotation from one of the thinkers of the lively "Warring States" period. It does not mean literally "a hundred" of anything but "free struggle" of ideas in general.

The idea of "unity of opposites" is especially manifest in the concept of Tao as depicted in the *I-Ching* (*Book of Changes*), the *Chuang-tzu* and other classics, and in symbols such as the *pa-kua*, or eight triagrams, and the more familiar *yin-yang*.

Tao is the Absolute that contains the total life force, or *T'ai Chi*. The halved circle, one side light, the other dark, indicates all the opposing stresses constantly being transformed and harmonized or synthesized in the Oneness of Nature: light (*yang*) and darkness (*yin*), male and female, dynamism and passivism, growth and decay—unity in division and a perfect dialectical symbol. Taoist symbolism permeates Chinese art, literature and science. Mao Tse-tung has frequently drawn attention to dialectical images in China's folklore in helping to popularize Marxism. Thus:

> All contradictory things are interconnected and they not only coexist in an entity under certain conditions but also transform themselves into each other under certain conditions; this is the whole meaning of the identity of contradictions . . . The innumerable transformations in mythology, for instance, Kua-fu's racing with the sun in the *Book of the Mountains and Seas*, Yi's shooting down of the nine suns in *Huai Nan Tse*, the Monkey King's seventy-two metamorphoses in *Pilgrimage to the West* . . . [are] transformations of opposites into each other as told in legends.[4]

All Men Are Brothers (*Shui Hu Chuang*) contains "numerous examples of materialist dialectics," according to Mao. He cites the episode of Sung Chiang's two attacks on Chu village and his two defeats due to his failure objectively to examine *all sides and all aspects* of the contradictions facing him. Sung Chiang then changed methods by

> conducting an investigation into the situation with the result that he learnt about the intertwining roads, succeeded in disrupting the alliance between the Li, Hu and Chu villages, and won final victory in the third battle after secretly infiltrating his own soldiers into the enemy's camp by a stratagem similar to that of the Trojan horse.[5]

Dialectical materialism used in analyzing any given historical situation—posing a thesis locked in a struggle of contradictions with an antithesis from which emerges a synthesis or continuity—is thus readily acceptable to Chinese minds conditioned by philosophical rather than theistic concepts. To Chinese Marxists, as to Marxists anywhere, the present stage of history (one of basic class antagonisms between the bourgeoisie owners and the working class nonowners) can end in unity only when the contradictions are resolved in a universal Communist society. Inside this mystique, history is not an aimless cycle of rises and falls, as in the Toynbeean mystique of chance "challenge and response," but a set of phenomena which behave in accordance with organic laws ascertainable through Marxism.

All that may seem tedious to pragmatists but it is probably impossible to comprehend contemporary Chinese thinking if it is ignored. This is what the innumerable political meetings and "study groups" are all about. The many millions of Chinese now accustomed to analyze events in this way are not likely to change heads in the visible future, or, as some Old China Hands still imagine, "return to normal" or begin "to think like the West."

In 1957, Mao concluded that the contradictions between the state and ex-capitalists and intellectuals and groups influenced by bourgeois thought were mainly "nonantagonistic" or "within the people." There was, nevertheless, a hangover of "antagonistic" (irreconcilable) conflict also. But in China those "antagonistic" groups had on the whole been benign patriotic citizens who now supported socialism. That is, their nationalist sentiments which coincided with Communist aims overbalanced their anti-Communist sentiments. It was dangerous to leave any contradictions unresolved, however. If they were not met and overcome in debate they might become predominantly "antagonistic" and result in tragedies such as Hungary.

"Marxists should not be afraid of criticism . . . Quite the contrary, they need . . . the storm and stress of struggle," said Mao. "Carrying out the policy of letting a hundred flowers bloom and a hundred schools of thought contend will . . . strengthen the leading position of Marxism. You may ban the expression of wrong ideas but the ideas will still be there. The bourgeoisie and petty bourgeoisie are bound to . . . stubbornly persist in expressing themselves in every possible way on political and ideological questions. We should not use methods of suppression . . . but should argue with them and direct well-considered criticism at them . . . Contradictory forces among the people are the very forces which move society forward."

But:

"The essential thing [for critics] is to start with a desire for unity . . . In 1942[6] we worked out the formula 'unity-criticism-unity' to describe this democratic method of resolving contradictions . . . inside the Communist Party." Now it was time to extend it to the whole people. "What is correct always develops in the course of struggle with what is wrong." However, one must begin debate "only to achieve a new unity on a new basis." "Without this subjective desire for unity, once the struggle starts it is likely to lead to . . . murderous blows."

Thus it was obvious enough that Mao did not intend to license "antagonists" or "evil-doers" to seek to oppose or dissent from the basic system of "democratic dictatorship" to achieve socialism. But how can a dictatorship be run democratically? Mao's explanation: democracy means "freedom for the people," *and* it means "dictatorship for the enemy of the people." That is a phrase which falls naturally from Chinese lips, since it is not derived from Stalin or Lenin or Ibsen or the Romans or even from Periclean Greece but from Ch'in times and earlier. But someone must *manage* the dictatorship for the people. "This freedom is freedom with leadership, and this democracy is democracy under centralized guidance, not anarchy." Said Mao:

"Within the ranks of the people democracy [stands relative] to centralism, and freedom [stands relative] to discipline . . . Our democratic centralism means the unity of democracy and centralism and the unity of freedom and discipline." [7]

It is easy to dismiss these paradoxes as sheer demagoguery. It is not so easy to recognize the underlying pretensions here to an ethical system of "distinguishing between right and wrong" which identifies party leadership with the traditional Chinese expectations of perfect righteousness in its rulers, representing the synthesis or Unity of Opposites.

We should remind ourselves again that Marxism in China was directly transplanted under Leninism and Stalinism, and not from Marx himself. Marx detested liberalism but he was influenced by the contradictory aims of liberal philosophers of his time; he sought to secure individual liberty through first establishing equality by revolutionary means. China did not have even the weak but important liberal tradition of nineteenth-century Russia, which somewhat affected Lenin but never Stalin. No government in China had ever been "liberal" enough to legalize an opposition. China felt little impact from the two centuries of liberating ferment which stirred Europe from Descartes through Mill, Hume, Rousseau, Proudhon, Comte and others. But China had its own humanist tradition which idealized harmony with nature, including the nature of power. Marxism made its strongest appeals to the Chinese desire for both individual and national equality (anti-imperialism); equalitarian social unity imposed at the expense of individual liberty or license was in the logic of Chinese philosophical tradition.

According to the *Gorgias*, when Socrates prevailed in debate with the three wisest men in Greece his concluding moral was that oratory and all activity "must be employed in the service of the right." Moreover, said Socrates, "if a man goes wrong in any way he must be punished and the next best thing to being good is to become good by submitting to punishment." Mao and Socrates might never have agreed on what *is* right, but for Mao also the "knowledge of right" carries with it the duty to "correct" what is wrong within oneself and others and to deprive evil of its freedoms.

These concepts are meant to apply to *both* party and nonparty people. In the published version of his speech Mao Tse-tung laid down six explicit "criteria" by which critics' "words and actions" could be "judged correct." * All of them left no doubt that to be accepted as "nonantagonistic," criticism must not "undermine" but must "help to consolidate all aspects of democratic centralism" and "the socialist path and the leadership of the Party."

Mao's speech was not printed until June 17, when press controls were restored and outspoken critics were beginning to be denounced as "rightists." In a prefatory note he acknowledged that he had made "certain additions." These almost certainly included the "six criteria." On the other hand many references to his speech in public criticisms by delegates to the National Congress who had heard him—comments published before Mao himself appeared in print—as well as in versions leaked abroad via Poland,[9] left no doubt that Mao's original remarks contained all the necessary warning against breaches of "socialist discipline" and "democratic centralism."

Mao had admitted that "some mistakes" had been made by the party. During the "suppression of counterrevolutionaries" there had been "excesses." He called for a comprehensive review of sentences and disfranchisements and asked that "wrongs be righted." He acknowledged that planning errors had resulted in "imbalances" between supply and demand and guaranteed a stabilization of the state grain tax at the existing level. He warned party members against "doctrinarism" and arrogance toward the people. He took note of recent "disturbances" (strikes and conflicts between farmers and cadres) and said that "the root cause of all disturbances was bureaucracy." What was "very bad" was the appearance among "many of our personnel" of "an unwillingness to share the joys and hardships of the masses, a concern for personal position and gain." Mao warned such cadres that "a considerable number of them will return to productive work"—out of the offices and into the farms and ditches.[10]

Mao's speech certainly invited the public to enter complaints against officials and party members guilty of "bureaucratic practices, dogmatism and sectarianism." For two months *after* he spoke that was the theme of countless meetings to discuss his meaning. The *People's Daily* and other papers summarized the "contradictions" theory and party functionaries everywhere made known its contents to a delighted but still skeptical public. "Bourgeois-democratic" parties summoned conferences and began to voice their criticisms. On April

* Mao wrote: "We believe that, broadly speaking, words and actions can be judged right if they: 1) Help to unite people of our various nationalities, and do not divide them; 2) Are beneficial, not harmful, to socialist transformation and socialist construction; 3) Help to consolidate, not undermine or weaken, the people's democratic dictatorship; 4) Help to consolidate, not undermine or weaken, democratic centralism; 5) Tend to strengthen, not to cast off or weaken, the leadership of the Communist Party; 6) Are beneficial, not harmful, to international solidarity and the solidarity of the peaceful peoples of the world." [8]

30, 1957, the Central Committee had issued a directive officially authorizing the beginning of an "evaluation-rectification" campaign to correct the party's "style of work." People were urged to criticize by the highest leaders.

Now the whole country broke out in a rash of forums called by newspapers, magazines, schools, factories, unions, all kinds of organizations, where party leaders listened and lesser party people and nonparty people spoke. The "three evils"—bureaucracy, dogmatism and sectarianism—were freely denounced by those who had become convinced that they could do so not only with impunity but *with approval*. In an access of euphoria some critics forgot that neither Mao nor the party had authorized "counterrevolutionary" demands for an end of "democratic centralism" itself. They put forward ideas for a "multiple party" system which exposed them as unreformed "bourgeois democrats."

At any rate Mao was not long in learning that not all his contradictors were "nonantagonistic"—not by a long shot.

52

---❖---

Wild Flowers

In Peking and elsewhere I spent many hours reading criticisms[1] published during the thaw and I talked to Chinese who had participated in the group "discontent" meetings. The great bulk of protests was hurled against the Communist party cadres, the functionaries, the bureaucrats—against their arrogance, sectarianism, dogmatism, doctrinarism and abuses of power as an entrenched elite. They ranged from "constructive" comment to outcries of bruised egos and from citations of grave injustices and inefficiencies to outright counter-revolutionary exhortations.

"Bourgeois-democratic" party leaders asked for the right to recruit students, peasants, workers and groups from other than the dying capitalist class to which they were obliged to confine themselves. A few proposed a two-chamber parliament and an end to "democratic centralism." Dr. Lo Lung-chi, vice-chairman of the China Democratic League and then minister of the timber industry, summed up the case of the displaced intellectuals:

> There are students of philosophy who work on the compilation
> of catalogs in libraries, students of law who take up bookkeep-
> ing work in offices, students of dye chemistry who teach lan-

guages in middle schools, students of mechanical engineering who teach history. Among the higher intellectuals there are also returned students from Britain who earn their living as cart-pullers and returned students from the United States who run cigarette stalls.²

Dr. Lo was a graduate of Wisconsin and Columbia universities, and now sixty-five; he had been a prominent prewar anti-Kuomintang critic. He was well known abroad. Now he led a number of forums of the League. He was later accused, along with Chang Po-chun, another anti-Chiang liberal, of trying to organize a "conspiracy against the State." What they did advocate was simply the right to form a legal parliamentary opposition party. That might indeed have ended the Communists' monopoly of power, but they went no further than verbalizing.

Not very many of the older and senior intellectuals made outspoken criticisms of the government or party, perhaps because of distrust of the promised immunity. But many thousands of younger "brain workers" vociferously voiced complaints. Scientists and teachers protested against nominal responsibility in positions where real authority lay in the hands of party incompetents. Editors and journalists protested against denials of access to officials and freedom to report facts. They cited the sterile press filled with official propaganda instead of news. Housewives complained that army officers' wives wore leather shoes and "put on airs." Artists protested against being obliged to turn out stereotyped works of "socialist realism."

Teachers hated the long hours required at Marxist study meetings. Students denounced arrogant party cadres who took charge of all activities and suppressed all opinions contrary to their own. Businessmen exposed disastrous orders from party administrators in charge of their plants or shops where they had to retain nominal responsibility. Religious leaders asked for freedom to propagate the faith without having their children excluded from Red Pioneer activities in the schools. Scientists, teachers, civil servants and all groups complained of unqualified people advanced to high positions solely because of party connections while competent nonparty men suffered in the inferior ranks. Instances were cited of heavy overwork and of women deprived of adequate rest before childbirth. Some small businessmen bitterly complained that allowances to them were not adequate to support their families.

All these attacks were published in government newspapers and periodicals or broadcast over the radio. For *six weeks* no attempt was made to answer or suppress them. The party's earnestness in seeking to know exactly what the "ten percent" thought of it is hardly to be doubted. Even demands for rights for "counterrevolutionaries" and threats of violent overthrow of the government appeared in the official *People's Daily*. Consider this sample—by a young lecturer at the China People's University—printed on May 31:

> I think that nothing can be wider apart than relations between the Party and the masses today compared with those in pre-liberation days . . . There is an acute shortage of pork and the common people find the commodity unavailable . . . Who are the people enjoying a higher standard of living? They are the Party members and cadres who wore wornout shoes in the past but travel in saloon cars and put on woolen uniforms now . . . Where has all the pork gone? The shortage is brought about by deviations committed in enforcing planned grain buying and marketing policy which make the common folk unwilling to breed hogs . . .

> China belongs to the 600,000,000 people *including the counter-revolutionaries*. [Italics added.] It does not belong to the Communist Party alone . . . If you carry on satisfactorily, well and good. If not, the masses may knock you down, kill the Communists, overthrow you.

Most protests did not sound like people seeking "unity" but people fed up with unity too long imposed by censorship. Some resembled standard out-of-office grumbling but with one very important difference. In China out-of-office means out-of-influence in practically every field of social endeavor where the individual can command prestige. There were many expressions of agonized frustration by men who aspired to rank and role from which they were barred by the monopoly of power held by the party elite, access to which was denied them except at a low level.

A basic resentment among older Western-educated people who had assumed that they had learned something was the discovery that in Communist eyes they were ignorant. Many knew nothing of Marxism and some were simply not interested in politics but only in their specialized tasks. They had been studying in college halls while Mao and his followers took their degrees with the peasants and organized Marxist study in the hills. Now they had to go back to school again. Not everybody is a Mao Tse-tung and they often had to play student to party dogmatists whom they considered their intellectual inferiors —and who often were their inferiors.

Second, nearly all the alien flowers that bloomed were variations of a single species: lack of freedom—to speak, to move, to publish, to disagree. Among students the demand for civil liberties was uppermost. Mass meetings were held all over the country. Mao himself was seldom attacked but Dr. Lo Lung-chi was quoted in the press as having said at a public forum on May 8: "Chairman Mao is a very shrewd and crafty man, much more ruthless than any other ruler in our history." [3]

Reprints of Lo's speeches and those of other Democratic League leaders were spread around the nation. Tientsin student posters described "present society" as a "place of total darkness." Party leaders were called "rotten eggs" and accused of "intellectual stagnancy." In the universities of Peking thousands of *ta tzu-pao*—wall papers— appeared. Many youths stopped attending classes to hear antiparty speeches and a few professors were attacked. Some students demanded the right to choose their own teachers and curricula; they wanted free food for all, and no more work in the countryside.

On May 25 Mao Tse-tung reminded a meeting of the Communist Youth League that *"All words and actions that deviate from socialism are completely mistaken."* Clearly, anyone opposed to the existing system would be following a dangerous line. Many seemed not to have heard or read what Mao said. But still the party did not counterattack. Letters and articles flooded into the press.

Children of landlord and capitalist families were later blamed for student agitation. Perhaps a few did take part but most of them were only too aware of thin ice beneath them. Many peasants are distantly related to former "great families," however; scratch a peasant and you find a landlord's cousin. The ten million landlords formerly denied voting rights in China have many millions of relatives. It would therefore be easy to establish "bad class background" in almost any case.

Some party youth leaders also joined the chorus of critics. A few protested against Soviet intervention in Hungary; at least one opinion was reported that if Russia's conquest of Hungary was justified then the U.S.A. had a right to intervene in Taiwan. (A poor defense for either one?) The chief of the Communist Youth League propaganda department at Shenyang Normal College was reported in the Shenyang *Daily* on June 11 as having uttered these profoundly antiparty sentiments at a forum:

> The suppression of counter-revolutionaries was necessary and timely but too many persons were put to death . . . Many were formerly military and political personnel of the so-called Manchukuo and Kuomintang and landlords but they were not guilty of heinous crimes . . .

> The cause behind the mistakes of the campaign for rounding up counter-revolutionaries will be traced to the Party centre . . . Now that the Party is in a privileged position Party members of mediocre talent are found everywhere occupying high positions. Old Party members, forgetting the tradition of working for the nation and the people, are fond of flattery and

loath to accept criticism. . . . The Press unanimously sings the praises to its meritorious service and virtue . . . Like two paper flowers the National People's Congress and the People's Consultative Conference decorate the facade of the democracy . . . All kinds of important questions are decided upon by six persons [the Standing Committee of the Politburo] . . . The destiny of 600 millions is directed by the pen of these six persons. And how can they know the actual situation? At best they can make an inspection tour of the Yellow River and swim the Yangtze. Even if they talked to the peasants the peasants would not tell the truth and could only say: "Chairman Mao is great." . . . The party has never criticized itself publicly since the founding of the Republic . . . The National People's Congress must be made an organ for exercising genuine power . . .

Although many critics thus took a "line" that actually *was* "rightist," or counterrevolutionary, in Mao's context, few objected to the socialist aims of the state. Relatively few complained of personal hardships, food shortages, or long hours of work. Many demanded trials of party men held responsible for wrongful punishment of alleged counterrevolutionaries. (Mao himself had called for a "re-examination.") Charges of general police brutality, corruption, bribery and immorality were rare. Some labor union members accused the party of "commandism" (coercion without discussion and persuasion) and cited demands for overtime work without pay. The "Hundred Flowers" was mainly a blooming among both party and nonparty intellectuals. It unfortunately evoked little direct testimony from the less articulate peasants, still the vast majority of the people—as well as the party! But "rightist peasants" were later to come in for a different kind of thought remolding which began with the communes.

There were many thousands of *ta tzu-pao* tacked on bulletin boards before schools, farms and factories of which only a few could see print. Many nonparty editors given freedom to publish what they liked must have retained themselves within self-imposed bounds of discretion.

Despite these limitations the party had by early June accumulated enough data to keep it occupied in rectifications both inside and outside the organization for many months to come. On June 8 the *People's Daily* launched a counterattack. It focused on critics accused of leaving the path of national "unity" and openly advocating a bourgeois-democratic system. That could mean a return to "class struggle" and lead to violence *à la* Hungary and far beyond the scope of non-antagonistic contradictions among the people. "Correct criticisms" were still invited but the publication of Mao's speech on June 17, with addenda including the "six criteria" of loyalty, left no doubt that many had already violated those sanctions.

The party turned the tide. Meetings continued to be held but their purpose now was to denounce "rightists" and to praise the party in "evaluations" with which "critical critics" had forgotten to sweeten their "evaluation-rectification" of "work-style."

53

Counterattack
and Paradox

One curious thing about the Hundred Flowers period was the intensity of the party campaign to evoke criticism of itself. It almost seemed that quotas had been handed out to selected groups of intellectuals, with bonuses for overfulfillment promised to the energetic. Suddenly criticism was the thing. Animadversions by sophisticated party members themselves led others in "speak frankly" meetings again and again.

"People have learned," said a former Chinese Ministry of Interior employee who published a book abroad called *Ten Years of Storm*, "to become double selves, an outer, superficial self which conforms to the demands of the Chinese Communists, and an inner moral self which remains hidden." [1] Chinese dissimulation is an immemorial art, of course, but in reading of this period one is sometimes left wondering whether the "inner moral selves" were speaking now any more than in past extravagances of praise emanating from the same persons.

Another puzzling aspect was that even after new criticisms were cut off in mid-June the government press and radio continued to broadcast attacks against itself. For months the "rightists'" speeches or essays were published while their authors were being haled into forums. The difference now was that they were met with counterattacks from party supporters. Here is one excerpt from a *10,000-word* open letter to Mao Tse-tung written by Yang Shih-chan, an obscure teacher of accounting in Hankow:

> During the campaign for the suppression of counterrevolution-aries in 1955 an untold number of citizens throughout the country were detained by the units where they were working (this did not happen to myself). A great many of them died because they could not endure the struggle [thought remolding] . . . This is tyranny! This is malevolence! . . . articles on human rights have become a kind of window-dressing to deceive people . . . I admit that in seven years . . . achievements are predominant. However, on the particular question of our policy toward intellectuals I should say our policy has been a failure. In the last seven years . . . the intellectuals who chose to die by jumping from tall buildings, drowning in rivers, swallowing poison, cutting their throats, or by other methods, were innumerable . . .[2]

The writer went on to express preference for the Nazi gas chambers or Ch'in Shih Huang Ti's "burial alive of the literati" to the "massacre" of intellectuals in China. In the context he meant psychological or moral destruction by means of "thought remolding" rather than physical "massacre," but the sweeping charges were sensational. Yet even at this late date (July 13) the editor of the government paper which published his letter merely commented at the end, "We can hear the warm applause from Taiwan!"

If that letter had been published before the restoration of official censorship it would be an understandable part of the editor's discretionary responsibility. But it was not easy to see what function it served *for the government* in the post-blooming period. I asked an official about it. His reply was, "If we did not publish the lies of the rightists how could the masses be aroused to the danger and take action?" How could he be so sure that the "masses" would recognize them as "lies"? His answer did not satisfy me but I should have to stay longer in China than I did to find an adequate explanation.

It would be simpler to write this story if one could merely affirm that "millions went to concentration camps, tens of thousands were executed." Such reports were published abroad but as usual lacked any documentation. That might be the answer of Hitler or Stalin but in China the aim of rectification is not to kill but to convert—to make the wrong-thinker see his moral error, to repent, and to seek "unity" with the party.

That the party's legions had been kept silent for so long a period doubtless intensified the severity of the response when it came. Prime targets were Lo Lung-chi and Chang Po-chun, the two most outspoken ideological critics and leaders of the Democratic League. There was no legal indictment. Instead, they were subjected to merciless attacks in meetings of their own peers which were fully reported in the press. Hundreds of students and intellectuals whose views were linked with those of Lo and Chang—who were accused of striving to restore bourgeois democracy and capitalism—were disgraced and called to account in public meetings.

Both Chang and Lo were obliged to make humiliating confessions of having held "incorrect views." An excerpt from Lo Lung-chi's *mea culpa* delivered before his peers in the National People's Congress must suffice to illustrate the nature of "rightism." He said:

> I am a guilty creature of the Chinese People's Republic. I have spoken and acted *against the Communist Party and socialism* . . . I am to be held culpable for egging on and adding fuel to the subversive acts of rightists and even reactionary and counter-revolutionary elements . . . I did not ask the *original Party organs* to reverse the wrongs done [against counterrevolution-aries] but worked for the establishment of *a new organ* to do it. Here I attempted to *negate the leadership* of the basic level of the party . . . I had attempted to . . . expand the organization and *raise the position* of the China Democratic League, thereby acquiring a relatively big voice in national affairs . . . This was where my dream stopped. I do not have and have never had any scheme for the overthrow of the Party and socialism or for the reinstitution of capitalism . . . ." [3]

Any critic who does not seek to help the party leadership, but opposes or competes with it, is obviously committing a crime. It is odd, of course, that anyone as sophisticated as Dr. Lo could have concluded otherwise from Mao's speech. But here is an anomaly. Neither Lo nor Chang ever admitted the charges of a "conspiracy against the state," which were eventually dropped. Indeed, Dr. Lo was permitted to go to Ceylon even after the antirightist campaign began; he would scarcely have returned if he had feared entrapment in a conspiracy. Both Lo and Chang lost their ministerial portfolios but both were restored to their positions in the Political Consultative Conference and took part in the discussion of a successor to Mao Tse-tung held in April, 1959.

Thousands of people who had gone beyond "seeking unity" were denounced as rightists in counterattack meetings led by party wheelhorses. Many who had allegedly "struggled against" the party's leadership were removed from positions of responsibility by "the masses" in the form of votes of no-confidence at meetings of their organizations led by Communists. Very often they were suspended from their posts or had to take inferior jobs while attending weekly study groups and expiating their guilt. Passage of the Law of August 17, 1957, also made it possible for those expelled by their organizations to be subject to "corrective labor." The timing of the legislation suggests that it may have applied to many "rightists" undergoing thought remolding. No complete statistics were published on the number of "rightists." In October, 1959, the government announced that the label had been lifted from 26,000—which I was told unofficially was "the great majority."

Some Western-educated intellectuals were denounced in such extreme terms, including "traitor" and "spy," that one would assume their public life over, yet many have since reappeared in their former positions. The case of a Harvard graduate and university professor, Ch'ien Tuan-sheng, is typical. He was accused of having established contacts (years earlier) with an "American spy-professor," John K. Fairbank (also an ex-State Department official), and of having considered fleeing China at the invitation of another American official. After confessing his sins in 1959, Ch'ien was in the year of my visit again sitting among delegates to the People's Consultative Conference. (It is an ironic fact that Dr. Fairbank was also a target in the late Senator McCarthy's aberrant campaign against those "conspirators in the State Department" who sold China to Russia. He is the only Harvard professor who has succeeded in simultaneously playing both left end and right end for the Crimson.)

Among "rightists" shifted by "their own organizations" to work in the communes was Hsiao Ch'ien, a British-educated novelist and editor who was an old friend of mine from Yenching University days. He had had the misfortune to be editor of the Wen Yi Pao, a literary paper which published some slashing attacks on party cultural leaders and their policies. I inquired about Hsiao Ch'ien when I met Lau Shaw (Hsu Shih-yu), whose Rickshaw Boy was a wartime Book of the Month in America. He had so far overcome that handicap that he was now vice-chairman of the Writers Union. He told me that Hsiao Ch'ien was "happily working in a commune" and "no longer much interested in writing," a change of character which I could not at all imagine. He insisted that only a "small minority" of members of the Writers Union had been sent to do farm labor.

On the other hand I met a writer less well known than Hsiao Ch'ien, who had completed his "restudy of the sources of art" in a commune and returned to Peking, sunbrowned and apparently enthusiastic, with a batch of manuscript under his arm. He said he had "never felt better, in every way." I also inquired about the woman novelist Ting Ling, who had been reported abroad as disgraced. If what I was told by a Very High Official is true, her exile from Peking may have had little to do with her writings and is a much more serious affair. Another old friend, a Russian-trained artist, had lost his job as deputy director of the Art Academy and was doing "research on an encyclopedia." I sent letters to two other former student friends; though I was told that they were in Peking I received no replies from them. After one visit to Yenching I gave up trying to contact Chinese professors I had known there. I was stiffly received by an administrator, and an English-speaking dean insisted on using an interpreter. Private conversation did not seem feasible.

By contrast, I dined in town with a group of students and professors I had known years ago; they were all in their forties or fifties now. I ran over a list of names of party and nonparty people. One was now a deputy mayor; one was a vice-minister; one was an ambassador; one was a publisher, another an editor; there was an engineer here, a doctor there, a few teaching, others retired, some killed in the war or dead from natural causes, four or five in Hongkong, and quite a number in the National Congress.

I inquired about Fung Yu-lan, the distinguished Chinese philosopher and historian, who had been reported imprisoned. I was told he was teaching at Pei-ta and that I could see him if I wished; I did not find time, but Dr. Fung was interviewed by Felix Greene, the British correspondent.[4] Another well-known American-educated professor I asked about was Hubert Liang, who had been a colleague of mine at Yenching. A former admirer of the Generalissimo who had returned to work in China, Liang had had the misfortune to be praised on the Taiwan radio, and was thereafter rumored to have been liquidated. In Peking I was told by Rewi Alley that he was teaching in Nanking University. I was also able to trace another former colleague of mine, Lu Kuang-mien, said to be in trouble. He was teaching in Kunming. Dr. Fei Hsiao-t'ung, a distinguished Western-educated social anthropologist, had written a report prematurely critical of the results of some agrarian policies. (Two years later the party press was making some of the same self-criticisms.) I was told that he had gone through *hsueh-hsi* but was not harmed, as believed abroad, and was still a member of the Academy of Sciences. The book *Ten Years of Storm* stated at length that Lin Piao had disappeared because he had aroused Mao Tse-tung's "jealousy."[5] Lin was actually hospitalized (and is still not well) but he is today Minister of National Defense and a member of the inner party secretariat. Rumor is not always "a pipe blown by surmises, jealousies, conjectures," but it is well to look twice to see who is playing it.

A Very High Official told me quite flatly that only persons engaged in counterrevolutionary "acts of violence" were arrested and that no mere dissenter, individualist or critic of party mistakes was punished. (That may depend on whether one considers public denunciation punishment.) According to him the promise of immunity was fully observed. In *The Hundred Flowers*, probably the most detailed study made of the available data, Roderick MacFarquhar offered no evidence of any executions during the period beyond those of three student leaders of a "revolt" near Wuhan. Accused of leading physical attacks on officials and police and attempts at organizing "armed rebellion" in the countryside, these students were executed before 10,000 people. MacFarquhar thinks that they were singled out because the government was more concerned about dissaffection among students—traditionally the leaders of popular discontent in China— than among any other group.[6]

There is nothing conclusive about all this, but from what I could learn in China I should say that it is not fear of physical liquidation or even of concentration camps which torments those intellectuals still unable freely to adhere to the party, but the far subtler and socially more complicated means of securing conformance. Thought remolding, or "brain washing" as it is called abroad, conducted not in concentration camps but by one's peers; a choice for stubborn "reactionaries" between social ostracism and the anguish of public recantation; a spell of down-on-the-farm at the recommendation of one's own organization; and various other measures which in the past would have been called public "loss of face": these are the main instruments of pressure. They can be as cruel to sensitive people as corporal punishment but they may leave open a path of reconciliation.

"You can have no idea how agonizing these self-criticism and group meetings can be," I was told by one American-educated intellectual who returned to China a decade ago and joined the party. "Everybody in my bureau from the office boy or scrubwoman up can tell me how bourgeois I am, criticize my personal habits, my family life, my intellectual arrogance, the way I spend my leisure, even my silences. I have to sit and take it." He paused to grimace. "Some people prefer suicide rather than submit to it. It took me years to get used to it but now I believe it has been good for me. I needed it—how I needed it! I am seldom a target any more. I am a lot humbler than I was. I value people more. I am better able to help others." And he, I repeat, was a party member in good standing. To some extent these meetings clearly serve the purpose of group or mass therapy and help older individuals adjust to a society which must seem normal only to the young.

A notable thing about the public denunciations of intellectuals during the rightist campaign is that they included very few, if any, senior scientists or academicians and practically no graduate scientists or engineers of any kind. That the party was especially scornful of Lo Lung-chi and other nonscientists—men with degrees in law, social studies and the arts—was doubtless partly because the leaders looked upon them as merely displaced politicians seeking power who had no remedy to offer except a return to the bourgeois ideology of the Kuomintang, which had already proved incapable of solving China's problems.

Conversely, it is certain that the "blooming" was genuinely intended by the leadership to induce "useful" intellectuals to express their grievances in the hope of reconciling them and drawing more such men into the party. In his speech "On the Question of the Intellectuals" Chou had admitted that:

> Certain irrational features in our present employment and treatment of intellectuals and, in particular, certain sectarian attitudes . . . have handicapped us. [To] overcome our shortcomings . . . is now the fundamental task for our Party on questions of intellectuals . . . According to available statistics there are now, in all, 3,840,000 intellectuals . . . The Party's policy toward [them] has not been properly carried out . . . 10% of our higher intellectuals are in posts for which they are not suited.[7]

He had said that intellectuals were required to attend too many meetings, their salaries needed adjustment upward, their social status was too low, their living conditions needed improvement, and scientists needed more time for research work. Intellectuals "criticize us for 'making great use' of them but giving them 'very little help.' Others complain that we approach them for three purposes only: 1) to transfer them to other work, 2) to ask them to clear up points in their past history, or 3) because they have committed some mistakes. These are sharp criticisms," Chou warned the party, and "we should pay attention to them."

Another paradox. Despite the external view that the entire period was a fiasco, it must be noted that it was not the end but the beginning of a most intensive and still continuing "Hundred Flowers" campaign—confined strictly to Mao's six "criteria" of "correct" discussion—to win the adherence of more intellectuals to the party. By 1961 this apparently had helped to increase overall party membership by 30 percent, as already reported, and doubled its percentage of "intellectuals." From the volume of denunciation poured forth against a mere handful of nonparty critics and "bourgeois democrats" it was evident that such people as Lo Lung-chi and Chang Po-chun furnished convenient pretexts for a major overhaul of membership in the party itself. *The rectification affected immeasurably more Communists than non-Communists* and reached as high as provincial governors and committeemen, many of whom were dismissed from their posts. Thousands of party members were denounced for the "three evils," as well as for "rightism." As many as one million cadres may have been put on probation.

In one province the governor, judges of the supreme court, an army general and even the first secretary of the party were removed. Statements published against them *by the open press* included a report that the first secretary had made publicly such utterances as "famine occurred continuously," "we are sitting on top of a volcano," "the problem of food production will not be solved in ten years," "the peasants are beasts of burden, human beings harnessed in the fields" and "girls and women pull harrows with their wombs hanging out." [g]

Final paradox. To this same province, a few months later, came Mao Tse-tung on a personal fact-finding tour, part of the time in Liu Shao-ch'i's company. Of all the consequences of bloom-and-contend and "search for unity" none was more momentous than this. Here in a province of party dissension there now began an experiment—the people's rural communes—which would in less than a year shake Chinese society more fundamentally than anything that had happened since the revolution.

Part Five

NORTHWEST:
OLD CRADLE
OF
NEW CHINA

☆

The party secretary in Honan province wrote an article in which he said that the attainment of communism for the "whole people" would some day be marked by the commune's ability to satisfy each person's ten basic needs; free supply arrangements covering all accommodations for marriage, birth, food, clothing, shelter, education, health, theater (entertainment), burial services—and "haircut," meaning cosmetics and adornment. Leo Tolstoy wrote a story called, "How Much Land Does a Man Need?" His penniless hero wandered to a tribe which possessed limitless grassland, and there the good-natured chieftain promised the visitor all the land he could walk around between sunrise and sunset. The poor man's greed far exceeded his strength; by sundown he had run so hard to complete his boundaries that upon his return he fell dead at the feet of the chief. He was buried in a six-foot plot of land, which was all he then needed.

In prophesying a time of "each according to his need" which would correspond to a "withering away of the state," Marx could not avoid, despite his hard-headed realism, the temptation to hold forth the image of man finally perfected, as have all great religious teachers. All the experience of modern civilization to date, whether under socialism or communism, tells us that the greater become the means of the attainment of equality among men, the greater becomes the necessity to curb and reform mankind's incessant greed and selfishness.

Yet one can of course envisage a distant Utopia where the "whole people" have become one with and consumed the entire state apparatus and its rulers into their selfless selves. That time would seem to await the day when men and women of great nations like China, Russia and the United States could amicably agree on the meaning of "how much" is "in accordance with need"—in simple matters like food, for example, or a haircut. The most encouraging fact in the list of the ten necessities was the omission of any kind of weapon.

54

Of Blue Ants
and White

Before investigating the people's communes one needs to see something of the hard logic of large-scale collectivization in China in relation to her fearfully difficult demographic problems. Overpopulation was not something invented by the Communists but was inherited. By greatly increasing mass employment and introducing the first effective rationing system ever known in China, the Communists have so far prevented the traditional annual harvest of deaths by mass starvation. The paradox is that imbalances between population and food supply seem to be intensifying everywhere in the world, almost in proportion to the success of measures to prevent disease, increase longevity, and improve conditions for legalized sexual activity. The dilemma at times makes one wonder, with Graham Greene, if God was entirely serious when he gave man the sexual instinct. (Mr. Greene reminds us that it was St. Thomas Aquinas who said that He made the world in play.) Whether we may regard the situation as tragic or merely amusing may depend upon whether the condition is permanent or temporary. Chinese Communists—perhaps fortunately for the rest of the world—believe that it can, in China at least, be remedied.

Overpopulation is a relative term. If China were as densely populated as England, Belgium, the Netherlands or Japan, there would be between three and four billion Chinese, or more than the present world population. *Studies on the Population of China, 1368-1953*, a remarkable book by Ho Ping-ti,[1] vividly suggests that this might well have happened if the Chinese had colonized the New World or otherwise escaped natural and man-made catastrophes. In his classic *Histoire de la Chine,* René Grousset gives census figures gathered in the Ming and Ch'ing dynasties as follows: 104,700,000 in 1661; 182,-076,000 in 1766; 329,000,000 in 1872.[2]

"Are the Chinese," many worried Malthusians asked me on my return to America, "doing anything at all about birth control?" The question reminded me of a remark General Douglas MacArthur once repeated to me. Paul McNutt, former governor of Indiana and at the time High Commissioner of the Philippines, had said to him pessimistically that the Philippines after independence would never have an honest election. "You're absolutely right, Paul," MacArthur responded, "but I'll tell you something else. The Philippines will have a more honest election than you ever had in the state of Indiana." The Chinese government may not be doing as much about birth control as it should, but it is doing a lot more about it than the government of the United States.

China is slightly larger in area than the United States. In 1870 the American population was 38,000,000. It has since increased by nearly five times while China's population merely doubled. Europe and China are almost equal in area. China had about 200,000,000 blue ants at the time the white ants of Europe began migrating on a mass scale. Since then Europeans have filled three "new" continents (and parts of a fourth) with an aggregate population of 420,000,000. If we combine that with the present population of Europe (including Russia) we get more than a billion people and see that the imperiled West has been doing its share of propagating. Today Chinese immigrants are virtually excluded from all those continents, although one of them, Australia, could accommodate several times its present population. What would be the long-range future of such a continent if it were inhabited by fewer than ten million brown men who wholly excluded immigrants from powerful neighboring states holding more than a billion *white* men?

In this perspective there is some irony in European fears of a yellow peril from a people that has taken five thousand years to fill out China's present frontiers on one continent while Europeans were seizing and populating most of the world. To the unreasonable Chinese this Western behavior looks more like imperialism than their own claims to Tibet, which was a tributary state of China several hundred years* before the North American Indians were subjugated by white invaders. The present Chinese increase, some 2 percent annually, is now about the same as that of the United States. But China's base

* Tibet was first formally annexed to China during the Yuan Dynasty, in 1253.

is so large that *les fourmis bleues* may number a billion by 1980. By then the white ants will be two and a half billion, however, if fruitful pullulation continues at current tempos.

Sir Thomas Malthus maintained that human ants of all kinds inevitably "multiply faster than the means of subsistence." If he was right, crowded stay-at-home peoples—the Indians, Japanese and Chinese—are doomed to famine or wars of expansion. Such catastrophes are not likely to be confined to the East. Before the revolution modern contraceptives were known and used by only an infinitesimal fraction of the Chinese population but "native methods" were practiced. Abortion was illegal but frequent; infanticide was the "guaranteed method" widely in use by the poor. In China, impoverished families had fewer children than "well-to-do," the reverse of the usual situation in the West.[3] More than a century ago Marx ridiculed Malthus, and Russian Communists have done likewise. Before taking power the Chinese party rejected birth control on Marxist grounds that man could produce his means of subsistence faster than he reproduced himself. After six years of effort to double the rate of food output compared to population growth, with erratic success, the Communists adopted a more realistic policy. In 1956, Peking recognized the practical necessity to limit births "in order to lighten consumption by nonproducers during the present period of socialist construction," as one advocate put it. A nation-wide campaign spread knowledge of modern "family planning" methods to every village and town. Graphic posters, picture books, movies and demonstration lectures carried the methods right into the peasant's home. After a trial period these efforts waned at a time which coincided with the development of commune plans.

From conversations with Women's Federation leaders I conclude that the campaign encountered mass resistance due to the following reasons: The peasants and some peasant-minded workers "weren't ready for it yet"; they still associated offspring with old-age security. (By law children are still obliged to help support their parents.) Sex and childbirth are matters of private management which people are reluctant to turn over to the state. Competent instructors were not yet available on a mass scale. Despite greatly lowered infant mortality rates, peasants still want extra children as insurance against the great number of deaths remembered from the past. Peasants ask how it benefits them to live in a welfare state if they don't use their right to reproduce. Latent sentiments of filial piety and centuries of male-ancestor worship cannot in one decade be submerged by the Marx-Engels concept of the family.

As with nearly everything else, party cadres overfulfilled their quotas on mass birth-control propaganda. Too much and too soon, it ran into the same kind of opposition met by earlier campaigns to enforce the new marriage law which legalized "on-demand" divorce. In the past divorce for women was practically unknown in China. Sudden party insistence on women's use of their new rights went to such extremes as developing "fronts" among husbands and wives, and calling "frank confession" meetings in public. After dissatisfied concubines had shed their aging bourgeois husbands and numerous men and women had dissolved misalliances arranged by their parents, divorce ceased to be popular. The campaign boomeranged until the marriage law became known as the "divorce law."

Contraceptives are on sale for both men and women. At various hospitals and clinics I found that standard devices were available at the equivalents of twenty to thirty American cents. I was told that they are supplied gratis when necessary. In remote Szechuan at a rather primitive clinic I was shown charts, demonstration equipment and plentiful supplies but was also told that the demand for instruction was "light." A pessary there cost thirty cents. Existing supplies would doubtless prove inadequate if the population applied en masse, but for those who presently "plan" there seemed to be no shortage.

Both abortion and sterilization were as easily available in China in 1956 during the "family planning campaign" as advice on contraception. While the advice is still disseminated through radio talks and literature, sterilization is now obtainable only through a doctor's recommendation and abortion is discouraged although still performed on the same condition. The extent to which people may submit to sterilization is indicated by experience in India, where significant cash inducements were offered together with free surgery. By 1960 only 22,000 cases were reported, or about one in 20,000.

A British-educated Indian demographer, S. Chandrasekhar, of the Institute of Population Studies of Madras, visited China in 1959. Like most travelers, he was "continually impressed by how clean and neat everything was," but he drew attention to the consequences for China's food economy. In the *Atlantic Monthly* of December, 1961, Mr. Chandrasekhar wrote that in 1959 the birth rate had attained forty per thousand while the death rate had been reduced to "twelve per thousand, an incredibly low figure for an Asian country. The infant mortality rate, a sensitive index to a community's level of public health, environmental hygiene, and total cultural milieu, was around fifty per thousand births per year." Mr. Chandrasekhar elsewhere says in effect that this represents a reduction of about 75 percent as compared to prerevolution estimates.

Mr. Chandrasekhar's figures would not apply to the country as a whole; as stated above, China's annual increase is about 2 percent, if the 1953 census was correct.[4] This figure was also given to me as "average" by Chou En-lai in 1960.[5] Even if China's increase dropped to as low as the current Japanese rate (1.01 percent;[6] the United States rate is 40 percent higher than Japan's) the result would be six to seven million more Chinese annually. India faces an even more serious problem than China, however, with the gap between her food output and the minimal survival needs of a third of her population widening each year. According to the Ford Foundation report already cited, India will by 1966 have 25 percent more people than she can adequately feed.

The dismissal of Ma Yin-ch'u from his post as president of Peking University in 1960 was attributed abroad to his espousal of birth control. The Peking authorities said he was retired because of "old age." He was seventy-six, but he had one of China's most active and independent minds and was in good health. A Yale graduate and a famous economist, Ma had made a deep impression on intellectuals when he decided to collaborate with the Communists. He did advocate birth control but he was not a Malthusian. In 1956 he published an original theory of "overall balance and proportional development" in economic planning which stressed the danger of retrogression by overdevelopment of industry at the expense of agriculture. For that he was strongly attacked, but he held his ground until party stalwarts forced his resignation. It is interesting that Mao Tse-tung nevertheless not only praised Ma's "eight point charter for agriculture" but had the party adopt it. In 1961 Ma still retained his seat in the National Congress. It was also significant that in 1961, Ma Yin-ch'u's "original theory" still remained unanswered.

Literature and radio broadcasts continue to publicize techniques of birth control and periodicals urge young people to use contraceptives for family planning. Many workers and peasants I questioned, as well as the college girls I have mentioned, said that they were "planning" for no more than two or three children. Party members told me that within the party "undisciplined" procreation is frowned upon. Most high-ranking party members have small families, although I know at least one who (somewhat embarrassedly) last year celebrated the birth of his seventh child in quest of a son! The two-child family is regarded as ideal and party functionaries receive no extra allowances* for more children.

A means of "planning" which might not work in another society but has produced a noticeable effect in China is the officially sponsored social approval for late marriages. For an ambitious student, early marriage can be a handicap, as in the West, and today everybody is supposed to be an ambitious student. The prestige of the party and the press behind marriage for men at twenty-five to twenty-seven and for women at twenty-one to twenty-three as "ideal" has made it stylish among the closely party-led youths. Their example may eventually impress the "outer-directed" peasant masses, who also do not like to

---

* Party and nonparty cadres or state employees are divided into eight "grades" which correspond to workers' levels in salaries and rations, but they get extra allowances, usually small, in accordance with the different demands of their tasks.

be found behind the times or "old-fashioned." The party does not "select brides and grooms," as reported abroad, but young people often consult group leaders as well as parents before they marry.

There was thus no "reversal" of policy, nor can anything like an increase-the-race campaign now be seen. What happened was that the Chinese realized that far more immediate solutions to problems of underemployment, underproduction, and maldistribution of man power were needed than family planning could provide. China's already existing millions are a fact of *Realpolitik* which cannot be changed by a command from Mao Tse-tung ordering half the population to drop dead; despite cynical Western notions to the contrary, he is not that omnipotent. Nor is it good politics, in China any more than elsewhere, to tell one's constituents that they should never have been born. That Mao and other leaders had repeatedly declared China's numbers to be her "greatest asset" also presented a contradiction to overdependence on birth control and spurred them on to seek other solutions.

No long-range adjustment can change the facts that more than 60 percent of China's vast territory stands above 6,600 feet and another 15 percent may prove nonarable because of climate and topography. Until advanced industrialization makes more extensive and intensive farming possible, the immediate problem will remain the overpopulation of China's available cropland. On the North China plain the average density is more than 1,000 per square mile. In parts of Szechuan and the Yangtze delta it reaches 3,000 per square mile. The national average is now not more than 0.39 of an acre of farmland per inhabitant (assuming a 1962 population of 700,000,000).

Yet China's agronomists by no means saw the outlook as hopeless. Brushing aside pessimistic views held in the past by Western experts on China, they were now convinced beyond doubt that the nation's agricultural output could be better than doubled by 1970 or earlier and provide more than adequate food. Was all this fantasy? Japan stood as proof to the contrary. With only about 8,000,000 acres of grain croplands (or scarcely more than half an acre per cultivator) Japan now turns out annually about 20,000,000 tons of basic cereal food, most of it rice.[7] If China could equal Japan's performance, her annual harvests (considering her higher percentage of multiple cropping) would indeed quadruple. If, furthermore, China's farmland can eventually be doubled—as her leaders now assert—she could not only satisfy her own needs but become a major grain exporting country for the first time in history.

Britain and West Germany have only half as much cropland per inhabitant as China; Denmark, the Netherlands, Japan and Belgium all have even less than that. Yet the per person income of China is from one-tenth or less to one-third or a fourth as high as in those countries. The difference is of course explained by the degree of industrialization, modernization of agriculture, and trade development. The farmers of

China are not less capable, and the I.Q. of its people is no lower than that of any other people; historically its society has demonstrated an efficiency higher than that of most nations. China's natural resources are now known to be not inferior to those of the countries cited above; they are markedly richer than those of Japan, where the effective organization of human labor has been the foundation of present wealth.

Japan achieves her gratifying grain output by the most intensive kind of scientific cultivation, including the use of ten or more times as much chemical fertilizer per acre as China, and by extensive application of power, mechanization, crop protection and government grain controls. (As in China, farmers in Japan are required to make fixed grain deliveries to the state.) By 1958 China's industry was not yet producing modern means of agriculture on anything like the scale required. In that year the Great Leap Forward and the organization of the people's communes were launched for a variety of reasons. Among them lay the hope that communes would reward the party's search with at least interim answers to the problem which plagues many countries besides China: too many people living on land producing too little to feed them.

55

Co-ops to Communes

On August 29, 1958, the party Central Committee published its earth-shaking directive which called for the establishment of People's Communes: "It seems that the attainment of communism in China is no longer a remote event. We should actively use the form of the people's communes to explore the practical road of transition to communism."

Up to this date China had not yet completed even the first stage of what Mao Tse-tung had called *semisocialist* rural cooperatives. Suddenly:

> agricultural cooperatives with scores of families or even several hundred families can no longer meet the needs of the changing situation . . . the establishment of people's communes with all-round management of agriculture, forestry, animal husbandry, sideline occupations and fishery, where industry, agriculture, exchange, culture and education, and military affairs merge into one, is the fundamental policy to guide the peasants to accelerate socialist construction, complete the building of socialism ahead of time, and carry out the gradual transition to communism.[1]

The directive demanded prompt merger of all producers' cooperatives into large units embracing whole townships (*hsiang*) each "comprising about 2,000 peasant households." Township governments and township party committees were to become commune governments and take control of former cooperatives.

Share funds were to be pooled and assets and debts consolidated. While some cooperatives were richer than others, the "cadres and masses" should "be educated in the spirit of communism" and "not resort to minute squaring of accounts, insisting on equal shares and bothering with trifles."

> The transition from collective ownership to ownership *by the people as a whole* may take less time—*three or four years*—in some places, and longer—five or six years or even longer—elsewhere . . . differences between workers and peasants, town and country and mental and manual labor . . . will gradually vanish. After a number of years . . . Chinese society *will enter into the era of communism* where the principle from each according to his ability and to each according to his needs will be practiced.[2]

Community dining rooms, kindergartens, nurseries, sewing groups, barber shops, public baths, "happy homes for the aged" and agricultural middle schools were to be organized. "Large-scale agricultural capital construction and more advanced agricultural technique and rural mechanization and electrification," and cooperation "which cuts across the boundaries between cooperatives, townships and counties," should be realized by the new commune governments with pooled labor, tools and resources.

In the whole history of the People's Republic there had never been such an abrupt and sweeping change ordered by so loosely worded a directive. Editorials and articles in the press offered much more radical and explicit authorization for the communization of remaining private property. In particular, the "Regulations" followed by the first people's commune to be publicized—called Weihsing (Sputnik) in Honan province—provided an exact prototype. In September the Honan party secretary wrote:

> Amid the high tide of water conservancy [building of dams, reservoirs, irrigation canals, by mass labor during the Great Leap Forward] and increased production, people in the whole province broke down the boundaries between counties, townships and cooperatives; extensive socialist cooperation involving millions of individuals was organized in the cities and countryside, and mountain areas and plains, brushing aside

personal considerations . . . and remnants of private ownership.[3]

The Honan "Regulations" required each village co-op to "turn
over all its collectively owned property." That included co-op shares
—which would "bear no interest"—and "privately owned plots of
farmland, house sites and other means of production such as livestock,
tree holdings, etc.," to be surrendered "on the basis that common
ownership of the means of production is in the main in effect."
Co-op members could "keep a small number of domestic animals
and fowls as private property" but no more.

Communes must build more irrigation works, apply more manure,
provide better seeds, breed animals, fight pests, "develop industry
as rapidly as possible," open up mines, iron, steel, farm tool and
fertilizer plants, build electric power stations and roads, establish
telephone and radio networks, take over education and the militia,
organize supply and marketing departments, deliver grain quotas to
the state at fixed prices, and control all trade for the whole system
of cooperatives. Everyone would be provided for "in accordance with
his work."

"The commune shall institute a system of centralized leadership,
with management organs at various levels, in order to operate a responsible system of production." Village co-ops were to be grouped as
production brigades under multiple-village "production contingents."
The production brigade was to become "a basic unit for organizing
labor" under commune direction.

The commune administration was to improve medical establishments
and build "housing estates" that would gradually replace individual
homes from which "bricks, tiles and timber" would be used by the
commune "as needed." Owners were not to be compensated for the old
houses or house sites or for their land used for public works. From
the yearly income, welfare funds "not exceeding 5 percent of the
total income" were to support cultural, health and public services, and
grain stocks "sufficient for one to two years" were to be accumulated.
All food would be supplied by the commune, with wages paid to
"ensure high speed of expanded production." When members reached
an average "living standard equivalent to that of well-to-do middle
peasants the rate of increase in wages should be reduced to ensure
the rapid growth of industry, the mechanization of farming and electrification of the rural areas in the shortest possible time."

Here was an ultimate program for the Absolute Welfare State—if
it worked! With land, labor, tools and agricultural resources placed
under the management of commune governments acting as agents for
central planning authorities, the program promised maximum control
and efficiency over all the basic means of rural production, distribution and investment of the national income.

Fantastic? No. Within the context of China's demographic and land problems, it was in theory highly logical. Even today it seems possible that the rural commune more or less as originally envisaged may eventually provide a rational solution for China. What went wrong?

What threw the communes for a great initial loss was the incredible haste with which they were established; the lack of adequate experimentation and preparation; the suddenness of the mass leveling imposed on prosperous villages and prosperous individual farmers when they were equalized with poorer ones; the lack of incentives to replace the drastic withdrawal of autonomous village control; the threat to home life before a broader community life had been fully established to replace it; the enormous technical responsibility and initiative demanded from inexperienced and poorly trained cadres; and the ruthless disregard of "the principle of voluntariness" by a vast army of township bureaucrats who mushroomed overnight and began to take charge of every hour of the people's lives. When unbelievably bad weather added its powerfully negative vote, the communes were rapidly driven back into a preparatory stage which the party had tried to jump over in 1958—at great cost to production.

Who was responsible for the hasty and euphoric directive of August 29? At first glance it looks like Mao Tse-tung. Yet with special reference to the organization of co-ops Mao himself in 1955 had repeated an old wartime slogan: "Fight no battle that is not well prepared, no battle whose outcome is uncertain." He said that "a great deal of spade work" was necessary before even producers' cooperatives could be accepted over all China.[4] As late as June, 1957, Mao still thought a period of *"five years or a bit longer"* would be required merely to "consolidate the cooperatives and end these arguments about their not having any superior qualities." He added:

As for social reform, cooperatives *after 1960* will gradually change, group by group and at different times, from cooperatives of a semisocialist nature to fully socialist ones. Only when socialist transformation of the socio-economic system is complete and when, in the technical field, all branches of production and places wherein work can be done by machinery are using it, will the social and economic appearance of China be radically changed. The economic conditions of our country being what they are, technical reform will take longer than social reform. It is estimated that it will take roughly *four or five* five-year plans [i.e., till 1972-75] . . . to accomplish, in the main, the technical transformation of agriculture on a national scale.[5]

Yet only a year later the party was leading the universal establishment of the ultraleftist communes (promising "ownership by the whole people" in three or four years), and Mao's name was being invoked to sponsor them!

This is one of many threads of mystery yet to be untangled. Before touching a few more of them a review of the main stages of agricultural transformation may help establish some perspective on the communes.

Remember, first, that 0.39 of an acre of farmland available per inhabitant! For the Communists the equalization of private land ownership was merely a first step to an end, and so their party program openly declared. To win "majority" support they had, for purposes of "agrarian reform," divided the rural population into great, middle and small landowning families, about 10 percent of the population; rich and middle peasants, 20 percent; and poor peasants, tenants and farm laborers, 70 percent of the population—the "have-nots."

By 1952 the landlords had lost most of their land, the owner-tillers had retained most of theirs, and 300,000,000 peasants (60 percent to 70 percent) had received 118,000,000 acres* or 45 percent of the cultivated land. Parcels handed out varied from only .15 to .45 acres per person.[6] The Communists thus sought to make allies of roughly 300,000,000 peasants, and to neutralize about 100,000,000 more. The Communists sought to win the vast majority of the population—not just "the proletariat" but "the people"—and then by stages educate them by the example of "correct" behavior and "right ideas" to accept socialism. "In the land reform we can and must unite about 92 percent of the households or about 90 percent of the population in the villages," Mao lectured the party cadres in 1948. "In other words, unite all the rural working people to establish a united front against the feudal system."[7] On the support of these millions of "rural working people"—and especially on the support of women and youths who shared in the distribution—the Communists heavily depended in every subsequent phase of the transition toward large-scale farming.

The new owners lacked good seeds, animals, livestock, fertilizer, tools, scientific methods—and capital. Individual earnings from fragmentary subsistence plots could never secure these necessities. Even before the land distribution was completed an all-China campaign began for mutual-aid cooperatives such as had been long established in the old Red bases in the Northwest.[8] Coercion was used by extending or withholding state loans and by state control of the market. Poor peasants who pooled labor, animals and implements in group cultivation and harvesting, and in general tasks of community interest, got maximum state assistance. Advantages were obvious and probably most peasants readily joined cooperatives in self-interest—as they did also in the next stage, conventional farm cooperatives.

From 1952 to 1956 rural cadres, using a combination of persuasion

* 700,000,000 *mou.*

and such coercive means as described, led the peasants from agrarian reform to mutual-aid teams to elementary cooperatives and finally to the stage of "advanced" producers' cooperatives. Under the elementary co-ops the villagers pooled their land, animals and other resources in exchange for shares which represented the value of their individual investments. Their income was based on share value plus their labor contribution. The "advanced" co-op was a whole village— sometimes several villages—of 100 to 200 families who elected a local council ("congress") which chose its own managers. The peasants turned in their deeds and resources, income was collectively owned and invested for the whole village, and wages were paid in accordance with work performed.

The advanced co-op had many advantages, particularly when several villages formed a big one. Council management could join small plots into large ones, decide what land was best suited for orchards, pasture, and irrigation, how much was needed for cash crops like cotton, how much for consumption, and how much to invest in new equipment and construction. All this had to be coordinated with plans at the township and county levels but the village retained much power of decision. Farmers still lived on land to which, although it was now held in common, they felt individual or ancestral attachments of ownership. They also retained their minuscule private garden plots.

All the advanced co-ops could do things beyond the reach of the individual farmer. But few were rich enough to buy modern tools or build good canals, power dams, roads, mines, cattle breeding stations, local railways, or establish farm equipment, fertilizer and consumer-goods industries. Only the larger multivillage co-ops could do those things. Villages with improved land forged ahead faster than those that had drawn poor land and the former did not readily enter into multivillage planning with the latter. Private plots seldom exceeded a twentieth of an acre but in prosperous villages the smart peasants got hold of the best gardens, lent money to other peasants, established a claim on their output or land and acquired livestock. They soon began to resemble small kulaks.

By 1957 about 120,000,000 households, or 96 percent of the peasantry, had pooled their cooperative shares (for which they had exchanged their former land deeds) and their means of production in common "ownership at the village level." They formed 740,000 advanced agricultural cooperatives. While the villages were thus in effect led into rural collectivization, China's machine and handicraft industry and trade and commerce had been put through the phased transformation from private to public ownership already described. By 1958 the state's control over both industrial and agricultural production and distribution was 99 percent complete. Control, but not absolute ownership—for farms were still collectively owned by the villages. Otherwise, one quarter of the people on earth had been added to the "socialized sector" of the world market.

That stage was reached in China in about a third of the time it took to collectivize Russia's farm economy. It is true that the Chinese Communists had benefited from Soviet experience and knew where they were going. But Russia, with its vast acreage which gave farmers good reason to believe private enterprise could succeed, presented a very different picture from the conditions we have seen which make collective effort appear to be the solution in China. Stalin's heavy-handed collectivization encountered no-planting strikes and mass sabotage followed by famines said to have cost the lives of 5 percent of Russia's population. In China such resistance would have meant 30,000,000 deaths. Nothing of the sort occurred.

There was considerable slaughtering of animals and recrudescent banditry led by rich peasants opposed to cooperatives in 1953, and again in 1956 and 1957 following the accelerated drive for collectivization. All that was relatively small-scale trouble. Some foreigners say that Chinese peasants are "too passive" to resort to violence. But China's history is stained with the bloodiest peasant rebellions of all time—by virtue of one of which, indeed, the present regime was founded. I believe there were no peasant strikes or rebellions on anything like a mass scale because the peasants themselves know that miniature private farms won't work and are mostly resigned to the inevitability of social ownership.

The speeded up collectivization in 1956 did cause considerable desertion from the land, however. Loss of incentive among the stronger peasants may have partly accounted for the disappointing 1957 harvest. Despite better weather than in the previous year the food crop increased only 1.3 percent, or less than the population growth. This brings us back again to the mystery of the communes and the way they were launched.

56

—◆·◆—

At Whose Demand?

Sophisticated observers abroad have ridiculed reports from China that the communes were "started by the peasants." To believe that widespread spontaneous demands by cultivators compelled the party to establish communes would of course be absurd. Yet late in 1957 the party actually moved to decentralize cooperatives and to halt more big mergers. On September 14 the Central Committee passed a resolution which stated:

> Experiences in different localities during the last few years have proved that large collectives and large teams are generally *not adaptable* to the present production conditions . . . all those that are too big and not well managed should be divided into smaller units *in accordance with the wishes of the members.* Henceforth a collective should generally be the size of a village, with over 100 households. . . . After the size of the collectives and production teams has been decided upon it should be publicly announced that this organization will remain unchanged in the *next ten years* . . .[1]

The hypothesis has been advanced by Western analysts that the origin of the communes lies in a kind of intraparty seizure of power by a left wing in China during the months June to November, 1957. Donald A. Zagoria expounds this theory in great detail in *The Sino-Soviet Conflict, 1956-61*.[2] The left (with Liu Shao-ch'i indicated as its mentor) is supposed from this date to have pushed the challenge to Soviet leadership in the Communist camp, and in foreign policy forced abandonment of the Bandung principles in favor of more militant struggle against colonial and bourgeois regimes, as well as against imperialism. Internally, according to this surmise, it adopted a more radical agrarian policy as an aspect of rivalry with the Soviet Union for world leadership of the party and as a demonstration of the power of people to build socialism without major Soviet aid.

The whole commune movement obviously had its exacerbating effect on Sino-Russian differences. That it began with that motivation is highly questionable. In foreign policy the theory that these leftist leaders (largely unnamed) sought to repudiate the Bandung principles is contradicted by China's continued pursuit of good relations with Burma, Nepal, Afghanistan and other Asian neighbors, by her conciliatory and compromise settlement with Indonesia despite the latter's superchauvinistic measures against Chinese residence, and by the extension of diplomatic and trade relations with a number of other bourgeois governments. China's dispute with India did not break out until two years later, after the Tibetan rebellion, and can scarcely be traced to any left coup in 1957.

External and ideological factors undoubtedly played a role in the decision to form communes. As may be seen from the above resolution, however (which Mr. Zagoria seems to have overlooked), the party was actually moving away from agrarian radicalism just at the time his hypothetical left "coup" should have been in power. Both communes and the ideological dispute with Russia were probably evolutionary developments, rather than sudden children sprung full-grown from any one man's head. The evidence suggests that the communes were—like many past Chinese Communist innovations—a synthetic solution, worked out collectively, to meet a set of circumstances which had not been foreseen in the particular combination that occurred, and that they were not adopted until prolonged argument had reconciled differences in a majority opinion.

A starting point in this set of circumstances was that the poor harvest of 1956 had forced an emergency hunt for means of stimulating rural production without reducing capital investment in industry. Among several possible solutions the first would have been new loans from Russia. In November Mao Tse-tung had gone to Moscow to attend the world conference of Communist parties. There he made proposals for a militant international strategy which would have made China more important to Russia and a candidate for additional economic as well as military aid, including atomic support. Mao's trip produced no cash. China was to have new trade credits but no capital. On the contrary, amortization installments due Russia necessitated continued output increases in the agricultural raw materials of industry, particularly cotton. Together with textiles, cotton had averaged the greater part of China's export payments for Soviet machines.

China had no other foreign sources of capital and all wealth had been utilized. Or had it? What about idle man power, the "poor and blank" millions whom Mao and other leaders had emphasized as China's greatest asset? In January, 1956, when Chou En-lai presented the draft Twelve-Year Agricultural Plan—to bring "food plenty" by 1967—he had pointed out that farm labor was underutilized. China's 120,000,000 rural households were capable of supplying 45,000,000,000 eight-hour labor days but only about 30,000,000,000 days were needed for farm tasks. Chou said that the plan would eventually use about 15,000,000,000 additional labor days which would be available when all able-bodied rural males worked 250 days a year and able-bodied females worked 120 days a year. (As early as 1925 a respected Western-trained economist had estimated China's combined unemployed and underemployed labor force as 168,000,000.[3])

There was also much urban underemployment. For years the party had opposed the "blind peasant drift to the cities," a phenomenon characteristic of newly industrializing nations. No measures had been able to halt a growth in the urban population of 23,000,000 in five years; in 1957 it had reached 94,400,000. But this rate of urban increase was two and one half times faster than growth of nonagricultural employment.[4] "Non-productive population in the cities too large and growing too fast" read a typical headline of July 27, 1957.[5] Housewives and other dependents of new industrial workers somehow had to produce goods in exchange for their food.

There was one other source of new capital. Resistance to the formation of collectives had come mainly from the "well-to-do" peasants. These included both the old owner-tillers whose land had been left untouched during the land reform, and the new kulak-type peasants who had benefited from the distribution. Certain whole villages, where an unusually large percentage of peasants had been owner-tillers, now belonged in this category.

"Rich peasants" and kulaks together were probably no more than 20 percent of the population. Many of them had, as former owner-tillers, lived on their land for generations. They differed from the poorer peasants who had been given land and who owed their improved status to the party. The "well-to-do" peasants (living at a prosperous share-crop level) resented anything that looked like loss of control over their savings, homes and land. But their farms and assets were in effect the last new source of wealth in the countryside which could still be socialized for investment.

It was against that background that the Central Committee on

September 24 issued another directive (by no means incompatible with the September 14 directive mentioned above) calling for mass mobilization of labor to construct public works. A month later the revised draft of the Twelve-Year Agricultural Plan was accompanied by slogans exhorting everybody to cut short the period by a couple of years. After the autumn harvest, from November onward, tens of millions of people were put to work repairing dikes, planting trees, digging reservoirs, making roads, collecting all kinds of organic and inorganic fertilizers, and starting small industries. This began weeks before Mao Tse-tung went to Moscow, and could have had nothing to do with the ideological stalemate which developed there.

The wave of socialist construction swept on into 1958, as millions leaped forward along the "general line" of "aiming high and going all out to achieve greater, faster, better and more economical results." Foreign visitors saw a countryside in convulsion, as armies of blue-clad peasants, drums beating and flags waving, attacked their joint tasks of cultivating, digging, building, as if committed to battle. Newspapers carried reports of people "eating and sleeping in the fields day and night" and of women cadres who "worked forty-eight and seventy-two hours without a rest." At this time twelve- and fourteen-hour work days in the fields were common and press reports told of people collapsing from fatigue. In less than six months China claimed to have more than doubled her irrigated lands. At least seventy million people worked at collecting fertilizer alone. Every machine was in use. To move earth to and from new dike works and canal reservoirs workers began to build miniature wooden railways. A few small native hearths were built to supply them with iron rail strips. The "back-yard" furnace movement began.

Mass feeding at canteens became common. Strong young women were brought into the work, and someone had to take care of their children and household chores; community services were organized. Swarms of office workers, students and intellectuals were sent from towns to help out; some of them set up spare-time schools for the illiterates. To maneuver masses of people on labor projects required organization and discipline, and local militia groups took charge. Common dining rooms, kindergartens, nurseries, sewing groups, cooperative industries, had all been introduced by the army and cadres during the civil war. Many urban factories, government and party organizations already had such arrangements. Now they spread to the countryside in the wake of "agricultural armies." Resemblance to the program of the *Communist Manifesto* and to Marx's description of the Paris Commune became striking. For example:

> Equal liability of all to labor. Establishment of industrial armies, especially for agriculture. [From the *Manifesto*.]

. . .

Combination of agriculture with manufacturing industries; gradual abolition of the distinction between town and country, by a more equable distribution of the population over the country . . . Combination of education with industrial production. [From *The Civil War in France.*]

It remained to define this new way of solving mass underemployment in the countryside with a reorganized village life and stamp upon it the name "commune."

The Great Leap Forward in production and new employment was not, of course, confined to the rural areas or the agricultural economy. According to a carefully documented and highly significant study of "Manpower Absorption" during this period made by John Philip Emerson, the nonagricultural labor force by 1958 reached 58,000,000, an increase of 43 percent in that year alone. Industrial employment increased by 15,500,000 while "construction and modern transport" absorbed another 5,000,000 persons.[6] A one-year 43-percent growth in nonagricultural employment makes sensational gains reported in industrial output for the Leap years—as well as subsequent farm labor shortage—somewhat more credible. (Much of this was, of course, unskilled or semiskilled labor on temporary location.)[7]

On his return from Moscow late in November of 1957, Mao had found preliminaries to the Great Leap Forward already in motion. The rectification campaign had subsided in the cities. In the villages it was directed against "rightist" peasants who resisted advanced cooperatives. In mid-winter Mao made a tour through the South, visiting factories, schools, and housing developments. During a "surrender your hearts" campaign, youth offered its "all-out" support to Mao and the big leap. Apparently reassured by these demonstrations of mass loyalty and enthusiasm, Mao settled down for a long investigation of farm cooperatives. In the early spring he spent a month in Honan.

We may now recall that one result of the Hundred Flowers was the revelation of a deep division in the Honan provincial party. A series of reports denouncing "rightist" leadership in Honan had been accompanied by a purge led by the central party supervisory committee under Liu Shao-ch'i himself. The new Honan secretary, Wu Chih-pu, further clarified the issue as a struggle which followed the dissolution of a number of large-scale cooperatives on orders of the former leadership:

Yielding to the demand of a small number of well-to-do middle peasants, a few rightist opportunists within the Honan provincial Communist party committee indiscriminately tried to compel all the large co-ops to split up.[8]

Throughout 1957 the rectification campaign had been "conducted in the cities and the countryside as to the two roads—socialism or capitalism," according to Wu. Advocates of collectivization had overcome "the onslaught of bourgeois rightists, [ex-] landlords, rich peasants and counterrevolutionaries" and "the spontaneous tendency toward capitalism among the well-to-do middle peasants." Thereafter the people had resumed their "march forward along the socialist path."

With resumption of the merger of small co-ops, public works projects were undertaken along lines already described—"socialist cooperation on a vast scale." Various welfare facilities were organized and "in the cities, too, an increasing number of factories were built and more and more community services" initiated. This was the urban commune in embryo. All through North China experimentation continued in the winter and early spring of 1957-58. When Mao reached Honan in April,

> . . . people were not yet aware of the real nature of the development. Only after Comrade Mao Tse-tung gave his directive regarding the people's communes did they begin to see things clearly, realize the meaning of this new form of organization that had appeared in the vast rural and urban areas, and feel more confident and determined to take this path.[9]

In August Mao made another tour of North China and "gave further instructions on the organization of people's communes, saying: 'It is better to run people's communes. Their advantages lie in that they can merge industry, agriculture, trade, culture and education and military affairs into one entity, and make it easier for leadership.' "[10]

Whether the communes had been discussed and already set up in Honan and elsewhere in advance of Mao's travels I do not know. When, in 1953, the party first published its resolutions calling for the creation of "primary cooperatives," thousands already had been formed on the basis of secret directives issued two years earlier.[11] Now, in any event, Mao Tse-tung was not openly credited with sponsoring the communes until July 16, 1958, in an article in *Red Flag*. Here it was asserted that in accordance with Lenin's advice to "Communists of Eastern countries" to apply Marxism "in the light of special conditions unknown to the European countries . . . realizing that the peasants are the principal masses," Mao Tse-tung had launched the Great Leap and the communes to speed up socialization and help to realize communism "in the not distant future."

This sunlit vision of a new society suddenly brought within reach seemed to share more of the charismatic dreams of the American Utopian, Edward Bellamy, than the plodding Marxism of Nikita Khrushchev, slowly struggling toward a goal of middle-class comforts "in accordance with work performed." In his novels *Looking Backward* and *Equality,* written nearly a century ago, Bellamy idealized community dining rooms, theaters, shops and services, all owned and managed by "industrial armies" whose guilds were to run America in our own time. His prophecies of a civilized society remain unfulfilled but his glimpses of future technological changes were uncannily accurate. Now, in China, men were daring to reach for the dream—before they had fully mastered the technology. Obviously annoyed by Chinese attempts to push ahead of Russia's own "stage of socialist development," Khrushchev told Senator Hubert H. Humphrey on December 1, 1958:

"You know, Senator, what those communes are based on? They are based on that principle, 'From each according to his abilities, to each according to his needs.' You know that won't work. You can't get production without incentive."

Feeling that he was "about to fall out of his chair," the Senator said: "That is rather capitalistic."

"Call it what you will," Khrushchev replied. "It works." [12]

The Soviet party seems to have had no advance warning of the Chinese commune program. This fact in itself lends some weight to the belief that it was a more or less spontaneous development and a name and form applied to conditions which grew out of the "leap forward." Moscow's reaction was at first cautious and then increasingly negative. Had not Russia in the earliest days tried a kind of agricultural commune and proved that it would not work? Anti-Stalin though Nikita Khrushchev might be, in this instance he soon made it clear that Stalin's views on premature egalitarian movements were his own. In a 1934 party report Stalin had declared:

The future agricultural commune will arise when the fields and farms of the artel are replete with grain, with poultry, with vegetables, and all other produce; when the artels have mechanized laundries, modern dining rooms, mechanized bakeries, etc.; when the collective farmer sees that it is more to his advantage to receive his meat and milk from the collective farm's meat and dairy department than to keep his own cow and small livestock . . . The future commune will arise on the basis of an abundance of products. When will that be? Not soon, of course. But be it will. It would be criminal to accelerate artificially the process of transition from the artel [cooperative, in which the incentive system prevails] to the future commune . . . The transition from the artel to the future commune must proceed gradually, to the extent that all the collective farmers become convinced that such a transition is necessary.[13]

How could China, more backward than Russia, attempt any such transition toward communism? The answer must be found in the party's belief that their people had already "changed fundamentally" even though the technology had not. In this they were to be proved mistaken, judging by the speedy retreat from claims that they were a means of *early* attainment of communism. Their appearance and continuation even in modified form, however, were to add greatly to the developing tension between Moscow and Peking. For the whole theoretical implication of the Chinese communes was that an *Asiatic form of Marxism* could develop more rapidly toward true communism than Marx, Lenin or Stalin had foreseen.

Not without reason had the Chinese named their prototype commune Sputnik—a pace-breaker of their own launched under "conditions unknown to European countries." One may thus imagine Mao's state of mind in the midst of the new "upsurge in the countryside," as he described it. Masses of men and women mobilized, performing prodigious feats, banners flying, seizing nature, changing it, turning rivers and mountains—the wealth of 15,000,000,000 labor days put to work at last. What should be done? Send them back to the villages as before the Great Leap? Decapitalize labor? Or make the tempo of the leap a permanent thing, provide a new social and organizational form for it—with a promise of early abundance as reward? Was not this the psychologically correct moment to build in everybody "the spirit of communism"? Only one more push would bring China into large-scale socialized farming and leave behind, forever, the "spontaneous tendency toward capitalism among the well-to-do peasants."

But where would the vast new array of administrators, accountants, technicians of all kinds needed at the township level, be found to organize communes? In 1955, to those who had objected that the cadres were "not prepared" to lead collectivization Mao had replied: "If we do not guide the peasants in organizing one or several producers cooperatives in every *hsiang* or village where will the 'cadres' experience' come from, how will the level of that experience be gained?" Leadership "should never lag behind the mass movement. As things stand today the mass movement is in advance of the leadership." Those were probably his answers in 1957, also.

And yet, when I asked a Very High Official the direct question, who did give the final "push" that launched the communes, his answer was, "The peasant masses started them. The party followed."

The transfer of much of the responsibility for rural modernization directly to an all-embracing authority offered advantages of decentralization. At the same time it focused political and economy control at a level much easier for the central government to manipulate. Third, the commune administrations would theoretically provide Peking planners with the means to universalize standards of farm production, to limit consumption, and to extract savings for investment on an increased scale. The communes would "make it easier for leadership," Mao had said. So it would seem—but did it?

57

Communes to Brigadunes

"If the Commune should be destroyed, the struggle would only be postponed. The principles of the Commune are perpetual and inde-structible; they will present themselves again and again until the working class is liberated."

—Karl Marx

Whatever doubts existed in the party must have been overcome mainly by widespread unpublicized organization of communes, with apparent success, throughout the spring and summer of 1958. When the open directive was issued in August, probably half the country-side was already in transformation. By November all the nation's 740,000 advanced agricultural cooperatives, embracing 99 percent of the peasantry, had been engulfed by 26,000 (later consolidated into 24,000) communes.

Management councils were set up by the former township govern-ments and party committees. In effect they became "organs of state power," or 24,000 "states within the state." Commune administrations took over direct management of trade and commerce, small industries, bookkeeping, banking, marketing and supply, education, communal dining halls and kitchens, housing, medical care, and the training and command of the militia as well as public works.

The mutation happened far too suddenly for all the technical problems and social implications to be understood even among the eight or nine million cadres of peasant origin, not to say the peasant masses. Many rushed ahead to establish "real communism" right away. Wu Chih-pu had reported a "free supply" system in Honan whereby the costs of "seven of the ten basic requirements of life are borne by the commune," namely: eating, clothing, housing, childbirth, education, medical treatment, marriage and funeral expenses. Accordingly, at least a few communes began unrationed "free supply" of food, clothing and other staples. They soon exhausted their reserves. Some commune leaders took command of the new militia to march and countermarch peasants to do jobs for the township, with long hours of work and inefficient food arrangements; in their ignorance they often interfered with harvesting and other work.

More experienced party leaders merely supervised local production and management and waited for the village production brigades to agree on plans for joint projects. Such communes showed great progress. Others at once began forming villages into barracks-like military reservations. Some communes turned all personal possessions into public property, right down to pots and pans; others did not. Many canteens and nurseries began mass operations before they had been through a trial period, and dissatisfaction followed. Prosperous peasants and villages leveled by the amalgamation were often the best and strongest farmers. For many of them the welfare advantages offered by the commune must have seemed poor compensation. Malingerers and weak peasants now got the same food and benefits as hard workers. Where was the incentive? The amount of fiscal chaos created by the wholesale pooling of village accounts under the township finance department may be imagined.

Very greatly increased agricultural production quotas were worked out between the state and the commune planners, in which peasants had little voice. Whereas in 1957 something like 89 percent of the net farm output was set aside for consumption and only 11 percent was used for accumulation and investment, close students of the economy believe that in 1958 plans may have called for an accumulation as high as 50 percent.[1] To maintain consumption at the 1957 level would have required an overall increase in output of about 80 percent! Did Peking really believe it possible? One reason for transfer of the statistical responsibility to the cadres was said to be impressions on high that well-to-do peasants had been cheating; the output of their farms and the tiny private lots was thought to be much larger than the statisticians had been reporting. With the pooling of all farms, plus gains from new waterworks, improved cultivating methods, more fertilizer, and anticipated mass enthusiasm for the communes, it may be that something like a planned miracle was actually expected. Held answerable for both quota fulfillment and statistics, the cadres provided them, many of them self-deceived.

Despite the gross exaggerations of the 1958 harvest figures, however, other aspects of disorder were already so abundant by the end of the year that the top party leadership abruptly ended the excesses and began what was to become a general retreat. Meeting in Wuhan,* the Central Committee adopted resolutions in which it definitely reversed itself on several points and on others cleared up the ambiguity of the August directive. The triple communiqué now pronounced the communes on the whole a rousing success; indeed, fantastic gains in agriculture (later repudiated) were attributed to the new order. But it was sharply made clear that communism was *not* just around the corner.

Even at a very rapid pace it would "take a fairly long time to realize, on a large scale, the industrialization of the country." Ownership "by the whole people" was no longer something to be attained in "three to five years" but had to await completion of industrialization. That would take "fifteen, twenty or more years." Until then China as a whole would remain in a stage of "socialist construction" —although as the communes built and financed public projects those would, of course, be owned by all. Meanwhile people would work indefinitely for wages; those who had begun a "free supply" system were wrong. Food was to be considered part of wages, payments for work would be divided into six or eight grades, and peasants would be supplied in accordance with skill and output. A system of rewards was to be enforced.

Other incentives were restored. The communes which had declared personal possessions—such as bedding, furniture, cooking utensils, bicycles—"public property" were ordered to rescind the proclamation; where such property had actually been seized it was to be returned immediately to its rightful owners. The working day was acknowledged to be too heavy. A guarantee of "eight hours of sleep and four hours for meals and recreation, altogether twelve hours" was declared a minimum, even in busy planting and harvesting seasons. The use of community dining rooms and nurseries and kindergartens became optional. Existing houses were to be restored to private ownership, and members could live in them "always." Decisions to build new housing could be taken only by the villages themselves. Such housing should be constructed so that "the young and aged of each family can all live together." The integrity of the three-generation family was thus reaffirmed.

* Between November 28 and December 10, the Sixth Plenary Session of the C.C.C.P.C. reached these decisions, which were made public on December 16, 1958.

Above all, misuse of the militia as a means of organizing production had to end at once. Many cadres had "misunderstood." What was described as "getting organized along military lines," said the directive, meant "getting organized on the pattern of a factory" or a factory farm—*not* an army where the member had no voice or vote. Commune chiefs could *not* be militia commanders. "It is absolutely impermissible to use 'getting organized along military lines' as a pretext to make use of the militia system—which is directed against the enemy—to impair, in the least, democratic life in the communes."

The most astonishing part of the December communiqué was the news that Mao Tse-tung had decided not to be a candidate for a second term as Chairman of the Republic in the elections due in 1959. Henceforth he would "concentrate his energies on dealing with questions of the direction, policy and line of the party and the state; he may also be enabled to set aside more time for Marxist-Leninist theoretical work." At the same time a reform and reorganization movement was launched to "tidy up the communes." As full-time Chairman of the party, Mao was now responsible for making the communes work.

It would take a long time to revive confidence and incentive. The need was further recognized by another and more fundamental decision taken by the Central Committee but not announced until March, 1959. New directives then greatly decentralized the commune. Now "three levels of ownership" were recognized: commune or township ownership; production brigade or village ownership; and ownership by the production team, or group of ten to twenty families. The commune itself owned only those factories, tractor stations, power plants, new schools, public buildings, reservoirs, railways, and such enterprises financed or built by the villages as a whole. These remain great achievements of regimented mass effort but many people were later to question the price paid for them.

"The basic level of ownership" was restored to the village or brigade—ownership over its land, farming tools, animals, forests, fisheries and local industries and schools built with village funds and labor. Ownership at the family level included houses, personal possessions, private plots, poultry, etc. In 1961 this system of ownership was "guaranteed."

Later on it was made clear that "ownership" carried with it rights of management. The brigade controlled its own labor, tools and animals. Commune authorities could no longer impose quotas or crop plans or commandeer village labor except in agreement with production plans of the brigade and the production teams of ten to twenty families. The latter were recognized as the "basic accounting units," with wide autonomy conceded to them in the use of their cash income and spare-time labor once collective quotas were fulfilled. With emphasis on collective "overfulfillment" reduced, the production teams were greatly stimulated (by local loans to buy breeding fowl, pigs, goats, and fertilizer) to increase "side-line farming" on family plots. It was noted that often the farmers who responded most enterprisingly to these incentives were also those who overfulfilled their brigade tasks.[2] In 1961, for example, one commune in which private plots were as large as .55 *mou* reported that private income accounted for 22 percent of the total earnings of the average family, while the collective economy—which remained "on a priority basis"—increased its grain harvest by 133,000 catties.[3] Here each family "ate on the average about 10 chickens and ducks that they themselves had raised"; during the same year each sold "an average of 15 domestic fowl" on the market. Families were reported maintaining from 66 to 77 fowl, and from one to two pigs each, largely fed on sweet potatoes grown on their private land.

With the Central Committee's directive of January, 1961, which envisaged "two or three years" of "consolidation" and of priority development of food production as the fundamental basis of the economy, rural capital construction merely for the sake of building was greatly curtailed. All new building henceforth had to contribute directly to immediate output, and state loans were decided by the principle of "letting the communes and the production brigades depend primarily on their own resources" to finance new enterprises. Beginning late in 1960 and in the austerity years 1961 and 1962, the state granted farm loans only to purchase "means of production commensurable with the material to be supplied" in exchange. Loans requested had to be kept within "50 percent of the commune's public reserves" in cash and materials in any given year.[4]

All this meant in effect a recovery of rights by the advanced agricultural cooperative. By the time I left China many village powers of self-management had been restored. The commune had become a loose federation of brigades. In 1961 the commune bureaucracy was reduced by 80 percent. Cadres "in overwhelming majority" were sent back to field work on the farms and villages.

Most of these changes were indicated in rectification directives following widespread self-criticism of errors and excesses in open press articles too numerous to require documentation, beginning especially in the latter part of 1960. A sense of reality was beginning to return to the countryside. Grain quotas were greatly lowered. Some communes were obliged to compensate peasants whose housing sites, private plots and crops had been expropriated. Commune institutions like nurseries, kindergartens, canteens and schools were turned back to village management. The brigade was guaranteed 60 percent of its product for consumption. State controls of the market were lifted or modified for all but five basic items and staples. Village fairs were revived, and families were encouraged to sell side-line produce and raise pigs, chickens and goats for private consumption or sale.

Thus the communes survived in part but it is the brigadunes that are now running them—with plenty of help from private initiative.

Rural France, Italy, Switzerland and other parts of Europe are still administered under townships called "communes." These trace to days of the French Revolution when men also dreamed of the ideal equalitarian society. Many such communes still own certain property in common but they have never been able to abolish inequality nor to establish the law of "to each according to his needs." Whether the commune in China will in "fifteen, twenty or more years" have attained that ideal state we cannot know. But it is still a very different society from anything ever seen in Europe.

58

Chairman Yen

Behind all the communes stood human personalities and countless small beginnings.

Yen Wei-chuan, chairman of the Yellow Ridge Commune, had started from one of those small beginnings. In July, I visited Yen and the farmers on Yellow Ridge's 9,300 acres of grain, vegetable and pasture lands, situated some twenty-five miles east of the city walls of Peking. This was a commune that had succeeded, for reasons which became clear.

Yen had been to Peking only once. He was attired in the peasant's blue cotton jeans, blouse and cloth-soled shoes, but he wore a badge of distinction, a cheap wrist watch—often given as an award to prize workers. His three-room, brick-floored, thatch-roofed cottage boasted a wall clock and several pieces of good Chinese furniture. He looked younger than his thirty-six years and younger than his wife, two years his junior, who was his assistant. He was stiff and shy when we first met but soon relaxed and occasionally smiled. His hands were heavily calloused and his head was shaved almost bald. He was all farmer, and fully at ease only when he talked his trade.

After I had listened for hours to the usual outpouring of facts, figures, dates, tributes to Mao Tse-tung, the "general line," the "eight-point charter for agriculture," and praise for the communes, he reluctantly answered some questions of personal history:

"My parents were poor tenant peasants of Yellow Ridge. From as early as I can remember we were hungry every winter. If there was a flood or famine we had to go into debt to survive. My mother died of sickness and starvation during the Japanese occupation. My father is still alive and a working member of the commune. When I was seven years old I began to do farm chores. I slept under my father's quilt till I was fourteen. At that age I became a full-time farm worker hired out to a local landlord [an indentured laborer]. Landlords and rich peasants owned about 80 percent of our land. About one family in three was part-tenant, part-owner. We belonged to the six families in ten who owned no land and were sharecroppers or laborers.

"Education? I had had two years of character study but had forgotten most of it by the time of liberation. I could not write even 'moon' or 'sun.' Since then I have become fully literate through spare-time study. I can read newspapers and books and of course have to know something about accounts. In ten years we have wiped out illiteracy among about 5,500 adult members of our more than 6,000 commune families.

"Was I a soldier, you asked? No. I have always been a farmer here. I did not take part in the revolution; I knew nothing about it. I became aware of the Communist party only just before the Kuomintang was driven from Peking. I was a farm laborer and a good one, but I earned just enough to eat, and owned nothing but a ragged cast-off coat and trousers. My wife did washing for 'the lord' and we lived in the stable.

"After liberation our landlord fled. I received my portion of land and began to eat better. Party cadres asked me to join a mutual-aid team with three other poor families. As master of my own land for the first time I was grateful and wanted to help. I had few tools and needed help, too. They chose me as team leader.

"The new village council gave us some seeds. I also received a rubber-tired cart and I took charge of transportation. At that time we had no other wheels. In 1951, our first year, our four families together made 160 yuan besides food—more cash than we had ever seen before. We bought some tools and better seeds. We recruited four more families and formed a small cooperative. I was again elected chairman.

"Our first year as a co-op was very tough. Floods destroyed both our spring and summer crops except on one farm—and by August we had nothing to eat. In this situation even brothers quarrel. It was a bad year everywhere [the Korean War?] and we could get little help from the government. Some wanted to leave the land for the city. We called a meeting and persuaded the one family with a surplus to lend the co-op seed and food instead of selling at a good profit. We had enough food to eat for one month. Very late in the season, then, we eight families, adults and children all working, planted our land in vegetables for one more try. Other peasants laughed at us; they thought we would never be able to bring in our crop. By intensive cultivation, luck and shock-brigade methods, we brought in a rich harvest in record time. That year our income increased by more than half. We were able to buy not only tools and seeds but eight bales of cloth to make winter clothes for every family and new shoes and new sashes, pay off our debts and still have a surplus. Seven of those families had never before owned a new suit of clothes.

"After our success, neighbors recognized the superiority of cooperative farming. More than fifty families asked to join. We took in twenty-five families and helped the others organize separately. The next year under poor conditions our income increased by 15 percent. In 1954 we took in the whole village, 106 families, and total income increased by about 60 percent. Already ten other co-ops existed in the whole district. In 1955 we took in another village and had altogether 296 families. We formed an advanced cooperative and I was still chairman.

"You want to know what our advanced cooperative was? Of course. We pooled all our land, tools, seeds and other resources and held ownership in common. Collectively we were able to organize labor more efficiently, to build roads, dikes, and canals, to dig wells, to buy equipment and seeds on joint credit, build many new homes, buy and sell to advantage. My father used to say, to perform miracles a man needs as many hands as a Buddha. Now he says our advanced cooperative was like a Buddha. By 1957 we had doubled our original assets.

"Since then—well, our co-op joined the commune, and you see the results all around. Great improvements we couldn't have dreamed about in the past—income up 20 percent in 1959 alone, and for us that was a year of floods."

"Results all around" included the Yellow Ridge first-brigade headquarters, a long, neat, one-story brick building in which we sat, a combined meeting hall and theater, in a tree-trimmed courtyard and flower garden. In one wing I had already visited a young girl, peasant by birth and a middle school graduate, who operated the brigade broadcasting station. Three other brigades owned stations and also broadcast to the commune's fifty-six villages, each with its receiving sets and amplifiers spreading music, news, lessons, orders of the day, exhortations and messages from local leaders. Another girl operated a switchboard; all villages were now connected by phone.

"—and 5,300 meters of high- and low-voltage electric wire, 370 electric water pumps, 11 tractors, 4 trucks, 500 rubber-tired carts, 1,500 horses and mules," said Yen, talking faster than I could write.

"That's what co-ops and communes have done for us. A clinic for every brigade, altogether 5 doctors, 44 medical assistants and nurses, 96 community dining rooms, our own factories making our own tools, fertilizers and building materials. Who could talk about machines and electric pumps in former times? What poor farmer ever heard of regular meals, good clothes, cash in the bank, schools and medical care for everybody? Even in good years we were hungry and in rags; in bad times our people died of starvation, sold their sons and daughters, or worse—"

"What about your children now? Working or in school?"

"They are in school, of course, and of course they work. Everybody goes to school now and everybody works. My oldest boy is in his second year in junior high school; he wants to be an engineer. My two daughters are in primary school. They do farm work in their spare time—just like Peking students who come to help us sometimes. My children already have a far better education than I had. Schools? We have twenty-three primary schools with 8,000 students; three middle schools, 1,800 students; a hundred and twenty kindergartens and nurseries, I forget how many little ones—but all our children go to school now. We also have four spare-time and technical schools for adults."

"And you're the elected head of it all—top man? In America they'd call you a self-made success."

Yen gave a puzzled glance at Shen Yao, the district party secretary, who had sat quietly listening through all this. They both looked at me curiously.

"You are making a joke," Yen decided. "I do not know how it is under capitalism but here nobody is 'self-made.' I am like everybody else, doing what work I can for socialism. How could I, an ignorant impoverished peasant, 'make myself' anything without the party, the leadership of Mao Tse-tung, the methods of Marxism and socialism? We owe everything to them."

"Yes, of course," I said. "I made a bad joke. Even a romantic poet said no man is an island. You in particular are a new kind of collective man, but all men are products of many minds and labors whether they belong to collectives or not. Einstein said something like that. Ever hear of Einstein?"

Yen looked lost, but Shen had read about Einstein. "He was a brilliant brain," he said, "but he would have been even more brilliant if he had been a Communist." That took care of relativity.

As for Shen Yao, he was not stupid, either. In his mid-forties, with short gray hair grizzled like a German Mecki doll's, a lined and deeply sunburned face, in dress a peasant, physically hard as nails, bright, quick, serious and confident in manner, not unpleasant, he was obviously a disciplined, well-trained party veteran. He studied me shrewdly and made occasional asides to a woman secretary who took notes on my questions. I told Shen I'd guess he was an old Eighth Route Army man.

"Right," he said. "I fought in the Wu T'ai Shan area."

Over a luncheon of local vegetables, fresh salad and chicken, I reminisced a moment about Wu T'ai Shan's wartime leaders—Generals Nieh Jung-chen, Tsai Chuan, Ch'en Keng—whom I knew years ago. Shen Yao warmed up. I learned that he was a primary school graduate and had been to party institutes besides having had military training. Child of a rich peasant family of Shansi, he had joined the Red partisans and worked as a peasant organizer for twenty years, the last eight of them in this district, where he had broken in Yen and other brigade leaders. Beside him, Yen was a boy. Shen Yao was the top brain and command of that whole commune.

59

A Commune That Worked

A subtle and vital relationship between the party man and the party-groomed local peasant natural leader, directly elected by the village, exists throughout China's 24,000 communes. (The village, brigade, and township or commune council chairman is usually, but not always, a party member; as a rule he is not the district party *leader*.) On the strength, intimacy and mutual confidence of this relationship largely depends the growth or failure of Chinese agriculture. When the local party leader is a "foreigner" his task is harder. He must know both peasant psychology and sound farming practice, make the party's directives understood and accepted by the people, organize enough support to prevent former landlords and able but antiparty peasants from taking dominance, and give the majority a feeling of pride of ownership and active management.

To expect to find 24,000 men at the township level and another 750,000 at the village brigade level, all of equal excellence in experience, intelligence and necessary flexibility in the implementation of generalized and often contradictory or ambiguous party slogans and directives, would be highly illusory. The leader must make orders fit local conditions; he must not go too far to right or to left. Misfits are inevitable; hence the continuous process of "rectification." (Western enterprises also have their annual toll of bankruptcies. The *Wall Street Journal*, February 14, 1962, reported 361,000 U.S. business failures in 1961, a year in which General Dynamics lost more than $400,000,000 on one bad guess on airplanes.)

Among the more than eight million party members of peasant origin are many commune, brigade and village team production leaders. The party deeply permeates the entire peasantry but of course the peasants are far from homogeneous. It would be a mistake however to visualize a few party men sitting on top of the peasants; millions sit beside them at all levels and are related to them by village and family ties. In many instances the district party secretary (or boss) is also the elected commune chairman. If such a chairman happens also to be a peasant of local origin who has grown quickly in both practical farming and political knowledge and competence, the chances for a high degree of success are enhanced—as I observed in several instances.

In Yellow Ridge 2 percent of the adult commune members—about five hundred men and a hundred women—were party members. Here the party secretary and the commune chairman (also a party member) obviously worked in harmony; they had been together for years and the secretary was one of the community. That this relationship was probably equally satisfactory throughout the brigades and teams was, I assumed, an important factor in this commune's prosperity.

More than 80 percent of the party members at Yellow Ridge were local people and seven in ten were actively engaged in production work, according to Shen Yao. They also served as functionaries under the commune management committee's various departments and subdepartments, which included the following: agriculture, industry, animal husbandry, public health and sanitation, culture and welfare, accounting and planning, public security and militia, justice, savings and banking, machinery management, and commerce or supply and marketing.

I was told that about 70 percent of the population had formerly been landless peasants; the rest were middle or rich peasants who had kept their property in the land distribution. Much of the area had been an imperial hunting park in the days of the Empire; half of it was low sandy marshland. During distribution many former tenant peasants got the worst land; the area flooded easily and needed extensive drainage work. When the advanced agricultural cooperatives were organized the "well-to-do" peasants, finding themselves in a minority, had had to contribute heavily to the common investment in rehabilitating the poorer land.

"Our investment in irrigation had been too small," Shen Yao explained. "Despite all our work our dikes failed to hold the local floods of 1959, the worst in a century. Four-fifths of the land was under water. It wasn't just one flood. We had had very good early crops but our autumn planting was ruined. Our seeds were washed away four times! In the old days that would have meant total ruin for the poorer peasants. They would never have been able to fight such floods as individual families. Those who were not affected would have opposed having their lands dug up into ditches and canals to save the poor families.

"Now it was a different matter. All our brigade leaders got together and drew up an emergency plan for the whole *hsiang*. We selected one half the land that was easier to drain and mobilized 'the whole people' to work on that alone—with the harvest to belong to all. It was very late in the season. By using all our machines, tools and labor, and a maximum of fertilizer, we managed to plant five thousand acres just in time. From then on we had excellent weather. By hard labor we brought in a bumper harvest—better than 1958. Even the prosperous peasants did better than ever. After the harvest we returned to the flooded lands. Again using all our resources we finally completed a whole new system of dikes, dams and drainage ditches. We rebuilt the villages with joint funds. We greatly improved the soil. What was once the poorer half of Yellow Ridge is now almost as good as the wealthy half."

What was the "bumper" year? Net income had risen from about 5,000,000 yuan in 1957 to 6,300,000 yuan in 1958. For the "bumper year" of 1959 it was 8,180,000 yuan ($3,350,000), a figure Shen believed would have been two million higher except for the floods. Target for 1960 was a 40-percent increase over 1959. Was 40 percent a realistic target? He said it was, because the flood menace was diminished by newly completed dams (at Miyun and elsewhere); drought currently affecting much of the North was not feared locally now because of an extensive system of deep wells and power pumps.

Distribution of income at Yellow Ridge is worth reporting in some detail because it indicates the very high rate of growth in profits and an extraordinarily rapid rate of capital investment and increase in assets which were fairly typical of *well-run* collective farms. After deductions for taxes, materials, depreciation, loan payments, all the costs of production and marketing—except wages—the net income in 1959 at Yellow Ridge, as stated above, worked out at 314 yuan per head or 1,362 yuan ($559) per family. The individual peasant-workers did not actually receive any such sums. Of the total collective profit the commune invested about 45 percent in new construction and equipment—including six more tractors, fifty carts, sixty horses, and seven power lathes. All these were held in common; each brigade or village had ownership rights to their use, and shared in the profits of enterprises. Eighteen percent was budgeted for welfare (loan fund, recreation, health, pensions, etc.) and reserves. Wages amounted to the balance of about 37 percent or 3,026,000 yuan. Shen Yao said that their welfare fund had never dropped below 10 percent. The 5 percent recommended by the Honan Sputnik commune had excluded several items voted for locally. Their reserves, excluding fodder, amounted to 5 to 8 percent of the product. These sums or credits, as well as wages, were distributed by the production brigades, "the basic accounting unit."

Some 10 percent of the wages was paid to outside seasonal and part-time labor (mostly in food). That left a theoretical balance of 454 yuan average income per village family. Some families with as many as four full-time adult workers easily earned as much as 1,000 yuan ($410) annually, according to Chairman Yen Wei-chuan. He asserted that he and his wife earned in labor points (combined administrative and field work) the equivalent of more than 800 yuan in 1959. The theoretical "income" of a family with only one actual wage-earner would be about 250 yuan. Wages were figured (as elsewhere) on a piecework rate. In a mixed farming economy such as that of Yellow Ridge, rates were highly differentiated, with various tasks ranked according to standards of skill and heavy or light work commonly agreed upon among the workers.

How much did the peasant see in cash? One-third of all wages was in the form of food for consumption supplied to members by the production brigades. This mainly took the form of grain. In Yellow Ridge, with a heavy truck garden output, all vegetables consumed were (then) free. Farmers also had miniature plots. Those I saw were planted in corn to feed the family chickens and a pig or two for local consumption or sale.

I was told that about 60 percent of the children of "able-bodied" (eighteen to forty-five) women were using the village nursery-kindergarten. Mothers living with their parents or in-laws usually left offspring at home. There was not now any compulsion to use the nursery facilities and Shen Yao insisted there never had been. Use of communal dining rooms was also not obligatory. In the beginning the commune had taken full charge of all dining rooms but now they were managed by the brigades. A new "brigade center" dining room was being built for mass use but people now used team (twenty-family) canteens. Nearly all families now cooked supper at home but workers ate noon meals in canteens. Members opted for public or private meals. In either case the ration for adults averaged "about forty pounds" of grain a month, and ten ounces of meat. The dining room I saw was serving wheat rolls, turnips, cabbage and spinach which looked adequate and wholesome. It was, I was told, a "meatless day." Meat days averaged four to six a month.

While the average family with one able worker nominally earned about 250 yuan, deductions for nursery and kindergarten costs and various contributions doubtless reduced it by another 10 to 20 percent. Furthermore, normally no more than half the wage was paid over monthly, the rest being credited to the member's savings account, theoretically accessible at the end of the year. Shen conceded that there was strong pressure on the peasant to accumulate, that withdrawals were made sparingly, and often only after discussion with the team leaders. (By way of comparison, a "poor commune where the soil is infertile and the economic foundation weak" was reported in February, 1962, as having provided for every family "70 yuan in cash on the average [apart from food and basic services]" in the previous year. There were 888 families; the whole commune had a "favorable balance" of 62,000 yuan in cash. Some members "wanted to buy good clothes" with their cash while others "wanted to buy expensive [!] goods." Cadres working in the brigade "repeatedly educated the masses in thrifty good housekeeping and love for the group, and penetratingly explained" the necessity to "self-finance" next year's development program. As a result, the peasants lent their bank one-half of their cash in order to construct a brick and tile kiln which would "bring in an income of 15,000 yuan in the first half of the year." The commune bank paid interest at state bank rates [2 percent] and guaranteed to return the borrowed sums "within a fixed period.") [1]

Again and again, and all over the country, I saw peasant homes with one or more of the following: wall clocks, radios, vacuum bottles,* furniture, lamps, abundant bedding, spare clothing, and even books and paintings—which owners told me they had bought with their savings. It would be a rare home that did not possess one such new "luxury." Obviously, however, the semiblocked savings accounts were a means for capital accumulation and investment in capital construction.

Even with a cash income of no more than 10 to 20 yuan per month, the families of Yellow Ridge were above average. Add to this their food, free rent (in most instances), welfare benefits, etc., and their standard was close to an urban worker's. Here young couples were permitted to build their own homes, small two- or three-room brick structures, which they financed (cost, about 400 yuan) from savings and money borrowed from the welfare fund. Here also, as in other communes, were some new one- and two-story multiple-family brick flats of one to three rooms. Most families still lived in old-style farmhouses and many preferred them, I was told.

"Our general plan," it was explained to me as we walked through the fields and villages, "is to organize the whole commune around four modern community centers. Each center will have administrative offices, schools, hospital, theater, playgrounds, parks, a factory zone, repair shops, hostels, clubs, lots of trees—the nucleus of a modern town. We are keeping the old villages and houses where they are worth improving, but the worst are being torn down as soon as new

* China's output of vacuum bottles in 1959 was 70,000,000; fountain pens, in 1960, 150,000,000.

housing is built. When small-plot farming changes into large-scale ranch-size farms and mechanization increases, we'll need fewer villages. The farm economy is changing to factory-farm economy. Already here in Yellow Ridge we are no longer a mere farm but a factory-farm."

Yellow Ridge leaders took me to see one of their community centers. Later, south of Shanghai, I saw a commune * in which similar community plants were very well advanced and highly successful, but those at Yellow Ridge were still under construction. A large square had been partly built up with new offices, stores and houses, dominated by a new building, seating capacity eight hundred, which would serve as a dining hall and theater. Bricks, windows and some fittings were locally made. The building would eventually have flush toilets, a distinct innovation in village life. General use of flush toilets in rural China would for some time be too wasteful even if it is more possible today; human manure is still much needed for fertilizer. The use of covered latrines is being widely enforced, however; sanitary squads collect the ordure in the manner already described. I saw such latrines in use here and on other farms, and I was told in Yellow Ridge by a clinic doctor that among some four thousand persons in his brigade only three cases of dysentery had occurred since 1958.

Near the civic center I inspected several new brick homes. Most residents were in the fields, but before a two-room cottage I met a lady of sixty-five working in her tiny garden of sunflowers and cabbages. She invited me in for tea and I sat beside a fine old Chinese table, several chairs and a teak chest. On the large brick family k'ang were piled clean, brightly colored quilts. She was a widow and her husband had been a poor peasant. The furniture had been acquired during the division of land—and landlord's furniture.

Rice simmered in a pot over a new brick cook stove in the tiny vestibule; water was available nearby from a new well. Here the old lady lived with her son and daughter-in-law, both then at work. Mme Wang was full of praise for the "new life better for all." For example, she and her husband were illiterates; just look at her grandchildren, both soon to finish primary school. What was more, her son and daughter-in-law were able to study at night school. Who could have saved in the past? Now her son could buy clothes for the children and make payments on a bicycle. Even she herself owned two coats, vests and trousers. Who would have fed a person unable to work in former times? Now she, an old lady, was fed by the brigade.

"You do the family cooking?"

"A little breakfast for everyone, yes. The children eat where they work. We have supper together in our team dining room. It's a great blessing, being able to take meals outside."

"In what way?"

* See Chapter 70, "Building, Building—."

"Ai-ya! In every way. No scrambling for fuel, preparing food, dish washing, pot washing, smoking up the house! Of course the cooking is not always the best. When we get tired of it we eat at home."

"Was there ever any attempt here to make your son and daughter-in-law live apart, in separate barracks—to divide men from women?"

My question had to be repeated and explained by the interpreter. The old lady looked at me in astonishment. Of course not. Could that be "human"? She wanted to know if it was practiced in my country.

Every commune has a history and so has every family in it. One was forever torn between spending hours to penetrate one wall, to identify a few trees closely, and the risk of not seeing the woods, or vice versa.

We went on to the older part of the village, with here and there a new brick house, until we reached a nursery-kindergarten and its seventy-two infants. It was (as often) located in a former landlord's home and was simply furnished with roughly made child-size chairs, stools, tables and benches. The little citizens were dressed in cotton playsuits and cloth shoes; there were a few runny noses and no overt signs of malnutrition.

They stood up, as usual, and cried in tiny-voiced chorus, "Welcome, Foreign Uncle!" Then they rendered a version of "Socialism Is Good," clapped hands and cheered. A smiling bobbed-hair doll handed me a large bouquet of yellow chrysanthemums picked from the school garden; thereafter she hung onto my hand. This performance, minus the flowers, was enacted in every nursery I visited. Usually I was able to bring some unexpected diversion into their lives by winding up and playing my miniature Swiss key-chain music box and holding it to the ears of children daring enough to listen in wide-eyed delight.

This nursery was better than average for a village, but its conditions were poorer than the standards of the well-run urban nurseries to which all aspire. Each child had the usual equipment: his own hooks for toothbrush, comb, washcloth, coat; he had a bowl of his own, chopsticks, and a place at the table and on one of the k'angs where all retired for morning and afternoon naps. Lunch was gruel and vegetables, and the infants had a ration of soya bean milk. Sanitary arrangements included Japanese-style johns, cut to size, and a lavatory through which ran a stream of fresh water in a long low stone basin used for ablutions. The sunny courtyard was equipped with homemade swings, slides and hobbyhorses.

Care and lunches here cost mothers three yuan a month for each child—deductible, however, from book earnings, not cash. There were no boarding children as in some nurseries; neighborhood mothers called for their charges each day after work. Attendants were four local women (one with bound feet) who were themselves all mothers, and who had had some rudimentary training in child care. Their leader was a primary school graduate, bright and energetic.

Of her efficiency I know no more than that she kept her charges remarkably clean, considering the circumstances, and reported complete toilet-training success with most of them at three, all by the age of four. A trained nurse visited once a week and was on special call. Vaccinations were complete and the health record for the year showed only minor ailments, principally colds.

Here again I could easily have invested the whole day with pleasure and profit, but I had just spent such a day at a nursery in Peking. As I had asked to see the brigade clinic, one of the new schools and a shop or two, I was hurried along through vegetable fields and acres of gladioli, chrysanthemums, and dahlias—Yellow Ridge grows flowers commercially for the nearby Peking market—until we came to the outskirts of Wei Hsien, the next big village.

"Teng Chia brigade includes fourteen villages of work teams—4,000 people out of our total commune population of 26,000." The speaker was the brigade deputy leader and party secretary, Chang Hsuan-hai. We got out of our car and scrambled through a large vegetable field.

"Our income is above average, you say? A little, yes. We have advantages of help from the city, we are more mechanized, with pumps and tractors, and we have good cash crops. We get three crops a year: spring vegetables; summer vegetables and wheat; autumn vegetables and corn. The whole commune averages two-thirds in vegetables, one-third in grain. We are also doing well with our tree nurseries and flowers; winter hothouses bring a good income. Two-thirds of our earnings come from the July crop, which looks very good this year."

Fields of tomatoes, peppers, fat cabbages and leeks were being weeded and sprayed by turbaned young and old women who plunged their embarrassed pink grinning faces into the vegetables when one turned and caught them staring. I inspected a made-in-Tientsin power pump tended by an elderly gentleman who was making bamboo cricket cages. From the earth there gushed up, to fill swift-running irrigation ditches, a sparkling output of pure water from which I liberally refreshed myself, to the consternation of my host. Chinese still feel safe only when drinking water near the boiling point—one possible reason (so my Norwegian cancer specialist friend had said) for a high rate of cancer of the esophagus in China. (Water from open streams is still liable to contamination, of course.)

I stopped to question some women gardeners but was interrupted by a sudden heavy shower. We took refuge in a farm hut set all by itself in the middle of the field. Inside, a young peasant woman and her teen-age brother welcomed us and a baby stared wide-eyed from the k'ang. The floor was of packed earth, the kitchen hung with drying onions and peppers. It was the house in which she had been born, said the woman; she liked it and had no intention of moving into any communal housing project. Her husband worked in a nearby factory. Her brother, who had been studying a textbook when we entered, said he had just completed higher primary school. How many village children got to middle school these days? About half. And what was he studying to be?

"Serve the needs of socialism. Obey the will of the masses."

"Yes, but *you*—what do you want to be if you have a choice?"

"I'd like to be a doctor." He had the bright eager face of hope and he grinned to hide his embarrassment.

"Why?"

"I want to be a soldier for my country," he replied. "In white uniform."

The rain ceased. We walked into the town and entered the brigade clinic, an old converted dwelling with rooms built round a courtyard now half flooded by the shower. A doctor in his early thirties was on duty, and a nurse was in charge of the dispensary. The equipment was crude, the brick floors and whitewashed walls clean.

Wu Chu-ying was a short-course (three-year) doctor—really an interne, under a township graduate physician. He hoped to continue his studies later. Dr. Wu was on call for all the villages of the brigade, each of which had a public health team and was now in touch with the clinic by telephone. Major diseases under control; no cholera, smallpox or other epidemics for some years; vaccinations, 100 percent; intestinal diseases down 80 percent since 1952. Colds, bronchitis, the usual complaints. Operable cases were referred to the county hospital or sent to Peking.

"Do you have many requests for instruction in birth control?"

"We provide it when required."

"Do you encourage it?"

Dr. Wu hesitated. "We don't oppose it. We advise it if the woman's health is affected or she already has enough children—three or four, for example."

"Are contraceptives available to unmarried people?"

The question produced a puzzled silence. Secretary Shen Yao had rejoined us. It was he who spoke up.

"Our people are always married when they have sex relations."

"Always? You never have any cases of premarital intercourse?"

This colloquy produced (as on a few other occasions) a distinctly uncomfortable if not painful atmosphere.

"This may be a problem in capitalist societies. It is not so here."

"Capitalism? I lived for several years in the Soviet Union. Premarital sex is about as common there as in any industrialized society. I know that in former times it was a rare thing among peasant women in China, when marriages were arranged early. Now, with women's rights, freedom of choice, sex equality—hasn't it changed any?"

"It has changed for the better. In feudal days young maidens frequently would be raped or seduced by landlords; sometimes the landlord claimed 'first rights.' That is gone. Now everybody can get married; the legal age is twenty-one for men and eighteen for girls; there is no need for sex before then. But I won't say it never happens. We have had only two or three cases that I remember, in the whole commune. Social opinion is strongly against it."

"What punishment is provided?"

"There is no law against it. We persuade people to get married."

"What if they simply don't want to get married?"

Shen Yao looked seriously at the others, who seemed depressed by this conversation.

"Usually they respond to education—their duties. I will say there was one such case. It was solved when the young man went to the city to work in a factory. Later, the girl moved to the city also."

"If a child were involved, what then?"

"The man would be held fully responsible as the legal father, of course. They would certainly be married."

"What if they were under legal age?"

"Special permission would be granted by the court."

"And adultery? Is that a crime?"

"It is not a crime unless the injured husband or wife wants to bring it to court. We had some cases at the time the marriage law went into effect but not in recent years. It is very rare now."

Before I left, Shen Yao asked me for criticism and suggestions. One is always asked. What could one say? From observation I knew that husbands and wives were not segregated, that the peasants were not starving, that the communes were not slave camps, that people were not living in barracks, that material and cultural progress was self-evident.

"If I lived and worked here a year I might have an informed comment. What can a tourist know of your internal tensions and problems of management? For example, how well satisfied are the peasants with their private plots? Would they like more? I don't know. How do they feel about the disposal made of their surpluses?"

"We have never taken private plots from the people—I know some communes have done so, but not here," answered Shen Yao. "Conditions vary. We have marginal land for those who want to work it. They can earn more by working the common lands; that is also their first duty. About management? It is in the hands of the production brigade. Commune management plans in consultation with the brigades and teams who know their own land best. We listen to the masses."

"Who actually owns the land, the commune or the village?"

"Here ownership is on three levels. The villages own the land, tools, housing sites, and some primary schools and nurseries and they manage all these things. But the brigades also have collective ownership. They exercise supervision and coordinate planning and management. The brigades collectively own the mechanized tools, horses, cattle, small reservoirs, pumps, brigade centers, and secondary schools, where investments were made in common. The commune owns large reservoirs, power plants, telephones, large factories, new technical schools and will own an agriculture college we are building. Basic ownership is at the brigade level and so is basic management."

"That's a very different picture from 1958, isn't it?"

He smiled. "We have to learn to walk before we can jump. All the means of production will eventually be owned by the commune. But that's a long way off. We have to wait. Poorer areas must be brought up to the level of the richer ones. We need far more mechanization, our political level must rise, everyone must understand. First, we have to learn a lot from experience. We make mistakes but we learn."

All these pages! Yet I have condensed only part of my notes and recollections of a visit to just one rural commune! I saw eleven. Yellow Ridge is far ahead of the average commune and benefits greatly from its nearness to Peking, yet it was not so prosperous as one I saw in the Yangtze Valley nor yet so advanced as another in Szechuan. I must content myself with the detailed story of only one more—where I spent three days far off the beaten track in the extremely poor country of north Shensi—before leaving this subject which still holds the key to Communist China's future.

60

Sian:

"Western Peace"

I wanted to see Shensi province again for several reasons.

By mid-September of 1960 the American press was beginning to publish seasonal famine reports about China from Hongkong. I have already described conditions in one serious drought area—Paotou. Another was said (in Hongkong) to be Shensi, where people were reported to be living on two meals a day of "watered rice." [1] Second, impressive though Manchurian industrialization might be, the impact of the new regime could be judged better, as I have said, in regions formerly little touched by modern life. Few had been more backward than hinterland Shensi and the middle reaches of the Yellow River Valley. I had made long treks across that province in wartime days of real austerity, and those fearsome old hills of loess still held a sentimental attraction for me. Finally, no foreign visitor had been back* to Yenan since the days when it was the mountain base and capital of Mao Tse-tung's guerrilla armies.

Having just completed a book, Rewi Alley was free to make the trip with me, bringing his deep knowledge of and pride in a part of the land to which he had made great personal contributions. He also brought along his never failing supply of Nescafé, one of Nestlé's

* Rewi Alley had been back, but Alley was a resident, not a visitor.

innovations which the Chinese had not yet equaled. We flew in a DC-3 from Peking to Taiyuan, in Shansi, and to Sian, the capital of Shensi; and on to the Yenan country in a smaller Chinese-made plane. We were to return from Sian to Peking by train, making leisurely stops at San Men Gorge, site of the great new Yellow River lower control dam; at Loyang, to see the tractor factory; and at Chengchow—altogether, a two weeks' journey.

It was clear, dry, crisp weather, beautiful for flying but not for autumn crops. All the way to Sian we were seldom out of sight of blue-water reservoirs and mountain catch basins. Most of them were very low and the irrigation life lines which reached out from them stopped far short of much of the thirsting grain, where peasants waited for a last-minute rain that did not come. The Yellow River itself, usually in flood by now, was a thin ribbon twenty feet below its normal level.

On the plane not one but two smartly dressed young army officers each carried a baby a few months old wrapped in soft padded quilts and sucking a pacifier, a public spectacle one would never have encountered in the past. Presently one baby dropped his plug and loudly announced his dissatisfaction with the state of affairs. I went to the man's aid by holding my miniature Swiss music box to his baby's ear; that stopped the bawling until the stewardess (having finished checking freight in the rear of the plane) could render more fundamental repairs.

"Where is your wife?" I asked the officer.

He explained that he had been transferred to a new post; his wife had gone ahead of him by train, taking their two other children. She already had a job and had to report for work. By the time he arrived she would have arranged for nursery care. In South China later I noticed several other baby-toting officers on planes and trains. Warriors seen in this homely role, so different from the Western caricature of the mad-dog, war-hungry Chinese—even as our military differ from the Chinese caricature of them—gave a sudden poignant sense of the profound pathos of man in uniform everywhere today, obsessed by the illusory pursuit of security for his loved ones through the perfection of the means of finally destroying himself and all he most cherishes.

Once we crossed over into Shensi the look of the land improved. Especially around the Wei River Valley, crops were lush and abundant. Here the economy was no longer purely agricultural. Where I remembered only straggling towns and villages along the river there were now forests of factory chimneys below, mazes of railway sidings, and substantial industrial towns.

"The Wei Valley has become a big base for heavy industry," said Rewi. "New iron deposits opened up, and coal all over the place. That's just a token of what is going on in Kansu and farther west.

Oil? Scads of it; China has plenty for her needs. Takes time to get the stuff out of the ground and then to get it out of the Northwest. So little to start with; had to build the railways, the roads. Takes man power and time, but they're moving fast."

China's geographical Northwest* is larger than India and formerly had less than a tenth of India's population, but the new regime has given high priority to its development. About two-thirds of the major enterprises begun during the First Five-Year Plan (1953-57) were centered in this vast region, and millions of technicians and workers have been coming in to complete them. Sian itself, a town of about 200,000 when I last visited it in 1939, was now seven times that size and spilled far beyond its ancient walls. Meanwhile it had been connected by rail with Turkestan via Lanchow to Urumchi;† with Siberia via Lanchow, Paotou and Ulan Bator; and with the upper Yangtze Valley via Chengtu and Chungking. A three-lane paved highway was being rapidly pushed westward from Sian to Lanchow.

"There it is!" cried Rewi as we lowered over the city. Long straight pennants of asphalt dotted with creeping trucks led into the western horizon and disappeared.

The region we had flown over is hallowed ground for the Chinese: the valleys of the Wei and Lo rivers, the cradle of their civilization. Great battles for supremacy were fought here thirty centuries ago, west of the bend of the Yellow River, between armies equipped with bronze spears and shields, riding in two-wheeled bronze chariots. Some of them were probably literate; writing similar to the present Chinese script was already in use. This was toward the end of the Shang Dynasty (c. sixteenth-eleventh century B.C.), which overlapped the Mycenaean civilization, a thousand years before the dawn of classical Greece. Following an interregnum the Wei civilization continued under the Chou Dynasty, which lasted at most another thousand years and held sway over a "Middle Kingdom" surrounded by unruly neighbors. After the period of "Warring States," the great imperialist Ch'in Shih Huang Ti (259-210 B.C.) prevailed and built his fabulous palace near Sian. When his vast realm fell apart in the hands of his son, successors founded the illustrious Han Dynasty (202 B.C.-220 A.D.) on the site of the present-day Sian—then known as Ch'ang-an (Long Peace)‡—and ruled China throughout the life span of the Roman Empire. These four centuries of enlightenment so impressed the people that they remained content, ever afterward, to call themselves *Han-jen,* Men of Han.

During the Han period notable advances were made in astronomy and medicine; tea cultivation and wine making began; and inven-

---

* Shensi, Kansu, Chinghai, Ninghsia, Sinkiang and part of western Inner Mongolia.
† The railway was eventually to extend to Alma Ata, the capital of Kazakhstan, but it was not known at this writing how far the Soviet connecting link through Kazakhstan and Sinkiang had progressed.
‡ *An* is usually translated "peace"; the more exact meaning is "tranquillity."

tions included the Han compass, water clocks, paper, glazed porcelain, and the humble wheelbarrow—which Europe did not import
for another thousand years. Sian was next the seat of the Sui Empire,
which sent colonists as far as the Penghu Islands (Pescadores) in
the Taiwan Strait and to Taiwan itself. On the foundations of the Sui
city arose the great capital of T'ang (618-906), and Sian entered
its golden age of art and literature.

Ch'ang-an was the center of the most brilliant empire of its period.
T'ang culture was imported bodily by Japan and a Tibetan monarch
united his throne with the dynasty by marriage. Foreign ideas, artists
and teachers—including Nestorian Christians—were hospitably received.

As a modern city, Sian dates largely from the Ming Dynasty (1368-
1644). I was glad to see the glazed-tile roofs and magnificent gold
and red pillars and lattices of the old Ming drum and bell towers
handsomely and faithfully restored. Streets had been widened, but
the ancient plan of thoroughfares radiating from these central towers
to the four great gates (one facing each direction) was kept intact.
Architects regard Sian as classical in its symmetrical design; it is one
of the few Chinese cities whose walls and gates are good enough to
be considered worth preserving as national monuments.

Interest in digging up the past has increased along with the digging of minerals, canals, reservoirs and foundations. Since 1952 more
than 2,800 tombs of the T'ang and earlier periods have been opened
or excavated in Shensi alone. Tons of porcelains, pottery, jades,
bronzes, weapons, tools and other artifacts have been unearthed by
engineers and construction crews briefed on how to identify and
preserve objects of historical value. China is overflowing with recently recovered historical and cultural treasures. More than three
hundred new museums have been opened, and many communes are
beginning to collect on their own.

In an old and neglected section of Sian, on a large mound of earth
where vegetables were growing, archeologists recently made a startling discovery. New construction is filling up most of the empty space
inside the walls, and this spot was chosen for the site of a large
housing project. Earth-movers who began to level the mound had not
gone far before they came upon what appeared to be a tomb. Following instructions, they summoned an archeologist. Careful excavation
revealed a complete neolithic village in almost perfect condition. It
has been named Po I-chih, is now roofed over in its entirety, and
stands at the summit of a long flight of stone steps flanked by buildings of a new museum.

Po I-chih is probably the best specimen of late-neolithic life yet
found here. There is a communal granary and a brick and pottery
kiln still in fair condition. The village was protected by a deep moat

which evidently connected with irrigation canals of surrounding fields. Igloo-shaped houses, half sunk into the ground and with a central hearth, resemble Igorot dwellings of the Philippines, except that walls and rounded roofs are made of baked mud bricks and straw. Numerous pottery utensils were found, and ornaments and toys. Buried in the walls were large well-turned earthen jars which served as coffins for children. Archeologists have fixed the age of the village as between five and six thousand years.

There was nothing neolithic about our commodious modern hotel: architecture in modified Chinese style, two hundred fifty rooms, modern baths, and good by any standards. Beyond my desk and all-wave radio stretched a park-like garden and a lawn where Chinese took setting-up exercises each day shortly after sunrise. A marble bridge led from my floor to a separate round-roofed pavilion which offered choice cuisine, but I never saw more than a dozen diners at once. Here was more housing for Russian advisers and their families, most of whom had departed leaving behind them industry of fundamental value.

Of the countless new and old structures in and around Sian I shall here mention three of interest to history: the Confucian temple, the Lintung pool, and No. 4 Textile Mill.

Sian's Confucian temple is considered one of the finest and its inner courtyards display the best surviving examples of T'ang architecture. These include an exquisitely roofed tea house about twelve hundred years old, with bell-hung eaves and perfectly balanced overall proportions. Now a state museum under the care of Academia Sinica, the temple area contains 30,000 cultural objects. Among the historical documents carved in enduring stone is a Nestorian tablet which records the presence in China of Byzantine Catholics. Introduced in 635, the cult flourished until it was involved in a rebellion a century later and suppressed.

Here also are four of the five world-famous Wei horses from the fifth century. The missing horse was stolen many years ago and today resides in the Philadelphia Museum of Art; Chinese now refer to this crime, as bitterly as if it had happened yesterday, as "another example of cultural imperialism."

Why Lintung? A pleasure resort ten miles outside Sian, Lintung has as its chief feature a large rock-lined pool and hot springs. It is famous in song and story as the retreat of beautiful Yang Kuei-fei, the most celebrated courtesan of the T'ang period. It was here, in 1936, that Chiang Kai-shek was taken prisoner by his own deputy commander in chief, Marshal Chang Hsueh-liang.

Rewi and I found it now a public park, where another museum portrays the Sian Incident, giving Yang Kuei-fei second billing as a current attraction. Chiang Kai-shek's bedroom (very simple) is intact;

the route of his flight barefoot up a steep stony slope, and the place of his capture by a soldier, are well marked. A glorious role is here ascribed to Chou En-lai and others who opposed demands for Chiang's execution at that time—with some details added which doubtless would be disputed by the Generalissimo as well as by the Manchurian army leaders who actually carried out the coup.

A large enclosed swimming pool was being built at Lintung. After its completion the park area was to be further expanded to include the tomb of Ch'in Shih Huang Ti—if tomb there was. Chinese archeologists awaited this attempted excavation, after 2,200 years, with intense interest. Legend has it that construction of the tomb occupied 700,000 men for eleven years and that a number of false entrances were made. Nobody could be sure whether the authentic vault would be found in the huge mound near Lintung that is said to be the resting place of the great emperor.[2]

No. 4 Textile Mill is a large new plant which in 1959 produced enough bolts of cloth annually to stretch around the equator and tie in a bow as wide as New York to Chicago. We drove to it over a well-paved road past numerous other new installations and factories in the suburbs. The plant spreads over fifteen acres and is self-contained, like many new satellite towns; it has a shopping center, schools, a theater and clubs, paved streets, and landscaped blocks of flats for its 6,000 workers—3,710 of them women.

This was an ultramodern plant: 3,240 automatic weaving looms and 100,000 spindles. The rooms were wide-aisled, glass-roofed, air-conditioned and so hushed and sanitized that one looked beyond white-gowned, gauze-masked operatives expecting to see "Hospital—Quiet" signs. Battery-driven rubber-tired trolleys provided the transport. Moving parts of the automatic machines were covered and one operator could manage more than a hundred of them.

"Every machine here was made in China," Manager Chao Ping said proudly. "The plant was erected in twelve months. Production? We make 44,000,000 meters of cloth a year. We make gabardine, sheeting, dress fabrics—600 different kinds of textiles. Sian has four other plants of about the same capacity." Other foreigners had visited these plants and found them operating a year earlier. How many were still producing in 1962 I cannot say. China's cotton and textile output fell drastically following crop failures in 1960 and 1961, but no figures are available.

I had been in Japan the year before and visited cotton mills in Osaka just as modern as this—and I have also seen mills in New England, where housing and living conditions, poor as they are for textile workers, are still considerably better than in either China or Japan. Japanese women work the same number of hours as women in No. 4, receive about the same wages and eat almost as meagerly.

They have some welfare benefits and can buy more clothes and other cheap consumer goods. One notable difference is that in a Chinese textile plant (and other state factories) husbands and wives work side by side, their children are cared for in community nurseries and schools, they eat together and their family life is tied in with their common work interests. In Japan, teen-age factory girls sleep on the premises and try to save a few dollars toward marriage and children, but they seldom marry "in the plant." As a rule there is no housing provision for married couples nor any community life built around the center of their work.

In No. 4 I visited dormitories which provided separate facilities for young unmarried women and men as well as two- and three-room flats for married couples. Bachelor quarters varied from small two-bed to larger four-bed and six-bed rooms. They were clean, austerely furnished, electrically lighted, and had group lavatories and washing facilities.

I never tired of looking into the way people were living. It was only after I had seen many instances that I accepted the fact that improvement was widespread though far from universal. To people who live in American ranch-style bungalows, all the new multiple dwellings in China would seem primitive. To workers in Shensi who were born in caves* or unlighted huts with no water and inadequate heat, the new life meant marked gains in basic comfort, aside from the new services and educational and entertainment facilities.

In one dormitory I met a woman of twenty-four reading Mao Tse-tung. It was her free day; in the evening she was going to a concert. She was a prize worker, earning 70 yuan a month, and showed me a bank book with deposits of 214 yuan saved over a four-year period. I visited a family flat during the noon hour and met a skilled worker who told me he earned 70 yuan a month and his wife earned 42. Their joint income was above average in a mill where apprentices started at 18 yuan and the median wage was 40 yuan. Rent cost them 8 yuan, utilities 2 yuan, food (for themselves and three children) 50 to 60 yuan, nursery care 6 yuan. After budgeting for clothing and miscellaneous items they saved 10 to 12 yuan a month. They owned a bicycle and planned to buy a radio.

Framed photographs hung over a table covered with an embroidered cloth. I noticed they were of groups by the seaside, and on inquiry learned that this worker and his wife were natives of Tsingtao. He had been working in a mill there when he was drafted to help open No. 4. Sixty percent of the employees here came from other provinces. Did they fare better or worse here? "About the same." Could they go back to visit their relatives? He said he had been back once. Would they have liked to stay in Tsingtao?

* Millions are, of course, still living in caves.

"No, we go where we are needed to help build socialism."

"But Shantung is a socialist province, too. Couldn't you have done just as good a job without leaving home?"

"Home? Shensi is home for all Chinese. Isn't that where China began?"

Nevertheless, I thought, few Americans would like being shifted about with little to say in the matter. Then I read a *New York Times* dispatch wherein Homer Bigart revealed, from Saigon, that the United States was helping in the "compulsory relocation" of thousands of Vietnamese supposedly infected by the Red virus.[3]

While I was writing these lines I also happened to hear a broadcast of a talk about the American family by Margaret Mead. In the course of it she remarked that 30,000,000 Americans had changed their domiciles (or "left home") since the end of the Second World War. That would be the equivalent of 110,000,000 migratory Chinese. The uprooting of populations everywhere and the breakup of large families are often not so much arbitrary political actions as consequences of increasing industrialization. But Americans move "voluntarily," it may be said; they go where "opportunity" lies. They also move where "the company needs them." Their children move elsewhere.

61

Museum of the

Revolution

We rose in our slow boxcar, a Chinese one-engine plane, and were soon flying over the reforested loess hills and marvelous works of terracing that are reclaiming these old badlands and helping to subdue the Yellow River.

"Probably there is reason to believe in man and his future, after all," said Snow in a banal philosophical observation. "When one looks down and remembers those people in that primitive neolithic village and the six thousand years of terrors and calamities that their children survived, until humanity finally discovered the riches of nature that were lying about here since the beginning, waiting to be opened—well, one almost believes in the indestructibility of man by man. A thousand years from now people may look down again and wonder how we could have had the courage to go on under our primitive conditions and despite all the ignorance which surrounds us today."

A young man whom I shall call Mr. Chao, assigned (not on request) by China Intourist to accompany us to Yenan, was genuinely shocked.

"How can you compare ignorant neolithic savages with enlightened socialism?" he demanded. "Men will always regard this time as the true dawning of civilization."

"Even a thousand—five thousand—years from now?"

"Long before then socialism will triumph throughout the world and people will live in paradise on earth. Eternity will be grateful to Mao Tse-tung for beginning the liberation right here in Shensi. There is no comparison possible with primitive times."

"Everything surely yields to comparison within the measurements of time," I said.

"Like those contour terraces down there," Alley broke in. "They brought that method over from Szechuan. Before the war you'd never see it around Shensi."

"Oh, you're wrong about that," said Chao, smiling agreeably. "That kind of terracing was invented by party experts right here."

A paved highway now ran toward Yenan and I congratulated Mr. Chao on that improvement. "There was nothing but a mule track there before liberation," he replied. Was that so? I had driven over the old dirt road in three days many years ago.

A little later I came out of a reverie to comment: "Faith and tenacity in human history are implacable things. When you think of that small band of Reds who arrived here a quarter of a century ago, freezing, half-starved, exhausted at the end of a six-thousand-mile retreat, and still being pursued by Chiang Kai-shek with all his might and prestige, it seems miraculous that they could have defeated Chiang ten years later."

"There are no miracles," intoned Chao. "What you foreigners call a retreat was in fact a great victory won under the banners of Marxism-Leninism and the correct strategy and wise leadership of Comrade Mao in advancing the people's forces to the Northwest to fight the Japanese. Victory was always inevitable. By the way, don't take any photographs without asking me first. Don't hesitate to ask questions."

So that's how it was to be. I gave Rewi a pained look. "Never mind," he muttered. "Enjoy the scenery." It annoyed me that on this trip into the deep hinterland (two hundred miles from a railway) I had to share the experience with a martinet.

Chao was twenty-nine, a native of Kansu, with thick black wavy hair, long nose suggesting Turkic traces, tight-fitting blue serge suit buttoned to the chin and the brain, and a perpetual false smile like Mona Lisa opened to full diaphragm—full of bowdlerized history, misinformation, the general line, misquotations from Mao, and with three fountain pens in his right breast pocket. I had known a dozen prenatally determined headmaster-bureaucrats like Chao in Russia, but he was the first I encountered in New China. Even Alley, a man of sainted patience, blistered under his condescension. He had no idea that Alley had helped build Yenan when Chao was still in split pants. We were to be stuck with him until our return to Sian—and he with us, poor fellow; we paid scant attention to his injunction against photographs once we had landed in Yenan.

Years ago I spent months riding and walking across north Shensi, Kansu and Ninghsia, through a weird surrealist beauty of hills and mountains pitted, slashed and scored by torrential rains that left behind bald peaks, deep ravines and slanting arroyos—an earth that might have been clawed and torn by herds of angry whale-size centipedes. The transformation that could now be seen from the air was beautiful to behold.

This is a region of the world's deepest and largest deposits of rich loess topsoil. Denuded of trees and overgrazed, the loess had been slipping toward the sea after every heavy rainfall, losing its fertility and filling the Yellow River with silt which piled up in its lower reaches and caused extensive floods. Shensi alone contributed 40 percent (half a billion tons) of the river's annual silt burden. The huge new Yellow River power and water conservation program required that the erosion be effectively ended.

Peasants began the tremendous task in the Yenan area soon after farm cooperatives were formed. With the beginning of the whole Yellow River project in 1956, a multiple-province plan was adopted which embraced all villages and townships in a systematic assault on nature gone awry. Now the results in north Shensi were already sufficiently dramatic to offer a scenic attraction for tourists. Thousands of square miles had been contour-terraced and interspersed with pines and other shade trees and extensive orchards and vineyards. Very steep gradients were brought under control and gullies and ravines sealed off by check dams, catch basins and soil banks, between hundreds of leveled-off shelves which stoutly retain and enrich useful land.

What the Swiss have done with stone-walled terraces (built over centuries) around Lake Leman, to preserve their precious vineyards, is now being duplicated here on a vaster scale by the use of mud and stone embankments six to seven feet high and one to two feet wide. Elaborate draining and control systems retain and guide moisture and silt, productivity of old fields has been doubled or trebled, new land has been won, flood dangers greatly reduced, and clean water reservoirs provided for human needs and for irrigation and power in the valleys. Scarified nature is being supplanted by an ordered work of man: range upon range of scalloped fields broken by young forests of pine and fruit and nut-bearing trees.

On the face of a high bluff overlooking Yenan today, large white characters proclaim from afar: "Make Green the Fatherland!" From all I saw of that grotesquely eroded and impoverished corner of the country I can say that it is well on its way to fulfilling that slogan, and recovering the lost ground of centuries.

New additions seen on the outskirts of Yenan, as our plane circled in over the old T'ang pagoda: two reservoirs nestling in the ravines; a medium-sized power plant and a number of factories; the stone-

walled Yen-hui Canal running from the hills through the city and beyond (where it irrigates four thousand acres); a war memorial with a
wide esplanade leading from the river into a mountainside. Our plane
lowered over the rebuilt city (intramural Yenan was almost totally
demolished by Japanese bombing) and I saw a new stone bridge.
I wondered aloud if it was true, as I had heard, that the bridge had
been ordered built after Chou En-lai, while fording the river, fell off
his horse and broke his arm.

"That's an imperialist slander," said Chao. "Premier Chou never
fell off his horse and there's nothing wrong with his arm."

I forebore quoting the Premier to contradict him.

Yenan has become a special municipality and the administrative
center of seven surrounding *hsiang* in the hills south of the Great
Wall. As an area under almost continuous Communist control longer
than any other—since December, 1936—it is a place of pilgrimage for
young Chinese. Nearly all China's Communist top elite lived and
worked here at some time under Mao's leadership. Men trained in
the wartime academies in the Yenan hills today enjoy the prestige of
veterans of Valley Forge. Here Mao mapped out, tried and perfected
the tactics and strategy which he followed to victory in the second
civil war, 1946-49. Yenan was occupied by the Nationalists in 1947,
but its reconquest by Mao the following year marked the beginning of
the end for Chiang Kai-shek.

At an elevation of about 2,500 feet, Yenan lies athwart the historic
invasion route from Mongolia to the Wei Valley; over millennia its
environs have seen hundreds of stormy battles. In this century, no
territory in China was fought over more continuously nor was more
impoverished as a result. Contests between bandits and warlords
were followed by class wars organized by Communist intellectuals and
army officers who sought refuge in a country ideal for guerrilla warfare; among them, Liu Chih-tan became most famous. Liu led partisan
fighting in Shensi for three years before the main Chinese Red forces
under Mao Tse-tung reached Shensi at the end of the Long March
from South China, in 1935, whence they had been driven following
the defeat of their first attempt to set up a Soviet state (1927-34) in
the Yangtze Valley. Killed in battle in Shansi, Liu is today the local
hero of Yenan.

By the time I reached Yenan, in June, 1936, the Red forces occupied
most of north Shensi, but Yenan was still garrisoned by Nationalist
forces under Marshal Chang Hsueh-liang. I have recalled how the
Communists had by then won over Chang to a secret truce which
ended in the Sian Incident. During that uprising the Red forces—then
numbering about 40,000—occupied Yenan and other surrounding territory, by agreement with Marshal Chang. After that, north Shensi became the main training base from which the Reds infiltrated the North

China plains and carried on guerrilla operations throughout the next eight years of the Sino-Japanese War.

By terms of the September, 1937, agreement between Chiang and Mao the old Red Army abandoned its name and flag and took the title Eighth Route Army under the Generalissimo's nominal command. It also abandoned overt class-war slogans in favor of policies of rent reduction and other "democratic reforms." In practice Mao was able to continue (in relative security) an intensified program of Marxist indoctrination which attracted thousands of young patriots and intellectuals, and prepared the peasant masses for future revolution while they were organized to resist Japan. It was during this period that the Reds in effect seized political control of the national anti-Japanese war in North China.

Unable to secure Mao's submission or to fight him during the war against Japan, the Generalissimo used 100,000 of his best troops to blockade the Reds from access to any outside aid. Immediately after V-J Day, forces of both sides rushed into and seized as much territory as possible as fast as the Japanese withdrew. By July, 1946, heavy fighting had spread to most of the country. Meanwhile, formal attempts to achieve a truce and create a coalition government preoccupied American policy makers in China until 1947. By then the two Chinese armies were locked irrevocably in a final struggle for power which engulfed the whole country.

On the Communist side, the brains and source of directives of the high command remained, until national victory was within grasp, concentrated in the inhospitable hills of north Shensi—which still seem an unlikely place to have sheltered the future leader of 700,000,000 people.

While in Yenan, it is appropriate to recall at least a few basic points in Mao's concepts of war operations which are highly relevant to any interpretation of his thinking about strategic and tactical policy on the "international front" today.[1] Years ago the "four principles" of guerrilla warfare which the Red Army evolved from its early struggles were elaborated by Mao Tse-tung in the following set of paradoxes:

> Defense, in order to attack; retreat, in order to advance; flanking, in order to take a frontal position; curving, in order to go straight. These are inevitable phenomena in the process of development of any event or material matter.

Such was the general strategy which Mao used to defeat Chiang Kai-shek's forces when they launched a major attack against Yenan in March, 1947. Under Hu Tsung-nan and other top commanders, picked Nationalist troops numbering 230,000 invaded the Red bases in north

Shensi, Kansu and Ninghsia. Most of the Red troops were east of the Yellow River, scattered across the North China plain to Manchuria, where Chiang had already suffered heavy reverses. Yenan had only 30,000 regular troops at its disposal and did not call for reinforcements from the east.[2]

One month before the Nationalists attacked, the Politburo and Central Committee decided to withdraw from Yenan if the enemy advanced in force, but to "defend and expand" the Northwest base as a whole; to keep army general headquarters in the hills close to the Yenan region; and to follow tactics of "wear and tear," "wearing down" and "completely exhausting" the enemy. Of Mao's "ten principles of operations in the Northwest" five may be noted as timeless guerrilla tactics* :

1. Attack small dispersed weak forces first, large strong ones later.
2. Seek to destroy enemy *forces,* not to capture or hold *places.*
3. Fight no battle unless certain of victory; never engage superior forces; use three to six times as many men as the enemy to win decision before the enemy can reinforce.
4. Replenish with captured arms and soldiers (up to 80 percent of men can be won over after capture) and not with local recruits (to avoid interference with production).
5. Thoroughly indoctrinate troops in the "new ideological education" (to which Mao attributed "unity with the people" and "invincibility").[3]

The enemy arrived well supplied but found a dearth of food, animals and able-bodied men in the towns. If he went foraging in the countryside and spread out he was ambushed and quickly wiped out. If he pursued in force the Reds broke contact, countermarched and bit off his tail. Four times the Nationalists circled the province chasing the Reds; each time they dropped a few more brigades isolated and outnumbered in sudden, surprise attacks. By the end of the year the tables were turned; the Reds had captured more than 100,000 men and considerable American arms; the enemy was completely defeated and withdrawing in great confusion. Back in Yenan, the Politburo began sending directives for general offensives on a nation-wide scale.

Despite its political importance, north Shensi was inhabited by extremely poor and backward peasants and Yenan itself had no power, modern industry or motor vehicles until after the war. Today, not surprisingly, Yenan city (population 60,000) has all such conveniences plus a few traffic cops (mostly women using megaphones

* Mao recently said, "We still follow guerrilla tactics."

to warn bumpkin pedestrians against underestimating the speed of trucks), some paved streets, a good provincial hospital, a comfortable hotel, clubhouses, theaters and—above all—museums. After visiting a dozen hallowed caves and other meeting places of Politburo members it seemed to me the place was already in danger of becoming another Benares.

"Merchants may make fortunes here some day selling old Politburo ink brushes, sacred hairs, or Chairman Mao's teeth, if this goes on," I said to Mr. Chao on impulse.

He was so upset that I immediately regretted my irreverence. It would have been all right to address that remark to Chou En-lai or even to Mao—but not to Chao. From then on my name was Dr. Mudd. I soon overheard Chao tell one of the museum directors not to ask me to enter the usual signature and comments in the guest book because I was "hostile to China." Nothing more was done for me that had not already been arranged; I could not meet a single Yenan official who could brief me on the city. The "Yenan style of party work" was a model constantly publicized throughout China and the Yenan party school would have been worth seeing. We passed it on the road twice and I had seen its exhibit in the town fair. But Chao insisted that it had been closed down; I could not get near it. A foreigner is always wrong in this kind of situation, I knew. Thereafter my behavior was entirely correct. But I never saw Mr. Chao smile again until we parted from him at the Sian station.

The Yenan fair was more interesting than any of the "museums of the living." It exhibited a variety and abundance of products unknown or rare here in the past, including fruits, grapes, walnuts, honey, and wild silk. I duly inspected an eighty-pound squash, corn fifteen feet tall, and fat fish from new hatcheries. Charts informed me that the Yenan region had afforested 830,000 acres of land and "basically completed" soil erosion work.

Items of some significance: 1) in 1952, when the area population was 677,000, there were only 266 steel plows in use; in 1960 (area population 919,000) there were 73,100 steel plows, a vast change for a region in which most families still live in caves; 2) 7,252 people were receiving pensions and 161 old people's homes were in operation; 3) illiteracy among local cadres admitted to the Yenan party school had declined from 26 percent in 1952 to zero in 1958.

Finally, *un morceau sentimental:* in a museum that was the former social hall where wartime foreign observers and occasional correspondents used to hobnob with Politburo members and their wives at Saturday night dances and entertainments, there now hang, in testimony to bygone days of comradeship, photographs of a smiling Chairman Mao, arms linked with his American and British guests in agreeable community. Among the faces I recognized Colonel David

Barrett, chief of the American mission. Colonel Barrett was denounced by Peking in 1951 for allegedly having aided and abetted an espionage center in the capital. In Yenan, at least, he still holds his place of honor with the rest.

62

Yenan Teachers College

Yenan had no institutes of higher study before it became the Red capital in 1937, when a wartime "university" was set up with dormitories and classrooms in hillside caves. Today's descendant of that improvisation is called People's Revolutionary University; it has more than 1,000 students and specializes in agronomy. There is also a Shenpei (North Shensi) College, as well as two middle schools and the party training institute. All these "plants" consist of whole buildings as well as half-structures with rear ends that reach into the clay cliffs and front ends conventional in appearance, with round-arched doorways and windows surmounted by several stories of terraced penthouses. They cost little to build, are inexpensive to maintain, and are not unpleasing to the eye.

In a morning at Shenpei College I learned something about the teacher-training program designed to spread middle school education across this whole desolate loess plateau. The nearest college formerly was in Sian, where Kuo Yi, chairman of Shenpei College, graduated from Northwestern University. He was now forty-six and had been working in Yenan since 1948. His assistant or co-administrator was Li Shen-kuei, at thirty-four already a party veteran. A former Eighth Route Army officer, he had been through middle school only. Both men were participating with student workers in helping to build the college, which was still uncompleted when I was there. All students spent ten weeks a year in productive labor.

Shenpei was organized in 1958 with a student body of 210. In 1959 the curriculum was enlarged and a two-year medical course was introduced. It was intended that by 1962 it would become a five-year medical college with a fully qualified faculty. Meanwhile, it had 36 teachers and 412 students. Of the latter, 85 were girls. About 80 in 100 students were said to be of peasant or working-class origin; the rest came from "bourgeois" families of mixed background. Tuition, books and rooms were free but food cost 12 yuan ($5) a month. Eighty percent of the students received a monthly stipend of 15 yuan.

"At present our main purpose is to train middle school teachers," Kuo Yi explained. "Courses include Chinese literature, mathematics, combined natural science (physics, chemistry, botany and zoology), and physical culture and politics."

A question about "politics" brought forth that it took up six classroom hours a week, and included study of political economy, Marxism-Leninism, and "special problems of immediate importance." Sixteen of the political hours were devoted to Mao's two theses on "Contradictions." The basic general reference work was Ho Kan-chin's *A History of the Modern Chinese Revolution*. Students spent nine hours a day in classroom lectures or study and were guaranteed eight hours of sleep. They were required to spend four hours a week cultivating the school gardens or at shop work.

Kuo Yi said there was an immediate demand for all graduates to help staff the "several score" agricultural and technical junior middle schools already opened or soon to be opened in north Shensi. Schools of this type began under the advanced cooperatives in the pre-commune period and by now have branched into a nation-wide half-study, half-farming system similar to the urban schools run for workers.

While the legal age for full-time workers in China is eighteen, I often saw youths who looked no more than fourteen and I found many at that age already doing full-time work on the farms (this is not unknown in the agricultural regions of other countries, of course, including the United States). Schools and teachers for all China's teenagers simply do not exist, even if the economy could spare their labor from production. Census data of 1953 indicate that China had 13,000,000 youths aged thirteen in 1960, a year when the draft economic plan projected a total of 4,000,000 students in ordinary full-time middle schools. There was a total of 37,000,000 in the thirteen-sixteen age bracket in 1959, according to a party spokesman, Lu Ting-yi.[1]

For the central government to provide facilities obviously would take many years. In line with general aims of decentralizing responsibility and utilizing latent skills and talents at all levels, the party called upon the commune or township councils to organize their own half-work, half-study schools for teenagers. What the Chinese Communists call "walking on two legs," in industry—which is what Western economists call "technological dualism," meaning high-ratio investments of capital in modern industry contrasted with high-ratio investments of labor in rural public works—was applied with great energy in spreading this innovation in people's rural education.

Such schools, called *nung-yeh chung-hsueh,* are now meeting some of the problems presented by millions of graduates of the primary educational system who do not qualify for the still largely town-focused regular middle schools. Their emphasis is on training youths in the techniques of a more modern and mechanized agriculture. In addition to generally more competent farming, special skills are needed. According to Lu Ting-yi, China will require 1,840,000 agricultural machine operators and 440,000 "technical farming cadres" by the mid-sixties.[2]

Half-study, half-work middle schools have flexible schedules, with "less study during the busy farming season, more during the slack farming season, occasional study during the busiest season and all-day study on rainy days." [3] Their curricula vary considerably, but generally resemble that of Shenpei College, with the addition of technical courses suited to needs of the local community, where 80 percent of the graduates will remain. As a rule, students in these schools spend five months a year in classroom work and five to seven in farm work.

Few agricultural middle schools yet earn all their expenses; most of them seem to be about two-thirds dependent on state and commune support and one-third self-sufficient. Their cost of operation is much lower than that of full-time schools, which in China is a small fraction of the expense of comparable education in the West. While it costs the state an average of 500 yuan ($200) to put one student through the full three years' training in a standard junior middle school, it has been reported that the annual cost per student is as little as 13 yuan for the state, plus no more than 38 yuan for the commune, in the agricultural middle school [4]—which is supposed to provide the equivalent education in four to five years.

The aim everywhere is to make half-work, half-study schools wholly self-supporting. Besides agricultural commodities, they commonly derive cash income from sericulture, fish hatcheries, pigs, rabbits, woven straw mats and ropes, the manufacture of insecticides, fertilizer and leather products, and the repair of machinery. In Tailing, Manchuria, I saw one such school which appeared to be paying its way entirely by part-time lumbering and forestry.

As with every "great leap" initiated by the communes in 1958, this one was launched with inadequate preparation and too much was attempted too soon. Dependent largely on amateur, volunteer, poorly paid or unpaid teachers and administrators, such schools ran into grave problems which not all were able to overcome. The party philosophy was that leadership had to "learn from the masses" by actual practice.

Some schools failed to operate in harmony with agricultural production, sometimes slowing it down and depriving it of needed labor, and were dissolved. The best of the survivors still provide only "second-best" secondary education of a largely improvisatory type.

Sampling some published self-criticism of middle schools one learns that "the quality of education is not good enough," that "examinations are learned by heart and without being understood cannot be properly applied," that "some students, afraid of hard work, do not want to take part in agricultural production," that "the idea that agricultural production is glorious and pleasant has not yet been firmly set up," and that "some experimental farms exist in name only." [5] Remedies advocated include improved training of young teachers "to take the Red and expert road. 'Redness' means support for the Party and for socialism. Expertness means serving socialist education with one's special knowledge . . ." To attain these ends, working and living conditions must guarantee that "teachers can spend five-sixths of their time on official duties." [6]

The foregoing criticisms were applied to a relatively advanced area, in Kwangtung province, and to full-day standard middle schools. One may surmise how still less satisfactory must be the quality of redness and expertness in half-time schools in so benighted a region as northern Shensi. Yet it may prove less significant in the long run that such weaknesses and low standards exist than that they are acknowledged; and more important that opportunity for higher education exists on an ever broadening scale for those who strive for it than it is that present levels still leave much to be desired. Anyone familiar with the stagnations of primitive rural life in Shensi in the past will recognize at once the meaning of a single instance of profound change. A certain Shensi village named Wei Tsun, with about two hundred families, which had never in history sent anyone to college, was recently honored for having produced ten youths who had passed their college entrance examinations—six of whom had already graduated.[7]

As normal colleges such as Shenpei provide better trained teachers for both full-time and part-time schools it is reasonable to assume that the rising cultural and technical level of the hinterland (where mere literacy was formerly a mark of distinction) will fairly rapidly eliminate the ancient gulf between town and country. Today it is believed that there are over 30,000 half-work, half-study agricultural middle schools—including as many as 10,000 which specialize in forestry, animal husbandry, tea-growing, fisheries, etc.—with a possible enrollment of 3,000,000.[8] In 1962 the Chinese press reported that "almost 100,000 agricultural middle school graduates" in Kiangsu province alone were "actively engaged on the production front." [9] By 1963 and 1964 such graduates may begin to provide large numbers of rural cadres qualified to cooperate, on a more scientific basis, with growing regiments of college-trained agronomists.

63

Pride
of Poor Men

Li Yu-hua, his face crinkled like the hills around him, was burned deep walnut and his hands were roots of the same tree. He wore the peasant garb of Shensi: white toweling around close-cropped hair, a white cotton girdle over old trousers wrapped with cotton bands at the ankles, and a worn jacket hung loosely on bent, broad shoulders, over a white T-shirt. He was fifty-five, a Red partisan farmer since 1935, a native of Hung Shan county, and a brigade leader of Willow Grove Commune, which covered twenty-five square miles of Yenan county.

"Hung Shan," I said. "That's the no man's land I crossed when the Red Army smuggled me back across the lines in 1936—down near Lochuan. Where were you in 1936?"

"I won't forget that year," he answered, suddenly animated. "You must have been there about the time I was arrested by the *mint'uan* [landlord militia]. Why? I joined the Poor Men's League when the Red Army occupied our district. After the Kuomintang came back with the landlords, many of us were arrested."

He had been imprisoned, half starved, and beaten repeatedly for refusing to talk. "I acted stupid," he said. Other peasants raised enough money to buy him out of jail, and he went back to work for the landlord again. He had to sell everything he owned and got into debt to pay back his friends. I broke in to ask what was the "bitterest" time in his life.

"That was it—that winter," he said. "We were barely alive. The worst moment was when my starving son said to me, 'Let me die, let me die. You are feeding me just enough to keep alive. Please let me die so that the rest of you can live.' That was bitter."

We were sitting in Li's cave, high on an elevation above a rice field in the valley. It was a large clean brick-floored room with a plastered arched ceiling and a wide arched window with paper panes. A two-burner stone stove stood under a pantry shelf lined with half a dozen glazed jars. Beside the stove were four earthen crocks filled with pickled vegetables. A heavy clothing chest stood beside the great k'ang where five quilts were neatly stacked. Through a connecting doorway which led to another cave I could see three pairs of children's rubber boots and a pair of sneakers beside another k'ang. Four chairs were squared round a teak table holding a giant wicker-covered vacuum bottle and a teapot and china bowls. It occured to me that several of those items would in the past have been seen only in a landlord's home; I could remember when Shensi bandits would have robbed you for the vacuum flask alone. On one wall hung eight framed photographs of Li and his family and friends, taken in younger days, and beside them were yellowed newspaper clippings which told of various honors won by Li's brigade.

After the Reds occupied Yenan, Li had made his way through the lines and over the hills to investigate. He went on:

"Everything was just as in liberated days in Hung Shan. I went back to report to my neighbors and in two days seven families were ready to leave. We had nothing to lose. I carried all the belongings of our family—we had four small children then—in one light bundle. All eight families got away safely at night and reached Yenan two days later." A pink-faced young girl in braids, who wore a pink-and-white-checked blouse and matching trousers, brought a plate of sunflower seeds and filled our teacups. "My youngest," said Li, casting an appraising look after her.

"So you got land when you came to Yenan?"

"Not then. We missed out on the first distribution but we got shelter and food. We got our land in the second distribution, in 1942—four *mou* [two-thirds of an acre]. Our eight families stayed together and organized as a cooperative in 1943. Yes, I was chairman. We did well, with the party's help—bought tools and fertilizer. In 1946 we produced as much as in the two previous years combined. We were able to buy sheep, pigs and a couple of cows."

"Then you lost it all during the Kuomintang occupation?"

"We lost the crop but we had a year's warning and had places fixed to hide our tools and seed grain. We lost our cows but drove most of the sheep and pigs to the hills, where our families looked after them. We came back the next year and had another good crop that autumn. Since then—well, we can talk about that when you see the farm."

Mrs. Li was her husband's age but still without a gray hair. She sat shyly hiding her bound feet; she must have been conscious that I had noticed them and she refused to be photographed with Li and their children. She had given him three sons and two daughters, and they had four grandchildren. "Only four?" I asked.

"What poor man could have seen three sons and four grandsons survive in the past?" he asked. "It was luck if a man lived to see one."

"So you weren't counting granddaughters? Women have the vote, women count equally now, don't they, Lao Li?"

He grunted. "Oh, they're equal all right. A woman earns as much as a man nowadays." As he walked through the doorway he said, "If you count girls, I've got five grandchildren from my eldest daughter alone." She was in charge of the kindergarten and nursery at brigade headquarters, where I met her later, with two of her own children— one of whom was the energetic leader of the chorus. Li himself could barely read, but all his children had been through primary school, and the eldest son was in part-time middle school. One son managed the brigade dining rooms; another worked in a chemical factory and a third was a work team leader in a nearby village.

I spent two days with Li and his brigade, ate meals with some of them, trudged up and down their hills and fields, heard their stories of triumphs big with meaning in their small world, listened to their dreams of the future—and I despair of making any of it mean anything to anyone who never saw north Shensi. I don't say that Willow Grove is any model of commune prosperity today. It is still wretchedly poor. What it does show is how wealth can be made from nature's scrap material. In this sense it offers hope that much of China lying fallow can yet be made fruitful.

To give meaning to Willow Grove I must repeat that north Shensi in the nineteen thirties was so ravaged a land that it was always astonishing to find people living in its crevices at all. The soil seemed worn down, worn out, the topography all against profitable farming: nine-tenths of it sloping and eroding, and the valleys so narrow that the good land there provided even landlords with no more than a poor living by our standards. Most of them were as illiterate as the peasants. This country was blighted worse than an Oklahoma dust bowl or the Texas badlands; there were very few trees, and it was arid except for swift summer floods and winter snows. Its best asset was a fine dry healthful climate. That alone probably explained why poor people could survive in their tumble-down caves infested by flies and rats (bubonic plague used to be endemic) and scratch an existence from scabby patches of grain planted on slopes sometimes as steep as 30 degrees, from which they were lucky to bring in three or four bushels an acre.

"Oh, this country always had possibilities," Alley cut in on my recollections. "You saw it at its worst. This loess soil is potentially very rich. It just needed work, water, fertilizer and organization."

We stood on the wide baked-clay terrace before Li's caves, overlooking a lower ledge where a man drove a herd of white goats down the hill to water. There was a view of a ravine on one side and on the other the green and gold of the valley, far down, where half a dozen of the fifty-nine villages of Willow Grove Commune were in sight—each consisting of old caves and two or three new one-story tile-roofed buildings. Several hundred sheep kicked up the dust of a new dirt and gravel highway. In the ravine a team of surveyors was laying out what would be a spur road to the new reservoir. Here a branch of the Yenan River fed into irrigation ditches watering rice fields. *Rice?* Millet and corn were the hardy annuals here, and wheat and vegetables for the good land. Rice was a delicacy I had seldom tasted on my first visit.

"Yes, old farmers said we couldn't grow rice here when we planted it," said Li. "Never been done before. We got expert help. It will run to two hundred catties a *mou* [twelve bushels an acre] this year but we'll double that next year. Our brigade will have rice for everybody."

Now, across the valley, climbing right to the tree-planted hilltops, lay tier on tier of terraces, with pools and catch basins built to hoard water and soil drawn in by well-engineered drainage systems. Mixed grain and giant squash were the hill harvest, but several lengths of the vast staircase were covered with something new, flowering tobacco plants. An experimental crop, said Li.

"Erosion?" He itemized the landscape: "See that young pine grove over there? See those apricot trees; they're bearing for the second year. We have planted 47,000 *mou* in pines, nut trees and orchards. Erosion? It's basically [how they love that word!] solved here. Our commune has dry-terraced 6,000 *mou* and terraced another 4,000 in guaranteed irrigation."

Their total land area was 65,000 *mou* (about 11,000 acres); they must have covered everything but the ridges and peaks.

"How long does it take to terrace a *mou* of land?"

"About seventeen man-labor days. We could do it in two or three with small bulldozers. We don't even have a tractor yet." With the hand labor of about 2,600 men and women members, Willow Grove had thus terraced 1,500 acres, a third of it since 1957.

We walked a mile through a ravine to see the No. 1 Dam, a well-built, deep-footed stone embankment about seventy feet high lying in the bed of a small tributary to a minor branch of the Yellow River. Beyond the causeway placid blue waters joined towering cliffs and made a lake half a mile long. Beneath one cliff, where a road was carved, some sun-clad children scampered under willows overhanging a shallow beach.

"Maybe you don't know what it means to us to have dams and reservoirs," said one of Li's young team leaders, earnest and enthusiastic, who had joined us. "We've got another dam bigger than this and seven more almost as large. People in these hills never knew the blessings of a good year-round water supply even for bathing, not to say irrigation or power. They hardly knew what soap looked like. It used to be said that a Shensi man bathed only twice in his life, when he was born and when he was married—and that was an exaggeration. Now our children even learn to swim. Our reservoirs are stocked with 640,000 fish! What peasant around here ever ate fresh fish? There's a good life ahead for our children!"

As a "commune," Willow Grove was in population hardly larger than a big brigade. What are called villages here are mostly small groups of ten or twenty families living in a cluster of caves. Level land is too scarce to be used for villages; even cattle and poultry are quartered in hillside caves. Willow Grove had only 1,592 families; 640,000 fish meant 400 for each family. Fish every day and two on feast days? No. These were commune assets on which to build for the future, and were being consumed only sparingly. The meat and fish ration per member was given as two catties (2.2 pounds) per month, supplemented by such poultry, pigs and goats as each family could maintain on its small private plot. Like most communes, and especially poor communes, Willow Grove was selling much of its meat and saving the proceeds to buy things needed for future development.

Although pork, lamb and beef were produced here in quantity, I saw none eaten. The Chinese prepare relatively little dried meat, and since the villages have no refrigeration systems, fresh meat (except poultry) is available only at slaughtering times. There was a packing plant in north Shensi. Much of China's tinned meat was exported to the U.S.S.R. and Eastern Europe to buy equipment.

Alley and I were Li's guests while at Willow Grove, on condition— to Mr. Chao's dismay—that no feast was spread. We ate *man-t'ou* made of millet, and potatoes, turnips, corn and squash. Yenanites had now learned to eat corn on the cob, in the past considered fit for pigs only. Everything was boiled or baked. There was a "shortage" of cooking oil. We had fresh tomato salad, also something new here, served with salt and garlic. We ate in the brigade headquarters canteen, at Willow Grove village, for which the whole commune was named. This canteen fed most of the village team at noon—about ninety families. At night it fed fewer, mostly unmarried party workers and young people; married couples ate at home with their children and parents.

The menu varied little from meal to meal except that breakfast was wet *hsiao-mi*, millet gruel. The food at Willow Grove was far better than the unvarying *mien t'iao* (millet noodles) I had eaten out of chipped enamel basins with the old Red Army—a diet which, like Grant's whiskey, did not interfere with winning battles.

Here, as well as anywhere, a brief digression on food values.

Chinese like meat and have no religious taboos against it, but in former times none but "rich men" ate meat more than three or four times (feast days) a year. Many Europeans and Americans seem to believe that without meat at least once a day a man cannot be properly nourished. The absence of meat is no hardship to habitual vegetarians; George Bernard Shaw and Gandhi proved that genius can thrive to a ripe old age on a noncarniverous diet. Many walrus tears shed abroad over the dying Chinese were inspired by ignorant mis-interpretations of reports that meat and fish were rationed at one to two pounds a month (true) and that the people, "reduced to starva-tion," were forced to substitute sweet potatoes for meat and grain (which in some areas was true).

One medium sweet potato contains nineteen times more vitamin A units than a whole orange, twice as much B_1, B_2, phosphorous and iron, and nearly three times more calories. One average Chinese yam (or large sweet potato) gives 200 times more vitamin A than a bowl (large cup) of cooked rice, one-third less B_1, nearly four times more B_2, six milligrams of vitamin C (rice has none), 40 percent more cal-cium, and about ten more calories. (It takes two yams to give equal protein value.) The yam has 10 percent fewer calories than its weight in beefsteak but many times more vitamins and minerals, except phos-phorous and iron. The humble dried pea contains five times more calories than its weight in steak, and three times more protein; it pro-vides four times more protein and nearly three times more calories than its weight in pork chops. One cup of Yenan squash contains five times more calcium, two-thirds as many calories, and 10 percent more vitamin A than one four-ounce serving of calf liver.

Monthly rations of wheat, millet, rice and potatoes here were said to average 34 catties (35.3 pounds) per person. This was supplemented by vegetables which are unrationed in season but rationed in winter. (Cabbage, turnips, etc., are stored in straw in caves or covered pits.) Members also keep a few fowl and a pig or two which can be consumed or sold on the market. The diet was austere and monotonous but cer-tainly provided well above 2,000 calories, more than "adequate." For a "basically poor" commune they were doing well.

Willow Grove already had one small power plant which lighted 120 buildings and supplied a telephone system that reached all its fifty-nine villages. (All the communes were now connected by tele-phone.) The brigades operated eleven small industries. I saw a slate and tile works, a transportation service (60 rubber-tired carts and 138 animals), a fertilizer plant, the largest brick kiln in Yenan county, a carpentry shop and a blast furnace.

I visited the furnace, which stood beside a small dam and pleasant reservoir in a village three or four miles from headquarters. It was a homemade but businesslike open hearth which turned out half a ton of iron a day—all consumed by the foundry where plows and tools were made. This was one of the many small native furnaces* that had been found practical and continued operations after the 1958 steel-making drive. Ore was conveniently right around the corner from the village and coal was also not far off. Both were of low grade but adequate for local needs. The village had no ore crusher and everybody, old ladies too, joined in hammering the ore from time to time. Under matted straw canopies I saw small children helping their mothers and thoroughly enjoying themselves. (What is more fun than hammering rocks?) Here I talked to a pretty schoolteacher from Szechuan; she had met a soldier in her native province, followed him back to his Shensi village, where he was a team leader, and married him. Did the Shensi natives accept Szechuanese as "people" now, or were they as "antiforeign" as ever?

"We don't have those old provincial prejudices any more," she answered, laughing. "I'm as much a *Shensi-jen* as anyone else, now that I've learned the dialect."

Toward noon I saw another team finish up an acre of squash and knock off for a siesta which lasted an hour and a half. Working hours during the harvest had been twelve or more a day but the harvest was practically over now and people were back to a nine-hour day. The frantic pace of '58 seemed left behind.

The notion that everybody in China is being madly pushed was not borne out by my observation. In Peking one day I stood at a window in my room in the Hsin Ch'iao and watched two women workers filling in and tamping earth over a drain newly installed in the Eye, Ear, Nose and Throat Hospital across the street. Every ten minutes they would stop and rest for an interval. One of them would go off and fetch a bowl of tea. They would resume work for ten minutes, pause, talk, laugh, have some tea, and so on. The stops were so frequent that I managed to get the whole sequence on one roll of movie film—while Stuart Gelder stood laughing with me at the "great leap forward."

At Willow Grove men got three or four holidays a month, as they do normally everywhere in China; women got four to six. In Old China the New Year, the equinoctial spring and autumn festivals, and occasional market days were as a rule the only holidays granted to working people. Now the traditional festivals are observed (with New Year's reduced to one day), but May First, several days on the October anniversary, weekly holidays, and annual vacations (normally ten days)

---

* Some of these had their crude beginnings in the Chinese Industrial Cooperatives Rewi Alley and his sons had started here, with overseas aid, as far back as the 1940's.

bring the total to many more rest days than the average person enjoyed in the past.

In another village I saw people building a new tile-roofed brick kitchen-canteen and meeting hall (stone foundations), and learned that the whole structure—seating capacity, 100—would cost no more than $1,700. As I watched, they dug up a sculptured T'ang memorial stone for which some Western museum would have paid a good price. I learned that there were sixty-three village dining rooms. People could eat in them or cook at home as they preferred. I saw families cooking and eating at home both in Willow Grove and in Yenan city.

When I first went to Shensi there were schools in county towns but none on the village level. Now there was one for every five villages in Willow Grove, where about 90 percent of children over seven were studying. Li claimed that 80 percent of people eighteen to forty here were now literate. Willow Grove village had the best primary school building and the largest: 183 students, eight teachers and a normal school graduate as principal. His wage was 47 yuan a month—the highest salary in the commune—plus board and lodging in a house, not a cave. As yet there was no commune higher school. But in the years 1958-59 Willow Grove had had 189 primary graduates accepted in Yenan middle schools, where the commune paid for their board—a not inconsiderable item on a small budget.

Willow Grove's home for childless aged people was a three-chamber cave on a terrace not far from Li's own hilltop castle. There I found eight gentlemen in their late sixties; one of them, with a white beard luxuriant for China, insisted that he was fifty-six. "He doesn't know when he was born," said one of the others, laughing at him. They were given food and a cook who looked after them and they had a few chickens and a tiny garden. None of them could read. What did they do with their time? When they felt energetic they strolled up to the new dam. (Had I seen it? Did we have such things in my country?) They played chess and they gardened a bit, but mostly they drowsed on the terrace or looked down at the familiar valley activity below. Communism? They knew nothing about that and were too old to learn. But the old folks' home? They repeated what I heard everywhere.

"Like it? Who doesn't like a rest after a hard life? Who would feed and shelter old men with no children in former times? Nothing to worry about! Simply unheard of! We'd all be dead."

I did not disturb these tranquil elders by telling them that they had been herded into camps and separated from their children, or so I had read abroad. Even the childless old ones were not forced into this home. Two individualists ("too old to change") here in Willow Grove lived in their caves alone, and wanted nothing to do with any "home" as long as they got food.

64

Willow Grove

The next day we sat for hours on benches beside a long table in the big cave that was the brigade headquarters and meeting room. Red banners flecked with stars hung on the walls, and photographs, slogans, charts, tables of production, posters, graphs and trophies. Li and two of his team leaders, the chairman of the women's work department, the doctor, the treasurer, the youth leader, were all there. Peasants drifted in, listened curiously to my questions, whispered among themselves, and sauntered outside to discuss answers.

Facts, facts, facts! In other times you couldn't get an exactitude from any peasant: his children were "several," the next town was "not ten *li* distant," the size of his farm was *"shang hsia"*—more or less. Now, whether it's the party secretary, a nurse, a cook or a student, he talks percentages, numbers of pigs and piglets, years and increases, high yields and average, things everyone discusses at meetings again and again: how much old Tsai should be paid for weeding, what counts as heavy work and what as light, how much cabbage for the old people's homes, how much wheat to be sold, eaten and reserved, how to increase fertilizer—and what to plan for in 1967! These people know their taxes to a decimal; they know their "four fixed" and their "three guarantees," and where their labor and money go. "Fixed" items are land, man power, animals and tools. "Guarantees" are quotas of production for taxes; state purchasing contracts; and "outside contract" sales and local consumption. "Rewards" are fixed bonuses for overproduction.

Li Yu-hua was only one of twenty-four brigade leaders in Willow Grove, but the commune took its name from the village where he organized the first cooperative, and he was the senior captain of them all. His "success story" was much like that of Yen Wei-chuan of Yellow Ridge: small beginnings, proof to skeptics that two heads are better than one, that cooperative labor was more productive; a gradual mass conversion which here reached over not one but two decades of effort. By 1955 the area had twenty-one advanced cooperatives which showed an increased production of more than 30 percent. Remaining skeptics then pooled their assets and joined.

"How did your commune begin?"

"We read Mao Tse-tung's article in June, 1958,[1] praising the Honan commune, and we discussed it. It made sense to us. We held meetings with other advanced co-ops and the *hsiang* and county officials and decided to organize as a commune."

"Led by the party, no doubt?"

"Led by the party."

Li had often seen Mao in his Yenan days and had talked to him. How much, I wondered, did Mao know about farming?

"He's a good farmer. He knows farming. He was right about cooperatives. He was right about communes. We followed his eight-point charter and it produced results for us."

This magic charter "everywhere held aloft" by the rural communes consists of: deep plowing and soil improvement; close planting; more fertilizer; water conservation; improved seeds; pest control; improved management; better farm tools.

"The charter sounds practical, if applied by practical men, Lao Li, but in what way did communes help you get the means to carry it out?"

"In every way: greater resources, greater income, greater economies, better use of labor, more money to invest—our dams, our irrigation works, our industries—"

At the risk of dropping some readers, I shall present "the facts" brought out to prove Li's contentions. An amendment to that: here are the facts which I extracted and had to fit together literally like a Chinese puzzle. These practical men of the field have no experience in presenting complex materials to an outsider; they assume background you don't possess; they are in no way prepared to impress the foreigner, and no public relations officer hands you a neatly packaged story.

There are dozens of technical traps. To cite one: you may end up with production and income figures per capita which don't tally at all with aggregates. Unless you can check your translator you may not realize that the speaker is talking about *chia* (family) income, not individual income. Despite man-woman equality, rural Chinese still lump husband-wife (and grandfather-grandmother) income as a unit and tend to use it interchangeably with "per capita" in conversation.

It is hard digging to get to the bottom of what's really going on. They pour out the pieces but you don't know which are relevant and which are not until you sift and pick, and if you haven't time to search again you come away with an unfinished puzzle. In Willow Grove I had the time and—the grain harvest being in—so did Li and his teammates.

Some vital statistics interested me. The total 1959 population of the commune was 6,254, of whom 3,655 were dependents, young and old. There were 1,582 families; the average couple had only two dependents. Of the 2,599 able-bodied workers, 1,592 were males, of whom only ten seemed to be still unmarried. The relative insignificance of this commune's industrial output is indicated by its full-time industrial labor force: only 181 workers (male and female) with 128 dependents. "Able-bodied" here meant from eighteen to retirement age. Veterans were encouraged to settle and there were many "immigrants" from other provinces. After 1948 the population of Yenan had sharply declined; thousands of youths trained by the party and the army left for the east, and very few of them returned.

In 1950 average output in this area was less than 5 bushels of grain an acre. By 1956 Li's advanced co-op had raised theirs to nearly 12 bushels. In 1959, a year after the commune was formed, culti-vated land had been increased from 3,500 acres to almost 5,000 acres by the twenty-four-brigade organization of labor, conservation works, etc. In the same year grain output averaged 19 bushels an acre. In 1960 weather in north Shensi was good (in contrast with drought in the south) and preliminary returns on the harvest, already in, showed an output for the whole commune well above their target, which was fixed at about 28 bushels of mixed grain (including livestock feed) an acre.

Even for mixed grain, those figures compare favorably with an American average wheat yield of 21.3 bushels per acre, but the in-vestment in labor power in China is still vastly greater. Peking economists recently pointed out that annual output per farm worker in the U.S. is about 1,000 bushels of grain. In China it required 300 days of labor to take care of 2.1 acres of crops. If China's labor productivity equaled that of the U.S. she would need only about 21,000,000 farm workers to feed the nation at its present level—in-stead of nearly ten times that number.[2]

Willow Grove's harvest included an average of 55 bushels on each of 1,650 acres of their best land, where a top yield of 118 bushels an acre was claimed. Such figures were phenomenal for north Shensi but they were not much more than average in Szechuan and China's rich delta areas. Near Shanghai a commune chairman told me he had established a record yield of 540 bushels (of mixed grain) an acre. I didn't believe it. I mentioned that figure to K. S. Kosambi, an Indian economist and agricultural expert of the Bombay government who was visiting China. Mr. Kosambi assured me that it was not only possible but that he had himself seen and tested harvest-ripe rice in the lower Yangtze Valley which would, by his own estimate, yield as much as 6,000 catties a *mou*—or better than 650 bushels an acre. These were, of course, only a few acres of high-yield demonstration plots.

Irrigation, terracing, steel plows, improved methods and heavy increases in fertilizer were paying off, said Li. Other investments of labor and capital were reflected in increases of Willow Grove's livestock population since 1957 as follows: pigs, 2,370, up 51 percent; cattle, 3,220, including 1,540 cows, up 10 percent; sheep, 14,690, up 42 percent; chickens, 8,000, up 25 percent.

I most certainly did not make a head count of the livestock but I can say that I saw literally thousands of sheep and goats, more than I remembered seeing in all north Shensi in the past. One dairy I visited had more than two hundred cows. If Mr. Li's figures were at all reliable this whole commune now had about one cow, nine sheep and five chickens per family, and three collective pigs for every two families. Comment on the pig: in China more than anywhere else he is not only wholly consumable except for the squeal, he is also a fertilizer factory worth almost more alive than dead. One pig produces enough manure to fertilize one *mou* of soil. Normally, according to Li, it takes fifty man days of labor to collect the equivalents in cattle and sheep droppings! Willow Grove's livestock was now supplying about half of its fertilizer.

One reason I took Li seriously was that he gave me such a very low figure on Willow Grove's 1959 net income. I was unable to get a clear answer from him about gross income, or percentage of actual output delivered on compulsory sales contracts to the state. He merely gave me to understand that taxes never exceeded "10 to 12 percent" and that the brigade was guaranteed a minimum of 60 percent of its output for consumption or "cash sale" at market prices.

A brief digression about taxes. Up to 1958 direct grain levies had not been as exorbitant as many supposed. According to Mao Tse-tung's report to the National Congress in 1957, output of food crops in 1949 was "only something over 210,000,000,000 catties." That would be 105,000,000 tons, perhaps the crop on which taxes were collected but likely not the full crop. By 1956 the harvest was claimed to be 360,000,000,000 catties or 180,000,000 tons—not far from correct, in the view of foreign economists. (The U.S. cereals crop in 1957 was 157,000,000 tons.) Said Mao in 1957:

The state agricultural tax is not heavy . . . only 30 billion catties [15 million tons] a year. Grain bought from the peasants at normal prices [he refers to compulsory sales of fixed percentages of the crop to state grain agencies] amounts to something over 50 billion catties a year. These two items together total over 80 billion catties. . . . We are prepared to stabilize over a number of years the total amount of grain purchased by the State at approximately something over 80 billion catties [40 million tons] a year.[3]

A tax of 15,000,000 tons on a crop of 180,000,000 tons (a bit more than 8 percent) and state grain purchases of 40,000,000 tons would bring the combined levy to roughly 30 percent of the crop. Mao left himself an escape clause in the "something over" but it is quite possible that in 1957 state taxes and purchases did not much exceed 30 percent. In 1958 and 1959, however, the combined tax and purchases may have been far higher than that figure, if the levies were based on the inflated harvest reports of those years.

Taxes on Willow Grove Commune in 1959 were stated to have been only 5.4 percent of output, whereas in Yellow Ridge they were 11 percent. In other areas I found variations from 6 to 14 percent, depending on prosperity. In 1960 many hard-hit cooperatives were forgiven taxes while fortunate ones paid much more heavily. The *People's Daily* for June 5, 1958, stated that average grain taxes for that year were to be 15.5 percent, based on the harvest of 1956 or 1957; this would have meant a low tax if the expected giant 1958 crop had materialized. But I was told by one Chinese official that some communes had so far overestimated their harvests that they paid up to 50 percent of their crop in taxes and obligatory sales. Afterward they had to appeal to the government for relief. Gilbert Etienne, a Swiss economist who returned from China late in 1961, gave me this variation of tax rates he collected in different communes he visited that year in the following neighborhoods: Hangchow, 19.19 percent; Wuhan, 7 percent; Nanking, 7.1 percent; Peking, 17 percent.

Because of unknowns in the ratio of taxes to "forced grain sales" and because commune claims on gross output even late in 1960 had still not been completely adjusted to reality, only *net income* had much meaning. To return now to Willow Grove and its earnings for 1959.

Wages are determined on a basis involving eight to twelve grades of farm tasks, each paid differently. Every team keeps daily and monthly records of the amount and kind of piecework accomplished by each member. This system might drive a chartered accountant mad but it seems satisfactory to Chinese farmers, who agree on fair rates among themselves. In Willow Grove Commune the income was figured in both cash and grain.

Mr. Li's "net income" figure for 1959 was what remained after operating expenses and payment of taxes and sales to the state— which may amount, as indicated, to more than 30 percent of output. Other deductions included "15 to 20 percent" for livestock feed and seed grain, "15 to 20 percent" for depreciation, reserves and welfare fund, and "about 10 percent" for new investments. Of the capital invested in new projects and equipment, 60 percent went to improvements in the land, industries, cattle, etc., owned by the brigades or villages, the rest went to commune projects under joint ownership.

After all these deductions the cash left for distribution amounted to only 187,800 yuan, which worked out at an average of about 72 yuan per worker. In addition each averaged an income of 830 catties in grain, including meat equivalents. Out of this grain income the commune set aside 390 catties (429 pounds) per inhabitant (including dependents) for consumption. The member worker was thus left with less than half of his 830 catties as book income. The "surplus grain" was "voluntarily" sold collectively at market prices, each member being credited with his proportion in "share ownership." The profit was added to capital funds for investment in brigade and commune projects and services.

Stated as take-home cash, the 72-yuan pittance sounds intolerable; but here the family paid no rent, nothing for utilities, nothing for nursery, kindergarten and schools (supported jointly by the commune welfare fund and the state), very little for medical care, no personal taxes, and his staple food was supplied. Members kept pigs or poultry and gardened an average family plot of .10 *mou* for consumption or supplementary income. (A pig sold for 40 yuan.) A strong worker could make much more than the average. I was introduced to one who earned 190 yuan ($72) in 1959. With a bonanza harvest in 1960, Willow Grove brigade leaders anticipated an income of 150 yuan cash per head.

Peasants here never used to see more than a yuan or two in cash at a time; their purchases were limited to salt, light oil, needles and thread, and occasionally a piece of cloth. Poor peasants were always in debt to usurers; now, if a peasant borrowed money to buy a pig or a bicycle it was from his mutual welfare fund and at no more than 3 percent interest. Not all peasant homes I saw in Willow Grove were as "richly furnished" as Li's, but even the poorest had chests of clothing and piled-up quilts. Even on such minimal cash they somehow managed to dress their children attractively and I was constantly surprised at the bright, clean clothes of the peasant girls one saw riding donkeys to and from town.

All the land, orchards, local dams, irrigation works, buildings, factories, and livestock were jointly owned by the brigades and village teams of Willow Grove. Mounting assets were thus considerably greater than the current cash income reflected. They might reasonably be expected to pay an increasingly higher return once the basic national construction program in agriculture and industry was completed and consumer goods output could absorb more cash. Since peasant members cannot sell their nominal share in the brigade's capital assets, their investment in it tends to keep them stabilized on the land; if they leave for another commune it may take them years as hired laborers to win acceptance as members with full rights.

The whole success of collective ownership depends upon maintaining peasant understanding of the reasons for self-denial and saving and on maintaining faith and enthusiasm about the system. Here in Willow Grove at least, the already realized tangible benefits, combined with visible evidence of the new wealth created by their collective labor, had produced a high degree of ambition for the fulfillment of plans. And every worker knew about these plans.

Lu Hsin-ming, the commune chairman and deputy party secretary (a local peasant leader of thirty), who came over to join the conversation at one stage, explained the charts and diagrams on display with great confidence and fluency. By 1967 grain production would double, orchards would increase from 130 acres to 250 acres, lumbering operations would be well along on 8,000 acres of afforested timberlands, livestock per person would number three pigs, three cows, twelve chickens and eight sheep. By then cultivation in the level lands would be mechanized. (The commune planned to buy its first trucks and tractors in 1962—two of each.) Eight more small power stations, a new middle school, one theater-opera house, and ten primary school buildings would be constructed. By that time cash income (in addition to free food) would increase to 500 yuan per person—or about $400 per family. That paradise was six years away, but looking back on changes since 1954, the peasants might well believe in it.

War could certainly interfere with fulfillment. Lu said they were not afraid of war. "China will not start a war and if the imperialists attack us we shall defeat them." This was an eternal truth—as useless to dispute as to argue the doctrine of karma with a Buddhist.

Before I left Willow Grove, I visited the kindergarten-nursery in a cave high on a bluff where Li's daughter, a Mrs. Chen, kept thirty-three infants busy learning the rudiments of socialist cooperation. A nursery in a cave? The Shensi *yao-fang* is not a hole in the ground but a "house in a hill." Except in external appearance a cave can be superior to the average farm hut, drier and cooler in summer, warmer in winter. Terraces dug from the fudge-colored loess provide a suitable façade; chimneys are put in at a slant; the rooms have vaulted ceilings and large arched windows give ample light. Frequently two or more rooms are linked into apartments. My old friend Dr. Horse used to have a large hospital, with operating chambers, built in a Yenan hill, and I had visited a wartime cave college for women in one of these hillsides (there were cave-men colleges, too). Plastered walls and bricked-over floors give ample clean quarters for the cost of little but labor.

Mrs. Chen proudly showed me around her premises. Most of the little ones were of kindergarten age; there was a separate room for nursery tots. On a k'ang in another room, five diapered babies stared as impartially as if I were just another man-giant, not an imperialist. In a third room stood a battery of children's toilet seats with an ingenious arrangement for flushing from a large barrel and a drain which led to a covered pit outside.

The rooms were clean, so were the children, and so were the grown-ups—down to fingernails. (Shensi peasants with clean fingernails? There has been a revolution here.) There used to be dysentery in nearly every family. Mrs. Chen said they had had no case for a year. A public health nurse called once a week; all children were vaccinated. I saw no sign of trachoma, formerly very common. The children looked well nourished and healthy and their behavior was energetic. They were dressed in cheap but attractive jumper suits differing in color and design; girls had slashes of red ribbons in their bobbed hair, boys had shaved heads and wide grins.

Taking charge of me, tugging at my hands and jacket, the kindergarteners dragged me to see their piles of squash and pumpkins, their purple corn; these they had tended and hauled up the hill themselves.

The usual rows of combs, toothbrushes, wash basins and towels were ranged under health posters, and each child had his bowl and chopsticks. Besides gruel, mashed vegetables and occasional eggs, there was even milk here twice a week—for nursery tots only.

Commune nurseries at Willow Grove were (as in many rural areas) operated only during the busy planting and harvesting seasons, when mothers work full time in the fields. Most of them were, like the kindergartens, day schools only. Parents left the children in the morning and picked them up after work.

Who cares what the hillbilly parents of these infants stashed in yao-fang think about their nurseries, kindergartens, schools, terraces, dining rooms, halls, dams, new rice fields—or whether bound-footed grandmothers sigh with envy as their daughters work beside their husbands, learning to read and talk like bold people with natural feet? Yet those who would heal the world must try to see the importance of these quick-learning peasants teaching their children sanitation and hygiene from infancy up, the uses of clean water and clean bodies, and the benefits of shared work, shared savings, shared pleasure and shared plans for a future in which any smart peasant child can attain the best education the land can offer. Why? They're all a bunch of Reds. Yes, that's true. What can all this mean to a woman reading a slick magazine in which a single trinket advertised may cost as much as a Willow Grove family can earn by hard, unceasing toil in five years? Conditioned by cold-war hates and fears, we may feel no real empathy with this distant scene, but its meaning should be understood. If the changes I saw in the caves of the Northwest can be achieved in a few short years then they may well reach into darkest Africa and the Andes sooner than many think.

I shall omit my conversations with peasants and school children. I shall skip three more cave-nurseries I saw in other villages. I shall merely mention that in Willow Grove's 42 nurseries and kindergartens 532 children from toddlers up were learning how to play, work, sing and dance together—in the midst of material conditions basically no worse than in Puerto Rican slums in New York.

I have described two communes that were more or less typical of nine others I visited except that Yellow Ridge was one of the richest and Willow Grove was the poorest. The best managed I saw was the Horse Bridge Commune near Shanghai, a very prosperous large ranch farm with yields as good as American ones. It was so much above average that to dwell on it at length would be misleading. For the same reason I have omitted here a detailed report of the highly mechanized state farm I saw at Chia Mu Ssu outside Harbin.

State farms are run like factories and employees on them are wage workers who have no private ownership rights. They are a stage beyond collectivization, in Communist theory; they are "owned by the whole people" and thus already have "elements of communism." Cultivators receive high cash wages comparable to those of factory workers, and the general standard of living is much above that of the cooperative farms.

A few model state farms were organized as long as ten years ago, in Manchuria—where great wheat domains and cattle ranches were first opened by White Russians—and later extended to virgin lands in sparsely populated Sinkiang, Mongolia and Yunnan. Since communes were formed such farms have about doubled in area, but by 1961 they still embraced only 12,500,000 acres, or less than 5 percent of China's cultivated land. Most of them were not affected by the drought that came late in 1960—a year when they reported a 2,500,000-ton harvest gathered by 2,800,000 workers. If the same rate prevailed everywhere China could show a crop of 550,000,000 tons (3.7 times the estimated 1960 output), need but 60,000,000 farm hands, and have an abundance of food as well as labor. The state farms' high productivity was explained by heavy use of chemical fertilizer and 28,000 tractors and 3,300 combine-harvesters; they are about five times more mechanized than the communes.

In both Honan and Paotou I saw country badly treated by nature, and generally speaking, I chose my own itinerary. I have faithfully described what I could see and learn about farm conditions very far from ideal or anywhere near Western standards of prosperity.

Yet what I saw and heard was less than one distinguished American columnist had already learned about China on a visit to Macao a year before. When I returned from Yenan to Sian I found a few letters forwarded from Peking. One enclosed clippings of some articles depicting conditions inside China in November, 1959. They were written by Joseph Alsop. Viewing the situation from the Portuguese colony, Mr. Alsop reported that "gnawing hunger, made worse by chain-gang work conditions, now prevails *in every region of the Chinese countryside.*" He went on to assert that "fats and proteins . . . were mere dreams of the past in the communes"—"many" of which were requiring "16 hours of work a day for at least half of each month." He also learned in Macao (which has Kuomintang as well as Communist propaganda centers) of "numerous cases of grass-eating . . . and leaf-eating" in China and of "peasants being driven to work *24 hours a day* for two to four days on end."[4]

I have had some experience in detecting starvation among wartime refugees. In famine areas of yore I personally saw hundreds of Chinese actually feeding on bark, leaves and even mud. But they were not working sixteen or twenty-four hours a day. They were dying.

After a swift visit to Hongkong and another peep at the bamboo curtain early in 1961, Mr. Alsop scored an even more important scoop over resident Hongkong correspondents. He cabled home the news that Chinese were now reduced to dining on human afterbirths.[5] Mr. Alsop attributed this refugee intelligence to "an obviously well-balanced trained nurse from North China."

65

---◆◆---

The Refugee
as Source Material

En route from Sian to San Men Hsia I wrote a few notes under the above heading which I may as well elaborate in a more serious evaluation of reports like the foregoing that have been coming out of Hongkong for many years predicting imminent collapse in China.

I first visited Hongkong and Portuguese Macao in 1930 and have been back often since then. I was in Macao again in December, 1959, a month after Mr. Alsop's appearance there the year before my return to mainland China. In Macao I saw scores of Chinese crossing the border to bring in vegetables and other food on which that colony has always been dependent. I also saw many crossing back into China again—something Mr. Alsop must have missed. Macao still derives much of its revenue, as in the past, from the sale of opium and its derivatives. I saw some dope-drunk addicts there, as any visitor can. Heroin and morphine were still sold more or less openly. Widespread opium consumption is also a commonplace fact about Hongkong, where it is smuggled in, these days, largely from Iran, Thailand, Laos and Saigon.* One might suppose that these and other readily observable conditions reflecting misery and despair in the slums of

* See Chapter 85, War and Peace in Vietnam.

Macao and Hongkong might occasionally be worth a line or two as variants to ditto about China, but perhaps they are too old a story.

It seems an anomaly that Portugal still recognizes Chiang Kai-shek's government on Taiwan and that there is a Nationalist consulate in Macao. Yet the People's Republic also owns a book and propaganda center in Macao and has trade representatives there. People wonder why China doesn't take back Macao, especially now that India has seized Goa without incurring any more displeasure than some huffs and puffs by *Time* and other friends of India against Krishna Menon—which popularized and helped re-elect him. In Peking I was told on what may have been good authority that the Portuguese had been angling for a guarantee of the security of their colony in exchange for a switch in their vote on China's place in the U.N. Thus far the offer had been ignored. Meanwhile Macao is, like British Hongkong, still as useful to China as a trading and "observation" center as it is to foreign intelligence.

Hongkong was taken by Britain in 1842 as a prize after the defeat of China in the first Opium War. Following China's humiliation in the Sino-Japanese War (1895), Britain demanded and secured a ninety-eight-year leasehold on large "New Territory" added to the Kowloon (Nine Dragon) Peninsula, across the bay from Hongkong, which China had been obliged to cede (1860) after her defeat in another war. The combined population of Kowloon and Hongkong is today about 3,200,-000, and 99 percent Chinese. Hundreds of Chinese with legal exit permits cross into Hongkong and Kowloon every day from China. As many as "a thousand to fifteen hundred Chinese a day go *to* China" from Hongkong, according to a recent CBS-TV news report which quoted a British border official.[1] Both Kowloon and the island of Hongkong are dependent on China for some food and some water. Britain lost no time in recognizing the People's Republic (January 6, 1950); today the latter owns and operates banks, department stores, shipping, airlines (flying some of General Chennault's planes), newspapers, schools and other interests there, and a powerful (if discreet) party organization infiltrates all sections of the population.

British officials are fully aware that the Hongkong-Kowloon colony exists on borrowed time. The small, largely Chinese police force and a handful of British troops could not prevail against a well-organized insurrection combined with a general strike and a cut-off of supplies and mainland trade. No armed invasion would be necessary. The British are anxious to secure from Peking at least a definite time period in which to prepare for an orderly withdrawal from Kowloon. So far the best assurance they have been able to get is their own knowledge that the free port is economically and politically valuable to China. Peking officials see the United States as the main imperialist culprit, and prefer to keep Britain divided from Washington on China policy rather than risk uniting the whole Anglo-Saxon world against them.

"We like to see Hongkong become rich," one Chinese government economist I know remarked privately. "All that wealth came from the labor and resources of our people and eventually it will return to us."

Much capital has recently been invested in Hongkong and Kowloon, where abundant cheap labor and duty-free imports of raw materials result in quick profits from the manufacture of bargain-price consumer goods sold to waiting markets in America. Most of the new capital is Chinese. Much of it originated from foreign-exchange accounts established by mainland capitalists who had the foresight to get out before the total collapse of the Kuomintang currency preceding Chiang Kai-shek's flight to Taiwan.

About 500,000 immigrants and refugees came into Hongkong during the Sino-Japanese and Chinese civil wars. By 1949, the year in which the People's Republic was founded, the Hongkong population stood at about 1,700,000. Since then (to 1962) it has increased by some 1,500,000. The natural, internal growth during those years has been estimated at about 700,000; immigration added 800,000. The flow of immigrants into Hongkong thus averaged 60,000 to 70,000 a year. Many of these people are "returned Overseas Chinese." Since 1959 more than half a million Chinese have been forced to leave Indonesia. Many thousands came to Hongkong but even more returned to the mainland.

There they have been relocated chiefly in the South, but I met refugee families from Indonesia as far north as Shenyang, Manchuria. More than 50,000 Chinese returned from abroad were reportedly settled on fifty-six state-owned farms in five southern provinces between 1960 and 1962. "The State invested Y.37,000,000 in the livelihood needs and productive capital construction"—quarters, factory buildings, warehouses, stables, nurseries, schools and water conservancy projects—according to the press.[2] These "Overseas Chinese state farms" were said to be already "40 to 50 percent self-sufficient."

Even if *all* the Hongkong immigrants came from mainland China they would, at the present rate per year, number less than one in ten thousand of the Chinese people. Compare this with the about five out of ten thousand persons of German birth who in 1959[3] chose to emigrate to the United States rather than stay in Europe (including West Germany), the three out of ten thousand Italians who made the same choice on leaving Italy, and the four in ten thousand persons born in Britain who did likewise. In 1951-60 more than 1,300,000 Europeans (excluding those from Eastern Europe) entered the United States from their native lands in the Old World. This omits millions who emigrated elsewhere. If Chinese had emigrated to the United States in the same proportion to their population as the Germans came, our country alone would have admitted more than 5,000,000 between 1951 and 1960.

Not long before Pearl Harbor the Chinese premier, Dr. H. H. Kung, gave me an estimate of 10,000,000 as the total Overseas Chinese community. From what terrors had they fled in those days and earlier? Without counting any postrevolutionary increment this community would by natural increase alone now number well over 13,000,000. That was the figure accepted in 1959 by Robert Elegant when he wrote *Dragon Seed,* an absorbing historical and contemporary account of the various Chinese migrations.[4] These have created a Chinese majority in Singapore and added as much as a fifth to the population of Thailand, where the native stock is close kin of the 600,000 Thais in southern China. Mr. Elegant does not include the Taiwan population among the Overseas Chinese, since Taiwan is a territorial part of China. The 2,000,000 mainland Chinese who retreated to Taiwan—including 600,000 Kuomintang soldiers involuntarily transported there by the Generalissimo—are not émigrés but constitute a regime whose sovereignty over the 8,000,000 native Taiwanese is recognized and protected by the United States.

Except for exiles who fled from northern China during the Japanese war, and during the 1947-49 civil war period—predominantly middle class, and a few score thousands at most—the native population of Hongkong is overwhelmingly Cantonese. Canton is really "Kwan-chou"; the province is called Kwangtung. By convention the river port city is spelled Canton by foreigners but "Cantonese" may mean a native of either the city or the province. Traditionally, Chinese emigrants have come almost exclusively from two southern provinces, Kwangtung and Fukien. The average hinterland Chinese peasant no more thinks of moving abroad than the average Kansas farmer thinks of emigrating to Australia or Europe. If we omit the Philippines, where Fukienese predominate, well over 90 percent of all Overseas Chinese are Cantonese. And of these the great majority come from only seven counties in the Canton delta. It is "people of the three rivers"—their confluence is the Pearl River which reaches the sea below Canton—who have largely populated the Kowloon peninsula and Hongkong. They look upon the colony not as a foreign land but as an extension of their own delta domains—which indeed it was, before the Opium Wars.

Kwangtung province is only 84,000 square miles in area and it has about 40,000,000 inhabitants, or four-fifths as many as Italy. The fertile Pearl River delta is saturated by a labyrinth of waterways and canals, grows all kinds of tropical fruits and vegetables, and produces rice, silk and tea in abundance, and babies more so. With more than 12,000,000 people living on a total of 2,890 square miles, there is today less than one-sixth of an acre of cultivated land per person. About 300,000 Cantonese who have spilled over into sampans and junks exist on the margins of land and water from birth to death.

For generations the fecund delta area has been sending children abroad. Scarcely a village in southern Kwangtung does not boast relatives in Hongkong, Southeast Asia, Hawaii, or the South Seas. Many families exported one or more children in each generation, as a kind of insurance. Some were slave girls, like Michener's Nyuk Tsin, who sent money home long after they became grandmothers abroad. Some built the railways in America's West, and died there. Some were penniless barefoot boys like Sun Yat-sen, who went to Hawaii from Choy Hang. A few became millionaires. The Canton delta is the Sicily of China. For tens of thousands of families the difference between relative prosperity and want was measured by remittances from overseas or from Hongkong.

Beginning with the Japanese destruction of Western empire in Asia, and increasingly during the last decade of rising young Asian nationalisms, all this drastically changed. Indonesia used to take many thousands of Chinese annually; now it has deported more than half a million, with more to follow. The Philippines Republic has effectively banned Chinese immigration. Australia admits no Orientals at all. Thailand, Malaya and other South Asian countries have also closed their doors to Chinese. South America takes a few who can raise the fare to get there. Europe will take virtually none. The United States legal quota has been 104 a year. Since Chiang Kai-shek went to Taiwan that island has admitted only 15,000 Hongkong immigrants—fewer than 1,300 a year.

Officially, the Chinese government welcomed Chinese refugees from Indonesia. Comparatively few could be resettled as communities on marginal and reclaimed lands in other provinces. Instead of thinning out its surplus humans by emigration as Europe does, and as was done in the past, Kwangtung in recent years has had to absorb many thousands into their old villages, while Overseas remittances have greatly shrunk. The party's ideological position nevertheless remained "more people, more production." In 1958 the theory was put to severe tests by the organization of communes. By 1960 the Cantonese commune appeared not only to have brought no appreciable improvement but, helped by the bureaucratic errors and disastrous weather, may have contributed to actual declines. For three consecutive years Kwangtung was one of three or four provinces hardest hit by alternate flood and drought. In the early spring of 1962 severe floods inundated much of the land. Meanwhile, in villages worried about summer crops, anxiety was deepened by the arrival of "more mouths." Party directives had ordered heavy cuts in construction activity and nonessential industries in favor of all-out efforts on the agricultural front, and many workers were sent back from the cities and towns.

Cantonese dialect is little understood in other provinces, the dialects of the delta are scarcely understood outside their own region, and these people do not readily acclimatize in cold-weather areas. For such reasons Cantonese peasants cannot be shifted elsewhere to alleviate local pressures as easily as northerners. In times of trouble people of the delta think of their relatives in Hongkong or abroad rather than of moving to the hinterland.

In May, 1962, mainland policy on migration from Kwangtung underwent a dramatic and apparently experimental change. Instead of permitting only small numbers of people to "visit relatives abroad" the Chinese authorities abruptly lowered the barriers to anyone who wished to cross the Hongkong frontier. The news spread rapidly. Thousands began to trek through the delta country, trampled down the barbed-wire fences along the twenty-three-mile border, and for a time overwhelmed the British guards. A total of about 70,000 were estimated to have attempted to enter the colony during the month of May, before British protests to Peking resulted in a restoration of restrictions which halted the flow. The great majority were turned back by the British. Chinese guards readmitted them and persuaded them to return to their homes.

There was lively speculation in the American press; many criticized the British for not welcoming all these people believed to be fleeing from Communist terror. Many American newspapers concluded that "hundreds of millions" of Chinese would also like to leave. No one suggested where they would be received. Hongkong is a tiny colony already almost as overpopulated as the delta itself. The whole episode did prove one thing quite clearly: that the outside world provides no answer even for the delta emigrants. But did it prove that hundreds of millions of Chinese wished to emigrate or were starving or that even those in the teeming delta were starving?

Reginald Maudling, British Colonial Secretary, on May 22 reported official intelligence from Hongkong to the House of Commons. He stated that "there was little evidence that the Chinese refugees attempting to enter Hong Kong were suffering from malnutrition," according to the *New York Times*. In the same journal an eyewitness dispatch from the colony on that day confirmed that "Few [of the refugees] have told stories of political persecution. Few have shown unusual symptoms of malnutrition or starvation." A long and detailed eyewitness report by Richard Hughes appeared in the *New York Times* in June. "After the initial shock of the mass influx, the next surprise for Hong Kong was that the great majority of the refugees was not starving or even seriously undernourished," wrote Mr. Hughes. When intercepted, "most of them were suffering only the normal hunger of people who had been one day without food while waiting to crash the border." Except for occasional signs of vitamin deficiency those refugees seen by Mr. Hughes indicated to him that "food rationing—to cope with three years of failing agricultural production and bungled corrective methods—has obviously served to ward off mass starvation." It was not true, he reported, that soldiers had joined the exodus. Not an instance was noted. Discipline in the army was as firm when the migrants were called back by the authorities as when they were passed to the frontier.

British "intelligence reports . . . agree that the Communist ideology as such had little influence on the escapees' motives and aspirations,"

Mr. Hughes continued. "Personally and symbolically, Mao Tse-tung still dominates the China scene" and is "revered as a great national leader and patriot." "One Hong Kong interrogator summed it up succinctly, 'These folk are seeking jobs and security; they aren't escaping communism.'" There was "no interest in Chiang Kai-shek" and it was "a singular fact that there is no record of any refugees having asked to be permitted to go to Taiwan." [5]

Some American congressmen now had second thoughts about granting asylum to those Chinese who wished to enter the United States. They began vociferously to oppose President Kennedy's modest humanitarian proposal to waive the quota limit of 104 annually and admit 5,000 to 6,000 Chinese at once. These were to be well-screened Chinese of means and education who had long been on approved United States waiting lists. That gesture could no more solve the basic problems of the peasants than missionary soup kitchens in Hongkong, but the congressmen did not want Chinese of any variety—"red, white, yellow or green," as one of them put it. Was that a point the mainland authorities had wished to make by opening the gates? If people had doubted them when told that there was "no room" for them abroad, they knew now. Lady Liberty held her torch toward Europe, not Asia. The American way of life, with its twelve acres per inhabitant, could not solve even the local Cantonese problem, with its six inhabitants per acre. China had to find her own answers to her oceanic dilemmas and she had to find them on her own land.

In Hongkong each immigrant has his own story of discontent or oppression. The educated who lost fortunes or status are a new kind of refugee but altogether they number far less than one percent of even the former owning classes. I have spoken to many of them and also to ordinary peasants who could be called exiles from misery. Few of the latter know much about China beyond the delta; one speaks to them only through Cantonese interpreters. For many, it is simply a tradition that some "mouths" should emigrate. But rich or poor, what makes Europeans emigrate makes Chinese emigrate too. Political oppression, religious intolerance, yes; but most of all they seek opportunities to make money, to win position, to attain economic security, to "better themselves."

In 1962 the additional impetus was the cumulative misfortunes of three years of poor crops which lay upon the land. By no means all peasants have lost their superstitions. (I met a peasant woman who thought the trouble started with the "year of the pig," 1959; bad luck always followed the pig year.) The gods had repeatedly failed them, but many also enjoyed ridiculing the earnest, bungling young cadres. The emigrants and would-be emigrants were not starving but they feared that famine might come.

Meanwhile, many thousands of Hongkong and Overseas Chinese businessmen have continued to go into and come out of China. A trickle of emigrants with places to go will be allowed to leave China. Others will slip across the frontier and disappear in Hongkong. A few will become prosperous; others will return to the motherland. It would be naïve to suppose that among those who emigrate with legal papers there are not government agents. Many are eager to satisfy the municipal or private benefactors who feed and try to house them. Nor is it only the virtuous who take wing; inevitably a certain number of criminals also slide out.

None of these observations is intended to minimize the discontent that certainly affects many in China who long for a return of the old ways and for whom "the new society" holds no interest or promise. In the Devotions it was said by John Donne,

> Every man is a peece of the Continent, a part of the maine; if a
> Clod be washed away by the Sea, Europe is lesse, as well as if
> a Manor of thy friends or of thine own were.

The immigrant-refugee is important even if his interviews are sometimes tailored to fit an alien audience. Without him, China is less. He is more of the truth than just his annual statistic of one in ten thousand. But how much more? Any species examined after it has been separated from the ecology which produced it may provide information of some value and yet leave a hundred basic questions in the realm of sheer speculation. In order to lift those questions from the speculative level to the level of observable evidence of scientific truth, it is necessary to see and compare some of the human species who are living and functioning organisms inside the mainland environment which is China. Serious students of the subject who are based in Hongkong are fully aware of this fact and treat the refugee as source material with appropriate reserve.

66

The Yellow River
Turns Blue

We took a night express from Sian to the new city of San Men Hsia, Three Gate Gorge, where man has at last put a throttle on the Yellow River. Some people consider this the most spectacular and significant single engineering achievement yet seen in eastern Asia.

If we think of the known history of China and its civilization as having had a life span of twenty-four hours, then Communist power has been in existence less than five minutes. By comparison, the longest single dynastic reign in China endured for almost five hours. Anyone who ever found anything admirable in this land or any part of its history need not be a Communist, therefore, to derive pleasure from two remarkable improvements in the landscape brought about mainly during the past "five minutes." These are best seen from the air: 1) the numerous blue-water reservoirs I have mentioned; and 2) the advancing forests of young trees flanking the sides of once barren hills, along rivers, canals, highways and railways, and pushing back the northern deserts.

Kuant'ing and Miyun reservoirs, which I had seen, and now the San Men, which we were nearing, were three of a score of major new water-conservation works that had been completed as part of a state program for more than four hundred principal dams which were in various stages of construction or planning. Within the decade since 1950, China had risen from twenty-fifth place as a power producer to seventh place in the world, standing just behind France. Meanwhile a myriad of hands had in twelve years built more than a million small reservoirs and ponds such as those at Willow Grove, and dug nine million wells. They had also developed new canals and storage basins which increased the irrigated area by 120,000,000 acres.

Between 1952 and 1960, China graduated more than 5,000 forestry experts and established a modern forestry service. In north Shensi I saw the southern edge of one great forest belt which stretches for 360 miles above the Yellow River to stop the silt-laden sandstorms from the Gobi. Above it, reaching from Inner Mongolia to the Manchurian provinces, another tree belt had been more than half planted over a length of 720 miles. Elsewhere most of the afforestation labor was provided by agricultural communes, but every able-bodied person had participated and was still planting his annual quota of trees. Most collectives and production brigades now have tree nurseries, and billions of seedlings and saplings have been nurtured and cultivated.

In the Northwest, extensive new resources and industries are being developed around the Tsaidam basin, where it was essential to reclaim marginal land in order to feed the incoming population. Since 1955, it is claimed, some 150,000 acres of land in that region have been successfully desalinized and already produce "grain yields of around two tons per hectare."[1] Altogether, "about five hundred state farms" have been created from "former wasteland in Northwest China," it was recently announced at a farm conference in Sian.[2] "Located in sparsely populated uplands," or on the edges of deserts and alkaline areas, they have "since 1958 increased by four times the total area cultivated by state farms in the Northwest," and "5,500 tractors have been added." In Sinkiang alone "more than 140 mechanized state farms have been set up since 1949 by demobilized army men and other young people." Much of the 30,000,000 acres of land brought into cultivation since the revolution lies in this area and in Mongolia. There have been massive failures at reclamation as well as successes. Farther west, an extensive forest shelter belt across the Tengri Desert is said to "account for nearly half the 260,000 hectares [650,000 acres] afforested in the Ninghsia Mohammedan Autonomous Region in China's Northwest since 1949."[3]

Over all China, it was claimed, more than 51,000,000 hectares—"an area twice as large as Great Britain"—had been tree-planted and reforested between 1949 and 1960.[4] Much of this is scattered acreage and includes urban as well as forest plantings.

In Peking's agricultural and industrial exhibition halls I had seen scale models not only of all the major conservation systems but of important projects I had never heard of, many of them already completed, in widely scattered areas. (One example: a dam in Turkestan almost as large as San Men, to be completed in 1961.) One Wellsian exhibit showed the long-range plan of a canal and river system which would virtually encircle China, reaching from the frontiers of Manchuria to Yunnan, and from Peking to Central Asia, bringing all corners of the realm within reach of motor vessels carrying cargo and passenger traffic. This involves no less than turning some of the headwaters of the Yangtze River from eastern Tibet into the Taklamakan Desert. It is easy to draw futuristic pictures, of course. What make these schemes notable are the steps already taken toward their realization. Many achievements publicized only locally, which the outside world never hears about, would be considered major events in small countries or even in a large country like India.

Rewi Alley had seen more of these "unknown" transformations in the hinterland than any other foreigner. While I was with him he kept up a continual discourse which would have been simply Sinbad tales to me if I had not already seen enough to modify a natural skepticism. In years past he had walked across more of China than most veterans of the Long March; his tireless interest in the fate of thousands of derelict families and children he had known kept sending him back to see how they fared. Recently he had retraced his old footsteps on new roads in a jeep. He spoke of scores of instances of lost waifs refound working as foremen, schoolteachers, nurses, engineers; of scrofulous mud towns never before penetrated by machines or power but now organized and cleanly rebuilt, operating mines, containing flood waters, turning from small blast furnaces to modern steel mills, making motors, generators, machine tools; of old canals redug and deepened and of floating pumps used to shoot water uphill, to make streams cross mountains; of places I could not myself readily locate on a map where he had watched people move in ten years from the Middle Ages to the threshold of modern life and its good potentialities. As I listened to Alley remember aloud these encounters with humble people risen to greatness in forgotten corners of the earth, he was so enthusiastic that no one could doubt his personal satisfaction in the fulfillment of his own dreams for his adopted homeland.

"Yes, yes, yes, San Men is a magnificent thing," he said as we came into the new city, "but it's the miniature San Mens going up all over the backwoods, like Yenan—and like Yunnan—each one representing untold struggles of little people who had to dream big—that's where you really see the creative force this country is releasing." Those who are worried about China's launching an aggressive war might find in Alley's new book, *China's Hinterland*,[5] and its thousands of true stories of unsung heroes at work, some interesting information about how that nation's vast human energies are presently being contained in building activities which should make the world rejoice—unless, of course, all growth in lands of the blue ants must inevitably lead to war, as it has done in the white-ant lands. (Nor can I affirm that it will not.)

In 1956, San Men City was a drowsy village known as Hui Hsin, on the Honan-Shensi border. Today it unexpectedly finds itself host to 170,000 workers, with many more to come. The village had an ancient history unknown even to its inhabitants. When excavations were made for a new railway station, workmen uncovered the tomb of a Prince of Kuai (seventh century B.C.). Evidently a sporting gentleman, he was entombed with four hunting chariots each drawn by two horses, and with hunting dogs and other interesting accessories of the chase. Nobody remembered who Kuai was until a Confucian scholar identified his father as a minor king of the warring states toward the end of the Chou Dynasty who was mentioned in Confucius' *Spring and Autumn Annals*. The chariots and skeletons were in good condition and the young Red official who met us at the station seemed no less pleased by the discovery of old Kuai than by the new city and the great dam beyond it.

Hui Hsin was the point nearest to the gorge accessible by railway and for that reason was chosen as base of operations. The Sian-Chengchow main line had to be relaid to touch here, and double-tracking of the whole Sian-Chengchow line as far as Lanchow was accelerated to accommodate workers on the dam and the reservoir as much as to facilitate access to the new oil fields in the Northwest. The reservoir backed up behind the big dam is 194 miles long, and reaches to the outskirts of Sian itself. I was told that it is now China's second largest lake.

Nothing was finished in San Men City, but it was laid out with wide, straight paved streets running through block after block of half-completed red-brick apartment buildings and on to many new structures: railway workshops, sidings, spur lines to the steel plant and car repair shops and various other industries I had no time to investigate. I had come to see the dam. We put up at a guest house in a group of modest buildings strung around a courtyard and flower garden with a teahouse in the center. The quarters were simple but comfortable and had modern plumbing. It was pointed out that sewers had not yet reached the large new hotel.

"You are in the oldest modern building in the city," said Mr. Chin, our guide. "It was built to house the first engineers who reached here and it's already three years old. Come back in a year or so and we'll show you something better."

After breakfast on ham and eggs we drove in a new Ford sedan across a rough dirt road which suddenly gave way to an excellent macadamized highway and immediately entered steep mountain country. The curves were sharp but well banked, the driver fast, the landscape breathtaking: drops to deep ravines on one side, highlands glimpsed on the other—cave dwellers, loess terraces high up, shepherds and cowherds silhouetted on the skyline. Suddenly I saw a group of perhaps a hundred men wearing white hoods and capes like Klansmen and I insisted on stopping. I wanted some pictures.

It is a major victory to get a Chinese driver to stop en route anywhere; he moves like a homing pigeon or a missile. This time I insisted. What were these men? Monks? Prisoners? Or were they women? We piled out and saw that about half of them were drinking tea. We went up to one sitting in the shade and quickly learned that they had been dynamiting and breaking up stone from a nearby ledge; their felt capes were to protect them from flying debris. When I told them I had thought they were monks, they all threw off their capes and began laughing. They were a work gang from the dam.

From then on our driver gave no quarter to the curves; for all the twenty-seven twisting miles I was driving, too. As we came out of the pass we entered a plateau of beautiful farmlands and soon afterward reached a bluff where we stopped. Mr. Chin motioned me out and led me to the precipice. A thousand feet below us, on either side of the wide new dam which had caught the Yellow River and belted it at its narrowest, lay vast expanses of shimmering water as blue as the Aegean.

"Our yellow dragon has changed color," said Mr. Chin, smiling. "He is tamed now."

67

The Grandest Coolie

Perhaps only a Chinese or someone who had seen something of the past rampages of the Huang Ho would have found the closing of the great gates of San Men particularly exciting. For all Chinese, whether pro- or anti-Mao, San Men was not just another barrage adding 1,200,000 kilowatts to the national power capacity; it was the beginning of a happy ending to an old tragedy.

"If the People's Government did nothing else, and if it perished tomorrow," someone wrote in the guest book at the dam, "the Chinese nation would gratefully remember it for a thousand years because of its conquest of the Yellow River!" San Men is No. 37—but the key control point—of forty-six step-dams in the giant staircase 2,500 feet high and 2,000 miles long, by means of which that conquest is being won.

The Yangtze is China's mightiest river, but the Huang Ho basin is more important agriculturally. It includes 60 percent of the nation's wheat fields, 57 percent of her cotton fields, and 67 percent of her tobacco fields. Starting in the highlands of Chinghai, near Tibet, the river runs eastward through Kansu, flows abruptly north to Inner Mongolia, drops southward through deep gorges which divide Shensi and Shansi provinces, and then marches toward the Northeast across the plains of Honan, Hopei and Shantung. Ending its travels of nearly three thousand miles south of Tientsin, the Huang Ho has at times added as much as fourteen square miles of new land a year to the coastline along the Yellow Sea. In places its silt burden has been twenty times that of the Colorado. It has changed its course twenty-six times in recorded history. During the past hundred years overflows occurred more than two hundred times, but probably the greatest new catastrophe before the revolution was man-made. When I was in Hankow in 1938, Generalissimo Chiang Kai-shek ordered the Yellow River dikes opened near Chengchow in a poorly advised effort to halt the southward advance of the Japanese army. The Japanese took Hankow in a few weeks, but all northern Honan was turned into a muddy sea and then a desert. Kuomintang officials at that time estimated that the flood and resultant famine cost 880,000 lives.

By 1950 the habits of the river combined with years of man's neglect and misuse of nature's own controls had created the staggering problems I have described: plateaus and farms of the Northwest gradually denuded of trees, overgrazed, and desiccated. Half the annual rainfall in this basin occurs in July and August, when each year sudden torrents would sweep more earth, natural phosphates and nitrates into the river and down upon the central plains. In Shantung the river bed was built up twenty to twenty-five feet above the surrounding countryside and I have watched junks sail overhead at that height. Prodigious amounts of labor were needed to prevent floods even in years of normal flow, and they were labors of Sisyphus repeated for ages past.

Part of the radical solution required to tame the Yellow River was foreseen years ago by American famine-relief engineers, notable among them being O. J. Todd. No Chinese administration ever undertook the gigantic task until 1954, however, when the Peking government established the Yellow River Planning Commission. Extensive surveys were made and a multipurpose Yellow River plan was completed in 1955; with the help of Soviet experts actual work began in 1956. By November, 1960, China could justly claim that it had (a year ahead of schedule) "basically" licked the River Dragon God, propitiated for many centuries past by superstitious peasants.

Victory came a few months too late. As early as the summer of 1960 the San Men dam could have stopped the Yellow River in flood—but that was not the problem. There was no flood; in the lower reaches of the basin, including the whole province of Shantung, with 57,000,000 people, there was for weeks simply *no river*. In 1960, North China suffered its worst drought in a century. By October, when I watched the lake at last filling up from a flow heavy with delayed autumn rains, the harvests had been lost in the parched plains below.

San Men is the Grandest Coolie and the Grand Coulee of China, and there is equal truth in either spelling. Compared to America's largest concrete dam, San Men is fundamentally a drought- and river-control project. It produces only 60 percent as much power as Grand Coulee but its reservoir holds 36,000,000,000 cubic meters of water, or more than Grand Coulee and Boulder dams combined. In 1960 it was the world's third-greatest reservoir. San Men will provide irrigation and prevent flood on 6,600,000 acres.

The second largest Yellow River dam, at Lanchow, in Kansu, will be operating by 1963; it will have the same power capacity as San Men. Three other major dams and reservoirs and forty-one smaller ones, some already built, will complete a system of reservoirs with a total water-reserve capacity exceeding the flow of the Yellow River for an entire year. The whole dam and power system was scheduled to be completed in 1967. When all generators are installed it should produce a total of 23,000,000 kilowatts, with an annual power output of 110,000,000,000 kilowatts. That is four times China's prewar power capacity and 40 percent more than that of India in 1960.

None of this plan would be fully practicable, however, nor could it ultimately double agricultural production on one-third of China's grain lands, as promised, if it were not for giant supplementary efforts. All the power dams and reservoirs would have a brief life if the erosion problem affecting a land area inhabited by 150,000,000 people were not simultaneously solved.

Antisilting and soil-rationalization measures began in some areas ten years ago. Labors of Hercules, mostly done by hand, the program includes: reforestation, afforestation, and orchard planting on 15,000 square miles; soil and water retaining, contour terracing, ditching and banking covering 22,000 square miles; soilbanking and dust-pan storaging (small ponds) on 4,000 square miles of steep slopes; grass-and-crop rotation on 3,300 square miles, and returfing and otherwise improving 50,000 square miles of pasture land.[1]

Battalions, whole divisions, of spade-armed peasants in this general area have been working on a plan which requires about 950,000 check dams, gully seals, and silt-precipitation basins, and 37,000 ponds and sumps with a total capacity two-thirds as large as San Men Lake. Many of these toy dams are already used for local power, irrigation and soil-restorative purposes such as I saw in Willow Grove. Precipitated silt is helping to reclaim wasteland and desert while the forest belts are beginning to halt the desert in the North. Irrigated land in the whole basin is to be extended sevenfold.

So massive a project as the Yellow River multiple-purpose plan, or even its lesser variations throughout the whole country, could never have been undertaken in China except by sustained, cooperative and highly organized effort. State outlays for *all* the above work involve only 5,324,000,000 yuan, or $2,240,000,000, about the cost of the

T.V.A. hydroelectric plants alone, which develop half as much power for the use of fewer than two million customers. The explanation here lies in countless contributions of cooperative labor, materials and techniques and the rule that whoever benefits from the program must work for it. With millions of vest-pocket farms owned by individual families operating independently of and indifferent to each other, or to any centralized plan or direction, such a project would probably have been unattainable.

The Yellow River control system can work miracles but it cannot make rain. In 1961 the Yellow River basin again got scarcely half its normal rainfall in season and the plains dried up for a third straight year. Even in good years the water flow is inadequate. Nearly 51 percent of China's cultivated land lies in the Yellow River basin, which gets only 7 percent of the nation's water flow, while the Yangtze Valley, which embraces 33 percent of the cultivated land, receives 76 percent of the annual water flow. In search of a solution to the water problem, Chinese engineers have completed surveys for a daring project to split the upper Yangtze and divert nearly two billion cubic meters of water into the Yellow River. This would about *quadruple* the volume of the latter, an increase which could easily be managed by the new control and reservoir system. Russian engineers who participated in the survey and planning work believe that the project is entirely feasible.

According to original building schedules, work should be well along on the great power barrages in the Yangtze gorges even before the Yellow River basin plan is fulfilled. The Yangtze plan involves the greatest engineering tasks in Asia. Four dams are to be built, each larger than San Men. Three Gorges Dam, between Ichang and Chungking, will serve multiple purposes of power, flood control, irrigation and navigation. It will have a power capacity of 4,000,000 kilowatts, larger than any existing plant in the world. The combined system, including a series of upstream barrages, would add a total of 18,250,000 kilowatts to China's capacity.

Both the river-splitting and the Yangtze barrages would be stupendous undertakings in any country. In China they will mean concentrations of capital and engineering resources on a scale which at present probably could be achieved only with considerable technical and material help from abroad. One of the major unpublished Chinese complaints behind the Sino-Soviet dispute was Moscow's decision to build the Aswan dam for Nasser on easy terms denied to China for the Yangtze and Yellow River projects. In the absence of such help, work on both projects was moving very slowly in 1962. Nothing better illustrates the vicious paradox of China's undercapitalized economy than that such basic solutions to agricultural problems must be deferred while technique and resources are diverted to overcome food crises by means which can provide little more than temporary relief.

Meanwhile, Chinese engineers had by 1958 already completed nine-teen other modern hydroelectric systems without Russian help. The largest was the 580,000-kilowatt plant in Chekiang, equipped with the first China-made giant generators, of 75,000- and 100,000-kilowatt capacity. Literally thousands of smaller thermal power stations are now installed every year by Chinese engineers using Chinese equip-ment. Most of them are rural plants of small capacity, but according to a study made by General Electric engineers, 184 such plants in 1959 were to have involved investments of about two million dollars or more each.[2] San Men's power plant of 1,200,000 kilowatts was planned to utilize eight generators, each with a capacity of 150,000 kilowatts. China had produced nothing so large and these generators were ordered from the U.S.S.R. Only one had arrived at the time of my visit. Growing Sino-Soviet tension made it doubtful whether the U.S.S.R. would fulfill future delivery schedules. Original specifications for the Lanchow and other power dams, however, were already based on expectations of China's capacity to make large generators for them. If Russia reneged on deliveries to San Men the power part of the whole Yellow River project would doubtless be delayed—along with other major works dependent on Soviet imports—but by 1963 China should be able to make even these very large generators herself.

So I was assured by the general administrator, Chou Yi-lin, who conducted me through the labyrinth of San Men. He had already told me that Russian engineers who supervised the construction work from its beginning had left in July, 1960. Work was being completed under a Western-trained chief engineer named Chang Wen-ping and four foreign-educated Chinese assistant chiefs. More than a hundred Chi-nese engineers were employed at San Men.

"San Men has been a field college of priceless value," said Mr. Chou. "In four years we've trained hundreds of engineers and tech-nicians who will be kept busy for the rest of their lives building dams and power plants and training others. China has a hydroelectric power potential of 500,000,000 kilowatts, second in the world only to that of the Soviet Union." [3]

There were 21,000 workers directly engaged on the San Men proj-ect, including 2,000 women. Kuant'ing, China's first large modern res-ervoir, which was built in 1954, is less than one-tenth the size of San Men Reservoir in area and power capacity. It required 60,000 workers plus assistance at one stage of an army division of diggers. Most of the skilled workers at San Men got their preliminary training at Kuant'ing, but now they had mechanized China-made equipment as well as machines and tools from all over Europe. One giant crane, on tracks nearly a kilometer long, came from Germany; I visited a Dairen crane factory where a copy of that crane had already been made and shipped for use on the Lanchow dam. Large diesel engines needed here were also imported at first; now they were being made locally, as were cement, rolling stock, small ships and power-plant equipment.

Wages for workers ranged from 40 to 100 yuan and averaged 60; the work day was eight hours. Engineers got from 150 to 250 yuan; part-time apprentices (half-study, half-work) began at 20. Rent, utilities, medical care, movies, opera and clubs were provided free of charge, as were workers' dungarees, helmets, goggles, shoes, etc. Their main expense was food, which cost 12 to 15 yuan a month.

Floodlights were strung everywhere, and work went on day and night. Amplifiers hung at strategic points and opera and symphonic music alternated with the noise of riveting and instructions from on high. Banners hung amidst steel girders, flags flew, squads of drums and cymbals now and then marched to present pennants to bonus-winning "overfulfillers." The steep mountain of concrete was formed, 350 feet high and three-fifths of a mile long: the dozen spillways, each with two gates, the 250-ton overhead sluice-gate controls operating, and the great steel flumes being placed now for the power plants.

"Quality First!" proclaimed one long banner raised high against a cliff for all to see. "Build for a Thousand Years!"

"When the Yellow River is controlled a genie will appear!" ran another slogan, quoting an ancient peasant axiom. "The genie has appeared: the Chinese people!"

The ancient "Three Gates" of the Gorge were narrows formed between stone eyots; they had been called Man's Gate, Gods' Gate and Dragon's Gate. Now the eyots had disappeared under the great jaws of the dam. So: "Where is the Gate of the Gods? Where is the Gate of the Dragon? Only the Gate of Man Remains!" declared another slogan hung from the bamboo stagings.

"Fulfill your quotas, comrades! Complete our job on schedule and help agriculture!"

Imagine Western steel workers responding to such exhortations. Imagine George Meany working for a pennant and recognition.

I stopped to take a color picture of a welder playing his bright torch on a silvery flume and then I asked him to remove his helmet. "He" was a grinning bobbed-haired girl, agreeably good-looking. Parents? Peasants in a commune. Like the work? Why not? She had tried hard enough to qualify for it. But she was doing spare-time study and hoped to become an engineer, as many had already done before her.

Then I asked to go up the giant crane to meet the slaves up there doing what looked to me like the most responsible job on the set; the lives of hundreds of men below depended upon their accuracy. Cheerfully Chou Yi-lin took me up a hundred feet or more in a fast elevator from which I stepped out to behold a splendid panorama of the whole barrage and the reservoir. Through one open sluice gate the imprisoned river surged and boiled, and now beyond it I could see a canal being dug through solid rock to by-pass the dam; it would permit motor ships to enter the upper lake through a series of locks. I stepped out on the catwalk and watched the great fist of the crane pick up a two-hundred-ton steel and concrete beam and place the load neatly between huge studs where fitters and welders perched far below.

When I went into the control cabin I found two twenty-two-year-old girls second and third in command of the crane. The smaller one was rather shy, a primary school graduate from Tangshan, homely but bright-eyed; short hair; unmarried. She had got her job by passing an examination and had worked at Kuant'ing a year before coming here. Father? A miner. "From the first time I ever saw a crane—it was in a movie—I knew I wanted to operate one. I studied, I learned the technique. There's nothing I'd rather do." The other girl, an orphaned daughter of poor peasants, felt exactly the same about it. I don't know how many women operate cranes in other countries, but they seem to be more trusted than men at the job in China.

During the two days I spent taking still and moving pictures at San Men, Chou Yi-lin devoted half his time to me. I was with him driving down to Ta An, the new workers' village, when I thought suddenly of the old people around us. On the cliffs and bluffs rising up on both banks of the river to the plateau three thousand feet high there clung hundreds of caves where peasants still lived—the same peasants who used to make annual sacrifices to the river dragon. A few years ago people in these rugged mountain fastnesses had never seen a motor. A movie about the making of San Men dam showed the first workers assembling on the heights and holding a solemn torchlight procession, then pledging themselves to battle in a great war against the river dragon. Old peasants were standing on the outskirts scowling and shaking their heads; no good would come of that, they seemed to say. Now they had seen miracles. Their sons were driving trucks and handling pneumatic drills; their daughters and granddaughters were marrying literate workers from other provinces. Some of the workers would settle here, others would go on to the next job. Time had moved ahead ten thousand years.

"Half a million people were displaced by the lake reservoir," said Chou. "We had to explain patiently the meaning of the slogan, 'One family leaves the valley to guarantee life for 10,000.' It was hard at first. But we found homes and land and jobs for all of them. Now there are fishing and boatbuilding industries and new towns are springing up along the lake. There will be plenty of fish, and canning factories—it will be a big thing. Our servicing industries will go on after we leave. Look at Ta An—nobody could have lived on this river bank before. Now it's already becoming an attractive lake port. It will be a pleasure resort and have commercial importance besides."

Ta An (Great Peace) was built from scratch to house the personnel for the dam, and it was no shanty town; a planning committee had supervised all building. The straight streets were still unpaved but sewers were being laid and telephones and street lights were working. In the center was a square with a shopping center, a theater, a post office, new schools, playgrounds; built around it were long rows of red-brick tile-roofed bungalows linked together like motels and divided by courtyards planted with vegetables and young trees beginning to give shade. With a population already numbering 27,000, Ta An was organized as a combination urban-rural commune which took in surrounding farm lands. High above the town, 6,000 people still lived in caves, now lighted also by Mr. Edison's magic lanterns.

In one flat I met a man of fifty-four who had been a railway worker all his life; after eight years of spare-time study he had just qualified as a graduate engineer and proudly showed me his diploma. In another place I flushed out two doll-like children to photograph. The prettier, a little girl with large saucy black eyes and beribboned hair her mother must have water-waved, refused to cooperate. "I just won't do it," she said with finality, hiding her face but bursting with laughter. Even Chou, who knew her parents, couldn't persuade her.

"She's always that way," he said good-naturedly, "but she's clever. Probably going to be an actress."

We dropped in on a young woman worker preparing a meal. She was at home nursing a leg injury acquired at the dam. As I talked to her Chou Yi-lin looked around and went over to a family-group photograph. "Is this man related to you?" he suddenly asked her. Yes, he was a cousin. Chou said he knew him very well, he worked in his bureau. Then he was off exchanging small talk with her about mutual acquaintances and when he left they seemed already old friends. A good politician. Somewhat the same thing happened when I stopped a bound-footed woman on the street who told me both her son and daughter-in-law worked on the dam. She greeted Chou warmly and I asked if he knew her.

"Yes," he said, "she's a clean-up woman in one of the engineering laboratories."

And who was Mr. Chou?

We had been so busy working together for two days that I had had no time to ask. He was in his mid-thirties, homely, thin and wiry, with jutting teeth and thick lips: a man I had found ready with precise answers to every question I asked him. It occurred to me that I had not once heard him mention American imperialism.

"Let me see if I can guess some of your personal history," I said as we sat down for tea in the canteen, while Rewi dozed in a corner. He looked amused. "You're a veteran, of course. Not old enough to be a Long March man, but a veteran. Had to shoot a few people, Japanese and maybe a few others. Known a lot of hunger—and old enough now to know the difference between wanting something and wanting to do something? Where did you come in?"

"Not bad guessing. Yes, I was in the army—wounded once—nearly died. My parents were small landlords but I had only three years in school. We were ruined by the Japanese. I joined the guerrillas under Lo P'ing-hui and fought all through the anti-Japanese war and then the civil war. I ended up at Canton as a regimental commander. After that the party sent me to school. I met my wife; she's a party worker, too. Then I was put in command of military units that helped build the Kuant'ing reservoir. That's how I became an 'expert' on dams." He laughed. "Of course I did study some engineering along the way. The party sent me here to San Men and I've been working at it ever since."

"Are you here as an army officer or party leader?"

"Both. My real boss is the Minister of Hydroelectric Works, Fu Tso-yi."

"So you're working for the general you defeated."

He smiled. General Fu Tso-yi was the last old North China warlord to surrender. He held onto Peking for a month while he bargained for a peaceful turnover and good conditions for his men and himself. (Peking, like Paris, is always surrounded first, then peacefully surrenders.) Not a mere display-window minister, like some of the ex-Kuomintang officials in the present government, Fu Tso-yi worked hard at his job and was widely respected as an able administrator.

Driving back to the city late in the afternoon we passed many detachments of young men and women carrying spades and farming tools, sometimes arm in arm, occasionally clinging to a tractor or a truck loaded with vegetables, sometimes marching battalion style and singing under waving banners. They were students and workers from technical schools and shops in the new city, doing their hsia fang or down-on-the-farm harvest labor. They looked strong and healthy.

We picked up our bags in town and drove on to the station. Halfway there we passed about twenty men carrying picks and shovels and marching down the street between two very young armed soldiers. I stared at them intently as we drove by. They did not look at us; they gazed straight ahead and they were not talking or singing. Their expressionless faces were entirely different from all those other groups I had seen that day. There were two or three youths among them but most of them were middle-aged men. They were not in uniform but were dressed about like any other workers, and they were physically sound, as far as I could see at a glance.

It does not matter what crimes a man commits, once he becomes a prisoner he ceases to be an enemy and evokes sympathy like a caged bird or an animal. I remember how it was always that way during the war; we hated the Nazis and Japanese still uncaught or unkilled, but prisoners were lost people in rumpled clothes, needing shaves, lonely, hanging onto torn photographs of girl friends or wives or children;

captivity made them pathetic humans again. All this flashed through my mind as I asked Mr. Chou whether these were political or ordinary prisoners.

"They're from a reform labor farm," he replied. "Some of them may be political; more likely not. They've been building roads."

"Do you use many prisoners around here?"

"Very few. Most of the time they work on the farm."

"Any on the dam construction?"

"Did you see any soldiers guarding our workers there?" No, I had not. "No, and you won't see any. Prisoners have to work, like everybody else, but not until they've been re-educated can they work with good citizens again. It takes time to reform them."

In fairly wide travels in twelve provinces and over many back-country roads I saw one other detachment of guarded prisoners doing field work—also a small group—as against countless men and women obviously not working under duress.

68

Loyang and Chengchow

Loyang is more than three thousand years old; it was the capital during several dynastic reigns beginning with the Chou. The old walled city with its narrow streets is still picturesque but now it is swamped by surburbs where most of Loyang's 600,000 inhabitants live and work in new enterprises. In 1948 Loyang had a population of 80,-000. There had been no modern industry here. Coal and iron resources are plentiful nearby, so it was decided to turn Loyang into a "major construction city." Mining machinery, ball bearings and tractors are among its principal products. Now 595 factories employed 140,000 workers, or so I was told by a city councilman who showed us around.

Largest and most significant is Loyang's Tractor Plant No. 1, which employed 23,000 workers. Around it a model new satellite town has been constructed replete with shopping centers, wide paved streets and sidewalks, and well-landscaped housing for 100,000 people. This is China's largest tractor plant and its assembly line was working well when I visited it. Output in 1959 was 15,000 tractors and the 1960 target was fixed at 30,000, or capacity. No. 1 was among the initial 156 projects built with the aid of Soviet machines and engineers.

Here, as in most factories, I saw enthusiastic workers—4,000 of them young women—vying with each other to create labor-saving and time-saving devices to "speed up production to help agriculture." Before the benches of "innovators" were red posters or flowers announcing their successes. (In an electrical meter factory I saw in Harbin each girl worker had a placard before her machine which briefly told the story of her "innovations," if any.) One worker here had been honored with "nine points" of improvement (out of a possible ten) and was hero of the day. All over China thousands of ideas pour in from workers and many of them prove useful. Rewards in cash are probably less incentive than the publicity, recognition and promotions. Many scholarships are offered as further inducement to "dare to think and dare to do"—a slogan few Communists would admit bears any resemblance to IBM's THIMK.

All parts of the tractor from tracks to engines were made in Loyang, where the assembly rate normally was one machine every nineteen minutes. "Now we are turning out one every few minutes," the director told me. There were two eight-hour shifts. The "East Wind" is a sturdy multipurpose tractor of 54 horsepower and has numerous attachments for hauling, water pumping, forging, etc. Some idea of current costs of production in motor-mechanized industry may be gathered from the "output value" (sales price) of 21,000 yuan ($8,400) which the director placed on an East Wind tractor.

Wages were lower here than in most state industries, but a 30-percent bonus was distributed for fulfillment of quotas. The average wage was given to me as 40 yuan, with a top, for engineers ("one to three per workshop"), at 280 yuan. An apprentice starts at 21 yuan. Rent in housing (modern, including tiny kitchen and shower for married couples) was only 60 cents a month. Food costs averaged 10 to 12 yuan per worker. Medical treatment was free to employees and half-rate to their dependents. Medical care, pensions and other benefits came out of the welfare fund to which workers contributed 1.5 percent to 3 percent of wages.

I saw only about a quarter of this very large plant, from which all Soviet engineers had departed. "Farewell Soviet Comrades" read signs. "We shall never forget you!" The director told me that Chinese engineers were able to duplicate No. 1. A copy of it would be finished in Paotou in 1962. Smaller tractor plants also existed in Shanghai and Manchuria, and I saw threshing machines made in Kunming on a low production basis.

One afternoon I visited a Loyang primary school where 1,180 students and 48 teachers worked in new brick buildings with a vegetable garden at the back. The director, a normal school graduate, took me through some of the twenty-four classrooms and five workshops, pointing out wall slogans along the way which echoed those in the factories: "Dare to think!" "Dare to do!" "Dare to invent!"

"Since we began to combine practical shop work with classroom

study in 1957," he said, "our superior students have risen from 79 percent to 93 percent. It has given them new incentives."

He cited the case of a student who was failing in three out of five
subjects. "He had a knife and he liked to carve characters on his desk.
He covered his own and then carved other children's desks. He didn't
respond to discipline. Then we opened the radio shop. He became the
best worker there. After he was chosen foreman his classroom marks
improved. Now he has superior ranks in all five subjects and has the
rank of a student hero."

Students aged nine or above were obliged to spend two hours a
week in shop but many volunteered for much more. It seemed to me
no different from the manual training and cooking classes we used to
have in Norman School in Kansas City, but it was a new idea in China.
There is a variety of work and students sell their products. Profits go
into the school welfare fund. Each class is led by an elected foreman.
Here I saw boys and girls making parts for small table radios and
assembling them, mixing and packaging a patent-medicine pain-killer
(under a teacher's supervision!), and making furniture and ceramics.
About half of them wore Red Pioneer kerchiefs. Each foreman made a
little speech of welcome to me. Like most Chinese schoolchildren they
gave an impression of good deportment, cleanliness and alertness.
There were no fat boys and I saw none starving.

Outside Loyang I visited a large rural production brigade called
Ku-ch'eng, made up of fifty production teams with about two thousand
members. It was part of Lo-pei township. This brigade was an old
advanced agricultural cooperative.

According to information given to me by the cadres, Honan had had
rain on only fourteen days of the past three hundred; the total fall was
less than 40 millimeters. It was the worst drought for fifty years, yet
Honan would have enough of a harvest to feed itself, they said. Ten
million *mou* of Honan were now irrigable by canals and well systems.
(Millions of Honan peasants were caught in areas without adequate
water, however. They did not simply sit there in the desert, waiting
to starve, as in the past. Commune organization permitted them to be
temporarily shifted to more fortunate farms, where they were put to
work on land improvement, construction, workshop and other tasks,
in exchange for their rations.) Ku-ch'eng itself showed lush crops. A
wide fast-flowing canal brought in from the Yi River pierced the
middle of the village and went on to power a small (48-kilowatt)
generator. Nine small power plants (the largest, 250 kilowatts) had
been built by this township since 1957.

In the middle of a tomato field I fell behind my hosts to take some
pictures of the canal. An old peasant, sunburned black, bare-chested
and with a jacket hung over a shoulder, stood watching me. Was he a
native? I asked. Yes. He had one brother. They had received land in
the distribution? He pointed across the canal where half a dozen men

and women were tilling a field of cabbage and spinach. That was it, right there. Good land?

"Very good. Between our families we had six *mou*."

"Now it belongs to the whole village?"

"It's part of the *tui* [brigade] land."

"Does it grow more or less than when you tilled it as a family?"

"Oh ho! Four times more! We didn't have the canal then, and who could buy fertilizer, get power and tractors?" At the tractor station I had seen six tractors and a combine—some of the thirty-four tractors and six combines owned jointly by the township.

"Married?"

He had married late in life, he said; they had two children. One was in middle school in the city. One was in primary school. What had happened to his family burial plot? He pointed to a grove of trees. On the whole, were things better or worse?

"I liked it better when we had our own land." He pulled on his jacket, shrugged and started to leave. Then he turned and added: "But of course all this—" His hand swept in the canal, the power plant in the distance. He grinned. "Without the canal we would be starving in a year like this. The young people are probably right. This is the only way." I took a picture of him.

The village cadres came hurrying back up the lane. I turned and met them on the way. As we went on toward the tractor station the party secretary politely cautioned me not to take photographs of people without asking their permission. They objected, he said, to an invasion of their privacy. They had their rights.

"If you mean that farmer back there," I said, "I did ask his permission."

"Hereafter it would be better if you asked me to ask their permission," he said.

"Of course," I said solemnly, determined not to let another Mr. Chao spoil my visit. A few minutes later he led me to the local tractor station and proudly offered some machines to be photographed, but I could not resist saying, "No, I think we had better not invade their privacy," and declined. He was miffed and soon turned us over to a more amiable cadre.

At a village kindergarten thirty or more inmates shrieked a loud welcome and immediately went into a song-and-dance act, accompanied on a battered organ. When I went through their earthen-floored playroom I saw that they had only one tricycle. Yes, the teacher answered me, each had his ration of time on it, and all had learned to ride it. I later bought another tricycle (50 yuan) and had it sent to the kindergarteners with a card from my children, Chris and Sian, wishing them success as "future tractor drivers of China." I never heard from them directly, but weeks later I received two exquisite copies of miniature T'ang horses from Loyang.

Going east, half a day beyond Loyang, we stopped for two days at ancient Chengchow, which was also being transformed. The city proper had a population of 700,000 (before the war, 150,000) and the greater municipality embraced five counties with 2,800,000 inhabitants. Now there were 221 modern factories, including a textile-machinery plant and several large cotton mills, in addition to 372 commune-run shops which employed 50,000 housewives.

I quote from my diary:

Chengchow, Sept. 27. Awoke at six with the aid of blue cadres singing cadres' blues. My hotel is headquarters for the cadres' autumn training. Their morning opens with party hymns, followed by exercise in the courtyard. There seems to be a choice between *t'ai chi ch'uan* and the conventional physical jerks.

Chengchow's housing development is the most successful I have seen here. The old wall is down completely. Most of the new streets are broad and the new buildings are set well back from them and generously spaced and landscaped. Principal highways are divided by parklike esplanades all of which are now being used as vegetable gardens. Nearly every inch of surface is planted in sunflowers, turnips, cabbage, corn and potatoes. Scattered along the margins are asters, roses, gladioli and hollyhocks. Four-fifths of the population is said to be living in new housing, mostly three- or four-story apartment buildings in brick, generally grouped around the new factories. Each zone has its own shopping and recreational centers. There are nine new theaters and six opera houses. On the streets are far more bicycles than in Peking and stores seemed well stocked.

Down a newly opened divided highway flanked by modern buildings come rubber-tired carts filled with bricks, bricks, and more bricks, mortar, sand, lime, bags of cement, carrots, cabbages, apples, potatoes, tomatoes, cardboard boxes, paper, steel reinforcement rods, chemical products, radios, bundles of cloth, household furniture, bathtubs, motors, toilet seats, television sets, coal—and small children! The pullers are students, teachers, workers, peasants, red-kerchiefed Pioneers, each with a rope around his shoulders, sometimes singing, sometimes following banners; housewives dragging their new commune-made goods to market; professionals with heavy loads, cushioned pads on their shoulders. Made-in-Manchuria trucks drag three or four trailers behind them, each carrying tons of produce from farms or factories—iron bars, agricultural tools, bales of cotton. A giant self-propelled crane, its kangaroo neck reaching 20 to 30 feet ahead of it, is preceded by boys laying down lengths of padded cloth before the tracks to save the pavements. Between bamboo-scaffolded uncompleted buildings graze flocks of sheep and goats and on small isolated ponds are clusters of ducks, indifferent to the oncoming town. Old ladies with bound feet ride donkeys in danger of being crushed by trolleys, trucks and carts. A long street of modern, almost California-Spanish architecture, with low brick walls and moon-gate doorways leading into gardens: casement windows—and flowers on the sills. Who lives there? "Intellectuals," said Shih, my Intourist guide.

After watching textile machines being made in a large (2,500 workers) factory, where the whole output was earmarked for export to North Vietnam, I stopped by to see some railway workshops. There I learned about an urban-commune quilt and clothing factory run entirely by women, and on request I was permitted to visit it. Most of the workers were wives of railway workers employed in the nearby locomotive repair shops. The lady in charge, a housewife named Cheng Chih-chi, told me that they had started work in 1958 with twelve sewing machines, eight of them owned by members and four purchased.

Their workshop was a white cement-block building originally designed for a neighborhood meeting hall in the new housing development in which they all lived. Now they owned 108 machines, employed more than two hundred women, and in 1960 output was valued at 28,000 yuan monthly—mostly work clothes, children's jumpers and leather jackets for railway workers. Their wages, on a piecework basis, averaged 22 yuan monthly per person. Here the women worked a full eight-hour day, eight to twelve and two to six.

Workers whose children were in nurseries or kindergartens paid 1.50 yuan a month each for their care, and 3 yuan a month each for their lunches. Kindergartens cost the same. Boarding children paid 6 to 7 yuan a month for food. This was about 40 percent less expensive than the best nurseries in Peking. The cost of their food was no more than at home. Nursery, kindergarten and community services were paid for from the commune's welfare fund set aside from income. This shop averaged 15 percent net profit from its output.

The women had a canteen but it was used by only one in five. The rest took their meals at home. About 80 percent of the "able-bodied" women in the neighborhood were now working but only about 30 percent were in commune shops. The rest were employed in state or municipal factories or services. There was no compulsion to work but most wives liked the extra income, said Mrs. Cheng, and conveniences like sewing service, laundry, and household care relieved them of "that drudgery." By pooling wages the average husband and wife could now save as much as 20 to 30 yuan a month. This had made it possible for most families to own at least one bicycle; several in her shop owned two.

I stopped to talk to a young woman worker behind a machine and asked her where her children were. She had two, both in kindergarten. Was she satisfied with their care? Very much so. They were healthy and learning to dance and sing; she could never have taught them that. She herself now also had time to attend spare-time literacy classes. What was her husband? He was a railway worker but he had won a scholarship for a year's study in Peking. He would be back in a few weeks. How could she live on 22 yuan a month while he was gone? They drew his full pay during his absence. She told me that in three years they had saved 500 yuan ($200)! She was doubtless rehearsed to say this? But I had picked her at random from among two hundred . . .

We visited one of the apartment buildings: brick, two-story, wooden floors, lights, plastered walls. I would not call it a "barracks." After knocking on several doors I found an old lady at home. She had bound feet, was aged sixty-six, and had an alert mind. Her son and daughter-in-law, with whom she lived, both worked in factories. They had two children, one in school and one in kindergarten. She had nothing to do but keep the two rooms clean, look after the children when they came home, listen to the radio and cook dinner. She was a peasant from the hinterland; when she was three her mother had died during a famine. Her father died when she was nine and she was brought up by her sister-in-law. I looked round her tiny flat. They had a sunny window and a tiny kitchen. There were two toilets on the floor. How did she like it here? *Ai-ya!* She threw up her hands. She spoke simply and I understood her Chinese.

"Before we came here we lived in one room in a mud house with a dirt floor. We had no running water, no lights, and we cooked on a mud stove. In winter we froze, in summer we roasted. We used to pay a landlord 5 yuan a month for that. My husband earned only 18 yuan. Here we get light, heat and water all for less than 5 yuan. There is simply no comparison. We don't have to worry about money. If we don't want to eat at home we just walk over to the neighborhood dining room and it's all ready. Good food? Yes, indeed, our women cook it themselves! Now they even get paid for making clothes for their men and suits for their children!"

If her speech was prepared for the chance visit of the one American who happened to be "legally" in China it was a remarkable piece of clairvoyance and rehearsing.

Before leaving Chengchow I saw one of the oldest rural communes. I shall not go into its finances but the irrigation system and the small hydroelectric power plants had transformed a backward farming area into a highly prospering community. Just a few miles farther north, on our way back to Peking by train, we crossed the Yellow River. Under the long newly double-tracked bridge the river was so low that one could have maneuvered an army division between the water and the towering earthwork dikes to which it normally attains at this season.

Along the way I saw numerous family burial mounds set in groves of old trees entirely surrounded by broad unbroken fields where collectivization had erased other traces of small-scale farming. India has her sacred cows, monkeys and rats which consume about a sixth of her annual grain crop, but fortunately the Hindus cremate their dead. North China's equivalent (in terms of lost production) has been the family burial plots; in parts of the Yellow River Valley, inhabited for thousands of years, the dead were said to remove as much as 10 percent of the land from cultivation by the living. Several years ago the party began a drive to consolidate the bones in common cemeteries. Many welcomed the change but some conservative peasants resisted and the pressure relaxed. As with birth control, time and education were needed to win general acceptance. More and more villages and towns in North China now cremate the newly deceased or bury them in wasteland set aside for collective cemeteries, however, as we do in the West and as has long been the custom in parts of South China.

Between ten in the morning and dusk we passed five or six wholly new towns, each centered on a small or medium-sized steel mill. They looked like well-planned industrial communities: electrified, with wide tree-lined streets dividing block after block of new two- or three-story apartments interspersed with gardens, schools, hospitals and shopping centers. Our express did not stop at them. But south of one new station, called Yuanshi, a town I don't remember from when I used to travel the Chengchow-Peking line in the past, our train came to a grinding stop in open country. Slowly we went into reverse. When the train halted Alley and I got out to investigate.

A man riding a bicycle had run into the tail end of our train when his brakes failed. A conductorette happened to see the accident and reported it to the engineer. The train's first-aid team got the injured man onto a stretcher and brought him aboard. They telephoned ahead to Yuanshi, where an ambulance waited when we made an unscheduled stop. (From the past I could recall seeing a truck not even pause when the driver hit a mere "coolie.") Our express was delayed half an hour by the incident.

I remembered once standing on Bubbling Well Road in Shanghai waiting for a taxi. A loud clamor came from a side lane, a burning wheel shot out, and I saw it was a man on fire. He collapsed almost at my feet. It was an entirely Chinese crowd around me and nobody made a move. I wrapped my coat around the man (mourning as I did so; it was a new camel-hair number) and put out the fire, but the man still smoldered. I called for water and a rickshaw coolie finally brought it to me. I managed to get an ambulance, and as I was leaving the scene, the coolie demanded *kumsha*. "You pay me watah, mastah!" What a change, I thought now after this incident on the train, from that sad moment for humanity back in 1930!

In the afternoon we passed hundreds of peasants who were gathering cotton from already rusting fields. Threshing machines were working in some villages; in others wheat was being winnowed by hand. Here and there tractors were turning freshly harvested soil; on other farms draft animals were used, and occasionally one saw men and women dragging heavy implements across the fields, as of yore. Golden corn and melons were piled mountain high in many fields. Before I went to sleep I looked out the window and beheld a whole village celebrating the harvest. Someone was playing an accordion and young women in costume were dancing on the earthen threshing floor, where flags waved around a circle of corn and pumpkins, lighted by huge bonfires.

Back in the capital I spent three weeks in Peking's glorious October weather and then told Rewi and other friends farewell. I turned southward to the Yangtze Valley for the last leg of my journey and an exit via Kunming.

Part Six

SHANGHAI
AND
BEYOND

☆

While I was in Loyang, Honan, I drove out over a new paved highway to see the world-famous works of art at Lung-men.

When Loyang was the capital of the T'ang Empire, Wu Tzu-t'ien, loveliest concubine of the enfeebled Emperor Kao Tsung, seized power in the year 660. She became the only female "emperor" in Chinese history, and ruled until 705. A highly talented woman, she was an enthusiastic Buddhist and was responsible for a great age of religious sculpture in China. She took for her lover a young monk whom she made abbot of the Lung-men monastery on the banks of the Yi River outside the capital. In this period, Wu Tzu-t'ien and her lover lavished funds on the gigantic and beautiful Buddhas which stand on the stone cliffs at Lung-men. Thousands of other Buddhistic sculptures, murals, and works in bas-relief decorate the nearby grottoes.

One of the Lung-men caves held two panels of exquisite bas-relief sculptures of graceful male and female figures from the Chinese Buddhistic pantheon. Both were stolen about thirty years ago by vandals hired by Yueh Pin, a notorious art dealer of Peking. At the gate of the shrine I saw enlarged photographs of these stolen friezes, one of which is on display in the Metropolitan Museum and the other in the Nelson Gallery in Kansas City. Mounted under glass beneath the photos were reproductions of contracts allegedly signed by Alan Priest, the Metropolitan curator, and Yueh Pin. Above them were emblazoned the words "American Cultural Imperialism!"

Chinese pilgrims who come here read the story and mourn their loss. As my student guide read me the details his voice shook with wrath.

"Egypt and Greece fared much worse," I said to console him. "You should see what Lord Elgin left of the Parthenon! After all, isn't it something to know that Americans who see these treasures will appreciate Chinese as artistic and talented people?"

"Who can see them? Only imperialists! How can imperialists like art if they hate people?"

Alas!

That night I dreamed that the Empress Wu, her lover, the sculptors, Yueh Pin the cultural bandit, the American cultural imperialists, and my guide all stood in a grotto before the Buddha, each defending his right to the disputed friezes glorifying the Eightfold Path. The Empress had murdered for them, her monk had sinned for them, the sculptors had labored to make them, the bandit had stolen them, the curators had paid for them, my guide had wept for them, and each demanded them. Gautama listened in silence. When they had finished he asked: "What has any of this to do with right knowledge, right intention, right speech, right conduct, right means, right effort, right mindedness, and right concentration?" Thereupon he vanished in a blinding light.

Left on the walls of the grotto were the words: Hatred does not cease by hatred at any time. Hatred ceases by love . . .

Tibetan shepherds in Chinghai. *(N.C.P.)*

Vet service, Inner Mongolia. *(N.C.P.)*

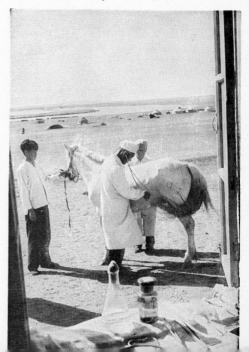

Mongol secretary, Precious Spring (dressed in her finest for the foreign guest), at New Wealth Springs, Pailingmiao, Inner Mongolia.

Women operators of giant cran
San Men Hsia irrigation and Yello
River power project.

Ho Hai, behind the Winter
Palace, where Dr. Ma steals a
swim after dark.
(*Felix Greene*)

The Peking Stadium seats 80,000. (*Felix Greene*)

Miniature railways run by diesel engines are becoming common in the countryside. (*N.C.P.*)

Rugged individualist: selling cricket cages in Peking.

Village poster agit-prop art.

Prisoners in Peking Municipal Jail (enameled teapots suppied by the management).

In this famous photograph it is Nationalist gendarmes shooting Communist suspects on the streets of Shanghai—but it has been reused to imply the opposite. (*Warren Lee, United Press International*)

Sunday throng in Pei-hai Park, Peking. (*Felix Greene*)

ice planting made easy. Premotorized mechanization: a "walking on two
gs" invention. (*N.C.P.*)

A handmade jacket for a grandchild? Beautiful but expensive, in a Shanghai specialty shop.

Henri Cartier-Bresson photographed these "impatient university students" who dragged tons of mud from a swamp "to make their own swimming pool instead of waiting for machinery," at Tsing Hua University, Peking. (*Cartier-Bresson* © *1961 MAGNUM Photos*)

Large new municipal pool, Peking. (*Felix Greene*)

Low-pressure water pumps made in Yunnan (Tungyung Machinery Works). (*N.C.P.*)

Tractor demonstration for Yi tribesmen in Szechuan. In 1949 farmers here used wooden plows. (*N.C.P.*)

Three types of vehicles now made in Yunnan, which formerly made no motor vehicles. (*N.C.P.*)

Brigadune chief. Li Yu-hua, chairman of No. 1 brigade, Willow Grove Commune, Yenan.

Retired timbermen in the Old Men's Home, Tailing, Manchuria.

Amateur art troupe performing Flowered Parasol Dance for workers on a Honan commune project. (*N.C.P.*)

69

Shanghai

Gone the glitter and glamour; gone the pompous wealth beside naked starvation; gone the strange excitement of a polyglot and many-sided city; gone the island of Western civilization flourishing in the vast slum that was Shanghai.

Good-by to all that: the well-dressed Chinese in their chauffeured cars behind bullet-proof glass; the gangsters, the shakedowns, the kidnapers; the exclusive foreign clubs, the men in white dinner jackets, their women beautifully gowned; the white-coated Chinese "boys" obsequiously waiting to be tipped; Jimmy's Kitchen with its good American coffee, hamburgers, chili and sirloin steaks. Good-by to all the night life: the gilded singing girl in her enameled hair-do, her stage make-up, her tight-fitting gown with its slit skirt breaking at the silk-clad hip, and her polished ebony and silver-trimmed rickshaw with its crown of lights; the hundred dance halls and the thousands of taxi dolls; the opium dens and gambling halls; the flashing lights of the great restaurants, the clatter of mah-jongg pieces, the yells of Chinese feasting and playing the finger game for bottoms-up drinking; the sailors in their smelly bars and friendly brothels on Szechuan Road; the myriad short-time whores and pimps busily darting in and out of the alleyways; the display signs of foreign business, the innumerable

shops spilling with silks, jades, embroideries, porcelains and all the
wares of the East; the generations of foreign families who called
Shanghai home and lived quiet conservative lives in their tiny vacuum
untouched by China; the beggars on every downtown block and the
scabby infants urinating or defecating on the curb while mendicant
mothers absently scratched for lice; the "honey carts" hauling the
night soil through the streets; the blocks-long funerals, the white-clad
professional mourners weeping false tears, the tiers of paper palaces
and paper money burned on the rich man's tomb; the jungle free-for-
all struggle for gold or survival and the day's toll of unwanted infants
and suicides floating in the canals; the knotted rickshaws with their
owners fighting each other for customers and arguing fares; the peddlers and their plaintive cries; the armored white ships on the Whangpoo, "protecting foreign lives and property"; the Japanese conquerors
and their American and Kuomintang successors; gone the wickedest
and most colorful city of the old Orient: good-by to all that.

Some of it has been carried by refugees to Hongkong today and
some of it, with strip-tease added, you may find in Tokyo. Shanghai
still holds more people than either city, if suburbs are included; in
1961 its population was 10,400,000. Foreigners still say it is the "one
place in China that really looks like a great city." The tall buildings
are there, but the International Settlement and the French Concession,* which used to be the heart of a modern megalopolis, are
strangely like a village now, and downtown after dark is as quiet as
Wall Street on Sunday.

There is plenty of heavy traffic in the new industrial suburbs, but
many downtown office buildings of the Settlement have been turned
into schools, dwellings and workers' clubs. Here bicycles, pedicabs
(not many) and trams move leisurely between shops selling necessities and a few luxuries to customers who give the impression of being
village tourists taking in the city where the wicked imperialists used
to rule. The once crowded Bund is a recreation center. Into it, each
morning and afternoon, the former office buildings debouch swarms
of little children to play and exercise in well-kept gardens along the
river. Elderly folk also gather there to read, drowse or play Chinese
chess; one of them told me he remembered a time when Chinese (and
dogs) were not admitted. So did I.

The Shanghai Club, once very exclusively for British gentlemen,
used to boast the world's longest bar. It is now run by the party as an
international seamen's club, where sailors may play games or read
books or see movies, but find no bedtime companions. Nearby, the
ponderous old Hongkong and Shanghai Bank building (the paws of

---

* Before the 1840's Shanghai was a fishing village on a mud flat on the Whangpoo;
its importance began with the Opium Wars in midcentury, after which Britain
and other powers acquired control of Shanghai as a treaty port. For a brief historical account of Shanghai see *Journey to the Beginning*.

its huge bronze lions still shining from many hands that touched them for good luck) is now a government bureau. The old American Club building has been put to the same use as the National City Bank in Peking; both house police headquarters.

I stayed at the Cathay Hotel, which stands at Nanking Road and the Bund and was once Asia's finest hostelry. It is now called the Peace Hotel and is exceedingly so: quiet, orderly, the restaurant little used and subdued compared to its former aggressive gaiety, its famous bar and night club extinct, its lobby shops closed at dusk, and few lights on after ten. One got the impression here, as at certain large and empty provincial hotels, that the Chinese had not yet quite decided how to utilize these rooms since the Russians left. But the Cathay is still a fine place to live, furnished much as it was when owned by Sir Victor Sassoon: the simulated Chinese décor a bit tarnished now but the plumbing super, cuisine ditto, and more new American cars for hire outside its doors than anywhere in China.

I was offered my choice of Sir Victor's suite, usually reserved for V.I.P.'s, or an ordinary double room about the dimensions of the *May-flower*. A single would do me nicely, I said, but I asked to see the suite. It was in the tower, high above the river, pseudo-Tudor, handsomely paneled and filled with light from wide leaded windows. The bedroom was sumptuously furnished with king-sized twin beds adjoining two large tiled bathrooms; there was a dressing room the size of a small flat, a private entrance foyer, servants' quarters, a bar, a kitchen and pantry, a private dining room with a fireplace, and a spacious living room with another fireplace.

"How much?" I asked the China Intourist agent.

"Thirty-five yuan a day."

"That's less than fifteen dollars. At the Waldorf it would cost me a hundred. Betraying incurable bourgeois romanticism," I said, "I'd like to wake up in the morning knowing how Victor Sassoon felt when he owned Shanghai. I'll take it for a night."

I did not rest comfortably. For a long time, as I looked down at the river life, I was filled with remembrance of things past in this city where I had invested or misspent some years of my youth, fallen in love and into a brief but eventful marriage, seen two wars and many men destroyed in futile combat, until, engulfed by China, I had turned abroad—to more wars. Returning to my present magnificence, I tried the first bed but could not sleep. Then I tried the other, soft and blissful, but had no better luck. I ended on the living room couch and woke up at dawn. If that was the way Sir Victor had felt when he owned Shanghai I did not envy him. Perhaps he had had better company than my thoughts.

At seven o'clock I went down to walk in the Bund gardens, which were already well populated. Eager young and middle-aged people were doing their *t'ai chi ch'uan* steps and some students wearing athletes' red sweat shirts and slacks were practicing sword dancing. Under a tree some small children were being led in song by their teacher. Everyone was much in earnest. I watched a family in a sampan eating a breakfast of rice and greens, waved to them, and they waved back, smiling. Encouraged, I sat down on a bench beside an elderly gentleman who looked my way. I spoke to him in Chinese.

"You are up early," I said.

"At my age you don't need much sleep."

"Your age? You don't look over fifty, Elder Born," I lied.

"Courtesy talk! I'm more than sixty. What does a man my age do in Russia, sir?"

"You take me for a Russian? No, I'm an American."

"American?" That's a dirty word in China now but they still use the old flattering term for it: *Mei-kuo,* the "beautiful country." He repeated it and I nodded. Now he began to speak in stilted but animated English. "You are certainly the first American I have seen for many years."

"I don't doubt that. How long is it since you spoke English?"

"Quite some years. I am forgetting it. You have been a long time in China? You speak Chinese."

I told him that I was a newspaperman and had once worked for the *China Weekly Review* in Shanghai. He remembered it; he had read it, he said. He had learned some English in his youth and had used it in business. Now he was retired.

"I take it you are not a Communist?" I said.

"Oh, no!" He grinned and showed half a dozen large teeth. "I'm a capitalist! That's what they tell me." He plucked at the sleeve of his dark blue padded jacket of worn silk. "I used to own a silk store."

"How do you live?"

"I get my interest-dividends like other merchants."

"But how is it compared to the past? Before *chieh-fang* [liberation]?"

"We eat better than most. We live in our old house, my wife and I, sharing now with some others. That's all right. Good people. Hardworking people. We don't need the rooms. My children are married and live away. What is your thinking of China?"

"Officials show me something, then always ask me that. They want criticisms. Now I'll ask you, what are your criticisms?" I repeated the word in Chinese.

"Oh, I know." He looked at me shrewdly. "Americans think we have a bad time, maybe? I can say the truth, I have lived much better. But poor people have lived much worse. Everything is for the people. We used to think America was for the people too but it not look so now, eh? Is America only friend of Chiang Kai-shek? How is this?"

"Suppose I oppose that. Can you criticize your government?"

"Oh, I know. It makes bad mistakes. Who is ever right? I could tell you stories of people who have a bad time. Myself too, but not much. China is a socialist country now. Property rights are not the same, you know. One thing: this is an honest government. Hard, but honest. It has made China one great country again. Chinese can hold up their heads in the world. We are not foreign slaves any more." He drew back proudly. "What do you think about that, sir? Maybe the government is too strong, sometimes too young to listen to others. But—it does good things for China and does not steal. We forget much against that. Nobody wants Chiang Kai-shek back again, no!"

"Your son? What does he do?"

"Two sons. One is a teacher, all right. The other is in Hongkong. He wants to come back but he should stay there. We are the old generations. We lost something. My grandchildren, they are the new life. They wear it. They like it. Things in China were too bad in old days. Well, they have ended the worst. I won't cry."

"Many people in jail—prison—arrested?"

"Very few I know. They convince you and convince. I see the point. All for China. You know old Shanghai? Everybody robbing, cheating. Crimes, gangs, bad men. Tu Yueh-sheng? You know him?* Bad man. Now you see the *hsiao hai-tzu* [children] telling us older ones not even to spit, to use the spit bucket. Not to throw dirty things on the streets, that's good. Everybody working, everybody reading. No more starving people dying. How is that? Better. Building, building, building more—but nobody getting rich. Why? All for China family. I see the point."

"Maybe you aren't telling me everything. Maybe you're afraid I'll tell the government?" I smiled but he did not.

"Ha! I say the truth. Why should—"

An acquaintance of his stopped and he stood up to exchange greetings. They strolled off together, but before the capitalist left he turned and bowed to me and said, "So much building. You must see."

I took scores of pictures at random of all kinds of people in the Bund gardens and along the waterfront and in various Shanghai streets. Like the pictures I took everywhere else in China, they showed people poorly dressed, none of them fat. They were all dying but apparently only at about the same rate people are dying everywhere; among them were no diseased beggars, no mangy infants, no policemen beating up anybody, no rice riots. These pictures got the same reception abroad that others taken by foreign visitors have got-

---

* Yes, I remembered Tu and had known him. He was for years Shanghai's No. 1 gangster, chief of the *Ch'ing Pang* (Green Circle Secret Society), which ran the narcotics, gambling and prostitution rackets. In 1927 his armed thugs helped Chiang Kai-shek (with aid from the International Settlement's Shanghai Municipal Council) seize power in the native city from the left-wing trade unions' militia. About 5,000 workers were killed. Later on Chiang Kai-shek rewarded Mr. Tu with a post on the Opium Suppression Bureau, which continued to run the narcotics traffic, and officially decorated him with the Order of the Brilliant Jade. For details, see *The Battle for Asia*.

ten. Editors thought they looked too "posed." They wanted to see "the real China." A few months after I left, the Swiss journalist Fernand Gigon photographed some summer-naked infants playing around a pile of coal balls. *Time* bought that, called it "scavenging children," and its readers got a full page of "the real China" at last. From the same source, N.B.C. picked up some movie film, spliced it in to freshen ancient shots of prerevolutionary China, and presented it under the title "White Paper on China." Included in it was a remarkable scene of street executions by Kuomintang gendarmes in Shanghai —presented in a context which left the audience with the misapprehension that it had witnessed Communists shooting down the people.

70

"Building, Building—"

Chang Yao-hui, secretary-general of the Shanghai People's Congress (which elects the municipal government and sends delegates to the National Congress), welcomed me "as an old resident." He was a man of about forty, strongly built, erect, son of a rich peasant family, and possessed of some higher education. As a student he had left his native Shantung and joined the guerrillas under Liu Shao-ch'i and Ch'en Yi. Like most veterans he was relaxed and easy to talk to; he ticked off answers sans the usual preliminaries about Mao and the general line.

"Gangsters? They weren't hard to eliminate once they lost their government protection and the people were free to expose them. Gangs are organized to make money for gang leaders; when they succeed they become capitalists no different from the others. The chief of one gang here was chairman of a bank; he fled to Hongkong. His successor published an ad in the papers, at our suggestion, dissolving the secret organizations. We've had no gangs since 1951. Pimps and prostitutes? Eliminated at the same time, but it took much longer to re-educate the women and find jobs for them. I won't say there are none left but they are rare cases."

Chang Yao-hui offered to show me anything I wanted to see in

Shanghai. I said I'd like to see some housing, the best and the worst.

"That's all right. But what about industry? Shanghai is a lot different from what you knew, and even from the Shanghai of ten years ago. Textile and other light industry used to account for 60 percent of total output here. Now we have a bigger textile industry than ever, but heavy industry amounts to more than half the output. We made more cotton spindles in Shanghai alone in 1959 than total British production. You never thought of Shanghai as a steel city, did you? Shanghai will smelt more than two million tons of steel this year. Look out on the Whangpoo. Most of those steel ships were made in China. Shanghai turned out vessels up to 10,000 tons this year. How much time do you have?"

"Five days."

He was disappointed. "Anyway, we'll show you more than most people see in ten days."

I was afraid of that. I was beginning to feel steel running out of my ears. I begged for a day to myself, just to walk the streets in search of forgotten places. Chang reluctantly agreed to this waste of time but he got me down for a tough schedule from then on, under the skilled guidance of an assistant, Li Yi-ming. A bright young Shanghai college graduate, Li spoke fast English and never missed a remark or a cue.

Strolling through the old shopping centers on my own I recognized places but not faces, and no shops I remembered were doing business at the old stands. I stopped at what used to be the Chinese-American Bookstore, where there was now a vast assortment of fountain pens, ball points and automatic pencils at a few cents to as much as three dollars each. I told a clerk that I'd like to see a good copy of a Waterman and she showed me a dozen varieties of Parker-type pens. She was an attractive girl in a Chinese gown and a bit of make-up. Shanghai women still display style and cosmetics which make them easy to spot among their country cousins.

"What I should like," I said, "is a flexible point that will write from medium to heavy."

The clerk patiently showed me all she had, but there was nothing suitable and I expressed my regret. "I know what you want," she quipped as I left. "You capitalists want the kind of pen good for signing checks. We Chinese like pens to write fine characters, we have no use for checks."

"One check," I replied, "is often worth ten thousand characters." At least she smiled as she turned to the next customer.

Consumer goods on sale made a poor contrast with the remembered glory of the silk blocks on Nanking and Bubbling Well roads. Shanghai produces more silk goods than ever and in magnificent designs and fabrics, both modern and traditional, but most of them are exported to buy machinery. (I sometimes thought of Omar, who wondered what the vintner bought one half so precious as the stuff he sold.) I priced rayon at the equivalents of $1.50 a yard, dark silk for $2.25 to $7, wool at $6, cotton at 75 cents to $2. Leather shoes ranged from $3 to $12, shirts were $2.50 to $5, socks 40 cents to $1.50 a pair, leather jackets $25 to $30.

All these prices were somewhat higher than those in Hongkong, where China-made consumer goods are sold (for foreign exchange) in an abundance unknown in Shanghai. But I also saw goods in greater variety and quantity and at lower prices in Chungking, Loyang and Kunming. The cloth ration (halved since 1959) allowed each person 16 feet (one-meter width) a year—the same for infants and adults. That was enough for two Chinese dresses, one and a half adult suits, or two or three children's outfits. Used clothing could be bought in second-hand stores without coupons, but prices were high. For instance: $15 to $25 for a woolen suit.

"Yes, we export a lot of materials," the Communists say. "But the average family has two to three times more clothing than it had in the past. If we stopped all our exports we might have perhaps only another suit or two per person. As for silk, let the capitalists wear it for a few more years. When we have all the machines we need we'll have plenty of silk, too."

The great department stores, Wing On's, Sun Sun's, and Sincere's, were still open; they displayed clothing, shoes, linen goods and cheap merchandise of a wide variety, including some off-ration tinned goods, beer (60 fen), wine (2 yuan), vodka (8 yuan), household equipment and toys and bicycles. A good bicycle cost about $60, two months' wages for a skilled worker. A few blocks beyond Sun Sun's I located the Shanghai Race Course and golf links, where I used to play a round twice a week with Frank Oliver, of Reuters. The whole place is now a park with a giant stadium and public mall facing Tibet Road and adjoining the old French Club, which is now a people's palace. The evening I arrived, a crowd of half a million gathered there to hear a concert in which ten thousand voices participated, including choruses from both factories and schools.

I walked to the site of a restaurant that used to serve a good light Chinese meal for about thirty cents, which was then too expensive for the average Chinese. It was now one of those state provision stores which handle odd lots of unrationed goods. "What's for sale?" I asked the last man on the line. He gave me a hesitant look, then shrugged his shoulders. "*Pu ch'ing-ch'u.*" He "wasn't clear"—nor was the woman in front of him. Who cared? Apparently anyone with the time to spend queued up first and learned what was for sale when he got to it—if anything was left. I stood long enough to see a customer squeeze out the door with a small bundle from which a sickly banana peered. One saw such queues in all the cities. They reminded me of wartime Russia, except that in Russia the queues were longer, more numerous, and for bread, not luxuries like bananas. It is a fair comparison to say that the food situation in China is generally very much better than in Russia when I lived there during the war years, 1942-45.

Some of the old foreign store fronts (such as Whiteaways) now exhibited shining lathes and other machines, and salesmen offered literature to prospective buyers—who were not only foreigners, as communes also send purchasing agents to the cities. In the old Kelly and Walsh bookstore most of the display space was occupied by a large model of a 100,000-kilowatt power generator made in Shanghai, where not even 100-kilowatt generators were made before the war. What we used to call "Petticoat Lane," a group of smart foreign shops, was now given over to a flea market filled with miscellaneous items, mostly second-hand, from clothing to machine parts, displayed on open stands or tables, where people hunted for bargains. One corner store nearby offered a neat window display of ready-made, well-tailored children's garments; prices seemed prohibitive ($5 to $15 for jumper suits), but sales were being made.

I looked carefully for signs of undernourishment but saw no certain indications. People were lean, but most Chinese were always lean; "fat men" and "moneyed men" were synonyms. I was told by a Chinese doctor in Peking that cases of beriberi and pellagra had appeared in Shanghai hospitals, and in the Bund gardens I saw what may have been a case of vitamin deficiency. A woman teacher permitted me to photograph some attractively dressed, laughing children in her care. They at once clammed up and posed. I asked them to look natural and go on playing. While I was with them I noticed that one child had severely blackened teeth. I asked the nurse about it and she insisted that it was from "eating too much sugar when he was younger." Then she turned abruptly and left with her charges. At a kiosk in the park plenty of sweets were for sale, but when I tried to buy some for other children playing nearby I couldn't do so. Candy, like sugar, was rationed and sold to Shanghai residents only, at twelve ounces a month —hardly enough to blacken your teeth.

There were only about a dozen pedicabs on Nanking Road. They charged a standard fare of forty fen (about sixteen cents) an hour, too much for most Chinese. I hired one for a brief trip and in the course of it asked the pedalist how much rice he was eating. "Six bowls a day," he said. Enough? "Not enough. I need ten." Six standard bowls are about a pound. He also got greens, he said. "*Yo fa-tzu, yo pan-fa,*" he added. "On my free day I work in a garden and get a few eggs." He was neatly clad and an energetic pedalist.

Shanghai was always an ugly city and no aesthetic values would have been lost if it had been erased and begun anew. The municipality is satisfied to repair, expand and touch up existing buildings which will eventually be replaced. Most new construction lies beyond the old city limits, in satellite towns or suburbs. Wide new highways are being cut through the city and around it, to link town and country. In the suburbs the effects of planned construction contrast favorably with the aimless and helter-skelter expansion of other Asian cities— the monstrosity that is rebuilt Tokyo, for instance.

"Shanghai had about 20,000,000 square yards of housing space," said Li Yi-ming. "We have added 6,000,000 to that since 1952. That still means crowded living. We need twice as much housing. I want to show you what we're aiming at."

We drove for a day through the outskirts, visiting one development after another. Each of these self-contained communities economically centers upon a sprawling new machine-building plant, a textile mill or some other factory among many dozens now built or under construction on a large scale. Some of the surrounding truck gardens, piggeries and poultry farms are owned and managed by the factories. Good highways and sidewalks lead to traffic circles with shopping areas, hotels and theaters. Radiating from them are blocks of three- or four-story apartment dwellings for the workers, some built around gardens and playgrounds for children who attend schools also newly set up for the neighborhood. Residents are all within walking distance of their work.

Six satellites of this kind had been completed and five more were under construction. Much of the labor was spare-time effort contributed by the residents. I spent some hours in three of these new developments.

Ming Hong was typical—a community of about 70,000 workers and their families, employed by small neighborhood factories making motors and farm machinery. More than a thousand Ming Hong buildings of simple construction had been completed in less than two years. The town plaza consisted of eleven brick and tile structures, one of which was a hotel, newly opened, where I stopped for tea. It had fifty-five rooms and was built in sixty-seven days. In external appearance it was comparable to any small Middletown hotel, and it was attractively if inexpensively furnished. The manager was a twenty-year-old party member who had been through a special training period. He already had a full house and a backlog of reservations— mostly relatives of residents, workers delegations, lecturers, teams of visiting technicians and athletes. A two-room suite with bath at the Ming Hong cost three dollars a day; a room for two, without bath, one dollar per person.

Strolling down a tree-planted street of new apartment houses I chose one to enter. From the outside these buildings looked comparable to American lower-middle-class suburban dwellings, but they were crudely finished inside: unpainted plaster walls, stairs of cement, corridors narrow and poorly lighted. They were somewhat better than

East Side or West Side New York tenements and better than much housing I remember in Moscow, as well as a great improvement over old Shanghai slums.

It was afternoon in Ming Hong; most people were at work. No one answered our knocks at the first three flats. At the fourth an elderly gentleman opened the door and invited us in. A living room, two bedrooms, tiny kitchen, toilet and shower; sparsely furnished, no carpets, clean floors, white cotton curtains.

"How many? We are eight persons here: my wife, myself, our son and daughter-in-law, and their four children. Comfortable? Yes, indeed. Before, we were all in one room the size of this kitchen. Now we have space to turn around in. Me? I am a worker but retired, now sixty-five, living on pension. Who would have paid me 50 yuan a month to be idle in the past? I would be starving."

Further probing elicited that his son and daughter-in-law earned about 75 yuan per month each, working in the factory. Their rent was 12 yuan a month. Light and water, 3 yuan. Food at home cost them 90 yuan a month, the son and daughter spent another 30 yuan on factory lunches. Clothing, fuel, incidentals, 30 to 40. He didn't know all the details but he said they pooled their income and saved 25 to 30 yuan a month.

The greater part of the population still lives in the old built-up areas of the former International Settlement and the French Concession, and in the so-called native cities: Nantao, Woosung, Kiangwan and Yangtze-poo. Their appearance remains largely unchanged, except that the war-damaged structures have been repaired, private vehicles have all but disappeared, retail shops have closed or been taken over by state distributive agencies, and the old night life has moved to Hongkong.

Next day we drove fifteen miles into the countryside to visit the Horse Bridge rural commune. Large: 48,000 people, 12,000 acres. Well irrigated: 29 power pumping stations. Advanced in mechanization: 23 tractors. Prosperous: output up from $900,000 worth in 1952 to $6,100,000 in 1959, when cash income was 85 yuan per capita. Literate: 91 percent able to read and write, excluding infants and old folks. Horse Bridge produced rice (1959 yield, 2.3 tons an acre), rape, cotton (just beginning), vegetables, pigs (30,000; mostly frozen and exported to Eastern Europe), ducks (100,000, for Shanghai consumption) and cows (220; milk sold to Shanghai schools), besides operating several small factories.

Food allowance: average adult, 34 pounds of grain per month; vegetables, 30 to 40 pounds. Members cultivated their private plots and the average person got 13 eggs and 6 ounces of meat per month. In 1959 an able-bodied worker could earn about 200 yuan per year, in addition to his food. But in 1960 output would probably barely equal 1959. There had been a three-month drought and a light autumn harvest. People here, as on most farms I saw, appeared to be eating better than city-dwellers; they had an ample supply of vegetables in addition to the basic grain rations and bonuses in accordance with work performed.

Horse Bridge Commune's five "town centers" were rural equivalents of the city's satellite towns. Center No. 1, which I visited, had thirty-two new brick structures, all built by commune workers with bricks made in their own kiln: a large school, a modern kindergarten-nursery, a hospital (four doctors, two operating rooms, x-ray equipment, 150 beds), telegraph and post office, broadcasting station, several shops and stores, dining rooms, a theater, a public bath, and brick flats thus far providing housing for 600 families. The flats were surrounded by trees and flowers. Rent was free, electricity 1 to 2 yuan a month per family. Medical examination was free; hospital beds cost 20 fen a day; childbirth, 3 yuan. (Whenever I inquired I was told that all deliveries by healthy, normal mothers are natural births; anesthesia is rare.) Maternity leave, before and after birth: 54 days.

Everyone looked well fed around Horse Bridge. When I visited the kitchen, women were peeling mountains of potatoes, preparing cabbages and carrots, and cleaning fish for the evening meal.

"How do I like it?" An old lady of seventy-eight I questioned in the brigade dining room where she was arranging benches gave me her answer. "Well, now, I have five sons, they all have families. What would I be doing if it weren't for the commune? Cooking, washing, mending, slaving in a smoky hut, taking care of their children. As it is, I have everything I need and have to beg to get to help out a little. It's a pity I don't have long to live now to enjoy my leisure and freedom."

A rehearsed speech? Who could possibly have had foreknowledge that on impulse I should choose to address her? Her old eyes were wet with tears as she spoke.

But as I have said, I have no doubt that Horse Bridge was far above average and that here I was merely a tourist. This was what a commune should be—what others were aiming at.

"All right, Mr. Li," I said when we left. "You've shown me the best, now let's see the worst."

"What's your idea of the worst?"

"I remember thousands sleeping under mats along the Soochow Canal, thousands sleeping in the streets. I remember a jungle of bamboo huts in the burned-out parts of old Chapei down by the railroad station. I've seen the canal; that's cleaned up now. Even the sampans looked sanitized. No more street-sleepers. What about that jungle?"

"It's still there—Pumpkin Town. We haven't had time to build new homes for those people yet."

We got back to the city at dusk and went to see the old crazy quilt of crooked paths and lanes between "homes" built of box wood, pieces of bamboo, matting, old oil cans and newspapers. Refugees of all kinds, people hanging on the edge of life, traditionally had camped in Pumpkin Town in squalor worse than the mud cliffs and filth where derelicts live outside Mexico City—or much like the mat-shed refugee huts in Kowloon.

Some of the shelters had collapsed or been torn down but thousands survived, with improvements like roofs, glass windows and dry floors. The lanes and the alleyways were clean now, young willows were planted everywhere, water had been piped in to public fountains, and there were few flies. The grinning kids were no longer in rags and covered with sores. It was still a slum, but there were health stations in its midst, and tiny nurseries. Various workshops were busy and I saw a reading room and a bookstore. We had not gone a hundred feet before a businesslike woman appeared, introduced herself as the lane committee chairman, and asked our business.

"Most of our families don't want to leave," she said. "They're all squatters but their ownership was confirmed after liberation. The city needs the land and they'll have to move sooner or later, but we're making it a decent place to live in the meantime."

Here I stopped in to talk to another family—my own choice. An old lady was getting supper ready in her one-room mat-floored shanty, which was clean as a pin. A small radio was tuned to music. Her son and daughter-in-law were away at work. That was a smart girl, her daughter-in-law, she said. "She's been through primary school." Her three grandchildren who clustered around were smart, too, learning to read and write. "Just show the gentlemen how you can write, An-tsai," she said to one, who blushed and hid. The daughter-in-law earned 68 yuan a month; her son earned only 60. They had no rent to pay. Food cost them 70 yuan; she did the cooking and was economical. Food? She pointed to a charcoal stove where rice was simmering. Look at their supper: a fish tonight! (A one-pound fish for six people, but a fish. Probably their meat-fish ration for a week.) Two kinds of rice, wet and dry: "Two kinds, just imagine." There seemed to be a series of bunks behind a curtain but some of them must have slept on the floor.

"Move? Why? We've got our own home here. Quite happy as it is. If we can just get a sewing machine—"

71

The Mayor of
Shanghai

Inescapably I overfulfilled my inspection quota of Shanghai industry. Industrial output here in 1960 was valued at 24,000,000,000 yuan or more than 10 percent of the national total. I saw only a few of its muscles at work, but I can tell you now that the city makes good steel converters, power generators, rolling machines, giant hammers, drills, forging presses, aluminum-foil-making machines, fertilizer plants, diesel tractors and rubber tires up to sixty tons in weight, not to mention antibiotic drugs, fine surgical equipment, x-ray machines, precision lenses, television and other cameras, and disposable diapers and baby bottles. It would take many pages to describe even one factory adequately, if the people were included. When you have seen a hundred factories they blur together like scenes remembered from a moving car.

I learned more at the Shanghai Industrial Exhibit, which is housed in a very large building of the conventional exposition type. Every big city has at least one. In Peking half a dozen permanent exhibits are filled with animated displays as entertaining and informative as the Chicago Field Museum. For the Chinese it's all new and exciting. Television sets, hi-fi and radio-TV consoles, pianos, refrigerators, electric shavers, stunning fabrics of all kinds, a wide variety of processed foods, fine porcelains and rugs—things you don't see in the stores. They are mostly for export or available in China only for collective use. Chinese must view these displays with pride and satisfaction mixed with some envy of countries where individuals can afford to buy them.

Li Yi-ming broke in on my musings. "I am sorry to tell you that Mme Soong Ching-ling won't be able to see you tonight." *

"I'm not surprised; I know she's been very ill."

"But the mayor has invited you to dinner."

I supposed that the courtesy was extended partly in compensation for my disappointment at missing Mme Sun Yat-sen, one of my oldest friends in China. The mayor had a reason of his own.

"I've known you a long time," he said when he greeted me, "even though we never met. Perhaps I had some influence on your life." To my questioning look he replied: "At the time you first went to the Northwest it was I who wrote that invisible-ink letter to Mao Tse-tung. I was then head of the North China underground. I wrote the letter for Professor Hsu Pin to give to you."

"It changed my life, all right. A lot of people have never forgiven me for making that trip."

Shanghai is a special municipality, like Peking, and with its sub-urban districts it is as important as a province. Mayor K'eh is a Polit-buro member and outranks most governors. A big man, powerfully built, with a shock of black hair and wide, searching eyes, he looked fortyish but was in his late fifties. He is direct and forceful in his speech.

"It's the revolution that keeps a man's hair black," he said. "I was a student in normal college in Nanking in the twenties, when I left to join the Nationalist revolution. I was the only student in my class who became a Communist. Not long ago I looked up some of my class-mates who were still in Nanking; several of them were teaching. They had been afraid of starving or losing their jobs and never joined the revolution. Well, they had not starved and they still had their jobs. But look, I said to them, you all have white hair while I am still black. Why? Being a revolutionary keeps you young."

K'eh Cheng-shih was born in Huangshan, Anhui, north of Nanking, in a middle-class landowning family. After Chiang Kai-shek led the counterrevolution in 1927, K'eh became a "political miner." He went underground for ten years, first in Shanghai, later in Peking. With Liu Shao-ch'i he ran the party underground (the North China Bureau), and when Japan invaded China they went into the villages together to organize guerrillas.

---

* Mme Soong, the revered widow of Dr. Sun Yat-sen, lives in her old home in Shanghai most of the time. Her chronic illness had reached a particularly acute stage, she wrote to me from her sickbed. Her letter expressed buoyant satisfaction with the regime and deep confidence in the future.

The mayor welcomed me in the former home of the Italian Consul General, in the erstwhile French Concession, a rambling old dwelling in well-kept gardens. It was now used as municipal reception chambers and K'eh had an office there. If all the powers ever recognize China there will be some frustrated house hunters. The British Consulate General on the Bund is the only former Western property still in "imperialist" hands.

Others present that evening were the vice-mayor, Tsao Tieh-chien; Chang Yao-hui, the secretary-general; and Li Yi-ming.

"Your theory about black hair doesn't seem to apply in the case of Deputy Mayor Tsao," I said impolitely.

"He was not as lucky as I," K'eh answered. "Comrade Tsao spent seven years in the old Ward Road Jail in Shanghai, imprisoned by the International Settlement authorities for Communist activities. That's enough to make anyone gray."*

The mayor said his evening was entirely free. I could ask any questions I wished; he'd try to answer. To begin, he'd make some prefatory remarks.

"Li Yi-ming has told me that you have two impressions. First, the old surface glamour and prosperity seem gone. Second, the moral tone of the city seems to have improved. Both impressions are correct. Many foreign visitors don't see what the change means. As an old resident you ought to know. A small percentage of rich Chinese and foreigners had more than enough; the glamour and the luxurious shops and hotels on Nanking Road were for them. In the dirty back lanes and alleys millions lived in hunger or on refuse or they starved. Now, nobody is rich but nobody starves and nobody lives in filth and rags.

"Does everybody have enough? Yes, enough. Do people want more? Of course. Wages and living standards in Shanghai are higher than in the rest of the country. Shanghai produces more; Shanghai should have a higher living standard. The average industrial worker's wage in Shanghai is 74.50 yuan. Rent runs from 4 to 15 yuan a family, utilities cost 3 to 4, food about 12 yuan a person. The average family has two wage earners. That leaves a lot of consumer purchasing power, a lot of pressure on us. Production of consumer goods admittedly is still low. We can't get too far ahead. We have 10,000,000 people here. Suppose we raise consumption by only 20 yuan per person. That means 200,000,000 yuan a year taken out of production of farm tools, irrigation machines, steel, all much more urgently needed elsewhere than Shanghai needs more leather shoes."

"Is this a social occasion, off the record, Mr. Mayor? If not, I'd like to take notes."

"Please do take notes. Anything I say is for the record." He went on:

---

* Tsao was fortunate. The Settlement police, for which Britain and America were largely responsible until 1937, arrested thousands of Chinese radicals. Many of them were turned over to local Kuomintang authorities and heard from no more.

"Shanghai makes more than enough textiles to give everybody extra suits and dresses. When you think of increasing living standards you have to think of six hundred seventy million times* whatever the increase is. To double the cloth ration we must double cotton output, textile machinery, factories.† You can't do it overnight.

"We ration food now for the same reason. This region grows plenty but we've had two bad-weather years in the North. Crop failures in other parts mean we have to feed them, too. Rations are fixed now at an adequate minimum we can maintain indefinitely. Foreign press reports mistake our careful rationing for famine. We don't have and we won't have famine. When output provides plenty for everyone we'll end rationing.

"You asked about rations here? Our monthly minimum is about the same as elsewhere: for adults, 27 pounds of grain, 6 ounces of meat, 26 ounces of fish, 33 pounds of vegetables.‡ Factory workers get 30 to 33 pounds of grain and heavy workers get 44 pounds. Artists and brain workers get the same, plus extra meat allowances. So do capitalists living on dividends; there are special restaurants for them. We try to give people what they consider their honest 'need.' Altogether, the municipality is feeding more than 800,000 people on those top rations. As for the peasants, they do better than that, of course, with their side-line production."

Mayor K'eh was full of instances.

"Not long ago I dropped in on a peasant family at dinnertime. They were eating five dishes: squash, scabbard fish, spinach, rice—and eggs! [This might well have been true, but if that was an ordinary meal they were no ordinary peasants.] Take cooking oil. They ladled it on with a spoon. Farmers used to oil the skillet with a radish, oil was so costly. Take eggs. Only landlords ate eggs. Poor farmers traded their few eggs for needles, thread, salt, necessities. Now they buy those things with cash and eat the eggs. The city can't buy enough eggs any more; we have to set up more and more municipal poultry farms. Take rubber shoes. What peasant in my home town ever wore rubber shoes? Now it's the thing: everybody must have them—and many have leather shoes.

"Take rice. There are two edible parts, the husk and the green, rich in vitamins but less calories, and there is the kernel. In the past the peasants ate husks and only a bit of the kernels, which were sold. Now everybody eats the whole rice. On a farm recently I met an old man who was collecting manure from the latrines. Did you ever think

* Mayor K'eh was the only high official who used that large a population figure in conversation with me, in 1960.
† In 1959 China's cotton textile output was 7,500,000,000 meters, nearly half of which was exported, chiefly to the U.S.S.R. If the same export ratio were maintained China would have to produce about 80 percent more than U.S. output of cotton textiles in order to double the cloth ration.
‡ K'eh used equivalents in Chinese catties.

you could tell peasants where to *ta-pien?* Well, they do it; the children scold them if they don't. About that old man who was collecting
manure. I asked him how things were.

"'See here,' he said, 'look at this.' He showed me the stuff in his
buckets. 'When we were eating nothing but husks the *ta-pien* was
whitish and fluffy, an unhealthy color. Now, you see, it is solid and
brown. *Ma-ti!* It's the right color. People are eating better.' What are
your questions?"

"You mentioned the Ward Road Jail," I said. "How many prisoners
now?" The mayor turned to Tsao, who supplied the figure. "Under
2,500. That doesn't include prisoners on our Reform-Through-Labor
Farm. That's in Supei, north of the river, two or three days from
here."

Had Tsao been back to the Ward Road Jail? Yes; he'd seen his
old cell but there was nobody there; the door was open. All the doors
were open. In his time prisoners were allowed out for exercise half
an hour a day and beaten if they spoke to each other. Now prisoners
had their recreation time, a library and reading room for use after
working hours. There was no difficulty in arranging a visit, and the
routine was much the same as in the Peking prison I have described—
except the absence of gardening. Incidentally, the prisoner who taught
the literacy class was Mme Wang Ching-wei, widow of the Kuomintang ex-premier who later headed the Japanese puppet government.

"How many prisoners on the Supei farm?"

"About 6,000," said the mayor. "I've been there. It's a good farm.
You wouldn't know it was a prison—there are very few guards. Prisoners built their own houses. They have a power plant, electric lights,
movies. There's a lot of pigs and livestock and their production is
above average. When men are trusted they can get leave for a week
or so to come back to visit their families—no guards go with them."

"They always come back?"

"So far, always. Some of them ask to bring their families in and we
have let them; they work better. Some prisoners like it so well they
stay on and work for wages after their terms expire. They have rights
like any other citizens."

"Mayor K'eh, I wouldn't believe a word you're telling me except that
I actually spoke to some women ex-prisoners in the Peking jail who
said they were staying on to work there out of choice. I'd like to see
this farm for myself."

"It's quite a trip. You'd have to wait for a boat and it takes two or
three days each way. If you've got the time we'll try to arrange it."

I should have taken him up at once, but a week or ten days then
would have meant dropping the rest of my schedule or requesting another visa extension, which I wasn't sure I could get. I was told I'd
have other opportunities near Hankow, Chungking and Kunming, but
I did not. I cannot, therefore, blame anyone but myself for not being

able to confirm or deny Mayor K'eh's account of the only "labor camps" to which China admits.

Calculating 8,500 prisoners to the Shanghai population of roughly ten million gives a prison rate of .0085 per thousand. If that rate prevailed over all China her prison population would be 595,000.* Interesting—if true.

"That's not very high, especially if it includes all prisoners, not just political," I said.

"It includes all, and the majority are not political prisoners," said K'eh. "But our actual crime rate today is much lower than that. You must remember that Shanghai had the highest crime rate in the country in the past. Right now we have trouble finding a case in the courts to show foreign visitors who want to hear a trial."

"I know. I was told in Peking there was not a case in the courts. They told me to try here."

"We will let you know if there is anything on while you're here. Crime is no real problem now. Ninety percent of the people support what we are trying to do. Only a few would actively oppose us—if they could. We have 6,000 policemen, including the Fire Department. That's not many for a city this size. How many policemen do you have in New York? † Most of ours are for traffic control."

"They used to say Shanghai had more police, more prisoners, and more prostitutes than there were students in the schools. That was an exaggeration, of course."

"Not much. You couldn't say that now. We have more than 2,000,-000 students in Shanghai. If you count the 1,300,000 people in spare-time schools, almost a third of the population are students. That's another reason the crime rate is low." He gave me these figures:

Colleges and institutes of higher learning: 31, with 56,000 students. Middle schools: 450,000 students. Primary schools: 1,629,000 students.

"That doesn't sound like Shanghai is being forcibly depopulated, as was reported a few years ago."

"That was never true. What we did do was to persuade thousands of college-trained people, professional men and technicians to start new schools and factories in the interior. We had two good medical colleges and far more medical personnel than the rest of the country. We split the colleges and sent personnel to open new colleges and hospitals in Anhui and Wuhan. Today we have two new medical colleges with far more students, hospitals with more personnel— 30,000 hospital beds. That's one example. Altogether, Shanghai has sent 1,600,000 professional people and technical workers into the in-

* The same rate in the U.S.A. would give a prison population of 161,500. In 1960 it was 207,000. Arrest rates in U.S. (2,612,000 in 1960) would doubtless be much higher in proportion to prison rates than in China, where the number of convictions closely approximates the number of arraignments.

† New York City police numbered 23,000 in 1960, exclusive of the Fire Department. Shanghai has far less traffic.

terior. Shanghai and Manchuria have been the biggest training centers for China's modernization." *

It was past midnight and K'eh was still going strong. For me it had been a long day. I made a tentative move to adjourn.

"There is one other thing," he said. "We haven't talked about your country." I saw the old ground rising up that I had been over so many times with others. In deference to mine host I nodded; I was after all the first American he had seen for many years.

"Do the American people support U.S. occupation of Taiwan?"

"Generally speaking Americans oppose anything that smacks of colonialism. They have never had an opportunity to cast a vote about Taiwan. People talk about giving the Taiwanese a plebiscite on whether they want to join China or not. What Americans need is a plebiscite for or against the Taiwan protectorate and for or against recognition of China."

"We also doubt that the people support U.S. aggression in Taiwan. We consider it a pity that because of American policy we have lost all contacts with the American people and cannot have friendship with them." I knew what was coming next and silently joined him in chorus, ". . . nothing against the American people, it's only American imperialism which we oppose."

He continued: "We can never restore relations with America as long as you hang on to our territory, of course, and that means we can't trade with you, either. We don't like your government but we aren't going to war to change it; that's your affair. We are socialists but we do business with West Europeans—British, Germans, Scandinavians, Dutch, Canadians and others. Look at the ships in the river. Shanghai will soon be a great world port again, as great as before, even far greater than before. Our port facilities are being modernized, as you have seen. Why aren't American ships out there carrying on a peaceful trade—but only American warships invading our waters and wasting your money? It's not our fault."

"Premier Chou En-lai has already reminded me that I am not the Secretary of State," I said, "but I shall gladly convey your message."

* In 1961 Shanghai and other cities sent millions of skilled and unskilled workers and their dependents to help farm production under emergency conditions. See page 586.

72

God and Party

Christianity was still proscribed in China when Emperor K'ang Hsi took the throne in 1665, but Jesuit priests were in charge of the Peking observatory. This paradox was chiefly the work of Matteo Ricci (1552-1610), whom John Fairbank has rightly described as "one of the greatest proponents of boring from within." No latter-day Comintern agent in China was as subtle in subverting traditional Chinese society as Ricci, who became "all-Chinese" and ingratiated himself with imperial scholars by preaching a Christianity fully reconciled with Confucian ancestor-worship, ethics and philosophy.

After K'ang Hsi had put down the serious Wu San-kuei rebellion in the South and defeated the Russians at Albazin with the aid of Jesuit cannon, a new tolerance was granted Catholicism. The young Jesuit François Gerbillon taught K'ang Hsi some Euclidian geometry and helped negotiate the Sino-Russian Treaty of Nerchinsk, which was highly favorable to China. In 1693 K'ang Hsi acknowledged these various services in an edict which opened China to Christianity.

Jesuits prospered in China until 1715, when Pope Alexander VII began an egregiously bigoted attack on Confucian "paganism and idolatry." K'ang Hsi himself wrote to explain that nobody really be-

lieved that Confucius and the Ancients were living in the ancestral stone tablets any more than Christians believed Jesus was living on the crucifix. How could the symbolical "Rites" of homage to their spirits be called idolatry? The Vatican never got around to answering K'ang Hsi's arguments. Disgusted, the Emperor placated his Confucian reactionaries by issuing a new edict in 1717 which withdrew imperial recognition from the Jesuits.[1]

No massive opportunity to Christianize China arose again until 1850, when the T'ai-p'ing revolution was launched under the leadership of Cantonese converts. Missionaries denounced the T'ai-p'ings as heretics and deviationists, but their armies were blessed with success from Canton to the gates of Peking. When the Manchu throne was saved by the intervention of Western armies, China was finally forced to legalize the importation of opium, Christianity and Western philosophy—including all forms of Protestant heresy and Marxism.

A few representatives of various Protestant groups have visited Red China; both the Anglicans and the Friends have issued recent reports on the state of the faith under the People's Republic.[2] It may be well to remember that filial worship, with its traditional tenets in Confucianism, always remained the native religion of China, if religion it may be called. Christianity never embraced more than a fraction of one percent of China's population, and its impact on Chinese society was felt less as a spiritual force than as a political invasion.

I attended services of Christian churches in Shanghai and Peking, and I spoke to one ex-missionary Englishwoman who was visiting some Chinese followers but who did not wish to be quoted about her mission. A young Chinese Anglican bishop whom I met at a state banquet in Peking assured me that the constitutional guarantee of freedom of worship was being upheld. He himself was a delegate to the People's Consultative Conference, as were certain other religious leaders.

Shanghai always had the largest concentration of native Christians in China and was the base from which both Protestant and Catholic missionaries operated. It was appropriate, therefore, that I should seek out the Chinese Catholic fathers quoted at length below. Their anti-Vatican charges are of course disputed in Rome, where the Church has a very different story to tell.[3] This occasion was, however, a unique opportunity to hear church problems discussed by men responsible for confronting and solving them on the spot.

"For the first time in history we Catholics are in charge of our own church in China. Always before we were under foreign bishops and domination from abroad."

That is what I was told by Father Chen Fu-ming, forty-eight, a sallow, thin-faced, tense pastor whom I interviewed at Ziccawei Cathedral in Shanghai.

"What about Bishop Yu Pin—now a cardinal, I believe?"

"Yu Pin?" If spitting were not unbecoming to a priest and a citizen of New China, one felt that the padre would have spat. "We don't recognize him as a Catholic and he has lost his right to be called Chinese. He is a national traitor."

"He is certainly a running dog," echoed Shen Pai-chih, a priest fourteen years younger than Father Chen. "Otherwise, why should he attack his country and flee China to work for American imperialism in Taiwan?"

Both men asserted that their views were identical with those of the acting bishop of Shanghai, Chiang Chia-hsu, who was then in another part of the diocese. Despite their strong rejection of Vatican ties, neither had been excommunicated.

Ziccawei is one of the oldest Chinese Christian churches. The seat of a bishopric, with some 40,000 Catholics in the city and 110,000 in the diocese, it had been one of the wealthiest parishes in China. In the former French Concession, and long run by French priests, it is a fine brick edifice encompassed by spacious lawns and gardens.

"Our final break with the Vatican occurred in 1958," said Pastor Chen. "In June, 1958, the Vatican issued an Encyclical Letter forbidding clergy and laity from participating in any activities backed by the Communist party. Priests were supposed to withhold blessings from such people. By implication the Letter demanded that we become a counterrevolutionary organization dedicated to the overthrow of the regime and the return of Chiang Kai-shek. It expressed the aims of American imperialism. Those bishops and priests who received the Letter were threatened with excommunication if they ignored it."

"I am not familiar with the Letter you mention. What was the response of the Church as a whole in China?"

"There is no Catholic church under a single head," said the pastor. "Each diocese operates autonomously." *

"And the response?"

"We ignored the order. We consider it a sinful violation of the Commandments, and immoral. Both Pope Pius and Pope John have openly prayed for the downfall of our country. Pope John supported the Tibetan counterrevolution and the Vatican denounced the communes. The Pope said, like Mr. Dulles, that their aim was to destroy the family. Of course that is a lie."

"Under present circumstances, in the eyes of Rome do you have the right to administer the sacraments?"

---

* Father Chen estimated the Chinese Catholic population as three million today, about the same as it was before 1949, when Protestant converts were no more than a million.

"We have the right, and we do so. The Vatican uses the threat of depriving us of the right but we ignore it."

They mentioned only three instances of excommunication. A priest named Li Ying-t'ao who had "comforted the wounded" during the Korean War (performed Mass and given absolution and communion at the front) was the first to be read out. Li Wei-kiang, now bishop of the Nanking diocese, was the second; he had supported the government's 1951 expulsion from China of Monsignor Ribberi, the Papal Nuncio. Tung Kuan-ch'ing, who permitted himself to be elected bishop of Wuhan at a meeting of clerics and laymen, had been threatened with "special excommunication," but the threat had not materialized.

"What is your view of the case of Bishop James Walsh, the American now imprisoned in Shanghai for alleged crimes against the state?"

"First of all," said Pastor Chen, "Walsh was not a true bishop of any church in China. He had no church. He was brought back to Shanghai and imposed here by Cardinal Spellman in 1948. We Chinese had nothing to say about that. We attended his trial this year, where the facts were brought out. He had put himself in charge of a Catholic Central Bureau which attempted to control us by issuing secret orders and collecting intelligence through the Hua Ming [interdiocesan press]. It propagated rumors against the government. There is no doubt that Walsh was serving imperialism. He and Father McCarthy were both sentenced in March, 1960. Father McCarthy was given a suspended sentence and permitted to leave the country. Bishop Walsh went to jail to seek martyrdom. We don't recognize him as a martyr but as an agent of foreign imperialism."

I emphasize again that this report expresses only the opinion of two Chinese Catholic clergymen, without prejudice to other facts with which the Vatican doubtless would contradict it. The State Department's report on the case of Bishop Walsh, recorded in the Appendix of this book, does not support allegations that he deliberately chose martyrdom.

According to these priests there was no discrimination against either clergy or lay Catholics "unless they used religion as a cloak for counterrevolution." Priests and Catholics had civil rights, including the right to be elected to office and hold seats, up to the national congress level. They could not, of course, become members of the party.

"We believe in God and redemption," said Father Chen. "Communists do not. We observe the Sabbath and believe in prayer. On matters of religion we differ profoundly but on secular matters we can cooperate. In practice, the Communists observe the other Commandments and the law respects them."

What about "Thou shalt not kill"? The government of course opposed murder; there were fewer crimes in China than ever before.

But what about execution of priests and other clerics? There had been cases of misuse of the cloth for espionage and counterrevolution, they said. The Church deplored and could never sanction killing.

"Under foreign domination our church went beyond religious matters in the past and sometimes served as a political instrument of imperialism. We have cut all ties with that past. There is today no use of force against Christians who observe the laws of the land."

Further questioning explained something of what all this meant in practice. All schools, orphanages, hospitals and other welfare activities formerly run by religious organizations were taken over by the government during early campaigns which sought to arouse public disgust with missionaries, nuns, priests and such acolytes as served them. Foreign superiors once accounted for about half the 13,000 Catholic priests, brothers and nuns in China: Jesuits, Dominicans, Franciscans, Marists and others, Europeans and Americans. "By August, 1954, 126 out of 143 dioceses had lost their superiors," according to one authority. "Of the 5,486 foreign religious leaders who were originally resident in China, less than 100 remained."[4] Highly vilifying reports of their conduct were published, some suffered painful imprisonment and died, and eventually nearly all foreigners departed voluntarily or were deported. Some Chinese loyal to them were also reported persecuted and killed.[5] According to Pastor Chen there were in 1960 two European priests still at the Sacred Heart Church, in Peking.

Judging from my interview, state policy may have had the active support of those Chinese Catholics as well as Protestants who shared the general antiforeign *revanche* sentiments held by many intellectuals against any and all kinds of past "imperialist" domination and who wanted a "purely Chinese" church more than Papal blessings. That the Church is still sharply split between "orthodox" and "progressive" (anti-Vatican) elements was clearly indicated at a meeting of Church leaders from twenty-six provinces summoned to a Catholic conference in Peking during the "Hundred Flowers" period. The press then reported that numerous bishops and priests were opposed to the Christian National Front and that one even "demanded the dissolution of the Communist party leadership and going over to capitalism."[6] Meanwhile Protestant Christian churches, far less united than the Catholics, proved unable to support effective opposition to the drive for ideological integration of church and state. Today their Chinese leaders "support socialism" under the National Christian Council.

Members of the Chinese Catholic Patriotic Association obviously hold opinions sharply at variance with those of the American Church about the way the situation on this earth looks in the eyes of God. The chairman of the association, Archbishop Ignatius P'i Shu-shih, recently condemned President Kennedy as a "hypocritical Catholic," for having "pushed military spending to a new high and actively expanded arms in preparation for a war while intensifying the exploitation of laboring people"; at the same time the President continued "to occupy China's sacred territory of Taiwan by force."[7] Protestant members of the National Front concurred in these views. Bishop K. H. Ting, president of the Nanking Union Theological Seminary, reportedly "denounced the U.S. reactionary authorities for their attack on progressive [American] religious figures." No matter what "high-sounding words about peace and democracy" Mr. Kennedy might utter, one should remember the words of St. Paul: "Even Satan fashioneth himself into an angel of light."[8]

One need not subscribe to this hyperbole in order to recognize that linkages of missionary activity in China with past imperialist aggression are indisputable facts of history. When the fanatical Boxer rebels rose in 1900 against Western domination, a number of missionaries in the interior were the only foreign devils available for revenge. Mark Twain's bitterly ironic and classic commentary, "To a Person Sitting in Darkness," reminds us that some European missionaries secured the retaliatory execution of hundreds of people during the Allied occupation of North China following the rebellion—an event also applauded by a few American evangelists.

While Westerners looked upon missionaries dispatched into the old cultures of the East as messengers of altruism and redemption, they often appeared quite otherwise to peoples whom they sought to deliver. To educated Chinese the arrival of missionaries was always associated with China's military defeats. It must be conceded also that anyone who sets out into an unknown country carrying the only true faith under his arm is not in a frame of mind exactly suited to objective study of conceptions of social living which he is predetermined to supplant. It should not surprise anyone that nationalistic Chinese tended to consider the missionaries' attitude as arrogant if not ignorant.

During this century and earlier both Protestant and Catholic missionaries introduced Western science, medicine and other good works, however, along with their dogma. I myself taught in a Christian-founded university and know how enlightened and liberal a philosophy of human brotherhood it sought to advance. That did not prevent many of its students from later joining the Communists—a phenomenon I have tried to explain elsewhere.[9] Services performed by Christian educators, doctors and nurses, who saved countless lives (including those of some Communists) and acted in the best spirit of their faith, brought few of them any monetary rewards or honors beyond the thanks of humble people. Some of their sons did enter business and make fortunes in China. A few closely identified themselves—and hence the Christian Church, in the eyes of the Communists—with Chiang Kai-shek, even to the extent of urging massive armed American intervention to save the Generalissimo in 1949. With some exceptions—notably Henry R. Luce and Walter Judd—former China missionaries and their children today exhibit little vindictiveness toward the Peking regime for the harsh, undiscriminating, sometimes brutal and certainly politically unwise expulsion of all foreign Christian missionary personnel from China. Most of these "counterexiles" still cling to the belief that traditional Sino-American friendship will and should be restored regardless of political differences.

Chinese Communist hostility toward Christianity had both ideological and traditional or nationalistic aspects. Most missionaries in China owned property, lived on a far higher standard than Chinese, and were bourgeois in status and outlook. Some Catholic missions owned quite large farms and vineyards and the Communists saw no difference between them and native capitalists and landlords. Much property owned by missionaries had been acquired under extraterritoriality rights that made it nontaxable, and the owners were answerable only to foreign authorities.

If the Communists were deeply anti-missionary, their sentiments were strongly reciprocated for many years prior to 1949 by the vast majority of missionaries.

Capitalists in Marxist eyes, and also under direct Vatican discipline and control, the Catholics even to many nationalistic Chinese seemed outright imperialists. Periodically, they had also been attacked by the Kuomintang. Much as the old scholars had seen the Jesuits as a threat to enforcement of uniformity of ritual worship and Confucian thought, so the Communists looked upon Christian teachers as subversive to the correct system of discipline and conformance. A similarity between Catholic and Chinese indoctrination methods has been noted by more than one Catholic.

"Just as in Christian morality no concrete action remains indifferent," wrote Eleutherius Winance, O.S.B., a former missionary in Chengtu, "so for a Communist there is nothing that does not have a political aspect. He needs Hsio-hsi [*hsueh-hsi*, study] till his last hour." This priest understood very well both the method and the purpose of "thought remolding." Chinese political study sessions, he said, "reminded me of my youth: back home in our Christian brothers' school we used always to begin the day with the catechism lesson." [10]

Although missionary educational and social institutions and all holdings in farmlands were expropriated by the state, churches and grounds as well as urban commercial real estate nominally remain the property of each Chinese Catholic diocese. The real estate is managed by the government, however, much like joint private-state enterprise. The clergy receive their stipends and rents or dividends through the "ministry of cults." Other sources of income are minimal: contributions from the laity, payments for Masses and other services, and sale of religious articles. I was told by the Ziccawei priests that they maintained their own shops to make religious articles and that the same was true in other churches.

The Bible has not been touched, but extensive revisions of prayer books are required and neither these nor catechisms were being printed in new editions as yet, according to Pastor Chen. The Church has practically no press. He cited one example of an "unsuitable prayer" which had to be revised because of a line stating, "This land is filled with calamities" (Fatima?). Father Shen agreed that certain statements "clearly opposed to socialism" must be changed.

Worship is permitted but not proselytization. Missionary activity is not permitted. The interdiction applies not only to private Catholic schools but to Sunday schools and any kind of organized catechismic teaching of youth, as well. Children are expected to learn the elements of faith from their parents.

"That is the way I acquired my faith," said Pastor Chen. Both he and Father Shen were born in Catholic families. "Religion is a matter of personal belief. No other private organizations run schools. Why should we?"

No Catholic seminary exists in China today. The pastor said that the Shanghai seminary was dissolved by the members themselves, not on government orders. Allegedly it had been poisoned by the control of Father McCarthy and Bishop Walsh. Father Shen had been a teacher there, after having gone through "political indoctrination" in a Hong-kong seminary, where he had been a refugee. In 1955 he returned to Shanghai, he said, where he had followed the instructions he received to help sabotage the regime. It was not until 1958 that he had "fully realized" that he was "working against his country."

Meanwhile, an attempt to organize the patriotic or national Catholic Church had been opposed by the former bishop of Shanghai, Kung P'ing-mei,* whom Shen now recognized as a "tool of that Vatican imperialist agent," Bishop Walsh. In 1958, Shen joined others in voting to dissolve the seminary because it was "riddled with past contaminating influences." He was now working out with other Chinese priests a suitable curriculum for a new seminary which would "unquestionably" be permitted to function when they agreed. The property was still theirs, waiting to be utilized.

How much of this was sincere, how much uttered for the ears of Mr. Li, the party representative who was present, how much both men still wanted what the Vatican would call the "free Church" of the past, I do not know. Both emphatically denied that they were doctrinal rebels or in any way wished to "reform" basic Catholic teachings.

"From what you have told me and from what I have observed for myself," I said, "it seems to me that your means of propagation of the faith are extremely limited. All children are taught atheism in the schools, while you cannot proselytize against it. Will it not be difficult to find young men to enlist in your seminary even if you reopen it?"

---

* Arrested in 1955 as a "counterrevolutionary."

"We do not think so," answered the pastor. "As long as there is freedom of conscience people will seek God. We are masters of our own house; we are independent. Our people like the new Church better than the old one; they are more sincere in their faith. In the past, opportunists joined the foreign-dominated Church seeking advantages in the courts and foreign protection. We attracted lots of rice Christians. We don't want that kind of people, but men of high moral and spiritual convictions. There is no conflict between socialism and the teachings of Jesus."

"You are more interested in applied Christian ethics than in propagation of the faith?"

Pastor Chen replied: "They should be one and the same. Under new conditions we can make them so. Our future is the future of the people."

Clearly this kind of nationalized church, dependent on the state, could offer no serious threat to it. With fewer than six Christians per thousand Chinese, the combined Catholic and Protestant churches never actually constituted such a threat except through their potent foreign connections. By breaking those connections, conflict between church and state was solved in a manner relatively simple compared to the problem in satellite Communist states of Europe, especially Poland, where Catholicism is part of the national culture. Religion had nothing like so powerful a hold in China. Even native Confucianism and Taoism exerted their influence mainly through ethical and philosophical teachings, and Buddhism was already moribund. The ancient surviving temples of Buddhism's past glory are regarded as state treasures today and have never been so well renovated, so well kept, and so empty. Chinese youths now visit them and stare at the great images as curiously as foreign tourists.

Islam is a different matter. Moslems are called *Hui-min* (Moslem people) and are recognized as a minority nationality. Islam has an ancient history in China through its ethnic ties with Central Asian peoples who entered the Northwest as invaders and were slowly assimilated culturally but kept their religion. Unlike Christians, Mohammedans may join the party. But they join as *Hui-min* rather than as members of *Hui-chiao* (Moslem religion). In China as in Russia, "good" Moslem Communists are atheists, though they do not eat pork and do not publicly renounce the faith. Moslem leaders are cultivated by Communists also because of significant links between them and the anti-imperialist Islamic world stretching across colonial and ex-colonial Asia and Africa. The combined population of the Hui Autonomous Region of Ninghsia and the Sinkiang Uighur Autonomous Region is about eight million, but Moslems are scattered elsewhere and altogether may number fifteen million, of varying degrees of orthodoxy.

Chinese Moslems are held in low esteem by those professing to be closer to Mecca. "The only thing Moslem about them," a Pakistani diplomat in Peking told me, "is that they don't eat pork—when they can't get it." It is only fair to add that in Arabia I heard exactly the same opinion expressed about the orthodoxy of Pakistani Moslems.

Perhaps news of my interview at Ziccawei preceded me to Wuhan. In that city I met a young Communist member of the city secretariat who, when we were driving back from Tung Lake, suddenly said:

"I hear you are a Catholic."

"You are misinformed. I was brought up as a Catholic but I lost faith in institutionalized churches many years ago."

"Do you believe in God?"

"God seems to be a human invention to comfort and control man in his ignorance and fears. I share every man's profound ignorance and his lonely fear of oblivion after death. The organized church exploits both for its own glorification and a power often misused. On the other hand, I agree with Einstein's observation that the universe surrounds us with evidence of a superior reasoning power. That is very far from being a Catholic, and accepting the Pope as God's vice-regent on earth. Do you believe in God?"

"Huh! Not in any sense. Belief in God and scientific Marxism are irreconcilable. I am a Marxist."

I mentioned the Shanghai padre's comment that Communists also respect and work for the Commandments—or most of them.

"If that is so it is for different reasons. You cannot be a Christian and be a Marxist," he replied. "Marxism is modern, scientific truth. Religion belongs to the past. There's no connection between them."

"Are you sure? If you reject the virgin birth of Christ can you believe in the autogenesis of Marxism? Isn't Marxism a product of many historical teachings—among others, the ethical ideals of Judeo-Christianity? Did you ever read Engels' essay comparing early Christian martyrs to early Communist martyrs? He saw a lot of connection between them. When Marx and Engels called religion the opiate of the people they did not mean the Christian ideals of universal brotherhood but the organized church as a capitalist institution participating in the exploitation of man by man."

"Religion is a class question. If one denies that then one isn't a Marxist. I can see that you are after all still a Catholic."

That would be news to Cardinal Spellman, I thought. Red or Christian, a dogmatist makes a dreary conversationalist. I dropped the discussion. But I was once more reminded by it that Chinese Communists are in general far less concerned with problems of reconciling socialism and religious thought than are Communists of the West.

In Kunming, some time later, I noticed on the wall of the old Seventh Day Adventist compound a large and recently repainted sign in white Chinese characters: "Jesus Saves Sinners." When I expressed curiosity at this "relic" of proselytization, my Eastern companion, a young professor of Kunming's new Institute of Minority Nationalities, refreshed my memory that *tsui-jen,* as the word "sinner" is translated, is also the Chinese word for "criminal." The language has no exact equivalent for the Western concept of sinner.

"We all believe in saving *tsui-jen,*" he added wryly. "The rains will eventually wash that sign away, as they will religion itself. In the meantime, it does no harm."

It is too early to be so sure about that, I thought. Marxism is in solid at the moment, but the rains are indifferent to the slogans of the religions they erase.

73

Literature and Music

Not much need be said about literature in the People's Republic to date; its condition is roughly analogous to that in the Soviet Union before the "thaw" of 1956. Writing is party-functional for most authors. At its best it involves readers in educationally useful facts; at its worst it is vulgar propaganda.

China has produced great literature in the past and will again. Meanwhile, no one but a fool would contend that writers are free to nonconform, and the last person to say so would be Mao Tse-tung. In his famous *Talks at the Yenan Forum on Art and Literature* in 1942, he made it quite clear that literary art for art's sake would not be tolerated in transitional stages of the revolution. The writer must be disciplined to "serve the masses"; that is, the party's linear view of the masses' needs.[1]

That is still the rule. Mao has privately said that absolute individ-ualist freedom of expression will be possible only in a classless world. Literally, he could be right about that; no such absolute yet exists anywhere outside mental institutions, and they also impose certain limits on exhibitionism. (Mr. Hearst finally had to silence Mr. Pegler.) Communists believe that all literature serves one set of class interests or another; objectively speaking, it makes no difference whether the writer is a conscious or an unconscious instrument. The world is flooded with as many bourgeois hacks as proletarian hacks, of course. But the view that only the party knows how to serve the masses in a socialist society makes no allowance for the role of the writer as the timeless conscience of humanity as a whole and the voice of dissent or protest against intolerable realities—an aspect of contradictions which exist between any people and its socially organized power. Mao himself has noted such contradictions in China.

New interpretations of past themes and history, such as Kuo Mo-jo's re-examinations of the characters and times of Wu Tzu-t'ien and Ch'in Shih Huang Ti, in opera and drama, are unquestionably art which could not have found any legal audience in the old China. Such works are essentially prerevolutionary in their inspiration, however; their black-and-white overstatements of the virtues of effigies burned in the former society have no comment to make on immediate truths of the new society. In the past we saw one side of the thing and now we see the reverse side, but even if the reverse side is more attractive, still it is not the whole thing. Both the revolutionary dictatorship and the counterrevolutionary dictatorship are highly subjective in their attitudes toward art; neither can permit anything good to be said on behalf of the devil any more than the religious order can.

Under Kuomintang society the writer of any importance was persecuted, driven underground, and sometimes killed. (A few were buried alive.[2]) While he breathed, his work had the meaning of an individual conscience. He helped to expose and reject despotic idiocies of the old order; he served by quickening general awareness of the "becoming" beyond the "being." The present society has corrected some of the ignorance pitilessly exposed by Lu Hsun and his disciples. Yet if Lu Hsun lived with the same courage in the same frail body today he would not be able to project life beyond the idiocies and tyrannies in the current set of value-realities—*not before the party itself begins to rectify them.* He would not be buried alive; probably he would not even be imprisoned, as happens periodically to Djilas, in Yugoslavia. But he would certainly be obliged to attempt thought remolding. The artist is thus condemned to silence or to the repetition of party truisms —until self-criticism works its way to the top and a new set of collective truisms receives official sanction.

Still less, however, have any Chinese writers in exile produced any noteworthy literature. Hongkong bourgeois Chinese periodicals and books, for example, are filled with the old prewar puerilities of China or they imitate slick Western prose and poetry just as irrelevant. It can hardly be otherwise, since these writers have left their own ecology. The writer in China meanwhile retains roots in a living society and will one day originate again.

Nonconformist art is an introspective luxury which only relatively affluent and stable societies can afford. Whether led by church or state, reformations are always bigoted. If revolution is a new birth, postrevolution inevitably involves growing pains and adolescence; the artist who was creative when he was helping to make the revolution cannot expect to find the child born with an understanding of his adult view of the human experience. The new society is still engaged in a war of survival, and the individual who breaks ranks can help to provoke collective disaster. "Those who know must lead"; if those who "know" are not those responsible for the newly organized power, the latter must nevertheless demand conformance even at the expense of contradicting themselves as fathers of the revolution—by silencing the very voices of dissent which might save them from tragic error.

In an epoch of this kind literature does have a prosaic but noble function, however. That is to teach, to educate, to enlighten the dark corners of imprisoned minds formerly denied both the simplest liberating truths of universal practical knowledge and an appreciation of classical art and literature. In this respect Chinese literature is of incomparably greater mass service than in the past.

Another means of world communication recently opened up in China is the widespread teaching of Western as well as Eastern music and technique. It is making contributions of lasting value, quite apart from the overlay of changing slogans of the time. A good way to sense the enrichment music is now bringing to Chinese culture is to spend a day at the Shanghai Conservatory. Apart from the cosmopolitanism of the medium itself, it was a pleasure to me to hear English and French freely spoken by so many Conservatory faculty members.

One of the attractions was Chu Ying-hu, a grave little girl violinist, aged twelve, who had first attended the conservatory's spare-time school for children three years earlier. Her father was a middle school teacher, her mother worked in an agricultural research institute. What was her ambition? "To serve the people—with good music." She played a Chopin étude very nicely, bowed and made way for Hsu Fei-ping.

Hsu Fei-ping was eleven, and he came from Amoy, in South China. His mother was a musician, they had a piano in their home—no average home—and he had begun to play when he was five. Fei-ping's teacher in Amoy had recommended him to the school, where he had been a boarding student for two years. He had already given two public concerts. He played a selection from Mozart with skill and dignity, then bowed to three girl *p'i-p'a* players who succeeded him. The *p'i-p'a* is a native Chinese instrument something like a zither.

Dressed in red corduroy slacks and white blouses, hair bobbed, they were a poised, charming trio. One was the daughter of a bus conductor and another came from an official's family; the mother of the third was a widow who worked in a silk filature. All three were born the "year of the flood," 1949, and had no memory of a presocialist China. Their exquisite performance would have brought down any house in the West.

One child followed another, and then a large chorus of them. "Socialism is good . . ."

Four sixteen- and seventeen-year-old girls in blue serge skirts, white silk blouses and black pumps played something from Handel on three violins and one cello. Applause won an encore of a Cantonese folk song arranged by a faculty member. The violins were made in the school workshop, tones true and clear. A Tibetan woman of twenty-two, Chaidan Choma, with a fine natural soprano, sang her own highland songs and then a fragment from *Carmen*. She was a large, imposing figure in her bright native costume hung with silver and turquoise ornaments under a smile and a pile of thick glossy hair.

"She was a serf," explained Tan Hsu-chen, vice-director of the conservatory, a violinist and instrument maker. "Her voice was famous among the peasants, she used to sing in the fields at work. One of our teachers sent her back to us. She could not read when she arrived two years ago. After another two years she will return to teach music in Tibet." The school had three other Tibetan students, as well as a dozen youths nominated for their talent by the Mongol, Li, Yao and Chuang minority peoples.

The Shanghai Conservatory was established by foreign sponsors early in this century and provided the nucleus for a prewar symphony orchestra which I used to hear under the leadership of an able Italian maestro named Paci. Tan Hsu-chen had been a violinist in that orchestra and at the outset was its only Chinese member. Old Shanghai had many private music teachers and was the music center of China. But those who could afford to study Western instruments found employment chiefly limited to hotels and dance orchestras. Beyond a few treaty ports, Western and even modern Chinese music had few audiences.

The Shanghai Conservatory of today, vastly enlarged and run on socialist principles, is still a leading school of the nation but it has a lot of new company. I have referred to a renaissance in the theater and performing arts. In the teaching of music and music appreciation the growth is so remarkable and widespread that anything I have to say on the subject can be no more than a footnote for comprehension. Even in small village kindergartens I saw pianos in use, and kindergartens which had none ardently aspired to them. China may become one of the great musical nations of the world; its music is already astonishing in originality and variety of style and its blending of techniques of East and West.

There are now literally hundreds of orchestras of Chinese and Western instruments fingering both scales and kinds of music, and at least a score of these are capable of professional symphonic performances. The armed forces, most large municipalities, universities and great factories (unlikely places such as shipyards and steel mills) have orchestras and choruses of varying quality. With a decade of teaching and practice behind them, some are now quite good. Europeans in Peking in 1960 who heard the Central Orchestra play Beethoven's *Ninth Symphony* acclaimed it as first rate.

To list some of the musical performers I myself heard: the Central (Peking) Experimental Opera Orchestra; the Central Symphony; the Shanghai Symphony; the Central Broadcasting Symphony; the Army Symphony; the Navy Symphony; the Yunnan Folk Music Orchestra; the Inner Mongolian Song and Dance Ensemble; the Folk Institute Orchestra of Peking; the Peking Chorus, the Shanghai Chorus, the Army Song and Dance Ensemble; the Children's Chorus of Peking; and—one of the most popular—the Chorus Corps of the Central Security Forces!

The Shanghai Symphony Orchestra, which is still sponsored by the conservatory, has the oldest tradition, dating from Paci's day, and its partisans call it the nation's best.

"We had fourteen pianos here at the time of liberation," Director Tan told me. "Today we have more than five hundred. Most of them are made in China. We make good pianos now, although our grands are not yet quite good enough for concert work. We need more pianos—and more space. That's why"—he pointed to an uncompleted four-story brick and stone building on the campus—"we're all working to finish the new hall over there. Besides our child students we have 700 students in a middle school and 650 enrolled in the higher institute of the conservatory for four years plus a year of graduate study."

From its original building on a small plot the conservatory has expanded to include more then ten acres of classrooms in converted residences—one of them Mme Chiang Kai-shek's—and new buildings constructed by student labor with some professional help. Mme Chang Hui-chih, principal of the children's school of music, is the wife of the conservatory director, who was off on a visit to Kiangsi with some students recording folk music. The conservatory is not only the home of the symphony orchestra and a folk music instrumental orchestra; it records, broadcasts, collects musical archives, experiments with new instruments, and revives and improves ancient Chinese instruments out of use since the Mongol Dynasty. Mme Chang herself is a violin maker. She showed me an exquisite miniature violin she had made as a model.

"Our children's school is the largest, but there is another such school in Peking and one in Kwangsi," said Mme Chang. "To qualify for entrance exams? Children must be recommended by primary school teachers. We take full-time students from the fourth grade on and have a current enrollment of 106. Those from out-of-town are boarding students; the majority are day students. Tuition? Free. All expenses are paid except food, 12 yuan a month; those whose parents can't pay may receive full scholarships. Difficult to qualify? Last year we had more than a thousand recommendations. We were able to take only 60."

Child students get a general education and must pass standard exams to graduate. They work long hours: 8:00 A.M. to 4:00 P.M. Besides basic instruction in music and composition they may specialize in piano, violin, cello, flute, or one of the standard Chinese strings: p'i-p'a, yang-ch'in, yueh-ch'in, and others. The full-time faculty in the children's school is thirty-five, including thirty instructors who also teach in regular schools. Graduation qualifies children to enter the middle school of music, where they spend seven years and then go into the conservatory's college.

Beginning at seven, children may take instruction in spare-time music classes held twice a week. Enrolled in such classes, at all levels, were 1,400 students, including adult workers and factory choruses.

I had intended to spend only a morning at the conservatory. By late afternoon I had seen only a small part of the "plant" and met only a few of the senior faculty members and advanced students. There were nineteen laureates among the faculty; a number had studied and won honors abroad. Li Shih-chiang, whom I encountered in a vegetable patch, was a pianist of twenty-three who had taken prizes in concerts at Vienna and Bucharest. In one studio I met Ho Chan-ho, co-composer of the violin concerto *Liang Shan-p'o and Chu Ying-t'ai*, based on the ancient and beautiful Ningpo operetta whose theme is comparable to that of *Romeo and Juliet*. Ying Shing-ching, a pianist of nineteen, was a prize-winner at Prague and Warsaw, where he played *Lucky River*, composed by a faculty member, Hsiao Pai. I did not at first recognize Wei Cheng-tung, China's greatest p'i-p'a player. When I asked him what had happened to the beard I remembered, he said he had cut it off after the revolution was successful, when he "began a second life."

Kao Shih-lan, nicknamed "Ch'i-tan Kao" (a delicious Chinese custard) for reasons obscure to me, sang a duet with Chaidan Choma. Miss Kao is one of China's two most celebrated sopranos. She may be remembered at Juilliard, in New York, under her maiden name, Chia Lan-ko. She studied there until her return to China in 1948. Her husband, a New York University graduate, is now a professor in Shanghai University.

Here an aside seems necessary, in view of Western notions that all Chinese singing is falsetto. Some leading roles in classical operas were taken by female impersonators when women were banned from the stage, but even before the war this practice was becoming obsolete. The trend in today's theater is "natural," with male and female parts played by men and women and sung accordingly, as anywhere else. An outstanding exception is the eccentric and traditionally all-female Ningpo Theater, which produces the Chinese *Romeo and Juliet* mentioned above. It is, curiously enough, closer to Western dramatic form and staging and more easily comprehended and appreciated by foreigners than most Chinese opera.

"Don't tell me you're a gardener, too." I was speaking to Chou Hsiao-yen, the other "most celebrated" soprano. Daintily clad and lovely to look at, in a black velvet gown, wearing modest make-up with a dash of lipstick emphasis, she seemed right out of a stage dressing room. She smiled agreeably and said, "You should see me in my working clothes on the farm. We all spend a month a year helping the peasants and learning from them. I was frightened to death of it the first time, but now we look forward to it as the best fun we have. We are better artists and composers and closer to the people."

It was hard to believe that many peasants would let Hsiao-yen soil her hands but I was told she had laid her quota of bricks on the new school dormitory. (In a fine gloved hand, no doubt; Chinese are not quite so impractical as to insist that artists and instrumentalists ruin their hands and fingers; they are given light tasks involving little danger of injury.) I had first heard her sing a new arrangement of Hsieh Hsing-hai's *Yellow River Cantata.* Then I met Meng Po, a composer and former director of the conservatory, who was now head of the Shanghai Cultural Bureau. It was at a performance of the operetta *Storm Over the Yangzte,* in which Mme Chou starred. When I expressed a wish to know her story, Meng Po had arranged my visit to the conservatory.

"My story? That's simple," she said now, "and brief."

Chou Hsiao-yen spoke English and French. A native of Hankow, she had studied in Shanghai until she met Nieh Erh,* China's greatest popular composer. She then joined Nieh's wartime traveling Troubadours, who pioneered modern music in China.

"In 1939 my family sent me to France for further voice study," she continued. "I was caught there in the war and couldn't escape. I lived with French friends in Biarritz until liberation; then I went to Paris and studied and did concert work. After our Shanghai victory I returned, in 1949. I met my husband here when I was making a picture at the Shanghai film studio. He's chief director there. Chang Chun-hsiang. He's a Yale graduate but in spite of that we lived happily ever after. That's about all—except that I'm terribly glad I came back. We have our problems, but right now this is the most exciting and creative place in the world to be. I wouldn't live anywhere else."

The Cultural Bureau chief, Meng Po, arrived and organized an

* Besides the operetta I heard, Nieh Erh's many stirring compositions include the "March of the Volunteers," which is now China's national anthem. He died at the age of twenty-four, a hero widely mourned by patriotic youth.

impromptu concert. He brought together a forty-piece orchestra and a women's string quartet, a violin soloist, a flutist, two piano soloists, a harpist and a girl *p'i-p'a* trio, with apologies for being able to offer no more on short notice. For two hours I heard brief selections from Bach, Chopin, Brahms and Prokofiev; after that, assorted works of Chinese composers—concertos, folk songs, love songs, political songs.

The mellow and dreamy playing of the Chinese flute enchanted me. I was introduced to Lu Tsung-lin, and learned that his name was famous among millions of radio listeners as the "pedicab flutist." He had picked up flute playing by ear in his youth, learned to make his own flutes, composed ballads, and endured constant scolding from an aging mother for wasting his time playing when he should have been pulling passengers to buy rice. Ten years ago a music teacher had heard him playing on the street, recognized his talent, and put him in the conservatory. An illiterate then, he was now a concert artist, instructor, and composer of duets widely played at home and in Eastern Europe.

Tan Hsu-chen took me to see his factory, which was stocked with carefully selected varieties of pine, redwood, lapwood, ivory, ebony and horn. He himself had studied violin making in his youth from an old master, and now he also taught a conservatory course on the subject. I saw about a hundred skilled workers and student amateurs who were making and repairing violins, violas, cellos, oboes, clarinets, brass instruments, reeds and strings. Chinese are among the world's finest artists in wood, ivory, bone and metal; there is no reason to doubt their ability to excel in the making of musical instruments. I was especially impressed with a room where four dragon-headed harps were taking their final coats of gold. Beside their refinement of detail, the French original, still used as a model, looked somewhat crude and jaded.

"French harps cost us about 2,000 yuan each," said Tan. "We make ours for, I think, about—" His eyes closed in his thin face while he calculated. "Yes, for a little more than half that—and we add minor improvements."

"I see for one thing," I said, "that you use rampant dragons for your crown piece instead of the conventional angels. Obviously you aren't going to try to sell those in America."

"Oh, no, they are for China." He grimaced. "Our harpists play Bach even better without the angels."

Over good Fukien tea with Tan and others I expressed my thanks and pleasure. Modern music had come a long way in China since that first performance of Hsieh Hsing-hai's *Yellow River Cantata* in Yenan, back in 1939. Fresh from Russia then, Hsieh was thirty-four, and it was his first major wartime composition. I happened to be in Yenan for its debut before an audience of roughly clad students and soldiers of the Eighth Route Army, and an overflow crowd of peasants.

"That was a weird orchestra Hsieh put together," I reminisced. "The Catholic church organ for a piano, two or three violins, a home-made cello or two, some Chinese flutes, clarinets, *yang-ch'ins* and *hu-ch'ins,* improvised instruments of some kind made of old Standard Oil tins with gut strung over them, a few pieces of battered brass, cymbals, army drums and trumpets. Did he also use a few cannon? Somehow he got his melody and his fugue out of them. Before he be-gan he told what the cantata was all about, scene by scene, move-ment by movement; the whole epic of the historic river down to the enemy invasion, the struggle to hold the banks, and the proph-ecy of victory, revolution, liberation. He was passionately sincere about it. The audience listened raptly to the mystifying half-Western, half-Asian noises. In that starlit night you could almost feel the Yellow River itself joining in the final roar of the cantata—and the Japanese were not far beyond. At the end of it people wept and cheered.

"I wish," I added, "that Hsieh could have lived to hear your mag-nificent full orchestration of his composition today."

"Hsieh was indeed a talent," one of them said quietly. "You West-erners taught a few of our bourgeoisie some music, but it was Hsieh and those who followed him into Yenan—and the students they trained—who were the first to bring modern music to the people. They were the bridge builders between Western and Chinese music."

Students and professors drifted in as darkness fell; our circle en-larged. They began to question me about American music. They were interested in everything: jazz, ballads, folk music, spirituals, ballet, operettas, musicals, modern and classical styles, trends, subjects, com-posers. By means of old and new recordings they knew of music and composers scarcely more than names to me. What they missed, they said, was contact with American artists.

"What a waste of this day you've made on me," I said. "There ought to be a whole team of Americans here recording, writing down your music and ideas—people who could really talk your language."

"That's true," said one, "we have a universal language."

"There ought to be a dozen teams: one for each of the arts, for science, medicine—"

"Yes, yes, yes!" a chorus approved. "We would welcome them. We'd like to send artists to America, too. Ah, but what *is* wrong with your government?"

"Do you know," asked Meng Po, "that we did invite many Ameri-cans to come to China? They did not come. Not one artist came. Is it not true that at that time your government forbade them to come?"

I had to admit the truth of that. Even today no American artist, educator or scientist could get a passport to come.

74

Crime and Punishment

The courtroom was in a former missionary compound in the Hongkew district of Shanghai, an area which China once offered as a territorial concession to the United States. (The U.S. did not wish to share in colonialism, outright; arrangements were made to transfer Hongkew to the British settlement, where American residents shared in the benefits of foreign rule as hitchhiking imperialists.) The room held about forty people, dressed in working clothes, who were already seated and quiet as church when the young judge, Mo Pen-wan, entered. He was accompanied by two "people's representatives" in their thirties, with whom the law requires a judge to confer before pronouncing sentence. I learned from my companion that Judge Mo was a machinist and labor union leader who had been given special training in a school operated by the judicial department to teach the relatively simple legal codes of the People's Courts.

Yang Kuan-fu was the name of the prisoner, aged thirty-nine. A lean, sallow-faced man with a receding chin, he was escorted into the room and stood at attention before the elevated bench. Yang and his defense lawyer listened as the prosecutor read his summation of the charges:

"You were arrested on September 14, 1960. As a former special policeman under the Kuomintang regime you intrigued with gangsters to blackmail, intimidate and rob citizens, having in instances beaten them. After liberation you stayed on in Shanghai, failed to report your past misdeeds, donned civilian clothes, and took a job with the light and power company. Your duties were to collect bills owed for repairs and maintenance. During the past two years you embezzled 1,527 yuan by falsifying receipts. These facts were first reported by your fellow workers. After your arrest an investigation confirmed the facts, to which you have confessed. Accordingly you are brought to trial under Article Three of the Legal Code. Do you admit your guilt and acknowledge your confession?"

After the prisoner had replied in the affirmative Judge Mo questioned him directly:

Q. "What did you do before Liberation?"

A. "I was a policeman in Chiang Kai-shek's Loyalty Gendarmerie, engaged in political and intelligence work. Aside from that I arrested and tortured people to extract money from them, part of which I kept for myself. I helped carry out some looting also. With others, I took part in a few highway robberies . . ."

This curious confession, indicating a reversal of roles between policeman and criminal, may be explained by conditions at the end of Kuomintang rule (to which I have referred earlier), when the gendarmerie seized, tortured and extracted gold and precious articles from prominent citizens before Shanghai was evacuated.[1]

Q. "When did you take your present job?"

A. "In 1957. I began embezzling on a small scale but soon took as much as thirty yuan at a time. My method was to write one figure on the top receipt but a different and lower one on the carbon copy."

Several witnesses appeared against the accused. Judge Mo instructed them briefly: "Tell the truth. Do not exaggerate. Do not try to protect the accused." The first witness was a worker who asserted that Yang had come to his factory thirty-five times to collect for repairs. A total of 487.82 yuan had been paid to him. The next witness, an accountant in Yang's office, testified that the accused had remitted only 109.34 out of the total mentioned. Becoming suspicious, he had gone to the factory, compared receipts, and discovered the discrepancy. Two more factory representatives provided similar evidence. Most of the audience consisted of men and women workers from the defrauded factories and organizations. They were attending the trial to see that justice was done and to report back to their groups.

When the defendant had admitted all the accusations the Judge asked him whether he realized that he had been robbing the working people and his own family, and whether he realized the seriousness of his crime. He said that he did, and added: "While the whole country is going forward I have been leaping backward. The government had given me a new way of life despite my corrupt past life. I was not satisfied with ample wages. I was greedy and wanted more."

The prosecutor then demanded maximum punishment in accordance with the law. The accused had not voluntarily confessed his crimes. Even after his fellow workers had discovered the first instance of embezzlement, the previous May, he had refused to help them by admitting his other crimes. Only after they had gathered all the evidence and had him arrested had he confessed to the police.

Judge Mo next heard from the defense attorney, who spoke in the following sense:

"The accused has confessed and expressed his regret. Article Three is two-sided. It provides for punishment but also for reform through education. With us it is a principle to be lenient to those who repent and to be severe with those who do not. After his arrest the accused did quickly confess and confess thoroughly. After a trip in the country-side he himself has seen how everyone is working to build the country up while he was tearing it down. This is true even in his own family. Now he feels ashamed. We should consider the corrupt life he formerly lived and make allowances. I consider his attitude relatively good. I would recommend leniency."

Judge Mo turned to the prisoner, who was visibly shaking. "Have you anything to say?" Yang replied in a quavering voice with one sentence only: "I shall do my best to carry out whatever punishment is given to me and to reform myself into a morally fit citizen."

Court was recessed while the judges conferred. It took no longer than a cigarette smoke. In the courtyard I spoke to a young electrician who knew some English. He had worked in the same office with Yang. I asked him what Yang had done with the money he stole.

"He spent it on expensive restaurants where capitalists go. Of course when someone saw him in those places we began to get suspicious. He got hold of some bad women, too, and he wanted money to sleep with them. Prostitutes? No. But there are still some women around who will make love for money."

Yang could have got ten years for embezzlement. I asked the worker what his group thought would be fair in this case. "If he had confessed to us when we first got the evidence on him he might have been given only a year. Now—he may get five years." When court reconvened, Judge Mo again reviewed the facts. Then he compared life in the corrupt Shanghai of the past with the present and said that allowances must be made.

"The crime was serious but the prisoner has now fully confessed and seems ready to rehabilitate himself. We consider that after some re-education he can still do something useful in society. Our sentence," he ended, "is three years."

The prisoner was notified that he had a right to file an appeal within ten days. The court then adjourned. Everyone seemed satisfied.

In a moment the place was empty. I stared at the gray brick walls of the old compound where missionaries probably had sung hymns and prayed for man's redemption in the past. Then I walked down the gray October streets past the gray Whangpoo River to Mr. Sassoon's former hotel.

75

The Triple Cities

At the Hankow airport I was met by Li Chao, a short, round, energetic party stalwart in his mid-thirties. He was evidently a kind of man Friday to Li Chih, a member of the city council and local party secretariat, with whom I had an interview over a pot of tea. Li Chih was the mayor's protocol chief; a college graduate, he knew some English and had a modest and agreeable way of speaking, less cluttered with political clichés than most.

Li Chao, "the Short," was a former "little Red devil." He told me he had joined the anti-Japanese guerrillas in Shantung at the age of twelve. Thereafter "the army was father and mother" to him. In 1949, Liu Shao-ch'i sent him with Li Chih and sixty other young men to begin the reconstruction of Hankow. "At that time living space was so scarce here all sixty of us lived in four rooms." Housing had "more than doubled" since then. Li Chao spoke of new factories, schools, hospitals and bridges with the pride of one who had personally built all of them.

The three mid-Yangtze cities of Hankow, Wuchang and Hanyang—collectively known as Wuhan—have indeed witnessed some startling improvements. None is more pleasing to an Old China Hand than the railroad and vehicular bridges across the Han and Yangtze rivers, which have their confluence at Hankow. The Yangtze bridge, just short of a mile long, is thoroughly modern and aesthetically satisfying. Completed in 1958 with Soviet aid, it connected North and South China by rail for the first time and provided an unbroken line from Siberia to Canton.

Hankow accounts for two-thirds of Wuhan's present population of about 2,100,000. Like Shanghai, Peking and other large cities, Wuhan is now a special administrative region which integrates industrial and farm economy. The whole greater municipality covers eight *ch'u** and includes some 8,400,000 inhabitants. In the *ch'u* called Ch'ing Shan, Green Mountain, is the mammoth Wuhan Iron and Steel Works. A few years ago Green Mountain consisted of three townships of farmland with a population of 10,000. By 1961 it was a city of 210,000 industrial workers and their dependents, and 30,000 farmers whose principal task was to feed them.

The Wuhan plant is possibly the largest of all the basic projects built with Soviet aid. Work on it began in 1955 and the first steel was poured from its modern furnaces in 1958. There had been a small iron and steel works in this neighborhood as early as 1908, based on the iron reserves near neighboring Tayeh, but production was negligible and operations entirely ceased during the war. Before that, however, the Tayeh mines produced as much as 900,000 tons of iron ore annually, which was shipped almost exclusively to Japan. Foreign and Kuomintang geologists rated Tayeh's reserves as rich (50 percent iron) but limited; after 1949, thorough surveys revealed new and far more extensive deposits. It was then decided to make Hanyang the center of mid-China's largest integrated iron and steel industry. Indispensable to this are excellent deposits of coking coal in Pinghsiang, a short haul to Hanyang, which is now also connected by electric railway to the modernized and partly mechanized Tayeh mines.

Huang Ming, general manager of the big works, took me on a tour of as much as one could see in a day of its workshops, furnaces, power and cement plants, laboratories, schools, housing and recreational areas. A Shansi University student who joined the Paluchun in 1937, Huang received postwar training at the Anshan steel works, where most of Wuhan's leading technicians were recruited. The Wuhan plant still suffered from a lack of skilled workers and technicians as well as engineers, he said. The gap would soon be filled by graduates of Ch'ing Shan's own Iron and Steel Institute, with about 5,000 full-time students (under the Ministry of Metallurgy), supplemented by spare-time technical training schools for workers.

Huang Ming gave the plant target figures for 1965 as 1,500,000 tons of steel and 1,500,000 tons of pig iron annually. Current output was stated to be already 800,000 tons each of pig iron and steel (with one main blast furnace and one giant open hearth operating), but a No. 2

* An urban administrative unit, roughly equivalent to a borough.

blast furnace was being completed well ahead of schedule which would bring output for 1961 above a million tons each. At this writing no official figures are available; curtailed capital construction investment and general industrial slow-down beginning in 1961 have kept Wuhan's output lower than expected, I am told by a more recent visitor.[1]

To a nonspecialist the Wuhan plant seemed at least as efficient in layout and operations as the modern plant of the Nippon Steel Company, of about the same capacity, which I visited near Tokyo in 1959. Rather superior to the latter, however, were the Wuhan works' arrangements for housing and integrated community facilities. Large blocks of well-spaced three-story apartments, divided by the usual tree-lined streets, provided more than a million square meters of living space. Buildings were of about the same standard as those I saw around many state factories; accommodations varied according to size of family and income. Monthly wages averaged 65 yuan per worker, ranging from 32 yuan for apprentices to 107 for skilled technicians and as high as 230 for engineers.

In this instance, I asked to see the apartment of an engineer's family. In a building which housed fourteen families I entered, late one afternoon, a flat (two bedrooms, tiny kitchen, toilet and shower) occupied by a family of six persons. One son, aged fifteen, was home from middle school; he wore a gray corduroy jacket, slacks, and serviceable shoes; beside him stood his grinning sister, aged seven, in a bright yellow sweater. Another son, of fourteen, was still at school, as was another daughter, aged nine; both were doing Red Pioneer duties, the mother explained. She described her husband as a graduate engineer of the Peking Iron and Steel Institute, who earned 175 yuan a month. She herself, a primary school graduate, worked part time in a commune factory where she was paid 24 yuan. They ate their noon and evening meals at canteens; they had breakfasts and Sunday meals at home. Their monthly budget: canteen food, 70 to 80 yuan (rations, 25 to 40 pounds each); nonrationed food and miscellaneous, 30 yuan; clothing, books, "extras," 10 to 20 yuan; rent, including utilities, 11 yuan; savings, 36 yuan. Why "36"? State savings bonds were 4 yuan each; they were buying nine bonds a month. Could they cash the bonds, I asked. "When we need the money," answered the mother. "Meanwhile, it helps build socialism."

Undoubtedly the greatest local consumer of Green Mountain steel was the Wuhan Heavy Machine Tool Factory, operating since 1958, when 46 sets of heavy machine tools were made. In 1959 output rose to 369 sets; the target for 1960 was 670 sets. "Heavy" meant such things as portal lathes weighing up to 480 tons and a metal cutter on a bed 125 feet long, which I saw in production. Milling machines, grinders, casters and many other cutting tools were being turned out on a scale entirely new for a city that could not make a modern machine tool of any kind when I had last visited it. Time permitted me to see only a small part of this plant, which covered 500,000 square meters and employed 7,500 workers.

Here I was told that 80 percent of all adult workers attended spare-time schools; their average age was twenty-three. The factory also operated a part-time school for 800 youths aged sixteen to eighteen. At seventeen they did two months in the shop, eight months in classroom work, and had two months vacation; at eighteen they worked half-time at the bench, half-time in school. Food, quarters and an allowance of 3 yuan monthly were provided until they became full-time workers, at eighteen. Wages began at 33 yuan, with a top of 107, plus the usual welfare benefits. The site of the plant was formerly a swamp; this now drained into a lake on whose shores were an auditorium where weekly dances were held (20 percent of the workers were women), a football field and a boating pavilion. Orchestras, bands, athletic teams, theatrical troops and various clubs were part of the organized social life. After a farewell party given to the last three Soviet experts on their departure, a few weeks previously, the big factory was now entirely Chinese run. Eighty percent of its machines were Chinese made, 20 percent imported.

As an industrial city Wuhan's requirements for education and health facilities were recognized in planning that is making it one of China's more advanced cities in those respects. Many new sanatoria and rest homes for workers have sprung up along the shores of Tung Ting, the nation's largest natural lake. The most significant additions to China's third-largest educational center are the T'ung Chi Medical College and hospitals. These are already the focus of a network of smaller hospitals and clinics and a new county health system. I found T'ung Chi's pediatrics hospital and general hospital graceful ultramodern structures; they had a staff of about 250 doctors, of whom 92 were women. With 150 full-time professors and lecturers, aided by nearly 300 part-time lecturers from Wuhan University, the T'ung Chi Medical College had a current enrollment of 3,200 students, besides 460 studying in night school and several thousand enrolled in pre-medical correspondence courses.

Wuhan's economic, cultural and political life are of importance far greater than the space devoted to it here might suggest, but many Western scientists and other specialists have published their observations about it. The city is after all on the main "tourist circuit"—Peking-Shanghai-Hankow-Canton.

76

Szechuan, "The Heavenly Land"

Chungking lies about 1,000 miles west of Shanghai as our four-engine Soviet plane flew it, and nearly twice that far if one travels by boat up the Yangtze. I had not seen Chungking since 1943, when it was China's war capital. It is the largest city (now about 2,200,000) in Szechuan, which is a simply fabulous land. If Szechuan were a separate continent instead of a landlocked province clinging to the eaves of Tibet, it might in itself be a world power. It has an extraordinary abundance of nearly all the resources required by a major nation and a variety of climate—Himalayan to subtropical—that makes it possible to grow any product cultivated anywhere in all China. Since the pre-Christian era Szechuan has been known to the Chinese as "the heavenly land," but man has often contrived to make it hell on earth.

Including Sikang (recently joined to Szechuan) the province is 220,-000 square miles in area,[1] or slightly larger than France. In 1957 its population was officially put at 72,000,000; in 1962 it probably reached 80,000,000, or more than that of Germany. Half again larger than Japan, it produces much more rice than Japan, or about one-fourth of all the rice grown in China. It has more rainfall and water than it needs—not always properly distributed—and it holds one of the world's great potentials of hydroelectric power. Blessed by numerous streams and rivers (*Sze-ch'uan* means "four rivers") it normally produces a large food surplus. If China's transportation system were adequate to effect speedy distribution, this province alone might export enough food to alleviate chronic shortages in the alternately typhoon-swept and drought-stricken areas of the East and South.

At the end of a twenty-mile drive over a macadam road from the Chungking airport—about the size of that of Dayton, Ohio—I was escorted by a China Intourist agent to Szechuan's new provincial House of the People. This assembly hall is surmounted by a massive reproduction of the Temple of Heaven, an architectural curiosity which creates in the viewer something of the same state of anxiety as a giant piece of patisserie or Mr. Wright's Guggenheim Museum. Beneath the double superstructure there is a two-story hotel, modern and comfortable. Here a room and bath, with a balcony view, cost three dollars; excellent Chinese food was comparably inexpensive. At the foot of broad steps below the edifice lay a wide plaza and opposite it was the building formerly used by Chiang Kai-shek as his state palace. It now serves as a city hall or mayor's office, where I was invited to tea and stayed to dinner the second day after my arrival.

Mayor Jen was fifty-five and bore the *ming-tzu* or given name Pei-kuo. A professional writer until 1938, he left his old master, Lu Hsun, to go to Yenan to join the Eighth Route Army. Another protégé of Liu Shao-ch'i, he was a member of the provincial party standing committee as well as responsible for the administration of West China's largest city. In reply to my request that he discuss his "most difficult problem," Mayor Jen said that it was the procuring of more food for export to needy areas of China and the means of getting it there. Peasants here were "eating too much" and "eating more than ever before"; there had been some drought but still Szechuan would have a surplus for export. I asked whether there was continuing trouble, as reported abroad, with Khamba tribesmen in the Sikang area, where the Tibetan revolt first started, in 1957. He said that the country was thoroughly pacified although isolated assassinations of Han officials still occurred.

Jen emphasized that Szechuan as a whole was still behind the advanced seaboard areas. He added, "Any fair-minded person who knew the old opium-soaked province of the past could not fail to agree that the people have changed fundamentally."

In a three-day visit I could not assess his statement nor do much more than observe transformations in Chungking and its environs. Americans who were here during the war may find difficulty in believing that it is now a relatively clean city. Paved streets have replaced dirty alleyways, and 250 miles of sewers, plus the efforts of sanitary squads in every block, have dethroned and almost eliminated the rats. Broken stone stairways down which one used to slip precariously, or ride in a human-borne chair to the river front, have been rebuilt and chairs disappeared along with rickshaws. A steep truck road leads to the pier and there is a new funicular railway. The large new gymnasium, a municipal stadium (capacity 50,000), and a park and a "palace of culture and rest," have given the hilltop something like a city center. Around it are scattered some twelve institutes of higher learning, ranging from the university to a medical college, with a total enrollment of 19,000. Middle school students numbered about 200,000, in addition to 30,000 enrolled in half-time agricultural middle schools operated in three suburban counties now included in greater Chungking.

Mayor Jen asserted that housing in the city proper had "more than doubled" in ten years. Much of the new is shoddy in appearance and bamboo structures still line the river bluffs. In the growing industrial suburbs one now sees quite large substantial brick apartment buildings, four to six stories high, surrounded by vegetable gardens and trees. From the outside they appear as good as similar conventional structures in the West but they are cheaply finished within. Vastly better housing than workers hereabouts knew in the past, such apartments are as yet available to only a small percentage of the population.

Beyond doubt the greatest single change in Chungking and the rest of the province is the shattering of Szechuan's traditional isolation by the opening up of modern communications. "Szechuan has probably been more hampered by inadequate transportation than any other single factor," wrote George B. Cressey in his prewar and still highly valuable study, *China's Geographic Foundations*. "The movement of agricultural and mineral products together with other commerce requires an abnormally large number of people . . . Animals are rare, carts unknown, railroads but dreams, canals impossible, and the rivers too swift . . . Overland traffic is usually borne on the backs of men, whether it consists of coal from the many mines, pigs en route to market, or pilgrims on their way to the sacred mountains of Omei Shan. The 'roads' are merely narrow trails, paved with slabs of stone about three feet wide . . . As Beach has said, man is 'the universal animal, the omnibus of commerce and the pack mule of the race. It is cheaper to wear men down than to keep the roads up.'" [2]

Surveys and plans to connect Chungking, the greatest river trading port (where the Chialing joins the Yangtze), with Chengtu, the provincial capital and center of the richest region in the Chengtu basin, were made more than fifty years ago. Except for a few miles of track laid by the former government, however, nothing had happened before 1949. Under the new regime the Chungking-Chengtu railway (300 miles) was constructed in two years and began operating in 1953. By 1956 the longer (415 miles) and far more difficult Chengtu-Paochi railway was opened for traffic. Involving tens of tunnels through the Min mountains, it connects Szechuan to the Northwest and all parts of northern China.

Other railways are being pushed southward. One traverses Kwei-chow province and is approaching Yunnan, to provide a route to the Vietnam frontier. The Chungking-Hankow railway, said to be about one-third completed, will eventually join Szechuan to the middle Yangtze Valley—until now accessible only by small river boats which shoot the precarious Yangtze rapids on a 780-mile journey to Hankow. Some highways were built under the Kuomintang; the 1949 total of 4,920 miles had been tripled by 1960. Most impressive of the new arteries is the 1,400-mile road from Ya-an, near Chengtu, to Lhasa, one of three China-Tibet highways built since 1949. Over it went the made-in-Chungking generators which established Lhasa's new power plant.

Although thousands of trucks, rubber-tired carts and railway cars now crawl across the face of Szechuan, man is still an indispensable pack mule. Ten times more road mileage is needed and ten times more wheels. Szechuan has been rapidly industrializing to provide these and other means of modern transport. Chungking and its environs are the major heavy industrial base but machinery is being manufactured in many other cities. Szechuan's lone steel plant produced a pre-1949 peak of 8,000 tons of steel. By 1959 the province claimed an output of 1,060,000 million tons of iron and 700,000 tons of steel.[3] Chungking is said to be the nation's largest producer of railway rails and is an important source of machine tools.

Szechuan may by 1970 be industrially self-sufficient. It is now believed to hold China's largest coal reserves; coking coal is plentiful and conveniently located near iron ore. Newly discovered deposits in Yenpien (near the Yunnan border) are reported alone sufficient to satisfy foreseeable iron requirements of local heavy industry.[4] Oil wells are being exploited in Neichiang and Yuehchih, where natural gas is abundant, and uranium deposits are probably second only to those in Turkestan. Szechuan has significant reserves of copper, lead and asbestos, all of which are now being mined; it has long been an exporter of salt.

Rewi Alley's description of an exhibit in Chengtu catches some of the atmosphere of popular awe and enthusiasm for dawning industrialization which I felt in many hinterland places—its paradox, its incongruity, its naïveté. "In the industrial exhibit there were queues waiting to enter," he wrote, "middle-aged and even old women with bound feet, country farmers with long blue gowns and white turbans, city folk and innumerable youngsters. They were fascinated with the exhibits, many of which were simplifications of machine tools which could be easily built by the communes." An "eager group was gathered around the shiny new bicycles made in Chengtu. One section was devoted to precision tools made by the Chengtu Precision Tool Works. There was one of the big boilers I saw the girls making a couple of days ago, and then again a section for musical instruments in which there were some beautifully polished dark wood pianos." [5] Elsewhere, Alley counted up seven different factories in Szechuan making accordions.

Mountain-rimmed by ranges which in the west reach to the lordly height of Minya Konka, at 25,000 feet, and in the northwest to the 10,000-foot Min Shan, Szechuan lowers on the south and east to hill ranges and upland folds which form the gorges of the upper Yangtze. The central part of the province is a basin which was once a vast lake. Here the rich alluvial soil is scores of feet deep, over a red sandstone base, and fertile and easily plowed. The "red basin" ranges from 1,500 feet above sea level in the valleys to 4,000 feet in the mesas or flat hilltops peculiar to the region, which gets 35 to 40 inches of rainfall annually. Frost is rare, the farming season is ten months, and double cropping is general. A recent report states that one-fifteenth of the area of Szechuan is now under cultivation and that 48 percent of that is irrigated. [6] Besides the staple rice and wheat, major crops are cotton, sugar cane, delicious citrus fruit—Szechuan is the home of the mandarin orange—bamboo, rape, tobacco and tung oil.

Even the sober Dr. Cressey, not given to superlatives when he eyes China's resources, described the Min plain in the red basin as "one of the loveliest garden spots on earth" and concluded that "nowhere in the world is there a more fertile, productive, or thickly populated agricultural area of similar size." [7] Characteristic of Szechuan, long stairways of rice terraces fall from hillsides as steep as 45 degrees, and the narrow flooded plots are a million mirrors flashing in the sun. Below them varied crops of green and gold in the valleys make a checkerboard pattern; innumerable waterfalls rain down from coniferous forests into fern and bamboo groves bright with exotic flowers and tropical birds. High overhead cloud-dimmed peaks beckon from the Tibetan plateau. Not surprisingly, Szechuan has produced painters and poets since ancient times.

"The region offers a magnificent home for a prosperous and progressive people," wrote Dr. Cressey in the thirties, "but like so many of the gifts of nature there are limits to its capacity . . ." He considered the population, then well under 50,000,000, already too dense to be sustained by the available land. And so it seemed. One reason: "Opium poppy is raised very widely," Dr. Cressey noted. In times of nominal "suppression" farmers were "fined . . . whether the opium was raised or not." [8] Opium consumption was almost universal; I have seen ignorant parents spread it on sugar cane and feed it to their children as a pacifier.

During the war, poppy cultivation was pushed away from areas where foreigners could see it, but when I traveled overland from Chungking to Sian in 1939 I saw opium sold in the native inns; doubtless it helped guests overlook the lice and rats. The towns abounded with scrofulous beggars. Swarms of lice-ridden and ragged or completely naked derelict children used to wait in the streets outside restaurants for guests to throw scraps from their tables and amuse themselves by watching the little beggars scramble like boys diving for pennies.

In the past one did not have to look for beggars; in self-defense, one tried to avoid them. There may be beggars in Szechuan today. I did not see any around Chungking. Waifs had disappeared from the streets. I saw no one in filthy rags although many wore patched clothing. In several other areas of China where I had seen poppies grown in the past (Paotou, Shensi, Hopei, Yunnan) there were none today. I never smelled opium in China in 1960, nor had any foreign diplomat that I asked about it. Rewi Alley, who has traveled in every part of the hinterland, told me that poppy cultivation disappeared after 1949. "There is too much need of the land," he said.

Sanitation and public health measures have brought results in Szechuan not far behind the rest of China. Chungking now had 300,000 members of "health defense" or physical culture associations. In a talk with the municipal director of sports at the central gymnasium I learned that all able-bodied persons were required to take ten minutes of exercises every day. Chungking had 20,000 basketball teams, he said. (Szechuan is Chu Teh's native province and he still plays the game, in his seventies.) There were 130,000 "qualified" (one of four grades) athletes and one of them had run the 100-meter dash in 10.3 seconds. Athletic instructors now begin to select "tall and able" children at primary school age for special instruction. I gathered that China expected to win all the Olympics; thus far, she is represented only by Taiwan. On the gym court I watched two teams of teen-age girls play some fast ball. China's national teams are now six-footers. These Chungking girls averaged five feet ten—giantesses among old Szechuanese—and short shorts and tight shirts revealed interesting anatomical progress. I asked to photograph them but I had no flash equipment and when they all trooped outside they had modestly covered themselves in pullovers and long cotton slacks. Thus I missed a picture of the best bare legs I saw in China.

Food output in Szechuan had more than doubled since the war, it was claimed;[9] at any rate food was more plentiful than elsewhere although urban rationing was strict. In Shanghai and Hankow I occasionally saw signs of malnutrition among children but I saw none in Chungking. Kindergartens and nurseries I visited at random were poorly housed and equipped (in one, a single hobby horse for twenty-two!) but the children were clean and looked healthy. At one day school I saw steamed rice and wheat rolls and soya bean milk being consumed for breakfast; in another I watched a lunch of noodles and two vegetables being served. None wolfed his food or seemed famished. Food here cost six yuan a month per child for two meals a day.

Szechuan has yet to prove that Dr. Cressey was wrong in his belief that "there are limits" beyond which population growth cannot stretch nature's bounty. Mayor Jen's comment left no doubt that the problem of urban food supply was his major headache. To extract more from the peasants, city-dwellers had to produce more things peasants wanted to buy. Nowhere else, except in Dairen and Kunming, did I see department stores as well stocked as in Chungking; a general drive to increase output for local consumption seemed to show results. Major Jen told me the "big change" was that Chungking was now "80 percent self-sufficient" in manufactured consumption goods, whereas before 1949 it had imported 80 percent of its needs.

"Needs" is here a relative term; no one should visualize Saks or Selfridge's. The largest Chungking department store was about the equivalent of the store owned and operated by the People's Republic in Hongkong, which is distinguished mainly for low prices on cheap goods. Many peasants who crowded the aisles in Chungking seemed well supplied with money. I saw a bound-footed woman buy a fur-trimmed silk brocade jacket for 60 yuan. Another consulted with her son about children's shoes, priced at 4 to 6 yuan, while she cast a side-long glance at suede shoes of good quality, offered at 14 yuan. Foreign-style printed cotton dresses were selling at 12 to 60 yuan and silk gowns at 25 to 70. Children's jumper suits cost 4 and 5 yuan, cotton shirts were 5 to 17 yuan and men's leather jackets were 90 yuan. Szechuan specializes in bamboo articles of all kinds, including paintings—in which a brisk trade was going on at prices beginning at 9 yuan.

Many of Chungking's consumer goods were being made in urban commune workshops which utilized the labor of housewives in an experiment widely tried throughout China from 1958 onwards. In Chungking, as elsewhere, the urban commune organization had its prototype in former neighborhood street committees. Many such committees had operated nurseries, canteens, clubs, household services and health stations before communes arose. These were consolidated under party leadership to form administrations covering areas as large as precincts or boroughs, much as township governments took charge of the rural communes of villages.

The principal innovation of the urban communes was the mobilization of unemployed household dependents, chiefly women, to work in handicraft or small machine factories. Most of them made consumer necessities or parts and supplies for existing state or municipal factories which they served as satellites. Very many able-bodied wives of factory workers were already employed. Commune labor was drawn especially from dependents of unskilled or semiskilled peasant workers who had drifted to the cities or been recruited during the construction drives of 1957-58. Many who had never handled a tool or machine were taught by individual handicraftsmen or small cooperatives of handicraft workers, or by workers from nearby state factories.

I saw a dozen or more urban communes all the way from Peking to Manchuria and down to Yunnan. Working conditions varied from poor to good. In Chungking I saw commune foundries smelting iron and casting metal parts in primitive unheated outdoor sheds and I very much doubted the ultimate usefulness of the product. In Manchuria I saw some efficient, well-lighted factories employing as many as several hundred women producing bicycles, precision meters, ball bearings and electrical parts that looked quite serviceable. Salaries ranged from as low as 20 yuan to 35 or 40 yuan per month. In most shops workers spent six hours at the bench and two to three hours learning characters and elementary politics, for six days a week. Sparetime elementary schools were thus integrated with productive work.

Use of communal dining facilities in Chungking was optional, as it was said to be elsewhere. The average commune family seemed to be eating the noon meal communally and the evening meal at home. Participation in theory was voluntary but strong pressure was probably brought to bear in some instances. Door-knocking in various places, I did meet stay-at-home mothers who preferred to do their own babytending and whose husbands earned good wages. For mothers with two or more children, the take-home pay, after payments for day care of their infants, obviously could offer small inducement in the poorer communes.

Seven Star Ridge Commune, in Chungking, was fairly typical of large urban communes I saw, although it was poorer than some in Shenyang, for example, where communes even operated large suburban vegetable and poultry farms. Seven Star covered the area of an average city precinct, with a total of 76,000 residents. Of these, 22,000 adults were already employed in state or municipal enterprises or services. The commune itself operated 36 small shops which employed 4,160 persons, some of them part-time, and some 1,400 of whom worked in nurseries, homes for the aged, kindergartens, health stations, dining rooms and services. Service centers did the workers' laundry, tailoring, mending and shoe repairs and sold small daily necessities and theater tickets. They also provided baby-sitters.

Seven Star's largest enterprise made electrical parts, employed about 100 workers, and had a monthly output valued at 40,000 yuan. Other shops made shoes, clothing, leather goods, bricks and bamboo products. Wages averaged only 23 yuan per person for a six-hour day, or less than half the average pay in a state factory. Seven Star, organized in September, 1958, was the second oldest urban commune in Szechuan. Its chairman showed me several shops, nurseries and restaurants, and two of its six clinics. Three graduate physicians managed the clinics and the commune's 146 health stations—really, first-aid squads. The clinics were crudely housed and the larger one had 31 beds. Services of acupuncturists and herbalists were used, as well as diagnosis and treatment by Western methods. Midwives presided over 80 percent of the births, which cost 2.50 yuan per patient, including prenatal and postnatal care. Hospital beds were 35 fen a day and food 40 fen. Both clinics I visited were stocked with contraceptives. These were displayed when I asked to see them. Pessaries cost the equivalent of thirty cents each and what are euphemistically known in America as "prophylactics, for the prevention of disease only" cost five cents.

In 1959 urban commune industries in all China were reported to have accounted for production valued at 2,000,000,000 yuan. In 1960 they were scheduled to have an output five times that large. In that year they may have employed as many as 4,000,000 women. Since then they have been reduced in numbers and output. With the sharp curtailment of state capital investment in 1961, the de-emphasis on urbanization of the economy at the expense of agriculture, and the adoption of the slogan "consolidation and improvement in quality" for industry, many commune shops were merged with municipal factories, or closed down. Between 10,000,000 and 20,000,000 people were reported shifted back from the cities and hundreds of county seats to the farms in 1961, in accordance with "priority given to agricultural production." [10] These no doubt included dependents of millions of semiskilled peasant laborers moved from urban building and other suspended construction programs.

Everywhere I inspected urban communes I was told that they were still in an "experimental stage"—in contrast to rural communes—and no one would predict a future for them. By 1962 hordes of cadres had been sent from urban centers to do farm labor and most of the commune social services and productive functions apparently had been skeletalized and placed under direct municipal administration. At this writing it is still impossible to say whether their state of arrested development is temporary or permanent.

I had a feeling of being more closely watched—or protected—in Chungking than in other places. Every time I attempted to take a walk by myself I was soon discovered by my China Intourist guide. The best I could manage was a few minutes' rummaging in stores and book stalls. I saw not a single other foreigner. Szechuan has long had a reputation for xenophobia, even toward outland Chinese, but I sensed indifference rather more than hostility. When I was introduced people were polite and often animated. But no stranger on the streets proffered me any more attention than an American tourist in provincial France gets from a Frenchman who has nothing to sell him.

77

A Few Words on Tibet

Tibet was a land I had often wished to see, but when I lived in China time and opportunity had never coincided. Now I could not make a strong case for a visit since I had already expressed a preference to retrace old paths and the Chinese knew I had never been to Tibet. Then Stuart Gelder came to Peking, to write for British papers. He was very anxious to see Tibet and we put in a joint petition for air accommodation.

It was October, heavy snow was already falling in Tibet and there was no regular plane service. China had few army planes equipped to carry passengers above the 20,000-foot level to clear the mountains safely. Chou En-lai told Gelder that if we insisted he would furnish a military plane but we might be held up weeks in Sikang by bad weather. He added that if Britain's Armstrong Vickers had been willing to sell China the high-altitude planes she had been trying to buy, the whole problem would have been simple. Gelder and I had to abandon our trip. I mention it now only because at the time I wondered why China didn't buy the planes from Russia. A few months afterward I read that Khrushchev had sold India high-altitude helicopters to patrol her Tibetan frontier. It was not until December, 1961, that Armstrong Vickers announced that five of its giant turbojets had been sold to China. The incident is one of several which suggest a curious Soviet indifference to China's side of the dispute with India over the Tibetan frontier—and Britain's quiet indifference to the American embargo against trade with China.

I could have learned little more by spending a few days in Lhasa as a guest of the Chinese authorities than Anna Louise Strong and a group of European Communist correspondents who went there in 1959, after the flight of the Dalai Lama. I had already read Miss Strong's book.[1] During her visit preparations were already under way for the land revolution, which the Communists moved up by several years after the lamas and landlords launched a rebellion. The serfs were freed and land and cattle were distributed among them—with collectivization the aim, as in China. A program for complete integration of Tibet with China is being pushed ahead with great speed.

One man in Peking could have told me a great deal about Tibetans: the Panchen Lama, or Erdeni. I saw him once at a state dinner, resplendent in his priestly yellow robes, but nothing came of my request to interview him before he returned to Tibet. The two living buddhas are the Dalai Lama and the Panchen Lama. After the Dalai Lama fled to India, the Panchen Lama, his ecclesiastical alter ego (as in times of the dual papacy), became the chief figurehead of the Chinese-organized preparatory committee for an autonomous government of Tibet.

Ever since the Manchus suppressed the great Tibetan rebellion of 1751 the ties of the Panchen have been closer to China than those of the Dalai. In that year the Emperor Ch'ien Lung sent an expedition to Lhasa after the lamas, led by the Dalai Lama, had murdered the two Chinese high commissioners—*ambans*—and massacred the entire resident Chinese population. Ch'ien Lung's retaliation was sanguinary. His troops also crossed the Himalayas and descended upon Nepal, where they defeated the Gurkas who had been raiding into Tibet. (Nepal remained a tributary state of Peking until the British established a protectorate there in the nineteenth century.) The Panchen Lama (Panchen Rimpoche) was first in the religious hierarchy of Tibet and was traditionally viewed as the direct incarnation of Buddha, whereas the Dalai Lama was the incarnation of a mere bodhisattva. Ch'ien Lung recognized the Panchen Lama as the principal figure in the political as well as the religious hierarchy, reducing the Dalai Lama to a secondary role in both departments. At that time Tibet's frontier on India, then under the loose control of the Mogul kings and their feudatory states, was roughly fixed by Ch'ien Lung near—in some places, far beyond—boundary lines claimed by China today. The subcontinent of Hindustan was then ruled by Moslem conquerors and their feudatory allies, and the united Indian nation of today, consolidated under the British, did not yet, of course, exist.

No foreign power seriously questioned China's sovereignty over

Tibet until the collapse of the Ch'ing Dynasty, when Tibetan authorities, with British encouragement, attempted a coup and proclaimed Tibet's fealty to China at an end. Chinese troops suppressed the rebellion, but in 1911, with British assistance, the Dalai Lama, returned to Lhasa from exile in India and, as the imperial power disintegrated in Peking, its *amban* was expelled from Tibet. The British never recognized Tibet as an independent state, but in 1913-14 they negotiated a tripartite convention with Chinese and Tibetan representatives at Simla. This conceded China's suzerainty over all Tibet but sought to establish the "autonomy" of Outer (western) Tibet. Peking refused to ratify the convention, however, regarding it as an infringement on claims to Tibet as "part of China." The agreement would also have settled the Indo-Tibetan border on the basis of the so-called McMahon line but its rejection left areas of the lofty frontier still undetermined.

Generations of Chinese attrition had resulted in the settlement of much of the grasslands and highlands of eastern Tibet which were loosely administered by petty potentates who divided their fealty between Lhasa and Peking. Much of Inner Tibet had thus been effectively Sinicized. During the Kuomintang period these vast regions were formally incorporated into "China proper" by the creation of two new provinces, Chinghai and Sikang, but the republican government's hold over Lhasa remained almost entirely nominal—the existence of a true national government of China itself being often in dispute.

During the Second World War China's suzerainty over Tibet was a subject of discussion between Britain, China and the United States. In an aide-memoire in 1943 the British Embassy in Washington conceded "formal Chinese suzerainty" but also wished to secure for the Lhasa government "the full enjoyment of local autonomy," and the right to "exchange diplomatic representatives with other powers."[2] In reply the State Department unequivocally declined support for the latter aim when it declared: "The Government of the United States has borne in mind the fact that the Chinese Government has long claimed suzerainty over Tibet and that the Chinese constitution lists Tibet among areas constituting the territory of the Republic of China. This Government has at no time raised a question regarding either of those claims."[3]

What has all that to do with the wretched existence of a million and a half[4] Tibetan peasants? Very little. The Tibetan would like to be free among his flocks and enjoy the fruits of his toil on the high windy plateaus of the roof of the world. Except for a brief romantic flurry, when Ronald Coleman disappeared behind the *Lost Horizon,* not many people in the West took much interest in the Tibetan's liberation or his lamas in the past. It cannot be said that the United States ever offered to send the Dalai Lama any foreign aid, technicians or even moral support when he was a subject of Kuomintang China. In any case, it is doubtful that the Dalai Lama would have let us carry out such work in competition with the system of taboos, nostrums, charms, belief in his divinity and other magic by which the lamaist hierarchy exorcised evil spirits, sold absolution, indulgences and prayer wheels, and kept their power.

The Tibetan theocracy was an anomaly which only its inaccessibility could have preserved till now. Absolute feudalism prevailed and most people were held in serfdom. The lamas and nobility owned nearly all the land, livestock and other wealth. Fear of devils and hellfire for the impious combined with barbaric torture and death for fugitives from the system kept the population in subjugation, as in other feudalisms.

None of that means that many Tibetans were not anti-Chinese and would not desire independence. They are no more likely to get it than Kashmir is likely to get a plebiscite on the same subject from India. Certainly a reform and an age of enlightenment under Tibet's own leaders was long overdue and might have salvaged something of Tibetan Buddhism, freed of its lamaistic corruptions. They waited too long for a palace revolt. Chinese Communists arrived first. They began at once to organize poor Tibetans against the lamaist system. Their aim unquestionably was the subversion of the whole ruling class. Foreseeing their inevitable doom, the lamas and landed nobles refused to play the role assigned to them in the "period of transition." They rebelled and fled into exile, thereby hastening their own downfall but not that of Tibet itself. The land, the mountains, the rivers and the people are still there—a proud people, rugged as their peaks, and likely to prove as obdurate. It would have been comforting to our consciences to think that one great nation might be spared the experience which our machine civilization has flung across the entire earth, but history admits no exceptions to its law of change. Now the Tibetans, too, must learn to adapt or perish.

Today Tibet is held by a large army and probably will be for some years to come. Former Tibetan serfs are being trained and armed and labor is being conscripted to construct public works. Schools and hospitals and barracks are being opened in the lama temples and homes, a modern Tibetan army is being trained, highways now link China and Lhasa, and the capital has its first power plant and steel mill. Tibetans who received land and property are being prepared for eventual socialization. Even without Marxism, however, mass literacy and access to science and knowledge of the modern world alone would have doomed the anachronistic Tibetan theocracy together with its prayer wheels and sorcerers.

Tibetan party members receiving technical school and higher education in China now number many thousands. Most of them began as illiterates. The great majority are being trained to teach in a mass education program in Tibet. It was only in 1962 that "the first group of Tibetan students of the preparatory specialty class of the Central

Minorities Institute [Peking] graduated" and took up "their posts in the building of a new Tibet." [5] (Most of them were geologists.) It was stated that "almost all the group" were children of serfs. Meanwhile, *Chinese* geologists, wasting no time, have been busily digging in the no longer inaccessible Tibetan mountains and have reported finding many valuable resources.

In 1954, India, having recognized the People's Republic, acknowledged its sovereignty in Tibet, as had the British government before it. Peking gave general assurances that it would respect the "autonomy" of Tibet; the manner in which it would do so was regarded as an internal affair of China. India's boundaries on Tibet remained undefined except as the British Raj had asserted claims there during and before the abortive 1914 tripartite convention. Some disagreement over frontiers looked inevitable as the two governments confronted each other for the first time in Himalayan areas formerly hard to reach. Yet China managed to define a border to the satisfaction of the little kingdom of Nepal, and also reached a boundary settlement with Burma in a give-and-take manner. Why did the Sino-Indian impasse rather suddenly assume a character seemingly as insoluble as India's prolonged impasse with Pakistan over Kashmir?

The Sino-Indian dispute had arisen when India challenged China's right to build a highway to link southern Tibet to Chinese Turkestan. The remoteness and unimportance of the frontier area are suggested by the circumstance that the Tibetan highway had apparently been completed for two years before India discovered it. It was not until 1959 that India made its protest, following a clash between Indian and Chinese patrols which resulted in some casualties. That incident had followed hard upon the flight of the Dalai Lama and a revolt which had some foreign backing and large Indian sympathy. It also followed new American loans to India. The United States, of course, continued to recognize Chiang Kai-shek's regime on Taiwan as the national government of all China. Since Tibet was part of China, the United States might, if it found effective means, actively encourage Chiang Kai-shek's ambitions to "liberate" Tibet. Reports of C.I.A. activity along the Tibetan border (including air drops of arms and money) may or may not have been true, but they were taken quite seriously in Peking. The Chinese leaders were probably also considerably provoked by Moscow's offers of new aid to Nehru's government just at this time. On the Indian side Mr. Nehru was under attack for following an appeasement policy toward China; a "strong stand" over Tibet was demanded by the exigencies of internal politics to restore the Congress party's then dwindling prestige. Putting all these things together, Peking asserted that India was following policies incompatible with the five principles of peaceful coexistence, that she was maneuvering to get both American and Russian aid in order to oppose the unification of the People's Republic.

In December, 1959, I had discussed the border dispute with Prime Minister Nehru in New Delhi at considerable length. Mr. Nehru had seemed more perplexed by some harsh attacks made against him in the Peking press than by the disagreement that had arisen over the frontier—an event he regarded more philosophically. Now, in October, 1960, during an official interview with Chou En-lai,[6] I said:

"Last year Prime Minister Nehru told me that perhaps the basic reason for the Sino-Indian dispute was that both were 'new nations,' . . . newly independent and under dynamic nationalistic leaderships. In a sense they were meeting at their frontiers for the first time in history. . . . In the past India was a colony and China a semicolony. The boundary was not so clear and for the administrative needs of that time the boundary did not particularly have to be clearly delineated."

Premier Chou replied that such was not quite the case. "China and Burma are also newly independent countries," he reminded me. Why had it "been possible for Burma to settle the boundary question" with China whereas India had not? He answered his own question: "Burma took a *positive* attitude . . . India doesn't want to settle the boundary questions. The real idea they have in mind is to turn China's Tibet region into a buffer zone. . . . They don't want Tibet to become a Socialist Tibet. That's why after the rebellion was quelled in Tibet they became more dissatisfied and shortly afterwards the Sino-Indian boundary question came to the fore.

"Our stand has been very clear. It is to maintain the status quo and seek a friendly settlement. Even in the case of the so-called McMahon Line [established by the British and claimed by the Indians] we haven't crossed to the south of it in spite of the fact that we don't recognize it. Neither have we put forward any territorial claims as preconditions to negotiations. But the Indian side is using the Sino-Indian boundary question as a card . . . against progressive forces at home [the Indian Communist Party] and as capital for obtaining 'foreign aid.' There is no conflict of basic interests between the Chinese and Indian peoples. We will be friendly to each other. The present situation is but a temporary phenomenon."

China could not seriously plan war over the uninhabited and frozen highlands of the Tibetan-Indian frontier. Khrushchev had made it clear that he would not sacrifice India's good will to back China's side in the quarrel. This knowledge may have encouraged India to turn her attention southward for the armed conquest of Goa in December, 1961—which may also have been intended to impress China with India's military efficiency and readiness to use force when it is "unavoidable," as Mr. Nehru put it.

An aggravating factor in Sino-Indian relations (which does not appear in the official exchanges over boundary disputes) is the growing cooperation between Nepal and China. A month after he signed a treaty of peace and friendship with Burma, in March, 1960, Chou En-lai visited Kathmandu, the Nepalese capital, and concluded a similar treaty there. This was accompanied by statements that Nepal intended to remain neutral—by implication not only in the cold war, but in any Sino-Indian disputes as well. As early as 1956, China had extended Nepal some 60,000,000 Indian rupees of credits for the purchase of machines and equipment; in 1960 another trade agreement increased the Chinese grant by 100,000,000 rupees, or nearly $20,000,-000. Subsequently, in the boundary settlement, China withdrew historical claims to the whole of Joma Lungma (Mt. Everest) and accepted Nepalese maps. These placed the border across the summit of the world's highest peak, which was divided between the two countries. Another treaty provision created a thirty-two-mile demilitarized zone along the six-hundred-mile frontier. This proved advantageous to China when Nepal enforced it by clearing out Khamba tribesmen who had used that area as a base during the Tibetan rebellion.

In British times Nepal was a *de facto* British protectorate controlled through a Hindu Rajput family who had kept the native kings virtual prisoners for a century. In 1951 the heir to the throne recovered power, however, and a constitutional monarchy was established. For several years local leaders of the Indian Congress Party had aspired to take power; they might have brought Nepal into the Indian republic. In 1960 the reigning monarch, Mahendra, dissolved the parliament, arrested the premier, and reoriented Nepalese policy toward complete independence based on strict neutrality. To the irritation of New Delhi, part of Nepal's credits with China have been used to construct a new highway linking Kathmandu and Lhasa, and built by Chinese engineers. King Mahendra further strengthened his ties with Peking during a state visit in 1961. He was also a state guest of New Delhi in 1962, but he did nothing to placate Indian Congress feeling when he merely reiterated his neutrality and his desire for friendship with both China and India on an equal footing. Many Indian nationalists believed that India had somehow been cheated out of Nepalese allegiance by Chinese intrigue, and what they fear may be a Chinese policy of ethnic attrition aimed at aligning the Tibetan-border states with China.

Meanwhile, China improved relations with Afghanistan by diplomatic treaties and the extension of trade credits. Between Nepal and Afghanistan lies the disputed Kashmir border. Adjoining Nepal is the principality of Sikkim, which separates Nepal from Bhutan. India holds a somewhat vague protectorate position in Bhutan and asserts suzerainty in Sikkim. Both areas also have populations of Tibetan ethnic affinity. Far to the east, north of Burma, are other undefined borders along tribal highlands which the British designated simply

"The Northeast Frontier Agency"—a rather ambiguous name under which to rally nationalist sentiment. There is in fact no nation, merely unsurveyed mountains.

On balance, it is clear that China has firmly returned to central Asia as a major Himalayan power for the first time in two hundred years. New Delhi obviously would prefer a softer frontier than she is now likely to get. It is certain, however, that neither India nor China can seriously plan to use major military means to win a "map victory" in largely uninhabitable wastelands of no real value to either power.

Apart from the facts summarized above, it is impossible for any outsider to judge the merits of claims made by either side in this remote war, but it is obvious that neither can hope to win an absolute diplomatic victory. The objective result so far has been the loss to China of much Indian good will demonstrated in the past, and a division which has been exploited by non-Asian powers in ways costly to both China and India, but more costly to China. A settlement by compromise is inevitable if the Bandung principles of coexistence are to be fulfilled, as they probably must be fulfilled, in any future scheme of an Asia run by and for Asians.

78

National Minorities

"Minorities" in China cover a lot more territory than Tibet. The province of Yunnan alone holds about four times as many non-Chinese as there are Tibetans in Tibet. In preparation for a trip to Yunnan I spent a day at the Institute of National Minorities in Peking. There I found 2,600 students of forty-seven different nationalities (including 900 Tibetans), who were using twenty different languages in the acquisition of more or less higher education and training as teachers and party cadres.

That large institution symbolizes the fact that more than 60 percent of China's area is "autonomous" homeland for non-Han peoples. If all the autonomous areas were put together they would about equal the size of Europe without Russia. Most of them are on China's frontiers, but minority communities are scattered all through China. Altogether they number about 43,000,000. (See the map of minority nationalities on page 770.)

Autonomous Inner Mongolia has more Mongols than its brother state of Outer Mongolia. Autonomous Sinkiang has five million Uighurs and half a million Kazakhs on the borders of Soviet Kazakhstan. In Yunnan live a million Shans closely related to the northern Burmans. Above Indochina are other Thai and Chuang cousins of the

Lao people of Laos and northern Thailand. Isolated civilizations among more than a hundred tribal and minority peoples of China varied from naked forest folk who had never built houses of any kind, to highly cultured and advanced societies. Not advanced by standards of Chevy Chase, Maryland, perhaps, but still people like the Shans, who had ruled an empire a thousand years ago which covered much of Yunnan and South Asia.

Shans are among the comeliest and most attractive people in the world. Not so far away from them live aborigines who moved forward very little for five thousand years. Generally speaking, all these minorities preceded the Han in eastern Asia and have been very slowly pushed southward by them. Ranging from tribal or semi-tribal to feudal and semifeudal societies, they had agrarian or mixed pastoral-agrarian economies. Some of the Yi people in Yunnan planted grain as the American Indians did. They took a sharp stick, poked it in the ground, dropped a grain of corn into the hole, and uttered a prayer for good weather.

Minority peoples did not readily intermarry with the Han and were hostile to them. The Han looked down on them as barbarians and aborigines. Ruling powers in China appointed chieftains among them and collected taxes and tribute when they could catch them. The Nationalists had barely begun attempts to gather them into the form of a larger Chinese state. Communists were the first to reach them with a fully integrated theory providing a place for them in a "China Union." With it began a real effort to proselytize on a mass scale.

In view of the record of thousands of years of Han coexistence with these non-Han peoples, current talk of genocide in China falls wryly from the lips of American officials whose ancestors seized a continent from native Indians and wiped out nations of them scarcely more than a century ago. The march of civilization? No doubt. But let us leave claims to moral superiority in the vestibule when we come to consider the present-day Han people's relations with aboriginal subjects whom their ancestors neglected to massacre.

At the Institute of National Minorities I was met by Professor Lin Yao-hua, director of the History Department. He was a former professor of history and ethnology at Peking University. A graduate of Yenching and Harvard (1941), he had returned to China in 1946 and begun to specialize in nationalities questions. He would not converse with me directly in English. With him was Chang K'ai-yu, a secretary in the dean's office. Chang was obviously the party representative and Professor Lin the responsible academician.

The Institute covers nearly two acres and has twenty-one buildings, including classrooms and dormitories. Four large halls with Chinese roofs face a newly tree-planted campus. Flanking the next garden are new homes for a faculty of 370, who manage four departments at the university level, a middle school and a primary school. All food, clothing and living quarters are supplied by the state and students receive a stipend.

The populations of Sinkiang, Inner Mongolia, Tibet, the Moslem regions and the Chuang area of Kwangsi account for about three-fourths of all non-Han peoples. In addition to those territories there are 54 autonomous counties and 269 autonomous districts of township size or larger. All these areas have local governments organized like the rest of China, but their school systems are generally more backward. The central nationalities institute exists to train new teaching personnel qualified both academically and politically to speed up progress and bring literacy and ideological development abreast of the country as a whole. Eight provinces have special training institutes but the central institute is the only university exclusively for the training of national minority party cadres. Non-Hans may and do enter ordinary Chinese schools on an equal footing. Peking has also built a striking multistory edifice called the Museum of National Minorities which offers any visitor a fascinating visual education on the whole subject. According to official statistics, students of minority nationalities increased as follows between 1952 and 1958: in primary schools, 943,000 to 4,240,000; middle schools, 40,000 to 395,000; technical middle schools, 5,000 to 64,000; institutes of higher learning, 2,000 to 22,000.[1]

The Chinese Communists carry out a policy of preservation and protection of distinctive cultural characteristics of the different nationalities, their languages, costumes, folklore, music, and traditions, just as in the U.S.S.R. It is a patriarchal relationship. The aim is to give the minorities self-governing socialist systems. Party membership among them in 1961 exceeded a quarter of a million; one non-Han (Ulanfu, a Mongol) had reached as high as the Politburo.

An informative colloquy I had with Professor Lin and Mr. Chang explained why there are no "autonomous republics" in China as in Russia. I have mentioned that China is constitutionally defined as a "unified multinational state" while Russia is merely a "multinational state." According to Professor Lin, since the Han Dynasty all peoples have been equally members of a unified China. For two thousand years China has not been an "imperialist" state. In the 1840's China became a semicolonial country and all its peoples were alike oppressed. They all finally became free only in 1949, in Professor Lin's theory.

Now Tsarist Russia, on the other hand, was an imperialist country which held many smaller nations in subjugation, Professor Lin continued. When revolution occurred it liberated both Russia's working class and the colonial nations. As these nations were already "bourgeois nationalist" states they had to be recognized as "autonomous republics" with national political autonomy. In China the minorities never reached the stage of "bourgeois nationalist" states. They are minority *nationalities* but minorities of the one *nationality* they share with the Han majority—that is, "Chinese."

That official rationalization is accepted by neither Soviet nor non-Marxist scholars. Chinese history is replete with occasions of aggressive expansion in no significant way different from more modern imperialisms. All China's frontier territories, including Manchuria, Mongolia, Sinkiang, Tibet and even Yunnan, are inhabited by non-Han peoples or tribes conquered, absorbed or minimized within the records of written history. It is also true that China was often the victim of aggression and for long centuries was dominated by barbarian conquerors who eventually lost their identity in China—most recently the Manchus. Meanwhile, those same neighbors themselves aggressed against weaker peoples—a notable example being the Vietnamese and Thai obliteration of the Khmers.

While armed conquests certainly did not end with the Han Dynasty, it might be said that the boundaries of China as we know it today were fixed in the Han *mind*, without yet having been completely fulfilled. (The conquests were mostly made by Ch'in, but the Chinese like to attribute them to the power of cultural attraction under the "enlightened peace" of Han.) That Chinese Communists do not admit to themselves that such a thing as Chinese imperialism existed or can exist today is perhaps easier to comprehend, in view of the lapse of centuries during which Chinese historians drew a kindly veil over the facts, than the conviction held among many intelligent Americans (in which category all congressmen may be included to avoid argument) that the United States has never been imperialistic, or overrun weaker peoples and their territories, despite quite recent events which flatly belie them.

In Kunming, Yunnan, I visited another "national minorities" school with 1,676 students of 22 different cultural-linguistic backgrounds. Six million non-Han people live in Yunnan alone. The Yi are the most numerous and the Pai (close to the Siamese) exceed 600,000. This province operated a number of party and normal training schools on the county level. Obviously the main emphasis in Kunming was on political training, but a full middle school curriculum was offered, with much music and dancing.

The Kunming Institute had a fine campus with a swimming pool, modern buildings, and an excellent library and science laboratory. Its faculty of 90 teachers included 55 non-Hans. Teachers and students to whom I spoke no longer believed in Buddhism, Lamaism, Islamism or Christianity. (Some of the Chins and Kachins among them had been baptized.) They were there solely to master Marxism and science techniques to carry back to their villages as leaders and preachers of the new gospel.

I happened to visit the Kunming school when students were preparing for an autumn festival. The girls wore silk and velvet costumes of vivid colors and sang and danced to orchestras of native instruments. They were as full of vivacity and excitement as teen-agers engaged in the same exhibitionism anywhere else. Their Communist teachers had not forgotten that man does not live by politics alone.

79

South of the Clouds

Kunming, capital of Yunnan province, was the only city in China where I was awakened by the sound of gunfire. At the airport, enlarged since General Chennault's Flying Tigers used it during the Second World War, I had noticed more than two hundred MIG fighters lined up— the only field I saw in joint use by civilian and military planes. Coming into the old city on a broad paved highway we skirted a collection of two- and three-story buildings, brown brick with brown tile roofs, spread over many acres. They housed a military academy for cadets of the army and air force. Around it lay extensive fields of grain and vegetables where soldiers could be seen operating tractors and combines. On a nearby artillery range daily target practice gave the city a reveille and a reminder that Yunnan borders on Vietnam, in the southern half of which are American air bases. "Imperialist planes," the Chinese alleged, frequently violated the air space of both North Vietnam and Yunnan.

The weather in Kunming was as perfect as I remembered, and the air as bracing. Kunming is called "the city of eternal spring," and it is. Just above the tropical zone, it has an elevation of 6,400 feet and is rarely too hot or too cold. Rainfall is adequate but the skies are clear most of the year; the Kunming plain, encircled by blue hills, is usually flooded with sunshine. Yunnan means "south of the clouds" and most of them do seem to stop abruptly where the plateau leaves Kweichow, to the north, shrouded in mists.

When I was twenty-four I traveled by caravan across Yunnan westward from Kunming to Tali Lake and then to the south, over the upper Mekong and Salween rivers, down to the Irrawaddy and Upper Burma (fascinating land of giant "singing" bamboos, parakeets, rhododendrons, camellias, azaleas, flame trees, wild monkeys and wild elephants). There were no roads and the steep trails over the ancient mountains were slow going; the 500-mile trek took six weeks. Much of the time we were in bandit country; we hired Chinese soldiers as bodyguards at one yuan a day, which generally went for opium. It was not until the anti-Japanese war that a motor road was opened to Burma. For long Yunnan remained cut off from the rest of China except by caravan trails.

Today new highways link all neighboring provinces and one sees trucks and buses far in the interior. The spectacular French-built railway from Haiphong and Hanoi, in Indochina, to Kunming, is being changed from narrow to standard gauge. There is still no direct railway connection to the China coast but goods from Kunming can take the roundabout route down to Hanoi and thence overland to Hanoi–Kwangchow-wan and Canton, on a line completed during the Vietnamese war of independence against the French. Two other railways are approaching Yunnan, one from Fukien province, on the seaboard, and the other from Szechuan via Kweichow.

Before 1949 there was virtually no modern industry in Yunnan. A traveler by air today observes some new towns built around small power and steel plants, with blue-water reservoirs nestling in the hills nearby. Amazingly, as far north as Loyang I had seen large lathes and other machine tools marked "made in Yunnan." The Yunnan plateau's rich agricultural land is limited to much less than 10 percent of the total area, but the province is well endowed with other natural resources: tin, copper, mercury, zinc, antimony, phosphorus, cinnabar, manganese, placer gold, vast hydroelectric potentials, forest reserves, and recently discovered coal and iron said to be adequate for regional industrialization. Yunnan's tin deposits are among the largest in the world and output already accounts for two-thirds of China's exports of the metal. Thus far Yunnan produces no oil; its military and civilian requirements are imported through the Vietnamese port of Haiphong.

The province has an area as large as Poland and East Germany and less than half (approximately 21,000,000) their combined populations. A multinational state in itself and an anthropological garden of Eden, about one-third of its population are aboriginal peoples who live in historical homelands now administered as autonomous areas. Much of the western region, of lordly mountains and great river divides, is uninhabitable. In the south, Yunnan's border territories are largely populated by hill peoples closely related to natives of adjoining northern Burma, Laos and Vietnam.

Kunming is full of outlanders now. Since 1949 its population had quadrupled, to reach nearly a million by 1961, and its area had tripled. New factories and apartments sprawled far into the suburbs; structures of brick and cement were rising everywhere. The old city walls seemed entirely gone. Streets were widened and paved and old buildings replaced and renovated so that I could recognize few landmarks except the stately beauty of the eucalyptus trees which still line the canal that used to fill a city moat. A broad main thoroughfare busy with trucks and buses led me into the wide plaza dominated by a three-story department store fairly well stocked with consumer goods.

A thing new to me: I saw on the clean streets (something new in itself, for Yunnan) white-clad women wearing gauze nose masks and pushing along carts from which they ladled out milk, half a pint to each child for the equivalent of four cents. When I tried to buy some I received an astonished stare; it was for children only. Popsicles were sold to both adults and children, however, and at the industrial fair there were Eskimo pies. In the evening, bookstores were crowded; I saw many cheap prints, lithographs, posters and even some postcard reproductions of Western art, but nothing abstract. Watching a young officer shyly studying a photograph of Rodin's "The Kiss," I wondered what he would think of *Playboy*. Stores were offering food, clothing and household articles in some abundance and at relatively low prices. Among items I noted as unusual were a brace of fat ducks for seven yuan, and a five-pound Yunnan smoked ham for ten. It was suggested to me that transportation and export to other provinces being still difficult and expensive, Yunnan's own products largely remained in the home market.

Approximately on this spot, I remembered, the old street fairs were held in the past. There you could buy native wares of all kinds: tribal embroideries; fine leatherwork; fanciful items made of old Standard Oil tins; native jade, amber, turquoise and lapis lazuli; silver and gold jewelry; and a wide display of opium pipes, some of them richly inlaid and expensive. Those markets were certainly more colorful, filled with men and women in tribal costumes, including many Tibetans, who used to ride their small shaggy ponies clear to Kunming to trade. Today it was less picturesque, but the people looked in better condition.

On my last visit to Kunming, in 1945, it still lacked a single good hotel. Now there were several, including the modern Western-style hotel in the eastern suburb where I had a large room and bath, with meals, for four dollars a day. Across the street stood a new municipal hall and around us were many new apartment buildings. A few blocks down the main street I visited the industrial exhibit, where I saw Yunnan-made buses, pumps, generators, textile machinery, telephone equipment, radios, motorcycles, cigarette-making machines, musical instruments, lathes, diesel engines, cranes, drills, small tractors, hardware and electrical appliances, scales, surgical instruments, perfume, toilet water, and a variety of textiles—including one cotton print with a design that mystified me: Christmas trees bearing electric lights (possibly for some of the Christian Min Chia people?). A bantam two-cylinder car was also displayed; I was told that production thus far was only 120 vehicles; they cost 4,000 yuan each. Near the gates of the fair I saw an attractive teenager dressed in velvet trousers and jacket of good material and took a picture of her. Of all the articles exhibited, I asked her, what would she like to buy? She pointed to an accordion in the instruments exhibit. Her *ba-ba* (papa) had promised her one if she got "five superiors" in her school work.

"Yunnanfu [Kunming] smelled of opium everywhere; pipes and lamps were sold in all the markets; the drug was as easy to buy as rice," I wrote in *Journey to the Beginning,* of the old city as it was when I first saw it. "Demoralization and impoverishment were especially apparent in the abuse of children, who are exploited all over China but nowhere quite so unconscionably as in Yunnan. 'There are probably half a million slaves in the whole province,' to quote from an interview I had with Richard Lankester, English headmaster of a mission school [for escaped slaves] run by the Church of Christ. 'They do all the drudgery in the stores, workshops and homes. Their masters and mistresses do as they please with them. They really are *ya-t'ou* or yoke-heads, as they are called.'

"In that home for slave girls I talked to . . . one child of nine [who] had been paralyzed from the hips down by a beating delivered with an iron rod. Another was nearly deaf from a blow on the head. A girl of fifteen had been bought and sold four times. Her last master had starved her for a week and then hung her up by the thumbs to punish her for 'laziness.'

"Alienation of the land to absentee owners proceeded apace; at that time fewer than one-third of the peasants on the Yunnan plain owned their farms. A girl sold outright on the local market then brought the equivalent of only five to ten dollars but that was more than a farm laborer, working for four cents (U.S.) a day, could save in a year. Poverty in other parts of China also obliged the very poor to sell their surplus daughters . . . but except in deep famine conditions they rarely sold their sons. In Yunnan large numbers of boys were in servitude.

"One of the most criminal uses of them was in the primitive tin mines at Kochiu, a semigovernment enterprise. [The sale of tin was a monopoly run by officials who also owned most of the mines.] Once there, the boys often developed rickets, scabies and beriberi. The shafts and tunnels in the mines were very small, hardly big enough for a boy to crawl in and out on his hands and knees, with the ore basket strapped to his back. As a result many became permanently deformed and were cast aside. An American missionary named Baker specialized in salvaging the little wrecks and he and his wife nursed scores back to health and taught them useful trades or handicrafts."

Poppy cultivation had greatly declined and opium paraphernalia were not so openly sold during the time of American use of Yunnan as an air base, but man's inhumanity to man had not much changed. Whatever evils the new regime has brought, all children now enjoy a fairly equal opportunity to make the most of what is offered: health care, education, recreation—and the "iron rice bowl." Goiter, which used to be widespread, has been eliminated by iodinization of the water; trachoma, smallpox and other epidemic diseases are, as elsewhere, disappearing. Instead of stunted naked runts, illiterate boy slave miners exploited in primitive mines, Kochiu is now run by modern methods and adult workers—who live in clean dry houses, marry, have families, send their own children to school—in a valley with electric trolleys and tramlines, where tin production is sixteen times the 1949 output.[1] In the hills there are sanatoria for workers, and hot baths and ultraviolet treatments are available. At the headquarters center there is a swimming pool and a theater auditorium. It may be a pity that it had to be a Communist regime which accomplished the reform but it cannot be said that history denied the same opportunity to their predecessors.

When I traveled through Yunnan in former times most Han-jen regarded the "barbarians," as they called the non-Hans, with contempt. Distrust and hostility were mutual. For the most part Chinese ruled the plains while the tribal folk lived in the highlands and forests, where Chinese seldom ventured alone. Do the non-Hans like Red Chinese any better? I could take no poll. I have mentioned the Kunming Institute of National Minorities, which symbolizes a very real and systematic effort to improve relations with the Yunnan aborigines. Chinese-speaking students trained there will become political and cultural leaders of four large autonomous districts and seven autonomous counties of the province. That does not mean that tribal peoples are being segregated. They do obviously share a new equality of opportunity. There is widespread integration; to see the Lolo mingling freely with Chinese in work and social activities is truly remarkable when one remembers the past. They have proportional representation in provincial and national government organs. Outsiders might have great difficulty in distinguishing Han Chinese from the others, but besides subtle variations in physiognomy and stature, their dress, coiffure and speech differ widely. Today this is demonstrated on stage, screen, television and in art, which are widely used to popularize tribal songs, dances, folklore and products throughout the nation.

A mixed community of Han and non-Han farmers operated the last commune I saw before I left China. This was in an autonomous administrative area of the Kuan-tu district, on the outskirts of Kunming. Of its 21,000 adults 62 percent were Min Chia (San Mei) and Lolo (Yi) and the rest were Han Chinese. The area was divided into four brigades. In the Ala Commune, which I visited, the chairman was a Han, the two vice-chairmen were Lolo, the party secretary was a Min Chia, and the head of the women's work department was a Lolo girl. Through an interpreter I asked the girl just who had elected her.

"My friends," she said. She was pockmarked, homely, and had an honest smile.

"Why do they like you?"

"Well, it may be like this. I worked hard. I was a serf in the lord's house here doing dirty work until I was eleven. I'm twenty-three now. After liberation I was given some land. I raised more cabbages than the others and was asked to lead a mutual-aid team. Comrades taught me to read and write characters. Then I began teaching others. I took an interest in politics and life became better. I am a hard worker and like to help others."

"What women's work do you do?"

"Many things. I see that women get their equal rights. For instance, we have three rules that must be observed for expectant mothers: no field work for fifty days, hot water for their feet, and special food such as spinach. What else? I propagandize among women. To do that I must study and understand government policies and be able to explain them to others. It's not easy to get understanding. Many women are timid and don't want to be involved."

Near the large village that served as brigade headquarters many men and women, some in tribal costume, some Han, were feeding grain into a small red threshing machine, which separated the grain and threw out straw that had to be stacked. It was a new commune purchase and more people were watching, fascinated, than working. According to the chairman the threshing machine had been paid for entirely by cash profits of the commune on its output of rice, wheat, rape and vegetables.

He went on to say that per capita income had increased from 95 yuan in 1957 to 114 in 1959; in 1960 they expected to reach "469 yuan per family." The term "income" here must be regarded as ambiguous. I had no time to enter into details which would doubtless have revealed qualifications. The same might be said for extraordinary claims made for an experimental "high yield plot" of 1.3 *mu* which was said to have produced 600 catties of wheat—some 61 bushels. That would be at the rate of about 300 bushels an acre. The chairman asserted that they had used the equivalent of nearly "eight *tan*" * of "base fertilizer" and thirty pounds of seed.

The village was rather dirty and seemed to be getting little attention—compared to the new poultry pens with electric incubators. A few hundred feet away from the commune clinic, which stood apart

* One *tan* = 113⅓ pounds. The average Chinese field gets two to three pounds.

from the village in a whitewashed mud and straw building, there was a surprisingly modern-looking structure of two stories, with balconies and a tile roof. I was told that it was new commune housing but no one seemed particularly anxious to show it to me. I went off by myself to photograph it and was followed by the party secretary. The building was divided into about forty apartments of one or two rooms each, with wooden floors. Most of the doors were open; in all the building I found only one flat occupied—by a Lolo woman with two small children.

"Nobody seems to be living here!" I said.

"Not many," the secretary responded.

"Why not?"

"Oh, there will be more. It takes time to persuade people to leave the village. They have to get used to the new ways slowly."

Here was a commune where it seemed obvious that somebody had gone ahead inflexibly following higher directives calling for communal housing; public opinion may now have been casting a belated veto. Dirty, dark, mud-floored as the old village huts were, they were "homes" and probably preferred, with their few chickens and pigs moored in the muddy back yards, to the strange new many-familied building—even if it did have glass window panes and a promise of electric lights.

It would be interesting to know whether those apartments are still empty, or now house newlyweds—or have, perhaps, been converted into a factory or a school.

Here, as occasionally elsewhere—though not universally—I sensed that the guarantee of a fixed abode on a fixed piece of land was more important to many conservative peasant families than all the modern improvements. The advanced cooperative was still able to satisfy that traditional attachment. The scrambling of land and dwellings in the early commune often threatened it before the peasants were psychologically prepared to accept personal de-identification with the land in exchange for identification with a broader structure of security. (It has after all taken generations to detach Americans from the land.) Commune reforms since 1959 have been directed largely toward restoring that sense of security in the peasantry. It will remain an important part of peasant incentive until a more advanced and stable industrialization can offer greater guarantees than at present.

I saw the new Kunming iron and steel works only from the air, as I left for Burma, and I do not know its capacity; judging from the products I saw displayed, and the construction I saw accomplished, it must already have been not inconsiderable. Rewi Alley told me that he had seen "dozens" of small iron and steel plants with bessemer furnaces of modest capacity in various hinterland towns of Yunnan. Near the end of my journey, and anxious to tell my story—for I had written nothing except my notes for five months in China—I did not take advantage of the opportunity offered to me to travel by bus from Kunming to Burma. Considered in retrospect that was a mistake.

At my hotel I did meet a number of Burmese army officers who had just come up that highway from Bhamo and from their accounts I gathered that western Yunnan was also being rapidly transformed. Hsiao-kuan, at the southern end of Lake Erh Hai, near Tali, was reportedly building a power plant with a 250,000-kilowatt capacity. Industries there included a small steel mill (output, 20,000 tons a year), a sugar refinery, an agricultural implements factory, and glass and cement works. Numerous dams have been constructed and small hydroelectric plants now provide power and light, generated by dynamos made in Yunnan, to many towns that a decade ago still depended on wicks burning rape oil, as when I first passed through them.

I should like to have visited the Democratic Republic of Vietnam, an area which I knew in the past and which now lay easily accessible by rail or by plane from Kunming. As far as Chinese and Vietnamese authorities were concerned that would have been quite possible, I was told. One might assume that the opportunity to "accredit" one legitimate American observer to that land which Americans know only by hearsay would appeal to the State Department at least as much as a proposal to send somebody in for the C.I.A. by other means. But passport regulations still prohibit nonclassified Americans from traveling in either North Vietnam or North Korea. The concession which permitted me to enter China with State Department sanction was not extended to cover her brother states, so that I am unable to offer any eyewitness report on either.

The secretary of the Kunming branch of the Peace Committee, a Mr. Chang, drove me to the airport late in November on another cool, blue-sky-perfect Kunming day. Above the buildings a light breeze snapped the five-starred flag of China as if in farewell to me. A customs officer unpacked my bags and stacked some 50 rolls of Kodachrome and several thousand feet of 8- and 16-millimeter film on the table. Most of it was unprocessed. In Peking I had been assured that I would be permitted to take out unprocessed film; I knew the same courtesy had been granted to Henri Cartier-Bresson* and others. I had taken hundreds of exposures without any record being kept of them—many were made during casual walks alone—and I had no special photographer's permit. Now that I looked at the collection it seemed quite a lot—for the needs of a historian. I expressed some apprehension to Mr. Chang.

"Don't worry," he said. He spoke a few words to the official, who gave me an appraising look. "American?" he asked. "You're the only one we've seen here in ten years!" I exchanged the few yuan (export of

---

* Conditional only on his promise that captions used on his photographs would present the facts they represented, rather than be distorted to suit cold-war propaganda needs. I made the same commitment.

which is strictly prohibited) I possessed, the officer replaced my belongings neatly in my bags, and I was cleared for departure. *"Yi-p'ing hao lu!"* he said. "Peaceful journey!"

"Please tell the American people," Mr. Chang reminded me gravely, "that we have the friendliest feelings toward them—always have had and always will have. It is only—"

"The American imperialist government that you detest?" I finished for him.

"That's right."

I thanked him for all he had done to show me around the city; he had been really helpful.

"To peace, then," he said as we shook hands.

"To peace," I echoed. "That is one commodity of which it may be said that the more we keep it ourselves the more we give it to others."

Mr. Chang held up his thumb enthusiastically. "That's good. You tell that to Washington!"

In three hours I was in Rangoon and the next day I was united with my family again, in Europe.

Part Seven

THE
LONG
MARCH
AHEAD

☆

Mao Tse-tung asserts that as long as he is alive China will never resort to international war as a means of settling disputes, but that China will always oppose the export of counterrevolution.

"We on our part will shoulder the responsibility of world peace," Mao told me he wished the American people to understand, "whether or not the United States recognizes China, or whether or not we get into the United Nations. We will not defy all laws, human and divine, like the Monkey King who stormed the Palace of Heaven. We want to maintain world peace. We do not want war. We hold that war should not be used as a means to settle disputes between nations. However, not only China but the United States, as well, has the responsibility to maintain peace."

One other thing—"for as long as I am alive." He said: "Taiwan is China's affair. We will insist on this."

"For all the errors, China's present plight should not be exaggerated . . . The truth is that the sufferings of the ordinary peasant from war, disorder, and famine have been immeasurably less in the last decade than in any other decade in the century. And when the People's Daily *claimed yesterday that the first foundations had been laid for building a modern economy in China it was quite right. But the modern economy will be a long time coming."*

—Editorial in *The Times* (London) April 18, 1962.

80

1962: The Year the Chinese Vanished

One consequence of cutting off communications between Americans and Chinese is that it is no longer necessary for us to think of each other as men and women subject to more or less the same limitations of human possibility. Not long before I returned to China I was told by a prominent American (now a high official dispensing information) that he had "absolute proof" that husbands in China were being forcibly prevented from sleeping with their wives (even their *own* wives). He was as certain that the Chinese Communists had no common sense at all as Mr. Khrushchev is that President Kennedy is Governor Rockefeller's puppet.

More and better scholarly research is being done on China today on an academic and scientific level than ever before in America, but very little if any of it reaches the public via the popular press. The American newspaper student by now has been conditioned to know that you can't believe a thing you read about China unless it is absolutely unbelievable. In normal situations, for example, nobody but Al Capp (equipped with plenty mockoroni) could report the disappearance of a whole nation without arousing a certain amount of skeptical comment. But many American editors printed without question Joseph Alsop's recent disclosure in "Matter of Fact" that the

Chinese people had suddenly vanished. For those who missed this announcement, the fact of the matter follows.

On September 13, 1961, Joseph Alsop reported in his column that Sir Cyril Osborne, an English M.P., had returned from China with the news that the "average Chinese" was being compelled to live on a diet of no more than "600 calories" of food intake a day. While this would represent some improvement over Mr. Alsop's earlier reports of a Chinese diet of grass, bark and afterbirths, the *Herald Tribune* columnist deduced from Sir Cyril's testimony that "the Chinese people are receiving just the same quantity of nourishment, day after day, and month after month, that the more desperate American dieters receive when they do their few days of Metrecal and nothing else." This was "a level of nourishment so low that American doctors require patients needing such severe diets to enter hospitals for the purpose."

Mr. Alsop went on to report that a person on 600 calories a day "can normally be expected to lose about 20 pounds a month." While admitting that this statement, which had come to Sir Cyril from a reliable but anonymous source, was disputed by another reliable but anonymous source, which put the average Chinese diet as high as 900 calories a day, Mr. Alsop concluded that in either case the truth was that "the population of China is starving. The starvation is methodical and rationed but it is not even very slow starvation." Certainly not slow, not at the rate of twenty pounds a month for the "average Chinese." Figures released by the Nutrition Board of the U. S. National Research Council give 702 calories as the minimum "adequate for maintenance" of a thirteen-pound (two- to six-month-old) baby! [1]

Thus if Mr. Alsop and Sir Cyril were correct, we should only have had to wait until about April, 1962, for the Chinese people—losing an average of twenty pounds per person per month—conveniently to disappear. What if there were still some Han remnants on the scene at that late date? "The memory of the people is unbelievably short." *S'arrangera*, no doubt. What could not so easily arrange itself, however, was the omission in Mr. Alsop's column of any reference to the date of Sir Cyril's statement about Chinese rations. It was originally made on November 10, 1960,[2] soon after he returned from China and almost a year before it became "Matter of Fact" in Mr. Alsop's column. Ever since that date the "average Chinese" presumably had been losing twenty pounds per month. The "average Chinese" weighs well under two hundred pounds. If each person lost twenty pounds a month (Mr. Alsop's reckoning), the entire Chinese population would have already vanished from the earth two or three months *before* his column appeared.

Sir Cyril visited Peking for a few days while I was there. He was, we gathered, promoting trade relations. It never occurred to any of us that he was investigating rations, which were certainly not confidential information, as anyone could have told him. *Chin-t'ien ni ch'ih shen-ma?*—What are you eating today?—was a common greeting in Peking. If you didn't believe officials or hadn't much time to observe for yourself what people ate, you could get the answers from any old man you might meet in a park, provided you didn't ask in a way to make him feel he was giving away state secrets. Perhaps Sir Cyril was not around long enough to learn that; in less than a week he left for Canton.

When I got back to Europe some of the British press was convinced that there was mass famine in China, and I had many queries about it. I replied what most foreign residents in China knew: the food shortage was severe; staple foods were closely rationed and well below Western standards of good nourishment; there was no visible starvation and the population was in good health and working condition. When someone sent me a clipping of Sir Cyril's "600 calories" story I was inclined to think he had been misquoted. In later correspondence with me he put the "average Chinese" intake at "between 600 and 700" calories. In an official news release he had said "700 calories." He had learned this from a "reliable source" in Peking, which he could not reveal; the person had to be protected.

The fact that the Chinese didn't really vanish ought to have been enough to expose the absurdity of the assertion, but it was too incredible to die so easily. Who is interested in a bit of elementary arithmetic?

Basic rations in China are figured in grain, and presumably that is what Sir Cyril meant. If he intended to include nongrain foods in his 600 calories the significance is indicated below. Take it in grain: 600 calories means about 156 grams of rice. Multiplied by 700,000,000 times 365 days gives you about 40,000,000 tons of rice, or somewhat more of wheat, somewhat more of sweet potatoes. Even the most skeptical Western economist had never placed output below 140,000,000 tons after 1952 nor below 160,000,000 tons since 1956. Foreign analysts generally accepted figures ranging around 200,000,000 tons for 1958 and 1959 (when Chinese claims were much higher). Crop failures in 1960 certainly reduced the output considerably below that. Considerably—but not as much as the 80 *percent* implied by Sir Cyril's figure.

China's 1960-61 net grain imports were less than 5,000,000 tons. Even if that much were equally distributed among the population for immediate consumption, such imports could add less than 70 calories daily. But if by "rations" Sir Cyril actually meant to include vegetables, meat, oil, sugar and fats, then China's total 1960 food output would have had to decline on the order of 90 percent. Catastrophe of such magnitude has been precedented only by Biblical tales of the Flood. If it had occurred in China the entire population might indeed be dead.

I continued to be puzzled by Sir Cyril until one day I belatedly read the *Hansards* report of a December, 1960, parliamentary debate in the House of Commons. The debate was on a vote of censure against the Government for "failure to press for the admission to the U.N. of the People's Government of China." An excerpt follows in which Sir Cyril, speaking for the Government, revealed information which for the first time offered a possible clue to the case of the 600—or was it 700?—calories.

MR. [SIR CYRIL] OSBORNE [LOUTH]: As a boy fifty years ago I was brought up in a very stern puritan home, but even my father would not have lived in the world of China today. There is a central control of the George Orwell type which imposes a fanatical puritan spirit on the people which is hard to believe unless one goes there and lives among it.

MR. HAROLD DAVIES: That is not true. Will the hon. Member give way?

MR. OSBORNE: I have just come back!

MR. DAVIES: I have been there several times too.

MR. DEPUTY-SPEAKER [Sir Gordon Touche]: Order.

MR. OSBORNE: I am trying to give hon. Members my impressions.

MR. DAVIES: The hon. Member always does this. He twists the truth.

[Mr. Osborne was asked to give way.]

MR. OSBORNE: No, I will not. The Chinese have this purposeful fanatical idea, for which I give them credit. When I got back from Peking I found the English newspapers full of nothing but *Lady Chatterley's Lover*. I would rather have the stern morality which I found in Peking than what I have found here. Unless one goes to the country frequently it is almost impossible to realize the determination of the Chinese to drive their people on to a better and finer world for themselves and their children.

[Sir Cyril was not opposed to China's admission to the U.N., but he wanted the Opposition to start off with the desire for unity with the Government and its policy toward the U.S.A. to "do all we can behind the scenes to persuade the Americans to the inclusion of Red China in the United Nations"; in short, not to force the Americans' hand but to use methods of thought remolding.]

MR. OSBORNE: While we are not going to kow-tow to the Americans—we are not doing that—it is foolish not to take note of American susceptibilities if we are to go to America for financial help in order to pull China out of her difficulties.

[There was an interruption as two hon. Members rose to their

feet. One of them rebuked the other, saying, "The hon. Gentleman is not observing the courtesy of the *house*."]

MR. OSBORNE: May I have your protection, Mr. Deputy-
Speaker? May I have protection from the remark that has just
been made, that I have not the courtesy of a *louse?*"

MR. DEPUTY-SPEAKER: I heard no remark from which the hon.
Member requires protection from the Chair.

MR. OSBORNE: I am entitled to defend myself.

MR. MELLISH: Further to that point of order. It is probably my
fault, Mr. Deputy-Speaker, but I said that the hon. Gentleman
was not observing the courtesy of the House—spelt *H*-o-u-s-e.

MR. OSBORNE: No!

MRS. HARRIET SLATER [Stoke-on-Trent, North]: That is exactly
what my hon. Friend did say.

MR. OSBORNE: If that be the case, which I accept, it must be
due to my advancing age. I am getting deaf. I apologize most
sincerely. I must now cut my remarks short.[3]

Hmm. He was getting deaf. Normally it is not cricket to refer to
anyone's afflictions, but the lapse may possibly be excused if it offers
a clue to so serious a matter as the disappearance of 700,000,000 peo·
ple doomed by 600 (or 700) calories a day. Now what, I wondered,
might that "reliable source" in Peking have said to Sir Cyril which
could have caused the misunderstanding. Could it be—could it possibly be—600 *celeries?* Consulting a dietetics chart, I found the facts
confirmed my suspicion: 600 *celeries* equal 2,850 calories. That must be
it. Unless somebody was pulling somebody's leg, any "reliable source"
in Peking which gave out such a figure for the average Chinese daily
rations—almost as gross an overstatement of fact as 600 calories is an
understatement—would very understandably wish to remain anonymous!

In the spring of 1962, Mr. Alsop returned to the Pearl River estuary
which, by his earlier calculations, should now have been choked with
the famished dead floating downstream from the nation that vanished.
He found things somewhat better: "The Chinese masses are now living
on near-famine rations *averaging 1,300 to 1,600 calories a day*." [4] Curiously, the *Herald Tribune's* famine specialist offered no explanation of
this unexpected doubling (or better) of "average rations" as compared
to the quick-starvation Metrecal diet of two years before. Nor did another staff correspondent of the same newspaper who reported from
Hongkong, only a few weeks later, that "last year's grain crops and any
other food Chinese could obtain provides them with only *1,950 calories
daily*." [5] In China, the worse things get the more they improve.

None of which means that we quidnuncs should not continue to regard official Chinese statistics with realism tempered by skepticism.

We shall be doing equally well if we take cold-war statistics improvised by anonymous reliable sources abroad with a pinch of salt with our calories—I mean celeries.

For many years before Sputnik shocked us out of our complacency the American press was filled with the work of professional mourners who made a good living by predicting famine, general collapse and counterrevolution in Russia for publishers eager to pay for good sound misinformation. Now a somewhat smaller group has gathered round the waiting tomb of China. There is nothing personal in my observations concerning Mr. Alsop, and it would be unfair to single him out for this much attention had he not made himself the most conspicuous of the wake-sitters and given the widest syndicated circulation to the childish exaggerations I have noted.

In a world that has advanced little since Voltaire wrote *Candide*, however, it should surprise no disciple of Dr. Pangloss that the Chinese have to be punished for declining to vanish in 1961 and 1962. The *Saturday Evening Post* (August 11-18, 1962) has joined in another stern warning written by Mr. Alsop, entitled, "The Coming Explosion in Red China"—and the prediction is not nuclear detonations there but the long-overdue counterrevolution and disintegration within. What is more, plenty of people believed it.

81

Facts About Food

Throughout 1959-62 many Western press editorials and headlines continued to refer to "mass starvation" in China and continued to cite no supporting facts. As far as I know, no report by any non-Communist visitor to China provides an authenticated instance of starvation during this period.[1] Here I am not speaking of food shortages, or lack of surfeit, to which I have made frequent reference, but of people dying of hunger, which is what "famine" connotes to most of us, and what I saw in the past.

While I was in China, *Look* kept sending me queries about "the famine" and I diligently searched, without success, for starving people or beggars to photograph. (Nor did anyone else succeed.) I realize that belief in mass starvation in China is now so widespread as a result of cold-war press indoctrination that statements by actual eyewitnesses may be dismissed as wholly irrelevant. Nevertheless, I must assert that I saw no starving people in China, nothing that looked like old-time famine, and only one beggar (among flood refugees in Shenyang); that I do not believe there is famine in China at this writing; and that the best Western intelligence on China is well aware of this. As we have seen, even in the special case of the emigrants attempting to enter Hongkong from the Canton delta, no starvation was observed and very few examples of malnutrition. Isolated instances of starvation due to neglect or failure of the rationing system were possible. Considerable malnutrition undoubtedly existed. Mass starvation? No.

In these assertions I am supported by fresh information from Western observers in China even more recently than I, including Gilbert Etienne, the Swiss economist and assistant professor at the Graduate Institute of International Studies, Geneva, whose impressions appeared in *Le Monde;*[2] Clare McDermott, currently Peking correspondent for *Reuters;*[3] and a member of the Swiss Federal Assembly, Dr. Armand Forel, who informed me on his return from China in June, 1962, that he was "allowed to roam the streets freely, saw nothing to indicate starvation, no begging, [and] one case of rickets." [4] The years 1960-61 were critical, but by 1962 the food supply began to approach normal. In September, Mr. McDermott reported that off-ration restaurants were again open in the cities and seemed well supplied.

On July 31, 1962, Richard Starnes reported in the *New York World Telegram*, immediately following a trip to Hongkong and Southeast Asia: "There is not one shred of evidence known to the West that famine threatens Communist China . . . Red China's army is still well-fed. There is no indication available to Western observers that the army is no longer loyal or would not fight, and fight very hard . . . The hard, simple truth is that American policy cannot prevail in Southeast Asia or anywhere else in the world as long as it is based on myth and wishful thinking."

Chinese officials nowadays take starvation very seriously; to believe that, one need not credit the party leadership with humanitarianism. Many Westerners do not understand that in order to maintain its own image of itself the party *must* see that people are fed. "People are China's asset," but if they do not eat they cannot study or work; if they do not study and work they cannot produce; if they do not produce there is no growth; if there is no growth the system is a failure—and that, to any Chinese Communist, is an impossible thought.

But the food shortage remains real. This is nothing new. "According to a study made from historical records," a Chinese scholar in exile recently wrote, "it was found that between 108 B.C. and 1911 A.D. there were 1,828 famines, or one almost every year. Potential or actual famine is so much a part of cultural expectation that official figures included a factor for famine in the normal death rate." [5] What is new is that millions of people are not starving, as they did throughout chronic famine in the twenties, thirties and forties. What is new is that an equitable rationing system has been enforced for the first time. What is nearly unbelievable is that a government exists in China which (whatever else history may charge against it) actually kept enough foreign currency out of the pockets of officials to be able to pay hard cash for millions of tons of grain imported after the harvest failures of 1960—rather than beg from the United States, as normal people do.

Agricultural recovery has been China's major preoccupation since 1961.

Were the 1960 calamities actually as severe as reported by Peking—"the worst series of disasters since the nineteenth century," as Chou En-lai told me? Weather was not the only cause of the disappointing harvest but it was undoubtedly a major cause. With good weather the crops would have been ample; without it, other adverse factors I have cited—some discontent in the communes, bureaucracy, transportation bottlenecks—made things worse. The impact on Chinese peasant psychology of three years of bad weather in *combination* with commune innovations was recognized by policy changes in 1961-62 which, as we have seen, abandoned ultra-advanced socialist aims and restored many incentives to individual enterprise.

Merely from personal observation in 1960 I know that there was no rain in large areas of northern China for 200 to 300 days. I have mentioned unprecedented floods in central Manchuria, where I was marooned in Shenyang for a week. Between Shenyang and Dairen I watched tens of thousands of people building levees to try to save part of their soya bean crop inundated by the Red River. While Northeast China was struck by eleven typhoons—the largest number in fifty years—I saw the Yellow River reduced to a small stream. In Shantung it virtually disappeared and about half the cotton and wheat crops were lost. Drought, flood, storms, frost, pests and plant diseases reportedly destroyed or affected 150,000,000 acres of crops in 1960, or more than half of China's cultivated area.

In surplus-burdened America we have no rainfall problem comparable to the vagaries of the Yellow River Valley. Bad weather over a few states brings no national hardships; indeed, a few years of New England floods or Midwestern drought might be regarded as a boon to swollen government granaries. For China, living very close to the margins of want, and where food cereals make up three-fourths to four-fifths of the average diet (compared to less than one-fifth in the United States), a harvest drop of 20 percent in a single year means immediate privation.

In the best year of her history, 1958, China probably exceeded American cereal output, running at low speed. In highly mechanized, deep-plowed American croplands, using 25,000,000 tons of chemical fertilizer, one farm laborer feeds thirty-six people; in China, with only 5 or 6 percent of her farmland mechanized thus far, and producing less than 3,000,000 tons of chemical fertilizer, one farm laborer can feed only three people[6]—if the weather cooperates. But comparisons between China and the United States—which alone accounts for nearly half the world's exports of grain—are less significant than comparisons between China and other less-favored nations.

Usually it takes China two or more years of normal crops to recover from one year like 1960. But 1959 had already been subnormal. In 1961 rainfall in the wheat areas of North China was only slightly better than in 1960. Many reservoirs and shallow wells dried up, the Yellow River again failed the people of Shantung, and other caprices recurred. In these years harvests were lost or minimized over such wide areas that large-scale famine would have been inevitable in earlier epochs. It was avoided only because yields in some favored provinces were extraordinarily good; because state grain collection and distribution was somehow accomplished despite still very backward transportation facilities; because a policy of maximum local self-sufficiency was promoted by utilizing marginal land either as private plots or collectively for emergency gardens, because a strict rationing system was effected with frugality and reasonable equity by people made fully conscious of a national emergency; and because in all these policies the state was able to utilize the interdependent and mutual-help system of collective or commune society.

Finally, in January, 1961, the government reversed itself—belatedly but just in time—on its cherished road of priority for the expansion of heavy industry. Having done so, it focused the nation's major efforts on an all-out attempt to produce adequate harvests—a goal which it had boastfully proclaimed solved, and which it now humbly admitted had not been solved, back in 1958.

What is the actual extent of China's harvest failures or successes, how does output compare with that of other nations in trouble, what is the average person now getting to eat, and what prospect of improvement is there, if any? I have already given scattered testimony to these questions; here it seems necessary to offer some general perspective. Any attempt of this kind is bound to involve the reader in rather heavy material, to follow the unraveling of a mystery story; it is worth the effort because China's food problem is a matter of cosmic proportions and affects the entire world.

What is an adequate diet? World health authorities do not agree that it is the 3,000 to 3,500 calories which the average American or Englishman is supposed to get. Unless he is expending extraordinary energy, any person consuming that much is overeating, a disease perhaps more common in the United States than malnutrition in China. The average middle-class American family probably wastes and throws away enough food every day to answer the minimal needs of an average Chinese, Japanese or Vietnamese family. For nongourmands a minimum of 2,000-2,200 calories in balanced diet is adequate[7] except for heavy workers; when average consumption falls below 1,750 calories over a considerable period, deficiency diseases develop. It has been calculated by both Western and Chinese specialists that to get this average the Chinese needs about 1,500 calories in grain, in addition to a minimum of 500 he is able to get from other food items.

To provide 700,000,000 people with 1,500 calories in cereals every day requires a gross annual crop of about 180,000,000 metric tons of grain or its equivalent in potatoes and soya beans. A smaller gross crop may suffice only if there is considerable reduction of normal allowances for fodder, seed grain, reserves, waste and nonfood uses or if other sources of food energy are widely developed—as has been the case in China.* Otherwise, a gross grain harvest of about 2,300 kilograms (one kilogram equals 2.2 pounds) per head would be about adequate today —and was much more than adequate in 1958, for a 625-650,000,000 population.

Has China been able to produce 180,000,000 tons? Here we tread upon ground highly speculative since the Great Leap began. The Bureau of Statistics' estimate of 108,000,000 tons output for 1949 is generally considered an understatement designed to indicate a high rate of growth in subsequent years, but most Western economists accepted the following official figures as approximately correct: 1953, at 156,000,000 tons; 1955, at 174,000,000 tons; 1957, at 185,000,000 tons.[8]

I have commented on the 1958 aberrations (which carried over to mid-1959) when "politics in command of statistics" brought results as near fantasy as inflated stock prices in relation to real values proved to be in Wall Street in May, 1962. Revisions of overclaims reduced official figures for 1958 grain output to 261,000,000 tons and, still later, to 250,000,000 tons; 1959 output was first put at 281,000,000 tons. Only a government stronger and more self-confident than any modern China has known before would accept the "loss of face" entailed by admissions of error on so humiliating a scale. Even these greatly reduced figures for 1958 and 1959 were indirectly recognized, in conversations I had with Chinese officials in 1960, as still involving serious overstatements.

Since the 1959 "anti-buoyant exaggeration" reform began in the Bureau of Statistics, no comprehensive agricultural returns have been released at all. Chou En-lai's statement to me that the 1960 harvest was poorer than 1958 and 1959 but "higher than 1957" has remained a principal clue which Western specialists in Chinese agrarian affairs have employed in arriving at recent estimates. On this basis one expert suggested that China's grain output in 1960 might have been "something on the order of 190,000,000 tons." [9]

I am able to offer some additional information which gives a much lower and, I believe, more realistic estimate of the extent of the 1960 setback. In my interview with Wu Chen, Vice-Minister of Agriculture, he referred to 1956 and 1959 as "bad years," indicating that the harvest increase, if any, fell below population growth on both occasions. It seems that 1959 not only did not exceed 1958 production but likely fell as low as 190,000,000 tons, or even less. Mr. Wu said that the 1960 grain tax of 24,000,000 tons was "based on a maximum of 12 percent tax on the 1958 crop." That would indicate a taxable crop of 200,000,000 tons

---

* As examples, the Chinese have learned to process an edible and highly nutritious dry biscuit from green leaves of certain trees and also from processed sea algae.

for 1958.* The grain tax was to be held fixed for three or four years. Mr. Wu added, "Even if the 1960 harvest should reach as high as 250,-000,000 tons the tax will still be only 24,000,000 tons." The intimation to me was that 250,000,000 tons was now regarded as a high aspiration yet to be attained.

Chou En-lai's comment, quoted above, was made on October 18, 1960. A visiting foreign economist who was consulted by Chou En-lai on statistical method in the formulation of crop estimates later told me that in his presence the Prime Minister had berated top statisticians for bringing him revised figures which showed that their earlier estimates had been *20 percent* above what now seemed the probable expectation. That was in mid-November. If 190,000,000 tons was something like their earlier estimates, a reduction by 20 percent would bring it down to 152,000,000 tons. That was my own guess for the probable 1960 harvest.

Such an estimate would correspond also with what Marshal Montgomery was told in a long interview he had with Mao Tse-tung late in 1961. "The normal grain harvest in China is about 180 million tons; in 1960 it was 150 million tons and the forecast for 1961 was ten million tons more," wrote Lord Montgomery in paraphrasing his conversation with Mao. "They had used up all their reserves of grain during the past *three years* to feed the nation; they now had to build up fresh reserves." [10] Mao's figures were much below estimates by the most skeptical Western specialists. Montgomery did not report whether Mao's figure included potatoes, but probably it did. As a rule Chinese use "grain" loosely as a synonym for "food crops" exclusive of vegetables but not of potatoes. Mao has followed that usage. It should be added that the taxable harvest is always lower than the gross output, however, as it excludes private plot and considerable above-quota peasant production and consumption.

Nevertheless, it thus seemed probable that China's grain product in 1960 was 17 to 20 percent below "normal grain harvest" and that the full extent of the inflated estimates for 1958 and 1959 had at last been fully recognized. The imperative necessity for a massive campaign to grow additional food by all means, and to halt most new capital construction while industry concentrated its output on improving the tools of agriculture, became obvious. Measures were initiated such as I have mentioned seeing used—private gardens, private poultry and pig raising, wide cultivation of marginal land for fodder (especially sweet potatoes) and for human consumption—as well as the return of certain acreages planted in cotton, hemp, tobacco and other "cash crops" to the production of food.

---

* In a conversation with Yung Lung-kuei, of the Bureau of Statistics, however, the "maximum" tax rate was given as 13 percent, which would give a slightly lower output for 1958.

Reports abroad have given somewhat distorted impressions of the amount of food exported by China. That seems to have been held to less than 2 percent, more than half of which was soya beans up to 1955, according to figures supplied by Ch'en Yun in a reply to questions raised in the second session of the National Congress. On August 15, 1959, Chou En-lai reported that up to that date the year's "exports of rice totaled only 792,000 tons while our pork exports were equivalent to only 1,400,000 pigs; this constituted less than one percent of last year's output of rice" and a similar percentage of the pig population.[11] In 1960, I was told by Yao I-lin, Minister of Commerce, that the grain export quota fixed for that year was 4,000,000 tons, or less than 2 percent of an expectation of 220,000,000 tons. I later learned from foreign diplomats that certain contracts had been annulled. Others were largely balanced by rice imports—chiefly from Burma and Ceylon, before heavy purchases from Canada and Australia began in 1961.

The rice China exported to Cuba—in exchange for much-needed sugar—and the small tonnages sent to a few other countries to fulfill barter contracts, altogether amounted to a bagatelle in relation to internal consumption. The nation has exported processed meat, eggs, dairy products and other foodstuffs; this is also small-scale compared to the total. (Even if the people consumed *all* their existing cattle, pigs and poultry those would provide less than 500 calories per day per person, for *one* year, as may be calculated from the food tables in the Appendix.) The fact is that China again became a heavy grain importer in 1961. Purchases of wheat and barley made her Canada's No. 2 customer and Australia's No. 1 customer in 1961. China bought outright 6,466,000 tons of foreign grain, for 1961-63 deliveries, at a cost of $367,000,000. New contract options drawn with Canada alone would enable China to double that purchase within the same period, *if necessary*.

Crop failures and the drain on foreign exchange to buy food abroad not only halted domestic industrial expansion but depressed a promising foreign trade. Agricultural products still contribute a little over one-third of the value of China's industrial output as a whole. About half the national revenue "comes directly or indirectly from agriculture," while "over 70 percent of the total volume of exports consists of agricultural products or processed agricultural goods [textiles, etc.]."[12] In 1950, China's exports and imports amounted to only $2,000,000,000; by 1959 they reached $6,000,000,000, and showed a growing balance in China's favor. Sixty to 80 percent of this trade has been oriented to the Communist bloc; in late years a slight shift to non-Communist countries resulted in an exchange of products valued at $1,500,000,000 in 1959. That alone is more than China's total world trade before the war. Until 1961 well over 90 percent of all China's imports had been machinery or other capital goods. The proportion of her own exports of industrial and mining products rose from 9 percent in 1950 to 27 percent in 1958, while her exports of agricultural raw materials and products fell from

58 percent to 36 percent. In 1961, however, trade with the U.S.S.R. declined 20 percent, and with most other countries fell off 50 percent or more.

Even if the Chinese in one year consumed all the grain so far delivered from abroad it would add less than 100 grams to the average daily diet. As I have emphasized, rations in China are not equally distributed, except among children. They are based on the amount and kind of work performed and, to some extent, on the estimate of his needs which every individual, after "examining his conscience," is required to make. Late in 1960 I was told by Yao I-lin that the national average minimum grain ration was 25 catties (27.5 pounds) a month for dependents and sedentary workers, and ranged to 40 pounds and up for heavy workers. "Senior intellectuals" were classified with miners and steel fabricators as "heavy workers," incidentally, as may be seen in the ration tables in the Appendix (pages 749-752).

Mr. Yao asserted that the monthly minimum of 25 catties (in whole rice, about 1,500 calories daily) could and would be maintained; in some areas it might temporarily fall below that. Dependents or non-producers in the cities were always the first to feel shortages of supply and cases of undernourishment generally were found in this category. Contrary to impressions abroad, peasants eat well (heavy workers' rations) unless they are in areas of grave underproduction or want. The dispersal of "nonessential" persons from the cities in 1960 and 1961 was a form of direct food relief; they went *hsia fang* to produce or earn their own food at the source.

Szechuan boasts that it alone can "feed five provinces," but it is a long haul from there to coastal Shantung or Canton. Inadequate transportation is a first handicap in fair distribution. Freight priorities on railways (with a mileage still about one-thirtieth as much per person as that in the United States) had heavily favored industrialization programs. Motor vehicles, even more inadequate, were likewise needed for the shipment of raw materials and finished products in accordance with industrial ambitions. The movement of food into the cities even from nearby suburbs was, as I saw, still largely accomplished by hand carts or human backs. Raising transport priorities for food and agricultural tools in order to meet emergency needs was in itself enough to impose a slowdown in industrialization.

One area least accessible is near the Canton delta which produces the Hongkong immigrants. "It seems clear," wrote John Watt, a British China specialist, in a study of the effect of transportation on famine prevention, "that there are areas lying east and southwest of Canton and between the East and West rivers and the coastline which are not well served by transportation and which, in the event of natural calamities and the exhaustion of local supplies, could not easily obtain relief from elsewhere." [13]

It is not generally known abroad that China has been publishing the results of nutritional surveys for several years. Only recently these have become available through translations distributed by the United States Department of Commerce. One foreign specialist in agrarian affairs has made a study of these surveys for the *China Quarterly,* a London publication sponsored by the Congress for Cultural Freedom, which is not a pro-Communist organization. After careful analysis his conclusion is that the Chinese data represent "results of their investigations in a manner free from political bias." [14] For example, one survey revealed the existence of protein deficiency ailments in 4 percent of the students of a Changsha secondary school who had been working "from 4 A.M. to 10 P.M., preparing for examinations." By contrast, surveys conducted in 586 commune canteens in 1958 and 1959 showed peasant intake averaging from 2,245 calories per head daily in August, up to 3,000 and 4,000 calories during the busy harvesting seasons. Proteins, fats, carbohydrates, calcium and vitamins were found generally adequate. The author's conclusion was that even in 1961 "the diet, though monotonous and lacking the protective foods considered essential in European consumption patterns, is sufficient to sustain the Chinese population in good health and working condition." [15]

An interesting fact brought out by China's nutritional surveys is that women engaged in productive work generally raise their food consumption at a higher rate than men. In 1960, in Peking, I was told by Mayor Wu Han that the "250,000 women added to the municipal working force since 1956" had caused demands for food much greater than anticipated. A Chinese woman put on "heavy duty" work increases her food intake by 900 calories a day compared to 670 calories for a man.

My own conclusion, based on observations in the field and available data, is that the minimum "average diet" of *urban* Chinese in 1960-62 —varying with the seasons—consisted of about 1,350 to 1,450 calories a day in grain or equivalents. This meant a drop in the basic grain ration to slightly below the level of the year 1952. Persons on minimum rations now had to get from 500 to 800 calories a day from increased production and consumption of vegetables, fruit, poultry, fish, eggs, fats, oils or substitutes which normally supply about 300-500 calories per person. Peasants ate much more, on the average 2,000 to 3,500 calories, with seasonal variations; many nonworker urban people got less than 2,000 calories. Whatever he was eating, the "average Chinese" maintained himself in good health, as far as anyone could see. Since 1960 the government has been "building up fresh reserves" of grain, as Mao Tse-tung stated; withholdings are more substantial than in the past.

"Statistics are made to conceal as well as to reveal," one Chinese citizen remarked to me when I complained of their former unreliability and current scarcity. Bearing this philosophy in mind, it is possible to decide that the present dearth of factual data conceals nothing but bad news. Obversely, it would be prudent not to overlook the possibility that the Chinese authorities have learned the lessons of self-deceiving claims in 1958 and 1959, that understatement is now in vogue, and that present austerity measures may reflect a determination first to establish food and industrial reserves sufficient to meet any future series of natural reverses—before announcing new gains to either their own people or the outside world.

Government officials know that China must not only catch up with 1958 output but considerably surpass it. "Now *here,* you see," said the Red Queen to Alice, "it takes all the running *you* can do, to keep in the same place. If you want to get somewhere else, you must run at least twice as fast as that!" By 1963 China will have added to her population, since 1958, more people than there are in Great Britain. If the "normal harvest" was 180,000,000 tons (as Mao told Marshal Montgomery) China should in 1962 have increased her output above 1961 by 13 per cent in order to get back to "normal." To catch up with population growth from 1958 to 1962 another 8 percent would have to be added to that. To "get somewhere else," and well ahead of her population increment, output in 1963 ought to exceed 200,000,000 tons.

The nation has suffered and learned the hard way, by experience acquired in do-it-yourself techniques. In their schematic overemphasis on heavy industry and certain other doctrinaire measures its leaders repeated some of the Russian errors. They have made others all their own. They have learned that too much haste makes waste; they now know a great deal more about what won't work; they are at least farther along than countries which are making no basic efforts to solve their own problems. What solutions emerge will be pragmatic and suitable to Chinese conditions. For various other reasons my conclusion is that, given peace and reasonable luck, somewhere between 1963 and 1967 China may astonish the world by demonstrating that she can comfortably feed her population. In this estimate I am assuming that China will continue the renewed emphasis, which began in 1961, on various means of curtailment of the rate of population growth, including mass distribution of the means of birth control and advocacy of the postponement of marriages to the age of twenty-one for women and twenty-three to twenty-five for men.

Until then, no one can contend that "socialist construction" has solved China's fundamental problems. What is more, no Communist country anywhere has yet produced anything like what Marxists call "food abundance." Over the whole decade 1949-59 China appears to have made more progress in that direction than Russia was able to make, despite its greater natural wealth, during the first thirty-three years of socialism. In his report to the Central Committee in 1953, Nikita Khrushchev complained that "although the Soviet population had increased by nearly 50 million and the world agricultural technique showed a great advance over 1916, there was less livestock in the

U.S.S.R. in 1952 than in 1916. Grain production in comparable areas could only show an increase of barely 5 percent since 1928."

Nor did Tito's "other road to socialism" in Yugoslavia, where most farmland has remained under private ownership, show results to impress China. In 1961 Yugoslavia had a harvest shortfall 30 percent below expectations. In 1962 the Yugoslavs were warned to prepare "for a harvest so bad that it could almost classify as a disaster." The nation's wheat crop again would be "less than 3,000,000 tons . . . nearly 1,000,-000 tons under Yugoslavia's annual consumption requirements." [16] In 1961-62 Tito received about 1,000,000 tons of grain from United States surpluses; now the same amount would have to be provided in 1963, to feed her 19,000,000 people. According to Senator William Proxmire, writing in the *New York Times* of June 22, the United States had by 1962 provided $2,000,000,000 in aid to Yugoslavia. Had Red China received per capita help on the same scale from the United States we would by now have dropped about $70,000,000,000 there.

India, where free enterprise, free-world aid and American philanthropy actively compete with Soviet help, certainly provides no viable alternative. India consumes so little meat that it is not even listed in her production; the staple food of the millions is almost wholly grain or equivalents. China's food supply has steadily improved compared to that of India. According to comparative studies made by Professor Etienne for 1952 and 1955, normal years in both countries, the per capita output in China was more than 30 percent higher than in India.[17] In 1958-1959, considered a good year in India, when the population was about 420,000,000 (today it is around 450,000,000), the grain harvest (potatoes, beans and lentils included) was reported at 75,500,000 tons.[18] The Indian figure might be reckoned as high as 85,000,000 tons, however, if Indian rice were weighed as paddy, or uncleaned, as it is in China. Even so, that would mean a per person gross output about 10 percent below that of China in the year of her disaster of the century, 1960. (Not counting soya beans, 5 to 10 percent of China's crop.) Nothing in China is comparable to the hunger and beggary one sees on the streets of Calcutta or the villages of Bengal.

But perhaps the American experience could solve China's agricultural problems? Yes, it might—if we could duplicate, in China, the present endowments of the United States system. One way to start might be to reduce China's population by 80 percent, or 550,000,000 people, thereby providing, for the surviving 150,000,000 Chinese, about the same acreage of cropland per person that America has. A less drastic way would be to expand China's croplands by 40,000,000 acres —to equal the United States' currently cultivated area—to increase China's fertilizer output by ten times, to increase her motor-mechanized agriculture by twenty times, and then to secure a yield some 400 percent better than the United States now harvests from *the same amount of land.* In the course of completing this altruistic demonstration we should also have to find gainful employment for about 200,000,000 Chinese farmers whose labor would be rendered superfluous by the change.

There is still another way in which the American system might work wonders for China. The United States and Canada have about a billion acres of idle croplands and grasslands. Perhaps the surplus Chinese (over and above the equivalent of United States land-per-acre population) could be imported to cultivate this land for their own consumption and export to hungry and poor lands only? The effect would be to quadruple or better the United States-Canadian food output, to provide an abundance not only for China but for the whole world, enormously to increase the wealth and importance of the entire Western hemisphere, to eliminate all future danger of war between West and East, dispose of the have-nots problem and incalculably enrich both Asian and American culture.

The trouble is, that is not realistic. How would that affect Senator Eastland, for example, and the quarter of a million dollars he has received as an annual reward for idling his thousands of acres of Mississippi land? What about Mr. Estes and his vanishing silos? And Texas? It does not seem likely that this solution will be adopted while Senator Eastland remains chairman of the Senate Judiciary Committee, and immigration inspector. Nor is it likely as long as Mississippi retains the championship for the lowest per capita income in the nation, an illiteracy rate some 30 percent higher than Japan's, a maternal and infant mortality rate higher than that of urban China, the highest percentage of native-born white citizens in America, and the lowest percentage of Negro voters.

These daydreams suggest that the United States will no more solve China's food problem by means of the American system than it will solve Hongkong's overpopulation problem by providing open house for surplus Orientals.

The Chinese are of course mistaken in suspecting that the United States has the Christian intention of reducing their population by 80 percent. But no leader, whether a capitalist nationalist or a communist socialist, could welcome even the possibility of having so radical a solution imposed on his nation. On the contrary, the Chinese must strive not only to feed and conserve their multitudes; they must at the same time build nuclear bombs, to ensure that any invading force will suffer at least a comparable reduction in numbers. This is what both common-sense American capitalist nationalists and common-sense Chinese communist nationalists agree to call Security.

82

China, the United States, Russia and the Bomb

On January 26, 1954, Representative Frederic R. Coudert, at a hearing of the House Committee on Appropriations, asked Walter S. Robertson, Assistant Secretary of State under John Foster Dulles:

Q. "Did I correctly understand you to say that the heart of the present policy toward China and Formosa is that there is to be kept alive a constant threat of military action vis-à-vis Red China in the hope that at some point there will be an internal breakdown?"

Mr. Robertson: "Yes, sir, that is my conception."

Q. "Fundamentally, does that not mean that the United States is undertaking to maintain for an indefinite period of years American dominance in the Far East?"

Mr. Robertson: "Yes. Exactly."

Testifying before the Appropriations Committee on February 10, 1955, Mr. Robertson further declared: "Our hope of solving the problem of China is . . . through action which will promote disintegration from within."

I "learned from informed sources" in Peking that in 1957 Mao Tse-tung said to a visiting Yugoslav official, "We aren't afraid of atomic bombs. We have a very large territory and a big population. Bombs *could not kill all of us. What if they killed even 300,000,000? We would still have plenty more. China would be the last country to die."*

Even if Mao did not say that, someone would have had to invent it. Such a thought is bound to occur to anyone seeking an explanation for the absence in the Chinese press of warnings of the awful might of nuclear arms and China's defenselessness against them. It is also said that "China is so poor she has nothing to lose" and "welcomes war." Poor as she is, China is far wealthier and more powerful than ever before, yet it is true that individual Chinese have nothing much to lose but their lives. But is fear of losing the wealth in private property of some of us in the West a greater deterrent against war than fear of losing all our lives?

Suppose that Mao does fear atomic war? Suppose that he does not believe in the peaceful intentions of American forces in Southeast Asia and Korea, on his threshold in the Taiwan Strait, in Taiwan itself, but imagines that they are preparing for a "sudden blow" of nuclear holocaust? What would he do? Imagine the reverse of the situation. If China were giving armed support to an American Communist general in Hawaii, if China had air bases in Canada and Mexico, if Chinese reconaissance planes were daily flying over American territory, and if China had the bomb and the U.S. did not, what would the President do? Would he demoralize the American people with accounts of the horrors of nuclear war, and the hopelessness of defense? Would he switch to communism? Or would he tell the people to fear not, to take heart, to leap forward, to win new allies, to have faith—and meanwhile get busy on the bomb?

In the summer of 1962 there began a repeat performance of the 1958 Taiwan crisis and brinkmanship contest. For weeks the Generalissimo clamored for support for an invasive action against the mainland. Chiang's Taipei press described the United States as "cowardly" and "short-sighted" for delaying a war of liberation. Again Chiang reinforced his isolated garrisons on Quemoy (Chin-men Tao) and Matsu with new American equipment (including howitzers designed to fire nuclear shells) which could be used for an invasion; again his commandos raided the coast; again his American planes dropped propaganda on the mainland promising liberation.

In 1958 both sides had contributed to the long buildup of tension; it was not easy to say exactly who initiated the crisis and for what purposes. 1962 was not quite the same. For many months Communist guns had shelled Quemoy Island only intermittently and with propaganda, not warheads. It seemed possible that Peking was remaining passive while waiting to see whether President Kennedy would act in accordance with his 1960 campaign speeches, which had called for United States "disengagement" in China's near waters.

Chiang's renewed agitation was probably based in part on the theory that he would now be welcomed by uprisings of "millions of starving people," and in part on speculation that Sino-Russian relations had so far deteriorated that Khrushchev would not repeat his 1958 guarantee of all necessary aid to China to repulse any United States–supported attack. China's large-scale mobilization on the coast, followed by Khrushchev's renewed offer of support "by the whole socialist world," demonstrated that the two "tests" the Generalissimo may have had in mind could not be undertaken without again inviting consequences perilous to all. It is now useful to recall further how the 1958 events strengthened China's determination to become an independent nuclear power.

In December, 1954, a year and a half after President Eisenhower had accepted a truce to end the Korean War, he signed a military alliance with Chiang Kai-shek. In effect this established a unilateral United States protectorate over the Taiwan area. While the Generalissimo had been technically "re-leashed" by the alliance, this recognition of his claim to leadership of China seemed to be meaningless unless he was eventually to be helped to recover the mainland from a sanctuary held inviolate by American forces. Chiang used his American naval and air weapons to harass Red China's shipping. Taiwan boasted of landing spies, saboteurs and armed bands of agitators on the coast. By 1958 the exiled dictator had massed more than one-fourth of his troops on the islands of Matsu and Quemoy, the latter less than five miles from the mainland and within easy artillery range of Amoy. Taiwan spokesmen announced "imminent" liberation.

While Chiang issued communiqués about "preparations" Peking had not been silent. Virulent protests had been made by the mainland government against American "aggression" in Taiwan. Demands were renewed that the U.S. fleet withdraw from Chinese waters and Chinese territory. In the summer of 1958 high officials in Peking declared their intention to remove Chiang's blockade of Amoy and Foochow, exercised through control of the offshore islands, and promised final liberation of Taiwan itself. Troops, planes and ships were mobilized.

During an earlier Quemoy crisis following signature of the alliance, President Eisenhower had asked for and been given (January, 1955) unprecedented powers by Congress to commit the nation to go to war, if necessary, to preserve the Generalissimo's control over the disputed area. Invoking that power now, he ordered the Seventh Fleet battle-mobilized in the Taiwan Strait and it was announced that the U.S. air force based in the territory had been issued atomic missiles. Few knew whether to expect a Nationalist landing in China or a Communist attempt on the islands.

On August 10, Secretary of State John Foster Dulles defined United States policy toward China in what Peking had to regard as highly aggressive terms when he declared that Americans were obliged to "do all that we can to contribute to [the] passing" of the Chinese People's Republic.[1] On August 23, Red batteries began an intensive bombardment of Quemoy, together with warnings of an "imminent" landing and demands for surrender. Chiang's guns replied and his planes engaged those of the mainland, while United States naval vessels were deployed to protect his convoys. On August 31, Moscow's official party organ, *Pravda*, warned the United States that any power which threatened China was "threatening the Soviet Union also" and that "in its just struggle" China would receive "the necessary moral and material help." On September 4, China declared a twelve-mile coastal zone to be national waters.[2] The same day, Secretary of State Dulles countered with a threat that the United States might be obliged to bomb China if a conflict with Chiang Kai-shek's forces endangered the inviolability of Taiwan and the Pescadore (Penghu) Islands.[3] The United States sent naval vessels within three miles of the coast.

On September 5, *Pravda* categorically threatened that a "counterblow" against any "new military adventure in the Far East" would not be restricted to the Taiwan Strait but would "put an end to U.S. imperialist aggression." On September 6, Premier Chou En-lai repeated his demands for United States withdrawal. At the same time he offered to reopen the suspended Sino-American ambassadorial talks (provided for by the 1954 Geneva agreement) at Warsaw, to seek a peaceful settlement. As an added inducement Premier Khrushchev the next day wired President Eisenhower that "an attack on China would be considered an attack on the Soviet Union," which would "do everything" required to defend its ally.[4]

In both his September 7 letter and a follow-up missive (September 19) to the President, Khrushchev implied that the Soviet guarantee was limited to a defensive war by China against any attack backed by the United States; apparently it did not extend to an offensive by China against American armed forces in the Taiwan Strait. If this clearly put a quietus on any hopes nurtured in Chiang Kai-shek that Mr. Dulles' promise of doing "all that we can to contribute to [the] passing" of the Peking government could include American force to invade China, it also declined Soviet responsibility for the consequences of a Communist advance into the Strait.

Following the establishment of this equilibrium of power the tension began to relax. Mutual bombardments and air battles between Nationalist and Communist planes continued for some weeks, but the focus gradually shifted toward disengagement measures after the United States and China reopened the Warsaw talks. Chiang Kai-shek abandoned his attempts to blockade Amoy and Foochow. Talk of imminent liberation subsided on both sides. After a cease-fire on

October 6, China reduced offensive action against Quemoy to token shelling "on odd days only"—usually preceded by radio warnings to the inhabitants. The reason given for this in China was that, in a continuing civil war situation, it maintained "living contacts" which emphasized the American role of armed intervention.

Very detailed syntheses of data covering the 1958 "brink" were made for the United States government by RAND Corporation intelligence analysts. Some results of these studies are available in Alice Langley Hsieh's book *China's Strategy in the Nuclear Era,* and Donald S. Zagoria's *The Sino-Soviet Dispute, 1956-1961,* both published in 1962. These are masterpieces of spoor tracking across mountains of translations of the enemy press. Their conclusions support Secretary of State Dulles' belief that he engineered the "failure of China's Taiwan venture" by brinkmanship—exercised at the end of the longest limb of United States foreign policy and at heavy and continuing expense. (Fleet mobilization in the Taiwan Strait alone reportedly cost $1,000,-000,000.[5])

Mrs. Hsieh and Mr. Zagoria agree that China probably never intended to attempt a landing on Quemoy but sought to interdict it by artillery fire and force a surrender. They see the "failure of China's Taiwan venture" as a result of United States nuclear threat and use of naval force in running the blockade, and of China's unwillingness to fire on American ships. In judging Mr. Dulles' success, however, neither Mrs. Hsieh nor Mr. Zagoria recollects the American promise of doing "all that we can" to bring about the "passing" of the mainland regime. They do not find it relevant to recall Assistant Secretary of State Walter Robertson's provocative statement that the United States' "hope of solving the problem of China is . . . through action which will promote disintegration from within." Both overlook the ominous interpretation which China had placed on the United States' rejection of Khrushchev's unexpected agreement (in the main) to a long-standing Allied disarmament plan.* They make no mention of the hardening effects on Chinese policy of the Taiwan alliance and of Dulles' studiedly uncompromising rejection of all Peking's overtures (from 1955 on) to open conversations on a ministerial level in search of a Taiwan solution.

Seen against that background of events, China's side of the "Taiwan venture" is more comprehensible. The result at least allayed Peking's fear that the Quemoy-Matsu islands could be used as a forward invasion base supported by the United States. Mr. Dulles' threat to bring about the passing of the People's Republic had now clearly been restrained or modified by Soviet counterthreats which placed precise limitations on the State Department's ambitions in that respect. The American success was further qualified by the cessation of Chiang Kai-shek's attempts to blockade China's ports. In cold-war analyses we

* See page 722.

necessarily see through a glass darkly, but if an acceptable explanation of an event is to be reached it is mandatory to remember that each of the two antagonists makes his contribution to the resolution. Opposite numbers of Mrs. Hsieh and Mr. Zagoria in the Institute of International Affairs in Peking, on the other hand, talked to me of the "failure of American imperialism's 1958 adventure," but ignored the fact that the paper tiger had once again frustrated China's "freedom of action" within her own territorial waters.

Any realistic analysis of the results of Taiwan must concur, however, in the general RAND conclusion that the Taiwan crisis also reflected internal duels between Peking and Moscow over joint means best suited to confront United States arms in the Far East. A number of articles and books have used the RAND analysis to explain disagreements inside the Chinese army and party and between them and Russia over access to nuclear weapons and their proper use in the overall strategy of Communist foreign policy. Those interested in the complex details should consult the originals; here I confine myself to certain aspects of the RAND analysis directly related to China's atomic program.

A basic assumption of the RAND papers (presumably taken seriously in the Pentagon and the State Department) has been interpreted to mean that there exists in China a "professional officer" class which tends to be in rapport with Khrushchev and in sharp conflict with "nonprofessionals" and party leaders. These differences began following the Korean War, when China's army was reorganized and mechanized with Russian aid. The "professionals" wished to free the army from party control. They also lobbied for greater priority for modern war (including nuclear) industries as against the requirements of a balanced industrialization.

Opposed to the "professionals" were the men of "guerrilla mentality." These were the "nonprofessional" marshals committed to party leadership and to Mao Tse-tung's general strategic concepts, which emphasize human or political factors as ultimately more decisive than initial mechanical means in any war. Atomic weapons were held by the "professionals" to be capable of deciding the outcome by eliminating the human base of political power in a lightning blow.

The RAND analysts suggest a Chinese army high command divided between professional generals and guerrilla generals; between those who believe nuclear weapons are decisive and those who do not; between party and nonparty or antiparty officers' cliques; between those who advocate reliance on conventional weapons and army democratic traditions and those who consider them obsolete; between those who advocate high-priority nuclearization and those who do not; and between "leftists" who want war and "rightists" who want to avoid it.

Is not that too oversimplified a view of the Chinese army? There is nothing in China closely comparable to the West Point or Annapolis elite in conflict with the nonprofessional, or to the contradiction between the Prussian Junker class and the "non-von" plebeian Nazi generals of the last war. (There is also nothing comparable to American intra-service pressure groups lobbying for General Motors vs. General Dynamics or Boeing vs. Consolidated Vultee.) Thus far China has no professional soldiers in that sense. She has officers' training academies, of course, but most cadets still rise from the ranks. In a manner very different even from Russia, party and army leadership in China have from the beginning been inseparable. In a literal sense all general officers in China are guerrillas, all are professionals, and all are party men.

"You can no more cut me off from Mao Tse-tung," General Chu Teh told Chang Kuo-t'ao in 1935, when Chang held him prisoner and demanded that he denounce Mao and break all ties with him, "than you can cut a man in half." [6] Three years later, and again united with his military alter ego, Mao declared, "Our principle is that the Party commands the gun, and the gun will never be allowed to command the Party." [7] This policy made it impossible for individual warlords to arise and break unity, just as it prevented any future *coup d'état* by politicians backed by army conspirators.

As already emphasized, seven of the eight marshals of the army are in the Politburo itself, and the senior marshal is traditionally in the Standing Committee. All of them are professional if by that is meant persons having had technical training of some kind; all of them are also guerrillas if by that is meant battle experience in irregular warfare. The same thing would apply to most majority officers given postwar training by the Russians. There are no nonparty commanders. An elite exists only in terms of prestige acquired as veterans of the Kiangsi campaigns, the Long March, the Patriotic War, the Liberation War and Korea. In both the Liberation and Korean wars the Chinese command displayed great skill in the deployment of large numbers of troops and the use of combined modern weapons of all kinds, first against Chiang's American-trained officers, then against American armies themselves.

That does not mean there are no disagreements in the high command. It does mean that differences must be seen as reflections of *party* disputes over the correct way to reconcile political objectives with available means. These contradictions can be resolved only inside the party, however, not in the army except as the party is the army. Those who persist in opposing the dominant central line are apt to be called "antiparty," but that does not make them professionals or guerrillas. From this it is evident that any clear knowledge of China's nuclear policies requires a study of party debates over national and international strategy. It is also evident that the heart of such debates must concern key problems of military relations with the Soviet party and the Red Army, of which few men possess details. Something may be inferred from history, however.

The People's Liberation Army has an independent character which sets it quite apart from European satellite forces. This history began in 1928, when native Communists confounded prevailing Comintern views by basing the revolution on the peasantry and forming an army which Moscow at first considered "bandits." Mao was expelled from the Central Committee but later successfully discredited Moscow's chosen leader, Li Li-san. In 1935-36 Mao finally consolidated "native" control over the Moscow-trained "returned students" and firmly integrated party command in the army. Soviet aid and detailed directives virtually ceased, except for one decisive intervention in 1936,[8] but Mao's leadership was accepted in Moscow.

In ensuing years the Chinese party built up vast irregular forces of far greater potential than Stalin realized. In 1947 Stalin advised Chinese party leaders to take a subordinate role in a coalition under Chiang Kai-shek.[9] They "agreed," but instead engaged in a major armed struggle for power and quickly won victory. Stalin had so far miscalculated history that in 1945 he stripped Manchuria—two years later the Chinese Reds' main base—of nearly two billion dollars' worth of machinery.

The Russians effectively restored the machine basis of Manchurian industry during the Korean War, when the Sino-Soviet alliance (signed in 1950) was first implemented (in a covert way). No outsider knows exactly who signaled that war. When it began, Soviet advisers were still in North Korea but when reverses occurred they quickly withdrew. It was only after President Truman established United States protection over Taiwan, and after two warnings from Peking that China would intervene if American troops continued their march beyond the Thirty-eighth Parallel toward Manchuria, that the "Chinese Volunteers" entered the war, as Chou En-lai has reminded us. Even high Chinese officials believed that they had won a victory against the Americans—and in a limited sense they had. If one may judge from the support given to Chou En-lai by the North Korean party delegation to Moscow in October, 1961, when Chou opposed Khrushchev's expulsion of Albania from the bloc, the Chinese party emerged from the Korean War with stronger influence in Korea than Russia.

Nothing that happened in Korea had caused the Chinese to hesitate to back Ho Chi Minh and the Vietnamese revolutionary war of independence against the French. Mao's influence on Ho was considerable, and to him the situation in Indochina at the time of Dien Bien Phu (1954) fitted the axiom, "When the enemy retreats, we pursue." Soviet views prevailed. The Communists' joint decision to work for peaceful or competitive coexistence (minimizing the danger of local wars escalating into world war) required a policy of compromise. The result was the Geneva Conference, where France finally recognized the complete independence of Vietnam but left it divided between resistance forces in the north, led by Ho Chi Minh, and a coalition regime in the south which took over from the French puppet, Bao Dai—an anomaly which we shall examine later. Meanwhile, since it frustrated the China-Vietnam aim to free Southeast Asia of Western colonial power, this arrangement was unsatisfactory; to Peking it meant the probability of gratuitously providing new bases for American imperialism to replace French imperialism in South Asia after it was already defeated.

This record suggests: 1) an adroit Chinese leadership capable of wide maneuver to achieve its objectives within the concept of a "socialist camp led by the Soviet Union"; 2) a series of Chinese victories won in subtle "compliant-defiance" of Moscow's judgment and yet strategically dependent on the implied Soviet shield for success; and 3) a series of restraints on China's political aspirations in East Asia probably rather flatly imposed in the national interests of the U.S.S.R.

China's military and economic dependence on Russia thus had continued to modify her political independence. By 1955 Moscow's policies had made Peking fully aware of the role of nuclear weapons in their relationship, and Russia must have been under constant pressure to supply the means to her ally. While waiting for a decision it is reasonable to assume that Peking's leaders debated three ways in which China could become Russia's nuclear partner: 1) to place their forces as completely under Moscow's command as the Warsaw Pact states; 2) to seek a Soviet-Chinese all-weapons joint command like NATO with an equal division of powers which would recognize China's manpower-strategic resources as balancing Soviet technological superiority; or 3) to attempt to build an independent nuclear arms industry.

These were basically political alternatives affecting overall party strategy. Debate in the army command doubtless found some "guerrilla-professional-party" generals on one side and some on another but in essence it was a political debate. The alternatives posed problems inherent in the unique position of China in the socialist bloc, which did not arise among the European satellites. In East Germany, for example, the presence of nuclear weapons is implied by the presence of Soviet command without in any way changing the political status of the East German government.

Thus the first choice, for the Chinese, would have meant the surrender of supreme military command and placing China in the role of a complete satellite. In view of the history cited, and especially since the period of decision coincided with post-Stalinist transitions and great instability in Moscow, the first choice was unlikely even if the Russians proposed it, as they perhaps did at one time.* The third

* I was so told by one Communist, and only one.

alternative fitted China's aspirations as a great power but it was a costly long-range solution unless Moscow provided the technical and material assistance on a major scale. The second alternative would seem the most practical solution and one which the Chinese may have pursued with great persistence.

Khrushchev wooed Peking leaders in 1956 and 1957 and committed Russia to new agreements to build key basic industries on a generous scale. During his touch-and-go struggles inside the Soviet party, and throughout the Hungarian and Polish crises, Mao's backing was important to him. The knowledge that China's armies were behind Khrushchev put a chill in Poland's "revisionists" and helped swing Gomulka into line, which in turn gave Khrushchev a tighter grip inside his own party.

While he was consolidating power and needed China's cooperation, Khrushchev may have encouraged hopes of an integrated command to buttress Peking's position in the Far East. Following the Soviet launching of the first ICBM and space satellite, Mao's famous speech in Moscow in November, 1957, stated that the "East wind was prevailing over the West wind" and contended that the strength of the socialist camp already exceeded that of the West. It made sense only on an assumption of close integration of Sino-Soviet military command and maximum *combined* use of Soviet military technology. China received nuclear reactor materials from Russia in 1956-57, many Soviet physicists were sent in as advisers, and there were unconfirmed reports[10] from Poland that Russia had agreed to supply China with atomic missiles. Such reports may have been inspired by Eastern European Communists in the hope of provoking Soviet denials, after Mao Tse-tung's return from the November conference in Moscow.

That conference had exposed serious but apparently still friendly differences between Khrushchev and Mao Tse-tung over questions of correct strategy and tactics for the exploitation of the great advances in Soviet nuclear and rocket technology. Their conflict of views and purposes will presently be examined in detail. In this context it may suffice to say that to Khrushchev the H-bomb and earth satellite meant primarily the attainment of near-absolute national security, which was bound to diminish his dependence on China. To Mao Tse-tung the gains meant the opening of broader possibilities for revolutionary initiatives in Asia under the shield of Soviet power. Peking's dissatisfaction with Khrushchev's intentions may have already been deeply aroused by December, 1957. The Taiwan crisis of 1958 was to provide the first clear test, however, of how far Mr. K. would commit his new power in support of both China's interests and the interests of world revolution—which Peking tended to see as identical.

On May 11, 1958, Foreign Minister Ch'en Yi declared that China would "soon" have atomic missiles. At the same time he announced support for Khrushchev's proposal for an atom-free zone in the Far

East. Quite possibly it was not until the Taiwan crisis in that year, when Khrushchev withheld nuclear protection for any offensive operations in the Taiwan area which might result in conflict with United States forces, that the Chinese party seriously embarked on a program to make nuclear weapons of their own.

Mao is not a man easily taken by bluff; he has used it too often himself. Anyone who has studied Mao's tactical doctrines may assume that he was not at all courting a nuclear war in 1958 but was convinced, and with good reason, that Mr. Dulles was using the bomb as blackmail on which he dared not make good if called. He *had* been called in Indochina, when the relative balance of political and nuclear forces was much more favorable to Mr. Dulles. In 1958 he was dangerously isolated from both Allied support and public opinion in the United States. Mao therefore must have been astonished and disappointed at what he would have considered Khrushchev's quite gratuitous and maladroit tip-off to the United States that the bomb would be withdrawn from Mao's hand if he followed through with an offensive to close down the Quemoy-Matsu bases.

Peking's decision to build a nuclear weapons industry was obviously related to both the leap-forward program of industrialization late in that year and the deterioration of Soviet-Chinese party harmony.

Contradictions between the new political, economic and social objectives of the communes and the technical needs of the military establishment found their expression, in 1959, in the replacement of Marshal P'eng Teh-huai as Minister of National Defense. P'eng is one of China's ablest party military specialists. A soldier all his life and a combat Communist since 1928, when he led an uprising of Kuomintang troops, he is an intrepid warrior with an impressive career. A native of Mao's Hsiang T'an county, he has loyally supported Mao in every test. In 1936 he emerged in Shensi beside Mao and Chou En-lai as leader of the armed survivors of the Long March, after which he held top command posts throughout war and revolution.

Early in the Korean War, P'eng replaced his subordinate, Lin Piao, as commander in chief of the Chinese Volunteers. Far from being a general of "guerrilla mentality," as some believers in the "guerrillas versus professionals" theory have suggested, P'eng is thoroughly familiar with the terms of modern combat. In Korea he fought first-rate armies equipped with latest weapons and learned much from his Soviet military advisers. He developed a new kind of tunnel warfare which used deep gun emplacements, complete ground cover and heavy tanks dug in as artillery in a type of battle quite different from the traditional mobile tactics of the past. Tunnel warfare is now taught in China's army training schools. P'eng also became keenly aware of China's dependence on Soviet material and technical aid. From 1957 onward he came to personify skepticism among party military specialists about innovations such as overuse of regular army units in commune labor, overextension of the militia system, and too much "politics in command" of training schedules.

P'eng favored continued long-term close technological reliance on the Soviet Union in order to lighten the burden of an independent all-weapons industry which China is now pursuing. It seems possible that he was held partly responsible for failing to win Khrushchev's agreement to set up a joint Far Eastern command in 1958. After Liu Shao-ch'i took over chairmanship of the government P'eng found himself increasingly ranged with the "rightist" minority in the Politburo. In 1959 he and his staff were replaced by Lin Piao, a more compliant and less colorful figure. Lin's task became the restoration, among party military specialists, of complete solidarity behind Politburo leadership in fulfillment of internal tasks and support of Mao's military doctrine and ideological challenge to Khrushchev. P'eng neither led any "conspiracy" against Mao, as reported abroad, nor was "arrested" (*Time*, February 9, 1962). The Chinese party leadership does not work that way. P'eng still holds his seat in the Politburo and may again assume an important role if warmer weather prevails between Russia and China.

By late 1958 Khrushchev's internal prestige was secure enough for him to begin to reassert some of the prerogatives of Josef Stalin as leader of the socialist camp. By 1959 he was in a position to offer crushing rejoinders to any "other party" aspirants to master-mind Soviet strategy toward the West. In 1960 the Sino-Soviet ideological dispute broke into the open. The Soviet Party Congress in Moscow in October, 1961, revealed even to the outside world that Mr. K. intended to retain his nuclear monopoly within the bloc. After the fifty-five-megaton explosion Mr. K. offered his most direct affront to Peking when he excommunicated the Albanian party, sole European supporter of Mao Tse-Tung's strategic concepts within the international Communist movement.

It is significant to recall an incident which probably further convinced Peking leaders, if any convincing was still necessary, that an independent nuclear capability was essential in order to secure equality of treatment for China as a great power. In 1959, Soviet Air Force pilots shot down a United States RB-47 that was allegedly flying reconnaissance inside the twelve-mile coastal zone claimed by the Soviet Union as its national waters. Mr. Khrushchev warned that future intruders would be met in the same way. Following that, no further American flights of that nature were reported in that area. Recalling this event, in contrast to American naval action around Quemoy, a Chinese official (quoting Mao) commented, "In order to get rid of the gun, we must first grasp it in our hand."

Meanwhile, China's own nuclear efforts have been intensified. In 1955, Russia had signed an agreement to assist China's atomic energy program "for peaceful purposes." Work in this field actually began much earlier. Chinese assistants were assigned to Soviet scientists in Sinkiang, where atomic test reactors were reported in 1951. When Sino-Soviet "joint companies" were dissolved in Sinkiang in 1955 some atomic equipment was rumored to have been given to the Chinese. Soviet exploitation of Sinkiang's uranium (discovered as early as 1944) may have been paid for in this way. Since then, especially rich uranium deposits have been found in Szechuan and eastern Tibet. A reactor of unknown capacity is said to be located in that general area.

China's only announcement of such facilities was made at the opening of a 10,000-kilowatt heavy water reactor north of Peking in June, 1958. By agreement Russia was to supply a second and larger reactor, which is now believed to be working in northern Manchuria. "All political power grows out of the barrel of a gun," observed Mao Tsetung, a philosophy with which existing nuclear powers obviously agree. Public statements by Chinese officials in recent years indicate that China aspires to produce plutonium in quantities sufficient to make her a nuclear power.

In the General Electric Corporation's comprehensive private study published late in 1960, its experts could see "no problems which the Chinese are not capable of solving" in the realization of that ambition.

According to this study, China possesses all the materials necessary and has more than enough scientists and engineers to carry on a program without further Soviet aid or any major diversion of domestic energies from other fields:

> China now (August, 1960) has approximately 210,000 engineers and 44,000 scientists, and of the scientists about 10,000 are physicists and about 15,000 are chemists. A program aimed at the production of plutonium bombs would require about 1.15 percent of the Chinese scientists, 1.5 percent of the physicists and 2.16 percent of the chemists. In the engineering field only about 0.65 percent of the total engineering personnel would be required.[11]

China's first announcement that uranium and thorium were being extracted from *domestic* ore was made by the Chinese Academy of Sciences more than four years ago. Not till 1959 did published plans call for the construction of a uranium plant, "although it would seem possible that such a plant would have been started a year or two earlier." Chinese output of 99.9 percent pure aluminum, seamless tubing and special steels required for bomb manufacture has greatly increased. China-made atomic laboratory equipment is being produced on a considerable scale, judging from displays of it I saw at several industrial fairs. Nuclear research facilities have been established at many institutes and colleges throughout the country.

Completion of a 500,000-kilowatt hydroelectric plant in Sinkiang in

1960 coincided with a ban on all travel by foreigners to that part of
the country. By 1961 visitors were also excluded from most of Manchuria, an area of relatively high concentrations of power, water and
transport. Severe strains were placed on the Chinese economy by
agricultural setbacks of 1960-61 but they give no reason for believing
that China's nuclear program was curtailed: "Based on China's production record to date and the fact that past predictions of a financial
crisis in China have not been correct it is . . . unwise to assume that
economic conditions in China will grossly hinder their progress in the
atomic energy field."

The highly detailed General Electric report concludes:

> Assuming no large delays in materials, and that all develop-
> ment, design, and construction work in support of the numerous
> facilities were done by the Chinese [without Soviet aid], it
> would take at least five and a half years, but more probably six
> years, before the first bomb would be tested . . . Thus, accord-
> ing to these calculations, if the Chinese started their nuclear
> weapons program at the beginning of 1958, they would explode
> their first bomb sometime in 1963 . . . and *they would become
> a nuclear power in 1966 or later.* . . . Then the words of Liu
> Ya-lou [commander of the Chinese Air Force], "By that time
> another new turning point will be reached in the international
> situation," may indeed be true. . . .[12]

From the time a nation explodes its first bomb to the time when it
accumulates sufficient uranium, plutonium, thorium and other supplies and facilities to become a "nuclear power" has been shown to be
about three years. France exploded her first bomb in 1959 but is not
expected to achieve "bomb plenty" until 1963. My own guess is that
China will not successfully test a bomb of her own before 1964 or
1965, and that the attainment of an abundance of bombs may be
achieved in about 1967-68.

The world presumably has four or five years to think over the possible consequences of that event. Will it decisively change the existing military balance of terror? Probably not. Did the French bomb
basically alter the East-West military balance? If the United States
could not prevent a revolution in Cuba is it likely that nuclear means
would provide China with packaged revolutions for export? Junior
membership in the club did not help frustrated France to restore her
lost colonial empire or even to satisfy her "legitimate needs" in North
Africa. Nor is senior membership likely to do so. It is unlikely that
Mao would (if still alive) begin any suicidal wars of conquest with a
few bombs in his pocket. People obsessed with Yellow Peril and
Blue Ant forms of paranoia may doubt this, but the record shows
that Mao has as lively a sense of self-preservation as any man who

ever survived forty years of war. If Peking were intent on provoking an apocalypse it already commands all the means necessary.

Aggressive as Mao Tse-tung's aims against imperialism may be, he defends only national or revolutionary wars of liberation; nowhere in his writings has he ever advocated *international wars* of conquest. He believes, like all Communists, that liberating *class wars* are not only "inevitable" but exist at all times inside capitalist societies, whether in the form of armed uprisings or by relatively nonviolent class struggles. It is the duty of the "liberated" countries, as all Communists see it, to assist "anti-imperialist struggles" wherever possible but that does not mean conquests by international wars. In this perspective the *psychological-political* impact of a China-made nuclear device would be incalculably great. It would mean for the first time an Asian Communist vote, a colored vote, a poor-man's vote, and an end of the white man's monopoly of the Terror and of its use as a threat against China or her allies.

Enforcement of any conceivable world agreement for control and inspection of nuclear arms manufacture could not be made effective without China's participation. This is unalterable official policy, spelled out by the Standing Committee of the National People's Congress on January 21, 1960, and repeated again in my interviews with Chou En-lai. Russia has repeatedly stated this as a fact. China has reiterated it. Nor could China join any such pact while she is excluded from the United Nations and from diplomatic relations with the U.S.A. Both Chou En-lai and Mao Tse-tung made it quite clear to me that no settlement between the U.S.A. and China is possible unless American bases are liquidated "on Chinese territory"—meaning Taiwan. It is thus unrealistic and illusory to expect results from disarmament talks while this problem remains unsettled. For officials to pretend otherwise is a kind of fraud.

Once China became a nuclear power the chances of any cessation in the build-up of weapons of world destruction would become even more remote. China would doubtless adopt the attitude of France that it is to her political advantage to defer any nuclear agreements until she achieves "adequate means" both in weapons and in systems of overseas deliveries. For these various reasons alone the prospect for the next five years is one of heavier and heavier expenditures for weapons that "cannot be used." If the United States is still in Taiwan after China attains nuclear "plenty" the prospect would seem to be more of the same for many years to come.

83

<hr>

China and Russia:
Point, Counterpoint

"In the last analysis," wrote Lenin on his deathbed, in 1923, "the out-come of the struggle will be determined by the fact that Russia, India, China, etc., account for the overwhelming majority of the population of the globe. And it is precisely that majority that, during the past few years, has been drawn into the struggle for emancipation with extraor-dinary rapidity. . . . In this sense, the complete victory of Socialism is fully and absolutely assured."

In 1960 a Chinese Politburo spokesman, Lu Ting-yi, wrote (of the "anti-Leninists" in the Kremlin?): "The modern revisionists are panic-stricken by the imperialist policy of nuclear-war blackmail. They de-velop from fear of war to fear of revolution, and proceed from not wanting revolution themselves to opposing other people carrying out revolution."

Agamemnon and Achilles argued bitterly over their beauteous war prizes, Chryseïs and Briseïs; while Achilles sulked in his tent for ten years Troy was safe. On the banks of the Danube the Tartar princes in the thirteenth century massed their invincible forces to invade Western Europe. A courier brought news of the death of their leader; they vio-lently split over the choice of a successor, called off their offensive, and

Christendom was saved from subjugation. Some people think a similar fatal collapse of collaboration between the two Marxist titans is now imminent.

Behind Greek disunity on the shores of the Hellespont were many issues besides jealousy over the distribution of female status symbols. From and between the lines of the *Iliad* one may infer differences over tribal interests, over interpretation of the oracles, and over strategy, tactics and objectives against the Trojans. The falling out of the Tartar princes was equally complex—and so is the Sino-Russian dispute of today.

Broadly speaking, differences between the two leaderships may be defined as rooted in the geographical, historical, economic, and psychological or cultural environments which determine the behavior of two large, multinational states. They find overt expression in quarrels over external strategy and tactics toward the non-Communist world, and over complicated problems of intramural management and cooperation. This discontent in turn invokes conflicting interpretations of Marxist-Leninist doctrine and class interests which the two nominally have in common. All these contradictions are called "ideological disputes."

The Tsarist empire spread to its present Asian frontiers in the Amur and Primoye region and in Far Turkestan less than two hundred years ago. China reached those frontiers or beyond them, including Korea, Siberia, Mongolia and Turkestan, from one to two thousand or more years ago and has since advanced or receded from them in periods of rise and decline. The frontiers of Russia are relatively recent and unstable compared to China's. The U.S.S.R. sprawls over a land area nearly two and a half times as large as China; it has 24 persons per square mile compared to China's 190 per square mile. If we call "Asia" everything east of the Urals, the greater part of the Soviet Union lies in Asia, and nearly a third of its population is Asian, or non-Slav. The Russian Union Republic alone is nearly twice as large as China; east of the Urals, Soviet territories might accommodate several times the present population. In Central Asia the Kazakh Republic, whose people have cousins in neighboring Chinese Turkestan, is a fertile steppe about one-third the size of China, with one-seventieth of China's population.

While advancing across the then largely nomadic lands of Asia to reach the Pacific—during roughly the same period the United States took Texas and California from Mexico and the Indians—the Tsars followed a fixed policy of nonalignment with the sea-power invasions of China. Russia reached the Pacific largely by a process of attrition. A cardinal aim of her policy has been to avoid head-on collisions with China, while encouraging her conflicts with invaders from the sea. In this respect, with the help of Western mistakes, Russia has been highly successful.

Since the expulsion of European colonialism from Eastern Asia, and China's recovery as a formidable continental power, however, her attention has begun to turn in other directions. Those who believe that China seeks living space in Southeast Asia fail to note that the area provides little room for expansion; most of its agricultural lands (particularly Vietnam) are as densely populated as China. Northern Laos, Thailand and Burma are relatively less crowded but mostly mountainous areas inhospitable to farming. The "empty" spaces are not on the coasts but inland, and Chinese are filling them up.

The main migratory movements inside modern China have been toward the north; today the state is also sponsoring mass settlements in the Far West. China has reached Sinkiang by rail and has begun modernizing the area with great vigor. She has linked it up with Tibet by roads that flank Soviet Turkestan, which the Romanovs formally incorporated into the Russian empire scarcely a century ago. The Kremlin has not forgotten that when the Mongols were overlords of Russia—for two centuries—Tashkent and Samarkand, as well as Moscow, paid tribute to Peking. Russian power has been eliminated from Manchuria, and China has recovered an elder-brother influence in Korea. Inner Mongolia is being rapidly populated and industrialized. China is seeking and winning cultural and economic influence in Outer Mongolia, in rivalry with her Soviet ally.

In the nineteenth century, Russian pressure on all these areas seemed irresistible; today it has been checked and conceivably may be reversed. The underlying geopolitical facts are possibly of greater long-range significance than the ideological gulf between Peking and Moscow. More correctly, the former may underlie and be inseparable from the latter.

To trace the origins of Sino-Soviet political rivalries one may recall first that in Marx's view national differences would disappear after proletarian revolution abolished social classes. Once the revolution overthrew capitalism the state everywhere would wither away. Marx foresaw this happening in more or less simultaneous world revolutions led by advanced European countries on about the same level of development. He gave no serious thought to the possibility of a victorious revolution in a single, isolated, and relatively backward semi-Asiatic state such as Russia. Lenin and the early bolsheviks believed also that no single socialist state, not even one as large as the Russian empire, could long coexist with a capitalist world. Either one or the other would perish because imperialist war was inevitable as long as imperialism (capitalism in its highest stage) existed. Hence arose the theory of the permanent or uninterrupted revolution—basically an offensive-defensive concept.

Only after repeated failures of revolutionary uprisings abroad did the Soviet government under Stalin embark upon a program of "building socialism in one country." While preparing for "inevitable imperialist war" the bolsheviks defensively built "the base of the world revolution," in isolation, on foundations of Tsarist empire. They took over the Tsarist colonial territories by extending dictatorship to them under the hegemony of the working class (led by the Russian Communist Party) in order to keep them out of the hands of counterrevolutionaries and imperialists. Although the Soviet system provided administratively for the existence of autonomous national republics, in practice the minority peoples were ruled paternalistically from the Kremlin, under the principle of "democratic centralism."

For nearly three decades Russia remained the only Communist-ruled country. As defenders of "the threatened base of the world revolution" and the "only homeland of the world proletariat," Soviet party leaders demanded and secured recognition from dependent foreign Communist minorities of the paramountcy of their interests over any and all "local" interests of other parties. In a short time this led, after Lenin's death and Trotsky's exile, to absolute Russian dictatorship, personified by Stalin, over the Communist movement as a whole. Thus the interests of a single socialist nation came to dominate the concept of international proletarianism. During Stalin's era any foreign party leader who openly questioned his infallibility by pointing out contradictions between Soviet national policies and the interests of world revolution, or who sought to place the national interests of his own party on the same level as Soviet interests, was likely to find himself in an act of heresy and be removed.

When the Stalinist pattern of power victoriously advanced into the political vacuum left in Eastern Europe by the defeat of Hitlerism, Russia had had no experience in operating a federative system in which other national parties could reconcile their differences as equals in a commonwealth of truly self-governing bodies. The absence of such an alternative, plus lack of popular support for a revolution imposed by foreign arms—which necessitated violent suppression of counterrevolutionary forces that had originally supported Hitler's invasion of Russia—placed the Eastern European countries in much the same relationship with Russia as the former Tsarist colonial territories. It was a paradox: revolutionary colonialism.

As remarked at the opening of this book, it was not difficult to foresee that Soviet absolutism was certain to be checked as soon as Communist leadership in another country won sovereign victory by its own national efforts and without direct Soviet armed intervention. Stalinist chauvinism led to nationalist thinking in other parties. This is what happened under Tito in Yugoslavia. When Stalin failed to discredit and overthrow Tito in 1948, a limit was set to the use of the world Communist organization as a means of extending Soviet national power. This event marked the beginning of heterodoxy in the world

Communist organization—an era which the Italian Communist leader, Palmiro Togliatti, a decade later called "polycentric communism."

Stalin's break with Tito resulted in the collapse of the Greek revolution, but Yugoslavia was too small a country to shake Soviet leadership on a world scale. Shortly afterward such a challenge arose in eastern Asia. The Chinese Communist Party emerged as the leader of a victorious revolution in a major nation with a population three times that of the Soviet Union. It was, moreover, unique in that it was the only fraternal party in the world that had for twenty years fought an independent armed struggle for power, built up its own armed forces, held administrative responsibility over wide areas, acquired an immense amount of political and military experience, and learned to apply Marxist doctrine in many pragmatic ways.

Stalin's intelligence on the Chinese Communist forces during the war against Japan was probably poor; he did not have military advisers or even observers with them for many years. There are indications that he and his Politburo simply did not believe that a party could win power by Mao's methods. The Russian bolsheviks themselves had seized the state apparatus at the center and then imposed social revolution on the Russian peasants after a fairly brief civil war. In their minds that became the classic formula for success. On the other hand, Chinese Communists had been defeated in the cities, fallen back on the hinterland, and organized their bases by gradually winning over the peasant masses. Only after many years, and only after uniting mixed class elements against an invading army, did they capture the leadership of the national patriotic war and mass support with which to encompass and take the cities. In this sense the Chinese victory may have been more democratic (popular) than the Russian.

Russia had been a great empire dominating many colonial peoples; China was a semicolonial country still struggling for independence. In spite of their common adherence to Marxist doctrine, differences in the practical political experiences of the two parties led the Chinese to make claims of uniqueness and greater experience than even the Soviet party. It was in 1943, *five years* before the Tito heresy, that Liu Shao-ch'i asserted:

> It may be said that within these twenty-two years our Party has witnessed more important changes and accumulated more experiences of the revolutionary struggle in various complicated forms (whether it be armed struggle or mass struggle, civil war or international war, legal struggle or illegal struggle, economic struggle or political struggle, struggles inside the Party or outside the Party) than *any other Communist Party in the world*.[1]

In 1946, and still two years before Tito had begun to speak openly of "different roads to socialism," Liu Shao-ch'i categorically claimed:

Mao Tse-tung's great accomplishment has been to change Marxism-Leninism from a European to an Asiatic form. Marx and Lenin were Europeans; they wrote in European languages about European histories and problems, seldom discussing Asia or China. The basic principles of Marxism are undoubtedly adaptable to all countries but to apply their general truth to concrete revolutionary practices in China is a difficult task. Mao Tse-tung . . . uses Marxist-Leninist principles to explain Chinese history and the practical problems of China. He is the first that has succeeded in doing so. . . . On every kind of problem —the nation, the peasants, strategy, the construction of the party, literature and culture, military affairs, finance and economy, methods of work, philosophy—Mao has not only applied Marxism to new conditions but has given it a new development. *He has created a Chinese or an Asiatic form of Marxism.* China is a semi-feudal, semi-colonial country in which vast numbers of people live at the edge of starvation, tilling small bits of soil. Its economy is agricultural, backward and dispersed. In attempting the transition to a more industrialized economy, China faces the competition and the pressures—economic, political, and military —of advanced industrial lands. This is the basic situation that affects both the relations of social classes and the methods of struggle towards any such goal as the national independence and a better, freer life for the Chinese. There are similar conditions in other lands of southeast Asia. The courses chosen by China will influence them all.[2]

When Christianity took an "Asiatic form" in China during the T'ai-p'ing revolution it developed for itself both the reality and the name for a unique leadership. From its capital at Nanking the Heavenly Peace Dynasty issued edicts in the name of a Trinity led by God; by Jesus Christ, the Divine Elder Brother; and by the Divine Younger Brother, Hung Hsiu-ch'uan, the T'ai-p'ing emperor. The Middle Kingdom today is not incapable of producing a man equal to any European, be he Marx or Lenin himself. Stalin may have held a different opinion.

Liu Shao-ch'i's statement (an unmistakable bid for Chinese leadership at least in Asia) was made in an official interview with Anna Louise Strong. Shortly afterward Miss Strong left for the United States and then in 1948 returned across Europe to Russia. En route she visited the new "people's democracies," where her interviews and her book *The Chinese Conquer China*[3] received acclaim—particularly in Yugoslavia. Upon her arrival in Moscow, Miss Strong found it impossible to get Russian permission to return to China via Siberia. Her arrest as a "spy" followed, and her expulsion from Russia. Publication of her work on China, including Liu's interview, was banned through-out Russia and Eastern Europe; yet it had already appeared in Chinese.

Following Liu's 1946 assertion, and throughout the 1949-51 post-revolutionary period, Chinese party spokesmen reiterated claims for the originality of "Mao's ideology" and upheld the Chinese revolution as the "model" for other semicolonial and colonial countries. The Soviet party press took no recognition of any ideological "new development" or "Asiatic form of Marxism." It continued to cite solely the fountain of all Marxist wisdom, Josef Stalin. China's claims ceased only after the outbreak of the Korean War—not to be openly revived again until 1958.

Besides underestimating Mao's chances of victory, Stalin thus had reason, before the end of the Second World War, to be skeptical of his ability to fit Mao into his pattern of revolutionary power. The alliance he signed with Chiang Kai-shek in 1945, the day after Russia attacked Japan in Manchuria, plainly advanced Russian national interests. It also advanced Soviet revolutionary interests by creating a regional situation favorable to an extension of Stalinist domination, similar to that in Eastern Europe. By terms of the treaty Chiang Kai-shek in effect abandoned China's claims to Outer Mongolia by agreeing to a Soviet-sponsored plebiscite. He agreed to restore Russia's former rights in Manchurian railways and enterprises which Stalin, to avoid a conflict, had earlier sold to Japan. The treaty even restored Russian control over the old Tsarist Port Arthur (Dalny) naval base on the Pacific. (The Yalta Pact had left Chiang Kai-shek small choice in most of these matters.)

In sponsoring this treaty the United States recognized a Soviet sphere of influence in Manchuria and tacitly drew a line at the Great Wall beyond which American nationalism might not intervene.

When Stalin recognized and agreed to support only Chiang's government in Manchuria, he probably foresaw events differently from the way they occurred. Sound strategy required that the Generalissimo return to power in eastern China after first smashing the Chinese Reds south of the Great Wall or driving them into Manchuria. In the event that Manchurian Communists then won any success, Stalin might have proposed to end the war by separating Manchuria from China south of the wall—a solution already favored by some American officers.[4] Manchuria would then have fallen under a transitional regime led by some local personality more tractable than Mao and, Stalin must have hoped, capable of reconciling Soviet and Chinese national *and* revolutionary interests. Against the advice of the commanding American officer in the China war theater, Lieutenant General Albert C. Wedemeyer,[5] Chiang foolishly attempted to take control of Manchuria before consolidating his rear, and while the Reds were still thoroughly saturating North China. Events then developed in reverse order. Manchuria became the independent base from which the Chinese Reds swept southward.

It is probable that in 1945 Stalin believed—as did most observers on the spot—both that Chiang Kai-shek's well-equipped 2,500,000-man army would quickly disperse the poorly armed and heavily outnumbered Communist troops, and that the United States would massively intervene to save Chiang from destruction, if necessary. Stalin's advice to the Communists to dissolve their armies and collaborate as a minority in Chiang's government was probably based on those beliefs.[6] Even in Manchuria, according to General George Marshall, who headed America's mediation mission in China, "In the opinion of all my advisers and intelligence, they [the Russians] were not supporting them [the Chinese Communist forces]." [7]

The swift and total disintegration of Chiang's armies following initial disasters in Manchuria, and the emergence of the Chinese Communists as victors over all China in 1949, made any regional Soviet hegemony in the north an impossibility. From the standpoint of amicable *national* relations with a united China, Stalin would have had no alternative but to shift his alliance from the Generalissimo to the "new power," even if no revolutionary sympathies had been involved.

No Soviet aid program to China got under way until after Mao Tse-tung's first visit to Russia; a modest loan of $300,000,000 was announced in 1950. During China's war against Japan the Kuomintang regime had received more than that in Soviet materials. But Russia herself was still bleeding from the war, having lost at least 10 percent of her population. The loan to China was anyway a start toward compensation for the equipment removed from Manchuria by the Red Army as "reparations" in 1945-46. Although at this time China signed a tripartite alliance with Russia and North Korea which probably had protocols providing for the modernization of the Chinese army, no developments prior to the outbreak of hostilities in Korea suggested that China was preparing for a large military operation.

What did Mao and Stalin think of each other when at last they met? There is no published record of their conversations. In all Mao's search for an "Asiatic form of Marxism" he had never openly criticized Stalin or expressed anything but admiration for his "leadership of the world revolution." If Stalin had made selfish mistakes in dealing with the Chinese party, he and the Russian Revolution had pioneered the road, provided spiritual ballast for the others, trained some of China's cadres, and fortified the party's faith in the attainment of the unattainable. Mao was proud of China's independent victory and he wanted no charity. But belief was then strong that the Sino-Soviet alliance was an earnest of large-scale future economic help rendered in proletarian solidarity which would surmount all differences.

By the spring of 1950 the United States seemed ready to write off Chiang Kai-shek and Taiwan also. The transitional policy was to "let the dust settle" in China, in the words of Secretary of State Dean Acheson; both he and General MacArthur went on record to the effect that neither Korea nor Taiwan was necessary for the defense of United States positions from the Aleutians through Japan, Okinawa and the Philippines. On January 5, President Truman himself had declared that the United States "had no desire to establish military bases on Chinese territory" and that "it will not provide military aid and advice to the Chinese Nationalist forces on Formosa." [8] American forces in South Korea were reduced to training groups. During that same spring Yugoslav and Indian delegates to the United Nations secured a verbal commitment from the United States delegate that he would accept the decision on a resolution in the Assembly to settle the dispute over China's seat as a "procedural" rather than a "substantive" question.[9] Procedural matters do not go before the Security Council. The seating of the Peking government therefore could be decided by an Assembly majority without occasion arising for the United States to enter a veto.

It thus appeared that America would accept a general disengagement from China, and the Russians were certainly informed of the Yugoslav-Indian formula. Suddenly the Soviet delegation was withdrawn from the United Nations. It announced that it would not return as long as Nationalist China was seated there. In June a general offensive was launched from North Korea against the South. Soviet Russian political and military advisers (not Chinese) had helped set up the North Korean regime and had remained in key positions. It is impossible to believe that a well-planned, well-supplied offensive could have been undertaken without prior consultation with and approval by Stalin. Owing to Soviet absence from the Security Council, President Truman was able swiftly to win sanction for large-scale American counteroffensive operations as a United Nations police action.

Was that wholly unforeseen in the Kremlin? It is difficult to imagine that Stalin could have doubted that United States prestige would require any less decisive a response than occurred. (The Chinese might conceivably have thought otherwise, being outside the U.N. climate.) Even had Stalin supposed that North Korea could successfully hold its conquest, he must have realized that the United States fleet would be obliged to move into Taiwan to cover that flank against any surprise attack by Russia's Chinese allies. It is often observed that Korea provided an Asian diversion from Russia's difficulties in countering Western pressure in Europe. Cynics have gone further, to suggest that the whole Korean adventure was Stalin's design to bring the United States into irreconcilable conflict with China. That probably credits Stalin with greater Machiavellian cunning than any one man can possess.

The fact remains that Russian advisers were withdrawn from Korea once the issue was fully joined, and were later replaced by Chinese troops. The end result was that Communist China was formally branded an "aggressor" by the United Nations and excluded from any early possibility of admission there. Peking's dependence on Russia greatly increased. Hostility between China and the United States was fixed for years to come. Soviet Russia avoided direct involvement in the Korean War and resumed her seat in the United Nations without incurring a vote of censure.

After the death of Stalin in 1953, a new era was cautiously introduced as Khrushchev emerged triumphant. Russia had recovered from the Second World War and developed nuclear weapons. Fear of capitalist encirclement diminished, and it was tacitly recognized that a holocaust threatened capitalism and communism alike. Instead of Stalin's offensive-defensive strategy of preserving "socialism in one country," the new leadership experimented with a more flexible policy aimed at establishing communism on a world scale while avoiding war.

Gradually the Kremlin moved to engage the capitalist powers in "competitive coexistence" in earnest. The Tito lesson of "different roads to socialism," including the parliamentary road, was absorbed by Khrushchev. He led a de-Stalinization movement which first relaxed tension and then shook bloc unity and ushered in polycentric communism. The logic of these developments required releasing more self-governing authority to party leaders in the satellite countries, a tendency interrupted by, but resumed after the suppression of, the Hungarian rebellion. Stalinist puppets fell in Eastern Europe. In Russia, Khrushchev ended rule by terror and concentration camp and sought broad popular support.

Among the effects of de-Stalinization in China was an enhancement of Mao's prestige as the leading Marxist theoretician, and demands for a greater role at both the Communist and world summits. Khrushchev in his speeches did accord China a special place beside the Soviet Union conceded to no other country. He extended Soviet aid in new ways. Like Russia, China needed time for internal consolidation and growth. China also supported peaceful coexistence. Following the Geneva Conference of 1954, Chou En-lai took a leading part in the 1955 Bandung Conference of twenty-nine nations (largely colonial and ex-colonial) of Asia and Africa. Its principles were noninterference in each other's internal affairs, mutual aid and trade, and mutual resistance to imperialism. China opened talks on an ambassadorial level with the United States—provided for at the Geneva Conference—in attempts at some settlement of the Taiwan issue. It soon became clear that the American ambassador at the Warsaw level had no authority to discuss basic issues or do more than repeat demands for what would amount to Peking's *de jure* recognition of the legality of the American armed protectorate in Taiwan.*

---

* The United States position demands a formal declaration by Peking not to use force in the Taiwan area, acceptance of which would concede the legality of United States intervention in China's internal affairs. Peking's position remains that the United States must recognize China's sovereignty in Taiwan *simultaneously*

The "Bandung spirit" led to closer Sino-Indian relations for a time. A loose "Asian-African" bloc put up a common propaganda front, but it produced few concrete results for China. American military power had already created a Southeast Asia Treaty Organization, to include three Asian nations, two bordering on China: Pakistan and Thailand. The Geneva agreement, whereby France recognized the independence of all Vietnam, had provided for unification of that country by a national referendum to be held no later than July, 1956. Despite another guarantee of the agreement—noninterference by outside powers in Vietnam's internal affairs—the United States gave military backing to South Vietnam before the year 1954 was out. Ngo Dinh Diem soon violently suppressed his Saigon opposition and established one-man rule of the Syngman Rhee type. He then refused to discuss national elections with North Vietnam; instead, he accepted protection extended through the United States.

China withdrew her troops from Korea and invited the United States to do likewise, with no result. China released what she asserted to be all the American prisoners of war in her custody. Peking invited some Americans to visit China and indicated a desire to reopen people-to-people communications. The United States adamantly defended its Taiwan protectorate and forbade Americans to travel in or trade with China. In 1955-57, China offered visas to some American newspaper correspondents and editors; Mr. Dulles forbade any of them to accept, under pain of prosecution. Washington sought the support of other nations to isolate and quarantine the mainland and thus achieve the "speedy passing" of the Peking regime. Mr. Dulles frigidly repulsed all Chou En-lai's efforts to open serious high-level talks following the release of American prisoners of war—which had been understood to be a precondition of negotiations. The Chinese leaders concluded that they had been tricked into concessions without receiving a *quid pro quo*. They saw that their conciliatory moves had been misinterpreted. They were being punished for their weakness.

By 1957 China's dissatisfaction with a relatively passive policy was deepened by developments which suggested to Peking leaders that the United States was overextending itself in an age when Western imperialism was actually weakening, rather than strengthening, its hold on the world. Colonial empires were in rapid disintegration from Asia to Africa. National liberation movements, winning all across the board, were facing a critical choice between bourgeois nationalist dictatorship and proletarian dictatorship. Failure to support effective leadership on the Maoist model in the newly emerging states seemed to be forfeiting dominance in them to imperialism—that is, to bourgeois nationalist satellites of American power. Did Khrushchev's fear

---

with a joint declaration rejecting the use of force in the settlement of Sino-American differences. See pages 91-92, 765-766.

of nuclear war leave Communists no alternative but a peaceful coexistence which led to peaceful surrender or inevitable war?

Climaxing all these doubts, two very important events late in 1957 decisively influenced Chinese Communist thinking. On August 26, Moscow announced that it had successfully launched the first intercontinental ballistic missile. Many had regarded it as an ultimate weapon. On October 4 the Soviet Union put into space the first earth satellite in history. In China this was news of even more stunning importance (as it turned out) than in Moscow. A "new stage" had been established in the world power balance. Party conferences were called and prolonged sessions worked out a new international strategy. Opinion in the Central Committee led by the Politburo oscillated from right to left, as always. It came to rest on a new center, with Mao Tse-tung still its spokesman—far to the left of the pre-1957 position.

Mao Tse-tung's basic estimate as presented at Moscow in November, 1957, was that Russia's lead in ballistic missiles and satellite systems marked a "new turning point." In Marxist idiom a "turning point" means a decisive change, both qualitatively and quantitatively, in any balance of power; a major reappraisal is indicated—in this case, in world strategy. Placing his usual emphasis on man as the decisive factor in all political struggle, Mao asserted during the conference:

> The whole world now has a population of 2.7 billion, of which the various socialist countries have nearly one billion; the independent, former colonial countries more than 700 million; the countries now struggling for independence or for complete independence, 600 million; and the imperialist camp only about 400 million . . .[10] I am of the opinion that the international situation has now reached a new turning point. There are two winds in the world: the East wind and the West wind. . . . I think the characteristic of the situation today is the East wind prevailing over the West wind. . . . *The socialist forces are overwhelmingly superior to the imperialist forces . . .*"[11]

Mao called for a new orientation of policy to recognize that the 700,000,000 people in the newly independent states, combined with the 600,000,000 people in areas "struggling for independence or complete independence" (including those now dominated by "Yankee imperialism" in Latin America), would decide the balance of world power. In this sector of humanity, where the average income was scarcely $100 per person per year, the aim of the Communists should be to outflank and encircle Western imperialism by leading "struggles" which should not shirk from use of force when confronted by force. Mao did not advocate any general assault but rather his old guerrilla strategy of concentrating where the enemy was weakest, and smashing him one by one. He went on:

In order to struggle against the enemy, we have formed the concept over a long period, namely, that *strategically we should slight all enemies, and tactically we should take full account of them.* That is also to say, we might slight the enemy as a whole but take full account of him so far as each and every concrete question is concerned. If we do not slight the enemy as a whole, we shall be committing the mistake of opportunism . . . But on concrete questions and on questions concerning each and every particular enemy, if we do not take full account of the enemy, we shall be committing the mistake of adventurism. In war, battles can only be fought one by one and the enemy can only be annihilated bit by bit . . . Strategically, we slight the eating of a meal; we can finish the meal. But when actually eating, we do it a mouthful at a time. It would be impossible for you to swallow the entire feast in a single mouthful. This is called one-by-one solution. And in military literature, it is called smashing the enemy one by one.[12]

If at first the Russians did not take Mao very seriously, they were soon to learn that he meant every word he said. In his strategy in the war of resistance against Japan he had foreseen three stages: 1) enemy invasion, Chinese retreat and preparation; 2) prolonged stalemate while China organized her man power, and internal and world support were mobilized; 3) counteroffensive and victory. In his view now, the balance had changed in favor of the socialist forces. Counteroffensive should begin before the enemy could entrench himself in the uncommitted nations and continue preparations for a new war.

To attempt to trace all the subsequent controversies would be impossible in this space. What happened was no less than a rerun of a debate that has been going on among Marxists for a century: between right and left, revisionists and dogmatists, fundamentalists and deviationists, bolsheviks and social democrats—and have-gots and have-nots. The big difference is that the arguments now are not in garrets or caves but in the great halls of giant nations, whose behavior can vitally affect the lives of all men. Readers interested in the enormously complex and enormously important details may find them documented elsewhere.[13] Here it must suffice to complete the barest outline of events.

In November, 1957, the Russians and their European comrades did not accept Mao's estimate of the situation. Neither did they believe that by his strategy he could safely walk between "opportunism" and "adventurism." They did not consider that a "turning point" had been reached nor that the socialist forces were now superior. At most they had achieved a deterrent against attack. It was impossible to determine "who is encircled and who is the encircler," in Khrushchev's words. Second, the main issue before the world was peace or war but peace was indivisible and it must not be combined with methods that could lead to world war. Third, the attainment of communism was still relatively far distant. Since nuclear war was unthinkable, the decision would be won principally by demonstrating the superiority of the socialist system in a relatively peaceful economic contest with capitalism, in which risks of provoking counterrevolutionary wars were minimized.

To sum up the Soviet position it could fairly be said that Khrushchev now believed in the possibility of reaching arms-limitation agreements with the West, and in the awareness of bourgeois leaders of the danger of mutual destruction. Ultimately they would see that there was no alternative but coexistence, while the two systems competed by diplomatic, economic and cultural means to win a world following. To promote or encourage revolutions prematurely could result only in provoking wider imperialist intervention at the risk of world war. Many local wars of liberation would inevitably occur; they could not be incited by one side without inviting intervention by the other side. One must support them, but mainly by diplomacy. Extremely militant policies might also throw mature bourgeois democracies into deep reaction; that could close the path to socialists seeking power by parliamentary means.

There can be no doubt that Khrushchev's line was a revision of Leninism. It also opened a door to the despised social democrats. But was not imperialism now obliged to work with socialism? The Chinese denied that. Imperialism had not basically changed in the nuclear era; it was only weaker and more desperate. No revision was admissible in rounding the "new turning point."

The issues were not resolved by the Manifesto of November, 1957, which was a compromise to maintain outer unity. It recognized that the danger of war existed as long as imperialism existed. Yes, there was also now a possibility of peaceful transition to socialism. It could be realized only by the combined struggle of "popular forces," in terms used by Chou En-lai in his interview with me as late as October, 1960.* The Chinese emphasized the manifesto's support for "just wars" of liberation.

By the time I saw Chou, the Sino-Soviet dispute had broken into semipublic view, after months of heated polemical exchanges interrupted by meetings which had only intensified differences. If the 1958 Taiwan crisis is seen in this context it may be said to have strengthened Khrushchev's determination not to be drawn into conflicts the outcome of which he could not control. In Peking in July, 1958, Mao and the Soviet leader had certainly argued over the obvious contradictions between efforts at a genuine *détente* with the West and Mao's belief that the bloc should "slight the enemy strategically" while taking him seriously in specific tactical situations, where local force should be met by local force and nuclear weapons could be avoided. Almost certainly, in

* See page 100.

Mao's opinion, the Taiwan crisis which followed was a test of whether Khrushchev understood the application of this principle, and Khrushchev had played a weak hand, for reasons already noted.

Late in 1958, Khrushchev also became fully aware of the inherent challenge to Soviet ideological prestige in China's adoption of communes as a short cut to communism. This aspect of the dispute demands a special study in itself. If Peking had succeeded in imposing the very "advanced" goals first set up for the communes it would have left Soviet society a stage or two behind China in programmatic development toward communism. Did Mr. K.'s objections influence the Chinese party decision in December, 1958, to retreat from its extreme positions? If so, the extension of Soviet credits in February, 1959, which would, over a period of several years, supply China with 78 additional complete industries worth five million rubles ($1,125,000,000), on a barter basis, may be regarded as a large Soviet reward to bridge the gap between them. (These were still merely trading credits, however; no gifts were involved.)

The apparent reconciliation did not last long. Continuing his pursuit of peaceful coexistence, Khrushchev visited President Eisenhower at Camp David to discuss a summit conference. This could not have failed to revive Chinese suspicions of betrayal of principle, if not of their own interests. On his return in October, by way of Peking, Khrushchev's reception there was colder than the weather. His published speeches and subsequent Chinese press comment showed wide differences concerning the objectives of peace negotiations with the West.

Since then Mao and Khrushchev have not met.

From this point on Peking increased its offensive with attacks on Mr. K., thinly veiled by the euphemism "Yugoslav revisionists," with whom China had quarreled over some of the same issues. Moscow organs retaliated with criticisms of unnamed "dogmatists" and "left-infantilists," with occasional asides concerning Trotsky's mistakes. At another party conference in Bucharest in June, 1960, there were bitter clashes. Khrushchev for the first time attacked Mao personally as a visionary and a dogmatist. The Chinese delegate, P'eng Chen, replied with a verbal assault on Khrushchev as a petit-bourgeois non-Leninist. Almost simultaneously with the Bucharest meeting, a conference of the Communist world trade unions federation met in Peking. Such extreme language was used that Soviet delegates left the hall. Neither meeting resolved anything, but an agreement was reached to hold the important Moscow Conference of November, 1960. In that stormy session the Soviet and Chinese delegates reviewed their differences. Each clung to his old opinions, reinforced by new data from recent events, to prove contradictory theses—before representatives of eighty-one Communist parties of the world.

Very many points of fundamental division had already resulted in conflicting policies. Peking was bidding for support in neighboring countries by offering trade credits on easier terms than Moscow. In some instances the Chinese made outright gifts (to Outer Mongolia, Korea, Vietnam, etc.), something Russia had never done. Yet China was herself still dependent on Soviet credits. China recognized the Algerian national government much in advance, and to the embarrassment, of Moscow. (Khrushchev found it difficult to encourage the rebels openly while seeking to avoid antagonizing De Gaulle in the hope of broadening the General's differences with the United States.) Peking disagreed with Khrushchev's policy of aiding bourgeois nationalist governments in Egypt, India and Indonesia while slighting China and other left-wing forces. Quarrels arose over correct policies in Iraq and over disarmament negotiations. In Chinese eyes, Soviet support for U.N. armed intervention in the Congo amounted to counterrevolutionary betrayal. Behind all these contradictions lay basic disagreements in evaluating the true strength of the world "socialist forces." The truth probably was also that Mao had not trusted Khrushchev as a political strategist since he had unnecessarily betrayed his hand during Mr. Dulles' "bluff" in the Quemoy-Matsu crisis of 1958.

At the Moscow Conference of November, 1960, the dispute became a duel of personalities as well as strategies. Neither side could yield outright. As the junior and weaker socialist power, China (represented by Liu Shao-ch'i) seemed to make most of the compromises. The final conference declaration seemed to adopt the main points of the Soviet party, now designated "the universally recognized vanguard"; in 1957 it had been "the head" of the world movement. The conference agreed that competitive and peaceful coexistence was the only alternative to war and massive destruction; the road to socialism was gradual erosion of the capitalist system rather than promotion of armed revolutionary struggle. But in underdeveloped areas the parties were to support "national liberation movements" in which Communists could play a legal role in governments of "national democracies" to be led, stage by stage, toward socialism. Wording of the resolution was still sufficiently ambiguous on many points to provide scope for an independent Chinese interpretation, however, particularly on ways and means of "struggle" for proletarian (Communist) hegemony over the liberation movements.

While Mao's leftist strategy was voted down, in the main, China had forced a number of concessions from Khrushchev. For the first time a Soviet leader had been obliged to confront an opposition before the entire world organization. Revolutionary interests beyond those of Soviet power were now clearly recognized as the responsibility of the "vanguard party" of world revolution. A precedent was set: major Soviet strategy decisions henceforth would require intraparty consultation. China's thesis had found wider support than Khrushchev anticipated. Albania was the only European party which openly espoused the Chinese position in 1960, but elements in other parties, including the Soviet, apparently, were in sympathy with it. As a whole, Asian parties attempted to steer a middle course.

Something else happened, the significance of which was probably not at once absorbed by the contestants. The struggle of wills proved Mao's theory of the persistence of contradictions even between socialist states and between socialist governments and their peoples. In attempting to reconcile them a process developed very akin to freedom of speech, assembly, conscience and even publication. How long could such methods be adopted at the summit without having contagious effects within the ranks of the nations themselves?

The debate doubtless inhibited Khrushchev's freedom in pursuing a *détente* with the West. Certain aggressive tactical moves—direct aid to Laos, formal North Vietnamese political leadership in the struggle against Diem, building the Berlin wall, rupture (if temporary) of disarmament talks—suggested that he sought to answer criticisms of his lack of militancy as the leading Communist strategist.

In Peking, I spoke of conflicting national interests and differences in the geopolitical environments of the two countries to a Soviet historian who was about to join other Russians in the general departure. At the end he said, "Yes, we are two large, socialist countries, both opposed to imperialism; on this matter we are united. But we have had independent national experiences and are at different levels of revolutionary development. China is going through some stages we passed thirty years ago. We wish she could learn from our mistakes but it can't always be so. We have a higher standard of living, our people need and demand more, and we can't get them to make the sacrifices the Chinese make. Not any more. We said, relax a bit; *the socialist world is secure.* But the Chinese won't have it so; they want three shifts a day and complain if our machines break down under the strain. They are very proud. They want equality in the world. We have won it; they are still struggling for it. They are going to get it their own way and by their own efforts—and their way may be best for them. We have a Russian proverb that sums up the situation. 'You can't fit one man's head on another man's shoulders.' "

Among the differences in Russian and Chinese national experiences none is more pertinent than the contrast in United States behavior toward the two revolutions. Following the bolshevik revolution the United States did not establish armed bases on Soviet territory in support of the defeated regime. (Although the Siberian expedition was at first misinterpreted in that light, the U.S.S.R. later dropped all charges.[14]) In 1920, when there was a mass famine in Russia, Americans responded by sending in wheat. (America has a large Slavic population.) In the twenties and thirties the Soviet government hired American engineers and bought American machines which helped lay the foundations of Soviet industry. Cultural contacts were never cut off, and after 1933 normal diplomatic and trade relations were restored.

Despite American antipathies for communism, discourse continued on every level. Views were exchanged and an awareness of each other as neighbors was maintained.

In 1941 the United States began to aid Soviet Russia against Hitler even before Pearl Harbor. The United States helped save the Soviet Union from destruction. This fact confounded all Marxist dogma, for by orthodox reasoning the imperialist powers should have united to carve Russia into colonial prizes. Quite the contrary. The Soviet command was authorized, in armistices signed by the United States, to remove from power all elements "hostile to the Red Army" throughout Eastern Europe. Russia not only recovered her lost territories but was rewarded by a vast extension of the pattern of Soviet power.

In the ensuing cold war the United States never broke off diplomatic and trade relations with the Kremlin. Instead, the Soviet Communist government won full and respectful consideration for itself at the tables of the capitalists. President Eisenhower invited the devil into his camp and made efforts to show him how the welfare state really works. Not surprisingly, Mr. Khrushchev believes that peaceful coexistence is possible.

The Chinese see these facts, however, as a reflection of only one thing: Soviet power. In their eyes American imperialism respects nothing but force. It rewards revolutionary strength and receives it as an equal. It despises and punishes weakness.

This harsh judgment is based on Chinese Communist experience with an American imperialism which behaved according to their classical expectations. Their struggle began in a part of the world where Japan was the only power free from Western domination. Throughout the joint war against Japan the impoverished Communist forces received no aid from America. The United States armed Chiang Kai-shek alone and continued to support him against the Communists during the civil war. In 1949 the Peking government invited recognition; the United States withdrew.

To the Chinese, their aid to North Korea was an act of self-defense. As firmly as Mr. Truman believes he prevented a world war by intervening there, Chinese Communist leaders are convinced that they not only saved North Korea and Manchuria from conquest but prevented an imperialist war. As long as imperialism exists—on Chinese soil, at least—and as long as they do not possess nuclear weapons of their own, Chinese Communists will not feel that "socialism is secure."

Frustrated from winning redress for these injuries to national pride, denied recognition as an equal and great power, Communist China naturally looks upon the removal of the American menace as a much more urgent matter than the Russians do. Unable to launch a direct assault on the "invader," Mao seeks to outflank him by stimulating revolutionary victories in the underdeveloped countries. No doubt many in Asia, the Middle East, Africa and Latin America are ripe for revolutionary leadership. People are ignorant, diseased and wretchedly impoverished. Many live under backward, reactionary, corrupt and feudal dictatorships which show little sign of maturing as modern societies within the visible future. The poor, the vast majority, might readily respond to leadership of the Maoist pattern.

In the *Communist International Program* adopted in the early days of the bolshevik revolution—a purely Leninist document—it was clearly recognized that successful proletarian-led revolutions in colonial and semicolonial countries "will be possible only if direct support is obtained from countries in which the proletarian dictatorship is established." The Chinese Communists received very little help during their lonely revolution—while their enemy always received support from the imperialists. Now they said that to deny it to the weaker and struggling young liberation movements would be pure "opportunism" and shirking of the great socialist powers' responsibilities.

But overt support of revolution today would bring counterrevolution and dangerous showdowns, Russia argues. The present Russian generation consists not of Lenins but of youths anxious to enjoy the fruits of their parents' sacrifices. Still "have-nots" by Western standards, the Russians are a "have-got" nation in the Communist region, and Khrushchev holds power by promising greater abundances than under capitalism. Obviously these cannot be won by dissipating Russia's resources in conflicts in remote lands, but only by peaceful economic expansion. Eastern European parties still more reflect the same sentiments. Their people dread any prospect of new sacrifices imposed to carry out faraway liberating missions—especially under a Chinese leadership which must increase, rather than break down, their isolation from the West.

All that was implicit in the debates of the 1960 conference, where the Chinese accepted the revisions of the manifesto for the sake of unity rather than from conviction. Mutual press recriminations ceased but the Chinese continued propaganda for their own anti-imperialist line, in preparation for a review of the whole program at another meeting promised for 1962. Before the 1960 conference, Volume IV of Mao Tse-tung's *Selected Works* had appeared in Peking. Afterward it continued to be the subject of even wider press comment and eulogy as part of a "cult" campaign to uphold Mao as the foremost authority on revolutionary strategy in colonial and semicolonial countries. Many of its themes—including "all imperialists and reactionaries are paper tigers," "imperialism will never change," "slight the enemy strategically, take account of him tactically," and "man is more important than guns"—reiterated old Chinese positions.

In action, China took no aggressive moves to violate peaceful coexistence and joined efforts to negotiate a Laos settlement with the United States. Inside the bloc she exercised freedom of intraparty relationships as well as continued agitation for a more militant strategy. What most infuriated Khrushchev was Mao's defiance of his attempt to isolate Albania. Albania had its own reasons for sympathizing with Mao. Like China, Albania was excluded from the United Nations. With Albania, as with China, the United States had cut off all communications. The party chief, Hoxha, reflected the fears and hates of his tiny nationalism; if Khrushchev won Yugoslavia back into the camp it might be at the price of Tito's domination of Albania. Peking opposed Tito as a strong "revisionist" influence pulling Khrushchev in the direction of a *détente* with the United States at the expense of China's interests.

When Russian advisers and equipment were withdrawn from Albania, Peking sent in Chinese technicians and supplies to replace them. Other behavior continued to challenge Khrushchev's authority. Suppose East Germany were to join the Chinese in a faction against him? Yet Peking's prestige was also at stake; it was bound to support equality of rights for the one European party that had spoken for Mao's views. In October, 1961, Khrushchev dramatically rebuked both China and Albania, when foreign delegates appeared at the Twenty-second Party Congress to hear the Premier announce the Soviet draft program and blueprint for the transition from socialism to communism.

During his opening speech Khrushchev attacked Albania for refusing to abide by the decisions of the Twentieth Congress (de-Stalinization) program. Unexpectedly, he demanded expulsion of its leadership and read it out of the bloc. This action was at once recognized as aimed at China, for setting up a bipolar leadership. The Chinese delegation, led by Chou En-lai, was the only one which did not applaud Khrushchev's long address. After replying the following day, when he criticized the Soviet leader for dictatorial condemnation of Albania without prior consultation with any other party, Chou left the Congress and promptly flew back to Peking. He was warmly welcomed at the airport by both Mao Tse-tung and Liu Shao-ch'i.

Khrushchev's action was clearly a warning that if China continued intransigent he would also read Mao out of the party. The gravity of the threat was already manifest in the economic sanctions Khrushchev had applied against China ever since the trade-unions conference in Peking in June, 1960. (Chinese Communists had begun anti-Khrushchev political indoctrination of some Russians in China.) Shortly afterward Khrushchev had withdrawn nearly all Soviet technical experts from China, leaving some major projects in an unfinished state. Chinese engineers might eventually complete them but their task was viciously complicated by the withdrawal also of many blueprints and specifications as well as by the withholding of vital parts. Given familiarity with the key weaknesses and shortages of Chinese industrial and scientific equipment, it was not difficult to know where denials would hurt most. Contracts were not canceled; operations merely paused to give Peking time to think it over. Trade slacked off. Rather gratuitously, the Russians openly announced the suspension of certain shipments because of China's negative barter balance. These sanctions coincided with the worst harvests China had known in this century, when far greater than normal cooperation was needed from the Soviet Union.

In 1961 it seemed that Peking had to throw in its hand or call Khrushchev's card. But could he actually play it? Even before the Twenty-second Congress was over Mr. K. had some second thoughts; the final Albanian resolution was much modified and left a way open for reconciliation. Representatives of Western parties endorsed Khrushchev's leadership by attacking Albania; their responses varied from warm satellite sycophantism to nominal support. But *all* the Asian parties, with the single exception of that of tiny Ceylon, totally abstained from any criticism of Albania. This meant that not only all of China's neighbors—Asian Russia's neighbors, too—and what amounted to one-third of the Communist parties of the world, based in nations with combined populations far exceeding the others, could not be expected to approve any attempt to expel China from the "international."

If Khrushchev, personifying the current Soviet party majority, thought to bluff Mao Tse-tung by these various means, he had misjudged the man, the nation, and the Chinese revolution—if not that part of the world revolution personified by Mao. Would this spokesman for "the poor, the vast majority," in whom still burned the heart of the youth who had defied Chiang Kai-shek's thousand-to-one superiority in firepower, who had ignored Stalin's advice, and later refused to be intimidated by the American paper tiger, now be taken on the right by a rich peasant riding an H-bomb? Not likely. China was now too big to be driven to surrender. If Khrushchev forbade all bloc trade with China it would still be possible for the nation to go into a severely autarchical economy; it was after all in a somewhat better condition now to do so than Soviet Russia had been in the dark early days of isolation and "socialism in one country." China had other alternatives.

Soon after Chou's return from Moscow, Peking gave its answer by extending increased economic aid to Albania. The Chinese press reprinted Albanian statements attacking Khrushchev as an "opportunist," and for "revisionism," "treachery," "lies, pressure and threats." Inside the party now, at even the lower echelons, the whole dispute was threshed out. With Khrushchev under open attack in China, even non-Communists abroad could receive letters through the mail from Peking which described the Soviet Premier as a "social democrat."

On an earth about to send visitors to other planets all these polemics may seem ludicrous. But Mao's view is far from parochial; he has his eye on the multitudes who will not be space men but still live in rat-infested villages and are fearful of disease and starvation. His view takes into consideration the coexistence in man's knowledge and condition of Telstars and human beasts of burden, of the infinity of space and matter and the brevity of human life, of a John Foster Dulles carrying a prayer book in one hand and an earth-cracking bomb in the other, of an African tribesman convinced that an electric lamp is god, and of the Tibetan aspiring to become a living buddha by way of prayer wheels blessed by the lamas.

Encompassing these changing levels of life there is a unity of purpose which in political terms may be seen as a four-pronged thrust for a new equality in the condition of man. Four cosmic events are occurring simultaneously: national revolution (former slave nations struggling for racial, color and creed recognition as equals); class revolution (poor men everywhere struggling for equality against the rich); technological revolution (backward societies struggling for equality with advanced ones); and international revolution (blocs of have-not nations struggling for equality with have-got powers). The key to political mastery over all these equations is seen by Mao to lie in the overwhelming majority of mankind identified with the poor people, as against a very small minority of the rich.

Heretofore the idea of any poor-man's government has been considered Utopian. Now two large nations and one-third of humanity are ruled by regimes where there may indeed be no more individual liberty than before, but where the rich have been eliminated by the abolition of private ownership of the means of production, and where relatively egalitarian societies have been established which aim ultimately to secure "from each according to his ability," and to satisfy "each according to his needs." That these societies work has been universally recognized. One of them, the possessor of nuclear weapons, has to be received as an equal by the rich men's nations. Moreover, direct rule by Western have-got nations over the inferior states has dissolved nearly everywhere before the four-pronged revolution. In "desperation," the monopoly capitalists are driven to alliances on a basis of equality with the minority rich classes which rule in the former slave or semislave states, where the poor are the vast majority.

Mao wrote an essay entitled, "A Single Spark May Start a Prairie Fire." He has seen a few dozen determined men convince the poor that they can get along without the rich. In scarcely more than twenty years he led a quarter of the earth's poor to turn the gun around and take power. He is convinced that other poor men can also master the means of completing the four-pronged revolution. There is nothing between them and their liberation but force controlled by the rich and very small minority.

Mao's belief is that the disintegration of the colonial world marked a "turning point" which required *immediate* action. If action were delayed too long, the rich minorities in the backward countries might become so entrenched, with the help of the have-got governments, that conditions of struggle "by the poor" would become extremely difficult. Then the have-got powers (the imperialists) might be able to build such firm bases throughout the lands of the 1,300,000,000 people in the former slave states that they could be turned toward counterrevolution and produce an imperialist war. To win victory and to prevent an imperialist war, the important thing now is to keep the imperialists on the defensive.

Since the poor are "the great majority" Mao never doubts that they will triumph. One may therefore "slight the enemy strategically"; history has already demonstrated that he cannot win. Even if the enemy had a monopoly on the bomb he could not win. But the poor man already has the bomb. The enemy cannot use the bomb strategically (against the socialist base defended by the bomb) because he himself will be destroyed.

But one must "take serious account of the enemy tactically." Current liberation struggles are not fought in the have-got countries but in underdeveloped ones. The more the imperialist assists the native rich to defeat the aspirations of the revolution the more he alienates large sectors of the intellectuals as well as the poor population and unites them in antiforeign nationalist sentiment. Can the enemy use the nuclear weapon tactically? Yes, he can. But in a social revolution the poor arm themselves mainly by capturing weapons commanded by the rich. If the enemy deploys nuclear tactical weapons against the revolution, then sooner or later they and their operators will be captured and used against him. That is what happened to Chiang Kai-shek's conventional American weapons. That is what happened to French weapons in the Algerian and Indochina revolutions, and that is what happened in Cuba. "Man is more important than the weapon."

Yet international war is not the way to change matters. "Socialist countries never permit themselves to send, never will send, their troops across their borders," declared the Chinese Politburo, "unless they are subjected to aggression from a foreign enemy." [15] (Soviet Russia did not attack Hitlerism; socialism was carried into Europe as a *counterattack* against Hitlerism.) "People who believe that revolution can break out in a foreign country to order, by agreement," said Peking, quoting Lenin, "are either mad or provocateurs . . . We know that revolutions cannot be made to order, or by agreement; they break out when tens of millions of people come to the conclusion that it is impossible to live in the old way any longer." [16]

And how shall they be helped to reach that conclusion? The "imperialists always have two tactics; the tactics of war and the tactics of 'peace'; therefore, the proletariat and the people of all countries must also use two tactics to counter the imperialists; the tactics of thoroughly exposing the imperialists' peace fraud, and striving energetically for a genuine world peace, and the tactics of preparing for a just war to end the imperialist unjust war when and if the imperialists should unleash it." [17]

Lu Ting-yi, of the Politburo, was more explicit about the strategy all parties should follow. "All the means of revolution and forms of struggle, including the illegal and the 'legal,' extraparliamentary and parliamentary, sanguinary and bloodless, economic and political, military and ideological—all these are for the purpose of unmasking the imperialists to a fuller extent, showing them up as aggressors, constantly raising the revolutionary consciousness of the people, achieving broader mobilization of the masses to oppose the imperialists and the reactionaries, developing the struggle for world peace, and preparing for and winning victory in the people's revolution and the national revolution." [18] Sufficient unto the policies followed by the imperialists should be the answer thereto. An eye for an eye . . .

It may thus be seen what Mao meant by a one-by-one strategy. The United States cannot send occupation forces to every country in the world which is about to have a social revolution. The more it intervenes on behalf of the rich minority the more it will be hated by the poor and revolutionary majority.

Now, if we recall Premier Chou's replies to my questions about Sino-Soviet differences we may see that he answered truthfully, if succinctly. The two countries differed "on theoretical questions and on ways of looking at things." There were, first: differences on "how to evaluate the situation with regard to war"; second, the fact that Russia's membership in the United Nations seated her in the Security Council and other bodies where the "Taiwan clique" is represented. "Proceeding from this point," Chou said, "the nations of the two governments cannot be the same in *many* respects." (Emphasis mine.)

Their divergent views on "theoretical questions" and "war" are now known. Differences over bloc policies in the United Nations arise not only because the Soviet delegate and delegates of ten other socialist countries are obliged to engage in limited collaboration with the "Taiwan clique" and thus give credence to the existence of "two Chinas"; inevitably they must also collaborate with an organization dominated by American policies whose aim is to foster counterrevolution, restore Western power on the Asian continent, and destroy Communist China.

With the failure of China's efforts to win recognition in the United Nations through the Bandung policy, or to dislodge the United States from Taiwan by negotiation, Peking undoubtedly re-evaluated the whole bloc relationship to that organization at the "turning point" supposedly reached in 1957. While membership in the U.N. was a good propaganda issue with which to win sympathy among the uncommitted nations and divide the Western allies, it was not a viable means of pursuing revolutionary aims now demanded by a new situation. Mao's experience leads him to believe that the West would never peacefully accept a socialist majority in the United Nations.

Some of China's minority peoples, like the Chuangs, are bigger nations in both population and territory than several small European powers and a dozen from other continents. What honor would it bring to giant China at this late date to be "recognized" as part of a minority by a change of votes among tiny states like Guatemala, the Dominican Republic, or Somaliland?

Yet there can be no doubt that Peking was dissatisfied with the Soviet failure to unseat the Nationalists and win recognition for China's sovereignty over Taiwan. It would be unnatural if Mao had not questioned whether the Soviet delegates had really done everything possible. China's distrust of U.N. disarmament talks which excluded her was manifest. One means by which some of the powers fence-sitting on the question of China's admission might be stampeded into an affirmative vote, whereby critical pressure could be imposed on the United States, would be to threaten permanent withdrawal of the bloc in order to form a rival organization including as many neutral and uncommitted powers as possible. This alternative was undoubtedly debated in Peking and Moscow.

Why aren't the Chinese satisfied merely to build toward communism in one backward land, instead of pushing the whole world toward revolution? First, they haven't yet united all China. Second, they do have neighboring states divided by the presence of American military power. Third, Mao is part Leninist, part Stalinist—and mostly Chinese. He believes in a strong, independent China; he also genuinely believes in its compatibility with an inevitable world revolution as the only way to order and peace. If he had lacked faith in the doctrine as a universal solution he could not have won victory for it as a national solution. Under present circumstances an "activist" world program serves Chinese national interests. But power politics operate on both sides of the curtain. It may be in Russia's interest to keep China embroiled with the American foreign devil, but not vice versa, with China calling the shots. The more the Soviet Union invests in China and revolutions under China's influence, the more Khrushchev's authority is modified by a rival leadership. Where does one draw the limit in using Soviet resources to serve Chinese national aims? Khrushchev studied that question under Stalin.

Following the failure of his bluff against Mao in 1961, Khrushchev continued to punish Albania. In December he broke diplomatic relations. Meanwhile, China was chastised in fraternal letters from East Europe which appeared in the Soviet press. They clearly warned against the consequences of "dogmatism" and disunity.

But much more than personal prestige and ideological differences were and are involved. Russian national interests are at stake. If China were driven to take her own road the whole Soviet Pacific flank might be in jeopardy. Cut adrift, China would surely intensify her struggle by direct appeals to non-Western as well as Western parties to join her in dissidence. Two socialist worlds might arise. China could reorient her trade and economic policies toward other nations ready to exchange with her. France, Western Germany and Japan, now in fierce competition with the United States for the world market, might be brought into closer relations with China by only slight shifts in emphasis of Peking's trade policies.

A final split might also conceivably lead to a division of the socialist world on racial and color lines, threatening the basic political stability of the Soviet Union as a Eurasian state. That large part of the U.S.S.R. lying within Asia might not remain immune to repercussions of such a break. Even China's preoccupation with the United States as the main enemy might veer elsewhere. Within the Soviet party itself the effects on Khrushchev's position could be immediate and serious.

We now begin to see the true complexity of the uterine growth of a "new society" struggling between viable birth and catastrophic miscarriage, and the difficult choices which face the Soviet party as midwife of the future. One can sympathize with Khrushchev. Powerful forces at home pull him to the right and away from deep commitments in far places which might condemn Russia to continued low standards of living for years to come. Yet more divisive drives in Poland pull still farther to the right (with Yugoslavia in the distance), in the hope that a *détente* with the West might open the road to close collaboration with the rising new Common Market and an independent power center of Western Europe, freed from *both* Soviet and American domination. On the East the wind blows hard to the left, demanding greater equality and greater common sacrifices to advance the cause of liberation from pressures of a kind unknown in Europe.

In the winter of 1961-62 both parties had second and third thoughts. Khrushchev must have seen that he could not hope to shake the solidarity of the Chinese leadership through any palace revolution. By spring there were signs that the crisis had eased. Chinese press attacks had ceased and so had Moscow's threats. Korean and Vietnamese mediators were busy. In April Russia sent a large trade delegation to Peking which was warmly received. New assurances for unknown but apparently substantial credits were announced—shortly after a session of the National Congress in Peking, where Politburo spokesmen known to have been most vociferous in their attacks on Khrushchev were reported absent from the assembly. When Chou En-lai summed up the nation's tasks, he emphasized continued priority development of agriculture as the foundation of the economy, and "consolidation" of past gains, with minimum investment in new construction. Ahead lay another year of strict austerity, but the food situation had begun to improve. No public reference was made to the Sino-Soviet dispute.

No one supposes that the inner wounds have been healed, but both parties had apparently recognized the peril and withdrawn from the precipice, at least temporarily. Chou had said to me that no amount of ideological difference between China and Russia could be allowed to affect their basic military alliance against imperialism; come what might, an attack on one would be considered an attack on the other.

This mutual need doubtless proved to be the cement that weathered the storm. As long as the basic antagonism of these two allies against the have-gots of the West remains greater than their own conflict of interests, they will settle on a "center" of strategy for mutual defense —even though a right and a left in the world organization will continue to compete for leadership in the strategy of the revolutionary offensive.

84

China and Japan

There are approximately 900,000,000 Asians living in lands other than China, and excluding Asians and Asian mixtures in the Soviet Union, Mesopotamia, North and South America and Europe. Together with China, these people total well over half of humanity. The People's Republic has trade and diplomatic relations with the great majority of them, including the non-Communist countries of Pakistan, India, Afghanistan, Nepal, Burma, Ceylon, Cambodia, Laos and Indonesia, and the Communist-controlled halves of Vietnam and Korea.

Since the Second World War the United States has established military bases on Taiwan, in South Korea and South Vietnam, in Japan and in Thailand. The immediate national-security objective of Chinese foreign policy is not only to prevent any expansion of what it regards as American military encirclement, but to outflank it, mainly by political means. Its second objective is to push Western military power out of the Far East altogether—and the United States is the only significant Western military power left there. China's third objective is to establish an Asian community run by Asians—a Monroe Doctrine for the Western Pacific. Its long-range objective is to lead the Asian community toward social revolution as part of a future "one world" united in a Communist society.

Traditional Chinese strategy teaches that a curve is often the shortest line between two points, and Japan is China's shortest line to American vulnerability. Asia's greatest industrial nation, linked to China by a common written language, by race and by ancient cultural ties, by geography and by complementary economic needs, the 93,000,-000 literate and technologically advanced people of Japan hold the ultimate balance of power in China's struggle to end American military dominance in the Western Pacific.

Japan hammered at China for sixty years, seized her territories, plundered and ravaged her people, and did her best to bring the giant under control. The Japanese ended by creating conditions which made Chinese Communist triumph inevitable, as Mr. Kennan has told us. Japan also destroyed the crumbling edifice of Western colonialism, in a vain effort to replace it with her own Monroe Doctrine, and at the cost of her eclipse as an empire. Objectively, Chinese Communists recognize that Japan unconsciously thus played a "progressive" role in history.

China suffered more damage from Japan, and fought her far longer, than any other power. The Nationalist Chinese government confiscated Japan's very large investment in China, which the People's Republic inherited. Peking was not consulted when the United States signed a peace treaty with the vanquished empire. Peking does not recognize that treaty, granted as a condition of a defense pact which obliged Japan to provide the United States with military bases and left Taiwan under American dominance. American occupation policies in Japan under General Douglas MacArthur nevertheless made it possible for Communist and other left-wing movements legally to become powerful voices in Japan. At the same time those policies were wise from the viewpoint of American power interests and Japanese political stability.

"Why, I could be shot," General MacArthur, the future board chairman of Remington Rand, told me at lunch in Tokyo in 1945, with Grove Patterson and Martin Sommers, "if I tried to do some of the things at home that I am doing over here. They'd call me a bolshevik if I pulverized Standard Oil or the U.S. Steel Corporation the way I have been pulverizing the zaibatsu monopolies here." He seemed awestruck by his audacity, which was nothing personal but obligatory under Allied directives agreed upon at Potsdam. "Of course I'm simply carrying out orders. But it's practically revolution, gentlemen, revolution!"

Japan was swiftly and totally disarmed, war industries were dismantled, principal war criminals were tried and punished, labor unions were legalized, and totalitarian propaganda was suppressed. Women attained equality of legal status and the Emperor was reduced to a symbolic figurehead. Proconsul MacArthur handed the Japanese a brand-new constitution which *forever renounced armed force as an instrument of Japanese national policy*. Japan, unlike Germany, was saved from a revival of the militarism that brought us to Hiroshima.

Two fundamental economic reforms laid a broad basis for a new economic democracy in Japan. Great private and government estates were broken up and millions of tenant farmers were helped to purchase land on easy terms. (In prewar Japan, 70 percent of peasant families were tenants.) Second, the few great monopoly capitalist families of Japan known as the zaibatsu—who owned the greater part of the nation's industrial assets—were required to dispose of their vast properties to new and supposedly diffuse ownership. The first reform created a new owner-peasant class that is today the backbone of the conservative Japanese Liberal Party. The reform of the zaibatsu was less enduring. The American authorities opposed state ownership or socialism. They also would not advance adequate capital or credits to small entrepreneurs to enable them to buy out the "pulverized" industries and restore production. The economy remained stagnant, reconstruction was difficult and unemployment mounted. The Socialist party steadily extended its following, with the Communists also growing, under the impact of revolution in China.

Ironically, the Korean War solved the zaibatsu problem. Suddenly, America spent billions in army procurement orders in Japan. Under the exigencies of war, laws were "re-reformed" to the benefit of the old owning families, new credit and capital became available, and restrictions against monopoly control were so relaxed as to permit production to be restored under the zaibatsu—much as happened to the Krupps in Germany. Japan's industrial economy has now resumed much of its prewar ownership pattern, but democratic rights have remained. Labor unions are powerful; so are peasant cooperative unions. Peasant and worker opposition to militarism and war is widespread. After the Korean War, American policy in Japan favored a revival of Japanese military power, as in Germany. Almost universal pacifist opposition has made it impossible to rewrite the Japanese constitution, however, to legalize any restoration of the army, navy and air force beyond the small gendarmerie.

When the Japanese-American treaty came up for reconfirmation in the Diet in 1960, protests against even the old terms of the alliance threatened the downfall of the Liberal government. Huge nation-wide demonstrations were organized. The Kishi Administration was compelled to cancel arrangements to receive President Eisenhower on a state visit; it could not guarantee his personal safety. A humiliation for the United States, these events were hailed as a great victory by Communists everywhere. They provided the Chinese Communists with a powerful argument in Moscow that November in support of their American "paper tiger" theme.

The Kishi regime fell, but not before it renewed the treaty—with no provision for Japanese rearmament. In the new elections the Socialist party failed to win a majority, but while the Liberal-Democrats remain in power they probably will not again seriously raise the question of rearming. Reactionaries inside and to the right of the Liberal party seek to link rearmament with repressive laws against labor unions, restrictions on civil liberties, restoration of emperor worship, and il-legalization of the Socialist and Communist parties. This minority is supported by the old secret societies and sons of ex-landlords who were formerly the main source of officers for the army and navy which led Japan to war. Japanese anti-Communist liberals do not need Peking propagandists to tell them that those who want to rearm also aim to make Japan a nuclear power, dispense with the one-sided alliance, and restore totalitarian militarism.

On a recent visit to Japan, my first since 1946, I found that China had become a major issue in internal politics. This is by no means con-fined to those influenced by the Japanese Communist Party, which has tallied as many as three million votes in the national elections but is still a small minority. Most Japanese would like to have normal trade and cultural relations with China. Their inability to do so increases resentment against the American alliance, the presence of American armed force in Japan, and American occupation of Okinawa.

The United States walks a tightrope in Japan. American civilians are warmly received but the uniform is not liked; it is, of course, a re-minder of Japan's defeat. Soldiers are confined strictly to army reserva-tions, and men on leave in the cities wear mufti. Great care is taken to avoid incidents between American soldiers and the civilian population. "A single spark can start a prairie fire." The Japanese in general seem grateful for an American occupation far more generous than they had expected, and for vital aid in reconstruction. But sentiment heavily favors neutrality. If American policies were to embroil Japan in war, the safety of American bases there could no more be guaranteed than the safety of President Eisenhower.

Peking is better informed on Japan than on the United States. As resident delegate of the Japanese Peace Committee and the Japan-China Friendship Association, there sits in Peking a very important and able friend in the person of Kinkazu Saionji. A Princeton graduate, and son of the revered Prince Saionji, he acts as liaison between his Chinese hosts and hundreds of visitors from Japan: politicians of all hues, including ex-cabinet ministers; writers and artists, publishers, housewives, women's leaders, labor union and peasant union delegates, M.P.'s, businessmen, financiers, Sinologues, scientists and intellectuals. Kinkazu Saionji's Chinese colleague on the Peace Committee, Liao Ch'eng-chih, spent some of his youth in Japan. China's minister of cul-ture, Kuo Mo-jo, is Japanese-educated and is well known there among intellectuals.

China is to Japan what Greece is to children of Western culture. Japanese go there not just as tourists but as pilgrims. Chinese Marxist thinking also has its Japanese disciples, and the Japanese party is closer to China than to Russia. Sanso Nozaka, the Communist party chief, spent some years with Mao Tse-tung in Yenan.

Few Japanese suffer any real sense of remorse about having made war on the European nations; they feel a secret pride at having dislodged them in Asia and they were after all beaten by America, not by Europe. Among Japanese who knew China, however, I found a curious sense of unexpiated war guilt. This is skillfully exploited by the Peking government, which receives its guests in a spirit of let bygones be bygones and expressions of desire to restore peace and unity in an Asian community of the future. As Mao Tse-tung took delight in his youth in Japan's victory over Tsarist Russia, so many Japanese see in both China's resurgent demands for Western withdrawal, and her back-talk to Russia, a continuation of Japan's own lost dream of an Asian co-prosperity sphere. A sense of unity in resentment against the white masters' dominance in their Asian world is always latent between them.

It would be as foolish to believe that Japan will fall into China's arms as it would be to imagine that she can be kept cut off from China indefinitely by American pressure. Japan is not afraid of being conquered by China. In Japan's hundreds of years of borrowing from China there was no attempt by China to invade Japan except by the Mongols, whose fleet was destroyed in a storm.

Japan is now run by hardheaded and hard-pressed businessmen. They know that they must export or perish. Dependent on imports for 20 percent of its food and 90 percent of its raw materials, faced with the necessity to provide a million new jobs every year in a land one-twentieth the size of Australia but with nearly ten times its population, Japan cannot afford to look at markets with an ideological monocle. Since the Korean War the United States has provided substantial subsidies and a highly profitable market, but lopsided dependence on America has not made for a stable economy. Japan's relative prosperity is possible because of zero expenditures for national defense—in a land which formerly spent 80 percent of its budget on armaments. As long as America continues to buy enough of Japan's goods or otherwise subsidize her economy sufficiently to keep the low mass standard of living from dropping to danger point, the businessmen's regime may remain in power. If unemployment and peasant discontent should reach critical proportions, however, *any* Japanese government would begin to explore every possibility of reopening trade with China. China may never again become Japan's most important market for investment capital, but it is not inconceivable that she might again become her greatest trading partner.

Building toward leadership for that day, Japan's Socialist party has adopted a foreign policy platform which was popular enough nearly to defeat renewal of the alliance. The Socialists promise to secure the withdrawal of American forces not only from Japan but also from Okinawa. They would recognize and trade with the Communist bloc, in competition with Western Europe. They desire to continue close relations with the United States, but with Japan a fully independent and neutral nation.

While he was a visitor in Peking, shortly before his murder by right-wing assassins in Japan in 1960, the chairman of the Japanese Socialist Party, Inejiro Asanuma, was told by Mao Tse-tung that China would like to sign a nonaggression and nuclear-free-zone pact with Japan. It would specifically exclude the use of Japanese facilities by United States air or naval forces for any aggressive activities against China. (American U-2 planes had reportedly flown over China.) In exchange Mao said that China would ask Russia to remove the reference in the Sino-Soviet pact which named Japan as their former enemy.

When China resumes her industrial advance during the Third Five-Year Plan (1963-67) more scope may be allowed for Sino-Japanese trade. Soviet economic withdrawal cost China heavily during the ideological rift; she may be expected to "lean less to one side" [1] in future trading. Nor can Peking ignore the significance of the Soviet trade drive which in 1961 made Japan Russia's most important customer in Asia, after China.[2] In Peking I was told by Dr. Chi Ch'ao-ting, of the Foreign Trade Ministry, that a sounder basis for exchange with Japan exists now, owing to China's greater capacity to exploit resources which Japan lacks. These include iron, coal, tin, lead, salt and agricultural raw materials of industry, which could be bartered for Japanese fertilizer, tractors, heavy machinery, scientific equipment and high-level technical assistance. Necessity appears to be compelling China to drop political strings attached to recent offers of a resumption of trade; in any case the impact of an important economic exchange would soon be felt on Japanese foreign policy.

The Japanese Socialists need to win about seventy more seats, out of a total of 467, to become Japan's majority party. If conditions were to give the Socialists parliamentary power, and they carried out their announced intentions, the United States would be faced with thorny problems. Washington may have to provide a profitable market or otherwise subsidize the conservatives indefinitely if it wishes to keep the air bases there secure. To counteract Socialist pressure, Japan's ruling Liberal-Democratic party in September, 1962, sent a senior spokesman, Kenzo Matsumura, to confer with Chou En-lai in Peking. Late that month Matsumura announced, on his return from Tokyo, that he had discerned "bright prospects" ahead for renewed China-Japan trade. He was then able to foresee trade developing "step by step" with, rather than awaiting the achievement of, political reconciliation.

In Japan, the cost of American forward positions does contribute to the production of useful goods and services, rather than materials of war. This cannot be said for Taiwan, where we have seen that about 80 percent of the budget goes for the support of Chiang's inflated army. In South Korea, where the per person annual income is less than

$80 a year, another army of 600,000 consumes 60 percent of the national revenues, in addition to direct arms support from the United States. Ten years after the end of the Korean War, the unemployed number "more than 20 percent of the work force in a country of 25,000,000." United States civilian expenditures alone were reported in 1962 at a quarter of a billion dollars or $10 per head of the population.[3] No intelligent nonpartisan observer would contend that in either Korea or Taiwan the present military dictatorship could win popular confirmation in an honest election.

Following the 1962 *coup d'état* in Seoul, the *New York Times* published an article entitled "Korea: Transition to a Democratic Regime." In it, Abe Rosenthal quoted the No. 2 man and head of security and intelligence forces under the army junta in South Korea, Kim Chong Pil, as saying to him: "Even if a country became as dictatorial as Hitler —not that we are, of course—but was still for America and against the Communists, it should still be an ally of the United States." Mr. Rosenthal himself concluded: "Some foreigners believe that 30 percent [of the Korean people] at most support the Government."[4]

Kim Chong Pil was only partly correct in suggesting that the United States would have no alternative in the cold war but to back even an openly Hitlerite dictatorship. He would seem fully correct if he had added that even if Korea became a *Communist* state—but *opposed* both China and Russia—the United States might support it for the same reason it supports Yugoslavia. In this truism we see revealed the inner paradox of the cold war. It is a war between nationalisms in which the power game is "the thing," while the principle becomes more and more obscure.

It was Korea's tragedy to be caught like a shuttlecock between Russian and American nationalisms. Both powers punished the unfortunate land for its weakness when, after forty years of Korean patriotic struggle for national unity and freedom from Japan, we liberated it by cutting it in half. Before we consider whether there is any peaceful way to unite Korea and end America's hot and cold running war with China, let us take a brief look at another Asian nation cut in two by its liberators.

85

War and Peace
in Vietnam

" 'All men are created equal . . . They are endowed by their Creator with certain inalienable rights. Among these are life, liberty, and the pursuit of happiness.'

"These immortal words are from the Declaration of Independence of the United States of America in 1776. Taken in a broader sense, these phrases mean: 'All peoples on earth are born equal; all peoples have the right to live, to be free, to be happy.' . . .

"These are undeniable truths . . .

"Nevertheless, for more than eighty years, the French imperialists, abusing their 'liberty, equality, and fraternity,' have violated the land of our ancestors and oppressed our countrymen. Their acts are contrary to the ideals of humanity and justice."

—Preamble to the Declaration of Independence of the
Republic of Vietnam, Hanoi, September 2, 1945[1]

"All people who are prepared for self-government should be permitted to choose their own form of government . . . without any interference from any foreign sources."

—Harry S. Truman, enumerating the "Four Commandments"
of United States Foreign Policy: 1945

I was in Vietnam shortly after that declaration of independence. For a few weeks then the country was united, for the first time in sixty years. It has since been divided successively by the British, the Chinese and the French—all assisted by the Americans. The heat of Chinese-American conflict today centers in Southeast Asia, and Americans are beginning to be killed there in increasing numbers. We are spending billions of dollars trying to shore up the Diem government, and we may end either by putting as many troops there as in Korea, or by finding a formula for neutralization of the whole country and getting out. It is probably a last test of the viability of ten years of the Dulles policy in the Far East; any solution found there is bound to be directly relevant in Taiwan, in Korea, and in our relations with China and the United Nations. Therefore it is important to conclude our visit to the other side of the river with an attempt to see what Vietnam is all about.

It is a very long story. I shall try to make it short by stating at the outset what Vietnam is not. The Republic was originally set up not by Communists of China or Russia but by native nationalists of various parties, in which native Communists were in 1945 still a small minority. They did not take possession of the country from the French; the French regime had surrendered to the Japanese in 1940. The United States has not claimed that there are Chinese Communist troops in Vietnam nor that North Vietnam has invaded South Vietnam. The Vietnamese never attacked the United States, and Vietnam was never American territory. The United States has no international mandate in Vietnam. How do we happen to be there, 12,000 miles from home, flushing peasants out of the jungles and waiting to see what North Vietnam, China and Russia are going to do about it?

Indochina is not exactly a "little country" and not a new nation. With Laos and Cambodia it is about 300,000 square miles in area, and more than 80 percent of its inhabitants are Annamites. Even without Cambodia (88,000 square miles) Indochina is as large as France. In the western mountains lies the heavily forested jungle kingdom of Laos —with 91,000 square miles but fewer than 3,000,000 inhabitants. Vietnam proper is a long, rippling dragon with a coastline of about 2,000 miles, 127,000 square miles of territory, and about 30,000,000 inhabitants. Many centuries ago these people migrated from southern China and absorbed or destroyed earlier inhabitants. Cambodians, like the people of Thailand and Upper Burma, are mixed descendants of the same stock as the Thai and other minority peoples of China. Laotians are indistinguishable from the Pai people across the frontier in Yunnan.

From pre-Christian times this whole area was under Chinese political and cultural influence. It was no perfect idyll; China has had frequent periods of aggressive imperialism. Annam won its independence in the tenth century but it was invaded once every hundred years or so to restore China's position as suzerain. (In turn, it dominated Cambodia and Laos.) During most of the post-Mongol period the kingdom of Annam was probably as independent as the Dominion of Canada. The loose suzerainty of China usually relied mainly upon cultural dominance—with the threat of military occupation as coercion. The written language, Confucianism, court ritual, houses, customs, were imported from China by Vietnam. The name Vietnam ("Distant South")* was probably Chinese in derivation—as was Japan, which means "Source of the Sun(rise)," or east of China.

French merchants, soldiers and priests began to take over Indochina after the Chinese empire was crippled by the T'ai-p'ing Rebellion and the Opium Wars. At first the Bible was foremost; after that followed the weightier artillery of *la mission civilisatrice*. In midcentury the French seized the Saigon area and the emperor of Annam called upon Peking for military aid. Rocking from Anglo-French invasions at home, the suzerain power could do nothing. The Book and the sword moved steadily northward. In 1882 the emperor of Annam again appealed to China and large forces were sent to his assistance. In 1885 China—again under French attack at home—withdrew in defeat. France had won the potentially richest colonial prize in her realm. After fifty-five years a pro-Nazi governor general, Admiral Decoux, surrendered control of Indochina to the Japanese without firing a shot.

During that brief half-century isolated Annam had been introduced to Christian civilization. The Annamites were backward, weak and childish; they had to be punished and taught. The French built modern docking facilities at Saigon and Haiphong, laid down a few military highways, built small modern garrison towns, ran the difficult modern railway up to the capital of Yunnan with an official eye to its annexation, established a monopoly of foreign trade, built themselves luxurious homes and clubs, provided employment for native servants, and kept law and order by executing peasants who sometimes became bandits rather than pay taxes for their own benefit. It all brought little return to the motherland, but it was profitable for a French *colon* community of some 40,000, at peak.

When I first saw Hanoi and Haiphong, as a youth, they were miniature French provincial towns at the center, surrounded by slums of cowed and undernourished slaves. The halls of the best hotels smelled of opium. The cafés and restaurants were excellent. There had been recent revolts that year (1930), and whole villages were bombed and wiped out in reprisal. The local press announced the guillotining of "rebel leaders," whose heads were displayed for salutary effect.[2] At that time one could literally buy a comely Annamite concubine for less than a hundred dollars, as lonely French *colons* often did.

In balance, French supremacy was doubtless a more enlightened rule than the native despotism which it replaced. It did bring a back-

---

* Vietnamese characters for the Chinese term *Yueh-nan*, which literally means "South of Yueh" (ancient name for Kwangtung), or China's southernmost (distant) province.

ward, secluded kingdom into contact with advanced knowledge and learning of the West. Quite a few Annamites got to France and studied there; they learned to think politically, as well as to appreciate French culture. French history, as well as their own, taught some to become revolutionaries. By the time the Japanese arrived, the French were operating eighty-one prisons, not counting labor-reform camps. But after only fifty-five years, 2 percent of the children were officially reported to be getting an elementary education, as many as one-half of one percent had leaped forward into secondary schools, and there was a university in Hanoi. In the puppet kingdom of Laos one native doctor had already been trained. Harold Isaacs reported in 1943 that "the colonial government spent 30,000 piastres for libraries, 71,000 piastres for hospitals, 748,000 piastres for schools . . . and 4,473,000 piastres for the purchase of opium distributed through the official opium monopoly." [3]

Before Pearl Harbor, China was still resisting Japan, alone. The Japanese navy blocked all the China coast and the only way left open was through Haiphong to Yunnan. The French collected heavy duties on China's imports. Then the Japanese spoiled things by demanding control. Governor General Decoux was an Axis sympathizer; in 1940, he obeyed the puppet Vichy government's order to place the colony at Japan's disposal. Symbolically, this act marked the end of Western empire in Asia.

Bringing in their armed forces, the Japanese allowed the French to remain as stewards. The colonial bureaucracy supplied the Japanese with rice and conscripted native labor for them. Using Indochina as a staging base, the Japanese then mobilized the forces with which, in December, 1941, they invaded all southern Asia and attacked the Philippines. Japanese demands became excessive; their unhappy stewards had to rob the peasants for them. During the war years, according to American estimates, more than 2,000,000 Annamites starved to death —8 percent of the population, or about four times all the Americans killed in both world wars. [4]

The Annamites always seemed to me the meekest people in the world, but even the meek revolt; in desperation, thousands joined the guerrillas. Some began to attack isolated French police posts. Individual soldiers in the puppet militia faded away with rifles. Patriotic intellectuals in the underground national revolutionary movement organized a united front. In 1943 they sent emissaries to the French timidly to suggest a joint *Résistance* to the Japanese. French officials coldly rebuked them; they were accused of seeking arms against France, not Japan. Throughout the war the Foreign Legion and Senegalese forces were busy hunting down Annamese patriots.

By 1945 the Annamite forces had occupied many villages and built small bases. In Yunnan, they had liaison with the Nationalist Chinese. Near the Chinese border a few American O.S.S. men contacted their guerrilla bands and, helped also by a few antifascist Frenchmen, brought them arms and other supplies. The slaves were rising, and the French *colons* were no longer useful. Just before V-E Day the Japanese arrested, disarmed and interned all French forces in Indochina. Except for a small detachment near the border, which crossed over into Yunnan, there was no resistance. After March 6, 1945, no substance or *gloire* remained of French colonial rule.

Now the Japanese belatedly turned to appease nationalist sentiment. The French governor general had been all-powerful, but there was always a window dressing of native rule, headed by a puppet emperor who functioned much like the native princes of British India. Emperor Bao Dai had been France's figurehead ruler since boyhood. Educated in France, he had spent much of his life on the Riviera. At home, his make-believe court of mandarins formed a ruling hierarchy who danced when Frenchmen pulled the strings. Bao Dai's ancestors had once ruled most of independent Indochina, but the French had broken it up for administrative and economic reasons, restricting the emperor to a shrunken state called Annam. In the south they created "Cochin-China," under direct French rule; in the north they created the "protectorate" of "Tonkin"; in the west they had the puppet kingdoms of Laos and Cambodia.

The Japanese now declared that they were restoring "unity and independence" under Emperor Bao Dai. They revived the pre-French name of the land, "Vietnam." Bao Dai was permitted to send envoys to claim Cochin-China and Tonkin, and even to contact the puppet monarchs of Laos and Cambodia. For the first time since French conquest, the country was nominally "unified." Behind this façade, the Japanese sought first to destroy, then to reconcile, the free Vietnamese armed forces. These latter were guerrilla groups led largely by the Vietnamese Independence League—Viet Minh, for short. Their partisans spread over extensive areas from north to south. The week of Hiroshima, a Viet Minh congress representing both north and south elected a provisional government for the whole country. They also used the historic name Vietnam. Conceding independence to Cambodia and Laos, the congress invited them to join a Federation of Indochina.

Then an unusal thing occurred: a peaceful transfer of power. Envoys of the Vietnam republic negotiated with the Japanese commanders. On instructions from Tokyo the Japanese agreed to let members of the Viet Minh enter the cities, including the capital, organize freedom parades, and convene assemblies.* Elections were held by different parties. In Hanoi a national assembly met and drafted a declaration of independence. On August 25 the puppet emperor (anxious to be on the Riviera) made a remarkable declaration "to abdicate and transfer

---

* Japan sought to win postwar good will by recognizing, before the Europeans returned, the independence of all the colonies she had overrun—no doubt hoping also to turn hostility from Japan back toward the old masters.

power to the Democratic Republican Government." He expressed regret that he had been "unable to help his country" under the French or the Japanese. He accepted a post as "Chief Counselor of State." The mandarins and other puppets wilted from the scene.

Within a few days Viet Minh forces peacefully occupied government buildings from Hanoi to Saigon, took over administration of the bureaucracy (already nine-tenths native), and held power nearly everywhere from north to south. Confined to their barracks, Japanese troops did not interfere and there were few incidents. Vietnamese political prisoners were released; so were Jews and antifascist Europeans. Only the Legionnaires and other French troops remained interned. Amazed French civilians sat unmolested in their cafés. One Frenchman was killed in a street fight; otherwise the Viet Minh police and new troops maintained admirable order. They treated the French politely but no longer obsequiously. Having proclaimed independence, the Republic of Vietnam sent telegrams to France, to the United States—to all the world capitals, impartially—seeking recognition, admission to the United Nations, and authorization to disarm the Japanese.

Here I must greatly condense the history of the amputation and subsequent tragedy that now befell Vietnam, and—while urging the reader to consult the abundant documentation available elsewhere[5]—rely largely upon eyewitness knowledge of the main events which threw the Republic into the Communist camp, brought Mr. Dulles to the "brink" at Dien Bien Phu, and sent our troops into the muddy rice fields for Ngo Dinh Diem.

At Potsdam it was agreed that France still owned Vietnam. The Allied chiefs also decided that something had to be done for Generalissimo Chiang Kai-shek, who was fretting because he was not getting much attention as the Big Fourth. The Chinese Nationalists were therefore given the satisfaction of disarming Japanese troops in Indochina north of the Sixteenth Parallel. In the southern half of the country the British were to do that job—in a shoehorn operation for the French, who would later on also "relieve" the Chinese occupational troops in the north. The Allies made no announcements to the Vietnamese that the French were returning.

Officials of the Republic in Saigon welcomed the first British contingent as their antifascist "allies." General Douglas Gracey set up his headquarters and at once conferred with the Japanese commander, General Terauchi. Gracey refused to see Vietnamese leaders who wished to negotiate terms of cooperation for disarming the Japanese. On British orders the Japanese released from internment some 5,000 Foreign Legionnaires. They were immediately rearmed. Gracey then declared martial law and ordered Vietnamese troops and police to evacuate Saigon. Before dawn on September 23 the rearmed Legionnaires staged a *coup d'état* and seized the city hall, seat of the new government. State buildings were taken by force, hundreds of people were arrested, and blood spattered the streets. The Vietnamese began to organize resistance in the suburbs. More British troops arrived. (I also arrived then, as a war correspondent, in an American air force plane ferrying O.S.S. and other observers from Thailand.)

Early in October, French troops disembarked from the cruiser *Gloire,* their arms and all their supplies furnished by the United States. Systematically the Saigon perimeter was extended. Instead of disarming the Japanese, General Gracey ordered them to assist in suppressing the Vietnamese. Terauchi's troops were put back on a war footing, with roles now reversed between the French and themselves. (Over in Tokyo later that year, when I spoke of these small ironies to General MacArthur, he surprised me with the passion of his response. "If there is anything that makes my blood boil," he exclaimed, "it is to see our allies in Indochina and Java deploying Japanese troops to reconquer these little people we promised to liberate. It is the most ignoble kind of betrayal.")

More American-equipped French forces poured into Saigon. These soon included thousands of Nazi prisoners of war who had enlisted in the Foreign Legion. Meanwhile, many former Vichyite officials were busily re-forming the colonial Sûreté and bureaucracy. I saw them herd hundreds of Vietnamese peasants—men, women and children— into open squares where the broiling tropical sun beat down and they waited days for interrogation and summary sentences to long imprisonment or execution. The road was slowly opened to Cambodia, and French protectorate power was restored in Phnom Penh. Soon France had 50,000 troops in the south, enough to relieve the British. Having finally disarmed and repatriated the Japanese, General Gracey washed his hands of what soldiers were already calling *la sale guerre*—the dirty war. He departed with the last of his men to the strains of "Auld Lang Syne."

France was never to recover full control even in the south. In the north, with no British Trojan Horse to lead them, the French first had to dislodge hostile Chinese Nationalist troops. Why "hostile"? All Chinese, Nationalist and Communist alike, preferred an independent Vietnam to a French Vietnam. Chiang Kai-shek had sent down one of the Yunnan "opium generals," Lu Han,* to collect back debts from the French as well as from the Japanese. Ho Chi Minh, leader of the new Republic, had long been getting some aid from the Kuomintang. From the day General Lu Han arrived, he permitted the Vietnam regime to

---

* Throughout the war, as before it, Yunnan had been the fiefdom of the regional satraps Lung Yun and Lu Han, who controlled the opium and tin monopolies. Lu Han had the greater army. In a double maneuver the Generalissimo dispatched Lu Han to Indochina, then quickly descended on Lung Yun and seized control of the rich province. Lung Yun later revenged himself on the Generalissimo by accepting Communist assistance to recover control of Yunnan, but his nominal rule there proved short-lived. Until his death in the spring of 1962, he was a supernumerary among the ex-Kuomintang generals in Peking.

develop its administrative and political life around Hanoi as its capital.

General Lu was interested in cash, and for cash the Vietnamese could even buy the Japanese arms General Lu collected. They were expensive. Lu imposed Chinese currency as official tender at an exchange rate ten times its purchasing power in China. Officers-in-business (rice, opium, anything at all) piled up black-market profits in the millions which by chain of command reached official pockets as far back as Chungking.[6] France was assessed $23,000,000 to cover China's cost of disarming the Japanese. (The United States would pay.) Large blocks of real estate fell to Kuomintang carpetbaggers. Following their generals' example, Nationalist troops helped themselves, impartially, to the contents of French and Vietnamese homes.[7] Desperate to be rid of the locusts, the French made a humiliating and costly "evacuation" agreement with the Generalissimo.

Postwar governments of France included men who sincerely wished to satisfy nationalist sentiment in the colonies. A new constitution had provided for a *Union Française*. The possibilities of self-determination within the commonwealth then envisaged seemed very real, assuming honesty in France and patience in the slaves. But what Paris said and promised and what the *colons* did on the spot were quite separate things.

"France cannot negotiate with a gun pointed at her head," said the unwelcome liberators. The French demanded that the gun first be turned around, so that negotiations could be conducted in a *legal* way. Alas, the Vietnamese had now also tasted the power that grows out of the barrel of a gun. It must be said on behalf of the intentions of many Frenchmen, including the French Communists of that day, that they simply could not believe that anybody who had ever enjoyed the benefits of French civilization, even when offered to them from behind the barrel of a gun, could voluntarily prefer an independent path. Nor was that belief peculiar to French colonialists alone.

The bitter truth was to be fully and finally ascertained in Algeria more than a decade later, under General De Gaulle (to his credit), but in 1946 the Great Illusion still prevailed in Indochina.

The Vietnamese no more wished to be bossed by Chinese than by Frenchmen, but China's withdrawal left them with not a single friend among all the powers. None had even acknowledged the Republic's communications. The United Nations did not answer appeals for recognition. President Truman replied by sending millions in American lend-lease and military supplies to the French in Saigon. As the Chinese prepared to be "relieved" by the French, the Vietnam government at Hanoi, to avoid prolonged war in an already starving land, sought the best possible bargain offering any hope of self-determination under France.

The French would not grant "independence." In the agreement France signed with Ho Chi Minh in March, 1946, the Republic of Vietnam was recognized as "A Free State, having its government, its parliament, its army, and its finances, and forming part of the Indochinese Federation and the French Union." Cambodia and Laos had already been detached as separate states, but the agreement provided for a popular referendum on "unification" of north and (again French-occupied) south Vietnam. The French were to send no more than 15,000 troops into the north, to share in garrison duties with 10,000 Vietnamese troops, until the referendum was held. Meanwhile, Indochina's international status (as a member of the French Union) was to be decided by negotiation.[8]

Statesmen in Paris believed they had solved the Vietnam problem. Indeed, Ho Chi Minh and the great majority of Vietnamese nationalists were content to remain within the French Union, if only as a guarantee against possible future Chinese aggression. But Paris was not the colonial mind and hand of French Indochina. As events in North Africa were later to make clear to the world, the colonial army and the colonial bureaucracy operated quite independently whenever they could. And in Vietnam they could and did.

Before the ink was long dry on the Franco-Vietnamese accord, the highest French army leaders in the colony issued orders (then secret, later exposed in France)[9] unmistakably aimed at the crushing of all Vietnamese resistance, full restoration of French military and political power, and the complete sabotage of the "Free State" agreement. By these orders the French military units which moved in to "relieve" the Chinese were required "in each garrison" to prepare and set in operation "plans . . . to transform the situation from a purely military operation to a *coup d'état.*"[10] Meanwhile, the Sûreté was to create teams of specialists to locate "all leaders" of the various parties in the government and to prepare for "the task of discreetly neutralizing these leaders as soon as the command considers it necessary . . ."[11]

Such was the mentality of the men who led France to disaster in Indochina. Some of them would end, in the final insane gesture of frustration in 1962, as leaders of the Secret Army whose noble task was the "discreet neutralization" not only of unarmed "natives" but of French housewives with babes in arms—murdered on the streets of Algiers and Oran. Not all the Nazis were in Germany.

French troops were admitted peacefully in the north, and permitted to garrison key points, but hostilities in the south never stopped. In May, 1946, the day after Ho Chi Minh and the Vietnamese delegation left for Paris to negotiate terms of national elections and relationships within the Union, the French in Saigon announced the formation of a separate government for the south. In August the French called a "Conference of the Federation" consisting of hand-picked delegates having no connection with the "Free State," and launched a *national* puppet regime. In Haiphong the French army seized control of the ports and customs without any agreement. Incidents followed in many areas as the French "established order" by arrests, by local coups and by disarming native police.

Despite agreements Ho Chi Minh signed in Paris which called for a cease-fire and guaranteed Vietnamese "civil liberties," incidents were provoked which everywhere gave pretext for arrests and wider French military action. The 15,000 limit on French troops was rapidly violated; air, naval and army units soon doubled and trebled that. In December the French seized Haiphong, which was systematically bombarded and pacified, with the cutting of many a throat. In the same month the generals took police control in Hanoi and demanded the evacuation of all Vietnamese troops. Shortly afterward Hanoi became the scene of the first open battle of the two forces, which French troops easily won.

Léon Blum's Colonial Minister (a Socialist) now arrived in Indochina. Ho Chi Minh was still anxious to confer with him to end hostilities. The Minister listened only to the generals. He refused to meet with Ho, and announced that "only a military solution of the situation was possible." [12] (The French Communist Party continued to remain in Blum's cabinet.) Leaders of the Republic of Vietnam were driven back to fight in the fields and the hills. War again raged from north to south.

We must now consider a frail wisp of humanity named Ho Chi Minh, whose allies Americans are committed to destroy in Vietnam today. How was it that he, acknowledged leader of the minority Communist Party of Vietnam (in 1946, 20,000 members; today, called the Lao Dong—Old Party—more than 500,000 members), came to be the unanimous choice of all the independence parties and groups which supported the Republic—the man best qualified to lead the struggle against the Japanese, the French, and finally the friendly Americans?

"When one recalls," wrote two American anti-Communist specialists on Southeast Asia, Virginia Thompson and Richard Adloff, "that during its first nine months of existence the Vietnam Republic was occupied by rapacious Chinese troops, whose commander favored the Dong Minh Hoi [Nationalists] above the Viet Minh [Communist-led coalition], and that millions of people within its confines were threatened by famine, the skill with which Ho maneuvered at this time can be better appreciated . . . Ho was able not only to win the National Assembly's agreement to the concessions he had made to French imperialism [the abortive 1946 agreement] but also to get the Dong Minh Hoi to share his responsibility . . . Ho's integrity, which has been recognized even by his enemies, suggests that he would not betray the cause [true national independence] to which he has devoted almost all his adult life . . . Ho's personal prestige, ability, and training are so outstanding that the course which his leadership charts seems to be the determining factor [of the] future." [13]

Ho Chi Minh, whose real name is Nguyen Ai Quoc, has a background somewhat comparable to Chou En-lai's. Now about seventy, he was

born in northern Annam, in a family whose ancestors were officials before the French conquest. Thin as a blade of grass, and small-boned like
most Annamite aristrocrats, he is a well-educated intellectual. As a
student he went to France to interpret for coolie labor hired to dig
trenches and latrines in the First World War. He stayed in France
four years. Both his French and his English are good. He also knows
Chinese, Russian and German. In 1920, he attended the meeting at
Tours where the French Communist Party was founded.

Is it difficult to understand why Ho and hundreds like him saw the
Communist party as the only means of national liberation? Review the
reasons which drew men toward the same cause in China. Double
them; Indochina was all colonial, China only semicolonial. If you detested being a slave and found one friend who promised freedom,
would you reject or embrace him? Like Sun Yat-sen, Ho Chi Minh had
eavesdropped at Versailles; he had found that Vietnam was not on
President Wilson's self-determination program. Not the Republican
party or the Democratic party, but only the Communists, and only
Russia after its revolution, offered help to subjugated nations determined to fight for equality against great odds.

As in China, the revolutionary task was to bring leadership and political action to an amorphous mass of peasants—90 percent of the
people, and 90 percent illiterate—who lived under similar or worse
conditions of overpopulation, disease (80 percent had intestinal parasites), despair, underproduction and servitude. Independence and
national unity were the powerful elementary aspirations in Indochina,
as in all colonies. And would things then be more "humane" than under
the French? Probably not for some time; the former have-gots would
be punished for their weakness, now that they had lost their French
protectors. Yet they were to suffer even more when French military
and political aggression became responsible for driving Vietnam into
the Communist camp—with major American aid.

In 1950, Russia and China recognized the Democratic Republic of
Vietnam, as it was now called. Following the Korean truce, Russo-
Chinese aid in guns, training and technical assistance reached proportions which began to counterbalance American help to the French.
Vietnam's armies multiplied and improved in efficiency. In the south
the French still held the upper hand, but in the north they had to go
over more and more to the defensive. By 1954 France had an Indochina
army of 250,000 men fully engaged in the attempted reconquest—and
had spent more there than all the Marshall Plan aid extended to Paris
since its liberation.

Then, in a great miscalculation, the heart of the French army cracked
at Dien Bien Phu. It was not a French error alone. American joint staff
officers were deeply involved, for they had approved the great Navarre
Plan which led to the disaster. Divining the French intentions (which
foundered largely on false assumptions of security of supply lines),

the Vietnamese commanding general, Giap, followed a "one by one" strategy, broke the back of the offensive, and succeeded in isolating and entrapping the bulk of the French forces. On March 20, 1954, the French chief of staff, General Paul Ely, arrived in Washington fresh from Indochina to say that France was near the end of her endurance. He asked for immediate direct American intervention to relieve the besieged armies. Without it, France would have to accept Vietnam's offer of a cease-fire in exchange for an international conference to negotiate terms of French surrender.

French revelations since then make it appear that the first American response was made two months before the Geneva Peace Conference opened. According to Georges Bidault (French Foreign Minister at that time), Secretary of State Dulles twice offered him the use of American atomic bombs against both China and Vietnam—to back up his verbal threats of "massive retaliation." As reported by Roscoe Drummond and Gaston Coblentz in their recent book about Mr. Dulles, Georges Bidault said that the first offer was "of one or more atomic bombs to be dropped on Communist Chinese territory near the Indochina border" to destroy China's supply lines to Vietnam. Bidault recalled a "second offer" of two atomic bombs to be used against the Viet Minh forces at Dien Bien Phu. The authors added, "There is no doubt in Bidault's mind that these offers were made." [14]

Realizing the somber implications of such a move, M. Bidault instead repeated General Ely's request for American nonatomic air strikes at Dien Bien Phu. Immediate army and naval air force intervention was then advocated by Mr. Dulles as well as by Admiral Radford, chief of the Joint Staffs. Before a final commitment was made General Matthew B. Ridgway, army chief of staff, made a detailed logistical study of what was involved. His report to the President showed that direct intervention could not be "successful" short of a great war of enormous cost. In his memoirs General Ridgway wrote:

> In Korea we had learned that air and naval power alone cannot win a war and that inadequate ground forces cannot win one either. *It was incredible to me that we had forgotten that bitter lesson so soon—that we were on the verge of making the same tragic error.*
>
> That error, thank God, was not repeated . . . The idea of intervention was abandoned, and it is my belief that the analysis which the Army made and presented to higher authority [Eisenhower] played a considerable, perhaps a decisive, part in persuading our government not to embark on that tragic adventure.[15]

If we are to understand where we have been and where we are going in the Far East it is unavoidable to interject what may seem some irreverent inquiry. Regrettably, it must focus upon a patriot who died in the service of his country and is not around to read a brief of explanation. I should therefore like to make it perfectly clear that I respected John Foster Dulles and had no personal encounters with him of an unpleasant nature.

The questions which concern us, however, are in the broadest sense not one man's responsibility but rather concern the collective conscience of a whole nation. It would be a mistake to believe that Mr. Dulles acted alone or arbitrarily. The power delegated to him came from the President; behind both of them all Americans who did not say them nay lent their support. John Foster Dulles was not in truth the driver of the cart (though he surely believed otherwise); he was the dray horse for others in the seat. By the end of his administration those "others" so alarmed even President Eisenhower that he devoted the most earnest passages of his farewell address to a sudden, impromptu warning against what he called "the military-industrial complex," and a "disastrous rise of misplaced power" which threatens to extinguish "democratic processes." We shall have occasion to quote his remarks more fully in the next chapter.

John Foster Dulles was a product of that "complex" and of the post-Korea hysteria which strengthened it. America was in a punitive mood and Mr. Dulles was the man best attuned to it emotionally. He was an obstinate and a righteous man. Like many good Christian reformers who had gone forth to redeem the heathen in the past, he had no occasion to reflect that Jehovah, as well as his adversary, can take many forms in many places. Mr. Dulles' speeches never convinced me that he had troubled to study the history or realities behind the issues in the Far East or that he understood anything about revolutionary China or Indochina. No one in Washington saw much evidence that he had ever given his full attention to anyone who might have enlightened him.

The rise of John Foster Dulles unfortunately coincided with the long agony of McCarthyism, which offered the world the spectacle of a great nation reverting to political infantilism—not just for a few days but for four critical years. Mr. Dulles' capacity for trusting infidels on the other side of the river was no more generous than McCarthy's opinion of his fellow countrymen at home. By fortuitous circumstance, McCarthyism so upset the normal administrative, legislative and even judicial equilibrium that the Secretary of State was quite free to do some rather egregiously absurd things.

Senator McCarthy never managed to expose a single one of the "hundreds of card-carrying Communists in the State Department" who he once alleged were there, but he was a highly useful man in the pursuit of a policy objectively aimed at isolating the United States from most of eastern Asia. One effect of McCarthyism was the rapid separation from the State Department of many of our ablest foreign service specialists on communism. By 1954, Mr. Dulles had found so many of McCarthy's "names" agreeably expendable that he was left without one experienced senior China expert on the policy-making level of his staff. The only crime proved against any of those experts was their prophetically correct wartime reporting on China.[16]

It was a grave matter that Mr. Dulles swiftly deprived himself of such valuable help just when he embarked upon his bold program, but it must again be emphasized that he was not alone responsible. The same thing may be said on behalf of the late Senator McCarthy. A patriotic but transparently psychotic demagogue, he would have been laughed down except that he was exploited by part of the "military-industrial complex," by much of the press, and even by civic institutions, for both infantile and coldly calculated, adultly profitable purposes.

Of all Mr. Dulles' (and "our") errors of commission not one was more costly than his success in tying the United States to Chiang Kai-shek on Taiwan, in a unilateral intervention and a wholly unequal alliance without precedent in American history. That is not a mere hindsight view of my own; it exactly corresponds to the estimate made by the Department of State in the year 1949, as recorded in an official "policy information paper" issued to explain why the United States would not establish a protectorate in Taiwan.[17] Against the basic interests of the American nation, and for no more tangible a reason than a desire to punish China (and China alone) for the Korean War, Mr. Dulles bought a heavy political, economic, and military liability. At the expense of condemning a whole nation for the policy of a government, and thereby uniting Communist and non-Communist sentiment alike behind Peking, Mr. Dulles secured an alliance which deprived the United States of all the flexibility needed to deal with the vast and ever changing revolution of Asia. Since 1953 his policy has left his successors with no alternatives but costly perpetuation and extension of the original mistake—or a Christian retreat in admission of excessive zeal.

In the most literal sense, it was that alliance which brought America into undeclared war in Indochina.

Now we may well ask what would have happened if M. Bidault had accepted Dulles' offer or if General Ridgway had not successfully opposed major intervention at that time. To what significant degree would the individual American citizen have shared in the responsibility? There now exist international laws, fixed at the Nuremberg criminal trials, which quite likely would have been applied to those who dropped the bomb near Dien Bien Phu or on China—assuming that they had lost yet survived. Had we overheard conversations among totalitarian leaders solemnly considering the fateful decisions I have mentioned, might we not have doubted their sanity—as many doubt the sanity of Mao Tse-tung? Mao dogmatically believes that "the American people have nothing to say about policy; everything is decided by the monopoly capitalists." If we read President Eisenhower's "military-industrial complex" for the Marxist cliché, does Mao seem so bereft of logic?

Quite apart from the universal holocaust which M. Bidault foresaw if the bomb were used, what moral law guided Mr. Dulles (and "us") to recommend the execution and maiming of thousands or millions of people (including innocent children) who were after all struggling on their own miserable land, in their own way, for their own freedom? Led by the wrong men, no doubt, and among them atheistic Communists who warmly returned Mr. Dulles' hatred, they may then have been punishing or even executing "reactionaries"—traitors, landlords, or even some Christians opposed to them and perhaps mistakenly judged "enemies of the people." Could we have saved the innocent by dropping the bomb or by massive intervention? Who would have been morally superior if either the Dulles or the Radford-Dulles advice had been followed?

Of course that did not happen, for which we may thank General Ridgway. But it might still happen elsewhere. Did not the Communists also recommend the same means? We do not know. Perhaps they did. If so, we may also thank *their* General Ridgway. In contrast to Mr. Dulles, however, the Communists have never been converted to the Book. Is it possible that we were taken unawares on the hindside by the dark adversary? Who could have beguiled Mr. Dulles, after he had memorized so many verses from the Bible that was always with him (together with Stalin's *Problems of Leninism*), to forget that "All our righteousnesses are as filthy rags; and we all do fade as a leaf," or that "the wrath of man worketh not the righteousness of God"?

But perhaps we are misled. Perhaps what we wanted all along was only a fair and open election to assure self-determination in Indochina? Perhaps accounts to the contrary now given out to the public are merely drawn from the arsenal of our own cold-war propaganda, in order to frighten the enemy, while in fact our gentlemen never had any such evil intentions? If we believe that—as in charity and self-esteem many Americans must—then we must hope that the people on the other side of the river fully understand also that there is not, and never was, and never will be, any danger of war launched by the United States. But what has since happened in Vietnam?

With Dien Bien Phu, the French people had had enough of the "dirty war." In a new election Mendes-France received a mandate to "end the war in twenty days." At the Geneva Conference, concluded in July, 1954, France unequivocally recognized the complete independence of *all* Vietnam. Separate treaties provided for independent kingdoms in Cambodia and Laos. All three states were to be neutral; they were to be free to have diplomatic relations with both East and West. All foreign troops were to be withdrawn.

Yet as it turned out, the Geneva agreements destroyed the unification which they so explicitly confirmed. As early as 1950 the French had combined Cochin-China, Annam and Tonkin into a single "State" over which they persuaded the ex-emperor, Bao Dai, to preside as Chief Executive. The State was still part of the French Union, however. Lacking true independence (as usual), Bao Dai had held no more than nominal sway within the perimeter of French arms—which covered only parts of the whole country.

Now, at Geneva in 1954, the agreement provided for a national election as soon as the French forces withdrew. In the first stage the French were to concentrate south of the Seventeenth Parallel, turning everything north of it over to the Viet Minh forces. Before 1956 they would totally withdraw also from the south. Heterogeneous native military groups (organized by the French for the Bao Dai government) south of the parallel were to police the area until the national election. The electoral procedure was to be negotiated in 1955 between Bao Dai's government and the Democratic Republic of Vietnam. The vote itself was to be cast not later than July, 1956. This election would choose an all-Vietnam government to complete unification.

For Vietnamese seeking unity, the Geneva accord developed two major flaws. First, it left no outside power committed to enforce the terms. France, having finally surrendered all sovereignty to an independent Vietnam, had no more authority there. Like Russia, China, Britain and other signatory foreign powers, she was merely bound not to interfere in Vietnam's internal affairs. Second, the 1956 date for a national election provided time for have-got antiunification elements around the Bao Dai regime to regroup, bid for American armed support, and refuse to carry out an election.

Ho Chi Minh was universally known and his following was overwhelming. As a good politician, Ho had minimized his leading Communist party role. He retained the title, President of the Republic, while others rotated as secretary of the party. His prestige as a national patriot first, and party man next, was well established. He was George Washington on the left. So sure of this were the Viet Minh that they were ready to exchange electoral inspectors between north and south, as well as international observers. Mendes-France realized that even in a fair and well-supervised election the D.R.V. (Democratic Republic of Vietnam) would win dominant power. Vietnam was not East Germany.

Mendes-France had no alternative to the treaty, however; his premiership depended upon concluding a peace. Having failed to prevent what looked to him like a sellout, Mr. Dulles had first boycotted the conference—where he turned his back on Chou En-lai's outstretched hand. But Vietnam, Russia and China would not accept a settlement which left the United States free to intervene in the south. Under great pressure from the NATO allies, Dulles finally gave back-handed recognition to the agreement. On the last day of the conference he stated that the United States would "not oppose" implementation of the instrument, "either by force or threat of force," and would view renewed "aggression" with "grave concern."

It shortly became apparent that the electoral arrangements were to be sabotaged, however, by a *de facto* United States military alliance with Ngo Dinh Diem, an ex-royalist violently opposed to unification with the D.R.V. In September, 1954, the organization of SEATO enabled Mr. Dulles to offer military protection to the nascent neutral states. In October, Mr. Dulles persuaded President Eisenhower to make a declaration of unqualified United States support for Ngo Dinh Diem personally—even though Bao Dai was still "Chief of State."

The strategic concept behind SEATO was to extend the armored arc around China stretching from Korea through Japan and Taiwan to Thailand and Eastern Pakistan. Vietnam formed a missing link. It was presumably now to be filled in. China would then "pass away."

The Geneva terms had forbidden new arms build-ups in any of the Indochinese states. Only replacements of worn-out equipment were permitted, subject to check by an international commission. The international commission reported that China and Russia were abiding by the agreement. But were their technicians not "aiding" North Vietnam? Why should not the United States extend "technical assistance" to South Vietnam? Especially when there were assurances that there was not to be any election or unification? Washington's pledge had sealed the bargain. Ngo Dinh Diem eagerly welcomed the Americans who quietly replaced French military technicians and brought in money and better arms.

Using SEATO as a façade (but without any authorization from other members to do so) Mr. Dulles' envoys urged military assistance on both Cambodia and Laos. Prince Sihanouk of Cambodia quickly halted the infiltration and reasserted his complete neutrality, after he discovered the intentions of Central Intelligence Agency operatives functioning under the direction of John Foster Dulles' brother Allen. (So did Burma.) The little monarchy in Laos was more pliable—also more naïve. Russia and China as yet had no aid program there. In violation of the Geneva covenants, C.I.A. and American Embassy personnel, later followed by uniformed army officers, began to bring military equipment into Laos.

There was no demilitarized Seventeenth Parallel dividing Laos. In the north there were small guerrilla forces under Prince Souphanouvong, who had fought the French in alliance with the Vietnamese. In the center there was Prince Souvanna Phouma, the neutralist premier of a viable coalition government. On the right there was Prince Boun Oum, who had collaborated with the French. (The "king" was a cipher.) Americans chose Prince Boun Oum. In a few years "we" dropped half a billion dollars in that toy kingdom on Cadillacs and other gadgets for the palace retainers of the king and on bribes to buy votes in the Laos assembly, but mostly on military supplies.[18] It was an amateur job. Unexpectedly, the left-wing elements won an election and "we Americans" found ourselves financing troops on the wrong side—sympathizers with the North Vietnamese.

Rectification was sought by building an army under General Phoumi Nosavan (a former French protégé), who was able to seize Vientiane, the capital, in a coup in late 1960. There his fortunes ended. Souphanouvong escaped from prison, went back to the north, and reorganized his disbanded guerrillas. He appealed for help from the North Vietnamese, and received some. In Vientiane there had been a leftist coup, led by a young parachutist, Colonel Kong Le (who had been a big hope of the C.I.A.). Now, driven from Vientiane, Kong Le went to Souphanouvong's support. The reorganized forces General Phoumi had tried to destroy—helped now not only by 10,000 Vietnamese but also by arms airdropped by the Russians—counterattacked Phoumi's army (estimated at 80,000). It dissolved, before much smaller numbers. By 1961, Souphanouvong's followers had reached far below Vientiane and opened a pathway to South Vietnam.

U.S. marines were landed in Thailand and the United States hastily agreed to another Geneva conference. While Phoumi's reverses continued, Averell Harriman worked out an agreement to make the best of a bad job, and a cease-fire was arranged. By terms of the 1962 Geneva treaty, the three Laotian princes were left to restore a coalition among themselves. All foreign intervention was to cease, and the United States now fully recognized Laos as a neutral and independent state.

For the first time the United States thus gave Peking de facto *and* de jure *recognition, when China (together with Russia) became a signatory to the Geneva treaty.*

Whether American operations in South Vietnam will end in a similar manner, or more tragically, remains to be seen. President Kennedy has told us that we are in for a long war there. Perhaps that is a bargaining position from which to impress Peking, Moscow and Hanoi—like Mr. Dulles' H-bomb threats? Perhaps not. If we want a long and losing war, Ngo Dinh Diem seems to be our man.

Would it not have been pertinent to inquire whether "the West" could expect to defeat "the East" in Vietnam by using (or being used by) a Catholic Easterner in a country more than 90 percent non-Catholic? (The Vatican itself had never taken sides in Vietnam.) Pertinent also was whether an anti-Communist military dictatorship could be forced upon half a people more successfully behind American bayonets than by French bayonets tried seven years against a whole people. Even more to the point was whether an aristocrat from the top shelf of the 5 percent have-gots (and somewhat tainted by past collaboration with French imperialism) could now impose, in a Viet-

nam already in revolution for a generation, a "family system" dictatorship of the kind that had already failed under Syngman Rhee and
Chiang Kai-shek—whose delusions of adequacy never seem to have
troubled Mr. Dulles? If the Secretary asked himself these questions
about Ngo Dinh Diem he must have speedily found the answers reassuring. This time he acted in a manner which opened him to no possible
veto from any Milquetoast chief of staff.

As a French-educated administrator, and a member of the prewar mandarinate, Ngo Dinh Diem once led the agonizing life of Bao
Dai's prime minister, obliged to carry out the decisions of the French
governor general. After the Japanese occupation he became a right-
wing factional leader in the Vietnamese Catholic League. (Nominal
Catholics may now number 2,000,000; many of them are also Taoists
and Buddhists. Perhaps two-thirds of them are in the south.) Ngo
Dinh Diem might have had a big role to play in the independent
monarchy as restored by Japan, but Bao Dai's speedy abdication in
favor of the Republic left Diem out of politics. His background of
service with Bao Dai opened for him no place of importance in the
Viet Minh coalition. Ngo Dinh Diem astutely refused further collaboration with the losing French, however. Not until Bao Dai was made
Chief of State for all Vietnam did he again join a French-sponsored
government. He was premier of Bao Dai's regime at the time of the
Geneva Conference.

From 1954 on, protected by the demilitarized Seventeenth Parallel,
and with solid Dulles backing, Diem* quickly became the strong man
and Bao Dai the petulant figurehead. Diem built around himself a staff
of anti-Communists, anti-federalists, and anti-Baodai-ists and anti-
Hochiminh-ists. Their handicap was that few had done anything to
recommend themselves as national or revolutionary patriots. Diem
distrusted anti-Communist nationalists and democrats who had been
guerrillas against the French; perhaps they made him feel inferior. He
tended to favor the Catholic minority, and especially northern Catholics. Many Catholics had also fought the French, but most had not.
Fearing persecution or having already suffered under the now Communist-dominated Republic, thousands of Catholics came down from
the north, during an official exchange of sympathizers. (There are
about 16,000,000 people in the north, 14,000,000 in the south.) From
these new arrivals Diem chose his closest collaborators outside his
own family. In Saigon itself he had some support among the few
wealthy Vietnamese—many of them French educated—and among
anti-Communist middle- and upper-class refugees from the north.
There were also the large landowning families of the south, threatened

---

* The practice of referring to Ngo Dinh Diem as "Diem" has now been so well
established by journalese that I follow it in order to avoid confusion. Ngo is the
surname. There are so many Ngos in his regime that use of the given name was
adopted to distinguish "Diem" from the others.

by the Republic's land equalization program; from them many of Diem's army officers were recruited.

Bao Dai, never a man to "struggle," soon lost control of his cabinet and hand-picked assembly to Diem and his "National Revolutionary Movement." Diem ignored all requests from Hanoi to restore postal, telegraph, rail and other communications. He refused to discuss national elections. He denounced the Geneva agreement—to which Bao Dai, as the "legal person" and heir of French rule, was morally bound. Moreover, as last survivor of a dynasty which once ruled all Vietnam, Bao Dai wished to see it whole again, as one real service he might perform. Ho Chi Minh (politician enough to realize Bao Dai's sentimental value) was prepared to support him in some symbolical role in the elections. Diem doubtless sincerely wanted to save his country (even as Chiang Kai-shek had); for that he needed power. In October, 1956, he staged a "national" referendum on the question of separation and of Diem against Bao Dai. (Less than 15 percent even of those allowed to vote participated.) He then became the new Chief of State. Three days later he proclaimed formation of a "Republic of Vietnam" and assumed office as its first president.

Diem now began to enjoy the role he had been unable to play as frustrated prime minister in the puppet monarchy. The Americans were not in the same position as the French. They could not dictate to him. Like Chiang Kai-shek, he convinced "us" that we had no alternative. Like the South Korean officer trained by the United States Army and quoted by Mr. Rosenthal,* even if Diem were as dictatorial as Hitler, Washington would have to back him. Was not Diem fighting for the Free World against Communist aggression? Was he not the avenging angel against atheism? And did he not have the complete confidence of the Dulles brothers?

One might suppose that in a country with only a handful of highly trained and educated persons, Diem would have made great efforts to reconcile any and all intellectuals who could be used. In Saigon, at least, many were anti-Communists. Just the opposite occurred, according to Philippe Devillers, an outstanding French (Catholic and anti-Communist) authority on Diem and the Viet Minh. Why should he try to use anyone opposed to him when he had fulsome American backing? He had no mass party to restrain him. Diem destroyed all the opposition which might have saved him—imprisoning many, driving others into exile or the jungles. An eyewitness to these events, M. Devillers observed: "This repression was aimed in theory at the Communists. In fact it affected all those, and there were many—democrats, socialists, liberals, adherents of the religious sects—who were bold enough to express their disagreement . . ."[19] The Cao Dai and Hoa Hao are backward but important sects peculiar to South Vietnam who had fought the French on religious grounds. Diem took savage

* See page 679.

reprisals against them (driving some toward the Communists) in ways embarrassing even to the Vatican.

That may fairly sum up Diem's policies toward intellectuals, political and religious freedom, and civil liberties. But after all, perhaps the nation needs a *strong* government? Aren't the really important people the peasants? One could assume that a man of Diem's intelligence would have read and learned something from China, from Korea, and from North Vietnam and the French experience before him. Where did the Communists get their support? From the "great majority"—the poor peasants, ready to die for them. Why? Peasants were not interested in revolution, Marxism, or theories. They wanted peace, rice, parcels of land, relief from their agonies, freedom from crushing debts, usury and taxes, and a chance for their children to learn to read and write.

The two billion dollars America invested in French attempts at reconquest could have financed peaceful national land reform. Now, here was a second opportunity, with another two billions of American money to invest. Surely with only half a country to handle that would be enough to make a new start?

To confound the Communists it was necessary immediately to provide land for the landless tillers, to show that the regime stood for *some* betterment of the have-nots. With a satisfied peasantry as its foundation the whole countryside might have been stabilized. The compensated landowners might have become a new urban entrepreneur class. From the new peasant landowning class, youths could have been trained to carry out an adequate program of farm cooperatives, irrigation, roads, cleaned-up villages, health centers, schools, hospitals, local self-government, and so on. Plenty of volunteers (cured of TB and parasites) might then have been eager to accept training and provide leadership for the protection of their stake against Communists or any other threat. Indeed, Communists might have been confined to intellectuals in the cafés and opponents of nuclear testing except by the Russians.

Diem did not even have to fight his way back, like the French; the countryside was quiet when he took over. Viet Minh regular armed forces had been withdrawn to the north, and in many places in the south, where Viet Minh leaders had raised volunteers to oppose the French and Bao Dai, rents and taxes had already been reduced. On some large plantations of absentee native and French landlords, the tenants had been given land before the local Viet Minh guerrillas disbanded in 1955. Some refugee landowners and peasants from the north were settled on government land, but Diem carried out no general equalization of ownership. A new law guaranteed a landlord up to 250 acres—many times more than could be tilled without tenant labor. Peasants who had divided the land under the Viet Minh naturally came under suspicion from a regime determined to destroy all influence of the veterans of the *Résistance* throughout the country-side. In many villages such peasants were herded out of the "infected areas" and transported, after the processing away of contaminated persons, to state reservations.

The Diem family-system government is headed by four brothers. Ngo Dinh Ngu, the President's chief "political adviser," is the only one who is married. Mme Ngo Dinh Ngu has become palace hostess, boss of the Assembly, and author of a "Family Bill" which virtually prohibits divorce. Another Ngo brother is the Roman Catholic archbishop of Hué, an important provincial capital. A third brother, Ngo Dinh Can, in 1957 took charge of Diem's own "dirty war" against the peasants. Other members of the Ngo clan are strategically placed in the government; one is ambassador to Washington.

The facts are hard to believe. Diem's theory was that wherever the Viet Minh had operated—and that was in most villages—there were bound to be Communists, traitors, spies, unreliable people. (The majority of the Viet Minh originally were *not* Communists.) Ngo Dinh Can began systematic large-scale and savage "mopping up" operations against hundreds of villages that had long been quiescent. "In 1958 the situation grew worse," according to Devillers. "A certain sequence of events became almost classical: denunciation, encirclement of villages, searches and raids, arrest of suspects, plundering, interrogations enlivened sometimes by torture (even of innocent people), deportations, and 'regroupings' of populations suspected of intelligence with the rebels, etc." [20] Many villages were burned to the ground; charred corpses littered the ruins. Thousands of families were separated and suspects forced into concentration camps.

It was not North Vietnam or even local Communists but Ngo Dinh Diem who finally drove the whole countryside into rebellion. Anyone seeking more recent confirmation of the facts should read a belated and restrained but detailed and lengthy report by Homer Bigart in the *New York Times* in July, 1962, written after he had returned from six months of life under Diem's dictatorship and was free of Saigon censors.[21]

In 1957, before Diem began his repressions, and the reprisal policy in the hinterland, his government policed and was able to collect taxes in nearly three-fourths of the villages. By 1962 he had lost effective control of nearly everything but Saigon, the principal provincial towns and cities, and main communications. Yet within those years his armed forces had quadrupled. Besides an investment rapidly approaching three billion dollars, the United States had now placed 10,000 army ground and air force personnel in South Vietnam to assist in training and combat operations of Diem's troops. By 1963, according to Homer Bigart, Diem would be using 350,000 men against no more than 25,000 armed partisans—"who have no anti-aircraft guns, no air power, no trucks, no jeeps, no prime movers, and only basic infantry weapons." Most of the latter had, as usual in guerrilla wars, been captured from government forces.

In a still later report in *Newsweek* entitled "Vietnam: The Unpleasant Truth," that journal's Saigon correspondent, François Sully, diagnosed the problem there chiefly as lack of leadership and popular support, quoting experts on the scene.[22] One of them dryly observed that an American marine is a superb pilot "but he simply cannot indoctrinate peasants with an ideology worth fighting for." Immediately after these mildly critical comments appeared, Diem had Sully deported. A more optimistic view was expressed in an account by Robert Shaplen (after a visit to South Vietnam), who was more impressed by the fortified-village technique than Bigart, Sully or Devillers. Mr. Shaplen eschewed political criticisms and predicted humane and effective economic and social measures once the Vietcong* military threat was removed. American estimates given to him of the probable time required to destroy the guerrillas ranged around five years, however—and that on the assumption that the D.R.V. did not intervene in support of the Vietcong forces as directly as the United States had intervened on behalf of Diem.[23]

M. Devillers has described very dramatically how partisan warfare was provoked and grew to its present proportions.[24] Since 1960 it has organized national leadership for a "People's Liberation Army," operating under a "People's National Front," with many well-defended bases and local partisan regimes. Most members of the "Front" are nationalists and not (yet) Communists. There is a wide underground network. Various anti-Diem parties and groups support it in the cities. It has sympathizers high in Diem's army. Its program is not Communistic, but bourgeois-democratic and nationalist. It calls for land for the peasants, autonomy for ethnic groups and religious minorities, and civil liberties. It is pledged to "progressive reunification of the country by peaceful means on the basis of negotiation between the two zones," and immediate restoration of national economic, cultural and postal communications.

What embarrassed United States forces was that they were nowhere engaged against "Chinese Communist aggressors," as they had expected to be. Instead, they found themselves hunting down (sometimes with wolfhounds imported from Germany) and helping to kill native South Vietnamese. How could that be? All that money and power and heavy equipment, and all those tough, well-trained and well-intentioned Rangers, now brought to bear upon barefoot, puny, skeletal, worm-infested peasants and their children (bellies bloated from malnutrition), fighting not in uniforms but in rags, and not in tanks but from behind trees in their native rice paddies, their hills, their jungles and their malarious swamps? How was it that to them the American liberators looked no different, in the service of Diem, than

---

* An insulting term for veterans of the *Résistance*, followers of the Lien-Viet, Viet-Minh, and now the "People's National Front."

the French imperialists before them? Or that Diem's American-uniformed troops—well-paid, well-fed, and glad to have the job and a rifle to sell when things get rough—seemed no different from puppets of the past?

None of these things were good for American morale. American soldiers are not stupid and they soon begin to see what is going on. Americans want to be not only liked but well liked—especially by people they have come to liberate. They soon learned that not all American aid was spent on arms to fight the Vietcong. It also included new cars and gasoline to run them, refrigerators, freezers, air-conditioning machines, food, medicines, tools, and many other things that are fine in their place. All these were distributed by President Ngo Dinh Diem and his followers in order to avoid corruption. Somehow they did not get to the anti-Communist peasants but to the generals or officials—sometimes, alas, to be resold at fancy prices. Americans brought in lots of money.

Scarcities developed in essentials; rents and prices soared; inflation moved in. Rent-gouged American officers complained and organized a boycott against native and foreign real estate operators who demanded more than $350 a month for a two- or three-bedroom bungalow. A peasant here does not see $350 in ten years, and not one Vietnamese in a thousand owns such a house. Those who did supported Diem and the war against the Chinese Communist aggressors. So did the merchants, although, to his credit, Diem has tried to stop the traffic in opium smuggled down from Laos and Thailand—where the police had long made a good thing out of a monopoly on exports.[25]

Where was Ho Chi Minh's army? North Vietnam's troops have never crossed the demilitarized and heavily policed parallel to aid the southern partisans. By 1962, however, small-arms aid was being increasingly carried across the southern border. Obviously, if North Vietnam's now formidable army were to move southward with its modern equipment and air support, 10,000 Marines and a few dozen helicopters could not prevent a speedy Dien Bien Phu. What are they waiting for? Paradoxically, international law would be on their side; it was the South that had torn up the only agreements internationally recognized. What signator could condemn the North for removing the outlaws? In such an event the United States would have no legal basis for its intervention. Supported by none of the NATO allies—least of all by France—it even lacked sanction from members of SEATO.

Why had North Vietnam declined to move? The answer is not that they are better Christians but that perhaps they are greater realists. We must refer again to the Sino-Russian dispute, and to North Vietnam's relation to it. Insofar as I was able to study this question in China and afterward, I shall summarize the main points of an explanation.

After United States intervention in South Vietnam and repudiation of the election agreement in 1956, the international commission (Poland, Canada, India) dissolved itself in disgust. China and Russia both now openly give military support to North Vietnam. Contrary to widespread belief in the West, however, neither North Vietnam nor northern Laos was occupied by Chinese Communist or Soviet troops. Russia and China do extend large-scale economic and technical aid to North Vietnam, however, and 1,500 foreign technicians include military experts from both countries.[26] China and Russia about equally influence the Vietnam party, and elements within it reflect both orientations. But Ho Chi Minh above all seeks to retain his independence.

At the start Ho clearly wished to strengthen his equilibrium by maintaining economic, cultural and diplomatic ties with the United States, as well as with the United Nations. This would have given him a two-world position, valuable in bargaining inside the Communist camp, but useful also in any struggle to assert Vietnam's sovereignty. Events made that course impossible.

North Vietnam is of course now under Communist dictatorship. The regime also embraces other parties and more bourgeois-democratic and intellectual influences than in China. There was land redistribution, establishment of cooperatives, and collectivization. By 1958 the nation had embarked on a Three-Year Plan aimed at rapid industrialization and modernization of agriculture. In 1960 it began its first Five-Year Plan. Where conditions are comparable to those in China—and most of them are—North Vietnam has followed a Chinese pattern. The same mistakes were made and the regime has much the same sources of strength. It is not purely imitative; like Mao, Ho Chi Minh seeks to adapt Marxism to local realities.

North Vietnam has made such progress in industry that it could now carry out industrialization of the south.[27] Its industrial impact may soon be felt throughout all Southeast Asia. (In basic industrialization, it is already far ahead of Thailand and Burma.) But the north very much needs the surplus rice of the south; in the past it was always dependent upon Saigon for one-fifth to one-fourth or more of its food imports—in exchange for the north's abundant coal and other raw materials. The whole economic and political viability of Vietnam rests upon a united nation—much as does that of truncated Korea. Unification would also greatly strengthen Vietnam as an independent state able to resist outside pressures against its national interests.

For these and more obvious reasons Ho Chi Minh genuinely hoped for the honest implementation of the Geneva agreements. When Diem ruled out peaceful unification, the D.R.V. faced a dilemma. It had no desire for an armed conflict which would further weaken Vietnam, but a permanent amputation of the south was impossible to accept.

Ho Chi Minh was torn between Chinese and Russian views on peaceful coexistence. Vietnam was an immediate case in point in their dispute over armed support to "people's wars of liberation." If Ho began open movements against the South it might lead to war with the United States, and then to Chinese counterintervention in Vietnam. Ho wanted neither. At the same time he desperately needed rice; increased output in North Vietnam was still 20 to 30 percent under requirements. In 1960 the harvest failure in North Vietnam exactly paralleled that of China—and China could not help.

After Diem's regime rendered even trade exchanges impossible, North Vietnam still did not activate the underground Viet Minh forces in the south. It was Ngo Dinh Can's terror against the villages that forced Hanoi to lead an intensified partisan campaign. Communists in the south were in danger both of being exterminated one by one, and of losing leadership over the anti-Diem resistance to the nationalists. In December, 1958, after twenty Vietcong leaders perished in Phui Loi, one of Diem's largest concentration camps, Hanoi finally openly demanded Diem's overthrow in a war which the southern (non-Communist) Veterans of the Resistance had already begun on their own.[28]

Meanwhile, the North Vietnam Communist Party leadership had been reorganized under a new secretary, Le Duan, who represented those favoring support for the Soviet position in the Sino-Soviet dispute. If war came, Ho Chi Minh did not want to be isolated, with China as his only ally. The D.R.V.'s new policy still did not call for violation of the Seventeenth Parallel. The strategy was not a North-South war, but a ubiquitous partisan war confined to the South. What, if not organized armies, could the North supply the South? Infiltration of technically trained leaders and the development of a well-coordinated program, backed by propaganda and money with which to buy arms and defectors among Diem's soldiers. "The enemy," Mao taught, "is our supply line."

Now division of the land is carried out in earnest, every village becomes a battlefield between have-nots and have-gots, and for those in the middle, who want only peace and rice, life becomes a nightmare. Ngo Dinh Can's answer is more "agrovilles," which are set up like Chiang Kai-shek's erstwhile models of "New Life" in Kiangsi. These may impress foreign visitors, but the countryside is a sea and a few costly display villages cannot halt the erosion of the vast waters around them. Therefore Diem demands that the Americans finance the construction of 8,000 fortified villages surrounded by moats and barbed wire—in effect the placing of all peasants under village arrest. But the peasants are divided between pro-partisan, pro-landlord, and pro-Diem factions, and fearful of reprisals by all. Many youths desert for the hills, the swamps and the jungles. More soldiers are needed to "protect" them in the fields, where cultivation tasks must go on. But how many soldiers per fortified village—each soldier a sitting duck for well-led guerrillas?

And all this has been tried by Chiang Kai-shek, by the Japanese, by the French. What next? There are all those peasants of North Vietnam groaning under the Communist terror. Why doesn't Diem start a counterpartisan war among them against Ho? Peasants won't fight for a return of the landlords and the *colons*. That also has been tried.

"The American hypothesis regarding the probable effectiveness of these new tactics [in Vietnam] is based upon a failure to appreciate the very essence of guerrilla warfare," wrote O. Edmund Clubb, our last consul general in Peking, and a Chinese- and Russian-language senior officer distinguished as a pioneer student of Asian communism. "Successful guerrilla warfare depends upon the general support of the population *in resistance to bad government*. It relies upon an understanding of the desperate plight of the people and the identification of the guerrilla with their needs and aspirations. As Chinese guerrilla leader (and later Peking Defense Minister) P'eng Teh-huai put it: 'The people are the water and the guerrillas the fish, and without water the fish will die.' It would be hard to imagine anything more like a fish out of water than an American guerrilla fighting in the Vietnamese countryside for Diem's dictatorial and reactionary government." [29]

If it takes 350,000 Diem troops to hold down the main arteries against only 25,000 partisans in 1963, will 700,000 be required against 50,000 partisans in 1964? If we must depend upon force alone, why not put the army directly in charge? Why—as American "technical personnel" see it—be hamstrung by a civilian President who insists upon directing and bungling all operations?

"Should the situation disintegrate further," wrote Homer Bigart in his *New York Times* report, "Washington may face the alternative of ditching Ngo Dinh Diem for a military junta or sending American combat troops to bolster the regime. No one who has seen conditions of combat in South Vietnam would expect conventionally trained United States forces to fight any better against Communist guerrillas than the French did in their seven years of costly and futile warfare. For, despite all the talk here of training men for jungle fighting, of creating counter-guerrillas who can exist in forests and swamps and hunt down the Vietcong, Americans may simply lack the endurance— and the motivation—to meet the unbelievably tough demands of jungle fighting."

Adoption of the junta solution might or might not make for increased military efficiency, but it *would* mean political defeat. It would end the pretense that South Vietnam represents, as an anti-Communist alternative, anything like free, democratic or self-determinative government. Large-scale use of American combat troops would even more expose the blatant travesty. Either course would intensify the cold war and neither could long be tolerated by North Vietnam and China.

For five years Ho Chi Minh had balanced himself between Khrushchev's "peaceful coexistence" strategy and Mao's more militant approach, which better fitted Ho's aspirations but not his means. In 1958, Ho adopted Mao's line by lending all his political prestige and leadership to the overthrow of Diem's regime by means mobilized within South Vietnam. At the same time he observed discreet limits, in obeisance to Khrushchev's line, by avoiding direct military action involving the North Vietnam government.

If, however, the United States were to deploy great forces over a long period, or directly attack North Vietnam itself, or if the Communist-bloc diplomatic offensive should fail to bring about any modifications in the American approach, internal pressures in Ho's own camp would compel him to extend direct military aid to the partisans. He would then have to depend upon the Chinese and other allies to help defend his base territory. This would be the response which General Ridgway earlier anticipated when he foresaw major American intervention in Indochina as a "tragic adventure." Could it be that, with all those bombs and the immensely greater moral force of which John Foster Dulles was so confident in 1954, the United States might have to ponder again the question whether man was more important than weapons?

Following signature of the Geneva agreement on Laos, in July, 1962, wherein the United States recognized Laos as a neutral and unified state, and for the first time took *de jure* (though not diplomatic) recognition of Peking, it became obvious that China as well as Hanoi had begun to place greater credence in possibilities of a similar solution in Vietnam. It is toward that end that Khrushchev's policy has long been aimed. The "National Revolutionary Front" in Vietnam is a means of forcing Washington to accept a Laos type of peace.

. Such a solution would indeed imply a great "turning point" in the East-West struggle—but not one in exactly the terms Mao Tse-tung had in mind when he noticed a changed balance of forces in 1957.

86

Childhood's End?[1]

1835:

"Of all armies, those most ardently desirous of war are democratic armies, and of all nations, those most fond of peace are democratic nations . . .

"Among democratic nations it often happens that an officer has no property but his pay and no distinction but that of military honors; consequently, as often as his duties change, his fortune changes and he becomes, as it were, a new man . . . war makes vacancies and warrants the violation of the law of seniority which is the sole privilege natural to democracy . . . Moreover, as among democratic nations the wealthiest, best-educated, and ablest men seldom adopt the military profession, the army, taken collectively, eventually forms a small nation itself . . . Now, this small uncivilized nation has arms in its possession and alone knows how to use them; for, indeed, the pacific temper of the community increases the danger to which a democratic people is exposed from the military and turbulent spirit of the army . . .

"No protracted war can fail to endanger the freedom of a democratic country . . . War does not always give over democratic communities to military government, but . . . it must almost compulsorily

concentrate the management of all things in the hands of the admin-
istration . . . All those who seek to destroy the liberties of a demo-
cratic nation ought to know that war is the surest and the shortest
means to accomplish it . . . The most effectual means of diminishing
that danger would be to reduce the army, but this is a remedy that not
all nations are able to apply."

—Alexis de Tocqueville, *Democracy in America*

1961:

"We have been compelled to create a permanent armaments indus-
try of vast proportions. Added to this, three and a half million men
and women are directly engaged in the defense establishment. We
annually spend on military establishment security alone more than the
net income of all United States corporations . . .

"Now this conjuncture of an immense military establishment and a
large arms industry is new in the American experience. The total influ-
ence—economic, political, even spiritual—is felt in every city, every
state house, every office of the Federal Government . . . Our toil, re-
sources and livelihood are all involved; so is the very structure of our
society . . .

"In the councils of Government, we must guard against the acquisi-
tion of unwarranted influence, whether sought, or unsought, by the
military-industrial complex. *The potential for the disastrous rise of*
misplaced power exists and will persist. We must never let the weight
of this combination endanger our liberties or democratic processes. We
should take nothing for granted. Only an alert and knowledgeable
citizenry *can compel the proper meshing of the huge industrial and*
military machinery of defense with our peaceful methods and goals,
so that security and liberty may prosper together." (Emphasis added.)

—President Dwight D. Eisenhower,
in his Farewell Address to the Nation

"Many will tell you with mockery and ridicule that the abolition of
war can only be a dream. . . . But we must go on or we will all go
under. And the great criticism that can be made is that the world lacks
a plan that will enable us to go on. . . . We must have sufficient im-
agination and courage to translate the universal wish for peace—which
is rapidly becoming a universal necessity—into actuality."

—General of the Army Douglas MacArthur

"What is it all," asked **Tennyson**, "but a trouble of ants in a million
million of suns?" In the timelessness of infinity what remains of the
earth will cool, and as that tiny spark dies a myriad of new stars will

burst into beginning. Meanwhile, said Emerson, "we must treat men and women as if they were real; perhaps they are." Assuming that people are real, we and the Communists have not much time left in which to learn to live the Confucian truth that "within the four seas all men are brothers"—not much time before the fuse either burns to the detonator or is plucked out to save man for a few more billion years.

Can we coexist with China? With Russia? With communism? Until tourist tickets are available for mass migrations to fairer planets, where else are we to live? Where else are we coexisting now?

It is no part of my intention to suggest that coexistence is easy, nor will anything in this book support the view that it is going to become easier in the future. The whole world is caught inescapably in the four-pronged revolution. Not just the "underdeveloped" but all of us are living through a historic end of childhood. Individuals can afford for a few more hours to deny it, but for the nations there is nowhere to withdraw, no way to turn man back from his inexorable course, and no way to prevent the have-nots from struggling for equality and attainment of things now possessed by the have-gots alone. There is no way to refute the most prophetic remark in President Kennedy's inaugural address: *"If a free society cannot help the many who are poor it can never save the few who are rich."*

The problems of coexistence with China cannot be solved apart from the world-wide four-pronged revolution. Yet China is a continent in itself, and neither can any world solutions work which exclude her. Perhaps it is thought that we are successfully ignoring her now? People frequently ask, "Should we recognize China?" The answer is that the United States does recognize China, and in far more costly and significant ways than ever before in history.

The State Department, the armed services, the C.I.A. and other paramilitary organizations profoundly recognize China not only in the Far East, the Middle East and Africa, but also in Latin America and at home. In Asia alone, the United States recognizes China by subsidizing and arming at least 1,700,000 native troops under military dictatorships in Korea, Taiwan, Vietnam, Thailand and Pakistan, in addition to powerful American air, naval and ground forces arrayed on her perimeter.[2] Never before has China received so much recognition and so much respect from the United States.

The cold war from the beginning has been a two-way affair, starting with the mistakes of ignorance which Stalin and Truman (and all of us behind them) made in such ways as to provoke the hostile responses necessary to revive the arms race. China was no exception. China is a big country, too. When it blunders it is on a scale almost as big as the United States or Russia.

We have seen how the Chinese revolution grew from internal and external conditions which finally left the nation no other way out. After twenty years of fighting in the hills and remote villages the Communists came down to the great plains and cities and took power among the world's most numerous and most homogeneous people. In the hinterland they had evolved a domestic program based on Marxism— a harsh and relentless program but workable because it broke the worst chains which bound the imprisoned energies of most of the people.

In international affairs, however, the Communists had only the notebooks of Leninist theory and Stalin's advice to guide them. True, Japan and the Western powers in China had heretofore behaved quite in accordance with Lenin's prophecies. America, backing the have-gots to the very last, seemed no exception. Suspicious of any bourgeois Chinese who understood the United States, the Communists would take no advice from them. They knew that "imperialists would never change." The United States was given no help by them to make an easy adjustment, but its forces did withdraw to legitimate lines of self-defense.

It was not simply that Peking immediately formed an alliance with Russia; after all, Chiang Kai-shek had also been Stalin's ally. The unsophisticated Chinese from the hills failed to understand internal conditions in the United States which in 1949 still sharply limited the reach of American nationalism. True, the United States was doing nothing to liberate Europe's Asian colonies, but neither had it made colonies of the countries it liberated. Important changes since Lenin's time were never fully analyzed. The Chinese Communists seemed to forget that the United States had been pulled into China involuntarily. From 1946 onward they insisted and really seemed to believe that Russia's last-minute occupation of Manchuria had defeated Japan. They did not see that it was not as important that the United States had (rather reluctantly) supported the losing side in China as it was that American forces did not attempt an all-out intervention. Fear of Russia, they said. No. Russia was then very weak.

The men from the hills did not consider that the great American army of fifteen million men had been demobilized, that democratic American civilian forces were in charge, that war industry was being dismantled, and that only actions which could be construed as overt attacks on the United States could bring armaments and the generals into commanding positions over the American economy and foreign policy. In common with Stalin, the Chinese Politburo forgot the lesson of Pearl Harbor, if they had ever learned it. The American tiger had already left Asia—but it could be yanked back in again by the tail. The Chinese Communists overestimated Soviet strength and under-estimated antiwar and anti-interventionist forces in the world and in the United States. In "leaning to one side" they unnecessarily isolated themselves from powerful neutral and middle interests and they leaned too far—as they were suddenly to realize only when Khrushchev pulled the props away, in 1960, in consequence of which China suffered a severe attack of national vertigo.

Stirred by their exciting new might, the Chinese Communists also overestimated the ripeness of the rest of Asia for China-type social revolution. They did not quite understand the weight of the response which could be provoked by prolonged hostile demonstrations against American prestige. Above all, they did not understand the difficulty of arresting the momentum of American rearmament, once it was invoked in earnest. How could they? Some mistook President Truman for Chiang Kai-shek. Yet China sent no troops beyond her frontiers. Calls went forth for all Asia to follow the Chinese example—and some parties struggled to do so—but there were no supporting Chinese invasions. Propaganda is one thing, action another. Not until the Korean War broke out was it possible to convince the American nation that Russia and China meant to spread communism by national wars of conquest.

Korea provoked and provided excuses for all subsequent American policies of armed intervention and encirclement of China—which paralleled the rearming of Western Europe. The latter development itself gathered momentum only after Stalin's blundering attempt to blockade Berlin in 1949. Yet that move must also be seen as part of a long chain reaction going back as far as President Truman's cut-off of all lend-lease aid to stricken Russia immediately after V-E Day—an action cruel in its abruptness to a wounded comrade-in-arms, but much worse because it was totally senseless. That error appears traceable to thoughtless advice from minor figures in the State Department, but the same charity cannot be extended to Mr. Truman's rejection of earlier recommendations from Henry L. Stimson.

Mr. Stimson, inherited from Roosevelt, had just proved himself the ablest Secretary of War in the nation's history. His prophetic insight concerning Russia and the atomic bomb has been remarkably fulfilled by history, as noted in recent studies by Walter Millis and Fred J. Cook.

Anticipating that unless Russia were at once brought in to share the knowledge and responsibility of atomic power there would inevitably begin " a secret armament race of a rather desperate character," the Secretary of War urged, in a memorandum to the inexperienced new President, that he go directly to Moscow, with British support, and obtain an agreement both to "limit the use of the atomic bomb as an instrument of war," and "to encourage the development of atomic power for peaceful and humanitarian purposes." With the insight of clairvoyance Stimson recognized that the bomb had begun a new age that upset all previous traditions of diplomatic bargaining, and that there was in truth "no secret" which could long be kept.[3] He therefore recommended that it be handled "with the naked lack of hypocrisy that it demanded," as Millis later observed in *Arms and the State*.[4] Mr. Stimson wrote:

". . . If we fail to approach them now and merely continue to negotiate with them, having this weapon rather ostentatiously on our hip, their suspicions . . . will increase. It will inspire them to an all-out effort to solve the problem. If the solution is achieved in that spirit it is much less likely that we will ever get a covenant we may desperately need . . . The chief lesson I have learned in a long life is that the only way you can make a man trustworthy is to trust him; and the surest way to make him untrustworthy is to distrust him and show your distrust." [5]

Stimson's view was rejected and it was his farewell appearance in the Cabinet. (Even though Stimson's advice was ignored, the Chinese could learn something by trying to reconcile the mere fact that it could have been offered by any Secretary of War, and monopoly-capital representative, with their own rigid conception of American imperialism.) It was not until after the Soviet "all-out effort" was well along that the seemingly "realistic" Baruch plan was advanced by Truman, *not to Russia,* but through the then completely American-controlled United Nations. This would have placed an intelligence inspectorate over Russia which even a novice such as myself knew to be totally unacceptable in the milieu of the Soviet government's well-founded paranoia. The chance—merely a chance, but the *only* chance —of avoiding the ensuing epoch of world terror was thrown away. We also got the Korean War.

In June, 1950, Soviet troops had already evacuated North Korea; only Soviet advisers remained. American troops had also all but evacuated South Korea. Although divided, all Korea was nominally an independent country. The American Joint Chiefs of Staff and Dean Acheson had declared that Korea as well as Taiwan was unnecessary to the strategic defense of American security in the western Pacific. China has had special interests in Korea for centuries; it is linked to her by race, language and culture. In 1894-95 China fought a war with Japan over Korea, to defend her position as suzerain. It was again from Korea that Japan launched her invasion of all Manchuria, in 1931. Both Nationalists and Communists of China had long secretly supported Korean revolutionary parties, in years when the United States did nothing to free Korea. The United States had supported Japan in Korea in her war against Russia. That neither Russia nor the United States now even considered giving China a role in the Allied occupation of Korea was considered by all Chinese a national insult. Some of the Korean Communists who took power in North Korea were close comrades of the Chinese, and were aided in their underground resistance against Japan in Manchuria and Korea all through the Second World War. The United States had backed Syngman Rhee in arresting and killing such men in South Korea.

Many Americans still believe that China started the Korean War. That is historically untrue, as Chou En-lai has reminded us (in Chapter 12). "The evidence indicates that China made no early plans to commit the PLA [People's Liberation Army] to combat in Korea," asserts a recent study made for the United States Air Force by Allen S. Whiting, a RAND Corporation intelligence analyst.[6] It would be naïve to suppose that the North Korean government began the war without China's knowledge. If China approved, that was obviously a disastrous decision based on faulty understanding of the United States. Yet there is no available evidence that China originally planned to intervene. "The initial decision [to intervene]," in the opinion of Mr. Whiting, was not made until "late in August." It was not implemented in combat until four months after the outbreak of hostilities—not until Mr. Truman had received two warnings* from Peking against sending troops north of the Thirty-eighth Parallel, and not until American (and U.N.) forces were hard upon China's frontier on the Yalu River, which American planes were bombing.

Combining emotional ties with historic fears and strategic national interest, the Peking high command probably had no real alternative but to "resist in self-defense." Transfer the scene to Mexico. Would the United States do nothing if a foreign army approached the Rio Grande? Peking had first officially looked upon the struggle as Korea's internal affair. When war reached Manchuria, the historic invasion route of China, the government regarded its own action as counter-intervention against an "American invasion."

To this day the Peking government maintains—and most of the people of China seem to believe—that South Korea began the attack at American instigation. I have seen no convincing proof of that, I do not believe it, and most of the world does not believe it. (If it should ever be proved, more than a decade of history would have to be completely rewritten.) But it should not be overlooked that the foolish Syngman Rhee and his generals did repeatedly threaten, and appealed for American support of, an armed conquest of the north. There had been numerous reports of border violations of the Thirty-eighth Parallel by Rhee's forces as well as by the Communists. It is in this sense—as a decisive counterattack—that the Chinese Communists

---

* The MacArthur-Truman exchanges at this time have not been fully revealed. Briefly, General MacArthur's intelligence informed the President that the Chinese were bluffing. MacArthur had earlier sought to bomb China's supply lines, but even after the intervention, Truman (hamstrung by the U.N.) denied him that authority. A clear victory being unattainable under such restrictions, MacArthur early favored armistice negotiations. Truman refused, the war dragged on, and an armistice was eventually negotiated on terms worse than MacArthur believed he could have won earlier. For details, consult the Truman and MacArthur papers. (See Bibliography, page 788).

undoubtedly rationalized their participation in the war as defensive. It must also be remembered that China was excluded from the United Nations and was not bound by its ukases. None of that was really assimilated by Mr. Truman and other Americans in 1950. To them, Korea was another Pearl Harbor, and the United States had no alternative (nor did the United Nations) but to oppose armed aggression with force.

Since then we have somewhat reversed the situation. That the United States might be similarly entangled in support of any one of its dozens of alliances is a thought which might now be worth pondering. If Chiang Kai-shek took the offensive against China, if Diem attacked North Vietnam, or if South Korea violated the demilitarized zone in renewed war with the North, what would the United States do? Let them perish? Not likely. In truth we had no moral basis for our earlier limited intervention against the Vietnam Republic except an alliance with France. When the United States unofficially supported an attack by General Phoumi's forces against the Pathet Lao in northern Laos, without having even made a formal alliance with him, and in violation of the Geneva agreement, who branded America an aggressor or tried to unseat her in the United Nations? Who put that label on Russia for Stalin's role in the Korean War? Were the British or French outlawed for the attack on Egypt?

This lengthy discussion of seemingly dead history is necessary in order to understand why the government of China is quite genuinely unable to see in events in Korea—from which Chinese troops years ago withdrew—any justification for America's continued hold on Taiwan, the embargo, and exclusion of China from the United Nations. That continued punishment of China on these grounds was in the national interest of the United States seemed to be gravely questioned by Adlai Stevenson, according to Theodore H. White's report of an interview with him in *The Making of the President*. Mr. Stevenson said then that we should have long ago ended "this mythology of Chiang Kai-shek's return to China." He denounced the Dulles policy as "one of the greatest political crimes of our times, for in 1955 we had a chance to talk to them [the Chinese], to begin to resolve some of the problems" tracing to "that whole program of stupidity starting with the 'unleashing' of Chiang Kai-shek to the collapse of the Summit." [7]

One therefore was moved by sympathy for Mr. Stevenson when, in 1961, he found himself in the United Nations serving the new Kennedy Administration, but still obliged to carry on with the old vengeful preservation of "this mythology of Chiang Kai-shek." As Ambassador Stevenson that day again branded China "aggressive by nature," a "warrior state," a "massive and brutal threat to man's very survival," some delegates felt as embarrassed for him as on the day he rose in the same chamber and solemnly denied all American complicity in the costly C.I.A.-sponsored invasion of Cuba.

What then must the People's Republic do to purge itself, redeem the right to seat a representative in the United Nations, and re-establish relations with the United States? Should it begin by confessing its error in Korea? Recognize the legality of the United States armed intervention in the Taiwan Strait? Cease supporting North Korea and North Vietnam, and withdraw from Tibet? Should it stop attempts to build an atom bomb, admit that it cannot defend itself against Russia and requires American armed support, confess that the nation is starving and must have millions of tons of free American wheat?

The Chinese are proud, still relatively weak, newly independent, and confronted by merciless problems, but they are strongly patriotic. Their leaders cannot make any such one-sided true or false confessions to "imperialists" or they would lose their mandate as Communists. China has an avowedly Communist government, but the United States does not have an avowedly imperialist government. Is there no way that the United States can demolish the myth that it is imperialist and make the Chinese people see that they are being misled by Mao Tse-tung, and change?

Yes, there are ways. For many years now United States policy has exactly corresponded to Mao's prophecies of imperialist behavior. One way quickly to confound him in the eyes of his countrymen, and to shake the foundations of nationalist faith in the doctrine that there is no way to talk reason to an imperialist except from behind the barrel of a gun, is for the United States to follow a policy *exactly the opposite* of what Mao expects.

President Kennedy had a great opportunity to make such an innovation when he first took office. "So let us begin anew," he said in his inaugural address, "remembering on both sides that civility is not a sign of weakness, and sincerity is always subject to proof." The United States was not under pressure by China; it was a good time to move "anew," from positions of strength. It would have been a great time to be tall.

Without vitally affecting a single aspect of American security, and without any special authorization from Congress, the President could have 1) announced to Chiang Kai-shek that within sixty days the protection of the Seventh Fleet would be withdrawn from China's off-shore islands of Quemoy and Matsu, and suggested that he remove his troops from this provocative forward base; 2) modified the "enemy trading act" and embargo against China; 3) canceled the United States ban on travel and communications with China; 4) opened the United States to visits by mainland citizens, including Mao Tse-tung; 5) declared it the United States' desire to see a peaceful conclusion to the Chinese civil war through direct negotiations between Taiwan and Peking;* 6) announced the readiness of the United States to

* Direct, unofficial negotiations between representatives of the Peking government and Chiang Kai-shek for an intra-national settlement of their differences have been

extend long-term credits to China for the purchase of American surplus wheat and other commodities.

Had such measures been taken without any conditions or political strings attached to them, a totally new climate would have been created in the Far East. Khrushchev's "peaceful coexistence" would have found allies in Peking. The effect would have been electrifying. Mao would have been obliged to rethink an entire strategy based upon the assumption that "imperialism will never change." Prospects for international peace would have immeasurably improved everywhere.

There is no doubt that President Kennedy is sincerely a man of peace, yet of course he did not and could not make any such magnanimous gestures. America was not yet that tall. It would be Utopian to expect more; the weak must be punished, not rewarded by trust. That is what all us Christians believe.

For the truth was that America's entire Far Eastern policy then still rested upon the protectorate in Taiwan, the maintenance of United States "dominance in the Far East"—as Assistant Secretary of State Walter S. Robertson agreed—and the dusty illusions of Mr. Dulles that armed pressure on the periphery of China and Russia could bring about counterrevolution. Any move which suggests the elimination of the keystone of this scheme, in Taiwan, endangers the entire edifice erected around it and necessarily must lead to the disengagement of the have-got and have-not nationalisms now locked in limited but perilous undeclared war.

For of course "beginning anew" would mean continuing an alternative course toward other ends. Encouraging the Generalissimo to negotiate for peaceful unification would result in eventual cancellation of the United States alliance, withdrawal of American forces from Taiwan, admission of China to the United Nations, neutralizing Korea and Vietnam as a basis for their unification and admission to the United Nations, and United States recognition of China as an equal with responsibilities as well as rights among her peers. By such means China's conception of American imperialism could be modified and by such means new and more fundamental solutions to the needs of the have-nots could be found.

All those things must come about anyway, to be sure, but only after many billions more are wasted, and bit by bit, so that each move is misunderstood and all the impact is lost. If we did anything so foolish now, according to the cold warriors, the Chinese would interpret it as weakness; they'd become more aggressive. Meanwhile, we can have more tries at driving the wedge deeper between Russia and China, says the "rigid defense" school of bureaucrats. Yet not so deep that

going on intermittently for many years. Since the Geneva agreement on Laos these talks have taken on renewed life. Terms of a possible Peking-Taiwan entente are discussed in the Appendix (pages 765-766), together with possible terms of a Sino-American *détente*, as viewed unofficially from Peking.

China breaks away altogether, follows an independent path, and finally confronts the United States with the necessity to use the bomb. For that would provoke a coup against Khrushchev and possibly a return to Sino-Soviet solidarity. Try lifting the embargo an inch by offering to sell China wheat now, says the "flexible defense" school of warriors. Wait a bit, says the other set; we've almost got a Soviet-American joint embargo working against China. This is the time to put on more squeeze. If China is starving (what do you mean, *if* China is starving, haven't we settled that yet?) now is the time of disintegration we've been waiting for. Ah, but suppose the new Mao fits completely into Khrushchev's pocket? Where will that leave *us*? And Tito? The thing to do is keep the nuclear talks going, but not so far that people will think we don't need the higher new defense budget. That's the safe thing. Call in one of the columnists. . . . And so it will go on until the Chief Executive is in a freer position to move. There is still more time. (But we never know how much time.)

The real reason why Mr. Kennedy could not make any such "beginning anew" was not hard to discern. It lay not only in one man's inability to alter the "military-industrial complex" which dominates American foreign policy and indeed all American society—as President Eisenhower warned in the words which preface this chapter. It lay in the fact that Mr. Kennedy would never have got his budget past committee in the first session of his Congress if he had taken even one of the initiatives suggested. It lay above all in the corollary that United States policy had thus far failed to evolve any adequate alternative to bombs, bombs and more bombs, in answer to the Communists' bid for leadership over the have-nots.

Mr. Kennedy has not yet cared to tell that simple truth to the American people or explain why the original objectives of United States cold-war policies have proved unattainable. Such a sudden blow to the stability of the American economy might be so disastrous as to bring impeachment. The tragedy of John Foster Dulles was that those "original objectives" were already unattainable even before he assumed office and futilely defined them in 1952. "Roll-back," "liberation," and similar long-since-abandoned slogans of the first Eisenhower campaign were always illusory, but totally so once Russia became a nuclear power, in 1949. Mr. Dulles discovered only in 1954 that massive retaliation was not practicable even in Indochina, much less in Europe. Since then the tangible effect of United States cold-war offensives has been the arming of numerous Eastern dictatorships and an enormous expansion of both the domestic and external consumption of American armaments production. Except for Japan—where Americans continue to aspire to correct MacArthur's postwar mistake of total disarmament—United States intervention has nowhere yet created a single viable new democracy, while it has resuscitated countless ailing dictatorships.

This was certainly never the intention or conscious will of the American nation. Neither did it evolve from original master blueprints laid down in the Pentagon itself. Today we are all caught in a trap which the people only partly helped to lay. It has different origins but is nevertheless very similar to the trap in which Japan found herself in the 1930's when her own military-industrial complex became the dominant influence in foreign and domestic policy and emasculated a vigorous postwar democracy. After the Japanese army seized Manchuria it soon became deeply involved in politics, subsidized and intimidated publications and editors, outlawed Communists first, then Socialists, then pacifists, and ultimately all anti-militarist opposition, by equating all with treason. It systematically frightened or cajoled religious leaders, scientists, union leaders and teachers into total conformance. Every town in the country became dependent on military patronage and on war industry. No one could speak the truth without endangering his livelihood if not his life. Yet Japan was not then under attack by China, any more than the United States is today. Support of the "defense effort" nevertheless became mandatory for each man's comfort, dividends, security and patriotic self-esteem. Gradually, Japan and its colonial markets became saturated with military tools. To consume the weapons output and maintain the economy more and more conquests became necessary—until major war was inevitable.

America has not reached that extreme, but what worried President Eisenhower was that the "military-industrial complex" even in his time had become far and away the biggest and most dangerous corporation in the United States. It is, moreover, a socialist corporation; everything is free for members and paid for by taxpayers who have nothing to say about its deployment abroad. It is what De Tocqueville called a "nation by itself."

"The Pentagon today owns more than 32 million acres of land in the United States," wrote Fred J. Cook in his remarkable and well-documented work, "Juggernaut: The Warfare State," "and another 2.6 million acres in foreign countries. Its total ownings are larger than the combined area of Rhode Island, Delaware, Connecticut, New Jersey, Massachusetts, Maryland, Vermont and New Hampshire. . . . In the eight years of the Eisenhower administration, more than 350 billion dollars was spent for defense. Out of the 80.9 billion 1962 budget as originally drafted (this is a mere historic curiosity now, of course), 59 cents in every dollar was allotted for military purposes. . . . Military assets are three times as great as the combined assets of United States Steel, American Telephone and Telegraph, Metropolitan Life Insurance, General Motors, and Standard Oil of New Jersey. The paid personnel of Defense is triple the number of employees of these great corporations, whose influence on affairs of state have so often worried observers." [8]

In 1961 one hundred top corporations alone got $21,000,000,000 of the army procurement orders, with General Dynamics leading the field at $1,260,000,000; 86.4 percent of all the army's purchases were awarded without competitive bidding. Influence peddling? "The Hebert investigating committee in 1959-60 found that more than 1,400 retired officers from the rank of major up were employed by the top hundred corporations, including 261 generals or officers of flag rank." [9] General Dynamics had 27 retired generals and admirals on its payroll, headed by Frank Pace, Truman's Secretary of the Army. His predecessor there had been General Joseph McNarney, general manager of the Defense Department during the rise of militarism in the Korean War days.

General McNarney "testified in March, 1956, that [in four years] he had drawn $324,500 in salary and expenses (plus, of course, his regular Air Force pension of $16,000 annually)." There were also guarantees of $675,000 in "consultant fees" over another fifteen years, and those fat stock options which are the cream of the general-to-millionaire pie.[10] (It should be added that there *are* generals who have refused to cash in on this kind of socialism. I don't seem to recall General Ridgway's name on General Dynamics' board of directors.)

Yet General McNarney was still far from the caviar side of the table compared, for example, to the good fortune of former Secretary of the Treasury George M. Humphrey, as revealed in congressional hearings of 1962. The share of Mr. Humphrey (and his son) in profits made by the Hanna Mining Company on contracts with the government for the purchase of nickel for defense stockpiles, amounted to $4,480,000 during his period in the Cabinet. There was nothing legally unsound about either the Humphrey or the McNarney hauls, of course. Such instances, scaled down to the pint-size level of the little man, were repeated hundreds of times. Think of the countless towns and cities imploring the government not to shut down armaments plants or army bases for fear of unemployment and recession.

"One of the most serious things about this defense business is that so many Americans are getting a vested interest in it: properties, business, jobs, employment, votes, opportunities for promotion and advancement, bigger salaries for scientists and all that . . . If you shut the whole business off now, you will have the state of California in trouble because such a big percentage of the aircraft industry is in California." [11] Those words are quoted from remarks by our former Secretary of Defense, General Motors' Charles E. Wilson. In Los Angeles "it has been estimated that fully half the jobs are dependent, either directly or indirectly, on continuance of the arms race." Defense expenditures in Los Angeles county alone in 1961 amounted to five billion dollars.

Elaborate publicity machines led by Madison Avenue talent now work for every branch of the defense forces, nearly all of them in competition. Lobbies for rival manufacturers get columnists and television stooges to blow the horn for the pet schemes and gadgets of officers who are perhaps not unmindful of future retirement berths at $75,000 to $100,000 a year. Generals and colonels permeate the civilian branches of the administration, to "clear it with the Pentagon." Newspapers, magazines, broadcasting networks and movies find themselves so necessary to the "defense effort" that many hesitate to communicate any information to the public which might disturb either the military-industrial complex or its allied advertisers.

Then we also get the feedbacks from monies expended for similar aims abroad. Foreign lobbies, working on funds of American origin to raise more of the same, hold discreet meetings with such congressmen as they can find unoccupied with domestic military lobbies. Most notorious among these feedbacks is the Nationalist Chinese money which has found its way from such unlikely places as an early $10,000 contribution to the campaign chest of Richard Nixon,[12] down to the offices of the nation's greatest hoax: The Committee of One Million Against the Admission of Communist China to the United Nations. The only figures published by the Committee up to 1962 showed 368 dues-paying members.[13] But count, among the sponsors listed in its full-page advertisements, the retired officers, congressmen and businessmen. Then pair the names with those serving in directorates of defense corporations, or as advisers to American-subsidized dictatorships in Taiwan and elsewhere abroad—or bidding for new war industries to be located in their constituencies.

Not that the "military-industrial complex" and its lobbies are undemocratically run; every member of it has a voice in the spending. True, no one outside the Establishment is ever consulted about whether troops go to Taiwan or Vietnam or a billion more goes to Diem or General Dynamics or whether we talk or don't talk with the Chinese, but that is beside the point. Let not the citizen deceive himself, however. With nearly fifty billion dollars in military largesse (not counting veterans' payments, foreign military aid and war-debt interest, amounting to more than ten billions) now dispensed annually, the entire nation is so geared to it that many a gas station owner, many a grocery store clerk, and even many a plate-passer in the churches feels a personal threat if anyone suggests that every golden river must end in the sea and that this cannot go on forever.

From the billionaire to the parson, our beneficiaries of arms spending are as convinced as the Chinese Communists that they are saving humanity from extinction. Not so long before he died I spent many hours with John Jay Hopkins, a veritable titan among the lethal-gadget-makers. He was an extremely smart (he hired Mr. Pace and General McNarney) and likable gentleman. Between the time he took over an obscure submarine factory in Groton, Connecticut, not long before Pearl Harbor, and the time I wrote a profile about him for the *Saturday Evening Post* (September 9, 1956), one dollar's worth of common stock in the parent company of what became the General Dynamics Corporation increased by more than thirty times. Hopkins' father was a Scotch minister and a fervent pacifist. When I casually asked Jay one day whether he felt any contradiction between his father's ministry and his own activity he nearly exploded in blue purple before my eyes. I learned that his entire career was a sacrifice on the altar of peace and the cause for which his father had worked (in a less practical way) all his life. "Our deterrents alone," he said with great sincerity, "have saved the world from complete destruction."

It was the Communists, he said; they had started it all. What can we do if they won't disarm? Certainly it takes two to make a fight, and the Communists have never been slow to burn. No one expects the United States to disarm alone. On May 10, 1955, however, Khrushchev launched a wholly unexpected change in Soviet policy which challenged all previous assumptions of cold-war strategists. On that date his delegate to the London disarmament conference suddenly accepted a long-standing Anglo-French-American proposal for conventional disarmament, for cessation of the manufacture of nuclear weapons, and for their conversion to peaceful purposes—all that to be supervised by United Nations inspectors from control posts in every country. The Soviet acceptances left unsettled only one key item: a final definition of "adequate guarantees" of inspection.

So stunned was the American delegation by this *volte face* that it made no attempt to reply; instead, the United States called for a three months' adjournment. After that, silence. The American answer did not come until the following September, when the unhappy Harold Stassen, again at the U.N., was obliged to announce what amounted to a new and negative policy which withdrew all previous American disarmament proposals—until a *perfect* system of "inspection" of nuclear weapons tests and manufacture could be agreed upon.

Not many Americans read newspapers which made them aware that the Russians had accepted United States disarmament proposals, or of the significance of American withdrawal from the commitment. Voices were raised in protest even in the United States Congress, but the press rallied to support a new policy first enunciated by Secretary of the Air Force Donald S. Quarles. In the *New York Times*, James Reston reported him as having frankly declared that the United States had no intention of disarming "in the old-fashioned sense" (of actually destroying weapons) and that it would not depend upon " 'foolproof' inspection systems," but on "mutual surveillance" and "the retention of overwhelming air-atomic power." For six years Washington refused to consider general disarmament. As late as February 8, 1960, Senator Joseph S. Clark told the United States Senate: "The United States is the only nuclear power which has not accepted total and permanent disarmament under adequate international safeguard as its goal and put forward a comprehensive plan to achieve that end. I think that is a disgrace. The British have done it. The Russians have done it. We have not done it . . ." [14]

Not until President Kennedy spoke before the United Nations in 1961 did the United States again raise hopes of general disarmament. But since then there has yet been no real decision and no answer to—and practically no press notice of—Premier Khrushchev's unqualified offer made in the aide memoire he personally handed to President Kennedy in Vienna. To Senator Clark we are again indebted for a suggestion. "The Soviet Government," read Khrushchev's note, "on its part is willing unconditionally to accept *any* Western *control* proposals if the Western powers accept the proposal for *general* and *complete* disarmament." Calling this unanswered proposal to the attention of his colleagues, Senator Clark added, "I suggest that the least we can do is put Mr. Khrushchev to the test." [15]

Since President Kennedy's United Nations speech, all disarmament talk has again been about different ways to legalize espionage—known as "adequate inspection." This has been made into an extremely complicated subject and no judgment can here be offered concerning the merits of the American and the Soviet arguments. The integrity of the Soviet total-disarmament proposals was widely questioned following Khrushchev's decision to renew nuclear tests, in 1961, in violation of an informal moratorium. After that, the United States' only course, some said, was to maintain its surplus kill-superiority in nuclear weapons. Soviet experts gave the excuse that France had never observed the moratorium, and that Americans were using the results of tests made by their French allies. Americans denied the charge. As long as Americans kept building bombs to maintain a two-to-one superiority, said other experts, Khrushchev could not sign a pact unless the United States agreed to reduce its weapons to a parity basis and then disarm simultaneously with Russia. By 1962, agreement had been attained among technicians but not among political leaders. The significant truth was that the whole question of inspection was now rapidly becoming irrelevant. Before any written accord was reached, the development of space satellite espionage and electronic detection devices had so far advanced that all essential information needed to guarantee against surprise attacks would soon be in possession of both sides.

Even when inspection becomes complete, however, the bombs will still be with us. The danger will remain for years to come, if it takes as long to dismantle weapons and disarm as it has to get past the preliminary talking stage. In 1961 Dr. Linus Pauling, the distinguished scientist and Nobel Prize winner, estimated that the United States possessed about 100,000 megatons of atomic and thermonuclear bombs, and the Russians had something like 50,000 megatons. Due to the vastness of the Soviet Union about twice as many bombs would be required to eliminate it as the United States; hence the two powers had about an equal destructive capacity.

Dr. Pauling's study showed that 10,000 megatons would be adequate to burn, fatally maim, poison by radiation, or otherwise kill every living person in the United States.[16] If the very best, deepest and most extensive shelter systems now conceivable were built (estimated cost $100,000,000,000) the Russians would have to use 40,000 megatons to kill every man, woman and child in the United States. The Americans would need 20,000 megatons to burn up a nonshelterized Russia, and about 80,000 megatons if it were profoundly shelterized. With these prospects, Dr. Pauling concluded that threats made by leaders of both countries could not be taken seriously, since an attack would mean suicide by certain retaliation.

But the danger of war, he added, would persist as long as "extreme militarism continues" because of the possibility of war initiated by "some psychological or technological accident." General Lucius Clay, no pacifist but a sober thinker, has expressed the same deep concern. Apart from bombs now available for American strategic aircraft, the nuclear equivalent of some 20,000,000,000 tons of TNT is also distributed in the form of thousands of smaller American rockets and missiles spread around the earth. The Russians have comparable equipment. A single major blunder of human miscalculation might lead, Dr. Pauling fears, to "some series of catastrophic events" such that even the wisest national leaders would be unable to halt "the destruction of civilization."

Many citizens may share Dr. Pauling's concern about "extreme militarism," but as long as the phenomenon is multilateral the answer obviously cannot be any one-sided dissolution of our armed forces. Nor can they be expected to abandon their legitimate responsibilities abroad until they can be transferred to a supranational police force. American freedom was won by armed struggle, and our armies have since loyally defended it. But the ideal of national service meanwhile need not be confined to training in the techniques of defense. Soldiers might also be proud to devote part of their period of service to such tasks at home as raising the literacy and educational level, improving public health, advancing the water and forest conservation work currently so badly neglected, and so on. Here also would be a way to give volunteer citizens, including unemployed and hitherto unemployable persons, new skills and a recognized role to play in community development.

Walt Whitman Rostow, an excellent and learned professor who has the confidence of President Kennedy and is policy planning director of the State Department (something akin to coordinator of anti-imperialist strategy in the Peking Foreign Office) has often been quoted as having told an Army War College audience that "communism is a disease of transition." By that he meant transition from a backward society to a mature, advanced society such as, for example, the United States. Possibly Mr. Rostow's remark has been over-simplified in journalistic interpretations. It must engage our attention in its literal form, however, because it reflects an innocence of thought still widely characteristic of a nation which has not taken a close and honest look at its economy for twenty years.

Since the Roosevelt era the United States has frankly faced very few of its own fundamental problems of transition. We have merely post-poned and intensified them by increasingly heavy doses of sleeping pills administered in the form of defense expenditure tranquilizers.

The United States is still the richest and most powerful nation and potentially several times greater and taller than it has yet discovered. That should never be confused with the notion that it is already a "mature" or a "finished" society immune from sudden and dramatic changes yet unforeseeable to any of us. Communism undoubtedly is a disease in the sense that it proves highly contagious to techno-logically backward nations. But one might as well observe that private plunder of public resources, unemployment, personal profit from socialized army expenditures, racism, General Walkers, Birchites, mo-mentary possession of superiority in deadly weapons, and chauvinism —above all—are equally diseases of transition.

The American problem of abundance or overcapacity to produce commodities and undercapacity to consume them may at first glance appear to be something on an entirely different order from the Com-munist countries' problem of scarcity, or of undercapacity to pro-duce commodities and overcapacity to consume them. On closer ex-amination both appear to be diseases of transition. The Communist countries are unable thus far to satisfy the capacity food demands of the producers. Yet they have been increasing their total industrial output at rates two to three times faster than the United States. They have no serious unemployment problems. The United States produces far more food than present purchasing power demands. Yet for the past decade or more it has—even with annual cold-war booster shots now close to the budgetary outlays of all-out war in 1941-45—proved incapable of taking up the slack in an industrial plant running at 30 to 40 percent below capacity. Minimal unemployment climbs close to 10 percent of the work force. Underemployment probably impoverishes another 20 to 30 percent of the able-bodied population.

Can it be said that we have a "mature" society when, in a starving world, we spend five to six billion dollars annually in bribing farmers not to grow crops—and about two million dollars a day for storage of surplus commodities? What is grown-up about an administration whose latest solution aims at further reducing farm labor by about one-half? Or by removing from production more than two-thirds of our farmlands? Or price supports by means of the destruction of bil-lions of pounds of fruit and other foods? How "advanced" is a society capable of making enough fertilizer, water pumps, pest-killers, tractors and plows to double or treble the food output of the nonindustrialized nations in a few years, which is yet incapable of offering any means of realizing such an operation—seemingly simple compared to hitting the moon?

Does it make adult sense to sit by while tens of millions of illiterate have-nots learn from Soviet and Chinese propaganda that they can get along without their have-gots, that there is a way, not to become rich, but to build a life which at least promises the minimal satisfactions of food, clothes to cover their nakedness, better health, some education and equality of opportunity for their children, employment and freedom from beggary—the socialization of poverty for a generation or two, no doubt, but freedom from hated enslavement to the financially privileged and the constant reminders of denial to their loved ones of any hope of attaining the adequacies of the rich? Or is it still supposed that bombs and a few thousand Rangers taught the tricks of guerrilla warfare, and some paltry charities or reforms urged upon the bought army elites in the impoverished lands, will long be enough to contain the force gathering behind the turning barrel of the gun—among "the poor, the great majority"?

What is "mature" about waiting for more thousands of wretched usurers, landlords and sheiks to be killed in a struggle over scrubby parcels of land in Asia, in the Middle East, in Africa, in Latin America? For a small percentage of the $400,000,000,000 the United States spent in ten years to prevent the spread of Communist revolutions, enough land could have been purchased to satisfy all the tenant farmers, a stable new class of owner-tillers established, capital created among ex-landlords obliged to invest in modern production, youths trained to destroy rats and lice in the villages, to organize cooperative farming, and to lay a new basis of public health, schooling and stable citizenship, and to complete technical surveys and the foundations of industrialization.

Am I suggesting that the United States finance an international peasant rebellion? Nothing so ambitious; the Communists are taking care of that. What I am asserting is something that Communists would see as possibly workable alternatives to violent class warfare but which they would dismiss in a kindly mood as mere Utopian dreaming, or in a more severe mood denounce as positive incitement to counter-revolution on the left.

Problems of land shortage and exploited tenants are by no means universally characteristic of underdeveloped countries. What I am asking is whether, where farm ownership is a revolutionary issue, it would not make good sense to encourage a nation to seek a peaceful transition by spending a few *millions* to equalize land ownership *before* spending *billions* to arm landlord armies—to provoke peasants to relieve them of their land *and* their weapons? I am asserting that while land redistribution may provide a temporary political solution it can offer no economic panacea for such countries, which can find stability only by far-reaching modernization.

The United States cannot order bad regimes to behave wisely but it can refrain from supporting and compounding their stupidities. It can make known to the world a desire for basic solutions, and offer help to achieve them. It can flatly decline to supply weapons for regimes bent upon their self-destruction. It can at least stop expanding the payroll of the millions now in sub-armies which render us ever more dependent on subsidized overseas arms markets, dangerously dislocate the American economy, and threaten the stability and life of the American democracy.

Had the United States taken the lead in such a world war against poverty, disease and ignorance it would itself have found some means of transition from the "military-industrial complex" escapism into which it has fallen. But aren't we already doing enough with the four to five billion dollars annually expended in foreign aid? Directly and indirectly, by far the greater part of such sums go into military hardware that is of no value to the poor and is often used as a means of repressing and reducing any chance of peaceful change. In machine-poor lands much of the rest goes into the pockets of military sycophants, profiteering merchants, landlords, politicians and the quick among the have-gots. It goes into cars and gasoline and freezers for the few. Too much of it tends to intensify class hatreds, the chasm between rich and poor, and dislike of the Yankees who bring gumdrops but not the means of work.

All civilizations of the past have been built on slavery, but the time of the human slave is nearing an end. That is certain not only because the human-slave societies cannot compete with the mechanical-slave societies but because the human slaves everywhere are aware of the means of their liberation. (Communists are taking care of that, too.) Apart from famine relief, "help" to backward societies is useless unless it directly contributes to their liberation from human slavery—chiefly by providing them with the means of producing mechanical slaves of their own.

Paul G. Hoffman, manager of the United Nations Special Fund, has classified eighty-two non-Communist member nations and "some 40 territories" as "underdeveloped"—which embrace "more than a billion people . . . undernourished and without the barest of health or educational facilities." Their national incomes are increasing at the rate of 1 percent a year, adding "not a third of a penny a day" to their per capita incomes of less than 35 cents daily per person. (The poor are not even getting the extra third of a penny, as Mr. Hoffman is talking about *per capita* income, or a statistical assumption that everybody earns equally.) "This rate of increase," said Mr. Hoffman, "*is too low —dangerously too low.*" [17]

Many billions a year for investment in productive purposes of direct benefit to the poor is one alternative to armaments races. The United Nations is one place to sponsor it. The United States cannot and should not provide more than its share, but it can initiate it and its share is large indeed in proportion to the world's wealth. Such a war against poverty cannot be adequately financed by the private capitalist sector of nationalism. It must be seen as an investment in world construction financed by United Nations bonds underwritten by the various governments, like state savings certificates. In any case only this kind of foreign investment will long be secure, especially in underdeveloped countries. American investments abroad now approach $75,000,000,000 and exceed by about $25,000,000,000 the private foreign investment in the United States. The tendency for capital-poor countries to nationalize foreign investments will increase rather than decrease. The United States cannot fight every nation which does that, particularly since the original capital advanced has usually long since been recovered. But no country can afford to isolate itself from a world government by repudiating debts incurred for low-interest, long-term, productive loans.

Much the same thing may be said for the Administration's "Alliance for Progress" program in Latin America. Historians a generation hence may ask themselves how sensible men could naïvely intervene halfway round the world, in a crisis far past conventional colonial solutions, when they had made no effort to read the revolutionary message left on the Cuban threshold of the United States itself. Not Vietnam but the Western Hemisphere—Brazil, Venezuela, Argentina, Chile and Mexico—ought to be the focus of the American war: the war against poverty, not against peasants. The eyes of Washington are on the wrong places and on struggles already lost.

In Asia it will be Japan and India which decide the balance, not Vietnam. While billions are sunk quixotically in Saigon, history is moving in on India: the food shortage has long since passed critical proportions and class tension is deepening. Yet the nineteenth-century-minded World Bank and other government agencies of international financial assistance raise the most absurd barriers to extending even credits needed to stabilize poverty at its present level—vastly below that of Alabama. India could absorb billions of capital investments for years to come, and perhaps solve her land and production problems in a nonviolent way. Congressmen grudgingly part with handouts of grain (the removal of which saves silo rentals) and think they have "done something about India." In what age are men living who cannot see that the former slave nations are no longer solely a dumping ground for American surpluses? They *must* build the means of production in order to produce and trade as equals.

How did we finance the Second World War, which resulted in an enormous growth in America's assets? That was the only moment in thirty years when unemployment disappeared, our productive and creative energies were in full use, and national morale reached a summit.

We fed virtually the whole world and remained a healthy nation. How have we been financing the cold war? Mainly by inflation, because the product is almost total waste and adds nothing to basic output for consumption. But a war against want could take up today's 30-percent slack in American industrial capacity, create new assets, put the land back into use, and increase the nation's gross national product by $150,000,000,000 to $200,000,000,000.

And how are the poor to pay? By their labor—and by their production. By labor all existing wealth was created and all indebtedness discharged. These poor nations are nearly all potentially self-sustaining. They are like unemployed and underemployed Americans; they are not in use. But the poor wish to work. They do not want charity. They want to learn. They want peace. They do not want war. No one wants to die. Imagine the desperate resolve it takes for a timid, illiterate, fearful Annamite peasant to separate himself from his family and the fragile but only margin of security he has known, in order to become an outlaw of the revolution, to kill and be killed? It is only a last-hope decision for any man, whether he be a Chinese Buddhist or a Hindu *ryot*. But if nothing else is offered he will take that step rather than condemn his children to starvation and inequality—once he becomes convinced that there is a way.

From where is the $20,000,000,000 coming which the government is now committed to spend to put men on the moon? (Probably $30,000,-000,000 before the decade ends.) That is quite a sum for firecrackers, but it is remarkable how much more readily Congress finds that money available, compared to raising a few dollars to help bright but poor youths go to college—not to say the heathen overseas. We must have a place on the moon, no doubt; we must catch up with the Joneseviches. It is even possible that our space scientists will eventually be able to do something to improve the weather here on earth, as they tell us. But we should not overlook the basic military aims and appeal of this project nor fail to realize that it makes international government all the more inevitable. It is another (and a large) factor which necessitates the establishment of world order and world planning. While the Soviet astro-twins were flying the equivalent of three trips to the moon, the United States Senate was locked in a prolonged filibuster which failed to defeat Mr. Kennedy's bill to bestow exclusive space rights upon private corporations rather than to reserve them for public domain. What the senators appeared to be overlooking was the evidence that the moon was about to go Red; unless agreements were reached with the Russians the corporations might have to buy their lunar leaseholds from Khrushchev.

Suppose, then, that instead of fighting this "disease of transition" with bombs alone, we try immunizing means such as increased credits and trade with the pariahs, to hasten them onto the high road to maturity? What about starting by easing the heavy arms load of both

Russians and Americans by ending insistence upon an unattainable "perfect" espionage system, and accept the best possible? Whatever it is, won't it work both ways? Why not end the tiresome, desperate game over Berlin—which everyone knows neither power would risk a nuclear war to possess—and jointly undertake an inevitable step toward an international police force?

What? "Give up" Berlin? We never "had" Berlin and we don't have it today, any more than we "had" China under Chiang Kai-shek. Berlin belongs to the Germans, and it was Germans who built the wall —starting with Hitler—and it is Germans who must take it down. They can and will find a way to coexistence themselves—mayhap their own "Laos-type" solution—but they won't do that unless we get out and the Russians get out by internationalizing the city and putting it under United Nations police until it is unified, with freedom of access guaranteed to all. Is it not political sterility to cling rigidly to an occupation which was temporarily set up seventeen years ago, as an expression of Soviet-Allied *unity* against Germany, while refusing to make any adjustment to vastly different realities of today? Berlin is useless as a war base; it is a propaganda base, and an excellent means to keep East Germany closed, not to open it. The joint liquidation of a base which is meaningless in the defense of either Russia or the United States is a small price to pay for giving priority to international interests in peace over cold-war nationalist interests in Central Europe. But shouldn't "free elections" be held? Yes, indeed, highly desirable. While the Germans work out a formula suitable to their conditions, why don't we first show the way by encouraging free elections among our allies in Vietnam, South Korea, Taiwan, Spain, or even Alabama?

"The [Soviet] General Staff," wrote Harrison Salisbury in *A New Russia?* after his return from a recent trip there, "was nervous about Khrushchev's inability to achieve a genuine relaxation of tension. They felt they had put Russia ahead of the United States in military capability but did not know how long they could maintain the edge. It was up to Khrushchev to cash in quickly on the opportunity which they had given him. There were men on the Western side, who also felt that time was running out . . .

"If peace could be preserved and strengthened; if the longed-for *détente* of Russia and the West could be achieved; then the forces for liberalization of Russia would be strengthened. The evolution would go forward. The balance would tip strongly in the direction of the West. The momentum toward democratization of the Soviet regime would gather speed. The hope of the Russian intelligentsia would be realized—and the world would be safer to live in. But if the great powers failed to solve their difficulties; if tension rose; if the Chinese view of the world was confirmed; if Khrushchev's foreign policy again proved barren; if his domestic problems piled higher; then the neo-Stalinists and the bullyboys would have their chance." [18]

What about going further, and fully reopening trade with Soviet Russia, including the means of more rapidly modernizing their agricultural and urban life?

But what about those Russians down in Cuba? What about those Americans in Turkey and Iran? The Cuban entente with the U.S.S.R. enables Americans to know how the Russians suffered from a nuclear inferiority complex while American bombers sat on their thresholds. But American senators who clamored for an invasion of Cuba did not appear to see any such analogy, nor any analogy with Chinese complaints against American bases in Taiwan—about the same distance from the China mainland as Cuba is from Florida—or against the Seventh Fleet's hovering around Quemoy and Matsu, which are nearer China than Staten Island is to Manhattan. Cuba gives us a practical demonstration of what has long been obvious: that forward bases abroad can always be outflanked by political means, and that no amount of such bases can prevent (indeed, they provoke) breakthroughs and counter-encirclement of the encircler.

Then, once more, what about China? There lies, in the mainland that officially still does not exist for Washington, the hungriest market in Asia. Given loans and long-term credits, China certainly could absorb limitless surpluses of American products such as tractors and automotive equipment, fertilizers and plants to make them, dynamos, and scientific facilities. Could China ever pay for all her import needs? Who knows? Have we ever really offered China trade and aid as alternatives to blockade and cold war? Until we explore such alternatives, how can we be sure they would not bring more civilized results than we get from heavy outlays for current dependence on bombs alone?

And what about the bomb? Scientists tell us there never was any real secret to it after 1945, and there is none at all today. Mr. Stimson was not a stupid man; he won the war for which he was our First Secretary, and that may be more than can be said for the cold war fought by his successors. (It must be admitted he won it fighting with the Russians, not against them.) We lost the one chance to avoid an arms race with Russia when we tried to "negotiate with them, having this weapon rather ostentatiously on our hip." China will get the bomb anyway—and after that, what? Until then, we have a second chance "to share the knowledge and responsibility of atomic power" in exchange for an agreement to ban the bomb which cannot be used and "to encourage the development of atomic power for peaceful and humanitarian purposes." Indeed, Chou En-lai has several times made such a proposal—dismissed by the State Department as "propaganda."

Obviously, such a decision could be made—I hasten to add before some literal-minded reader (not you) misapprehends me—only as part of a comprehensive accord reached with China for a "new beginning" and, of course, accompanied by necessary provisions for mutual legalized espionage known as "adequate inspection." None of that can happen while we are punishing China and playing cold-war games. But if we made such an agreement with one poor nation, should we not then have to make it with all the others who desperately need atomic power and other peaceful nuclear utilities? Indeed we should—and there is no way of avoiding it if we are to halt the spread of the arms regatta. Right now, if we are seriously seeking an agreement with the Russians, there could be no surer way of accelerating it than by holding a few preliminary talks on the general subject with Chairman Mao.

But what about the blue ants, the yellow peril? It is silly to speak of birth control while holding an atomic rifle on China or any other nation. Obviously, sane opinion about limited parenthood cannot prevail while nationalism continues to dominate all political thought and no alternative exists in real world government or world planning. Only if and when the rich powers emerge with solutions and offers to help the poor on the emergency basis outlined here—and in the works of thoughtful scientists far better informed than I am—can the means and practice of effective population control be universalized. It can never be imposed on the assumption that the poor nations must remain poor and have fewer children while the rich white races that settled the fairest parts of the New World a few years ago continue to proliferate.

The Chinese, the Indians, the Japanese, nearly all the overpopulated nations, are not opposed to reducing the population increase; several of them are far ahead of the United States in accepting this necessity. Tens of millions of us are still bound by archaic laws which make it a criminal offense to interfere with the operations of physical nature in this one respect—while in every other respect we control and direct nature's rich disorder every day. In America this is an absurdly taboo subject. One consequence of our self-imposed silence is that even Catholics are often unaware that Vatican pronouncements against birth control are not at all fixed dogma, but policy decisions which can be changed when the interests of the Church require it.

For what seem to me good reasons I have stressed American more than Chinese responsibility for the present isolation from each other of two nations whose peoples total nearly a third of humanity. The United States is far richer and more powerful. In 1949, American government and society existed in stability and maximum security. The United States had not just emerged from a century of invasion climaxed by a revolution and an acute sense of persecution. The United States initiated the formal cut-off in communications. Being an American, I have an incurable tendency to expect the United States to grow slightly up.

But I do not wish to minimize the heavy contributions made to the conflict by the stubborn pride, self-righteousness, ignorance of the

United States, and an understandable but childish desire for retribution in the Chinese leadership. I cannot predict that the Chinese will turn the other cheek, but I do know that they have long been in a mood to respond to another approach by the United States. I need not recapitulate their mistakes in domestic policy, which have been candidly reported here. There will be more. Suffice it to say that they have learned that while it is a difficult thing to win a revolution with the help of men ready to fight for farmland, it is even more difficult—once that land is put into the community chest of socialism—to find other incentives to maintain mass enthusiasm. To inspire that, without private ownership, they must constantly create other means—satisfactory to the whole people, not just the party—to guarantee equality of rights in all aspects of life. That is something new. It involves no less than the physical and psychological reconstruction of what used to be regarded as the most conservative society on earth.

China's internal tasks will fully occupy her for at least another generation. It will be equally long before China could ever seriously undertake to attack the internal security of the United States. The aggressiveness of her propaganda and policy lines are at least as defensive as offensive, as I have shown. Yet they have gratuitously supplied ammunition to the American "military-industrial complex" with which to frighten many people about China's intentions and vastly exaggerate her capacity to do evil. Mao Tse-tung's greatest blind spot is his inability to conceive of United States society as it really is. The United States government's great error is not to have invited him, and if need be the whole Politburo, to visit this country for an extended tour to see what it looks like—how people live, talk and act, and to engage in a few balcony arguments, *a là* Khrushchev. The longer the isolation the greater the distrust, the fear, the doublethink, the suspicion and the conspiracy and counterconspiracy.

The Chinese have done little to make it easier. Wounded in their prideful isolation, they have somewhat puffed themselves up with too much faith in "politics in command." Temporarily fooling others, they have often fooled themselves most of all. Obsessed with the size and power of their reunited nation they have tended to forget that though large in numbers they are a minority in the world as a whole, and smaller still in comparative wealth. Remarkable as have been their assimilation and adaptation of an imported philosophy, they have not been able altogether to avoid the fundamentalism which inevitably makes the convert to a faith more orthodox than men born to it.

They know the United States is not made up of 90 percent peasants and 10 percent landlords. Yet much of their propaganda about American life reflects an assumption that most Americans are illiterates with no influence, no brains, and no power. It is true that the American press is 99 percent against them and probably will be for some time to come. They are right in assuming that most of the press speaks for the interests of its millionaire owners and the advertisers. They are right in their skepticism about "people's capitalism" in a nation where less than 10 percent of the people own any corporate stocks at all, and about 10 percent control most of the productive assets. But they are wrong in assuming that the other 90 percent are have-nots, in ignoring class mobility in the United States, and in failing to see that the nation is evolving toward an exclusively middle-class society with guarantees of satisfaction for the "ten basic needs" for which Chinese communes are just reaching. (That in itself is not particularly reassuring, of course; it would be hard to find anything more chauvinistic and offensive to non-Americans than the middle-class slogan, "The American Century." But the point is: ordinary journeymen guaranteed $8 to $10 an hour on defense projects, and farmers paid more for idling land than cultivating it, are not exactly oppressed peasants and proletarians. Some re-visions are needed.)

The Chinese Communists are mistaken in assuming that the people of the United States always think and behave the way they are told to think and behave by the press or even by the "military-industrial complex." They misunderstand the time lag between public opinion in favor of a restoration of communications with China (as expressed in the Gallup Poll) and the press and government policy opposed to it. They forget that 80 to 90 percent of the same press was always violently against Franklin Delano Roosevelt—and that he was the only President ever elected for three terms and the only one ever elected for four terms. Full of awareness of contradictions in their own camp, the Chinese Communists have failed to exploit the contradictions in an American society far more complex than they conceive. Nor have they listened either to their own people who know something about the United States or to strangers speaking in a different idiom who might translate some facts for them.

Perhaps even the Russians have sharply differed with Peking on such matters; if so, the Chinese need not suffer to hear more of the same from a bourgeois journalist. But it is past time for them to reopen inquiries (in their own interest) on other key questions that have been swept under the carpet. Why *did* American imperialism support Russia instead of joining Hitler? Why did the United States *not* invade China—or even occupy Cuba? (Perhaps the Chinese leaders should listen now and then to that girl engineering student in Peking who answered the same questions, when I asked her, by saying, "The American people would not have supported such a thing.") Why did the United States not only disarm Japan but make it into a pacifist nation? It is also necessary for the whole Korean War to be publicly re-examined on the Chinese side. It is time to take a more realistic view of the results of Hiroshima and to correct propaganda in China that Russia alone defeated Japan and Hitler. (Very probably this credit will soon be withdrawn, in any case—but for different reasons.)

China could herself do some positive things to reach "the American people" as apart from the imperialist government. In the sense that President Kennedy might shake Mao's certainty that imperialism will never change (and thereby go far toward shaking Mao's hand), Chairman Mao could also alter the American nation's conviction that it is impossible to coexist with China. The People's Republic could take the following steps, "toward friendship with the American people," and without any political strings or trading with the State Department: 1) release the four Americans now serving long prison sentences, in a special amnesty; 2) publicly renew invitations to visit China to friendly American scholars, teachers, scientists, engineers, doctors and nurses—some of them Christian missionaries—who were formerly acknowledged by Communists themselves to have served the people of China selflessly and without participating in "imperialist exploitation"; 3) publicly renew offers of visas to reputable writers for leading American news media; 4) have an "American People Week" in China (sponsored by the International Peace Committee) which would show, in its truthful paradox and complexity, a nation capable of electing a man to lead it for four terms against the veto of the foremost publishers—and its achievements in science and education despite some slightly prehistoric congressmen—along with its failures to solve the economic contradictions I have indicated.

Why should the American prisoners be released if they were guilty? Because it is unjust, in time of peace, to impose prolonged punishment on a few individuals for actions for which a whole government and a whole society are responsible. It is more than unjust; it is stupid to detain them as hostages and pawns for diplomatic bargaining. But the American reporters sent to China would write only what their publishers want to hear? Yes, that is partly true; yet there are some honest publishers and many honest reporters. They will know nothing of old China and misunderstand what they see? Yes, those who did not know the degradations of the past will see only the poverty of the present. But they could be sent, and the American prisoners with them, in the company of the Old China Hands I have mentioned; they will then learn what has happened. None of that would hurt China. Particularly if the visitors were received in the spirit of Colonel Stimson's axiom that the only way to make a man trustworthy is to trust him, and in the tolerance of Mao Tse-tung's dictum that if a man's work is 70 percent right and only 30 percent wrong then his performance is satisfactory.

But the State Department would never permit it? Perhaps not. Not at once. But the news would reach the nation, and it would make a deep impression upon the people. In time it could not fail to have a salubrious impact on the ossified cold-war bureaucracy and change thinking in the Congress itself.

I cannot predict that the Chinese will remold their thinking in that way. Mao Tse-tung himself can no more change a nation's pace and direction all alone than President Kennedy can. I do know that some Chinese leaders have long been prepared to respond to a "let us begin anew" approach by the United States. Too proud to say so directly, they were obviously hopeful that my visit might help to re-build a bridge or two. That is what they told me in various ways—always with the knowing added note that my imperialist government was not interested in bridge-building.

I thought they exaggerated the resistance of Washington to the in-troduction of useful information. When I returned to the United States, however, I had to revise my opinion; the official wall was a great deal more solid than I had supposed. After a brief colloquy with Dean Rusk, the newly appointed Secretary of State, I was left with the impression that the Chinese had been right.

Yet on reflection I felt sympathy for Mr. Rusk, himself (like all of us) a prisoner of the "complex" President Eisenhower mentioned. He was as helpless as Mr. Herter before him to change anything alone. Nor could President Kennedy himself have done anything with fresh in-formation from Mao Tse-tung, at that moment. It will take a long time and very much hard work by the "alert and knowledgeable citizenry" to break out of the trap. That it will change, that it is gradually chang-ing on both sides, is becoming evident.

When Averell Harriman first went to Geneva to discuss getting us out of the Laos mess inherited from the Dulles brothers he had to wire Washington for specific permission even to shake hands with Foreign Minister Ch'en Yi, although they were sitting at the same table every day. (Mr. Dulles' precedent of back-turning would no longer work but the ban on hand-shaking was still in effect.) Since then Mr. Harri-man has had several private talks with Ch'en Yi. On July 26, 1962, Harriman went so far as to say that there seems to be "a less aggressive spirit in China now." That could be, of course, because there seemed to be (as a result of the Laos agreement) a less aggressive American spirit now. It could also be because Averell Harriman has learned a great deal about the world since he began studying it in earnest from the other side of the river in Moscow, back in the days of the Second World War.

There will be strong counterattacks against agonizing attempts to reach an objective understanding, which will be denounced as appease-ment. The way ahead is hard but the bridges can, and ultimately must, be built.

All that I have been saying means that the cold war is not only a dead end, it may end us all dead unless we put an end to it. The alternatives to mounting military expenditures are no certain cure, even if they were adopted in toto and put into immediate effect. I have no illusions that they will be. They also involve risks, perhaps great risks, but nothing comparable to the risks of relying solely on present means. The truth is simply that the atomic era manifestly made a continuation of the anarchy of nationalism impossible for any prolonged period. Today we are suffering through its last stages.

Of course no one imagines that the national form of cultural and social life will not persist just as the infinite variety of nature itself persists. It would be a dull world if different ethnic groups ceased to compete and grow and add to the common fund of civilization. But nationalisms as warfare states, whether right or left, must surely soon yield their sovereign killer capacities to a higher concept of federated world authority based upon the common realization that the security of all nations against attack is henceforth the only reliable condition for the security of any nation to develop in freedom.

Communist prophets at least recognized the necessity to unite the world—of workers. The result up to now has been to bring the conflict of nationalisms to its greatest crisis—and turning point. We speak of Communist imperialism and they speak of capitalist imperialism. What we really have are nationalisms of the relative have-nots struggling against nationalisms of the relative have-gots, and even differences of principle between them seem to grow ever less distinct.

The United States, somewhat hysterically anti-Communist and anti-socialist at home, abroad supports Communist governments in Yugoslavia and Poland and hopefully looks elsewhere for more anti-Soviet deviationists. It has rebuilt a France and an Italy in which Communist parties have far larger mass following than any rivals. It has pampered a Germany where the "Socialist" party may soon come to power. It supports what it considers socialist regimes in Britain and India and would even ship free wheat to China if Peking would come begging. All the anti-Communist dictatorships armed and financed by the United States are in varying degrees totalitarianisms maintained for the benefit of socialized consumption by the small military elite. Russia meanwhile aids deviationist Yugoslavia, and bourgeois-nationalist regimes in India, Burma, Indonesia, Iraq and elsewhere. Russia also heavily invests in Nasser's fascist government, which puts Communists in concentration camps. At the same time Khrushchev is not above applying severe economic sanctions against Communist China. China itself has advanced loans to semifeudal monarchies in Nepal, Afghanistan and Yemen, aids other monarchies in Cambodia and Laos, and backs nationalistic Algeria and other bourgeois regimes.

Behind all these maneuvers are the vestigial characteristics of power politics and nationalism, cloaked in the deadly clichés of the cold war, but also the beginnings of inevitable international unification. While mankind groans under burdens of more than $150,000,000,000 in labor effort wasted every year on bombs as useless as pyramid-building, but far more deadly, we hear also the parting knell of nationalism and the beginning of world planning, which must end in a certain pooling of world resources. For now it is either childhood's end or the end of all children.

Am I dreaming? I have company among the realists. In 1961, as a guest at my niece's graduation from Briarcliff College, I heard Dr. Edward Teller deliver the commencement address. Dr. Teller is Dr. H-Bomb himself, and a believer in more and better shelters. If he had had something to say to encourage the shelter-seekers he might have made the covers of *Time-Life* that week, but as it was the press ignored his remarks. I do not think it was only because Eleanor Roosevelt was there that he said a few words about world government. In the most solemn tones he made two declarations, one of which would have called mockery upon him a few years ago, and the other of which shocked a young clergyman, who afterward expressed his fear to me that Dr. Teller might not be a religious man. Dr. Teller's first comment was that within the lifetime of the students there assembled we would be probing far distant planets to discover the secrets of infinity and God. His other prophecy was that East and West would, within an even shorter period, be united under a single world government and world law, with a world police force, and a world economic planning board. "There is," he said quite simply, "no other way."

But is it not preposterous to suppose that President Kennedy, even if he agreed with any of these modest suggestions, could possibly win acceptance for them in the United States Congress? Of course it is. Can one imagine that such ideas could prevail in a Congress which rejected even a medical-aid bill so inadequate that it would scarcely buy eyeglasses for the old folks to enable them to read the President's speeches? According to a study made by the Franklin D. Roosevelt Foundation, 19 percent of all our urban "consuming units"—more people than the combined populations of Finland, Norway, Denmark and Switzerland—live at levels "below prevailing standards of minimum adequacy." [19] Less than half of our brightest high school students get to college, 20 percent do not finish high school at all, and half a million of our most talented young people annually abandon higher education, mostly for financial reasons. Would a Congress which steadily refuses to take any serious responsibility for education, or shore up crowded and dilapidated school buildings—and at the same time forces half a billion dollars on an unwilling President to buy arms even the Pentagon can't use—be expected to propose that the United States initiate an all-out war against poverty even at home, not to say abroad? Or make peace with China? Naturally, not.

The Congress is far behind the sentiment of the American nation,

however, and opinion is not dead, it is momentarily asleep. If war is
"too serious an affair to be left in the hands of generals" world peace is
too imperative a need to be entrusted entirely to politicians. Soon our
congressmen may be forced to listen to somebody besides the oil
billionaire lobbies, the A.M.A., the corporations, the army lobbies
and the veterans bureaucracy. Many millions of American housewives
and mothers (and househusbands and fathers) are beginning to demand some guarantee of peace and assurance that their children won't
be exterminated or be born deformed. Pressures will mount. In time
it may be realized by more and more American voters that they are
not getting a fair shake. People will begin to know that it is not enough
to demand disarmament and peace; they must help their representatives find ways of promoting *production for peace.*

No administration to date has proved capable of stunting the growth
of the "military-industrial complex." It is not expected that any one
President can turn it off like a faucet; another tap must be turned on
before the old one can be shut off. The people themselves must make
a start toward recovering control over foreign policy and the machines
and setting both to work on new projects. "Only an alert and knowledgeable citizenry can compel proper meshing of the huge industrial
and military machinery," President Eisenhower warned, "with our
peaceful means and goals." And only that same citizenry can compel
Congress to begin at home the necessary support for modernization
and re-education of our own nation in preparation for commencement
exercises in the years immediately ahead.

That there are enough intelligent Americans to do just that, I do
not really doubt. The people are not so dull as the high-pressure public
relations mills suppose. In a recent tour of the whole country, when I
spoke to thousands in colleges, forums and civic groups, I found men
and women (young and old) eager for some *facts,* and full of a
healthy new skepticism. (To get the truth they read Art Buchwald,
not the editorial pages.) They don't take the straight cold-war scare
propaganda any more. They know the other side gets even more doc-
tored information but they also know they seldom hear the other side
over here. Even if the government isn't giving them all the facts, as
William Lederer tended to demonstrate in *A Nation of Sheep,* they
are going to be harder and harder to lead to the slaughter. One day
they will wake up and changes will begin—because they have to
begin.

But I am not trying to leave anyone with the impression that it is
possible for Americans alone to do much more than make it easier for
other people to behave in accordance with their best interests, and to
keep up with the world rather than fall dangerously behind it. Only
one man in thirteen is an American and very few others live as Americans do. Nothing is more preposterous than the assumption that the

"American system" can be exported to solve the problems of nations in very different circumstances. We can do no more, essentially, than cooperate with the attempts of others to find decent pathways of their own. As it was naïve to speak of an American Century so it is blindness not to see that unilateral American military dominance over much of the earth is rapidly waning. The United States is in no serious danger of eclipse by any one power but it cannot forever hold its overwhelming lead in economic development over all powers—particularly by the policies now being pursued.

New centers of world power are already clearly established. Europe has its independent Common Market. De Gaulle is cutting Germany loose from United States dominance and may soon lead Europe into federation. Another power center growing around the Soviet Union in the great heartland of Eurasia is also developing much faster than the United States. Latin America is beginning to stir with a new consciousness of its regional common interests and enormous potentials. In the Far East, China must rather sooner than later be seriously accepted as a responsible and leading nation which will find greater mutual interests with all eastern Asia, including Japan. This continent has infinite room for internal growth in the vastness of the United States, Canada and Mexico. Abroad, the United States can build strong and profitable trade and cultural relationships with all these natural regional groupings. It can do little more than that.

Whichever "system" prevails, no single pattern can exist everywhere on the same level nor can any one power control it. Here one must subscribe completely to the views of George Kennan, already quoted. The American system has numerous alternatives to exhaust before it would consciously embrace socialism; perhaps the only serious sign of weakness it has exhibited to date is the suppression of the American Communist Party. Itself a negligible minority, the party's martyrdom has given it symbolic importance in the general decline of dissent, opposition and freedom of controversy that has robbed the democratic process in America of much of the vitality it possessed in Roosevelt's day. Communism or socialism is not about to happen in the United States tomorrow or even the day after that, but to maintain some sense of proportion in public thought it seems useful to remind ourselves that even if it did happen the country would not be run by China or Russia or anybody but Americans. Nor would the change eliminate rivalries and competition or clashes of national interest nor even necessarily make them easier to keep under peaceful control. Russia has been unable to dictate to China. China does not rule Vietnam or Korea. Any United States system inevitably would be "deviationist"—and patriots inevitably would find any American system best.

The prospects of a readjustment in American dominance need not arouse undue anxiety in good Americans. Perhaps we shall be able to see this clearly only when we are relieved of excessive armaments (together with others) and relinquish police control to a larger world organization. Perhaps only then may we mature in planning for our own nation, so badly in need of fundamental modernization in many areas (slums, urban reconstruction, anarchy of traffic, education, housing, prison reform, archaic laws, etc.) ever since the bomb dropped on Hiroshima. In the end it will be what we do here, and not what we do or say to other peoples, that will create a civilization others wish to emulate.

Perhaps the greatest illusion was that America was ever in full charge at any time.

All plans are important only as indications of a general direction and only if they generally cooperate with the likely. Great events of the transition are quite beyond the compass of any single power, right or left, and often they seem to move independently of all. When we glance back at the postwar years we see that few of the really majestic changes followed the plans of the Pentagon or the State Department. It was not their planning that freed the subcontinent of India and released Europe's other colonies in Asia. Nothing that the United States did ordained the turning loose of Africa. China went Communist despite all that the United States government did to save the Nationalists. Even Cuba slipped away despite much that Washington did for Batista. Communism did not disintegrate from within, as Mr. Dulles planned that it must; both China and Russia are far more formidable competitors, not weaker, than a decade ago. The secret of the bomb on which so much strategy was based was after all no secret. Nor did we plan to fall so far behind in space flight that we would now like to share information with the Russians. (Possibly Mr. Stimson was right about that time ahead and a "covenant . . . we may desperately need.")

With equal impartiality history also upset Communist plans and prophecies. Stalin least expected a successful revolution to occur in China; in postwar Western Europe high hopes of Communist victories were completely frustrated. All Moscow's efforts to defeat the Marshall Plan seemed only to increase its success in reviving European capitalism and stabilizing the NATO alliance. Russia's sealing off of the satellite states hastened the formation of the Common Market, with the consequence least desired by Moscow: the exclusion of the U.S.S.R. from Western Europe. Stalin's monolithic Communist superstructure was designed to avoid what it now appears to have done most to create: polycentric communism. And despite the grand strategy of the left, most of the newly emerging states are thus far following a bourgeois path of development.

Seen in perspective, end events are always more complex than any plan can foresee, and the synthesis is certain to be a compromise quite

different from, and sometimes the very opposite of, anything consciously desired by even the most powerful nations which set in motion
forces to contain or direct history.

Inscribed on the tomb of the Earl of Devon and his wife (d. 1419)
in England is an Epitaph which seems to sum it up:

> What wee gave, wee have;
> What wee spent, wee had;
> What wee kept, wee lost.

For of course the United States has made numerous and noble contributions to world recovery. Among these are many constructive actions of first importance, but of them all perhaps the greatest, in the
eyes of history, is that the United States did pass by numerous opportunities to misuse its vast postwar power to launch a final world holocaust. Over the half-century which has seen two world wars and
their aftermath, the policies of the United States in Asia, as in
Europe, have been the product both of responses to the aggressions
of others and of challenges which helped provoke them. More than a
century ago De Tocqueville observed of Russia and the United States
that "each of them seems marked out by the will of Heaven to sway
the destinies of half the globe," and his prophecy has been fulfilled by
the rapid westward expansion of one and the eastward expansion of
the other. Viewing the world over that period one discerns an inexo-
rability in the transoceanic movement of the vast energies generated by
Europeans in the New World into the Orient, there to confront the
great Eurasian land power in a rendezvous destined to break forever
the isolation of East and West and to create the foundations of a modern international society.

We can still learn from our mistakes and continue to adjust peacefully to an insurgent world in which we shall always have a voice—and
a big voice—but not the only voice, and increasingly a more contested
voice. I assert again: we do stand at the threshold of childhood's end.
We shall be obliged to follow the general direction of accommodation
for the irresistible demands I have mentioned. One cannot say when
each step will be taken but taken it will be, if not in one year then in
another. It may never be that we shall say that on such and such a day
war ceased in the world. It may be rather more like the way Rome
stopped the practice of watching gladiators murder each other and
of feeding Christians to the lions. No law was ever passed but, after
Nero, men all at once became revolted with the spectacle and moved
on to a higher stage of barbarism.

Toward the end of the fifteenth century the last of the Crusades simply disintegrated, under King Peter, from lack of enthusiasm and plain
boredom. There was no edict or encyclical which banned Crusades but
no more were begun, and one reason men could no longer be rallied

to the old holy-war cries was because, a few years after King Peter's fiasco, Columbus discovered America. Merchants thought they had found a new trade route to the East and the Holy Land was no longer so strategically important. During the next four hundred years the aggressive energies of Europe were largely absorbed in the exploitation of new continents and conquests of nature and savage infidels. Today we are being forced into a race for the planets which may prove analogous.

Or again it may be that humanity's triumph will be comparable to the events depicted by Tolstoy in *War and Peace*. Napoleon seemed to win all the battles, the French army was invincible, the nation was conquered, and yet the Russian people were victorious. The fine tactical and strategic plans drawn up by the Polish and Austrian and Prussian staff professionals repeatedly came to naught; nothing ever happened the way they anticipated because they did not understand the general direction of events. To their mounting fury, General Kutuzov ignored them and saw logic and moral triumph even in the seeming defeat at Borodino. The old man somehow understood that far vaster and more complex forces than the outcome of any battle would decide everything. Kutuzov rode the storm with his people, in the moments of their greatest defeats he understood that they were winning, the French army perished, and the storm subsided.

We must have faith that the American nation also has a better sense of the general direction of history and in the end will have more to say about the future than some of the strategists of the moment, so large with great plans for small ends. Whether we shall eventually carry the republic and the union onto the higher ground of a victory shared with all men depends, of course, upon the ability of our "alert and knowledgeable citizenry" to see beyond immediate selfish interests, and act far more objectively than they have ever been required to do before.

Wars will face us for many years, and for the first time in history there is no prospect but defeat for the victor in any attempted armed conquest of one nation by another. Dr. Hugo Boyko has reminded us that the whole world has now shrunk to a state smaller in time dimensions than Israel was three thousand years ago, when it took fourteen days to travel from the northern border to Elath. Tomorrow our entire planetary system will be reduced to less space than the world of Ulysses' Aegean Islands. Between men who inhabit this earth there are no more seas; there are only rivers.

Appendix

Communist Party, People's Government and Science Organization

OFFICERS OF THE COMMUNIST PARTY OF CHINA

CHAIRMAN OF CENTRAL COMMITTEE

Mao Tse-tung

VICE-CHAIRMEN

Liu Shao-ch'i	Chu Teh
Chou En-lai	Ch'en Yun
Lin Piao	

SECRETARY-GENERAL

Teng Hsiao-p'ing

POLITICAL BUREAU (*Politburo*)

Mao Tse-tung	P'eng Teh-huai
Liu Shao-ch'i	Chu Teh
Chou En-lai	Ch'en Yun
Teng Hsiao-p'ing	Lin Piao
Tung Pi-wu	Liu Po-ch'eng
P'eng Chen	Ho Lung
Lo Jung-huan	Li Hsien-nien
Ch'en Yi	K'eh Cheng-shih
Li Fu-ch'un	Li Ching-chuan
T'an Chen-lin	

ALTERNATE MEMBERS

Ulanfu	Chen Po-ta
Chang Wen-t'ien	Kang Sheng
Lu Ting-yi	Po Yi-po
Teng Tsu-hui (?)	

OFFICERS OF THE PEOPLE'S GOVERNMENT OF THE PEOPLE'S REPUBLIC OF CHINA

CHAIRMAN OF REPUBLIC

Liu Shao-ch'i

Vice-Chairmen of Republic

Mme Soong Ching-ling   Tung Pi-wu
(Mme Sun Yat-sen)

National People's Congress

Chairman of NPC Standing Committee

Chu Teh

Vice-Chairmen

Lo Jung-huan	Chen Shu-tung
Shen Chun-ju	Saifudin
Kuo Mo-jo	Ch'eng Ch'ien
Huang Yen-p'ei	Panchen Lama
P'eng Chen	Ulanfu
Li Wei-han	Ho Hsiang-ning

Liu Po-ch'eng

Secretary-General NPC Standing Committee

Hsieh Chueh-tsai

Chief Procurator

Chang Ting-cheng

Council of National Defense
(1 chairman, 14 vice-chairmen, 100 members)

Chairman

Liu Shao-ch'i

Vice-Chairmen

Marshal P'eng Teh-huai	Marshal Hsu Hsiang-ch'ien
Marshal Lin Piao	Marshal Lo Jung-huan
Marshal Liu Po-ch'eng	Marshal Nieh Jung-chen
Marshal Ho Lung	Marshal Yeh Chien-ying
Marshal Ch'en Yi	Cheng Ch'ien
Teng Hsiao-p'ing	Chang Chih-chung
Fu Tso-yi	Marshal Chu Teh

State Council

Premier

Chou En-lai

Vice-Premiers

Ch'en Yun	Li Fu-ch'un
Marshal Lin Piao	Li Hsien-nien

Marshal P'eng Teh-huai   Marshal Nieh Jung-chen
Teng Hsiao-p'ing   Po Yi-po
Teng Tzu-hui   T'an Chen-lin
Marshal Ho Lung   Lu Ting-yi
Marshal Ch'en Yi   Lo Jui-ch'ing
Ulanfu   Hsi Chung-hsun

INTERNAL AFFAIRS   Chien Ying
FOREIGN AFFAIRS   Marshal Ch'en Yi
DEFENSE AFFAIRS   Marshal Lin Piao
PUBLIC SECURITY   Lo Jui-ching
STATE CAPITAL CONSTRUCTION COMMISSION   Ch'en Yun
STATE PLANNING COMMISSION   Li Fu-ch'un
STATE ECONOMIC COMMISSION   Po Yi-po
SCIENTIFIC AND TECHNOLOGICAL COMMISSION   Marshal Nieh Jung-chen
FINANCE   Li Hsien-nien
FOOD   Sha Chien-li
COMMERCE   Yao Yi-lin
FOREIGN TRADE   Yeh Chi-chuang
AQUATIC PRODUCTS   Hsu Teh-heng
METALLURGICAL INDUSTRY   Wang Ho-shou
CHEMICAL INDUSTRY   Peng Tao
MACHINE BUILDING 1ST MINISTRY   Tuan Chun-yi
MACHINE BUILDING 2ND MINISTRY   Liu Chien
MACHINE BUILDING 3RD MINISTRY   Chang Lien-kuei
PETROLEUM INDUSTRY   Yu Chiu-li
COAL INDUSTRY   Chang Lin-chih
GEOLOGY   Li Su-kuang
BUILDING   Liu Hsiu-feng
TEXTILE INDUSTRY   Chiang Kuang-nai
LIGHT INDUSTRY   Li Chu-chen
RAILWAYS   Teng Tai-yuan
COMMUNICATIONS   Wang Shou-tao
POSTS AND TELECOMMUNICATIONS   Chu Hsueh-fan
AGRICULTURE   Liao Lu-yen
LAND RECLAMATION   Wang Chen
FORESTRY   Liu Wen-hui
WATER CONSERVATION AND ELECTRIC POWER   Fu Tso-yi
LABOR   Ma Wen-jui
CULTURE   Shen Yen-ping (Mao Tun)
EDUCATION   Yang Hsiu-feng
PUBLIC HEALTH   Li Teh-ch'uan
PHYSICAL CULTURE AND SPORTS COMMISSION   Marshal Ho Lung
NATIONALITIES AFFAIRS COMMISSION   Ulanfu
OVERSEAS CHINESE AFFAIRS COMMISSION   Liao Ch'eng-chih
COMMITTEE FOR CULTURAL RELATIONS WITH FOREIGN COUNTRIES
Chang Hsi-jo
SECRETARY-GENERAL OF STATE COUNCIL   Hsi Chung-hsun

ORGANIZATION OF SCIENCE*

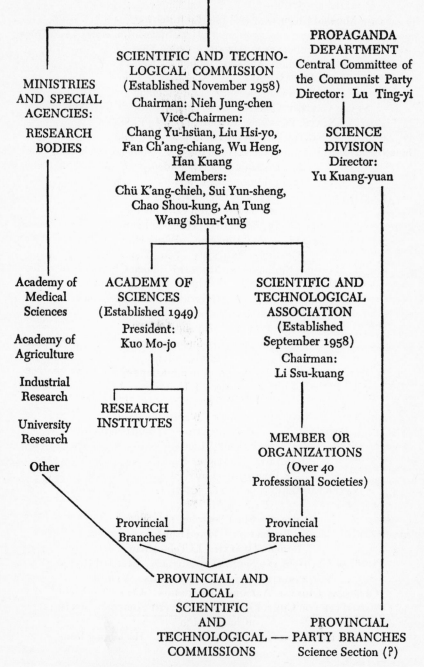

STATE COUNCIL
Premier: Chou En-lai

PROPAGANDA DEPARTMENT
Central Committee of the Communist Party
Director: Lu Ting-yi

SCIENTIFIC AND TECHNOLOGICAL COMMISSION
(Established November 1958)
Chairman: Nieh Jung-chen
Vice-Chairmen:
Chang Yu-hsüan, Liu Hsi-yo, Fan Ch'ang-chiang, Wu Heng, Han Kuang
Members:
Chü K'ang-chieh, Sui Yun-sheng, Chao Shou-kung, An Tung Wang Shun-t'ung

MINISTRIES AND SPECIAL AGENCIES:
RESEARCH BODIES

SCIENCE DIVISION
Director:
Yu Kuang-yuan

Academy of Medical Sciences

Academy of Agriculture

Industrial Research

University Research

Other

ACADEMY OF SCIENCES
(Established 1949)
President:
Kuo Mo-jo

SCIENTIFIC AND TECHNOLOGICAL ASSOCIATION
(Established September 1958)
Chairman:
Li Ssu-kuang

RESEARCH INSTITUTES

MEMBER OR ORGANIZATIONS
(Over 40 Professional Societies)

Provincial Branches

Provincial Branches

PROVINCIAL AND LOCAL SCIENTIFIC AND TECHNOLOGICAL — COMMISSIONS

PROVINCIAL PARTY BRANCHES
Science Section (?)

* From "The Organisation and Development of Science," by John M. H. Lindbeck, *The China Quarterly*, No. 6, April–June, 1961.

Food and Agriculture

Thanks are expressed for permission to reprint the following five tables, compiled by William Kaye and published in the *China Quarterly*, April-June, 1961.

TABLE 1

China—Farms and Farmers

	1950	1955	1956	1957	1958	1959	1960
Peasant Households (millions)	105.50	119.20	120.00	121.50	123.20	(125.00)	n.a.
Mutual Aid Teams (millions)	2.70	7.15	n.a.	none	none	none	none
Agricultural Producers "Co-operatives" (000)	0.02	633.70	764.00	784.00	negl.	negl.	none
lower level	0.02	633.20	276.00	84.00	none	none	none
higher level	0.00	0.50	488.00	700.00	negl.	negl.	none
People's Communes (000)	none	none	none	none	26.00	24.00	(24.00)
Households in Mutual Aid Teams (millions)	11.30	60.40	n.a.	none	none	none	none
Agricultural Producers "Co-operatives" (millions)	0.00	16.90	117.80	119.50	negl.	negl.	none
lower level	0.00	16.90	10.40	4.50	none	none	none
higher level	0.00	0.00	107.40	115.00	negl.	negl.	none
People's Communes (millions)	none	none	none	none	(122.00)	(124.00)	n.a.
State Farms (000)	1.20	2.24	2.25	n.a.	n.a.	n.a.	n.a.
Sown Area of State Farms (000 hectares)	155.00	394.60	587.50	n.a.	n.a.	n.a.	n.a.
Employed on State Farms (000 hectares)	43.00	134.00	206.00	n.a.	n.a.	n.a.	n.a.
Tractors (15 h.p.) on State Farms (000)	1.20	2.80	4.40	n.a.	n.a.	n.a.	n.a.

Sources: Official Chinese Statistics ( ) = estimated. n.a. = not available.

TABLE 2

China—Livestock Population

	1949	1955	1956	1957	1958	1959	1960
			millions				
Horses, Donkeys and Mules	15.8	21.4	20.8	19.8	n.a.	20.0	n.a.
Cattle and Buffaloes	43.9	65.9	66.6	65.8	(65.5)	65.4	n.a.
Pigs	57.8	87.9	97.8	145.9	160.0	180.0	243.0
Sheep and Goats	42.3	84.2	92.1	98.6	108.9	112.5	n.a.

TABLE 3

China—Crop Acreages, Production and Yields

	1949	1955	1956	1957	1958	1959	1960
	million hectares						
Acreages							
Rice	25.7	29.2	33.2	32.3	32.7	29.4	31.0
Wheat	21.5	26.7	27.3	27.6	26.6	24.1	27.5
Other Grains and Pulses	47.4	52.4	52.7	50.6	45.7	49.2	44.0
Potatoes	7.0	10.0	11.0	10.5	16.3	16.3	(17.5)
Total Grains and Potatoes	101.6	118.4	124.3	120.9	121.3	109.0	(120.0)
Soya Beans	8.2	11.4	12.0	12.6	12.9	(13.0)	(13.0)
Total Foodcrops	109.8	129.8	136.3	133.5	134.2	(122.0)	(133.0)
Non-Foodcrops	(21.2)	21.3	22.9	23.7	22.1	(20.5)	(21.0)
Total Area sown	(131.0)	151.1	159.2	157.2	156.3	(142.5)	(154.0)
Total Area cultivated	98.0	110.2	111.8	111.8	107.8	105.0	(110.0)
Multiple Cropping Index	133.8	137.2	142.3	140.6	145.0	135.3	(140.0)
Harvest	million metric tons						
Rice	48.6	78.0	82.5	86.8	113.7	n.a.	n.a.
Wheat	13.8	23.0	24.8	23.6	28.9	n.a.	n.a.
Other Grains and Pulses	35.8	54.9	53.4	52.7	62.0	n.a.	n.a.
Potatoes *	9.8	18.9	21.8	21.9	45.4	n.a.	n.a.
Total Grains and Potatoes	108.0	174.8	182.5	185.0	250.0	270.0	297.0
Soya Beans	5.1	9.1	10.2	10.0	10.5	11.5	(12.5)
Total Foodcrops	113.2	183.9	192.7	195.0	261.5	281.5	(309.5)
Yields	metric tons per hectare						
Rice	1.90	2.67	2.47	2.70	3.47	n.a.	n.a.
Wheat	0.64	0.86	0.91	0.86	1.09	n.a.	n.a.
Other Grains and Pulses	0.76	1.05	1.02	1.04	1.35	n.a.	n.a.
Potatoes *	1.40	1.88	1.99	2.09	2.80	n.a.	n.a.
Total Grains and Potatoes	1.06	1.46	1.42	1.54	2.03	2.48	(2.47)
Soya Beans	0.62	0.80	0.88	0.80	0.81	0.88	(0.96)
Total Foodcrops	0.86	1.22	1.21	1.24	1.67	1.97	(2.01)

Sources: Official Chinese Statistics.

* in grain equivalent.   n.a. = not available.   ( ) = estimated.

TABLE 4

China—Grain Imports 1961-63

	000 million metric tons				*Total (Commodity Weight)*
	Rice	*Wheat*	*Barley*	*Flour*	
from Burma	0.35	—	—	—	0.35
from Canada	—	5.89	1.28	0.03	7.20
from Australia	—	2.08	0.30	0.04	2.42
from Europe	—	0.03	—	—	0.03
Total	0.35	8.01	1.58	0.07	10.00

TABLE 5

China—Food Balance 1960-61

	Gross Domestic Production	Non-Food Uses	Net	Food Kilos per head	Supplies Calories per head per day
		million metric tons			
Grains	140.0	46.0	94.0	145.0	1,430
Potatoes	40.0	17.0	23.0	35.0	90
Pulses	10.0	6.8	3.2	5.0	50
Soya Beans	8.0	4.8	3.2	5.0	50
Sugar	1.5	0.2	1.3	2.0	20
Fruit and Vegetables	80.0	40.0	40.0	60.0	50
Meat and Poultry	5.7	0.5	5.2	8.0	65
Eggs and Fish	5.0	1.1	3.9	6.0	15
Fats and Oils	3.0	0.4	2.6	4.0	90
Total Domestic Imports					1,860
Grains	2.5	0.5	2.0	3.0	30
Sugar	0.5	—	0.5	1.0	10
Grand Total	—	—	—	—	1,900

Sources: Official Statements.
Estimates.
The figures in these tables have been compiled from numerous sources over the years.

FOOD RATIONS

The following table of official government rations was supplied to me, together with the appended comment, by a foreign doctor in China at the time of my visit, whose access to realistic information was exceptionally good.

Category	Daily Equivalent of Calories
Steel and other heavy workers	3,000
Medium workers	2,500 to 3,000
Light (sedentary) workers	1,800
Senior intellectuals	2,000 to 2,500
Intellectuals	2,000
Students (including children)	2,000
Housewives (non-producers)	1,500 or less
Lower office employees	1,500 to 1,800

"These are high rates; that is, in the small towns, and in Szechuan; in Peking the rations are badly done and would probably rate 300 calories lower for every individual. In Canton they are also very badly handled. There is no famine, not as you and I saw before, but there is malnutrition in the cities; and in some stricken areas there is avitaminosis and disease. To alleviate: each institution, factory, school, grows its own vegetables, rears its own pigs, and leases space in a commune or enters into direct contract with a commune for food. I have seen flower pots now planted with cabbages and tomatoes. City workers are going to the countryside; 46 percent of all cadres are going to the communes to 'help,' but also to eat. Hundreds of people have told me, 'One eats better in the commune.'

"Transport is the big snag, each institution must be responsible for transport of its own food, and has a transport team that goes down to the countryside once a week to haul (sometimes on their backs) food for the employees. All terribly difficult!

"But the communes were absolutely necessary; the cadres were necessary; whatever the attendant evils, China could never have done what she has done so far without the organization, discipline, and rigid indoctrination of the last ten years. I am convinced of this and that is why I still think that they have done 90 percent right. The difference is that whereas before millions died without a voice being raised, now the slightest grumble anywhere is magnified and sometimes out of proportion."

(Army rations are 3,200-3,400 per man. See page 289.)

This table by Allan J. Barry appears to me closely approximate to official rations generally, but not universally, observed. Permission to reprint it from the *China Quarterly*, April-June, 1961, is gratefully acknowledged.

	PER MONTH		PER ANNUM	
	Light	*Heavy*	*Light*	*Heavy*
	Workers		Workers	
Grains	25 lbs.	40 lbs.	135 kilos	218 kilos
Sugar	4 oz.	4 oz.	1.35 kilos	1.35 kilos
Meat	12 oz.	12 oz.	4.10 kilos	4.10 kilos
Vegetable Oil	12 oz.	12 oz.	4.10 kilos	4.10 kilos

American Prisoners in China

DEPARTMENT OF STATE
Washington

October 6, 1961

IN REPLY REFER TO
FE/CA

Dear Mr. Snow:

I refer to your letter of September 15, 1961, to the Assistant Secretary of State for Far Eastern Affairs, requesting information regarding Americans in Communist China. The Department of State shares your interest in reporting these facts accurately to the American public. For convenience, the answers to your questions are listed in the order in which you posed them.

1. An estimated fifty-seven American citizens are believed to be residing still in mainland China. This figure does not include an undetermined number of persons of Chinese race who may have a valid claim to United States citizenship.

2. Approximately twenty of the known resident American citizens are married to Chinese spouses.

3. There are now four American citizens known to be imprisoned in Communist China, although we cannot discount the possibility that there may be others. The four are:

John Thomas Downey, of New Britain, Connecticut, a Department of the Army civilian employee with the Far East Command, who was a passenger aboard an aircraft which disappeared on a regularly scheduled flight from Korea to Japan on November 29, 1952. The fact that he was in Chinese Communist hands was for some time concealed by Peiping when the issue of repatriation of Americans was discussed at Geneva in the talks between United States and Chinese Communist consular representatives which began on June 5, 1954. On November 23, 1954, the Chinese Communist radio announced that Mr. Downey had been sentenced to life imprisonment on charges of "espionage."

Richard George Fecteau, of Lynn, Massachusetts, a Department of the Army civilian employee, disappeared together with John Downey and was arrested presumably under identical circumstances. Mr. Fecteau was sentenced in November, 1954, to twenty years imprisonment on charges of "espionage."

Hugh Francis Redmond, Jr., of New York, an employee of an American import-export firm in China, was arrested on April 26, 1951, and sentenced on September 12, 1954, to life imprisonment on charges of "espionage."

James Edward Walsh, of Cumberland, Maryland, Roman Catholic Bishop who had been engaged for many years in missionary activity in China, was arrested in October, 1958, and thereafter held incommunicado for seventeen months with no charges having formally been placed against him. On March 18, 1960, he was sentenced, after a "showcase" trial, along with fourteen Chinese Catholic clergymen, to twenty years imprisonment on charges of "espionage" and "sabotage," having been branded a "veteran United States spy."

There was a fifth prisoner, to whom you refer in your letter. He was Robert Ezra McCann, a businessman and lifelong resident of China, who was arrested on June 14, 1951, and subsequently sentenced to fifteen years imprisonment for "espionage," and "crimes against the Chinese Government." Mr. McCann was released from his imprisonment on April 5, 1961, with virtually no prior notice and precipitately removed from Communist China for what the Peiping regime chose to describe as "humanitarian" reasons. Upon arrival in Hong Kong he was found to be in the terminal stages of lung cancer, having been subjected to what American physicians described as "skillful neglect" at the hands of his captors. I might add that Mr. McCann was not the first American to have been released from Chinese Communist captivity in moribund condition, thus leading to the suspicion that the sole Chinese Communist motivation in releasing the individuals concerned was to escape the onus of having them die while in Communist hands.

4. Your query with respect to United States prisoners of war touches upon a matter concerning which there has been a great deal of public misunderstanding. We have no reliable information to indicate that American servicemen from the Korean conflict are in fact being held prisoner. We have, however, attempted to elicit from the Communists at Panmunjom, at the ambassadorial-level discussions at Warsaw, and through other means, a satisfactory accounting (in accordance with their obligations under the provisions of the Korean Armistice Agreement) for American military personnel whom the Department of Defense has reason to believe may have been held by the Communists at some time during the hostilities in Korea. There were originally 944 Americans listed in this category, along with several thousand Republic of Korea and various other United Nations troops. Largely through the efforts of United States Graves Registration teams working in Korea, the number of unaccounted-for Americans has now been reduced to 389. We believe that the Chinese Communists must have knowledge of the fate of at least some of these men, but they have met all our questions on this subject with evasion and have refused to enter into meaningful discussions on the matter.

5. There were originally twenty-one prisoners of war from the United States armed forces who refused repatriation at the end of hostilities in Korea. Of these, one has died in China, ten have returned to the United States and ten remain in Communist China. The following persons remain:

Clarence C. Adams, of Memphis, Tennessee, formerly a corporal in the United States Army, is reportedly studying Chinese at Wuhan University.

Howard G. Adams, of Corsicana, Texas, formerly a sergeant in the United States Army, was last known to be working as a chemist in Tsinan.

Albert C. Belhomme, although a Belgian national, was a sergeant in the United States Army at the time of his capture. He is reportedly employed as a metal worker in Tsinan.

John R. Dunn, of Baltimore, Maryland, formerly a corporal in the United States Army, was last reported to be living in Peiping, unemployed and in poor health.

Scott L. Rush, of Marietta, Ohio, formerly a sergeant in the United States Army, was last known to have been working as a lathe operator in Wuhan.

Lowell D. Skinner, of Akron, Ohio, formerly a corporal in the United States Army, was last known to have been working as a lathe operator in Tsinan.

James G. Veneris, of Hawthorne, California, formerly a private in the United States Army, was last known to have been working as a lathe operator in Tsinan.

Harold H. Webb, of Fort Pierce, Florida, formerly a sergeant in the United States Army, is reportedly studying at Wuhan University.

William C. White, of Plummersville, Arkansas, formerly a corporal in the United States Army, is reportedly studying Chinese law at People's University in Peiping.

Morris R. Wills, of Fort Ann, New York, formerly a corporal in the United States Army, is reportedly studying classical Chinese at Peking University.

With respect to the query contained in the penultimate paragraph of your letter you may recall that, as a result of agreement achieved in the early sessions of the United States-Chinese Communist ambassadorial-level discussions in Geneva, the representatives of both sides on September 10, 1955, issued parallel statements in the form of an "Agreed Announcement" concerning the return of civilians. The Chinese Communist declaration stated: "The People's Republic of China recognizes that Americans in the People's Republic of China who desire to return to the United States are entitled to do so, and declares that it has adopted and will further adopt appropriate measures so that they can expeditiously exercise their right to return." This wording was specifically designed to cover all categories of Americans known to be in Communist China, including those in prison.

The American declaration concerning Chinese in the United States was similarly worded, and provided for implementation through the good offices of the Indian Embassy in Washington: "If any Chinese in the United States believes that contrary to the declared policy of the United States, he is encountering obstruction in departure, he may so inform the Embassy of the Republic of India in the United States and request it to make representations on his behalf to the United States Government. If desired by the People's Republic of China, the Government of the Republic of India may also investigate the facts in any such case."

Today three Americans who were covered by the provisions of these joint declarations are still in Chinese Communist prisons. As for the United States, any Chinese is free to leave this country for any destination of his choosing, and not a single one has been refused exit. The scrupulous manner in which the United States has implemented its announced pledge can be attested to by the Indian Embassy, which continues to assist, through financial aid and travel arrangements, Chinese nationals who desire to return to the mainland. The Indian Embassy has never cited a single instance of United States interference with the departure of any Chinese for Communist China. Chou En-lai's allegations to the effect that Chinese nationals are being detained here are entirely without basis in fact.

I hope that the foregoing data may be of assistance to you.

Sincerely yours,

Joseph A. Yager
Director for Chinese Affairs

THE JUDGMENT OF JOHN THOMAS DOWNEY AND RICHARD GEORGE FECTEAU

The Ministry of Foreign Affairs in Peking furnished, at my request, the following excerpts from "Judgment of the Military Tribunal of the Supreme People's Court of the People's Republic of China," proclaimed November

23, 1954, against two of the four Americans now imprisoned in China whose release (according to Premier Chou En-lai) has repeatedly been set forth as a precondition for negotiations toward a settlement of the "Taiwan dispute" by the United States representative in the Sino-American ambassadorial talks at Warsaw. I have no means of determining the accuracy of the purported facts disclosed in the judgment, and offer it merely as a matter of information, heretofore unpublished in the United States.

Excerpts from Judgment of the Military Tribunal of the
Supreme People's Court of the People's Republic of China
(November 23, 1954)

John Thomas Downey, the defendant, joined the U.S. Central Intelligence Agency, a United States espionage organization, in June, 1951, and was transferred in December of the same year to the Atsuki (Japan), espionage organization of the U.S. Central Intelligence Agency. Richard George Fecteau, the defendant, joined the U.S. Central Intelligence Agency in June, 1952, and was transferred in October of the same year to the Atsuki (Japan) espionage organization of the U.S. Central Intelligence Agency. Both defendants have undergone special training in terrorist subversive activities and armed riots against the Soviet Union and the people's democracies. In the spring of 1952, John Thomas Downey together with another U.S. agent, on orders of the chief of the Atsuki espionage organization, selected special agents from the agent training center of the U.S. Central Intelligence Agency on Saipan Island and brought these agents to a secret training camp in Chigasaki, Japan, of the Atsuki espionage organization. John Thomas Downey also transferred there Wang Wei-fan and radio operator Niu Sung-lin and Chung Tien-hsin from another agent training center of the U.S. Central Intelligence Agency. John Thomas Downey organized Chang Tsai-wen, Hsu Kwang-chih, Yu Kwan-chou, Niu Sung-lin into a team called "Team Wen," and secretly air-dropped them from a U.S. C-47 plane into Kirin Province of Northeast China in July, 1952. John Thomas Downey also organized Luan Heng-shan, Wang Wei-fan, Wang Chin-sheng, Chung Tien-hsing and others into another team called "Team Shen" and secretly air-dropped them from a U.S. B-17 plane into Liaoning Province of Northeast China in September, 1952. Besides, he had Li Chun-ying air-dropped from a U.S. plane into Kirin Province in October, 1952, to keep in contact with the other agents and to conduct subversive activities. In August, 1952, John Thomas Downey himself secretly intruded into Kirin Province of Northeast China in a U.S. plane to air-drop food and supplies for the agents of "Team Wen," who had been air-dropped into Kirin Province. Finally on the night of November 29, 1952, John Thomas Downey and Richard George Fecteau secretly intruded into the territorial air of Northeast China in a U.S. C-47 plane and again made contact with and provided supplies to the agents that had been air-dropped into our country. They also attempted to pick up the agent Li Chun-ying to give them a report of work so as to continue the air-dropping of large numbers of special agents into our country. The plane in which they came, however, was shot down and John Thomas Downey and Richard George Fecteau were captured.

All the defendants in this case have admitted the crimes committed by them after their capture. Their crimes are also borne out by a vast amount of captured material evidence such as weapons, ammunition, radio sets, maps, parachutes, equipment for air-dropping special agents, forged passes of the Chinese People's Liberation Army, certificates for wounded soldiers, as well as gold, paper currency and other instruments for conducting espionage activities. In view of such conclusive evidence of their crimes, it is beyond doubt that the defendants were air-dropped into Chinese territory to conduct espionage activities seriously jeopardizing the security of China in an attempt to carry out the scheme of the American aggressors to extend U.S. aggression against China and undermine China's cause of people's democracy.

John Thomas Downey, the defendant, actively assembled and trained special agents and had them secretly air-dropped into Chinese territory to conduct subversive activities. He also personally intruded into China's territorial air to carry out criminal activities. He is the chief criminal in this case and should be punished without leniency. The defendant Richard George Fecteau who assisted John Thomas Downey in intruding into China to conduct espionage activities should also be severely punished.

In accordance with Articles 6, 3, 7, 11, 14 and 16 of the Law of the People's Republic of China for the Punishment of Counter-revolutionaries, judgment is hereby passed:

(1) The defendant John Thomas Downey is sentenced to life imprisonment.

(2) The defendant Richard George Fecteau is sentenced to 20 years' imprisonment.

Second Interview with Chou En-lai:
October 18, 1960[1]

My text has already covered the lengthy interview I had with Premier Chou during our trip to Miyun. Further conversations I had with him in his Winter Palace offices remain the most complete statement available of the Chinese official view on several questions. Following is the official on-the-record part of my report as it appeared in *Look* magazine, January 31, 1961:

Snow: "Against the background of China's policy as already explained by the Premier, it seems probably that mere withdrawal of U.S. armed forces from Taiwan would not be sufficient to stabilize peaceful U.S.-China relations, or to remove from the United States the stigma of Enemy No. 1 for China. Would not U.S. forces also have to be withdrawn from South Korea as well as from South Vietnam, and would not U.S. bases have to be given up in Japan and SEATO dissolved? As such events could only occur as a part of general disarmament agreements, would China be prepared for step-by-step disarmament carried out simultaneously with the U.S.A. and other powers in this part of the world?"

The Premier: "In this question, you have mixed several things together, but I will deal with them separately in my answer. I know why you have put them together. It is because the U.S. Government, starting from the days of [the late Secretary of State John Foster] Dulles and up to the present-day [Secretary Christian] Herter, has all along thought that U.S. armed forces cannot be withdrawn from Taiwan; if they were withdrawn, it would lead to a chain reaction in which U.S. troops in such other places as South Korea, Japan, the Philippines, Thailand and South Vietnam would all have to be withdrawn. There is, of course, this possibility.*

"If the United States adopted the same attitude and concluded similar treaties first with other Asian countries rather than China, to respect their sovereignty, territorial integrity and independence, withdraw its troops and liquidate its military bases there, would not these countries then really attain independence and freedom? In spite of the treaties concluded between China and these Asian countries, should the United States still have apprehensions, thinking that these treaties with China are not sufficient, and be thus unwilling to withdraw from Asia and the Far East, then a peace pact could be concluded between the four powers—China, the Soviet Union, Japan and the United States—to jointly guarantee the peace and security of this region. This was the suggestion of Japanese friends. Or there is the alternative to let every country take part, which is our proposal to conclude a peace pact of mutual nonaggression among the countries of Asia and those bordering on the Pacific. Would not the peace and security of the Far East, of Asia and the Pacific region be thus ensured?"

Snow: "Was Inejiro Asanuma, the late chairman of the Japanese Socialist party, included among the Japanese friends mentioned by the Premier?"

The Premier: "Yes. Not only the Socialist party, but other progressive parties and popular organizations of Japan have entertained the same idea.

* Here, Chou briefly renewed complaints already recorded in our first interview, against the U.S. policy of rimming China with bases "set up under the pretext of preventing Communist expansion," and again contrasted it with China's five-principled policy of peaceful coexistence as incorporated in treaties with neighboring countries.

"But, up to now, the U.S. Government is still unwilling to do so. Clearly, it wants to dominate Asian countries and places wherever it can, and continue with such domination. It is unwilling to withdraw troops and liquidate military bases anywhere. On the contrary, it wants to increase its troops, expand its invasion and occupation, and set up military bases where none existed before. In Laos, for instance, the United States is trying to get military bases through military 'aid.' It will inevitably arouse the opposition of the local population. So, you see, the people of these countries are opposed to U.S. imperialism, not only because the Chinese people are opposing U.S. invasion and occupation of China's Taiwan, but mainly because of what the United States itself has done in these countries, which is to encroach upon their sovereignty, to bully the people and increase their burdens.

"Can it be said that the struggle of the Japanese people was caused by the Chinese people, that the struggle of the South Korean people was caused by the Chinese people, that the struggle of the Turkish people was caused by the Chinese people, that the struggle of the South Vietnamese and Laotian peoples was caused by the Chinese people? No. These struggles were caused by the policy of aggression which the U.S. Government has pursued there, and by its aggressor troops.

"It is the imperialist policy of the U.S. Government, and not merely the fact that U.S. troops have invaded and occupied China's Taiwan, that has put the U.S. Government in the position of being the enemy of these peoples. The invasion and occupation of Taiwan can only make the United States the enemy of the Chinese people. [It was suggested that the word "intervention" would be better understood to describe American action in civil-war situations in Taiwan, Korea, Vietnam, etc., rather than "invasion" and "aggression." The suggestion was stoutly rejected. Otherwise, throughout these formal interviews, the interviewer deemed it his proper function to record, not to debate.]

"Only when other countries have suffered similar acts of invasion and occupation will they become hostile toward the United States, and only then will the people of these countries consider U.S. imperialism as their common enemy. This is the fundamental reason why the people of these countries are opposed to the United States. If the U.S. Government agreed to withdraw its troops from Asian countries and to liquidate its military bases there, friendship between the people of the United States and these Asian countries could be developed, and, moreover, the possibility would arise of realizing peaceful coexistence between the U.S. Government and these Asian countries.

"Looking at the development of the over-all situation, even if the United States doesn't withdraw from the Taiwan region and no breakthrough occurs there, breakthroughs will occur elsewhere, leading also to a similar chain reaction so long as the U.S. Government persists in its present policies of aggression and war. Because in bullying and oppressing other peoples, the United States will inevitably arouse their opposition and suffer ultimate defeat. It is only a matter of time. As to where the breakthrough occurs first, this depends on the development of the struggle.

"What I have said above deals only with relations between the United States and the Asian countries. In your question, there is also the point of Sino-U.S. relations. On our way to the Miyun Reservoir, we discussed this question at length, and I have made our position quite explicit. [The Premier briefly reviewed China's position on Taiwan, already emphasized, and then continued.]

"The third part of your question is about disarmament. We support the proposal for general disarmament, but it goes without saying that any disarmament agreement would not be binding on China if it was reached without the participation of, and was not signed by, the official Chinese representative. This we have declared on many occasions.

"You put the above three questions into one. I have dealt with them separately, though I admit there is some connection between them."

Snow: "Would China refuse to sit in the United Nations as long as any kind of Taiwan government were allowed to represent Taiwan separately there?"

The Premier: "This question is relatively simple. If the so-called 'Taiwan Clique' is to appear in the United Nations, under whatever form and in whatever name—be it the Chiang Kai-shek clique or some other clique—we shall definitely refuse to take part in the United Nations and sit together with them, so as not to create a situation of 'two Chinas.' This applies also to our participation in other international organizations and conferences."

Snow: "How *soon* does China expect to be making nuclear weapons of its own?"

The Premier: "I can briefly state that I myself don't know when we will be making nuclear weapons."

Snow: "The two U.S. Presidential aspirants, Richard M. Nixon and John F. Kennedy, waged a debate as to whether the United States would 'go to war' to 'defend' Matsu and Quemoy, China's offshore islands. Would an announcement by the United States that it was withdrawing its 'protection' from those islands in any way encourage in China a belief that the United States does not have aggressive designs on China and desires a peaceful settlement of the Taiwan issue?"

The Premier: "In an election campaign, the two U.S. political parties invariably choose some international questions to make campaign material. In our view, the two U.S. parties have no basic differences on China policy.

"As to Quemoy and Matsu, whether or not Chiang Kai-shek's troops withdraw from these islands is China's internal affair; it is an issue of civil war between the Central Government of New China and the Chiang Kai-shek clique. Even Chiang Kai-shek said that U.S. Senator Kennedy had no right to meddle in this question, to interfere in China's domestic affairs. This I read from the statement of a spokesman of the so-called foreign ministry of the Chiang Kai-shek clique. In my previous interview, I told you that, by suggesting a 'Sino-Formosan nation,' Chester Bowles was testing out the plot of manufacturing 'two Chinas.' Kennedy's statements are intended to follow the same line of the 'two Chinas' plot. It is opposed even by Chiang Kai-shek. Even Bowles himself admitted that it was opposed by the Chinese people on the mainland, by Chiang Kai-shek and by the Chinese in Taiwan. The United States has pinned its hopes on a handful of people like Hu Shih and Lei Chen, hoping that they would manage to set up a so-called opposition party, but they are getting nowhere."

Snow: "The U.S. Government is reported to be considering the imposition of an embargo against trade with Cuba. Imposition of a trade embargo had the effect of stimulating industry in China until now China is able to make items on the embargoed list for itself. If Cuba desired, could China now supply such items to Cuba in the event of an embargo, and would it do so?"

The Premier: "Having established diplomatic relations with China, there will, of course, be the possibility of expanding trade with Cuba. The embargo list of the United States applies only to U.S.-Chinese trade or U.S.-Cuban trade; it cannot apply to Sino-Cuban trade."

Snow: "There is talk now in the United States of imposing an embargo on Cuba. What I mean is that it would be an ironical situation if China were able to export to Cuba those very products which China, stimulated by the embargo on it, can now produce itself."

The Premier: "The policy of embargo is bound to go bankrupt. But in each country, the course of development is different. It is decided primarily by the forces within the country, and then comes foreign assistance. We hold that a U.S. embargo against Cuba will go bankrupt, as did the one against China. China is not the only country which will be helping Cuba. A U.S. embargo against Cuba will first of all arouse the opposition of the Latin-American countries, who, sharing the same destinies, sympathize with each other. The 220 million people of Latin America are the next-door neighbors of the United States. Their sympathies and support are on the side of the Cuban people. The U.S. Government invariably underestimates this strength of theirs, and on this account alone, the U.S. will meet defeat in its embargo against Cuba."

[At this point, Premier Chou concluded his remarks on relations with the United States, and the interview took up China's relations with its neighbors and its economic affairs.]

Snow: "Without going into China's policy in Tibet or the question of China's sovereign claims there, could you explain to me why Tibet is not an 'autonomous republic' (as in the case of Kazakhstan and Kirghizia in the U.S.S.R.), but an 'autonomous region'?"

The Premier: "You asked why we called Tibet an autonomous region. We not only call Tibet an autonomous region, but set up organs of self-government wherever fraternal nationalities live in compact communities. For instance, in Sinkiang [Turkestan] there are a number of nationalities, of which the Uighurs are most numerous. So there is the Sinkiang Uighur Autonomous Region. In addition, we have the Inner Mongolian Autonomous Region and the Kwangsi Chuang Autonomous Region. Besides autonomous regions, we have autonomous *chou* (special administrative areas) under provinces, for example, the Yenpien Korean Autonomous *Chou* under Kirin Province. And we also have autonomous *hsien* under the districts. Formerly, we had autonomous *hsiang*. All these have evolved in accordance with the actual conditions and historical development in China.

"The state structures of other countries have been evolved in accordance with their actual conditions and their historical development. The Soviet Union has various forms of organization, including the autonomous republics and the autonomous regions.

"You said quite rightly that China and the Soviet Union were both Socialist countries, that they were the same in nature, being both dictatorships of the proletariat. But the state structures are not necessarily the same and need not be entirely identical. Actually, the rights and privileges of our autonomous regions are stipulated in our Constitution, to which you may refer. In Western countries, you also have different state structures. In the United States, the subdivisions are called states, while in France, they are known as provinces. This is related to historical development."

Snow: "Last year, Prime Minister [Jawaharlal] Nehru told me that perhaps the basic reason for the Sino-Indian dispute was that they were both 'new nations,' in that both were newly independent and under dynamic nationalistic leaderships, and in a sense were 'meeting' at their frontiers for the first time in history; hence it was natural that a certain degree of conflict should be generated before they could stabilize their frontiers. Would you agree with this generalization and agree with him that there is no dispute between China and India which cannot be settled peacefully?"

The Premier: "You said that Prime Minister Nehru said that China and India being both new nations and meeting for the first time at their frontiers, the boundary dispute between them was therefore difficult of settlement. With regard to such a statement, I don't feel that it is the case. China and Burma are also newly independent countries. Why has it been possible for Burma to settle the boundary question?"

Snow: "I did not *quote* from Prime Minister Nehru; I was paraphrasing. I may have misinterpreted him, but he made a similar statement in Parliament. He said that both nations were very dynamic and filling out, and now they were meeting as modern nations on the borders. In the past, there were buffer zones between the two countries; both sides were remote from the borders. Now that they have met, the borders must be stabilized. In the past, India was a colony and China a semicolony. The boundary was not so clear, and from the administrative needs at the time, the boundary did not particularly have to be clearly delineated."

The Premier: "I don't agree entirely with what you have said. You said that, in the past, one was a colony and the other a semicolony; and that, under the rule of feudalism, the boundary was not so clear, that it was not de-limited. This was the actual situation. . . ."

Snow: "And there were buffer states between them?"

The Premier: "What 'buffer states'?"

Snow: "Like Nepal, the Northeast Frontier Agency, Bhutan?"

The Premier: "The boundary is not clear—this is one aspect of the situation, an aspect we inherited from history. There is another aspect, one imposed on us by imperialism. For instance, India and Burma were formerly ruled by British imperialism, and it was from there that British imperialism invaded and occupied many places of semicolonial China and concluded secret treaties in collusion with the local authorities of China. The best-known example of this is the so-called MacMahon Line. This MacMahon not only brought about a secret treaty between India, Burma and the local authorities in Tibet, but he also drew another MacMahon Line between Afghanistan and Iran, bringing a loss to Afghanistan. Having attained independence, we, the countries concerned, should take the stand of Asian countries and settle outstanding questions left over from history on the basis of the Five Principles of peaceful coexistence. Burma took a positive attitude toward the settlement of the boundary question. Although the Sino-Burmese boundary question was only settled this year, after more than five years, it was settled very well.

"But India doesn't want to settle the boundary question. It does not admit that there is a Sino-Indian boundary question. The real idea they have in mind is to turn China's Tibet region into a 'buffer zone,' a 'buffer state' as you just put it, and to maintain in Tibet the former system of serfdom. They don't want Tibet to become a Socialist Tibet, as had other places in China. Why are they acting like this? If they want to oppose socialism, why come to China's Tibet to oppose it? It is interfering in China's domestic affairs. That's why after the rebellion was quelled in Tibet, when the Dalai Lama had run away and democratic reforms were started in Tibet, they became more dissatisfied, and shortly afterwards, the Sino-Indian boundary question came to the fore.

"Our stand has been very clear. It is to maintain the *status quo* and seek a friendly settlement. Even in the case of the so-called MacMahon Line, we haven't crossed to the south of it in spite of the fact that we don't recognize it. Neither have we put forward any territorial claims as preconditions to negotiations. This was also our attitude in settling the Sino-Burmese boundary question.

"But the Indian side took a different attitude. It is using the Sino-Indian boundary question as a card against progressive forces at home and as capital for obtaining 'foreign aid.' The Indian Government doesn't want a settlement. Having no case for the eastern sector, it went to the western sector, laying claim to that tract of territory (the greater part of which is in Sinkiang and a smaller part in Tibet), which for many years has been under Chinese jurisdiction, saying that this territory was the territory of the former Ladakhi kingdom of Kashmir. If accounts are to be squared going so far back into history, the world will be thrown into a turmoil. Using this method, the United States would have to be returned to British rule, because the United States has only been independent for less than 200 years, while we have been administering this area of Sinkiang [Turkestan] for several hundreds of years."

Snow: "The United States should be turned back to the American Indians?"

The Premier: "Right. You have put it more correctly. But, of course, the United States should recognize the right of the Indians to national equality.

"We hold that the boundary question can only be settled by maintaining the *status quo* while seeking a friendly solution. The Sino-Burmese boundary question was settled in this way. After signing the boundary treaty, we can change the way the Sino-Burmese boundary was drawn on our maps, and corresponding changes can be made on Burmese maps. But the maps cannot be changed unilaterally. India has been independent for thirteen years, during which it has made continuous changes in its maps. The boundary was first marked as not clear, then as boundary undefined, and finally as boundary defined. This was the case with regard to the eastern as well as the western sector. How can this be permitted? The Indian Government then produced its 1954 map as the final version, claiming that this was the boundary, the unalterable boundary. How can a friendly settlement be reached with such an attitude?

"The Chinese side is still striving for a friendly settlement to the boundary question and is maintaining the *status quo*. To prevent clashes, we are not sending patrols to the border, so that there can be no contact between the patrols of the two sides. We believe that the peoples of China and India want to be friendly with each other, and now that an example has been set by the Sino-Burmese boundary treaty, the day will come when the Sino-Indian boundary question can also be settled. There is no conflict of basic interests between the Chinese and Indian peoples. We will be friendly to each other for generations to come. The present situation is but a temporary phenomenon.

"But it must be pointed out again that there is this idea among the Indian ruling class that, in order to consolidate their rule, they must seek provocation along the border with which to attack progressive forces at home and as capital for getting 'foreign aid.'

"Now, I will answer some of your specific questions on economic affairs."

Snow: "1960 has been an exceptionally grave year, in which natural calamities have severely handicapped agricultural production. In former times, under such circumstances, many would face starvation. Will China be able to show any increase in agricultural production this year, despite these reverses?"

The Premier: "Natural calamities have been particularly severe this year, and, moreover, it was the second consecutive year of them. The collective strength of the people's communes has played a great role in recouping the situation and in struggling to overcome the difficulties. But in spite of this, the total value of agricultural production this year may be less than that of last year. That natural calamities cannot be fully overcome holds throughout the world, and of this you are aware."

Snow: "I have been told that this year's drought is China's worst since the nineteenth century."

The Premier: "That is true. But agricultural output will still be higher than that before 'the Great Leap Forward,' that is, higher than 1957."

Snow: "Can you tell me how much 'free aid,' apart from published agreements covering credits and trade exchanges, China has received from the U.S.S.R.?"

The Premier: "You asked whether the Soviet Union gave China any aid without compensation. Generally speaking, no. But in a specific sense, one can say yes. For instance, no patent fees are charged for blueprints. For technical data, we are charged only for the cost of the paper, of printing, of the designing fee and of shipment. In this sense, they are given to us free of compensation. In our technical aid to the countries of Asia, Africa and Latin America, we also do the same."

Snow: "China's population was in 1957 reported as 650 million. It has been said that the birth rate now is 2.4 percent, or 15 million annually. Will it be correct to say, in 1961, that China's population has reached 700 million?"

The Premier: "The 2.4 percent was for a year of maximum increase. The average is around 2 percent."

Snow: "Is the trend now downward or upward?"

The Premier: "It wavers around that figure."

Snow: "Can you tell me what percentage of China's land is still cultivated by human power alone, as distinct from horsepower or tractor or other mechanical means?"

The Premier: "The degree of mechanization is still extremely low. We still depend mainly on man power and animal power. A considerable period is needed before China can surpass the norm with regard to mechanization and semimechanization, irrigation and the use of chemical fertilizers. This is indeed one reason Chinese peasants have wanted to set up people's communes, to leap forward and to shake off their backwardness with a high speed of development."

Snow: "With a per capita income of 800 dollars a year (say 2,000 yuan, or Chinese dollars), China would be able to exceed present U.S. gross national production. Could you tell me when you think that figure might be achieved? Could you also estimate China's current total gross national product?"

The Premier: "We are not very clear about the gross national product of the U.S. as compared to the national income."

Snow: "The gross national product of the United States is running around 500 billion dollars. My point is that, China's population being about 700 millions, if its per capita income were the equivalent of U.S. $800, that would mean a G.N.P. roughly equivalent to that of the United States' G.N.P. But if the per capita income of China were equal to that of the U.S., then China would have a G.N.P. three and a half times as large as ours: about 1,750 billion dollars."

The Premier: "This cannot be done in a day! A long time is required. We cannot begin to compare with your production now. Our target was to catch up with Britain in about ten years, and that not in terms of national product per capita, but in terms of major industrial output. But a feature of China is that individual *incomes* are not far apart, and there is no unemployment. This is because we have a different system with which you have nothing to compare."

China, Taiwan and the United States

Both Communist and Nationalist officials foresee that restoration of diplomatic relations between China and the United States will be conditioned by an accompanying or prior agreement between the People's Republic and the National Government on Taiwan. A declaration by the United States that it would not oppose a peaceful settlement of the Chinese civil war and the unification of China would probably result in the open resumption of negotiations which were suspended after the formation of Chiang Kai-shek's government on Taiwan.

No such declaration by the United States is on the horizon, but the possibility of a change in conditions always exists. As long as the United States continues to give him generous financial and military protection, and does not support, or at least announce a hands-off policy toward, negotiations with mainland China, Chiang Kai-shek probably will not compromise with Peking nor assume (as he has been offered) high office in the People's Government, which still nominally retains the form of a political coalition in which a left-wing Kuomintang group is represented. Neither will Chiang be likely to declare the independence of Taiwan or agree to any form of a "two Chinas" solution, such as has been urged in some quarters. That would permanently detach Taiwan from China's sovereignty and make Chiang a traitor in the eyes of most Chinese, left or right.

The future of Taiwan remains ambiguous. Chiang Kai-shek is in his late seventies; reportedly, he has undergone two operations in recent months and is in failing health. General Chen Cheng is Chiang's premier and vice-president and is therefore technically the No. 2 man in Taiwan. Chen's rival is Chiang's son, Chiang Ching-kuo (educated in Russia and married to a Russian), whom Chiang uses to balance the power of Chen Cheng. The latter commands most of the army, but it is permeated with security forces answerable to Chiang Ching-kuo, as his father's deputy, and he also controls the political and administrative machinery through command of the secret police. When Chiang Kai-shek leaves the scene, a struggle for power between Chiang Ching-kuo and Chen Cheng is expected.

General Chen Cheng is about seventy and Chiang Ching-kuo is in his early fifties. The United States protectorate seems hardly likely to last throughout Chiang Ching-kuo's life expectancy. Among Kuomintang representatives who have continued to hold secret conversations with the Communists, those working for Chiang Ching-kuo are most active. They doubtless seek to reach an understanding with Peking which could be utilized in the event that the United States withdrew protection from Taiwan or threw its support behind Chen Cheng as the Generalissimo's successor.

A Hongkong newspaper owned by Chiang Ching-kuo, the *Cheng Pao*, has published a number of stories which imply the existence of negotiations. On July 29, 1962, Chiang's paper carried a report that Mao had recommended to the Politburo that better terms be offered to Taiwan. That report implied that Peking might "continue" the disrupted Kuomintang-Communist negotiations which had been conducted with General Li Tsung-jen, the last "legal" President of the National Government in China. When, after his defeat in North China, Generalissimo Chiang resigned as President, he turned over that office to Vice-President Li Tsung-jen, authorizing him to negotiate an internal peace. After he fled to Taiwan the Generalissimo formed a rump National Government, however, and resumed office as President while General Li was in the United States in consultation with President Truman. Li has been in the United States ever since, has not resigned his office, and maintains that he is the legitimate chief of the Nationalist state. One implication of the Hongkong story is that Chiang Ching-kuo might seek to use General Li by recognizing him as the legal president in order to prevent Chen Cheng from taking power. General Li would probably be willing to resume that role as a peace negotiator if all parties desired it, and particularly if he believed his efforts would lead to a betterment of relations between China and the United States. Li is known to be a man of peace and is on good terms with all the parties.

Terms of a settlement rumored to have been discussed, but *totally lacking any official confirmation* (and, naturally, denied by Taiwan at this stage of the game), include: 1) Taiwan to be permanently recognized as an autonomous region within the Chinese state; 2) Nationalist armed forces to withdraw from the offshore islands but remain on Taiwan and the Pescadores; 3) the Nationalist president to become a vice-chairman of the People's Republic and concurrently deputy commander in chief of the armed forces of the Republic; 4) the Kuomintang to be reorganized to include the Kuomintang Revolutionary Committee, now in Peking, and to form a coalition Taiwan regime represented in the mainland National Congress and cabinet; 5) the People's Republic to assume all diplomatic representation abroad; 6) Taiwan to control its defense forces for ten years but gradually to reduce them to provincial status; 7) for a specified period (ten years? twenty years?) Peking would send no armed forces to Taiwan but would provide training and supplies for the existing forces.

Following any Taiwan-Peking agreement, or concurrently with it, Taiwan would request the dissolution of the United States alliance and the withdrawal of U. S. forces. The United States would be asked to make a joint declaration with the People's Government, in which the United States would recognize the sovereignty of the People's Republic in Taiwan; both powers would guarantee not to use military force as a means of settlement of any disputes between them; and China would guarantee not to send any military forces into Taiwan except on the terms of the Taiwan agreement.

As time begins to run out on the exclusion of mainland China from the United Nations, the bargaining power of Taiwan may be expected to weaken. For this reason periodic rumors of Kuomintang-Communist negotiations* may have to be taken more seriously than in the past, when they have generally coincided with demands by Chiang Kai-shek for increased American aid, or rumors of a change in United States policy toward China.

* For example, the London *Observer* of August 12, 1962, in a dispatch from Singapore, reported that a "secret agreement" had actually been reached between the Chiang family and the Communists in Peking. Some but not all of the terms described in the *Observer* story were similar to those outlined above.

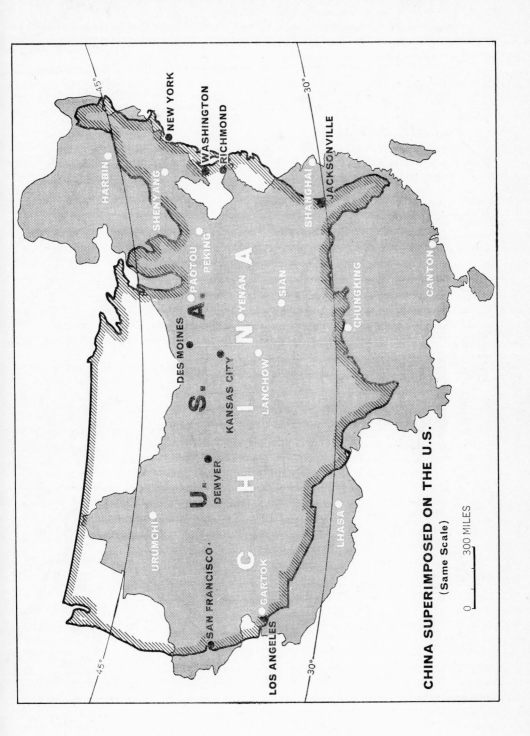

CHINA SUPERIMPOSED ON THE U.S.

(Same Scale)

0   300 MILES

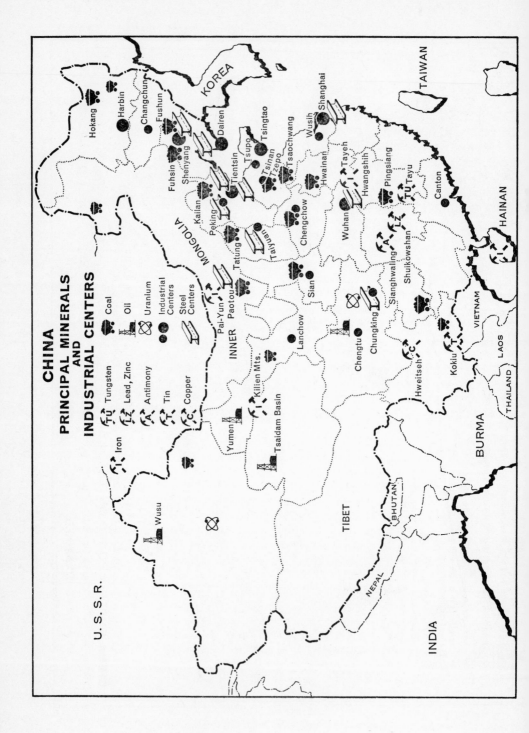

CHINA
PRINCIPAL MINERALS
AND
INDUSTRIAL CENTERS

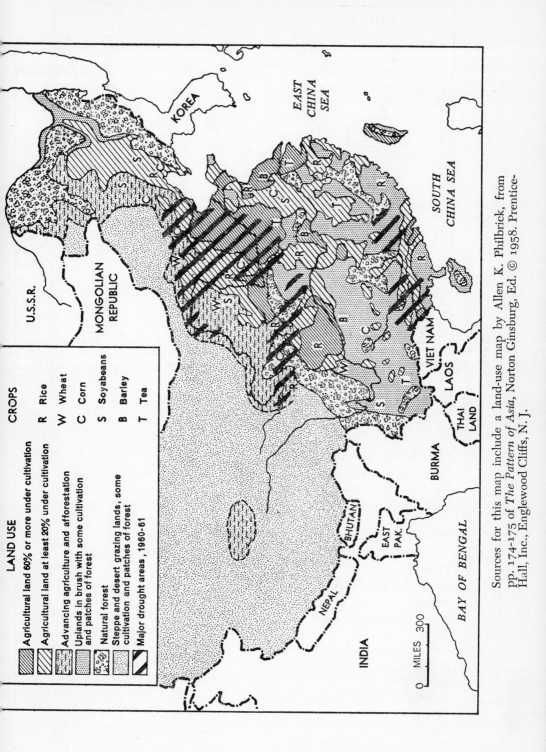

LAND USE

- Agricultural land 60% or more under cultivation
- Agricultural land at least 20% under cultivation
- Advancing agriculture and afforestation
- Uplands in brush with some cultivation and patches of forest
- Natural forest
- Steppe and desert grazing lands, some cultivation and patches of forest
- Major drought areas, 1960-61

CROPS

- R Rice
- W Wheat
- C Corn
- S Soyabeans
- B Barley
- T Tea

0 __ MILES __ 300

U.S.S.R.

MONGOLIAN REPUBLIC

KOREA

EAST CHINA SEA

SOUTH CHINA SEA

BAY OF BENGAL

INDIA

NEPAL

BHUTAN

EAST PAK.

BURMA

THAI LAND

LAOS

VIET NAM

Sources for this map include a land-use map by Allen K. Philbrick, from pp. 174-175 of *The Pattern of Asia*, Norton Ginsburg, Ed. © 1958. Prentice-Hall, Inc., Englewood Cliffs, N. J.

National Autonomous Regions

Inner Mongolian Autonomous Region: Mongols
Kwangsi Autonomous Region: Chuang
Ninghsia Autonomous Region: Mohammedans (Hui)
Sinkiang Uighur Autonomous Region: I-li (Kazakh), K'e-tzu-le-su
    (Khalka), Ch'ang-chi (Hui)
Tibetan Autonomous Region: Tibetans

Larger Provincial Minority Autonomous Districts (*Chou*)

Hainan
South: Li and Miao
Hunan
West: Tuchia and Miao
Kirin
East: (Yen-pien border): Ko-
   rean
Kweichow
Southeast: Miao, Tung
South: Puyi, Miao
Szechuan
West (Kan-tzu, A-pa areas):
   Tibetan
South (Liang-shan): Yi

Tsinghai
West (Kuo-lo, Yu-shu): Ti-
   betan
Northwest (Hai-hsi): Mongol,
   Kazakh, Tibetan
East (Hai-pei, Hai-nan, Huang-
   nan): Tibetan
Yunnan (Shan)
South: Thai, Chingpo, Hani, Yi
Northwest: Lisu, Tibetan
West: Pai, Thai, Chingpo, Chu-
   ang, Miao
Central: Yi

Notes

---◄ ► ►---

Abbreviations used are as follows:

C.Q.: *China Quarterly*, London.
C.R.: *China Reconstructs*, F.L.P.
F.L.P.: Foreign Languages Press, Peking.
J.T.T.B.: *Journey to the Beginning*, Random House, N.Y., 1958; Gollancz, London, 1959.
N.C.N.A.: New China News Agency (*Hsin Hua Hsin-wen Shih*).
P.D.: *People's Daily* (*Jen-min Jih-pao*), official newspaper, Peking.
P.R.: *Peking Review*, F.L.P.
R.S.O.C.: *Red Star Over China*, Gollancz, London, 1937; Random House, N.Y., 1938; reprint, Grove Press, N.Y., 1961.
S.W.: *Selected Works of Mao Tse-tung*, Vols. I, II, III and IV. F.L.P., 1961.
T.B.F.A.: *The Battle for Asia*, Random House, N.Y., 1941.
T.Gl.Y.: *Ten Glorious Years*, 19 articles and speeches by leaders of the party and government. F.L.P., 1960.
T.G.Y.: *Ten Great Years*, Statistics of the Economic and Cultural Achievements of the People's Republic of China, Compiled by the State Statistical Bureau, F.L.P., 1960.

Many but not all of my excerpts from translations of the Chinese press and magazines derive from services published by the United States Consulate General of Hongkong, namely: *Survey of the China Mainland Press* (*S.C.M.P.*), and *Current Background and Extracts from China Mainland Magazines.*

INTRODUCTION

1. N.Y., 1958; London, 1959.
2. London, 1937; N.Y., 1938, 1961.
3. George F. Kennan, *Russia and the West Under Lenin and Stalin*, Boston, 1961, p. 276.
4. Before the Seminar on the American Character, at the Center for Study of Democratic Institutions, Washington, May 29, 1961. Quoted in *I. F. Stone's Weekly*, June 5, 1961.

PART ONE · *Rediscovering China*

Ch. 1. Arrival in Peking

1. See *T.B.F.A.*

Ch. 4. Confucius to Mao

1. *T.G.Y.*, p. 8: area 9,597,000 sq. kil.

2. U.S. Statistical Abstract, 1961, p. 618.
3. For a brief, excellent review and evaluation of Chinese civilization consult Derk Bodde, *China's Cultural Tradition*, N.Y., 1957.
4. *Chinese Thought from Confu-*

cius to Mao Tse-tung, Chicago, 1953; reprint, N.Y., 1960, p. 32.
5. R.S.O.C., p. 134.
6. S.W., Vol. IV.
7. Kennan, op. cit., p. 275.

Ch. 5. Paotou Retrospect

1. See Alley's *Sandan*, Caxton Press, Christchurch, N.Z., 1959, for his story of an inspiring adventure in creative education.
2. J.T.T.B. contains an account of my adventures with Mr. Wu.

Ch. 6. Steel in Mongolia

1. See R.S.O.C.

Ch. 7. White Cloud

1. Mr. Alley's *China's Hinterland*, F.L.P., 1961, covers his latest travels through eighteen provinces and is an enormously informative guide to recent changes.

Ch. 8. Mongol Commune

1. See "Cultural Changes in Inner Mongolia," by Li Fang, in the P.R., Feb. 10, 1961.

Ch. 9. Why China Went Red

1. Some passages in this chapter have been borrowed from J.T.T.B., with no apologies to the author.
2. Edgar Snow, *Random Notes on Red China*, Cambridge, Mass., 1957.
3. For interesting comparisons between present-day Chinese Communist philosophy and bureaucratic sanctions, and Confucian and neo-Confucian techniques of power, consult *A History of Chinese Philosophy*, by Fung Yu-lan, translated by Derk Bodde, Princeton University Press, 1952; and *The United States and China*, by John K. Fairbank, Harvard University

Press, Cambridge, 1948, 1958.
4. T.B.F.A., p. 290. Cf. "That 'Agrarian Reformer' Myth" in J.T.T.B.
5. J.T.T.B., ibid.

Ch. 10. Aboard the Premier's Special Train

1. T.B.F.A.
2. Ibid.

Ch. 11. New Shores on Ancient Mountains

1. Cressey, *China's Geographic Foundations*, N.Y., 1934.
2. T.G.Y., p. 128.

Ch. 12. Chou En-lai and America

1. *United States Relations With China*, With Special Reference to the Period 1944-49, Washington, August, 1949.
2. See Allen S. Whiting, *China Crosses the Yalu: The Decision to Enter the Korean War*, N.Y., 1960.

Ch. 13. Table Talk

1. S.W., Vol. IV, p. 99.

Ch. 14. Sino-Russian "Differences"

1. Some obsolete material is here omitted. For full text of this interview see *Look*, January 31, 1961.
2. H. Arthur Steiner has made some interesting contributions on this point, e.g., "Ideology Vs. National Interest in Chinese Foreign Policy," a paper presented at the University of Hongkong Golden Jubilee Congress, Sept. 11-16, 1961.

Ch. 15. New China Hands

1. *When Serfs Stood Up in Tibet*, New World Press, Peking, 1960.
2. Mr. Greene's book, *Awakened China*, was published in 1961 by Doubleday, N.Y.

PART TWO · *Where the Waves Beat*

Ch. 16. The Big Change

1. In a speech made in Peking, July 1, 1951, as reported in *Current Background*, No. 89, July 5, 1951. Italics added.

Ch. 18. Flashback to Pao-an

1. *An Analysis of Classes in Chinese Society* (1926), F.L.P., 1956.
2. *Report on An Investigation Into the Peasant Movement in Hunan* (1927), F.L.P., 1953.
3. *Ibid.*
4. See, for example, exchanges between Prof. Benjamin Schwartz and Dr. Karl August Wittfogel in *C.Q.*, Nos. 1, 2, 3.

Ch. 19. The Long March

1. *On the Tactics of Fighting Japanese Imperialism* was a series of political lectures delivered in Pao-an in 1935 (F.L.P., 1953); a year later Mao evolved the military strategy in another series of lectures published in Yenan, May, 1938: *Strategic Problems in China's Revolutionary War*, followed shortly by *On the Protracted War*, (1938), both published by F.L.P., 1953. *On Coalition Government*, 1945 (F.L.P., 1955), completed Mao's major writings during the Patriotic War.
2. Mao rewrote this poem in the more classical form in which it appears, entitled, "The Long March," in his *Poems*, Peking, 1959.

Ch. 20. Power Personality

1. *S.W.*, Vol. IV; and Anne Freemantle, *Mao Tse-tung: An Anthology of His Writings*, "Strategic Problems . . . ," N.Y., 1962, p. 77.
2. *S.W.*, Vol. IV, p. 380.
3. *S.W.*, Vol. IV, pp. 185, 202, 215.

4. *Report on an Investigation . . . ,* p. 10. The virtues listed were attributed to Confucius by a disciple.
5. *S.W.*, Vol. III.

Ch. 21. Mao at Home

1. Considerable confusion has been created concerning the account of Mao Tse-tung's early life story as told to me, which was Part Four ("Genesis of a Communist") of *Red Star Over China* (London, October, 1937; N.Y., January, 1938). To clarify: I wrote up part of my notes of my trip to the Northwest late in 1936, and early in 1937 gave copies of my newspaper articles to Chinese professors in Peking who brought out a volume in Chinese called *Chung Kuo Hsi-pei Yin-Hsiang Chi*, or *Impressions of Northwest China*. In July, 1937, I gave a copy of the completed manuscript of *R.S.O.C.* to a team of Chinese professors and writers who were members of the National Salvation Association, to which I granted translation rights gratis on condition that book earnings were to be contributed to the Chinese Red Cross. The translated volume, called *Hsi-Hsing Man-Chi, Travels in the West*, appeared in 1937 and is the only authorized Chinese version of *R.S.O.C.* The book was immediately pirated in China—in English, as were most foreign books in those days. Later on (1938), Part Four of *R.S.O.C.* was pirated in a Chinese version, which appeared in Canton under the title *The Autobiography of Mao Tse-tung*. Some Western scholars have translated the Canton piracy back into English, and thus established for themselves "a new source." For example, *Mao Tse-tung and I Were Beg-*

gars, by Saio-yu (published in the United States in 1959), contains a long commentary by Robert North which, alternately quoting (unauthorized) excerpts from *R.S.O.C.* and from the so-called *Autobiography of Mao Tse-tung*, states that the latter is a quite independent "source . . . in the Chinese language." (I was placed in the awkward position of appearing to be stealing material from one self without giving acknowledgment to

the other self—or pirating a piracy of my own work.) Mao Tse-tung has never written an "autobiography" nor authorized any "life" account except my own. Both authorized and unauthorized versions of *R.S.O.C.* are out of print in China, although copies are occasionally found in bookstores.

2. Mao Tse-tung, *Poems*.
3. *On the Correct Handling of Contradictions Among the People*, F.L.P., 1957.

PART THREE · *Socialist Construction*

Ch. 22. Steel Decade

1. T. J. Hughes and D. E. T. Luard, *The Economic Development of Communist China, 1949-1958*, (London, 1959), p. 24, put the prewar average at two-thirds of an acre.
2. Quoted in Ygael Gluckstein, *Mao's China*, Boston, 1957, p. 23, from *Chinese Farm Economy*, Chicago, 1930.
3. Quoted in George Babcock Cressey, *op. cit.*, p. 100.
4. Hughes and Luard, *op. cit.*, p. 6.
5. "On Cooperatives," N.C.N.A. Peking, July 31, 1955.
6. U.S. Statistical Abstract, 1961, pp. 318, 619, 207.
7. Betty Feinberg, "Report on the AAAS [American Association for the Advancement of Science] Symposium [on the Sciences in Communist China]," *C.Q.*, No. 6, April-June, 1961, pp. 93-94. Italics added.
8. *T.G.Y.*, p. 14.
9. *Op. cit.*, p. 8.
10. *Foreign Affairs* magazine, N.Y., April, 1960.
11. Special Supplement No. 59, March, 1960. U.S. Dept. of the Interior, Bureau of Mines, Washington, D.C. Italics added.

Ch. 23. Reeling, Writhing and Arithmetic

1. *Atlantic Monthly*, Dec., 1959.

2. Charles Bettelheim, *Economic Weekly*, Bombay, Nov., 1958.
3. René Dumont, *Le Monde*, Paris, Oct. 12, 1958.
4. T'ang Ming-chao and Dr. Ch'i Chao-ting.
5. Dr. Chen Han-seng, a Harvard graduate and normally a cautious scholar, summed up his observations after a tour in Kansu province, early in 1960, as follows: "The ten-year socialist reconstruction of our country has eliminated *all three factors* that gave rise to the widespread grain-hunger under Kuomintang rule." The "three factors" listed by Dr. Chen were "low productivity, irrational distribution, and *natural calamities.*" *China Reconstructs*, July, 1960. Italics added.
6. W. W. Hollister, *China's Gross National Product and Social Accounts, 1950-1957* (Center for International Studies, M.I.T., Boston), Glencoe, Ill., 1958, p. xix.

Ch. 24. Of Leaps Forward

1. Li Fu-ch'un, "The First Five-Year Plan," *Ta Kung Pao*, Tientsin, Sept. 16, 1953.
2. U.S. Statistical Abstract, 1961, p. 872.
3. Hollister, *op. cit.*
4. Tibor Mende, *China and Her*

Shadow, N.Y., 1962, p. 35.

5. *P.R.*, Nov. 24, 1959.
6. Li Hsien-nien, *P.R.*, April 5, 1960.
7. *T.G.Y.*, p. 103.
8. Hollister, *op. cit.*, p. 4.
9. *Ibid.*, p. 5.
10. *Ibid.*, p. 141.
11. *Ibid.*, p. 132.
12. Chairman Liu Shao-ch'i in *T.G.Y.*, p. 2.
13. Quoted in Li Choh-ming (Univ. of California, Berkeley), "The First Decade: Economic Development," *C.Q.*, No. 1, Jan.-March, 1960.
14. *P.R.*, April 5, 1960.
15. The *N.Y. Times*, July 4, 1961, in a report by Harry Schwartz, quoted *Ekonimicheskaya Gazeta*, Moscow, on the Chinese industrial output figures for 1960 which are used here.
16. *T.G.Y.*, p. 95.
17. *N.Y. Times, op. cit.* Earlier, Peking officials gave the figure 18,450,000 tons (*P.R.*, Jan. 27, 1961), which was the exact target for 1960. The British Iron and Steel Institute estimate of 17,000,000 tons was reported in a UPI dispatch from London in the *N.Y. Herald Tribune*, March 24, 1961.
18. *N.Y. Times, op. cit.* All 1960 figures quoted here are from this source unless stated otherwise.
19. Western European and U.S. figures from *N.Y. Herald Tribune*, Paris, July 5, 1961.
20. *T.Gl.Y.*, p. 62.
21. The 1959 figures are from Li Fu-ch'un, *op. cit.*; the 1960 figures are from the *N.Y. Times*, *op. cit.*
22. *N.Y. Times, op. cit.*

Ch. 25. And Leaps Backward

1. A. Doak Barnett, *Communist China and Asia: Challenge to American Policy*, N.Y., 1960, p. 402.
2. "U.S. Government Foreign Grants and Credits," U.S. Statistical Abstract, 1961, pp. 875-879.
3. *N.Y. Times*, May 9, 1962.
4. Li Choh-ming, *op. cit.* Italics added. Li Choh-ming's *The Statistical System of China* (Berkeley, 1962) helps to explain Chinese overestimates of capacity to invest in capital construction in 1959-61 as well as reasons for the 1958 aberrations. It appeared too late for its assessments to be fully reflected in this volume.
5. *Ibid.* Italics added.
6. Li Hsien-nien, *op. cit.* Budget figures here are from Li Fu-ch'un, *op. cit.*, and Li Hsien-nien.
7. *P.R.*, Jan. 27, 1961.
8. *Ibid.* Italics added.

Ch. 26. Yao Wei and Private Enterprise

1. *S.W.*, Vol. IV, p. 207. Italics added.
2. *Ibid.*, p. 209.
3. Hughes and Luard, *op. cit.*; and Robert Loh, *Atlantic Monthly*, Dec., 1959, p. 84.
4. *S.W.*, Vol. IV, p. 203.
5. See Hughes and Luard, *op. cit.*, pp. 83-95, for a more extended discussion of "The Treatment of Private Enterprise."
6. *Ibid.*
7. *Ta Kung Pao*, Hongkong, June 1, 1961. *S.C.M.P.*, No. 2552.
8. See *J.T.T.B.*, p. 17.
9. *Atlantic Monthly*, Dec., 1959.

Ch. 27. Manchuria: Industrial Heartland

1. Charles B. MacLane, *Soviet Policy and the Chinese Communists, 1941-46*, N.Y., 1958, pp. 235-238; and Edgar Snow, "Honorable Spoils Rot in Japan," *Saturday Evening Post*, June 14, 1946.
2. "The United States and China," an address given before the China Institute, New York City, May 18, 1951. Reprinted by the Committee of One Million, 1961.
3. René Grousset, *Histoire de la Chine*, Paris, 1941, pp. 178ff.

Ch. 29. High Society

1. Hu Chang-tu, editor, *China, Its People, Its Society, Its Culture,* New Haven, 1960.
2. *P.D.,* Oct. 6, 1959.

Ch. 30. Science and Education

1. General Electric Co., *TEMPO: Science and Technology in Communist China* (RM60TMP-72), by John Berberet, Santa Barbara, 1960, p. 110. An excellent general compilation of materials on education and scientific capabilities.
2. John M. H. Lindbeck, "The Organization and Development of Science," a report presented to the Symposium on the Sciences in Communist China, sponsored by the American Association for the Advancement of Science, Dec., 1960. *C.Q.,* No. 6, April-June, 1961.
3. General Electric Co., *op. cit.,* p. 57.
4. Olga Lang, *Chinese Family and Society,* New Haven, 1946, p. 73.
5. On August 26, 1960.
6. *Professional Manpower and Education in China,* U.S. Government Printing Office, 1961, p. 13. Includes tables on educational enrollment at all levels, names and locations of institutes of higher learning and scientific research, specializations offered in those institutes, regulations governing enrollment, detailed outlines of examinations held in various branches of mathematics and the sciences, evaluative surveys of professional man power and its distribution, and of population and the available labor force. Mr. Orleans' work is mandatory reading for any deeper study of a cultural revolution which must soon engage the close attention of pedagogues throughout the world. If the reader who consults this source finds contradictions between its figures, estimates and judgments and my own, the explanation is at least partly indicated in Mr. Orleans' prefatory notes and side remarks concerning the difficulties of reconciling and unifying various sets of Chinese statistics.

7. U.S. Statistical Abstract, 1961, pp. 921, 942.
8. During the Great Leap Forward, in 1958, it is said to have fallen as low as 40 percent.
9. N.C.N.A., May 12, 1960. Italics added.
10. Peking, May 7, 1961.
11. Joseph C. Kun, *C.Q.,* No. 8, Oct.-Dec., 1961, contains a more detailed study of "Higher Education: Some Problems of Selection and Enrollment."

Ch. 31. "Ministry" of Spare-Time Education

1. Quoted in Ygael Gluckstein, *op. cit.*
2. N.C.N.A., Aug. 10, 1955, quoted *ibid.*
3. Jan. 21, 1955, quoted *ibid.*
4. N.C.N.A., June 26, 1956, quoted *ibid.*
5. *P.D.,* April 9, 1960.
6. *On the Correct Handling . . . ,* pp. 60-61. Italics added.

Ch. 34. Swan Lake in Peking

1. Chinese title for *R.S.O.C.*

Ch. 35. Doctor Horse

1. *R.S.O.C.* and *J.T.T.B.*

Ch. 36. Sino-American Romance

1. For a dramatic account of Dr. Bethune's life and work, see Ted Allan and Sydney Gordon, *The Scalpel and the Sword,* Boston, 1952.

Ch. 40. The Family: Fact and Fancy

1. Quoted in Lang, *op. cit.,* p. 112ff., from Hu Shih, *The Chinese Renaissance,* Chicago, 1934.

2. *Ibid.*, p. 113.
3. Now in English. See Bibliography, Chinese Publications.
4. Lang, *op. cit.*, p. 108.
5. *Ibid.*, p. 16.
6. Hu Chang-tu, *op. cit.*, p. 173.
7. *Ibid.*
8. *United States Relations with China,* With Special Reference to the Period 1944-1949, Washington, 1949; and *Foreign Relations of the United States, 1943, China,* Washington, 1957.
9. Denis Lazure, M.D., "The Family and Youth in New China: Psychiatric Observations," *Canadian Medical Association Journal,* Montreal, Jan. 27, 1962, Vol. 86.

Ch. 41. Medical History, Personal and Otherwise

1. *Lancet,* London, Nov. 9, 16, 23, 1957.
2. For Dr. W. Y. Chen's condensed report, from which all these quotations are taken, see "Medicine and Public Health," *C.Q.,* No. 6, April-June, 1961. Italics added.
3. Dr. R. K. S. Lim and Dr. C. C.

Chen, "State Medicine," *Chinese Medical Journal,* 1937. Cited in Dr. W. Y. Chen's report.
4. The figure "467,000 beds" probably included those of many primitive commune clinics and health stations. In 1959 Premier Chou En-lai reported only "775 hospitals and sanatoria with over 34,000 beds; in addition there were over 14,000 clinics and health centers" (*T.Gl.Y.*, p. 44). But in 1960 the State Statistical Bureau reported that "maternity clinics established in the countryside by the people's communes" had by the end of 1958 reached "134,000, with 416,000 beds [!!]." (*T.G.Y.*, p. 221).
5. *New Scientist,* London, Dec. 31, 1957.

Ch. 42. From John D. to Acupuncture

1. W. Y. Chen, *op. cit.*
2. *Ibid.* Italics added.
3. *Ibid.*
4. *Observer,* London, Oct. 22, 1961.
5. *Ibid.*

PART FOUR · *The Democratic Dictatorship*

Ch. 43. State and Superstructure

1. *S.W.,* Vol. II, 2nd ed., Peking, 1952.
2. *S.W.,* Vol. III, Peking, 1953.
3. See *Electoral Law of the People's Republic of China,* F.L.P., 1953.
4. *On the Correct Handling* . . .
5. A brief biographical sketch and an account of Mme. Sun's activities in the Communist revolution appear in *J.T.T.B.*
6. This is a rough estimate used by Communist officials. For detailed discussion of scientifically and technically trained personnel available in China at the time of the take-over in 1949 see John M. H. Lindbeck, *op. cit.*

Ch. 44. The 800

1. Speech delivered before the Eighth National Congress of the C.C.P., Sept. 16, 1956. F.L.P., 1956. Italics added.
2. *Ibid.* Italics added.
3. *The Historical Experience of the Dictatorship of the Proletariat,* F.L.P., 1959. The first article was published in the *People's Daily,* April 5, 1956, some weeks after the Politburo meeting on which it was "based." The second originally appeared Dec. 29, 1956.
4. See Nym Wales, *Inside Red China,* N.Y., 1939, and *Red Dust,* Stanford, 1955; Agnes Smedley, *The Great Road,* a

biography of Chu Teh, N.Y., 1956.

5. "From that time on to the defeat of the first great revolution [1927] Liu Shao-ch'i led the revolutionary trade union movement in China," according to an official sketch in Liu's *Internationalism and Nationalism*, F.L.P., 1951, N.Y., 1952.

6. *S.W.*, Vol. IV, pp. 231-232.

7. Both published, along with other writings of Liu Shao-ch'i, by F.L.P., 1951; also *On Inner Party Struggle*, N.Y., 1952.

8. F.L.P.

9. N.C.N.A., Nov. 23, 1949.

Ch. 45. The Party and the People

1. In an address commemorating the 40th anniversary of the C.C.P., *P.R.*, No. 26-27, 1961.

2. "Almost all [expert analyses] yield a 1958 population estimate within the range of 650,000,000 plus or minus 25,000,000," according to John S. Aird of the U.S. Bureau of Census. Cited in *C.Q.*, No. 7, July-Sept., 1961.

3. Report before the Eighth National Congress of the C.C.P., Sept. 16, 1956. F.L.P., 1956, p. 91.

4. Li Hsien-nien, *P.R.*, April 6, 1960. Italics added.

5. Li Fu-ch'un, *op. cit.*

6. See example in "Report of the Northeastern Bureau, C.C., C.C.P.," *P.D.*, Jan. 24, 1952.

Ch. 46. Security

1. My correspondence on this subject with *Time* and the State Department is open to inspection.

Ch. 47. "Slave Labor"

1. Forced Labour, Supplement: Report of the I.L.O. on Forced Labour, Geneva, 1957.

2. Hu Chang-tu, *op. cit.*, pp. 304-306.

3. *P.D.*, Aug. 4, 1957, contains the full text of the law.

4. *P.D.*, Aug. 26, 1954.

5. *P.D.*, Sept. 7, 1954.

6. *White Book on Forced Labor in the People's Republic of China*, Commission Internationale Contre le Régime Concentrationaire, Paris, 1956.

7. *Ibid.*, Vol. II, pp. 193-194.

8. *J.T.T.B.*, pp. 52-53.

9. Lang, *op. cit.*

10. *Foreign Relations of the United States, 1943, China*, Washington, 1957, pp. 391-393.

Ch. 48. Hsueh-Hsi and Reform-Through-Labor

1. R. J. Lifton, *Thought Reform and the Psychology of Totalism: A Study of "Brainwashing,"* N.Y., 1961.

2. "Thought Reform: Ideological Remolding in China," *Atlantic Monthly*, Dec., 1959.

3. Allyn and Adele Rickett, *Prisoners of Liberation*, N.Y., 1957.

4. Harold W. Rigney, *Four Years in a Red Hell: The Story of Father Rigney*, Chicago, 1956.

Ch. 50. Prelude to the Hundred Flowers

1. See Roderick MacFarquhar, *The Hundred Flowers*, London, 1960 (published N.Y., 1960, under the title *The Hundred Flowers Campaign and the Chinese Intellectuals*). This compilation is a basic and invaluable reference work of the period.

2. *P.D.*, April 11, 1955. Italics added.

3. N.C.N.A., Jan. 29, 1956.

4. Lu Ting-yi, *Let a Hundred Flowers Blossom, a Hundred Schools of Thought Contend*, Peking, 1958. Lu's original speech was delivered May 26, 1956.

5. March 26, 1956.

6. N.C.N.A., July 17, 1956. Italics added.

7. May 17, 1956.

Ch. 51. Unity-Criticism-Unity

1. Tung Chih-ming, *An Outline History of China*, F.L.P., 1958, p. 403.
2. *On the Correct Handling . . . ,* pp. 9-10.
3. *The Way of Chinese Painting,* by Mai-Mai Sze (N.Y., 1956; reprint, N.Y., 1960), contains a brilliantly lucid discussion of these analogies.
4. *On Contradiction* (1942), F.L.P., 1958.
5. *Ibid.*
6. In *Rectify the Party's Style in Work*, which launched the party rectification movement of Feb., 1942, Mao wrote: "Our party members must realize the truth that they are always a minority compared with non-party people . . . [It is] utterly impossible to . . . attain the goals of the revolution unless the Communists are united with the non-party cadres and the people." F.L.P., 1953; see also *S.W.*, Vol. III.
7. Extracts are all from *On the Correct Handling. . . .* Italics added.

8. *Ibid.*, pp. 55-56.
9. See Sydney Gruson's Warsaw dispatch to the *N.Y. Times,* June 13, 1957.
10. *On the Correct Handling . . . ,* pp. 66-67.

Ch. 52. Wild Flowers

1. I am especially indebted to Clare McDermott, Reuters correspondent in Peking, who made available his file on the period.
2. *P.D.*, March 23, 1957.
3. N.C.N.A., Aug. 6, 1957.

Ch. 53. Counterattack and Paradox

1. Chou Ching-wen, N.Y., 1960.
2. *Ch'ang Chiang Daily*, Hankow.
3. *P.D.*, June 16, 1957. Italics added.
4. The interview was reported in Mr. Greene's book, *Awakened China,* N.Y., 1961.
5. Chou Ching-wen, *op. cit.*
6. MacFarquhar, *op. cit.*
7. F.L.P., Jan. 14, 1956.
8. *People's Daily*, Kaifeng, July 4, 1957.

PART FIVE · *Northwest: Old Cradle of New China*

Ch. 54. Of Blue Ants and White

1. Cambridge, Mass., 1959.
2. *Op. cit.*, p. 353.
3. Lang, *op. cit.*, p. 153.
4. Hu Chang-tu, *op. cit.*, p. 54.
5. *Look,* Jan. 31, 1961. p. 921.
7. Selected data from Japan Statistical Year Book, Bureau of Statistics, Tokyo, 1959.

Ch. 55. Co-ops to Communes

1. *People's Communes in China,* "Resolution of the Central Committee of the C.C.P. on the Establishment of People's Communes in the Rural Areas," F.L.P., 1958.

2. *Ibid.* Italics added.
3. *Ibid.*, Wu Chih-pu, "From Agricultural People's Communes Producers Cooperatives to People's Communes."
4. *The Question of Agricultural Cooperation,* July 31, 1955, F.L.P., 1956, p. 34. Italics added.
5. *Ibid.*, p. 34. Italics added.
6. *T.G.Y.*, p. 27. *Cf.* figures in Hu Chang-tu, *op. cit.*, pp. 337-340.
7. *S.W.*, Vol. IV, 1960, p. 229.
8. See *T.B.F.A.*, p. 322.

Ch. 56. At Whose Demand?

1. *People's Handbook* (for 1958), Peking, 1958. Italics added. This excerpt is taken from the article "The First Decade: Economic

Development," by Li Choh-ming, *C.Q.*, No. 1, Jan.-March, 1960, to which I am much indebted for both facts and interpretation in discussing this period.

2. Princeton, N.J., 1962, pp. 66ff.
3. Quoted in Ygael Gluckstein, *op. cit.*, p. 23.
4. N.C.N.A., July 25, 1957.
5. Quoted in John Philip Emerson, "Manpower Absorption," *C.Q.*, No. 7, July-Sept., 1961. Italics added.
6. *Ibid.*
7. From 1958 to 1961 "the population in the cities and in the industrial and mining districts . . . increased by 20 millions." *Ta Kung Pao*, Peking, Feb. 2, 1961.
8. *People's Communes . . .* , Wu Chih-pu, *op. cit.*
9. *Ibid.*
10. In *People's Communes . . .*
11. *The Question of Agricultural Cooperation.*
12. *Life*, Jan. 12, 1959.
13. J. V. Stalin, "Report on the Work of the Central Committee to the 17th Congress of the CPSU." *Selected Writings*, N.Y., 1942, p. 343.

Ch. 57. Communes to Brigadunes

1. Li Choh-ming, *op. cit.*
2. *P.D.*, Nov. 5, 1961.
3. *Ibid.*
4. *Ta Kung Pao*, Peking, Feb. 22, 1962.

Ch. 59. A Commune That Worked

1. *Ta Kung Pao*, Peking, Feb. 22, 1962.

Ch. 60. Sian: "Western Peace"

1. *Wall Street Journal*, Aug. 20, 1960.
2. A dispatch in the *N.Y. Herald Tribune* datelined Tokyo, March 22, 1962, quoted a N.C.N.A. report that the capital of the Ch'in Dynasty had been unearthed six miles northeast of the modern city of Sienyang, fifty miles from Sian.
3. April 3, 1962.

61. Museum of the Revolution

1. *S.W.*, Vol. IV, will be of interest to those who want a full discussion from Mao himself.
2. *S.W.*, Vol. IV, p. 130, contains abundant data on Mao's directives in this period.
3. These were basic tactics used by Cuban revolutionary leaders; internal evidence in Che Guevara's book, *Guerrilla Warfare* (N.Y., 1960), suggests that he and Castro were both students of Mao's works.

Ch. 62. Yenan Teachers College

1. Quoted in Robert D. Barendson, "The Agricultural Middle Schools," *C.Q.*, No. 8, Oct.-Dec., 1961, which provides a historical review and much general data.
2. *Ibid.*
3. *Ibid.* For more recent information see "New Developments in Agricultural Middle Schools in China," N.C.N.A., Nov. 24, 1961.
4. *Ibid.*
5. *Nan-fang Jih-pao*, Feb. 15, 1962.
6. *Ibid.*
7. N.C.N.A., Feb. 7, 1962.
8. Barendson, *op. cit.*
9. N.C.N.A., Jan. 11, 1962.

Ch. 63. Pride of Poor Men

1. From charts used by Adelle Davis, "Table of Food Analysis," *Vitality Through Planned Nutrition*, N.Y., 1949; and "Nutritive Value of Selected Foods," U.S. Dept. of Agriculture, World Almanac, N.Y., 1961.

Ch. 64. Willow Grove

1. In "Introducing a Cooperative," *Red Flag*, June 1, 1958, Mao Tse-tung discussed views which must have been formed during his Honan tour in April. He did not use the word "commune," but here employed the now famous "poor and blank" metaphor. China's people, said Mao, are

"first of all poor and secondly blank. This seems a bad thing but in fact it is a good thing. Poor people want change, want to do things, want revolution. A clean sheet of paper has nothing on it, so that the newest and most beautiful words can be written and the newest and most beautiful pictures painted on it."

2. See "Balance in Agriculture and Industry," by Yang Chien-pai and Hsu Ping-wen, Tientsin *Ta Kung Pao,* May 22, 1961.
3. *On the Correct Handling . . . ,* p. 37.
4. *N.Y. Herald Tribune,* Nov. 19, 1959. Italics added.
5. *Ibid.,* May 12, 1961.

Ch. 65. The Refugee as Source Material

1. Quoted in Felix Greene, *op. cit.,* p. 335.
2. N.C.N.A., March 16, 1962. *S.C.M.P.,* No. 2704.

3. U.S. Statistical Abstract, 1961, pp. 93-94.
4. N.Y., 1959.
5. *N.Y. Times,* June 2, 1962.

Ch. 66. The Yellow River Turns Blue

1. N.C.N.A., March 4, 1962.
2. N.C.N.A., Feb. 6, 1962.
3. N.C.N.A., Feb. 10, 1962.
4. See Chang Chao, "China's Fast-Growing Tree Cover," in *China Reconstructs,* Peking, Sept. 20, 1960.
5. F.L.P., 1961.

Ch. 67. The Grandest Coolie

1. For further details see Teng Tse-hui, *Report on the Multiple-Purpose Plan for Controlling the Yellow River and Exploiting Its Resources,* Peking, 1955.
2. General Electric Co., *op. cit.*
3. U.S. output in 1960 was 174,-998,000 kilowatts, that of the U.S.S.R. 59,140,000. Figures from World Almanac, N.Y., 1961.

PART SIX · Shanghai and Beyond

Ch. 72. God and Party

1. Grousset, *op. cit.*
2. The Quaker report on China is available from the Society of Friends, Philadelphia or London.
3. In 1961 the International Fides Service of the Vatican reported: "A very feeble number of priests surround the 35 illegitimate ["Patriotic Chinese Catholic"] bishops. Certain ones seem to be completely blinded and drawn by false patriotism but others are suffering and would turn back if they had the occasion or the courage." U.P.I., Rome, Sept. 13, 1961.
4. Hu Chang-tu, *op. cit.*
5. *Ibid.*
6. MacFarquhar, *op. cit.,* p. 253.
7. N.C.N.A., Jan. 23, 1962.
8. *Ibid.*

9. See *J.T.T.B.*
10. *The Communist Persuasion: A Personal Experience in Brain Washing,* N.Y., 1958. See also further comment by Mary C. Wright, *Pacific Affairs,* N.Y., April, 1960.

Ch. 73. Literature and Music

1. F.L.P., 1956.
2. See *J.T.T.B.*

Ch. 74. Crime and Punishment

1. See, for example, *China Shakes the World,* by Jack Belden, N.Y., 1949.

Ch. 75. The Triple Cities

1. Gilbert Etienne, of the Graduate Institute of International Studies, Geneva, in a conversation in

Nov., 1961. See his *La Voie Chinoise*, Paris, 1962, for details.

Ch. 76. Szechuan, "The Heavenly Land"

1. Wu Chun-hung, *A Simple Geography of China*, F.L.P., 1958, puts the area at 570,000 square kilometers.
2. Cressey, *op. cit.*, p. 320.
3. Rewi Alley, *China's Hinterland*, p. 422.
4. Wu Chun-hung, *op. cit.*, p. 183.
5. Alley, *op. cit.*, p. 423.
6. *Ibid.*, p. 422.
7. Cressey, *op. cit.*, p. 317.
8. *Ibid.*, p. 316.
9. Alley, *op. cit.*
10. Private letter from Clare McDermott, Peking.

Ch. 77. A Few Words on Tibet

1. *When Serfs Stood Up in Tibet*, New World Press, Peking, 1960.
2. *Foreign Relations of the United States, 1943, China*, Washington, 1957, p. 728.

3. *Ibid.*, p. 630.
4. The 1953 census gave the population of Tibet as 1,273,000, but there were 2,755,000 Tibetan-speaking persons, including 800,000 in Sikang (now part of Szechuan), 450,000 in Chinghai, and 200,000 in Kansu. The Tibetans have had a written language since the seventh century and have "one of the best developed cultures among the national minorities of China." Theodore Shabad, *China's Changing Map*, N.Y., 1956, pp. 40-44.
5. *Kuang-ming Jih-pao*, March 3, 1962.
6. *Look* magazine, Jan. 31, 1961. For full text of my second interview with Chou En-lai, see Appendix, in this volume, p. 758.

Ch. 78. National Minorities

1. *T.G.Y.*, p. 199.

Ch. 79. South of the Clouds

1. Alley, *op. cit.*, pp. 391-400.

PART SEVEN · *The Long March Ahead*

Ch. 80. 1962: The Year the Chinese Vanished

1. Home and Garden Bulletin, No. 72, U.S. Dept. of Agriculture. World Almanac, N.Y., 1962.
2. In a speech at Leicester. Communiqué issued by the Press Dept., Conservative Central Office, Westminster, London, Nov. 10, 1961.
3. Parliamentary Debates, Vol. 632, No. 30, Dec. 12, 1960. Italics added.
4. *N.Y. Herald Tribune*, April 16, 1962. Italics added.
5. *Ibid.*, May 31, 1962. Italics added.

Ch. 81. Facts About Food

1. There was certainly some starvation in the first years of the P.R.C.; after 1954, no further incidents were reported, until 1957. In June of that year it was revealed by press reports that 14,700 Kwangsi peasants caught in a severe drought in 1956 had been transported but not until 550 of their number had died of starvation. It was a major public scandal; senior officials of the province and responsible party members were reported dismissed and punished for concealing the facts.
2. While noting signs of possible malnutrition such as "ballooning stomachs," "thin breasts" and "meagre bodies" of the "Asian norm," Mr. Etienne wrote: "It may be said at the outset—and it is one of the rare points where we have the pretension to be

categorical—that it is false to speak of 'general famine.' The dolorous times of the Kuomintang, when millions of human lives were eliminated for want of minimum subsistence, have not reappeared." *Le Monde*, December 12, 1961.

3. In personal letters.

4. Personal letter, Nyon, Switzerland, June 27, 1962. Dr. Forel comes from one of Switzerland's distinguished families. He is also a Communist.

5. Hu Chang-tu, *op. cit.*, p. 397.

6. "Proportional Relationship Between Industry and Agriculture," *Ta Kung Pao*, Peking, Feb. 2, 1961.

7. William Kaye, "The State of Nutrition in Communist China," *C.Q.*, No. 7, July-Sept., 1961.

8. *T.G.Y.*, p. 119.

9. William Kaye, "Communist China's Agricultural Calamities," *C.Q.*, No. 6, April-June, 1961.

10. *Sunday Times*, London, Oct. 15, 1961.

11. "Report on China's Economic Plan," F.L.P., 1960.

12. "Proportional Relationship . . ."

13. *C.Q.*, No. 6, April-June, 1961.

14. Kaye, "The State of Nutrition . . ."

15. *Ibid.*

16. *N.Y. Times*, June 10, 1961.

17. Gilbert Etienne, *De Caboul à Pékin*, Geneva, 1959, Ch. IV.

18. *Eastern Economist*, New Delhi, May 1, 1962.

Ch. 82. China, the United States, Russia and the Bomb

1. U.S. Policy Statement on China, *N.Y. Times*, Aug. 10, 1958.

2. *N.Y. Times*, Sept. 5, 1958.

3. *Ibid.*

4. *N.Y. Times*, Sept. 9, 1958.

5. Demaree Bess, *Saturday Evening Post*, March 21, 1959.

6. Agnes Smedley, *The Great Road*, N.Y., 1936, p. 331.

7. S.W., London, Vol. II, p. 272, as quoted in *T.Gl.Y.*, p. 86.

8. For a discussion of Moscow's role in the release of Chiang Kai-shek in 1936, see "New Data on the Sian Incident," in my *Random Notes on Red China*, Cambridge, Mass., 1957, pp. 1-11.

9. See Dedijer, *op. cit.*, p. 322.

10. *N.Y. Times*, Aug. 18, 1958.

11. General Electric Co., *op. cit.*, p. 110.

12. *Ibid.*, p. 123. Italics added.

Ch. 83. China and Russia: Point, Counterpoint

1. Quoted in S. B. Thomas, *Government and Administration in Communist China*, N.Y., 1953, p. 79, from Liu Shao-ch'i, *Liquidate the Menshevist Ideology Within the Party*, F.L.P., 1951, p. 1. Italics added. Chinese original, Yenan, 1943.

2. Anna Louise Strong, "The Thought of Mao-Tse-tung," *Amerasia*, June, 1947. Italics added.

3. N.Y., 1947.

4. *United States Relations with China*, Wedemeyer's report to President Truman, p. 767.

5. *Ibid.*, p. 131.

6. Dedijer, *op. cit.*

7. *Institute of Pacific Relations Hearings*, etc. Washington, pp. 1653-54. But the Red Army did not *interfere with*, and probably facilitated, disarming of Japanese troops by the Communists in some areas.

8. *N.Y. Times*, Jan. 6, 1950.

9. Ales Bebler, later foreign minister, at this time headed the Yugoslav delegation at the U.N. In a conversation in April, and subsequently in May, he told me the substance of what is related here.

10. N.C.N.A., Nov. 18, 1957.

11. Mao Tse-tung, *Imperialism and All Reactionaries Are Paper Tigers*, F.L.P., 1958. Italics added.

12. *Ibid.* Italics added.

13. See *A Documentary Analysis of the Sino-Soviet Dispute*, pub-

lished as a supplement to the *C.Q.*, London, 1961; Zbigniew, Brzesinski, *The Soviet Bloc: Unity and Conflict*, Cambridge, Mass., 1960; and Donald A. Zagoria, *The Sino-Soviet Conflict, 1956-61*, N.Y., 1962. Mr. Zagoria's work is a comprehensive and expert compilation and interpretation of basic data. An objective historical understanding of the subject also requires study of it in the broader context of Communist response to American initiative, which has of course an offensive (as well as defensive) character often ignored in the reconstruction of events by cold-war scholarship.

14. The United States sent 7,000 troops to Siberia to expedite the transfer of Czech troops to Europe but not to support the counterrevolution, although President Wilson was under Allied pressure to intervene. The expedition was withdrawn in 1920. It was largely U.S. pressure which secured the subsequent withdrawal of more than 70,000 Japanese troops from northeastern Asia. The Soviet government became completely satisfied that the expedition was not politically interventionist in character. In 1933 Maxim Litvinov officially withdrew all claims "of whatsoever character . . . arising out of the activities of the military forces of the United States in Siberia." George F. Kennan, *Russia and the West Under Lenin and Stalin*, Boston, 1961, p. 113.

15. "Long Live Leninism!" *P.R.*, April 26, 1960.

16. *P.R.*, April 26, 1960, from Lenin, *Selected Works*, Vol. VII, p. 414, N.Y., 1936.

17. *P.R.*, April 26, 1960.

18. *Ibid.*

Ch. 84. China and Japan

1. In 1949, Mao Tse-tung said that China must "lean to one side"

in foreign policy, meaning toward Russia. Traditional Chinese diplomacy is to "use one barbarian to destroy the other barbarian."

2. Soviet-Japanese trade for 1961 was valued at $172,700,000. *N.Y. Times*, July 16, 1962.

3. *N.Y. Times*, May 28, 1962.

4. *Ibid.*

Ch. 85. War and Peace in Vietnam

1. Quoted in Harold R. Isaacs, *New Cycle in Asia, Selected Documents on Major International Developments in the Far East, 1943-47*, N.Y., 1947, p. 163.

2. See *J.T.T.B.*, pp. 42-46.

3. Harold R. Isaacs, *No Peace in Asia*, N.Y., 1947, p. 144.

4. *Ibid.*, p. 169.

5. For example, Philippe Devillers, *Histoire du Vietnam, 1945-51*, Paris, 1952; Virginia Thompson and Richard Adloff, *The Left Wing in Southeast Asia*, N.Y., 1950; Harold Isaacs, *New Cycle in Asia*, N.Y., 1947, and *No Peace in Asia*, N.Y., 1947; Anna Louise Strong, *Cash and Violence in Laos*, published officially in Peking, 1961.

6. Isaacs, *No Peace in Asia*, pp. 168-169.

7. *Ibid.*

8. Isaacs, "Agreement Between France and Vietnam," *New Cycle in Asia*, p. 169.

9. *Ibid.*

10. *Ibid.*, pp. 172-173.

11. *Ibid.*

12. *Ibid.*, p. 174.

13. Thompson and Adloff, *op. cit.*, pp. 32, 49.

14. Roscoe Drummond and Gaston Coblentz, *Duel at the Brink*, N.Y., 1960, pp. 116-123.

15. Quoted in Drummond and Coblentz, *op. cit.*, p. 119, from Matthew B. Ridgway and H. H. Martin, *Soldier: Memoirs of Matthew B. Ridgway*, N.Y., 1956. Italics added.

16. See *Foreign Relations of the United States, 1943, China,* especially "Political Conditions in China," pp. 191-457, and reports by John Carter Vincent, John Paton Davies, John Stewart Service, George Atcheson, Jr., and Ambassador C. E. Gauss, all of whom were senior China specialists, and all of whom were separated from the foreign service under McCarthy's pressure except George Atcheson, Jr., and Ambassador Gauss, who died prior to Dulles' tenure and the breakup of the China service.

17. In the "State Department Policy Paper" on China released in September, 1949, Formosa was described as having "no special military significance." The principal reasons given therein for rejecting the suggestion that the United States establish a protectorate position in Formosa are here summarized for the sake of brevity. It was stated that such a policy would: a) accomplish no material good for China or its Nationalist regime; b) involve the United States in a long-term venture producing at best a "bristling stalemate" and, at worst, possible involvement in open warfare; c) subject the United States to a violent propaganda barrage and to reaction against American "militarism, imperialism and interference" even from friendly peoples, and particularly from Chinese, who would be turned against the United States anew; and d) eminently suit the purposes of the U.S.S.R., which would like to see the United States "substantiate" its propaganda, and dissipate the energies and weaken the effectiveness of American policies generally by such action.

18. Fred J. Cook, "The CIA," *The Nation,* Special Issue, June 24, 1961, pp. 557-561. Mr. Cook presents many other details concerning this episode, including C.I.A. use of refugee Nationalist troops in northern Burma, Thailand and Laos. See also O. Edmund Clubb, "The Lesson of Laos," *The Progressive,* Madison, Wisc., May, 1961.

19. Philippe Devillers, "The Struggle for Unification," *C.Q.,* No. 9, Jan.-March, 1962.

20. *Ibid.*

21. *N.Y. Times,* July 25, 1962.

22. *Newsweek,* August 20, 1962.

23. *The New Yorker,* August 11, 1962.

24. Devillers, *op. cit.*

25. Darrell Berrigan, "I Saw the French Losing in Indochina," *Saturday Evening Post,* March 18, 1950.

26. "Total Soviet economic assistance to North Vietnam now stands at U.S. $365 million compared with offers worth more than U.S. $450 million made by China (of which roughly half is in the form of free grants and half credits). Total Soviet bloc aid offered to North Vietnam since 1955, including contributions by East European members of the bloc, amounts to more than U.S. $900 million." Some 1,500 technicians from bloc countries are implementing the program. While there is evidence of Sino-Soviet rivalry for Annam's allegiance, "Sino-Soviet cooperation cannot be ruled out." North Vietnam's total output in 1960 was believed to include $570,000,000 in industrial goods, $1,000,000,000 in handicraft products, and $2,700,000,000 in agricultural products. Coal, 2,-500,000 tons; electricity, 254,-000 k.w.; and rice, 4,400,000 tons. William Kaye, "A Bowl of Rice Divided: The Economy of North Vietnam," *C.Q.,* No. 9, Jan.-March, 1962. Italics added.

27. *Ibid.*

28. Devillers, *op. cit.*

29. O. Edmund Clubb, "Trap in

Vietnam," *The Progressive*, Madison, Wisc., April, 1962.

Ch. 86. Childhood's End?

1. With apologies to Arthur Clarke, astronomer, and author of one of the best space-fiction books ever written.
2. Korea, 600,000 troops; Taiwan, 600,000; Vietnam, 300,000; Thailand, 120,000; Pakistan, 100,000.
3. Maj. Gen. Leslie A. Groves's famous "error" in officially publishing the Smyth Report on the Manhattan project had in 1945 already released vital information necessary to construct the bomb which was of incalculably greater value than the trivial data obtained by the Rosenbergs, for which they were executed. General Groves himself later won renown before the Un-American Activities Committee as an expert on "atomic espionage."
4. Quoted in Fred J. Cook, "Juggernaut, the Warfare State," *The Nation*, Special Issue, Oct. 28, 1961, p. 293.
5. *Ibid.*
6. *China Crosses the Yalu: The Decision to Enter the Korean War*, N.Y., 1960, p. 126.
7. Quoted in Fred J. Cook, *op. cit.*, p. 307.
8. *Ibid.*, pp. 281-282.
9. *Ibid.*
10. *Ibid.*
11. *Ibid.*, p. 302.
12. Charles Christian Wertenbaker and the *Reporter* staff, "The China Lobby," *The Reporter*, April 5, April 19, 1952.
13. "United States China Policy," *War/Peace Report* (monthly), July, 1961, p. 4.
14. Cook, *op. cit.*, p. 213.
15. *Ibid.*, p. 320. Italics added.
16. Linus Pauling, "Why I Am Opposed to Fall-out Shelters," *Liberation*, Nov., 1961.
17. Paul G. Hoffman, "Economic Development: The United Nations and Business Partnership," United Nations Office of Public Information, PR SPF/6, April 20, 1959.
18. Harrison Salisbury, *A New Russia?*, N.Y., 1962, pp. 134, 136.
19. *Characteristics of the Low-Income Population and Related Federal Programs*, U.S. Government Printing Office, Washington, 1955.

Acknowledgments

———◆———

I am indebted to many authors for permission to use excerpts from their works and to their publishers for granting me the same privilege, especially:

Harvard University Press, Cambridge, Mass., for permission to quote from John King Fairbank, *The United States and China*. Copyright, 1948, 1958, by the President and Fellows of Harvard College.

The *China Quarterly*, London, for permission to quote from several articles that have appeared therein.

Cambridge University Press, New York, for permission to quote from C. P. Snow, *Two Cultures and the Scientific Revolution*, The Rede Lecture, Copyright, Cambridge University Press, 1959.

Yale University Press, New Haven, for permission to quote from Olga Lang, *Chinese Family and Society*. Copyright, 1947.

General Electric Company, for permission to quote from *TEMPO: Science and Technology in Communist China*, by John Berberet, Santa Barbara, 1960 (RM60TMP-72).

James K. Hotchkiss, for permission to quote from *Russia and the West Under Lenin and Stalin*, by George F. Kennan, Boston, 1961.

I also wish to thank Mr. Aldous Huxley, Miss Harriet Mills, Mr. Fred Cook and Dr. Denis Lazure for personal permission to quote from their articles, and Mr. Harrison Salisbury for permission to quote from *A New Russia?*

O. Edmund Clubb read the manuscript of this book with his customary meticulous and scholarly care, and his many valuable suggestions have contributed to whatever merit the result may possess.

My wife, Lois Wheeler, somehow contrived to combine management of our household with typing most of the manuscript; that did not lead to divorce, but solely because she is a special kind of angel.

I am indebted to Chang Hsin-hai, Chang Siang-mei, Harriet Mills and Philip Kuhn for careful readings and helpful suggestions.

To Mary Heathcote, of Random House, I am most grateful for editorial advice and never-failing help, but

> Not for these I raise
> The song of thanks and praise;
> But for those obstinate questionings
> Of sense and outward things . . .

Bibliography

It is impossible for me to trace all the sources of works by Chinese as well as non-Chinese writers in a bibliography which would adequately express my indebtedness to others during the many years of reading and study that have contributed to the making of this book. Periodical and newspaper sources are in the Notes and Index. In the brief selected reading list below I have included in the first section works by foreign students of China, or by Chinese abroad, as well as a second section of publications of the Foreign Languages Press of Peking, which have all been of immediate and varying degrees of help which I wish to acknowledge. It would also be presumptuous of me to offer an extensive bibliography on China when so many comprehensive ones have been compiled on the various subjects which I have briefly touched upon. These are available from various university presses and from the publications intelligence services of the State Department.

An excellent summary of basic books about ancient, modern and Communist China may be found in "Suggested Reading" at the back of *The United States and China*, John K. Fairbank, Harvard University Press, Cambridge, 1958. Harvard's Center for Chinese Social and Political Studies has also prepared extensive bibliographies of works on nearly every subject and period of contemporary and historic China. "A Selected Bibliography," in *China: Its People, Its Society, Its Culture*, compiled by Hu Chang-tu, HRAF Press, New Haven, 1960, together with a "Bibliographic Note" in Doak Barnett's *Communist China and Asia*, Harper, 1960, give comprehensive references to available literature in English and some other languages. Li Choh-ming, in *Economic Development of Communist China*, University of California Press, 1959, provides a bibliography of current mainland publications in the Chinese language which is impressive for its scope and its demonstration of vast fields of information now open to scholars. In September each year the *Journal of Asian Studies*, New York, devotes an entire issue to current publications on Asia which includes not only important new literature in English and Chinese but in other languages of the Orient as well as in principal European languages.

I have had the advantage of reading two excellent books written by Western journalists who recently visited China: *Awakened China*, by Felix Greene (N.Y. 1961), a colorful and highly readable account by an unusually discerning and intelligent observer; and *China and Her Shadow*, by Tibor Mende (N.Y., 1962), an equally informative, skillfully analytical and well-documented study. Both are important contributions to our knowledge of contemporary China as seen from the inside.

I am also indebted to Gilbert Etienne of the Institut Universitaire de Hautes Etudes Internationales de Genève for helping me to bring my information on China up to date in 1962. His reports in *Le Monde* (11/30/61, 12/1/61, 12/3/61 and 12/4/61) are especially useful in assessing the widely published, more sensational accounts of the same period by M. Gigon, another Swiss writer who traveled through China for a few weeks during M. Etienne's longer visit, late in 1961.

Adler, Solomon, *The Chinese Economy*, New York, 1957.
Barnett, A. Doak, *Communist China and Asia: Challenge to American Policy*, New York, 1960.
————, *Communist Economic Strategy*, New York, 1959.
Belden, Jack, *China Shakes the World*, New York, 1949.
Beloff, Max, *Soviet Policy in the Far East, 1944-51*, London, 1953.
Bodde, Derk, *China's Cultural Tradition*, New York, 1957.
Boorman, Howard L., Eckstein, Alexander, Mosley, Philip E., and Schwartz, Benjamin, *Moscow-Peking Axis: Strengths and Strains*, New York, 1957.
Brandt, Conrad, Schwartz, Benjamin, and Fairbank, John K., *A Documentary History of Chinese Communism*, Cambridge, 1952.
Brine, Lindsay, *The Taiping Rebellion*, London, 1862.
Buck, J. Lossing, *Land Utilization in China*, 3 vols., Chicago, 1937.
Buck, Pearl, *All Men Are Brothers*, trans. of the *Shui Hu Chuan*, 2 vols., New York, 1933.
Callis, Helmut G., *China, Confucian and Communist*, New York, 1959.
Chiang Kai-shek, *China's Destiny*, notes by Philip Jaffe, New York, 1947.
Chou Ching-wen, *Ten Years of Storm*, New York, 1960.
Compton, Boyd, *Mao's China: Party Reform Documents, 1942-44*, Seattle, 1952.
Creel, H. G., *Chinese Thought from Confucius to Mao Tse-tung*, Chicago, 1953.
Cressey, George Babcock, *China's Geographic Foundations*, New York, 1934.
Delza, Sophia, *Body and Mind in Harmony, T'ai Chi Ch'uan*, New York, 1961.
Drummond, Roscoe, and Coblentz, Gaston, *Duel at the Brink, John Foster Dulles' Command of American Power*, New York, 1960.
Dumont, René, *Revolution dans les Campagnes Chinoises*, Paris, 1957.
Elegant, Robert, *Dragon Seed*, New York, 1959.
Epstein, Israel, *The Unfinished Revolution in China*, Boston, 1947.
Etienne, Gilbert, *De Caboul à Pékin*, Geneva, 1959.
————, *La Voie Chinoise*, Paris, 1962.
Fairbank, John King, *The United States and China*, new and rev. ed., Cambridge, 1958.
Fei Hsiao-t'ung, *Peasant Life in China*, New York, 1939.
Fitzgerald, C. P., *China: A Short Cultural History*, rev. ed., New York, 1954.
Foreign Relations of the United States, 1943, China, Washington: U.S. State Department, 1957.
Freemantle, Anne, *Mao Tse-tung, An Anthology of His Writings*, New York, 1962.
Fung Yu-lan, *A History of Chinese Philosophy*, Vols. I and II, trans. by Derk Bodde, Princeton, 1952, 1953.
Gelder, Stuart, *The Chinese Communists*, London, 1946.
Greene, Felix, *Awakened China*, New York, 1961.
Griswold, A. Whitney, *The Far Eastern Policy of the United States*, New York, 1938.
Grousset, René, *Histoire de la Chine*, Paris, 1942.
Guillermaz, Jacques, *La Chine Populaire*, Paris, 1959.
Ho Ping-ti, *Studies on the Population of China, 1368-1953*, Cambridge, 1959.

Hsieh, Alice Langley, *Communist China's Strategy in the Nuclear Era*, Englewood, New Jersey, 1962.

Hu Chang-tu, ed., *China, Its People, Its Society, Its Culture*, New Haven, 1960.

Hudson, G. F., Lowenthal, Richard, and MacFarquhar, Roderick, *The Sino-Soviet Dispute*, London, 1961.

Hughes, T. J. and Luard, D. E. T., *The Economic Development of Communist China, 1949-1958*, London, 1959.

Isaacs, Harold R., *New Cycle in Asia*, New York, 1947.

———, *No Peace for Asia*, New York, 1947.

Kennan, George F., *Russia and the West Under Lenin and Stalin*, Boston, 1961.

Kuo Ping-chia, *China, New Age and New Outlook*, rev. ed., New York, 1959.

Lang, Olga, *Chinese Family and Society*, New Haven, 1946.

Lattimore, Owen, *The Desert Road to Turkestan*, New York, 1929.

Lifton, R. J., *Thought Reform and the Psychology of Totalism: A Study of "Brainwashing,"* New York, 1961.

(MacArthur, Douglas, see Willoughby.)

MacFarquhar, Roderick, *The Hundred Flowers*, London, 1960 (published N.Y., 1960, under the title *The Hundred Flowers Campaign and the Chinese Intellectuals*).

Marx, Karl, and Engels, Friedrich, *Basic Writings*, Lewis S. Feuer, ed., New York, 1959.

McLane, Charles B., *Soviet Policy and the Chinese Communists, 1931-46*, New York, 1958.

Meadows, T. T., *The Chinese and Their Rebellions*, London, 1859.

Mende, Tibor, *China and Her Shadow*, New York, 1962.

Needham, Joseph, *Science and Civilization in China, Vol. II, History of Scientific Thought*, London, 1956.

Orleans, Leo A., *Professional Manpower and Education in Communist China*, Washington: U.S. Government Printing Office, 1961.

Peffer, Nathaniel, *The Collapse of a Civilization*, New York, 1930.

Rickett, Allyn and Adele, *Prisoners of Liberation*, New York, 1957.

Rigney, Harold W., *Four Years in a Red Hell: The Story of Father Rigney*, Chicago, 1956.

Romanus, C. F., and Sunderland, R., *Stilwell's Mission to China*, Office of the Chief of Military History, Department of the Army, Washington, 1953.

———, *Stilwell's Command Problems*, Office of the Chief of Military History, Department of the Army, Washington, 1956.

Saeki, P. Y., *The Nestorian Documents and Relics in China*, Tokyo, 1951.

Shabad, Theodore, *China's Changing Map*, New York, 1956.

Simmons, Ernest J., *U.S.S.R.: A Concise Handbook*, Ithaca, 1947.

Smedley, Agnes, *The Great Road: The Life and Times of Chu Teh*, New York, 1956.

Tawney, R. H., *Land and Labour in China*, London, 1932.

Thomas, S. B., *Government and Administration in Communist China*, New York, 1953; rev. ed., 1955.

Thompson, Virginia, and Adloff, Richard, *The Left Wing in Southeast Asia*, New York, 1950.

Tocqueville, Alexis de, *Democracy in America*, Vols. I & II, New York, 1961. The text used is the Phillips Bradley edition published by Vintage Books, with notes, etc., added to the Henry Reeve translation of the French original, Paris, 1835.

Truman, Harry S., *Memoirs*, 2 vols., New York, 1958.

United States Relations with China, With Special Reference to the Period 1944-49, Washington: U.S. State Department, 1949.

Wales, Nym, *Inside Red China*, New York, 1939.

———, *Red Dust*, Palo Alto, 1952.

Walker, Richard L., *China Under Communism: The First Five Years*, New Haven, 1955.

White, Theodore H. and Jacoby, Annalee, *Thunder Out of China*, New York, 1946.

Whiting, Allen S., *China Crosses the Yalu: The Decision to Enter the Korean War*, New York, 1960.

Willoughby, Charles A., and Chamberlain, John, *MacArthur: 1941-1951*, New York, 1954.

Williams, S. Wells, *The Middle Kingdom*, 2 vols., New York, 1891, 1904.

Winance, Eleutherius, O. S. B., *The Communist Persuasion: A Personal Experience of Brainwashing*, New York, 1959.

Wong K. Chimin and Wu Lien-teh, *History of Chinese Medicine*, 2nd ed., Shanghai, 1936.

Zagoria, Donald S., *The Sino-Soviet Conflict, 1956-1961*, Princeton, 1962.

Chinese Publications in English

Since it is now legally possible to purchase Chinese publications in the United States, it may be of service to list those books and periodicals which I have found especially interesting or useful in the preparation of this volume. Many works in this bibliography are basic documents of which Western scholars and intelligence research analysts have long made intensive use. References to a few others will be found in my Notes. A complete catalog of publications issued with the approval of the Chinese government by the Foreign Languages Press of Peking may be obtained from the authorized distributing agency mentioned below.*

Geography of China: Peoples and Regions

A SIMPLE GEOGRAPHY OF CHINA, Wang Chun-heng. Charts, maps and illus. covering all regions of China. 256 p. 1958.

PEKING. China's capital city in photos of today and yesterday, reproductions of ancient paintings in color. Captions in Chinese with English translation in accompanying booklet.

Water Control and Climate

REPORT ON THE MULTIPLE-PURPOSE PLAN for Permanently Controlling the Yellow River and Exploiting Its Water Resources, Teng Tse-hui. Map, 49 p. 1955.

China in Transition

THE PEOPLE HAVE STRENGTH, Rewi Alley. Description of a New Zealander's travels through many parts of China in the early days of the People's Republic. 281 p. 1954.

* Foreign Languages Press publications are distributed by the Guozi Shudian, P.O. Box 399, Peking, China. United States distribution is handled by China Books and Periodicals, 334 Schiller Street, Chicago, Ill.

Miscellaneous

CHINESE THERAPEUTICAL METHODS OF ACUPUNCTURE AND MOXIBUSTION. Academy of Traditional Chinese Medicine. Illustrated. 18 p. 1960.

EMBROIDERY DESIGNS OF THE MIAO PEOPLE OF CHINA. People's Fine Arts Publishing House. 40 illustrations. 50 p. 1956.

CHINA'S HINTERLAND IN THE LEAP FORWARD. Rewi Alley. Peking, 1961.

Chinese Agriculture

THE QUESTION OF AGRICULTURAL CO-OPERATION, Mao Tse-tung. Report delivered July 31, 1955. 39 p. 1956.

THE DRAFT PROGRAMME FOR AGRICULTURAL DEVELOPMENT IN THE PEOPLE'S REPUBLIC OF CHINA 1956-1967. 44 p. 1956.

PEOPLE'S COMMUNES IN CHINA. Articles and documents. 90 p. 1958.

History of China

AN OUTLINE HISTORY OF CHINA, Tung Chi-ming. From Peking Man to 1949 A.D. Table of Dynasties. Illustrated. 469 p. 1959.

A RECORD OF THE BUDDHIST COUNTRIES, Fa-hsien. Being an account of his travels through Central Asia and India in the 5th century. Chinese Buddhist Assoc., Peking. 94 p. 1957.

THIRTY YEARS OF THE COMMUNIST PARTY OF CHINA, Hu Chiao-mu. 99 p. 1954.

A HISTORY OF THE MODERN CHINESE REVOLUTION, Ho Kan-chih. From the May 4th Movement in 1919 to the first half of 1956. A detailed analysis of recent Chinese history. 627 p. 1959.

International Relations

IMPORTANT DOCUMENTS CONCERNING THE QUESTION OF TAIWAN. Cairo Declaration, reports by Chou En-lai, etc. 184 p. 1955.

OPPOSE U.S. OCCUPATION OF TAIWAN AND "TWO CHINAS" PLOT. A selection of important documents. 162 p. 1958.

1960: DOCUMENTS OF THE SINO-INDIAN BOUNDARY QUESTION. Exchange of letters between Chou En-lai and Nehru. 144 p. 1960.

THE DEMOCRATIC REPUBLIC OF VIETNAM. An Official Report of the Government of the D.R.V., F.L.P., Hanoi. 157 p. 1960.

TWO TACTICS, ONE AIM. "An Exposure of the Peace Tricks of U.S. Imperialism." Inst. of Foreign Affairs. 146 p. May, 1960.

LONG LIVE LENINISM. Contains the much publicized articles from *Hung Chi (Red Flag)* and *Renmin Ribao (People's Daily)* on the danger of war and the struggle for peace and co-existence. Also an article by Lu Ting-yi. 106 p. Revised ed. Aug., 1960.

TIBETAN INTERVIEWS, Anna Louise Strong. 210 p. 1959.

IMPERIALISM AND CHINESE POLITICS, Hu Sheng. 1955.

China's Economy: The Five-Year Plans

REPORT on National Economic Development and Fulfillment of the

State Plan of the People's Republic of China in 1954. With Statistical Summary. 48 p. 1956.

First Five-Year Plan, 1953-1957. Documents on Capital Construction, Heavy Industry, Agriculture, Transport and Communications, Commerce, etc. 231 p. 1956.

China Will Overtake Britain, Niu Chung-huang. Plan to Surpass British Industrial Level within 15 Years. 66 p. 1958.

The Second Five-Year Plan Fulfilled in Two Years. Charts and photographs of the development of the national economy in 1959. Brief text. 40 p. 1960.

The Socialist Transformation of the National Economy in China, Hsueh Mu-chiao, Su Hsing, Lin Tse-li. 287 p. 1960.

Labor

Labor Laws and Regulations. Trade Union Law, Constitution of the Trade Unions, Labor Insurance, Award for Inventions & Tech. Improvement, Spare-Time Education, etc. 86 p. 1956.

Political Reports and Documents

Proposals of the 8th National Congress, C. P. of China for 2nd 5-Yr. Plan (1958-62). Report by Chou En-lai. 105 p. 1956.

Constitution of the Communist Party of China. Report on the Revision of the Constitution of the Communist Party of China by Teng Hsiao-ping, Sept. 16, 1956. 110 p. 1956.

Historical Experience of the Dictatorship of the Proletariat, Editorial in *Renmin Ribao* of April 5, 1956, on the 20th Congress, C. P. of the U.S.S.R. 64 p. 1959.

The Victory of Marxism-Leninism in China, Liu Shao-ch'i. 36 p. 1959.

A History of the Modern Chinese Revolution, Ho Kan-chih, Peking, 1960.

Thirty Years of the Communist Party of China, Hu Chiao-mu, Peking, 1959.

"Let a Hundred Flowers Blossom, a Hundred Schools of Thought Contend" (1956), Lu Ting-yi. 37 p. 1958.

Books, Articles and Speeches by Mao Tse-tung

(Date of original issue is given in parenthesis if earlier than date of publication.)

Analysis of the Classes in Chinese Society (1926). 17 p. 1956.

The Chinese Revolution and the Chinese Communist Party (1939). 43 p. 1959.

Combat Liberalism (1937). 6 p. 1956.

Comrade Mao Tse-tung on "Imperialism and All Reactionaries Are Paper Tigers." 32 p. 1958.

On Contradiction (1937). 55 p. 1958.

On the Correct Handling of Contradictions Among the People (1957). 70 p. 1959.

ON METHODS OF LEADERSHIP (1943). 10 p. 1955.

ON THE NEW DEMOCRACY (1940). 84 p. 1955.

ON PRACTICE (1937). 26 p. 1953.

ON THE PROTRACTED WAR (1938). 140 p. 1954.

ON THE QUESTION OF AGRICULTURAL COOPERATION (1955). 39 p. 1956.

ON THE RECTIFICATION OF INCORRECT IDEAS IN THE PARTY (1929). 19 p. 1953.

OUR STUDY AND THE CURRENT SITUATION (1944). 116 p. 1955.

QUESTIONS OF TACTICS IN THE PRESENT ANTI-JAPANESE FRONT (1939). 38 p. 1954.

RECTIFY THE PARTY'S STYLE IN WORK (1942). 29 p. 1955.

REFORM OUR STUDY (1941). 19 p. 1955.

REPORT OF AN INVESTIGATION INTO THE PEASANT MOVEMENT IN HUNAN (1927). 64 p. 1953.

A SINGLE SPARK CAN START A PRAIRIE FIRE (1930). 22 p. 1953.

STRATEGIC PROBLEMS IN THE ANTI-JAPANESE WAR (1937). 55 p. 1954.

WHY CAN CHINA'S RED POWER EXIST? (1928). 17 p. 1953.

SELECTED WORKS OF MAO TSE-TUNG, Vol. I, 1952; Vol. II, 1952; Vol. III, 1953; and Vol. IV., 1961, contain most of the foregoing material published as separate pamphlets or books.

Commentary on Mao Tse-tung

NOTES ON MAO TSE-TUNG'S "REPORT OF AN INVESTIGATION INTO THE PEASANT MOVEMENT IN HUNAN," Chen Po-ta. 88 p. 1954.

Classical Literature

ANCIENT CHINESE FABLES. From the 4th century B.C. to the 5th century A.D. Illustrated. 60 p. 1957.

THE DRAGON KING'S DAUGHTER. Stories of love and the supernatural from the Tang Dynasty (618-907). 178 p. 1954.

Verse

THE PEOPLE SPEAK OUT. Ancient and modern popular songs and poems translated by Rewi Alley. Illustrated. 107 p. 1954.

POEMS, Mao Tse-tung. 1959.

Literature and Philosophy

A BRIEF HISTORY OF CHINESE FICTION, Lu Hsun. From the beginnings to the 20th century. 462 p. 1959.

A SHORT HISTORY OF CLASSICAL CHINESE LITERATURE, Feng Yuan-chun. From the beginnings to 1919. 132 p. 1958.

TALKS AT THE YENAN FORUM ON ART AND LITERATURE (1942), Mao Tse-tung. 51 p. 1956.

Modern Fiction

THE FAMILY (1931), Pa Chin. In a feudal household a younger generation breaks with tradition. Illus. 323 p. 1958.

Spring Silkworms (1932-1943), Mao Tun. 13 stories dealing with the collapse of China's rural economy, the Japanese Invasion, Chinese industrialists, etc. 278 p. 1956.

Uncle Kao, Ouyang Shan. The struggle to develop a village consumer's co-op in the northern Shensi area. 297 p. 1957.

Modern Drama

Chu Yuan, Kuo Mo-jo. 5-Act Tragedy of the ancient poet of the third century b.c. with a modern meaning. 126 p. 1953.

The Long March, Chen Chi-tung. 6-Act Epic. 99 p. 1956.

Chinese Opera

Peking Opera, A Traditional Chinese Art. Brief history, training of actors, performances and costumes. 82 photos & illus. 102 p. 1957.

Chinese Language

English-Chinese Conversation. For beginners. 176 p. 1959.
Reform of the Chinese Written Language. 70 p. 1958.

Periodicals in English

China Pictorial. Semimonthly. The day-to-day story in pictures of life in modern China. Many photos in color.

China Reconstructs. Illustrated monthly. Popular articles on China's economic, social and cultural development. Language corner, reader's comments, modern art, stamps.

Peking Review. Weekly journal. Authoritative analysis and commentary on international relations and Chinese news and views. Cultural calendar of events in Peking.

Chinese Medical Journal. Monthly official organ of the Chinese Medical Association. Research, surgery, etc.

Index

ABOUT THE AUTHOR

EDGAR SNOW is a native of Missouri who went to the Far East when he was twenty-two. He made his home in China for twelve years, studied the country and the language, and lectured at Yenching University in Peking, where he made friendships with students who are among China's leaders today. As a foreign correspondent in China, Burma, India and Indochina he worked successively for the *Chicago Tribune, New York Sun, New York Herald Tribune* and *London Daily Herald.* Then, as associate editor of the *Saturday Evening Post,* he reported wartime and postwar events in Asia and Europe, and became its widely quoted specialist on China, India and the U.S.S.R. He is the author of ten books, including *Red Star Over China, The Battle for Asia, People on Our Side,* and *Journey to the Beginning.*

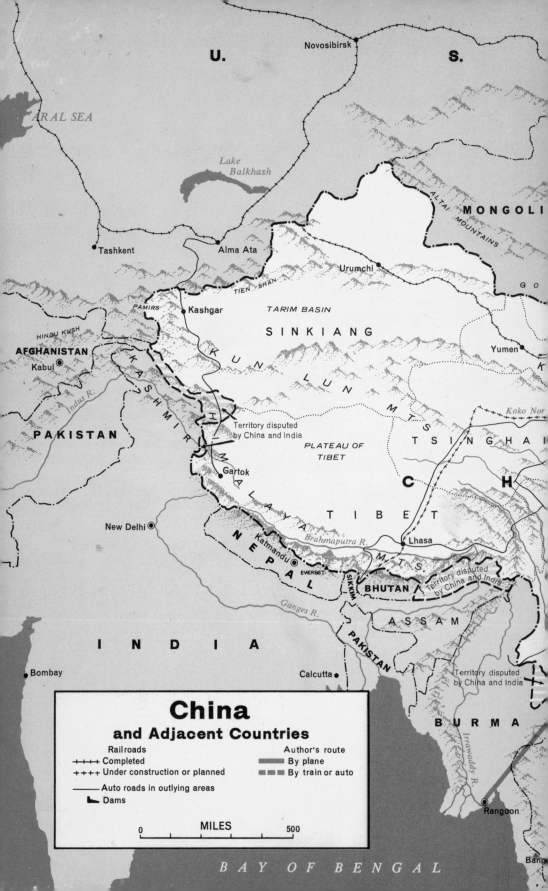

China
and Adjacent Countries

Railroads

+++ Completed

+++ Under construction or planned

—— Auto roads in outlying areas

⌐ Dams

Author's route

━━ By plane

━ ━ By train or auto

```
0            MILES            500
```

U. S.

Novosibirsk

ARAL SEA

Lake Balkhash

Tashkent

Alma Ata

Urumchi

MONGOLI

ALTAI MOUNTAINS

GO

TIEN SHAN

Kashgar

TARIM BASIN

SINKIANG

Yumen

K

PAMIRS

HINDU KUSH

Koko Nor

AFGHANISTAN

Kabul

K U N L U N M T S

TSINGHAI

KASHMIR

Indus R.

Territory disputed by China and India

PAKISTAN

PLATEAU OF TIBET

C

H

Gartok

H I

M A L A Y A

TIBET

New Delhi

Katmandu

Brahmaputra R.

Lhasa

NEPAL

EVEREST

M.T.S.

Territory disputed by China and India

SIKKIM

BHUTAN

Ganges R.

ASSAM

Bombay

Calcutta

PAKISTAN

Territory disputed by China and India

INDIA

BURMA

Irrawaddy R.

Rangoon

Bang

BAY OF BENGAL

Edwin N. Strickland